VOLKSWAGEN

GOLF, PO

SCIROCCO, CORRADO
WORKSHOP MANUAL

CW00734668

by
Lindsay Porter

Ring this number to find your nearest Volkswagen dealer in the UK – 0800 711 811.

CONTENTS

Detailed Contents are shown at the start of each Chapter.

FACT FILE

'LEFT' AND 'RIGHT' SIDES OF THE CAR

• Throughout this manual, we refer to the 'left' and 'right' sides of the car. They refer to the sides of the car that you would see if you were sitting in the driver's seat, looking forward.

First published in 2001 by:
Porter Publishing Ltd.
The Storehouse • Little Hereford Street
Bromyard • Hereford • HR7 4DE • England

Tel: 01885 488 800
Fax: 01885 483 012
www.portermanuals.com

British Library Cataloguing in Publication Data.

A catalogue record for this book is available from the British Library.

ISBN 1-899238-40-9

Series Editor: Lindsay Porter
Layout and Typesetting: Pineapple Publishing, Worcester • Printed in England by The Trinity Press, Worcester

CHAPTER 1: FACTS & FIGURES

*Please read **Chapter 2, Safety First** before carrying out any work on your car.*

This chapter provides you with all the information you will need about your car, especially in connection with servicing and repairing it. First, you'll need to identify the engine type. If you don't know it already, see **Chapter 6, Engine**. Before buying parts, be sure to take your vehicle's chassis and engine numbers with you - ***PART G: IDENTIFICATION NUMBERS*** in this chapter.

CONTENTS

IMPORTANT NOTE:
→ Many detail changes have taken place over the years, and there have been many different special editions and options available.
→ The following information will be true of most cases but can only be taken as a general guide.

→ Volkswagen's quoted torque settings and other information sometimes vary between publications. The figures shown here are the latest available to us.
→ If in any doubt, consult your local Volkswagen dealer for confirmation.

Part A: Major Milestones

CORRADO
Corrado: 1989 to '96. 3-door Coupe. 1781cc, 1781cc G60 Turbo, 1984cc 8V and 16V, 2860cc VR6.

GOLF
Golf Mk 1: 1974 to '83. 3-door hatchback. 1093cc, 1272cc, 1457cc, 1588cc and 1780cc petrol/gasoline engines. 1471cc and 1588cc diesel engines.
Golf Mk 1 Convertible: 1979 to '93. 1.6 and 1.8 petrol/gasoline engines.
Golf Mk 1 Van: 1980 to '84. 1.1 petrol/gasoline or 1.6 diesel engine.
Golf Mk 2 and Jetta (saloon): 1984 to '92. 1043cc, 1272cc, 1595cc and 1781cc petrol/gasoline engines. 1588cc diesel with Turbo option from 1985.
Golf Mk 2 Van: 1984-on.
Golf Mk 2 Caddy Pick-up and Van: 1987-on. Caddy to '92. Has rear chassis and leaf spring rear suspension.
Golf Mk 3 and Vento (saloon): 1992 to '97. 1391cc, 1595cc, 1598cc, 1781cc, 1984cc and 2792cc V6 petrol/gasoline engines. 1896cc diesel engine available normally aspirated, TD and TDi versions.
Golf Mk 3 Convertible: 1994-on.
Golf Mk 4: 1998-on. 3-door and 5-door hatchback and 5-door estate from 1999-on. 1390cc, 1595cc, 1781cc (turbo version available), 1984cc and 2324cc V5 cylinder petrol/gasoline engines. 1896cc, including TDi diesel engine.

POLO
Polo and Derby: 1976 to '81. 2-door. 895cc, 1093cc engines.
Polo: 1981 to '90. 3-door hatchback and Coupe. 1043cc, 1093cc and 1272cc petrol/gasoline engines.
Polo Classic: 1982 to '87, 1093cc and 1982 to '90, 1272cc petrol/gasoline engines.
Polo: 1990 to '94. Hatchback, Coupe and 2-door saloon. 1043cc, 1272cc and 1272cc supercharged engine fitted to G40 model.
Polo Van: 1992 to '94. 1043cc engine.
Polo Caddy Van and Pick-up: 1992-on. 1390cc and 1595cc petrol/gasoline engines. 1896 diesel engine.
Polo: 1994 to '99. 3-door and 5-door hatchback, 4-door saloon and 5-door estate. 1043cc, 1296cc, 1390cc, 1598cc and 1595cc petrol/gasoline engines. 1896cc diesel engine.

SCIROCCO
Scirocco Mk 1: 1974 to '81. 1471cc petrol/gasoline engine.
Scirocco Mk 2: 1982 to '92. 1487cc, 1588cc and 1781cc petrol/gasoline engines.

Part B: Vital Statistics

Wheels and Tyres

ENGINE SIZE (cc)	RIM WIDTH & TYPE	TYRE SIZE	TYRE PRESSURES			
			NORMAL		LADEN	
			Front	Rear	Front	Rear
Golf 1/Jetta 1/Scirocco						
1093 & Diesel	4.5 J x 13 steel	145 SR 13	1.7 bar/25 psi	1.7 bar/25 psi	1.8 bar/26 psi	2.2 bar/32 psi
engine models	5.5 J x 13 steel	155 SR 13	1.7 bar/25 psi	1.7 bar/25 psi	1.8 bar/26 psi	2.2 bar/32 psi
1272, 1457,	5J x 13 steel	155 SR 13	1.7 bar/25 psi	1.7 bar/25 psi	1.8 bar/26 psi	2.2 bar/32 psi
1471, & 1588	5.5J x 13 steel	175/70 SR 13	1.7 bar/25 psi	1.7 bar/25 psi	1.8 bar/26 psi	2.2 bar/32 psi
1588 Injection	5.5J x 13 steel	175/70 HR 13	1.7 bar/25 psi	1.7 bar/25 psi	1.8 bar/26 psi	2.2 bar/32 psi
1588 Injection	5.5J x 13 alloy	175/70 HR 13	1.7 bar/25 psi	1.7 bar/25 psi	1.8 bar/26 psi	2.2 bar/32 psi
1781 Injection	5.5J x 13 alloy	175/70 HR 13	1.7 bar/25 psi	1.7 bar/25 psi	1.8 bar/26 psi	2.2 bar/32 psi
1781 Injection	6J x 14 alloy	185/60 R 14 H	1.7 bar/25 psi	1.7 bar/25 psi	1.8 bar/26 psi	2.2 bar/32 psi
Golf Convertible						
1457, 1588,	5J x 13 steel	155 SR 13	2.0 bar/29 psi	2.0 bar/29 psi	2.2 bar/32 psi	2.5 bar/36 psi
1595,1781,	5.5J x 13 steel	175/70 SR 13	2.0 bar/29 psi	2.0 bar/29 psi	2.2 bar/32 psi	2.5 bar/36 psi
(carburettor),	5.5J x 13 alloy	175/70 SR 13	2.0 bar/29 psi	2.0 bar/29 psi	2.2 bar/32 psi	2.5 bar/36 psi
1588, 1781,	6J x 14 steel	185/60 R 14 H	2.0 bar/29 psi	2.0 bar/29 psi	2.2 bar/32 psi	2.5 bar/36 psi
(injection).	6J x 14 alloy	185/60 R 14 H	2.0 bar/29 psi	2.0 bar/29 psi	2.2 bar/32 psi	2.5 bar/36 psi
	6J x 15 alloy	195/50 R 15 H	2.0 bar/29 psi	2.0 bar/29 psi	2.2 bar/32 psi	2.5 bar/36 psi
Spacesaver (spare)	3.5J x 14 steel	105/70 R 14	4.2 bar/61 psi	4.2 bar/61 psi	4.2 bar/61 psi	4.2 bar/61 psi
Caddy						
All engines	5J x 13 steel	165 SR 13	1.8 bar/26 psi	2.7 bar/39 psi	1.8 bar/26 psi	2.7 bar/39 psi
Golf 2 /Jetta 2						
1272	5J x 13 steel	155 SR 13	1.8 bar/26 psi	1.8 bar/26 psi	2.0 bar/29 psi	2.4 bar/35 psi
1595 & diesel	5.5J x 13 steel	175/70 SR 13	2.0 bar/29 psi	1.8 bar/26 psi	2.0 bar/29 psi	2.4 bar/35 psi
	6J x 14 alloy	185/60 R 14 H	2.0 bar/29 psi	1.8 bar/26 psi	2.0 bar/29 psi	2.4 bar/35 psi
1781 carb.	5.5J x 13 steel	175/70 SR 13	2.0 bar/29 psi	1.8 bar/26 psi	2.0 bar/29 psi	2.4 bar/35 psi
	6J x 14 alloy	185/60 R 14 H	2.0 bar/29 psi	1.8 bar/26 psi	2.0 bar/29 psi	2.4 bar/35 psi
1781 injection	6J x 14 steel	185/60 R 14 H	2.0 bar/29 psi	1.8 bar/26 psi	2.0 bar/29 psi	2.4 bar/35 psi
	6J x 14 alloy	185/60 R 14 H	2.0 bar/29 psi	1.8 bar/26 psi	2.0 bar/29 psi	2.4 bar/35 psi
	6J x 15 alloy	195/50 R 15 H	2.0 bar/29 psi	1.8 bar/26 psi	2.0 bar/29 psi	2.4 bar/35 psi
Spacesaver (spare)	3.5J x 14 steel	105/70 R 14	4.2 bar/61 psi	4.2 bar/61 psi	4.2 bar/61 psi	4.2 bar/61 psi
Golf 3/Vento						
1391	5.5J x 13 steel	175/70 TR 13	1.8 bar/26 psi	1.8 bar/26 psi	2.0 bar/29 psi	2.4 bar/35 psi
1598	5.5J x 13 steel	175/70 R 13	2.1 bar/30 psi	1.9 bar/27 psi	2.1 bar/30 psi	2.4 bar/35 psi
	6J x 14 alloy	185/60 HR 14	2.0 bar/29 psi	1.8 bar/26 psi	2.0 bar/29 psi	2.4 bar/35 psi
1781 carb	5.5J x 13 steel	175/70 SR 13	2.0 bar/29 psi	1.8 bar/26 psi	2.0 bar/29 psi	2.4 bar/35 psi
	6J x 14 alloy	185/60 HR 14	2.0 bar/29 psi	1.8 bar/26 psi	2.0 bar/29 psi	2.4 bar/35 psi
1781 injection	6J x 14 steel/alloy	185/60 HR 14	2.0 bar/29 psi	1.8 bar/26 psi	2.0 bar/29 psi	2.4 bar/35 psi
	6J x 15 alloy	185/60 HR 15	2.0 bar/29 psi	1.8 bar/26 psi	2.0 bar/29 psi	2.4 bar/35 psi
1896 D	5.5J x 13 steel	175/70 TR 13	2.0 bar/29 psi	1.8 bar/26 psi	2.0 bar/29 psi	2.4 bar/35 psi
1896 TD	6J x 14 steel/alloy	185/60 HR 14	2.2 bar/32 psi	2.2 bar/32 psi	2.0 bar/29 psi	2.4 bar/35 psi
1896 TDi	6J x 14 steel/alloy	185/60 TR 14	2.3 bar/33 psi	2.1 bar/32 psi	2.3 bar/33 psi	2.9 bar/42 psi
1984	6.5J x 15 alloy	195/50 VR 13	2.0 bar/29 psi	1.8 bar/26 psi	2.2 bar/32 psi	2.6 bar/38 psi
	6.5J x 15 alloy	205/50 VR 15	2.0 bar/29 psi	1.8 bar/26 psi	2.2 bar/32 psi	2.6 bar/38 psi
2792 V6	6.5J x 15 alloy	205/50 VR 15	2.6 bar/38 psi	2.4 bar/35 psi	2.8 bar/41 psi	3.2 bar/46 psi
2861 V6	6.5J x 15 alloy	205/50 VR 15	2.5 bar/36 psi	2.2 bar/32 psi	2.7 bar/39 psi	3.0 bar/44 psi
Polo/Derby 1						
895	4.5J x 13 steel	135 SR 13	1.54 bar/22 psi	1.54 bar/22 psi	1.82 bar/26 psi	1.96 bar/28 psi
1043	4.5J x 13 steel	145 SR 13	1.47 bar/21 psi	1.47 bar/21 psi	1.68 bar/24 psi	1.89 bar/27 psi
1093	4.5J x 13 steel	145 SR 13	1.47 bar/21 psi	1.47 bar/21 psi	1.68 bar/24 psi	1.89 bar/27 psi
1272	4.5J x 13 steel	155/70 SR 13	1.47 bar/21 psi	1.47 bar/21 psi	1.68 bar/24 psi	1.89 bar/27 psi

ENGINE SIZE (cc)	RIM WIDTH & TYPE	TYRE SIZE	TYRE PRESSURES			
			NORMAL		LADEN	
			Front	Rear	Front	Rear
Polo 2						
1043	4.5J x 13 steel	135/70 SR 13	1.8 bar/26 psi	1.8 bar/26 psi	1.9 bar/28 psi	2.3 bar/33 psi
		145/70 SR 13	1.7 bar/25 psi	1.7 bar/25 psi	1.8 bar/26 psi	2.2 bar/32 psi
1272	4.5J x 13 steel	145/70 SR 13	1.7 bar/25 psi	1.7 bar/25 psi	1.8 bar/26 psi	2.1 bar/30 psi
		155/70 SR 13	1.7 bar/25 psi	1.7 bar/25 psi	1.8 bar/26 psi	2.1 bar/30 psi
1272D	4.5J x 13 steel	145/70 SR 13	1.7 bar/25 psi	1.7 bar/25 psi	1.8 bar/26 psi	2.1 bar/30 psi
		155/70 SR 13	1.7 bar/25 psi	1.7 bar/25 psi	1.8 bar/26 psi	2.1 bar/30 psi
Polo 3						
1043	4.5J x 13 steel	135/70 SR 13	1.7 bar/25 psi	1.7 bar/25 psi	2.1 bar/30 psi	2.4 bar/35 psi
		145/70 SR 13	1.6 bar/23 psi	1.6 bar/23 psi	1.9 bar/28 psi	2.3 bar/33 psi
		155/70 SR 13	1.7 bar/25 psi	1.7 bar/25 psi	1.9 bar/28 psi	2.3 bar/33 psi
	5.5J x 13 steel	165/65 SR 13	1.7 bar/25 psi	1.7 bar/25 psi	1.9 bar/28 psi	2.3 bar/33 psi
1272	4.5J x 13 steel	145/70 SR 13	1.6 bar/23 psi	1.6 bar/23 psi	1.9 bar/28 psi	2.3 bar/33 psi
		155/70 SR 13	1.7 bar/25 psi	1.7 bar/25 psi	1.9 bar/28 psi	2.3 bar/33 psi
	5.5J x 13 steel	165/65 SR 13	1.7 bar/25 psi	1.7 bar/25 psi	1.9 bar/28 psi	2.3 bar/33 psi
(1272 G40 Supercharged - Not covered)						
Polo 4						
1043	4.5J x 13 steel	155/70 R 13	1.8 bar/26 psi	1.8 bar/26 psi	2.1 bar/31 psi	2.4 bar/35 psi
	5.5J x 13 steel	175/65 R 13	1.8 bar/26 psi	1.8 bar/26 psi	2.2 bar/32 psi	2.6 bar/38 psi
1296	4.5J x 13 steel	155/70 R 13	1.8 bar/26 psi	1.8 bar/26 psi	2.1 bar/31 psi	2.4 bar/35 psi
	5.5J x 13 steel	175/65 R 13	1.8 bar/26 psi	1.8 bar/26 psi	2.2 bar/32 psi	2.6 bar/38 psi
1390	4.5J x 13 steel	155/70 R 13	1.8 bar/26 psi	1.8 bar/26 psi	2.1 bar/31 psi	2.4 bar/35 psi
	5.5J x 13 steel	175/65 R 13	1.8 bar/26 psi	1.8 bar/26 psi	2.2 bar/32 psi	2.6 bar/38 psi
1598	5.5J x 13 steel	175/65 R 13	2.1 bar/30 psi	2.1 bar/30 psi	2.2 bar/32 psi	2.6 bar/38 psi
1595	5.5J x 13 steel	175/65 R 13	2.1 bar/30 psi	2.1 bar/30 psi	2.2 bar/32 psi	2.6 bar/38 psi
1896D	5.5J x 13 steel	175/65 R 13	2.1 bar/30 psi	2.1 bar/30 psi	2.2 bar/32 psi	2.6 bar/38 psi
Corrado 89 - 96						
1781 16V	6J x 15 alloy	185/55 VR 15	2.6 bar/38 psi	2.3 bar/33 psi		
(1781 G60 Supercharged - Not covered)						
1984 8V	6J x 15 alloy	195/50 VR 15	2.4 bar/35 psi	2.1 bar/30 psi		
1984 16V	6J x 15 alloy	195/50 VR 15	2.6 bar/38 psi	2.3 bar/33 psi		
2860 V6	6.5J x 15 alloy	205/50 VR 15	2.5 bar/36 psi	2.2 bar/32 psi		

Weights and Dimensions

All weights in kg. All sizes in mm. NB Maximum load capacity = (Maximum Laden Weight) minus (Unladen Weight). Trailer weights are maximum loaded weight. * = depending on model.

Weights

MODEL	UNLADEN WEIGHT	MAXIMUM LADEN WEIGHT	UNBRAKED TRAILER	BRAKED TRAILER
Golf 1;				
1093 2-door	750	1200	400	800
1093 4-door	775	1250	400	800
1272 2-door	780	1240	400	1000
1272 4-door	805	1240	400	1000
1457 2-door	780	1250	400	1000
1457 4-door	805	1250	400	1000
1471 2-door	780	1250	400	1000
1471 4-door	805	1250	400	1000
1588 GTI 2-dr	810	1230	400	1200
1457 Diesel 2-dr	805	1250	400	800
1457 Diesel 4-dr	830	1250	400	800
1457 Auto 2-dr	805	1250	400	1000
1457 Auto 4-dr	830	1250	400	1000
1781 GTI 2-dr	840	1280	400	1200
Jetta 1;				
1093/1272	830	1260	400	800/1000
1457/1471	850	1300	400	1200
1588 injection	890	1300	400	1200

MODEL	UNLADEN WEIGHT	MAXIMUM LADEN WEIGHT	UNBRAKED TRAILER	BRAKED TRAILER
Caddy;				
Petrol	1000	1625	400	800
Diesel	1020	1625	400	800
Convertible;				
1457/1471/1588	960	1350	440	1200
1781	975	1350	500	1200
1781 injection	995	1350	460	1200
Golf 2;				
1272 2dr/4dr	845/865	1360	460	1000
1588 2dr/4dr	870/890	1400	470	1200
1781 2dr/4dr	880/900	1400	470	1200
1781 GTI 2dr/4dr	920/940	1430	490	1200
GTI 16-v 2dr/4dr	960/980	1430	510	1200
Jetta 2;				
1272 2dr/4dr	875/895	1400	460	1000
1588 2dr/4dr	900/920	1440	470	1200
1781 2dr/4dr	910/930	1440	470	1200
1781 GTI 2dr/4dr	990/1010	1470	510	1200
Golf 3/Vento				
1391 2dr/4dr	960/985	1470	500	800
1598 2dr/4dr				
1781 2dr/4dr	1020/1045	1550	500	1200
1896D 2dr/4dr	1020/1045	1525	500	850
1896TD 2dr/4dr	1055/1080	1585	500	1000
1896TDi 2dr/4dr	1085/1105	1625	500	1100
1984 2dr/4dr	1035/1060	1565	500	1200
2792V6 2dr/4dr	1155/1180	1680	600	1200
2861V6				
Polo 1/Derby				
895	685	1100	380	600
1100/1300	685	1100	380	650
Polo 2/Derby				
1043	700	1130	380	600
1100/1300	710	1130	390	650
1043 Diesel	810	1230	410	650
Polo 3/Derby				
1043	730/750*	1170	400	650
1272 Carb	750/770*	1170	410	650
1272 Inj.	775/785*	1170	410	650
1272 Diesel	800/810*	1230/1250*	410	650
Polo 4/Derby				
1043	765/780*	1230	410	650
1272 Carb	780/795*	1230	410	650
1272 Inj.	780/830*	1230/1250*	410	650
1391 Diesel	805/820*	1250	410	650
1722	780	1230	410	650
Corrado 89 - 96				
1781 16v	1100	1550	500	1200
1984 8v	1100	1550	500	1200
1984 16v	1100	1565	500	1200
2860 V6	1240	1650	600	1200

Maximum roof load - 75 kg (all models, except Caddy- 50 kg, Convertible n/a)
Maximum weight on towball, when fitted - 50 kg.

Dimensions   *depending on model

MODEL	OVERALL LENGTH	OVERALL WIDTH	WHEEL BASE	FRONT TRACK	REAR TRACK	HEIGHT (UNLADEN)
Golf 1	3815	1630	2400	1390/ 1404*	1358/ 1372*	1410/ 1395*
Golf convertible	3890	1640	2400	1404	1372	1410/ 1395*
Jetta 1	4195/ 4220*	1610/ 1630*	2398 1404*	1390/ 1372*	1358/ 1395*	1410/
Scirocco	3885	1624	2398	1390/ 1404*	1358/ 1372*	1309

MODEL	OVERALL LENGTH	OVERALL WIDTH	WHEEL BASE	FRONT TRACK	REAR TRACK	HEIGHT (UNLADEN)
Caddy	4370	1640	2625	1390	1375	1430
Golf 2	3985	1665	2475	1413/ 1427*	1408/ 1422*	1415/ 1405*
Jetta 2	4315	1665	2475	1413/ 1427*	1408/ 1422*	1415/ 1405*
Golf 3	4020	1695	2475	1450/ 1478*	1434/ 1462*	1425/ 1405*
Golf Convertible	4380	1695	2475	1450/ 1464*	1450/ 1462*	1425/ 1405*
Vento	4380	1695	2475	1450/	1448 1464*	1425
Polo 1/Derby 76-82	3605	1559	2330	1296	1312	1344
Polo 2/Derby	3655	1590	2335	1306/	1332/ 1320*	1355 1346*
Polo 3/Derby	3655	1580	2335	1306	1332	1355
Polo 3 Saloon	3975	1600	2335	1320	1346	1355
Polo 4/Derby	3765	1570	2335	1306/ 1320*	1332/ 1346*	1350/ 1375*
Polo 4 Saloon	4030	1600	2335	1320	1346	1350
Corrado 16V	4050	1676	2470	1429/1435*	1422/1428*	1320
Corrado VR6	4050	1676	2470	1430	1432	1320

Part C: Capacities

All fluid figures are given in litres.

ENGINE OIL: Multigrade, to V.W. Standard 50101, SAE 15W/50 or 20W/50
MANUAL GEARBOX AND FINAL DRIVE: Gear oil, API-GL 4, SAE 80
AUTOMATIC GEARBOX:
Gearbox - ATF Dexron
Final drive - Gear oil, API-GL5, SAE 90.
POWER ASSISTED STEERING: ATF Dexron
BRAKE FLUID: to specification FMVSS 116 DOT 4
COOLING SYSTEM: V.W. G11 antifreeze additive, to specification TL-VW 774A

FUEL TANK: Mk 1 Golf/Jetta - 40
Convertible/Scirocco(1/84-on) - 55
Mk 2 Golf/Jetta - 55
Mk 3 Golf/Vento - 55
Caddy - 60
Polo/Derby 76-82 - 36
Polo/Derby 82-90 - 42
Polo/Derby 90-94 - 42
Polo/Derby 94-00 - 45
Corrado - all models - 55

COOLANT CAPACITY INC. HEATER:
Golf 1/Scirocco/Jetta 1/Caddy (with expansion tank) - 6.5
Golf 1/Scirocco/Jetta 1/Caddy (w/out expansion tank) - 4.5
Golf 2/Jetta 2 - 6.3
Golf 3/Vento - 6.3
Polo/Derby 76-82 - 6.5
Polo/Derby 82 - on - 5.6
Polo/Derby Diesel - 6.5
Corrado - 5.5
ENGINE OIL CAPACITY - WITH (WITHOUT) FILTER CHANGE:
Golf 1/Jetta 1/Scirocco - petrol - 3.5 (3.0)
Golf 1/Jetta 1 - diesel 4.5 (4.0)

Caddy - petrol - 4.0 (3.5) - diesel 4.5 (4.0)
Golf 2/Jetta 2 1.05/1.3 litre - 3.0 (2.5)
Golf 2/Jetta 2 1.05/1.3 litre (hydraulic tappets) - 3.5 (3.0)
Golf 2/Jetta 2 1.6/1.8 litre 3.5 (3.0) to 8/85, 4.0 (3.5) 8/85-on
Golf 2/Jetta 2 diesel 4.5 (4.0)
Golf 3/Vento - petrol 6 cylinder - 6.0 (5.0)
Golf 3/Vento - All other petrol - 4.0 (3.5)
Golf 3/Vento - Diesel - 4.5 (4.0)
Polo/Derby - 3.5 (3.0)
Polo/Derby - Diesel - 5.0 (4.5)
Corrado - All models except VR6 - 4.0 (3.5)
Corrado VR6 - 5.5 (5.0)

TRANSMISSION:
Manual:
Type 020 4-speed - 1.5
Type 020 5-speed - 2.0
Type 084 - 2.2
Type 085 - 3.1
Automatic:
From dry - 6.0
Final drive - 0.75
Automatic - '95 on:
From dry - 5.3
Final drive - 0.75

STEERING GEAR:
Rack (all models) - 1kg grease
Power steering rack - 0.7 to 0.9 ATF

CV JOINT CAVITIES AND BOOTS:
All models - 90g grease

BRAKE FLUID:
Full bleed - 2.0

Part D: Service Data

All settings in mm. unless stated otherwise.

ENGINE

FIRING ORDER (Petrol models): 1-3-4-2

INJECTION ORDER (Diesel models): 1-3-4-2

DISTRIBUTOR POINTS GAP (Non-Electronic types only): 0.4

DWELL ANGLE (Non-Electronic types only): 44 to 50 degrees

IGNITION TIMING in degrees Before Top Dead Centre - BTDC:

Golf 1/Jetta 1/Scirocco/Caddy:
1093cc - 2 degrees
1093cc Formel E - 3 degrees
1272cc - 3 degrees
1471cc - 7 degrees
1457/1588cc - 4 degrees
1588cc (EG engine code) - 6 degrees
1781cc - 5 to 7 degrees

Golf 2/Jetta 2:
1272cc - 4 to 6 degrees
1595cc - 17 to19 degrees
1781cc (carb.) - 17 to 19 degrees
1781cc fuel injection - 5 to 7 degrees

Golf 3/Vento:
Ignition timing is controlled by ECU no basic settings can be quoted.

Polo 2:
All engines - 4 to 6 degrees

Polo 3:
All engines - 4.to 6 degrees

Polo 4:
999 - 5 to 7 degrees
1043i & 1296i - 4 to 6 degrees
1598i(Code AEA) - 4 to 6 degrees
1598i(Code AEE) - 5 to 7 degrees
1598i(Code AFT) - Ignition timing is controlled by ECU no basic settings can be quoted.
1598(Code 1F) - Ignition timing is controlled by ECU no basic settings can be quoted.

Corrado:
1781 Fuel Injection - 5 to 7 degrees
1984 8V Fuel Injection - 5 to 7 degrees
1984 16V Fuel Injection - 5 to 7 degrees
2891 Fuel Injection - 6 degrees

SPARK PLUG TYPES AND GAPS

Engine capacity (c.c.)	Champion	NGK	Gap (mm)
895/1093/1272	N7BYC/N7YCC		0.7/0.8
999		BUR6ET	0.7/0.9
1043 to '94	N7BYC		0.7/0.9
1043 '94 on		BUR6ET	0.7/0.9
1272 (3F code)	N6BYC		0.7/0.9
1298		BUR6ET	0.7/0.9
1390		BUR6ET	0.7/0.9
1390 (AFH code)		BKUR6ET	0.7/0.9
Engine capacity (c.c.)	Champion	NGK	Gap (mm)
1457/1471	N9YC/N9YCC		0.7/0.8
1588	N7BYC/N7YCC		0.7/0.8
1588 (EG engine code)	N6YC/N6YCC		0.7/0.8
1588 (from 9/85-on)	N9YCC		0.8
1598 (AEA & AEE code)		BUR6ET	0.7/0.9
1598 (AFT code)		BKUR5ET	0.7/0.9
1598 (1F code)		BUR5ET	0.7/0.9
1781 (not 16-valve)	N7BYC/N7YCC		0.8
1781 (16-valve)	C6BYC/C6YCC		0.8
1984 (2E engine code)	N7BMC		0.7/0.9
1984 (ADY engine code)		BUR6ET	0.7/0.9
1984 (9A engine code)		BUR6ET	0.7/0.9
1984 (2E engine code)	N7BMC		0.7/0.9
2861 (12valve)		BKRSEKU	0.7

IDLE SPEED:	RPM	CO CONTENT AT IDLE (MAX) %
Golf 1/Jetta/Scirocco/Caddy - carburettor:		
Engine code FH, FP, JB, FD, FR, FN	900-1000	2
Engine code FX	850-950	1.5
Engine code FR with Solex 2B5 carb - with Bosch K-Jetronic fuel-injection;	850-950	1.5
UK spec (with contact breaker points)	900-1000	2
UK spec (with electronic ignition)	750-850	2
US spec	850-1000	2
US spec (California) Golf 2/Jetta 2 - carburettor;	880-1000	1.2
1272cc	750-850	2.5
1588cc, engine code RF	700-800	1.5
1588cc, engine code EZ	900-1000	1.5
1781cc - with Bosch K-Jetronic fuel-injection;	900-1000	1.5
8-valve (to 9/84)	900-1000	1.5
8-valve (9/84 on)	800-1000	1.5
16-valve - with Digifant fuel-injection	900-1000	1.5
8-valve -with Digijet fuel-injection (to 7/89)	750-850	1.5
	750-850	1.1
(7/89 on)	880-980	1.5
-with Mono-Jetronic fuel injection	750-950	1.2
1984 8-valve - with Digifant fuel injection	770-870	1.2
1984 8-valve - with Simos fuel injection	830-930	0.5
1984 16-valve - with Bosch KE Motronic	800-1000	0.5
2861 12-valve - M2.9 Motronic	650-750	0.5

VALVE CLEARANCES (mm):
(Check when engine cold)

	Inlet	Exhaust
Petrol engines:		
Rocker finger type; 1093/1272cc (to 8/85)	0.10-0.15	0.20-0.25
Non-hydraulic bucket tappets; 1457/1471/1588/1781cc	0.15-0.25	0.35-0.45
Diesel engines:		
1457/1588cc	0.15-0.25	0.35-0.45
1896cc	Hydraulic tappets	

Diesel Engines

INJECTOR SETTING PRESSURE: 120-138 bar (Turbo-diesel 140-158 bar)

INJECTOR PUMP WITH NO. 1 PISTON AT TDC, COMPRESSION STROKE: Piston travel - 0.83mm

IDLE SPEED:

Bosch injection pump:

1457/1588cc (to 9/81)	800-850 rpm
1588cc (9/81-on)	920-980 rpm
1588cc Turbodiesel	920-980 rpm
1896cc	870-930 rpm
1896cc Turbodiesel	860-940 rpm

Polo

1896cc	920-960
1896cc Turbodiesel	870-930

CAV injection pump:

with hydraulic governor	760-860 rpm
with mechanical governor	920-980 rpm

MAX. FREE RUNNING ENGINE SPEED:

Bosch injection pump:

1457cc	5500-5600 rpm
1588cc	5300-5400 rpm
1588cc Turbodiesel	5050-5150 rpm
1896cc	5150-5250 rpm
1896cc Turbodiesel (to '94)	5100-5300 rpm
1896cc Turbodiesel (94 - on)	ECU Controlled

Polo:

1896cc	4950-5150 rpm
1896cc Turbodiesel	5150-5250 rpm

CAV Injection pump:

with hydraulic governor	5450-5650 rpm
with mechanical governor	5300-5400 rpm

VALVE CLEARANCES: (mm)

Check when cold:	Inlet	Exhaust
1457/1588cc	0.15-0.25	0.35-0.45
1896cc	Hydraulic tappets	

Other settings

CLUTCH ADJUSTMENT: Pedal free play: 15 to 20 mm

BRAKE DISC PAD MINIMUM THICKNESS: Front and rear (including backplate): 7mm

BRAKE SHOE FRICTION LINING MINIMUM THICKNESS: Including shoe: 5mm

Part E: Repair Data (engine sizes 895cc to 1595cc)

Dimensions in mm unless stated otherwise

Engine 'bottom end'

	895cc	999cc	1043cc	1093cc	1272cc	1298cc	1457cc	1471cc	1588cc	1588ccFI /16valve	1588cc diesel	1595cc diesel
BORE:	69.5	67.11	75.0	69.5	75.0	76.50	79.5	76.5	79.5	79.5	76.50	81.0
STROKE:	59	70.60	59.0	72.0	72.0	70.60	73.4	80.0	80.0	80.0	86.40	77.4
MAX. BORE TAPER OR OVALITY:	0.08	0.08	0.08	0.08	0.08	0.08	0.08	0.08	0.08	0.04	0.10	0.08
PISTON SIZES: Standard:	69.48	67.01	74.99	69.48	74.98	76.47	79.48	76.48	79.48	79.48	76.48	80.98
1st oversize:	69.73	67.33	75.23	69.73	75.23	76.72	79.73	76.73	79.73	79.73	76.73	81.23
2nd oversize:	69.98	67.58	75.48	69.98	75.48	76.97	79.98	76.98	79.98	79.98	76.98	81.48
PISTON CLEARANCES IN BORE: (max)	0.10	0.10	0.10	0.07	0.07	0.10	0.07	0.07	0.07	0.07	0.07	0.07

PISTON PROJECTION ABOVE BLOCK AT TOP DEAD CENTRE:
(Engine codes CR, CY, JK, 0.67-1.02 , code CK 0.43-1.02)

	895cc	999cc	1043cc	1093cc	1272cc	1298cc	1457cc	1471cc	1588cc	1588ccFI /16valve	1588cc diesel	1595cc diesel
PISTON RING CLEARANCES - RING-TO-GROOVE: (wear limit)	0.15	0.15	0.15	0.15	0.15	0.15	0.15	0.15	0.15	0.15	0.15	0.15

PISTON RING END GAP:
Compression rings: All engines 0.30-0.45
Oil scraper ring:
1-part - 0.25-0.40;
2-part - 0.25-0.45;
3-part - 0.25-0.50

CRANK MAIN JOURNAL DIAMETER:
All engines: 54.0 (standard)
Undersizes: 53.75, 53.50, 53.25

CRANK, BIG-END DIAMETER:	895cc	999cc	1043cc	1093cc	1272cc	1298cc	1457cc	1471cc	1588cc	1588ccFI /16valve	1588cc diesel	1595cc diesel
	42.00	42.00	42.00	42.00	42.00	47.80	46.00	46.00	46.00	46.00	47.80	47.80
1st undersize:	41.75	41.75	41.75	41.75	41.75	47.55	45.75	45.75	45.75	45.75	47.55	47.55

Engine 'bottom end'

	895cc	999cc	1043cc -	1093cc	1272cc	1298cc -	1457cc	1471cc -	1588cc -	1588ccFI /16valve	1588cc diesel	1595cc diesel
2nd undersize:	41.50	41.50	41.50	41.50	41.50	47.30	45.50	45.50	45.50	45.50	47.30	47.30

MAIN BEARING CLEARANCE: All engines - 0.17

BIG-END BEARING CLEARANCE:												
	0.095	0.095	0.095	0.095	0.095	0.13	0.12	0.12	0.12	0.12	0.12	0.12
CRANKSHAFT END FLOAT: (max)												
	0.20	0.20	0.20	0.20	0.20	0.26	0.37	0.37	0.37	0.37	0.37	0.37

Engine 'top end' and valve gear

INLET VALVE HEAD SIZE:												
	31.6	31.0	32.0	31.6	34.0	32.1	34.0	34.0	34.0	34.0	39.5	38.0
EXHAUST VALVE HEAD SIZE:												
	28.1	26.0	29.0	28.1	28.1	29.0	31.0	31.0	31.0	31.0	32.9	33.0

VALVE SEAT RE-CUTTING ANGLE: 45 degrees, (all types)
VALVE FACE RE-CUTTING ANGLE: 45 degrees (all types)

Cooling system

All figures in degrees Celsius unless stated otherwise.
THERMOSTAT:

Starts to open:												
	85	84	84	92	92/87*	84	87	87	87	87	87	85

*hydraulic-tappet engines

Fully open:												
	100	98	98	108	108/102*	98	102	102	102	102	102	102

Valve travel: All models - 7mm   *hydraulic-tappet engines

PRESSURE CAP RATING: (bar)
Caps with part no. suffix A: 0.9-1.15
suffixes B&C: 1.2-1.35;
suffix D: 1.2-1.5
COOLING FAN - Switches on:
Low: (All models) 93   High: (All models) 98
COOLING FAN - Switches off:
Low: (All models) 88   High: (All models) 93
WATER TIGHTNESS PRESSURE CHECK: Using tester handpump, should hold pressure of 1.0 bar

Clutch

LINING, OUTER DIAMETER (mm):
020 gearbox (4-speed): 190
020 gearbox (4+E): 200
020 gearbox (5-speed): 210
084 gearbox: 180
085 gearbox: 190

Brakes

(Thicknesses when new in brackets)
MINIMUM ALLOWED FRONT DISC THICKNESS (mm):
8 - (10)
10 - (12)
18 - (20)
MINIMUM ALLOWED REAR DISC THICKNESS - when applicable - (mm):
8 - (10)

MAXIMUM ALLOWED BRAKE DRUM INTERNAL DIAMETER - when applicable - (mm): (Diameter when new in brackets)
181 - (180)
201 - (200)

Running gear/suspension - front

CAMBER:
Golf 1/Jetta 1/Scirocco/Caddy (in straight ahead position): +20' ± 30, except 1.8 fuel-injection engine: + 20' ± 20'
Golf 2/Jetta 2 (in straight ahead position): -30' ± 20, except Golf GTI and Jetta GT: -35' ± 20'
FRONT CASTER ANGLE (not adjustable): 1 degree 50' ± 30'
TOE ANGLE (not adjustable): (at 20 degree lock to left and right) -1 deg 30' ± 30'

Rear suspension

CAMBER (not adjustable):
Golf 1/Jetta 1/Scirocco: -1deg 15' ± 35, except 1.8 fuel-injection engine: -1deg 15' ± 25'
Golf 2/Jetta 2: -1deg 40' ± 20'
TOE-IN (not adjustable):
Golf 1/Jetta 1/Scirocco: 20' ± 20'
Golf 2/Jetta 2: 25' ± 15'

Part E: Repair Data
(engine sizes 1781cc to 2861cc)

Dimensions in mm unless stated otherwise

Engine 'bottom end'

	1781cc diesel	1781ccFI	1896cc diesel	1896cc t/diesel	1984cc	2792cc	2861cc
BORE:	81.0	81.0	79.50	79.50	82.50	81.0	82.0
STROKE:	86.4	86.4	95.50	95.50	92.80	90.30	90.30
MAX. BORE TAPER OR OVALITY:	0.08	0.08	0.10	0.10	0.04	0.04	0.04
PISTON SIZES: Standard:	80.98	80.98	79.47	79.47	82.49	80.99	80.99
1st oversize:	81.23	81.23	79.92	79.92	82.73	81.49	81.49
2nd oversize:	81.48	81.48	79.97	79.97	82.98	81.99	81.99
PISTON CLEARANCES IN BORE: (max)	0.07	0.07	0.15	0.15	0.05	0.05	0.05

PISTON PROJECTION ABOVE BLOCK AT TOP DEAD CENTRE:
(Engine codes CR, CY, JK, 0.67-1.02 , code CK: 0.43-1.02)

PISTON RING CLEARANCES - RING-TO-GROOVE: (wear limit)

	1781cc diesel	1781ccFI	1896cc diesel	1896cc t/diesel	1984cc	2792cc	2861cc
	0.15	0.15	0.15	0.15	0.15	0.15	0.15

PISTON RING END GAP:
Compression rings: All engines 0.30-0.45
Oil scraper ring:
1-part - 0.25-0.40;
2-part - 0.25-0.45;
3-part - 0.25-0.50

CRANK MAIN JOURNAL DIAMETER:
All engines: 54.0 (standard)   Undersizes: 53.75, 53.50, 53.25

	1781cc diesel	1781ccFI	1896cc diesel	1896cc t/diesel	1984cc	2792cc	2861cc
CRANK, BIG-END DIAMETER:	47.80	47.80	47.80	47.80	47.80		
1st undersize:	47.55	47.55	47.55	47.55	47.55		
2nd undersize:	47.30	47.30	47.30	47.30	47.30		

MAIN BEARING CLEARANCE: All engines - 0.17

	1781cc diesel	1781ccFI	1896cc diesel	1896cc t/diesel	1984cc	2792cc	2861cc
BIG-END BEARING CLEARANCE:	0.095	0.095	0.12	0.12	0.12		
CRANKSHAFT END FLOAT: (max)	0.37	0.25	0.37	0.37	0.25	0.25	0.25

Note: On petrol engines with Aluminium blocks the crankshaft must **not** be removed. If crankshaft main bearing wear is suspected, the crankshaft and cylinder block must be renewed complete. There is no data from the manuafacturers for these engines.

Engine 'top end' and valve gear

	1781cc diesel	1781ccFI	1896cc diesel	1896cc t/diesel	1984cc	2792cc	2861cc
INLET VALVE HEAD SIZE:	38.0	38.0-32.0	36.0	36.0	39.5	39.0	39.0
EXHAUST VALVE HEAD SIZE:	28.1	28.1	31.5	31.5	33.0	34.20	34.20

VALVE SEAT RE-CUTTING ANGLE: 45 degrees, (all types)
VALVE FACE RE-CUTTING ANGLE: 45 degrees, (all types)

Cooling system

All figures in degrees Celsius unless stated otherwise.

THERMOSTAT:	1781cc diesel	1781ccFI	1896cc diesel	1896cc t/diesel	1984cc	2792cc	2861cc
Starts to open:	92	92/87*	87	87	87	80	80
Fully open:	108	108/102*	102	102	105	105	105

*hydraulic-tappet engines

Valve travel: All models - 7mm
PRESSURE CAP RATING: (bar)
Caps with part no. suffix A: 0.9-1.15
suffixes B&C: 1.2-1.35;
suffix D: 1.2-1.5
COOLING FAN - Switches on:
Low: (All models) 93   High: (All models) 98
COOLING FAN - Switches off:
Low: (All models) 88   High: (All models) 93
WATER TIGHTNESS PRESSURE CHECK: Using tester handpump, should hold pressure of 1.0 bar

Clutch

LINING, OUTER DIAMETER , mm:
020 gearbox (4-speed): 190
020 gearbox (4+E): 200
020 gearbox (5-speed): 210
084 gearbox: 180
085 gearbox: 190

Brakes

MINIMUM ALLOWED FRONT DISC THICKNESS (mm):
(Thickness when new in brackets)
(10) - 8
(12) - 109
(20) - 18
MINIMUM ALLOWED REAR DISC THICKNESS
- when applicable - (mm):
(10) - 8
MAXIMUM ALLOWED BRAKE DRUM INTERNAL DIAMETER -
when applicable - (mm): (Diameter when new in brackets)
(180) - 181
(200) - 201

Running gear/suspension - front

CAMBER:
Golf 1/Jetta 1/Scirocco/Caddy (in straight ahead position):
+20' ± 30' - except 1.8 fuel-injection engine + 20' ± 20'
Golf 2/Jetta 2 (in straight ahead position):

-30' ± 20' - except Golf GTI and Jetta GT -35' ± 20'
Golf 3/Vento (2ltr Models) GT -40' ± 20'   L,CL & GL -36' ± 20'
All other models: GT   -36' ± 20'   L,CL&GL -30' ± 20'
Polo/Derby 76 - 82 20' ± 30'
Polo/Derby 82 - 90 20' ± 30'
Polo/Derby 90 - 94 20' ± 30'
Polo/Derby 94 - 98 -25' ± 20'
Corrado up to 3/90(in staight ahead position) -40' ± 20'
Corrado from 4/90 (instraight ahead position) -1 deg 20' ± 20'
FRONT CASTER ANGLE (not adjustable): 1 degree 50' ± 30'
Polo/Derby 76 - 82 (not adjustable) 1 degree 50' to 2 degree 50'
Polo/Derby 82 - 94 2 degree 20' ± 30'
Polo/Derby 94 - 98 1 degree 20' ± 30'
Corrado VR6 +3 deg 25' ± 30'
TOE ANGLE (not adjustable):(at 20 degree lock to left and right) -1 deg 30' ± 30'

Rear suspension

CAMBER (not adjustable):
Golf 1/Jetta 1/Scirocco: -1deg 15' ± 35'
- except 1.8 fuel-injection engine -1deg 15' ± 25'
Golf 2/Jetta 2: -1deg 40' ± 20'
Golf 3/Vento -1 deg 30' ± 10'
Polo/Derby 76 - 82 ?
Polo/Derby 82 - 90 -1 deg 40' ± 20'
Polo/Derby 90 - 94 -1 deg 30' ± 10'
Polo/Derby 94 - 98 -1 deg 40' ± 20'
Corrado up to 3/90 -1 deg 40' ± 20'
Corrado from 4/90 - 1 deg 30' ± 10'
TOE-IN (not adjustable):
Golf 1/Jetta 1/Scirocco: 20' ± 20'
Golf 2/Jetta 2: 25' ± 15'
Golf 3/Vento 20' ± 10'
Polo/Derby 76 - 82 ?
Polo/Derby 82 - 90 25' ± 15'
Polo/Derby 90 - 94 20' ± 10'
Polo/Derby 94 - 98 20' ± 10'

Part F: Torque Wrench Settings

Key to engine types and sizes:

Golf 1, Jetta 1, Scirocco
A: 1093 & 1272cc
B: 1457, 1471, 1588cc
C: 1588 & 1781 Fuel injection
Diesel engines
D: 1471 & 1588
Caddy
E: All engines
Golf 2, Jetta 2
F: 1595, 1781cc except 16-valve
G: 1781cc 16-valve
Golf 3, Vento
H: 1598cc & 1396cc
I: 1781cc
J: 1984cc

Diesel Engines
K: 1896cc
Polo/Derby 1
A: 895, 1093 & 1272cc
Polo 2
L: 1043cc
Polo 3
A: 1272cc
L: 1043cc
Polo 4
H: 1598cc
M: 999cc, 1043cc, 1296cc & 1390cc
Diesel Engines
N: 1716 & 1896cc

Corrado 89-92
G: 1781cc 16V
Corrado 93-96
J: 1984cc 8V
Corrado 92-96
O: 1984cc 16V DOHC
Corrado VR6
P: 2793cc & 2861cc

ENGINE

ENGINE	ENGINE TYPES																Torque (Nm)
	A	B	C	D	E	F	G	H	I	J	K	L	M	N	O	P	
Main bearing cap, bolt	●	●	●	●	●	●	●	●	●	●	●	●	●	●	●	●	65
Connecting rod, fixing nut	●						●	●	●	●	●	●			●	●	30+1/4 turn
Connecting rod, fixing nut		●	●	●	●	●						●					45
Camshaft bearing cap, fixing bolt	●	●	●	●	●			●	●	●			●			●	20
Camshaft bearing cap, fixing bolt							●						●		●		15
Camshaft bearing cap, fixing bolt												●					6+1/4 turn
Camshaft sprocket, fixing bolt	●	●	●		●	●		●	●	●		●				●	80
Camshaft sprocket, fixing bolt													●				20 + 1/4 turn
Camshaft sprocket, fixing bolt				●							●			●			45
Camshaft sprocket, fixing bolt							●								●		65
Camshaft cover, fixing nut	●	●	●	●	●	●	●	●	●	●	●	●	●	●	●		10
Ball-head screw (valve clearance adjustment)	●																90
Toothed belt guard, (rear), fixing bolt	●	●	●	●	●	●	●	●	●	●	●	●		●	●		10
Crankshaft toothed belt sprocket, fixing bolt (M12x1.5)		●	●	●	●	●	●	●	●	●	●	●	●	●	●		80
Crankshaft toothed belt sprocket, fixing bolt (M14x1.5)		●									●				●		180
Crankshaft toothed belt sprocket, fixing bolt													●	●			90 + 1/3 turn
V-belt pulley, fixing bolt	●						●	●	●	●	●						80
V-belt pulley, fixing bolt		●	●	●	●	●	●	●	●	●	●				●		20
Vibration damper, fixing bolt			●	●	●						●				●		20
Toothed belt tensioning roller, securing nut		●	●	●	●	●	●	●	●				●	●	●		45
Toothed belt cover, upper, fixing bolt/nut	●	●	●	●	●	●	●	●	●	●	●	●	●	●	●		10
Water pump to crankcase, fixing bolt	●	●	●	●	●	●	●	●			●	●	●	●	●	●	10
Water pump drive pulley, fixing bolt	●	●	●	●	●	●	●	●			●	●	●	●	●	●	20
Water temperature thermostatic switch	●	●	●	●	●	●	●	●	●	●	●	●			●		25
Radiator cooling fan, thermostatic switch													●	●		●	35
Water temp. gauge sender unit	●	●	●	●	●	●	●	●	●	●	●	●			●	●	10
Oil pressure switch													●			●	20
Oil pressure switch	●	●	●	●	●	●	●	●	●	●	●	●			●	●	25
Oil pump to crankcase, fixing bolt (short/long)		●	●	●	●	●	●	●	●	●	●	●			●	●	10/20
Oil pump to crankcase, fixing bolt	●																10
Oil sump to crankcase, fixing bolt (hexagon head)	●	●	●	●	●	●	●	●	●	●	●	●			●	●	20
Oil sump to crankcase, fixing bolt (hexagon socket)	●	●	●	●	●	●	●	●	●	●	●	●			●		8
Oil sump drain plug	●	●	●	●	●	●	●	●	●	●	●	●	●	●	●	●	30
Oil filter mounting bracket, fixing bolt	●	●	●	●	●	●	●	●	●	●	●	●		●	●	●	25
Oil pick-up pipe to oil pump, fixing bolt	●	●	●	●	●	●	●	●	●	●	●	●			●	●	10
Oil cooler retaining nut														●		●	25
Pressure pipe, union, (oil cooler to filter housing)			●														50
Water pump to crankcase, fixing bolt		●	●	●	●	●	●	●	●	●	●	●			●	●	20
Alternator mounting bolts	●	●	●	●	●	●	●	●	●	●	●	●		●	●		25
Fuel pump to cylinder head, fixing bolt (carb engines)	●	●			●	●					●						20
Crankcase front cover, fixing bolt	●	●	●	●	●	●	●	●	●	●	●	●			●		20
Crankcase rear cover, fixing bolt	●	●	●	●	●	●	●	●	●	●	●	●			●		20
Crankshaft sealing flange, front fixing bolt	●	●	●	●	●	●	●	●	●	●	●	●			●		25
Distributor clamp, fixing bolt	●	●	●	●	●	●	●	●	●	●	●		●	●	●		20
Thermostat housing, fixing bolt													●	●			10
Thermostat housing, fixing bolt	●	●	●	●	●	●	●	●	●	●	●	●			●		20
Spark plugs, petrol models	●	●	●		●	●		●	●	●		●	●		●	●	20
Injectors				●							●						70
Glow plugs														●			15
Glow plugs				●							●						25
Glow plugs (engine AEF)														●			25
Injection pipes				●							●			●			25
Flywheel, fixing bolt	●	●	●	●	●	●	●	●	●	●	●	●			●		75
Lambda probe (catalyst-equipped cars)				●	●	●	●					●		●	●	●	50
Cylinder head bolts (engine cold) (M10 bolts):																	
Stage 1	●																40
Stage 2	●																55
Stage 3	●																65
Stage 4	●																+ 1/4 further turn
Cylinder head bolts (M11 bolts):																	
Stage 1	●															●	40
Stage 2	●															●	60
Stage 3	●															●	+ 1/2 further turn
Stage 4	●															●	+ 1/2 further turn

	ENGINE TYPES																
	A	B	C	D	E	F	G	H	I	J	K	L	M	N	O	P	Torque (Nm)
Cylinder head bolts:																	
Stage 1		●	●	●	●	●	●	●	●	●	●	●					40
Stage 2		●	●	●	●	●	●	●	●	●	●	●					60
Stage 3		●	●	●	●	●	●	●	●	●	●	●					+ ½ further turn
Cylinder head bolts (Aluminium Block 999cc)																	
Stage 1													●				30
Stage 2													●				+ ¼ turn
Stage 3													●				+ ¼ turn
Cylinder head bolts (Cast iron block not 999cc)																	
Stage 1													●	●		●	40
Stage 2													●	●		●	60
Stage 3													●	●		●	1/2 turn
EXHAUST	A	B	C	D	E	F	G	H	I	J	K	L	M	N	O	P	Torque (Nm)
Exhaust system joint clamp, fixing bolt	●	●	●	●	●	●	●	●	●	●	●	●	●	●	●	●	25
Downpipe to exhaust manifold, fixing nut, single pipe	●								●								20
Downpipe to exhaust manifold, fixing nut, twin pipe	●																30
Downpipe to exhaust manifold, fixing nut (M8)		●	●	●	●	●	●					●					25
Downpipe to exhaust manifold, fixing nut (M10)		●	●	●	●	●							●	●	●	●	40
CLUTCH	A	B	C	D	E	F	G	H	I	J	K	L	M	N	O	P	Torque (Nm)
Drive plate to crankshaft, fixing bolt	●							●	●	●		●	●	●	●		60
Drive plate to crankshaft, fixing bolt			●		●	●	●					●					100
Drive plate to crankshaft, fixing bolt		●															30 + ¼ turn
Flywheel to crankshaft	●							●	●	●	●	●	●	●	●	●	60 + ¼ turn
Flywheel to driven plate, fixing bolt		●	●	●	●	●	●										20
Flywheel to pressure plate (Diesel engine with two part flywheel)													●				13
Flywheel to presure plate													●	●		●	20
Flywheel to pressure plate, fixing bolt	●							●	●	●	●						25
FRONT SUSPENSION	A	B	C	D	E	F	G	H	I	J	K	L	M	N	O	P	Torque (Nm)
Road wheel, fixing stud	●	●	●	●	●	●	●	●	●	●	●	●	●	●	●	●	110
Wheel bearing housing to suspension strut, fixing bolt	●	●	●	●									●	●			upper - 80, lower - 60
Wheel bearing housing, fixing locknut					●	●	●	●	●	●	●				●	●	19mm - 80, 18mm - 95
Tie rod end to wheel bearing housing, locknut	●	●	●	●	●	●	●	●	●	●	●	●			●		30
Lower ball joint to control arm, fixing bolt	●	●	●	●	●	●	●	●	●	●	●	●			●		35
Front wishbone to body clamp fixing, with bonded rubber bush, fixing nut and bolt	●	●	●	●												●	65
Shock absorber top nut													●	●			60
Shock absorber bearing to body, fixing nut	●	●						●	●								20
Anti-roll bar bush, clamp, fixing nut	●	●	●		●	●	●	●	●	●	●	●				●	25
Wishbone to body mounting, fixing bolt	●	●	●		●	●	●	●	●	●	●	●			●	●	100
Strut to swivel hub mounting(nut/bolt)													●	●			95
Rear control arm bush, fixing nut						●	●								●		25
Control arm to crossmember, fixing bolt						●	●								●	●	130
Front wheel hub, fixing nut	●	●	●		●												230
Front wheel hub, fixing nut							●	●							●	●	265
Front wheel hub, fixing nut									●	●	●						90 + ⅛ turn
Suspension strut to top bearing, self-locking nut	●	●	●		●	●	●	●	●	●	●	●			●	●	60

*Data for diesel models as for equivalent petrol-engined version

GEARBOX AND DIFFERENTIAL

Type 084, 4-speed	Torque (Nm)
Oil filler plug	25
Magnetic drain plug	25
Bearing cover, fixing bolt	35
Bolt for relay lever	35
Drive flange, fixing bolt	25
Gearbox to engine, fixing bolt	55
Driveshaft to drive flange, fixing bolt	45
Reversing light, switch	30
Shift rod clamp, pinch bolt	20

Type 020, 4-speed	Torque (Nm)
Oil filler plug	25
Reversing light switch	30
Bearing cover plate, fixing bolt	40
Gearbox end cover, fixing bolt	15
Locking screw for selector shaft	20
Reverse shaft securing screw	20
Driveshaft to drive flange, fixing bolt	45
Gearbox to clutch housing, fixing bolt	25

Type 020, 5-speed	Torque (Nm)
Gearbox housing cover, fixing screw	25
Gearbox housing to differential, fixing screw	25
Selector shaft end cap	50
Oil filler & drain plugs	25
Relay lever bracket, fixing screw	25
Reversing light, switch	30
Driveshaft to drive flange, fixing bolt	45

Automatic gearbox	
Drive shaft to drive flange, fixing bolt	45
Converter to drive plate, fixing bolt	30
Gearbox to engine, fixing bolt	55
Bonded rubber bush to body, fixing bolt	40
Bonded rubber bush to gearbox, fixing bolt	55
Selector lever, cable clamp	8
Gearbox to final drive, fixing bolt	30
Side cover plate, fixing bolt	30

REAR SUSPENSION

	A	B	C	D	E	F	G	H	I	J	K	L	M	N	O	P	Torque (Nm)
Bushed axle mounting to body, fixing nut	•	•	•														45
Rear axle to body, fixing bolt				•		•	•								•	•	70
Anti-roll bar to axle, clamp, fixing bolt	•	•	•	•		•	•							•			30
Lower shock absorber to rear axle, fixing bolt	•	•	•	•													45
Lower shock absorber to rear axle, fixing bolt						•	•								•	•	70
Leaf spring, rear fixing bolt				•													65
Leaf spring, front fixing bolt				•													95
Damper, fixing bolt				•													40
Upper shock absorber to rubber bush, fixing nut	•	•	•														35
Upper shock absorber to rubber bush, fixing nut						•	•								•	•	25
Pivot bolts								•	•	•	•				•	•	80
Pivot bolts													•	•			65
Mounting bracket retaining bolt								•	•	•	•				•	•	70
Stub axle/backplate retaining bolts								•	•	•	•				•	•	60
Suspension strut:																	
Upper mounting Bottom Nut								•	•	•	•				•	•	15
Upper mounting Top Nut								•	•	•	•				•	•	25
Lower mounting bolt								•	•	•	•				•	•	70
Spring retaining plate								•	•	•	•				•	•	15
Shock absorber top nuts													•	•			15
Strut lower mounting nut													•	•			55
Strut upper mounting nut													•	•			25

STEERING

	A	B	C	D	E	F	G	H	I	J	K	L	M	N	O	P	Torque (Nm)
Steering wheel to column, fixing nut	•	•	•	•	•			•	•	•	•		•	•			50
Steering wheel to column, fixing nut						•	•					•			•	•	40
Steering column tube, fixing screw	•	•	•	•	•	•	•					•			•	•	20
Steering ball-joint to tie rod, locknut	•	•	•	•	•	•	•	•	•	•	•						50
Steering ball joint to tie rod, locknut												•	•	•			35
Steering gear to body mounting, fixing locknut	•	•	•	•	•	•	•		•				•	•			30
Power steering (when fitted) pump to engine, fixing bolt																	25
Steering column universal joint, pinchbolt	•	•	•	•	•	•	•	•	•	•	•	•	•	•	•	•	30
Power steering (when fitted) pressure pipe unions																	20

BRAKING SYSTEM

	A	B	C	D	E	F	G	H	I	J	K	L	M	N	O	P	Torque (Nm)
Wheel cylinder to brake backplate (where fitted), bolt	•	•	•	•	•	•	•	•	•	•	•	•	•	•	•	•	10
Brake master cylinder to servo, fixing nut	•	•	•	•	•	•	•	•	•	•	•	•	•	•	•	•	20
Brake carrier (rear discs) where fitted, fixing bolt	•	•	•	•	•	•	•								•	•	65
Brake backplate to stub axle & axle beam, fixing bolt	•	•	•	•	•	•	•								•	•	60
ABS retaining bolts (where fitted)													•	•	•	•	10
Brake and clutch pedal to bodywork, fixing nut						•	•	•	•	•	•	•			•	•	20
Brake and clutch pedal to bodywork, fixing nut													•	•			25
Brake servo, fixing nut						•	•	•	•	•	•	•			•	•	20
Front caliper guide bolts	•	•	•	•	•			•	•	•	•	•					40
Front caliper, self-locking bolts						•	•	•	•	•	•	•			•	•	35
Front caliper mounting bolts													•	•			25

COOLING SYSTEM

	A	B	C	D	E	F	G	H	I	J	K	L	M	N	O	P	Torque (Nm)
Radiator securing bolts	•	•	•	•	•	•	•						•	•	•	•	10
Cooling fan motor to radiator cowl, fixing nuts	•	•	•	•	•	•	•					•	•	•	•	•	10

SEATBELTS

	A	B	C	D	E	F	G	H	I	J	K	L	M	N	O	P	Torque (nm)
Anchorage point, fixing bolt	•	•	•	•	•	•	•	•	•	•	•	•	•	•	•	•	40
Seat frame anchorage point, fixing bolt	•	•	•	•	•	•	•	•	•	•	•	•	•	•	•	•	50

Part G: Identification Numbers

The Identification Plate

G1: Golf MARK I MODELS Polo Mk 1, 2 & 3: The plate is on the right of the front lock carrier plate (**1A**) near the bonnet lock.

Golf MARK II MODELS: The plate is in the engine compartment, on the right-hand side panel (**1B**) or, on the same side but in the plenum chamber (**1C**).

Polo Mk4: The plate is on the engine compartment bulkhead or on the bonnet lock carrier.

Engine Numbers

The engine number will be found in one of two locations:

ENGINES UP TO 1.3 LITRES: The number is below the distributor on the left-hand end of the block (**2**).On some models after 1980 the number is stamped on the flat surface of the cylinder head instead of below the distributor.

ALL LARGER ENGINES: The number is on the front of the block, just beneath the joint between the block and the cylinder head. On diesel engines the number will be found on the front of the cylinder block next to the injection pump.

Vehicle Identification Number (Chassis Number)

This is stamped on the rear panel of the engine compartment - see illustration **G1**, position 3.

Vehicle Data Sticker

On all models, the sticker is on the left of the rear panel in the luggage compartment. The sticker contains the following information:

G2: EARLIER MODELS:

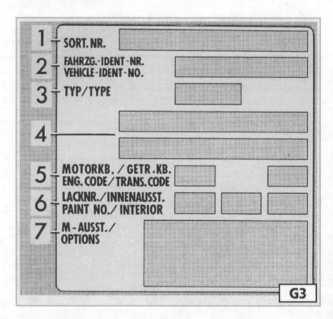

1 Chassis Number
2 Model code number
3 Engine and gearbox code letters
4 Paint number/interior trim code
5 Optional extra numbers

G3: LATER MODELS:

1 Production control number
2 Vehicle Identification Number
3 Model code number
4 Model explanation
5 Engine and gearbox code letters
6 Paint number/interior trim code
7 Optional extra numbers

CHAPTER 2: SAFETY FIRST!

Please read this chapter before carrying out any work on your car.

You must always ensure that safety is the first consideration in any job you carry out. A slight lack of concentration, or a rush to finish the job quickly can easily result in an accident, as can failure to follow the precautions outlined in this manual.

Be sure to consult the suppliers of any materials and equipment you may use, and to obtain and read carefully any operating and health and safety instructions that may be available on packaging or from manufacturers and suppliers.

GENERAL

RAISING THE VEHICLE SAFELY

• ALWAYS ensure that the vehicle is properly supported when raised off the ground. Don't work on, around, or underneath a raised vehicle unless axle stands or hoist lifting pads are positioned under secure, load bearing underbody areas. If the vehicle is driven onto ramps, the wheels remaining on the ground must be securely chocked to prevent movement.

• NEVER work on a vehicle supported on a jack. Jacks are made for lifting the vehicle only, not for holding it off the ground while it is being worked on.

❒ **1**: ALWAYS ensure that the safe working load rating of any jack, hoist or lifting gear used is sufficient for the job, and that lifting gear is used only as recommended by the manufacturer.

• NEVER attempt to loosen or tighten nuts that require a lot of force

to turn (e.g. a tight oil drain plug) with the vehicle raised, unless it is safely supported. Take care not to pull the vehicle off its supports when applying force to any part of the vehicle. Wherever possible, initially slacken tight fastenings before raising the vehicle off the ground.

• ALWAYS wear eye protection when working under the vehicle and when using power tools.

• Follow the instructions in *Chapter 4* entitled *Using a Trolley Jack*.

WORKING ON THE VEHICLE

• ALWAYS seek specialist advice from a qualified technician unless you are justifiably confident about your ability to carry out each job. Vehicle safety affects you, your passengers and other road users.

❒ **2**: DON'T lean over, or work on, a running engine unless it is strictly necessary, and keep long hair and loose clothing well out of the way of moving mechanical parts.

• Note that it is theoretically possible for fluorescent striplighting to make an engine fan appear to be stationary - double check whether it is spinning or not! This is the sort of error that happens when you're really tired and not thinking straight. So...

• ...DON'T work on a vehicle when you're over tired.

• ALWAYS work in a well ventilated area and don't inhale dust - it may contain asbestos or other harmful substances.

• NEVER run an engine indoors, in a confined space or over a pit.

• REMOVE your wrist watch, rings and all other jewellery before doing any work on the vehicle - and especially when working on the electrical system.

• DON'T remove the radiator or expansion tank filler cap or other openings when the cooling system is hot, or you may get scalded by escaping coolant or steam. Let the system cool down first and even then, if the engine is not completely cold, cover the cap with a cloth and gradually release the pressure.

• NEVER drain oil, coolant or automatic transmission fluid when the engine is hot. Allow time for it to cool sufficiently to avoid scalding you.

• ALWAYS keep antifreeze, brake and clutch fluid away from vehicle paintwork. Wash off any spills immediately.

• TAKE CARE to avoid touching any engine or exhaust system component unless it is cool enough not to burn you.

RUNNING THE VEHICLE

• NEVER start the engine unless the gearbox is in neutral (or 'Park' in the case of automatic transmission) and the parking brake is fully applied.

• NEVER run a vehicle fitted with a catalytic converter without the exhaust system heat shields in place.

• TAKE CARE when parking vehicles fitted with catalytic converters. The 'cat' reaches extremely high temperatures and any combustible materials under the car, such as long dry grass, could be ignited.

PERSONAL SAFETY

• NEVER siphon fuel, antifreeze, brake fluid or other potentially harmful liquids by mouth, or allow contact with your skin. Use a suitable hand pump and wear gloves.

• BEFORE undertaking dirty jobs, use barrier cream on your hands as a protection against infection. Preferably, wear suitable gloves.

• WEAR IMPERVIOUS GLOVES - disposable types are ideal - when there is a risk of used engine oil or any other harmful substance coming into contact with your skin.

❒ 3: Wurth produce a huge range of workshop products, including the safety-related items shown here.

• WIPE UP any spilt oil, grease or water off the floor immediately.

• MAKE SURE that spanners/wrenches and all other tools are the right size for the job and are not likely to slip. Never try to 'double-up' spanners to gain more leverage.

• SEEK HELP if you need to lift something heavy which may be beyond your capability. Don't forget that when lifting a heavy weight, you should keep your back vertical and straight and bend your knees to avoid injuring your back.

• NEVER take risky short-cuts or rush to finish a job. Plan ahead and allow plenty of time.

• BE METICULOUS and keep the work area tidy - you'll avoid frustration, work better and lose less.

• KEEP children and animals well away from the work area and from unattended vehicles.

• ALWAYS tell someone what you're doing and have them regularly check that all is well, especially when working alone on, or under, the vehicle.

HAZARDS

FIRE!

• Petrol (gasoline) is a dangerous and highly flammable liquid requiring special precautions. When working on the fuel system, disconnect the vehicle battery earth (ground) terminal whenever possible and always work outside, or in a very well ventilated area. Any form of spark, such as that caused by an electrical fault, by two metal surfaces striking against each other, by a central heating boiler in the garage 'firing up', or even by static electricity built up in your clothing can, in a confined space, ignite petrol vapour causing an explosion. Take great care not to spill petrol on to the engine or exhaust system, never allow any naked flame anywhere near the work area and don't smoke.

❒ 4: There are several types of fire extinguisher. Take advice from your accredited supplier to make sure that you have the right type for workshop use. Note that water fire extinguishers are not suitable for workshop or automotive use.

PRESSURE

• DON'T disconnect any pipes on a fuel injected engine or on an ABS braking system without releasing residual pressure. The fuel or brake fluid may be under very high pressure - sufficient to cause serious injury. Remember that many systems retain high pressure for sometime after last use. If necessary seek specialist advice.

FUMES

• Vapour which is given off by petrol (gasoline) and many solvents, thinners, and adhesives is potentially very harmful and under certain conditions can lead to unconsciousness or even death, if inhaled. The risks are increased if such fluids are used in a confined space so always ensure adequate ventilation. Always read the supplier's instructions and follow them with care.

• Never drain petrol (gasoline) or use solvents, thinners, adhesives or other toxic substances in an inspection pit. It is also dangerous to park a vehicle for any length of time over an inspection pit. The fumes from even a slight fuel leak can cause an explosion when the engine is started.

MAINS ELECTRICITY

❐ 5: Avoid the use of mains electricity when working on the vehicle, whenever possible. Use rechargeable tools and a DC inspection lamp, powered from a remote 12V battery - both are much safer. However, if you do use mains-powered equipment, ensure that the appliance is connected correctly to its plug, that where necessary it is properly earthed (grounded), and that the fuse is of the correct rating for the appliance. Do not use any mains powered equipment in damp conditions or in the vicinity of fuel, fuel vapour or the vehicle battery. Always use an RCD (Residual Current Device) circuit breaker with mains electricity. Then, if there is a short, the RCD circuit breaker minimises the risk of electrocution by instantly cutting the power supply.

IGNITION SYSTEM

• Never work on the ignition system with the ignition switched on, or with the engine being turned over on the starter, or with the engine running.

❐ 6: Touching certain parts of the ignition system, such as the HT leads, distributor cap, ignition coil etc., can result in a severe electric shock or physical injury as a hand is pulled sharply away. Voltages produced by electronic ignition systems are sometimes very high indeed and could prove fatal, particularly to people with cardiac pacemaker implants. Consult your vehicle's handbook or main dealer if in any doubt.

COOLING FAN

• On many vehicles, the electric cooling fan can switch itself on even with the ignition turned off. This is especially likely after driving the vehicle immediately before turning off, after which heat rises to the top of the engine and turns the fan on, suddenly and without warning. If you intend working in the engine bay, it's best to do so when the engine is cold, to disconnect the battery, or keep away from the fan, if neither of these are possible.

BATTERY

• Never cause a spark, smoke, or allow a naked light near the vehicle's battery, even in a well ventilated area. Highly explosive hydrogen gas is given off as part of the charging process.

• Battery terminals should be shielded, since a spark can be caused by any metal object touching the battery's terminals or connecting straps.

• IMPORTANT NOTE: Before disconnecting the battery earth (ground) terminal read the relevant information in **Chapter 10** regarding saving computer and radio settings. When using a battery charger, switch off the power supply before the battery charger leads are connected or disconnected. If the battery is not of the 'sealed-for-life' type, loosen the filler plugs or remove the cover before charging. For best results the battery should be given a low rate trickle charge. Do not charge at an excessive rate or the battery may burst. Always wear gloves and goggles when carrying or when topping up the battery. Acid electrolyte is extremely corrosive and must not be allowed to contact the eyes, skin or clothes. If it does, wash with copious amounts of water. Seek medical advice if necessary

BRAKES AND ASBESTOS

• Obviously, a vehicle's brakes are among its most important safety related items. ONLY work on your vehicle's braking system if you are trained and competent to do so. If you have not been trained in this work, but wish to carry out the jobs described in this manual, we strongly recommend that you have a garage or qualified mechanic check your work before using the vehicle.

• Whenever you work on the braking system: i) wear an efficient particle mask; ii) wipe off all brake dust from the brakes after spraying on a proprietary brand of brake cleaner (never blow dust off with compressed air); iii) dispose of brake dust and discarded shoes or pads in a sealed plastic bag; iv) wash your hands thoroughly after you have finished working on the brakes and certainly before you eat or smoke; v) replace shoes and pads only with asbestos-free shoes or pads. Note that asbestos brake dust can cause cancer if inhaled; vi) always replace brake pads and/or shoes in complete 'axle' sets - never replace them on one wheel only.

BRAKE FLUID

• Brake fluid absorbs moisture rapidly from the air and this can cause brake failure. Never use a previously opened container of brake fluid.

ENGINE OIL

• Always wear disposable plastic or rubber gloves when draining the oil from your engine. i) Note that the drain plug and the oil are often hotter than you expect. ii) There are very real health hazards associated with used engine oil. Use barrier cream on your hands and try not to get oil on them. Always wear impermeable gloves and wash hands with hand cleaner soon after carrying out the work. Keep oil out of the reach of children; iii) NEVER, EVER dispose of old engine oil into the ground or down a drain.

PLASTIC MATERIALS

• Be aware of dangers in the form of poisonous fumes, skin irritants, and the risk of fire and explosion. Do not allow resin or 2-pack filler or adhesive hardener to come into contact with skin or eyes. Read carefully the safety notes supplied on the can, tube or packaging.

FLUOROELASTOMERS

• Fluoroelastomers are commonly used for oil seals, wiring and cabling, bearing surfaces, gaskets, diaphragms, hoses and 'O' rings. If they are subjected to temperatures greater than 315 degrees Celcius, they will decompose and can be potentially hazardous. Some decomposition may occur when a car has been in a fire or has been dismantled with the assistance of a cutting torch.

• According to the Health and Safety Executive, "Skin contact with this liquid or decomposition residues can cause painful and penetrating burns. Permanent irreversible skin and tissue damage can occur". Damage can also be caused to eyes or by the inhalation of fumes created as fluoroelastomers are burned or heated.

• After a vehicle has been exposed to fire or high temperatures:

1. Do not touch blackened or charred seals or equipment.

2. Preferably, don't handle parts containing decomposed fluoroelastomers, but if you must do so, wear goggles and PVC (polyvinyl chloride) or neoprene protective gloves while doing so. Never handle such parts unless they are completely cool.

3. Contaminated parts, residues, materials and clothing, including protective clothing and gloves, should be disposed of by an approved contractor to currently applicable national or local regulations. Oil seals, gaskets and 'O' rings, along with contaminated material, must not be burned.

WORKSHOP

• Always have a fire extinguisher of the correct type at arm's length when working on anything flammable. If you do have a fire, DON'T PANIC. Direct the extinguisher at the base of the fire.

• NEVER use a naked flame in the workplace.

❐ 7: KEEP your inspection lamp well away from any source of flammable materials.

• NEVER use petrol (gasoline) to clean parts. Use only a proprietary degreaser.

• NO SMOKING. There's a risk of fire or of transferring dangerous substances to your mouth.

• BE METHODICAL in everything you do, use common sense, and think of safety at all times.

ENVIRONMENT FIRST!

• The used oil from the sump of just one car can cover an area of water the size of two football pitches, cutting off the oxygen supply and harming swans, ducks, fish and other river life.

❐ 8: When you drain your engine oil - don't oil the drain! Pouring oil down the drain will cause pollution. It is also an offence.

OIL POLLUTES WATER USE YOUR BRAIN- NOT THE DRAIN!

• Don't mix used oil with other materials, such as paint and solvents, because this makes recycling difficult.

• Take used oil to an oil recycling bank. Telephone FREE in the UK on 0800 663366 to find the location of your nearest oil bank, or contact your local authority recycling officer.

CHAPTER 3: GETTING THROUGH THE ANNUAL TEST

This chapter relates mostly to the UK where vehicles need to pass the 'MoT' test but also has relevance for those in other countries with a similar annual test. Obviously, you won't be able to examine your car to the same degree of thoroughness as the MoT testing station. But you can reduce the risk of being among the four out of 10 who fail the test first time!

The checks shown below are correct for the MoT Test in the UK at the time of writing but they do tend to become stricter! Your local testing station will have the latest information. DON'T BE TURNED AWAY! The vehicle, when presented for test, must be reasonably clean. Testing Stations can refuse to test vehicles that are very dirty and have excessive mud on the underside.

CONTENTS

Part A: Inside the Vehicle

STEERING WHEEL AND COLUMN

❑ 1: Try to move the steering wheel towards and away from you and then from side to side. There should be no appreciable movement or play. Check that the steering wheel is not loose on the column and that there are no breaks or loose components on the steering wheel itself.

❑ 2: Lightly grip the steering wheel between thumb and finger and turn from side to side. Vehicles with a steering rack: free play should not exceed approximately 13 mm (0.5 in.), assuming a 380 mm (15 in.) diameter steering wheel. Vehicles fitted with a steering box: free play should not exceed approximately 75 mm (3.0 in.), assuming a 380 mm (15 in.) diameter steering wheel.

A-2

❑ 3: If there is a universal joint at the bottom of the steering column inside the vehicle, check for movement. Place your hand over the joint while turning the steering wheel to-and-fro a little way with your other hand. If ANY free play can be felt, the joint must be replaced.

❑ 4: Steering security and locking devices (where fitted) must be in working order.

ELECTRICAL EQUIPMENT

❑ 5: With the ignition turned ON, ensure that the horn works okay.

❑ 6: Check that the front wipers work.

❑ 7: Check that the screen washers work.

❑ 8: Check that the internal warnings for the indicator and hazard warning lights work okay. When ABS brakes are fitted: Make sure that there is an ABS warning light that illuminates and that the lamp follows the correct sequence.

CHECKS WITH AN ASSISTANT

❑ 9: Check that the front and rear side lights and number plate lights work and that the lenses and reflectors are secure, clean and undamaged.

❒ 10: Check the operation of the headlights and check that the lenses are undamaged. The reflectors inside the headlights must not be tarnished, nor must there be condensation inside the headlight.

❒ 11: Turn on the ignition and check the direction indicators, front and rear, and the side markers.

❒ 12: Check that the hazard warning lights operate on the outside of the vehicle and at the internal warning light.

❒ 13: Check that the rear fog light/s, including the warning light inside the vehicle, all work correctly.

❒ 14: Check that the rear brake lights work correctly.

❒ 15: Operate the brake lights, side lights and each indicator in turn, then all at the same time. None should affect the operation of the others.

SAFETY FIRST!

• Follow the Safety information in *Chapter 2, Safety First!* but bear in mind that the vehicle needs to be even more stable than usual when raised off the ground.

• There must be no risk of it toppling off its stands or ramps while suspension and steering components are being pushed and pulled in order to test them.

FRONT SCREEN AND MIRRORS

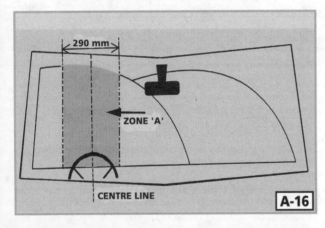

A-16

❒ 16: In zone 'A' of the front screen, no items of damage larger than 10 mm in diameter will be allowed. In the rest of the area swept by the screen wipers, no damage greater than 40 mm in diameter will be allowed, nor should stickers or other obstructions encroach on this area.

❒ 17: Check that the exterior mirror on the driver's side is in good condition.

❒ 18: There must be one other mirror in good condition, either inside the vehicle or an external mirror on the passenger's side.

BRAKES

❒ 19: You cannot check the brakes properly without a rolling road brake tester but you can carry out the following checks:

❒ 20: Pull on the parking brake. It should be fully ON before the lever reaches the end of its travel.

❒ 21: Knock the parking brake lever from side to side and check that it does not then release itself.

❒ 22: Check the security of the parking brake lever mountings and check the floor around them for rust or splits.

❒ 23: Check that the front brake pedal is in good condition and that, when you take hold of it and move it from side to side, there is not too much play.

❒ 24: Push the footbrake down hard with your foot. If it creeps slowly down towards the floor, there is probably a problem with the master cylinder. Release the pedal, and after a few seconds, press down again. If the pedal feels spongy or it travels nearly to the floor, there is air in the system or another dangerous fault with the brakes.

❒ 25: Check the servo unit (when fitted) as follows: Pump the brake pedal several times then hold it down hard. Start the engine. As the engine starts, the pedal should move down slightly. If it doesn't the servo or the vacuum hose leading to it may be faulty.

SEAT BELTS AND SEATS

❒ 26: Examine all of the seat belt webbing (pull out the belts from the inertia reel if necessary) for cuts, fraying or deterioration.

❒ 27: Check that each inertia reel belt retracts correctly.

❒ 28: Fasten and unfasten each belt to ensure that the buckles work correctly.

❒ 29: Tug hard on each belt to ensure that the inertia reel locks, and inspect the mountings, as far as possible, to ensure that all are okay.

A-29

IMPORTANT NOTE: Checks apply to rear seat belts as much as to front ones.

❒ 30: Make sure that the seat runners and mountings are secure and that all back rests lock in the upright position.

DOORS AND DOOR LOCKS

❒ 31: Check that doors latch securely when closed and that they can be opened and closed from both outside and inside the vehicle.

Part B: Outside of Vehicle

ELECTRICAL EQUIPMENT

See *Part A: Inside the Vehicle* for checks on the operation of the electrical equipment.

❑ 1: Examine the wiper blades and replace those that show any damage.

VEHICLE IDENTIFICATION NUMBERS (VIN)

❑ 2: The VIN (or chassis number on older vehicles) must be clearly displayed and legible.

❑ 3: Number (licence) plates must be secure, legible and in good condition with correct spacing between letters and numbers which must be of correct size and style.

BRAKING SYSTEM

❑ 4: Inside the engine bay inspect the master cylinder, servo unit (if fitted), brake pipes and mountings. Look for corrosion, loose fitting or leaks.

STEERING AND SUSPENSION

❑ 5: While still in the engine bay, have your assistant turn the steering wheel lightly from side to side and look for play in steering universal joints or steering system mountings and any other steering connections.

❑ 6: If the vehicle is fitted with power steering, check the security and condition of the steering pump, hoses and drivebelt, in the engine bay.

❑ 7: While your assistant turns the steering wheel more vigorously from side to side, place your hand over each track rod end in turn and feel for playing. Inspect all of the steering linkages, joints and attachments for wear.

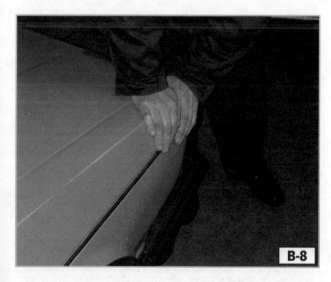

B-8

❑ 8: Go around the vehicle and 'bounce' each corner of the vehicle in turn. Release at the lowest point and the vehicle should rise and settle in its normal position without continuing to 'bounce' of its own accord. If not, a shock absorber is faulty. Always renew in 'axle' pairs or sets.

BODYWORK STRUCTURE

❑ 9: Any sharp edges on the external bodywork, caused by damage or corrosion will cause the vehicle to fail.

❑ 10: Check all load bearing areas for corrosion. Open the doors and check the sills inside and out, above and below. Any corrosion in structural metalwork within 30 cm (12 in.) of seat belt mounting, steering and suspension attachment points will cause the vehicle to fail.

WHEELS AND TYRES

Tread wear indicators

B-11

❑ 11: To pass the test, the tread must be at least 1.6 mm deep throughout a continuous band comprising the central three-quarters of the width of the tread. The Tread Wear Indicators (TWI) will tell you when the limit has been reached, on most tyres. (They are not coloured on 'real' tyres!)

IMPORTANT NOTE: Tyres are past their best, especially in wet conditions, well before this point is reached! (Illustration courtesy of Dunlop)

❑ 12: Check that the front tyres match and that the rear tyres match each other - in terms of size and type but not necessarily make. They must be the correct size for the vehicle and the pressures must be correct.

❑ 13: With each wheel off the ground in turn, check the inside and the outside of the tyre wall for cuts, lumps and bulges and check the wheel for damage. Note that tyres deteriorate progressively over a period of time and if they have degraded noticeably, replace them.

Part C: Under the Vehicle

You will need to support the front of the vehicle off the ground with the rear wheels firmly chocked in both directions.

❑ 1: Have your helper turn the steering from lock to lock and check that the steering turns smoothly and that the brake hoses or pipes do not contact the wheel, tyre or any part of the steering or suspension.

❏ 2: Particular attention should be paid to evidence of corrosion at the steering rack or steering box fixing points.

❏ 3: Have your assistant hold down the brake pedal firmly. Check each brake flexible hose for bulges or leaks. Inspect all the rigid brake pipes underneath the front of the vehicle for corrosion, damage or leaks and also look for signs of fluid leaks at the brake calipers. Rigid fuel pipes also need to be checked for corrosion, damage or leaks.

❏ 4: At each full lock position, check the steering rack rubber gaiters for splits, leaks or loose retaining clips.

❏ 5: Check the track rod end dust covers to make sure they are in place and are not split.

❏ 6: Inspect each constant velocity joint gaiter - both inners and outers - for splits or damage. You will have to rotate each wheel to see the gaiters all the way round.

❏ 7: Check all of the suspension rubber mountings, including the anti-rollbar mountings (when fitted). Take a firm grip on each shock absorber in turn with both hands and try to twist the damper to check for deterioration in the top and bottom mounting bushes.

❏ 8: Check that the shock absorbers are not corroded, that the springs are in good condition and that there are no fluid leaks down the body of the shock absorber. Renew if necessary

❏ 9: Check the front of the exhaust for corrosion and secure fixing at manifold and mounting points.

C-10

❏ 10: Grasp each wheel at 12 o'clock and 6 o'clock positions and try rocking the wheel.
FRONT WHEELS: Look for movement at suspension ball joints, suspension and steering mountings. Repeat while grasping each wheel at 3 o'clock and 9 o'clock.
ALL WHEELS: At the wheel bearing, look for movement between the wheel and hub.

❏ 11: Spin each wheel and check for noise or roughness in the wheel bearing and binding in either the wheel bearing or the brake.

❏ 12: If you suspect wear at any of the suspension points, try levering with a screwdriver to see whether or not you can confirm any movement in that area.

❏ 13: Vehicles fitted with other suspension types such as hydraulic suspension, torsion bar suspension etc. need to be checked in a way that is relevant to the system, with the additional point that there must be no fluid leaks or damaged pipes on vehicles with hydraulic suspension.

❏ 14: Inspect the rear springs for security at their mounting points and for cracks, severe corrosion or damage.

❏ 15: Check the rear shock absorbers in the same way as the checks carried out for the fronts.

❏ 16: Check all rear suspension mounting points, including the rubbers to any locating rods or anti-roll bar that may be fitted.

❏ 17: Check all of the flexible and rigid brake pipes and the fuel pipes just as for the front of the vehicle.

❏ 18: Have your assistant press down firmly on the brake pedal while you check the rear brake flexible hoses for bulges, splits or other deterioration.

❏ 19: Check the fuel tank for leaks or corrosion. Remember also to check the fuel filler cap - a correctly sealing filler cap is a part of the MoT test.

❏ 20: Examine the parking brake mechanism. Frayed or broken cables or worn mounting points, either to the bodywork or in the linkage will all be failure points.

❏ 21: Check each of the rear wheel bearings as for the fronts.

❏ 22: Spin each rear wheel and check that neither the wheel bearings nor the brakes are binding. Pull on and let off the parking brake and check once again to make sure that the parking brake mechanism is releasing.

SAFETY FIRST!
- Only run the car out of doors.
- Beware of burning yourself on a hot exhaust system!

C-23

❏ 23: While you are out from under the vehicle, but with the rear end still raised off the ground, run the engine. Hold a rag over the end of the exhaust pipe and listen for blows or leaks in the system. You can then get back under the vehicle and investigate further if necessary.

❏ 24: Check the exhaust system mountings and check for rust, corrosion or holes in the rear part of the system.

❏ 25: Check the rear brake back plate or calipers (as appropriate) for any signs of fluid leakage.

Part D: Exhaust Emissions

TOP TIP!

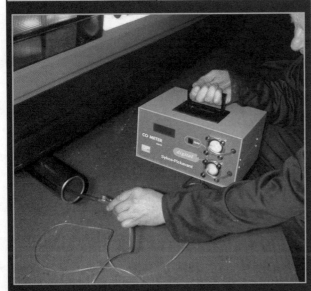

• This is a Sykes-Pickavant CO meter.
• If you don't own a CO meter, you could have your testing station carry out the emission part of the test first so that if it fails, you don't waste money on having the rest of the test carried out.

FACT FILE

FACT FILE: VEHICLE EMISSIONS

The information shown here applies, at the time of writing, to the UK. For information applicable to other territories, or for later amendments, check with the relevant local testing authorities.

PETROL/GASOLINE ENGINED VEHICLES WITHOUT CATALYSER

Vehicles first used before 1 August 1973 - visual smoke check only.

Vehicles first used between 1 August 1973 and 31 July 1986 - 4.5% carbon monoxide and 1,200 parts per million, unburned hydrocarbons.

Vehicles first used between 1 August 1986 and 31 July 1992 - 3.5% carbon monoxide and 1,200 parts per million, unburned hydrocarbons.

PETROL/GASOLINE ENGINED VEHICLES FITTED WITH CATALYTIC CONVERTERS

Vehicles first used from 1 August 1992 (K-registration - on, in the UK)

• All have to be tested at an MoT Testing Station specially equipped to handle vehicles fitted with catalytic converters whether or not the vehicle is fitted with a 'cat'.

• Required maxima are - 3.5% carbon monoxide and 1,200 parts per million, unburned hydrocarbons. There will be a further check to make sure that the catalyst is in working order.

TOP TIP!

• Because 'cats' don't work properly at lower temperatures, ensure that the engine is fully warm!

DIESEL ENGINES' EMISSIONS STANDARDS

• IMPORTANT NOTE: The diesel engine test puts a lot of stress on the engine. It is IMPERATIVE that the vehicle's engine is in good condition before you take it in for the MoT test. The tester is entitled to refuse to test the vehicle if he feels that the engine is not in serviceable condition.

Vehicles first used before 1 August, 1979
• Engine run at normal running temperature; engine speed taken to around 2,500 rpm (or half governed max. speed, if lower) and held for 20 seconds. FAILURE, if engine emits dense blue or black smoke for next 5 seconds, at tick-over.

Vehicles first used on or after 1 August, 1979
• After checking engine condition, and with the engine at normal running temperature, the engine will be run up to full revs between three and six times to see whether the engine passes the prescribed smoke density test. (2.5k for non turbo vehicles; 3.0k for turbo diesels. An opacity meter probe will be placed in the vehicle's exhaust pipe.) Irrespective of the meter readings, the vehicle will fail if smoke or vapour obscures the view of other road users.

MULTI-FUEL VEHICLES

• Vehicles which run on more than one fuel (eg petrol and LPG) will normally be tested on the fuel they are running on when presented for test.
• There is a slight difficulty with LPG vehicles and unless the testing station analyser has the facility for conversion, the mechanic will have to do a calculation. The machine is set to measure propane, but LPG power gives out hexane. The analyser will have a 'PEF' number shown. This is used as follows: 'propane' reading ÷ PEF no. = hexane value.

CHAPTER 4: WORKSHOP TOP TIPS!

Please read Chapter 2 Safety First! before carrying out any work on your car.

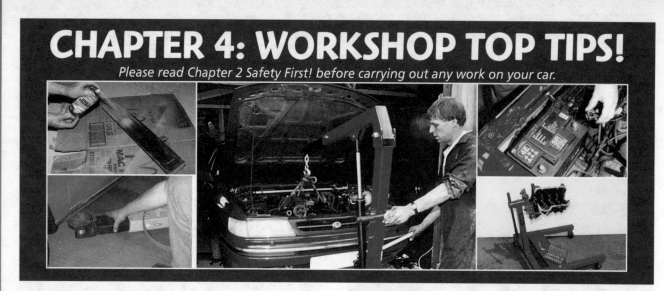

Here are a few *Top Tips!* to help keep things running well in the workshop.

1: DON'T LOSE IT! Buy sandwich bags and store small items in them, in groups, as they are removed. Keep the bags in a box or boxes, and keep the box/es in the vehicle if you have to go off and do something else. If you leave stuff lying around you'll lose some of it - right?

LOOK ON THE BRIGHT SIDE! Don't always assume the worst. That misfire - could it be the ECU? Highly unlikely, so try all the small stuff first. Engine running faults in particular are caused, 90% of the time, by failures in simple components such as spark plugs, leads, loose terminals and so on. So don't be a pessimist!

DON'T BE A BLUEBOTTLE! Work methodically; don't whizz around from one thing to another. Make a resolution to finish one thing before starting the next - even when you hit a tough patch, work through it! You'll finish jobs more quickly and you'll lose less stuff!

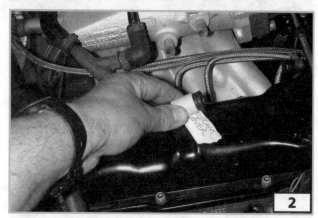

2: LABEL IT! Even in a manual like this, it isn't possible to cover every possible variation of wiring and pipework layout. If you assume that you WON'T remember how every single part goes back together - you'll almost certainly be right! Use tags of masking tape stuck on the ends of all removed connections, and label or number the matching parts. You'll save ages when it's time for reassembly!

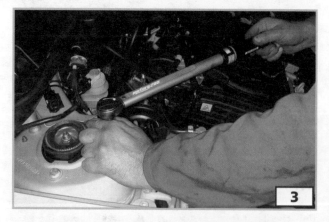

3: TIGHTEN RIGHT! Under-torquing and over-torquing threaded fixings is all too common. Some mechanics pride themselves on being able to judge the correct torque 'by feel'. They can't! Yes, they can get closer than a raw amateur, but the demands of modern components leave no room for guessing.

➔ Under-torqued fixings can come loose, or allow components to 'work' or chaff; over-torqued fixings can be even worse and can fail catastrophically or distort essential parts. Always check that threads run freely, and use a torque wrench!

❒ **4:** KEEP TORQUING! **Sykes-Pickavant** advise that their torque wrenches - and it actually applies to all makes - will read accurately for much longer if backed-off to the ZERO position before putting away, after each use.

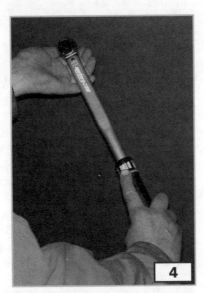

CHOOSING AND USING A HOIST

The best way of raising a vehicle off the ground - almost essential if you intend making your living or part of your income from working on vehicles - is to use a hoist. There are several types available, and the pros and cons are explained here by leading vehicle hoist manufacturer, **Tecalemit**:

➔ **FOUR POST:** This type of hoist is the least expensive, it's stable and capable of taking the greatest weights, but it's also the least versatile. With a post in each corner, the vehicle is driven onto ramps which raise the whole of the vehicle off the ground. The ramps do get in the way and the suspension is compressed by the weight of the vehicle. This restricts access in the wheel wells. On the other hand, it is possible to use a cross-beam from which you can jack specific parts of the vehicle - essential when vehicle testing. A four-post hoist is also useful if it's essential to raise a dangerously rusty vehicle off the ground.

➔ **TWO POST:** A post each side of the vehicle each carries two legs. The legs are swung so that a foot on the end of each leg is positioned under each end of the vehicle's body, usually under the normal jacking points. The great thing about these hoists is that they are 'wheels free' - the wheels and suspension hang down, providing almost ideal access to the underside of the vehicle. A two-post hoist should never be used on a vehicle that is dangerously rusty, because it will be raised on body parts which may collapse if the corrosion is very severe.

➔ **SINGLE POST:** This type has a single post, and swing-out legs reaching right under the vehicle. The advantage gained from the 'loss' of a post is offset by the intrusion of the extra-long support legs. The legs impede under-car access; the second post of a two-post hoist doesn't.

➔ **OUR CHOICE:** Without hesitation, we fitted a **Tecalemit** two-post hoist into the Porter Manuals workshop. Excellent service life from this famous-name manufacturer, and easy access for our mechanics, authors and photographers have made the hoist a wise choice!

❒ **5:** The legs can only be swung into position when they are fully lowered. They are extended, as necessary and aligned beneath the lifting points of the main body tub of the vehicle. As soon as they begin to raise off the ground, the legs are locked into position.

❒ **6:** Access to the vehicle's underside is ideal and, because there are no ramps - and no depressions in the floor, as is often the case with 4-post hoists - there is plenty of room to drive another vehicle beneath the one on the hoist for overnight storage.

❒ **7:** These **Tecalemit** hoists can run from 3-phase or 1-phase electrics, and can be fitted with a converter to enable a domestic level of current supply to power the hoist. In such cases, there will be a momentary delay while the converter builds up the power to the level required.

☐ **8A:** When a vehicle is raised on a hoist, it's perfectly safe, PROVIDED that the hoist has received its regular maintenance check by the suppliers. The **Tecalemit** two-post hoist is raised by screw threads and the legs are locked immovably when the motor is not being operated.

TOP TIP!

☐ **8B:** • Put a piece of tape on the post when you've established your best working height.
• Now you can raise the vehicle with the legs lined up with this mark every time!

8B

RAISING THE VEHICLE - SAFELY!

Read this section in conjunction with the essential safety notes in *Chapter 2, Safety First!*

For those who don't have access to a pro. hoist:
→ NEVER work beneath a vehicle held solely on a jack, not even a trolley jack. The safest way of raising a vehicle may be to drive one end of it up onto a pair of ramps. Sometimes, however, there is no alternative but to use axle stands because of the nature of the work being carried out.
→ Do not jack-up the vehicle with anyone on board, or when a trailer is connected (it could pull the vehicle off the jack).
→ Pull the parking brake on and engage first (low) gear.
→ WHEELS ON THE GROUND SHOULD BE CHOCKED AFTER THE VEHICLE HAS BEEN RAISED, SO THAT THE VEHICLE CANNOT MOVE.

USING RAMPS

Make absolutely certain that the ramps are parallel to the wheels of the vehicle and that the wheels are exactly central on each ramp. Always have a helper watch both sides of the vehicle as you drive up.
→ Wrap a strip of carpet into a loop around the first 'rung' of the ramps and drive over the doubled-up piece of carpet on the approach to the ramps. This prevents the ramps from skidding away, as they are inclined to do, as the vehicle is driven on to them.

→ Drive up to the end 'stops' on the ramps but never over them!
→ Apply the parking brake firmly and put the vehicle in first or reverse gear (or 'P' in the case of auto).
→ Chock both wheels remaining on the ground, both in front and behind so that the vehicle can't move in either direction.

USING A TROLLEY JACK

On many occasions, you will need to raise the vehicle with a trolley jack - invest in one if you don't already own one. Ensure that the floor is sufficiently clear and smooth for the trolley jack wheels to roll as the vehicle is raised and lowered, otherwise it could slip off the jack.
→ Before raising the vehicle, ENSURE THAT THE PARKING BRAKE IS OFF AND THE TRANSMISSION IS IN NEUTRAL. This is so that the vehicle can move as the jack is raised.
→ Reapply brake and place in gear after the raising is complete and chock each wheel to prevent vehicle movement.
→ Always remember to release brake and gear and remove chocks before lowering again.

☐ **9:** Axle stands also need to be man enough for the job. These inexpensive **Clarke** stands have an SWL of 3 tonnes. Make sure that the axle stands will each be placed beneath a reinforced part of the body, suitable for jacking from, or a main suspension mounting. Never place the jack or axle stand under a moving suspension part.

9

SAFETY FIRST!

• Whenever you're working beneath a vehicle, have someone primed to keep an eye on you!

• If someone pops out to see how you are getting on at regular intervals, it could be enough to save your life!

• Be especially careful when applying force to a spanner or when pulling hard on anything, when the vehicle is supported off the ground.

• It is all too easy to move the vehicle so that it topples off the axle stand or stands.

TOOLS AND EQUIPMENT

This section shows some of the tools and equipment that we have used while working on the vehicles that have been photographed for this manual.

You'll never have a complete set of tools; there will always be something else that you need! But over the years, if you buy equipment a little at a time, as you need it, you will accumulate a surprisingly large range.

When buying tools, it certainly pays to shop around. Tools that you won't need to use regularly, such as an impact screwdriver or a rubbing block for use with abrasive paper can be picked up for a song.

When it comes to larger and more expensive and specialised items, it pays to stick to a known maker rather than to take a chance with an apparently cheap tool whose make you may never have heard of.

❏ **10:** The **Clarke** 'Strong-Arm' engine hoist has the added advantage of being able to be folded into a really small space for storage.

❏ **11:** This engine stand, from the same manufacturer, is remarkably inexpensive. The engine is held at a comfortable working height and can be turned through 360 degrees. Recommended!

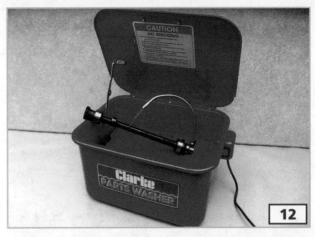

❏ **12:** When you've stripped components down, the most effective way of getting them clean is with a parts washer, this one from **Clarke** again.

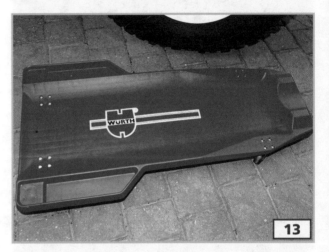

❏ **13:** Sliding beneath the vehicle will be a hundred times easier with a good quality car crawler, such as this plastic moulded crawler from **Wurth**.

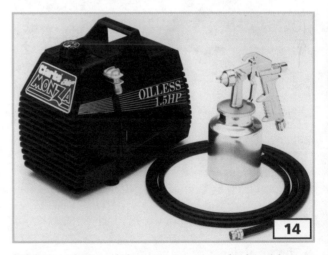

❏ **14:** Another tool that you can scarcely do without is a compressor. At the bottom end of the range, both in terms of price and performance, is a compressor such as the **Clarke** Monza. This tiny compressor will power a spray gun sufficiently for 'blowing-in' a panel and you'll also be able to inflate tyres and carry out all sorts of other lightweight jobs.

15

16

15: A compressor such as this 60 c.f.m. unit is the smallest needed by the serious amateur or semi-pro.. It won't run larger air tools, except in shorter bursts, but it's fine for the air wrench, for instance.

16: The Air Kit 400 provides a very useful and remarkably low-cost set of basic air tools capable of being powered by even the smaller compressors. Clockwise from top-left:
→ The engine cleaner gun works much better than a brush.
→ The spray gun is basic but effective.
→ Air hose is suitable for all smaller compressors.
→ Wear goggles when using the invaluable air duster.
→ Double-check tyre pressures with a hand-held gauge when using this tyre inflator and gauge.

17: Another use to which you will be able to put your compressor is spraying cavity protection wax. This **Wurth** injection gun is dual-purpose. It takes disposable **Wurth** screw-on canisters and also has its own large separate canister for injecting any protection wax that you may want to use 'loose'. Hand-

17

powered and cheap-and-cheerful injectors simply don't atomise the protection wax or blast it far enough into nooks and crannies to be useful.

18: Another invaluable tool is an angle grinder. This is the **Bosch** PWS7-115. This piece of equipment is perfect for using with grinding and cutting discs but, when used with this twisted-wire brush (available from

18

bodyshop suppliers), scours paint and rust off steel in seconds. Always wear goggles and gloves with this tool.

19: Another power tool which has a lot of domestic uses as well as being invaluable when working on a vehicle is something like the Jet 3000 Power Washer. It's a marvellous tool for removing mud, oil, grease and grim before stripping down body or mechanical parts

19

and it is also extremely useful around the outside of the house.

20: If your budget – or workshop space – won't run to a stand-alone pillar drill, the **Bosch** drill stand will turn your mains-power drill (this is the **Bosch** PSB with powerful 750W motor) into a perfectly adequate light-user

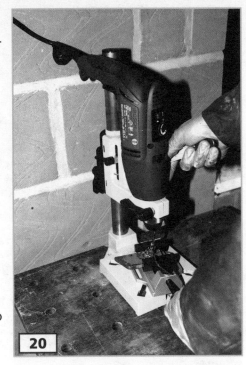

version. The same company also offer the hand vice which is an essential piece of equipment for gripping small pieces.

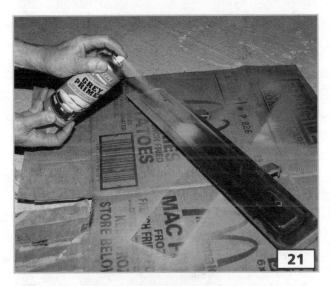

21: Aerosol cans of paint are extremely useful for small items, such as this number plate backing plate, mainly because there's no cleaning up to do afterwards. For large areas, aerosol is prohibitively expensive and you won't find the depth of paint or the quality as good as you would get from a spray gun. There's always a place for aerosol, however, and the **Hycote** range includes all the various types of primer and finish coats that you could want, as well as offering a range of mix-and-match aerosol paints which are mixed to the shade you need.

22: There is a wide range of tool boxes and chests available from **Sykes-Pickavant**. They're made of tough heavy gauge steel, are lockable, and contain separate 'filing cabinet' type drawers for tool storage. Most of the units are stackable.

23. Increasingly, the kind of work described in this manual requires the use of special tools. **Sykes-Pickavant** produce a complete range of regular workshop tools and equipment and also special tools for most purposes.

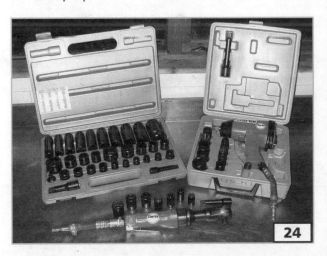

24. An air wrench can save a heck of a lot of time on dismantling and reassembly – although you should always finish off with a torque wrench, where appropriate. The **Clarke** 3/8 in. drive is 'wieldy' enough for engine bay work while the 1/2 in. drive wrench and sockets will cope with most heavy duty jobs. Note the flexible 'tail' we add to each tool to protect the female connector on the air line.

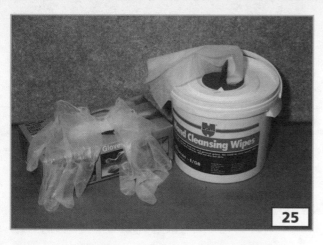

25: You'll need hand cleaner - the sort with granules shifts heavy grease best. **Wurth** also produce these hand wipes - useful if you need to touch upholstery in the middle of a job - and packs of disposable gloves.

26: Wurth produce a huge range of workshop products including electrical connectors and that wonderful 'shrink-fit' wire insulation tubing – slide it on, heat it up, and it 'shrinks' into place and can't come unwrapped.

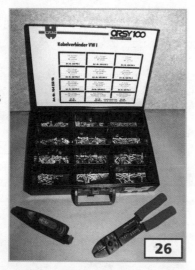

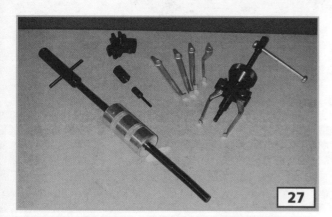

27: It's sometimes necessary to use pullers to remove 'stuck' bearings or other interference fit items. This **Sykes-Pickavant** set includes a variety of arm sizes and types, and a slide hammer to supplement the usual screw-type puller.

28: With these three **Sykes-Pickavant** kits, you can check (from left to right) many of the engine's most basic functions:
→ Cylinder compression tester - essential for a whole range of mechanical diagnostics, without the need for engine dismantling. Different testers are available for Diesel engines with their very high compression pressures.
→ Battery tester - essential for eliminating or confirming the battery as a source of problems.
→ Oil pressure tester. When combined with the cylinder compressions tester, this is capable of providing virtually a complete picture of the 'inner health' of any engine.

29: Last in this Chapter, but first job before carrying out vehicle dismantling: disconnect the battery! Beware of radio sets, alarms and ECUs that need a continuous electricity supply. See *Chapter 10, Electrical, Dash, Instruments* on preserving a battery feed.

CHAPTER 5: SERVICING

*Please read **Chapter 2 Safety First** before carrying out any work on your car.*

HOW TO USE THIS CHAPTER

This chapter contains all of the servicing Jobs recommended by Volkswagen for all models covered by this manual. To use the schedule, note that:
• Each letter code tells you the Service Interval at which you should carry out each Service Job.
• Look the code up in the Service Intervals Key.
• Each Service Job has a Job number.
• Look up the number in the relevant part of this chapter and you will see a complete explanation of how to carry out the work.

SAFETY FIRST!

• Please read the whole of *Chapter 2, Safety First!* before carrying out any work on the car.
• There are many hazards associated with working on a car but all of them can be avoided by adhering strictly to the safety rules.
• Don't skimp on safety!

SERVICE INTERVALS

Each service should be carried out at EITHER the recommended mileage OR the recommended time interval, whichever comes first.

SERVICE INTERVALS: KEY

A - Every week, or before every long journey.

B - Every 6 months, or 5,000 miles.

C - Every 12 months, or 10,000 miles.

D - Every 24 months, or 20,000 miles.

E - Every 2 years, or 40,000 miles.

F - Every 80,000 miles.

CONTENTS

JOB 1: ENGINE OIL - *check level.*	A
JOB 2: COOLING SYSTEM - *check level.*	A
JOB 3: BRAKE FLUID - *check level.*	A
JOB 4: BATTERY - *check electrolyte level.*	A
JOB 5: SCREEN/HEADLIGHT WASHER FLUID - *check level.*	A
JOB 6: TYRES - *check pressures and condition (road wheels).*	A
JOB 7: LIGHTS - *check/change bulbs.*	A
JOB 8: ENGINE OIL AND FILTER – *change.* Petrol engines	C
Diesel engines	B
JOB 9: ENGINE – *check visually for leaks.*	C
JOB 10: CRANKCASE VENTILATION – *check.*	C
JOB 11: VALVE CLEARANCES – (NOT engines with hydraulic tappets) – *check/adjust.*	D
JOB 12: CAMSHAFT TIMING BELT – *check.*	D
JOB 13: CAMSHAFT TIMING BELT – *change.*	F
JOB 14: COOLING SYSTEM – *check.*	C
JOB 15: ENGINE COOLANT – *change.*	E
JOB 16: MANUAL TRANSMISSION OIL – *check level.*	D
JOB 17: MANUAL TRANSMISSION OIL – *change.*	F
JOB 18: AUTO. TRANSMISSION FLUID AND FINAL DRIVE OIL – *check levels.*	D
JOB 19: AUTO. TRANSMISSION FLUID, FILTER, FINAL DRIVE LUBRICANT – *change.*	E
JOB 20: DRIVESHAFT GAITERS – *check.*	B
JOB 21: CLUTCH (manual adjusting type, not hydraulic) – *check/adjust.*	C
JOB 22: SPARK PLUGS – *check/gap.*	C
JOB 23: SPARK PLUGS – *change.*	D
JOB 24: CONTACT BREAKER POINTS GAP – *check.*	C
JOB 25: CONTACT BREAKER POINTS – *replace.*	D
JOB 26: IGNITION TIMING – *check.*	D
JOB 27: DRIVE BELT/S – *check/adjust.*	D
JOB 28: ELECTRIC FAN OPERATION – *check.*	C
JOB 29: IGNITION/INJECTION – *run diagnostic test.*	C
JOB 30: FUEL PIPES – *check.*	C
JOB 31: EXHAUST SYSTEM – *check.*	C
JOB 32: AIR FILTER – *check.*	C
JOB 33: AIR FILTER – *change.* Petrol engines	E
Diesel engines	D
JOB 34: DIESEL FUEL FILTER – *drain.*	C
JOB 35: FUEL FILTER – *change.*	D
JOB 36: IDLE SPEED AND EMISSIONS – *check/adjust.*	C
JOB 37: EMISSIONS CONTROL SYSTEMS – *check/adjust.*	

JOB 38: FRONT WHEEL BEARINGS – *check*.	C	
JOB 39: FRONT SUSPENSION – *check*.	C	
JOB 40: STEERING COLUMN, RACK AND TRACK ROD ENDS - *check*.	C	
JOB 41: POWER STEERING FLUID – *check*.	C	
JOB 42: REAR WHEEL BEARINGS – *check*.	C	
JOB 43: REAR SUSPENSION – *check*.	C	
JOB 44: WHEEL BOLTS FOR TIGHTNESS – *check*.	C	
JOB 45: FRONT AND REAR BRAKES AND PARKING BRAKE – *check*.	C	
JOB 46: BRAKE PIPES – *check*.	C	
JOB 47: BRAKE HYDRAULIC FLUID – *change*.	D	

JOB 48: HINGES, LOCKS, AND CHECK STRAPS – *lubricate*.	C
JOB 49: SLIDING ROOF - *lubricate rails*.	D
JOB 50: SCREEN GLASS – *check*.	C
JOB 51: SEAT AND SEAT BELT MOUNTINGS – *check*.	C
JOB 52: HEADLIGHT ALIGNMENT – *check*.	C
JOB 53: UNDERBODY – *check*.	C
JOB 54: SPARE TYRE – *check*.	B
JOB 55: WIPER BLADES – *check*.	B
JOB 56: AFTER EVERY SERVICE - *road test and final check*.	

FACT FILE

ENGINE BAY LAYOUTS

- The following diagrams provide a guide to the location of components in typical Polo and Golf engine bays.
- There are very many different layouts – these are typical of most.
- Not all of the components shown are fitted to all vehicles.

TYPICAL GOLF MK1

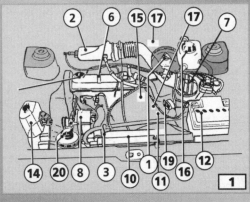

TYPICAL GOLF MK2

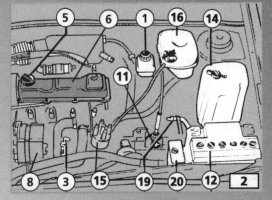

TYPICAL GOLF AND VARIANTS 1992-ON

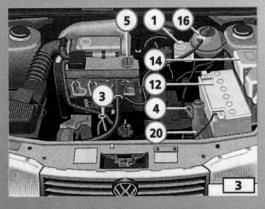

TYPICAL DIESEL

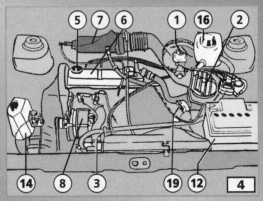

TYPICAL POLO UP TO 1994

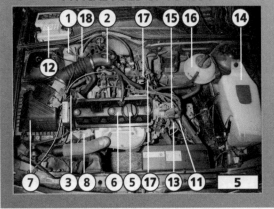

TYPICAL POLO 1994-ON

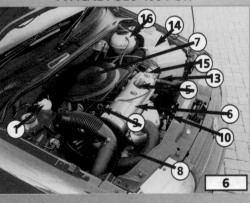

Annotations for all Engine-Bays

1 - brake fluid reservoir
2 - carburettor/ injection
3 - engine oil dipstick
4 - fuel pump
5 - oil filler cap
6 - camshaft cover
7 - air cleaner
8 - alternator
10 - radiator
11 - clutch lever
12 - battery
13 - thermostat housing
14 - screenwash container
15 - distributor
16 - coolant expansion container
17 - coil
18 - brake servo
19 - auto. transmission dipstick
20 - power steering reservoir

JOB 1: ENGINE OIL - *check level.*

Check the engine oil with the car on level ground and engine turned off for several minutes to let the oil drain into the sump.

JOB 2: COOLING SYSTEM – *check level.*

SAFETY FIRST!

• Check coolant level ONLY with engine COLD.

❏ **2A:** On some models, the expansion tank is built into the radiator. Some have their level marks on the outside of the tank, as shown. Others have the upper and lower level marks inside the tank.

❏ **2B:** On most vehicles, there is a separate expansion tank. Never allow the coolant level to fall below the lower (minimum level) mark (arrowed).

TOP TIP!

• A 50% mix of anti-freeze additive with water is normally sufficient protection, although you can use up to 60% additive.

JOB 3: BRAKE FLUID – *check level.*

SAFETY FIRST!

• If brake fluid should come into contact with skin or eyes, rinse immediately with plenty of water.
• If you let dirt get into the hydraulic system it can cause brake failure. Wipe the filler cap clean before removing it.
• You should only ever use new brake fluid from a sealed container. Old fluid absorbs moisture and this could cause the brakes to fail.

❏ **3:** On all models the brake fluid reservoir is positioned in the rear of the engine bay. There are two marks on the reservoir, sometimes with the words MAX (**a**) and MIN (**b**) marked on them.

Turn the cap without allowing the centre section to turn. Place the cap and float to one side - take care not to drip fluid from the float - and top up with fresh brake fluid.

Check the brake fluid-level warning-light - see illustration *3, item c*. With ignition key ON, press down the button between the two terminals on the reservoir cap. The warning light on the dash should light up. If no button is fitted, unscrew and raise the cap to check warning light.

JOB 4: BATTERY – *check electrolyte level.*

BATTERIES WITH REMOVABLE CAPS: Check the electrolyte level in the battery. Top up each cell ONLY with distilled or de-ionised water.

JOB 5: SCREEN/HEADLIGHT WASHER FLUID – *check level.*

The single reservoir for front screen, rear screen and headlights (as appropriate) is situated in the engine bay on most models.

On some early models, the reservoir for the rear screen is separate - on the right in the luggage compartment.

JOB 6: TYRES – *check pressures and condition (road wheels).*

Check the tyre using a reliable and accurate gauge. Also check for wear or damage.

JOB 7: LIGHTS - *check/change bulbs.*

See *Chapter 10, Electrical & Instruments.*

JOB 8: ENGINE OIL AND FILTER - *change.*

□ **8A:** The sump drain plug is on the under-side of the sump. Allow the oil to drain for at least ten minutes before replacing the sump plug.

□ **8B:** On all engines, the oil filter (arrowed) is mounted low on the front of the engine block. Use a strap or chain wrench to unscrew the old filter. To prevent the rubber sealing ring on the

new filter from buckling or twisting out of shape while tightening, smear it with clean oil.
Screw the new filter onto the stub by hand. When the rubber sealing ring contacts its seat, continue to turn the filter a further 3/4 of a turn, *by hand only.*

Always use a new sump plug washer, when fitted. Before refitting the plug, wipe around the drain hole with a piece of clean cloth to remove any dirt.

Pour in the correct quantity of **Castrol** engine oil (see *Chapter 1, Facts and Figures*) and check the level against the dipstick.

JOB 9: ENGINE - *check visually for leaks.*

Check for leaks, both in the engine bay, beneath the engine and on the ground over which the vehicle has been standing. Also check all hoses and hose connections for cracks, porosity or perishing. Replace if necessary.

JOB 10: CRANKCASE VENTILATION - *check.*

Check the condition of the breather hose from the engine to the air cleaner.

JOB 11: VALVE CLEARANCES (NOT engines with hydraulic tappets) - *check/adjust.*

See *Chapter 6, Engine.*

JOB 12: CAMSHAFT TIMING BELT - *check.*

□ **12:** Unclip the top of the camshaft belt outer cover and pull it away. Examine the belt for wear.
→ If there is any cracking, or if the toothed side

appears worn, or any 'teeth' are missing, replace the belt straight away.
→ If the belt breaks the valves may collide with the pistons, causing serious engine damage.
→ If you can twist the belt through more than 90 degrees at the centre of its longest 'run', it needs re-tensioning. See *Chapter 6, Engine.*

JOB 13: CAMSHAFT TIMING BELT - *change.*

See *Chapter 6, Engine.*

JOB 14: COOLING SYSTEM - *check.*

Examine the cooling system hoses, looking for signs of splitting, chafing and perishing. Squeeze the top and bottom radiator hoses. Any hard, brittle areas or crackling sounds tell you that the hoses are decomposing from the inside - replacements needed!

14: If Volkswagen hose clips are fitted, use a pair of pliers or self-lock grips (or preferably, the correct clip pliers!) to grip the two projections.

Check the heater tap. Make sure that it's not seeping and the tap moves freely. Lubricate, but keep oil and grease away from rubber parts.

JOB 15: ENGINE COOLANT - *change*.

See *Chapter 8, Cooling System*.

JOB 16: MANUAL TRANSMISSION OIL - *check level*.

16A: Check the level with the car on level ground.

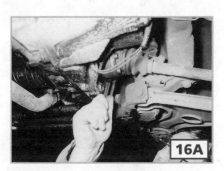

16B: This is the 5-speed 1.4/1.6 litre gearbox. Wipe around the filler plug with a rag to prevent dirt contamination. Top up if necessary, until oil just dribbles from the filler hole. Refit the plug.

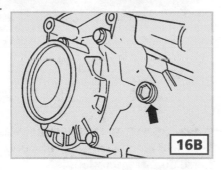

16C: This is the filler/level plug (arrowed) on the transmission fitted to engines, such as 2.0/2.8 litre and 1.9 Diesel.

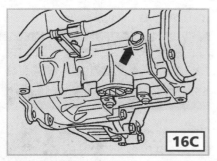

JOB 17: MANUAL TRANSMISSION OIL - *change*.

17: To change transmission oil:
➔ Do so only when the gearbox oil is warm.
➔ Clean around the drain plug, being pointed to here, before removing it.

➔ Leave for 10 minutes to drain completely, and refill with the correct grade of transmission oil.

JOB 18: AUTO. TRANSMISSION FLUID AND FINAL DRIVE OIL - *check levels*.

EARLIER MODELS: Automatic transmission fluid should be checked with car on level ground and engine at normal running temperature.

18A: Wipe the dipstick (arrowed) only with a lint-free rag to avoid clogging up transmission valves.

18B: Check the ATF level with the engine idling and the gear selector in the 'P' (PARK) position. If necessary, fresh ATF should be poured in

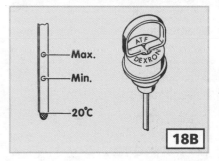

through the dipstick tube, using a funnel in the tube or by using ATF from a dispenser with a small spout.

IMPORTANT NOTE:
If you run the engine with no ATF in the transmission unit, the unit will be damaged.

LATER MODELS: ➔ On later Golf/Vento models the level plug opening is on the right-rear of the bottom of the transmission cover.
➔ The filler hole plug is on the front of the transmission, above the cover.

❏ **18C:** The level is checked by removing the ATF level plug (arrowed) from the oil pan using a socket extension. A small amount of fluid in the overflow pipe will run out.

18C

❏ **18D:** Lever off the cap on the filler plug (arrow and inset) with a screwdriver. Some locking caps are use-once and must be renewed; others have a spring retainer and are re-usable.

➜ Pull the plug out of the filler pipe.

➜ Inject ATF into the filler hole (**a**) until some runs out of the level hole (**b**).

➜ Refit the plug and the sealing cap.

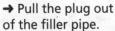
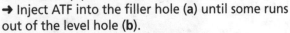

18D

FINAL DRIVE UNIT

Unlike manual transmission models, the final drive oil is separate on automatic models.

❏ **18E: EARLIER MODELS:** The filler/level plug (arrowed) is adjacent to the driveshaft on all earlier models.

18E

❏ **18F: LATER MODELS – GOLF/VENTO 1992-ON:** Clean meticulously around the speedometer drive (**a**), remove it. Refit drive, remove once again and check the level is between the **Min** and **Max** levels.

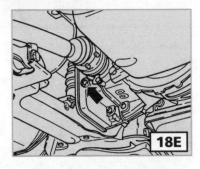

18F

JOB 19: AUTO. TRANSMISSION FLUID, FILTER, FINAL DRIVE LUBRICANT – *change*.

IMPORTANT NOTE:
Take very great care not to allow any dirt or grit to get into the transmission unit.

Always drain the fluid when the transmission is warm. Allow ten minutes for complete drainage.

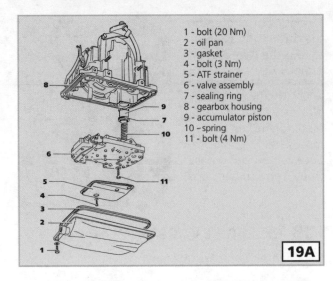

1 - bolt (20 Nm)
2 - oil pan
3 - gasket
4 - bolt (3 Nm)
5 - ATF strainer
6 - valve assembly
7 - sealing ring
8 - gearbox housing
9 - accumulator piston
10 - spring
11 - bolt (4 Nm)

19A

❏ **EARLIEST MODELS: 19A: 3-SPEED TRANSMISSION:** *Items no. 1 to 5* are the relevant components of the 3-speed auto-transmission. You do not need to dismantle any further in order to change fluid and replace filter.

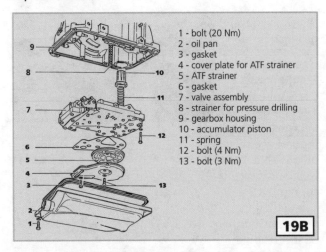

1 - bolt (20 Nm)
2 - oil pan
3 - gasket
4 - cover plate for ATF strainer
5 - ATF strainer
6 - gasket
7 - valve assembly
8 - strainer for pressure drilling
9 - gearbox housing
10 - accumulator piston
11 - spring
12 - bolt (4 Nm)
13 - bolt (3 Nm)

19B

❏ **19B: 4-SPEED TRANSMISSION – EARLY TYPE:** *Items no. 1 to 5* are the relevant components of the 4-speed auto-transmission.

TOP TIP!

• Later sump pans are not fitted with a drain plug.
• Loosen all of the bolts, until the pan hangs down at one end only, so the old ATF can be tipped out in a controlled way.

❏ **19C:** Remove the sump pan, remove the filter and fit the replacement. Use a new gasket.

19C

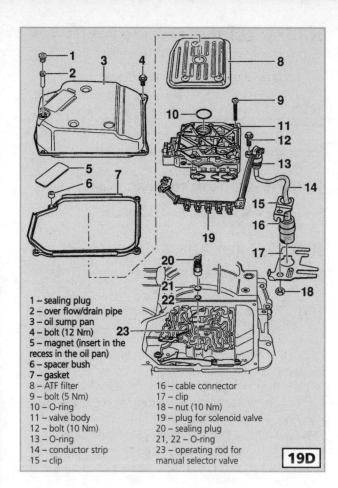

1 – sealing plug
2 – over flow/drain pipe
3 – oil sump pan
4 – bolt (12 Nm)
5 – magnet (insert in the recess in the oil pan)
6 – spacer bush
7 – gasket
8 – ATF filter
9 – bolt (5 Nm)
10 – O-ring
11 – valve body
12 – bolt (10 Nm)
13 – O-ring
14 – conductor strip
15 – clip
16 – cable connector
17 – clip
18 – nut (10 Nm)
19 – plug for solenoid valve
20 – sealing plug
21, 22 – O-ring
23 – operating rod for manual selector valve

19D

❒ **19D: LATER MODELS: IMPORTANT NOTE:** This Volkswagen drawing shows the transmission components 'upside down' when compared with the way in which they will be seen still fitted to the car.
→ There are minor differences between models but the basic principles remain the same.
→ Drain the fluid by first levering out the sealing plug (**1**) and then unscrew the over flow pipe (**2**) which allows the ATF to drain. When drained, replace the over flow pipe as far as its stop.
→ Take out the securing bolts (**4**) and remove the oil sump pan (**3**), taking care to retrieve the spacer bushes (**6**) as the gasket is removed.
→ When refitting the oil pan sump, press the spacer bushes into the gasket then fit a new gasket.
→ Insert a new O-ring (**10**) into the valve body (**11**) and press the new filter (**8**) on to the valve body.
→ Refit the oil sump pan and gasket and top up with the correct quantity of ATF.

❒ **19E: FINAL DRIVE UNIT:** The transmission unit will need to be supported from beneath the vehicle while the mounting (**a**) is removed. Remove oil pan (**b**), drain the oil, refit with a new gasket. Fill up to the correct level.

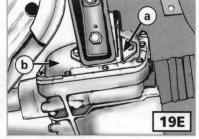

19E

JOB 20: DRIVESHAFT GAITERS – *check*.

❒ **20A:** Grasp and turn the inner drive-shaft and gaiters, checking for signs of gaiter splitting or damage that could allow grease out or - worse still - water in. Ensure the gaiter clips are secure.

20A

❒ **20B:** Check the outer gaiter as well. This moves over a greater range and is more prone to damage and splits.

20B

TOP TIP!

• When inner drive shaft gaiters leak, they put an oil stain on the drive shaft. Look out for it!
• Change a split, or damaged gaiter as soon as possible after discovering it.

JOB 21: CLUTCH (manual adjusting type, not hydraulic) - *check/adjust*.

FACT FILE

Cable-Operated Clutch: adjustable or non-adjustable?

• Earliest vehicles had an adjustable cable-operated clutch, while later ones are self-adjusting.

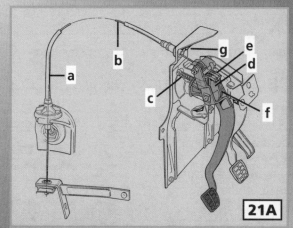

21A

❒ **21A:** • The self-adjusting type looks like this - note the absence of an adjuster screw on the conduit (**a**). The coil spring (**f**) is designed to ensure that the quadrant (**d**) maintains slight tension in the clutch cable.
• Keep the operating mechanism well lubricated on all cable-operated clutches, and grease the adjuster threads on adjustable clutches.

CABLE OPERATED CLUTCH:

❏ **21B:** 'Work' the clutch pedal a few times, then measure the free play at the pedal, which should be between 15 and 20 mm. If not, adjust the clutch pedal free play at the nut (arrowed) on the end of the cable, at the clutch lever on the gearbox...

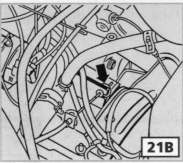

❏ **21C:** ...or at the end of the clutch cable conduit (arrowed), on the vertical-type of manual adjuster.

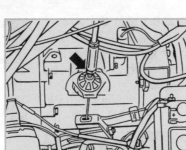

SAFETY FIRST!

• Read *Chapter 2, Safety First!* before carrying out any work on the ignition system.
• Stroboscopic timing requires the engine to be running - beware moving components!

JOB 22: SPARK PLUGS - *check/gap.*

Spark plugs should need no attention except for being checked and changed when necessary:
→ Spark plugs should be changed rather than cleaned.
→ Wire brushing spark plugs can harm their efficiency.
→ If heavily contaminated, there is an engine fault, and/or plugs are beyond their 'change-by' date.

JOB 23: SPARK PLUGS - *change.*

❏ **23:** Spark plugs 'tire' and lose efficiency over a period of time, even if they look okay.
→ Ensure that the plug threads in the head are clear. Use a Sykes-Pickavant thread chaser if necessary.
→ Screw the plug in by hand until it is fully seated.
→ To compress the washer, new plugs with flat seats are turned a further 90 degrees.
→ Already-used flat-seat plugs and conical seat plugs are both turned by only 15 degrees.

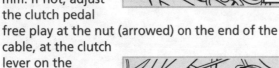

JOB 24: CONTACT BREAKER POINTS GAP - *check.*

See *Chapter 9, Ignition, Fuel & Exhaust.*

JOB 25: CONTACT BREAKER POINTS - *replace.*

See *Chapter 9, Ignition, Fuel & Exhaust.*

JOB 26: IGNITION TIMING - *check.*

See *Chapter 9, Ignition, Fuel & Exhaust.*

JOB 27: DRIVE BELT/S - *check/adjust.*

See *Chapter 6, Engine.*

JOB 28: ELECTRIC FAN OPERATION - *check.*

Check that the fan is working properly:
→ Drive the car until it is at normal operating temperature.
→ Park outdoors and, with the gearbox in neutral (or 'P' in the case of an automatic) leave the engine running.
→ At just above normal temperature the electric cooling fan should come on, and then go off again when the temperature drops. Refer to the gauge, if fitted.
→ If the fan doesn't behave, you will need to check the thermo-switch on the radiator, along with all connections and wires in the fan motor circuit.

JOB 29: IGNITION/INJECTION - *run diagnostic test.*

See *Chapter 6, Engine.*

JOB 30: FUEL PIPES - *check.*

Check fuel lines and hose clips from fuel tank and into the engine compartment, looking for chafing, splits and perishing of the rubber and plastic parts.

JOB 31: EXHAUST SYSTEM - *check.*

Examine the silencer and exhaust pipes and joints for corrosion and signs of leaking. Also check the condition of the rubber 'hangers'.

JOB 32: AIR FILTER - *check.*

❏ **32A:** The circular-type of filter has over-centre spring clips...

32B: ...while the rectangular type may have a variety of clips, depending on model: over-centre (**a**), lift-up clips (**b**)...

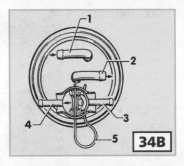

32C: ...and, with this type, the rear clip has to be removed to release the rear housing.

It is essential, when reassembling the filter, to ensure that all seals are in good order and are correctly reassembled. With the circular-type of filter, ensure that the two arrows - one on the housing and one on the lid - are aligned.

JOB 33: AIR FILTER - *change*.

33: The filter element should be removed, checked and renewed if necessary.

JOB 34: DIESEL FUEL FILTER - *drain*.

IMPORTANT NOTE:
→ Some models are fitted with a water-in-fuel sensor. Drain the filter when the warning light comes on. Unplug the sensor from the base of the filter, first.
→ Do not allow Diesel fuel onto your skin. Wear impermeable gloves.

The fuel filter is located in the rear of the engine compartment. Water accumulates in the bottom of the filter.

34A: FILTER WITHOUT DIESEL FUEL PRE-HEATING: Loosen the vent screw (**A**). Place a receptacle under the filter, then unscrew the knurled tap at the bottom of the filter (**B**) by a couple of turns and drain out about 100 cc (approx. a cupful) of fuel. Tighten the drain screw and the vent screw.

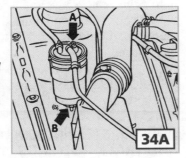

34B: FILTER WITH DIESEL FUEL PRE-HEATING: Pull off the retaining clip (**5**).

34C: With the clip removed, the control valve (arrowed) is now removed, but the two pipes are left connected to the valve.

34D: Unscrew the knurled tap at the bottom of the filter by a couple of turns and drain out about 100 cc (approx. a cupful) of fuel. Tighten the drain screw and refit the control valve.

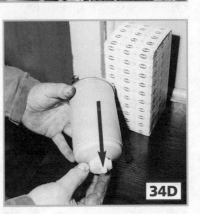

TOP TIP!
• Avoid fuel spills by pushing a piece of plastic tube on to the stub (arrowed) on the base of the drain tap.

BOTH TYPES: Check for leaks. Accelerate the engine several times, then check that the fuel flowing through the transparent hose is free of bubbles with the engine idling.

JOB 35: FUEL FILTER - *change*.

SAFETY FIRST!
• Work out of doors, in case of fuel leakage.
• Disconnect the battery negative lead before starting work.

CARBURETTOR MODELS:

❏ **35A:** Make sure that the arrow on the replacement filter body is pointing in the direction of fuel flow.

FUEL INJECTION (PETROL/GASOLINE) MODELS:

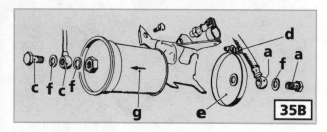

❏ **35B:** The fuel is filtered just before it enters the fuel metering/distribution unit.

➜ Undo the fuel supply pipe union (**a**) and remove the pipe.

➜ Undo and remove the pipe union (**c**) feeding the distribution unit.

➜ Undo the retaining clip screw (**d**), take off the clip (**e**) and remove the filter.

➜ Use new union washers (**f**) when fitting the new filter.

➜ Fit the new filter with the arrow on the body (**g**) facing towards the outlet union.

CLAMP-ON FILTERS:

❏ **35C:** Drain the filter. Disconnect the hose from the fuel tank (**A**) and the hose to the injection pump (**B**). Undo the clamp and remove. Fill the new filter with Diesel fuel and fit the hoses in their correct positions.

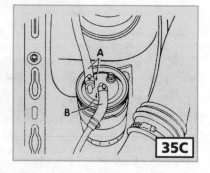

DIESEL MODELS WITH FUEL PREHEATING: Refer to illustrations **34B, C** and **D.**

➜ Empty the fuel filter. Pull off the spring clip (**5**) and detach the control valve but leave the return pipes connected to the stubs (*items 3* and **4**).

➜ Detach the return pipes from the stubs on the filter (*item 1* - from fuel tank, and *item 2* - to injection pump).

➜ Fit a new O-ring to the control valve when fitting the new filter.

➜ Fill the new filter with fuel, fit it, refitting the control valve and locking clip and refit the return pipes to the stubs on the filter - in their CORRECT locations!

JOB 36: IDLE SPEED AND EMISSIONS - *check/adjust.*

See *Chapter 9, Ignition, Fuel & Exhaust.*

JOB 37: EMISSION CONTROL SYSTEMS - *check/adjust.*

See *Chapter 9, Ignition, Fuel & Exhaust.*

JOB 38: FRONT WHEEL BEARINGS - *check.*

Rock the wheel about its centre, feeling for excess bearing play. Also, try spinning each wheel, feeling for rough rotation.

TOP TIP!

• If a wheel bearing is worn, you will normally hear a noise on the outer, loaded bearing when cornering.

JOB 39: FRONT SUSPENSION - *check.*

SUSPENSION OUTER BALL JOINT

➜ Jack up the car underneath the wishbone and support on an axle stand, so that the wheel is just off the ground.

➜ Use a long lever and carefully 'jog' the wheel upwards while a helper checks the lower balljoint for vertical movement.

➜ Also, examine the ball joint gaiter for any damage or leakage of grease.

WISHBONE INNER BUSHES: Further raise the car and support it on an axle stand under the subframe so that the suspension on the side being checked can hang free. Lever between the inner end of the wishbone and the subframe, looking for excessive movement of the front and rear wishbone bushes. Some cushioned flexing is normal.

SUSPENSION STRUT/SHOCK ABSORBER: Examine the shock absorber, which is enclosed inside the coil spring, for leaks, looking for signs of a 'damp' oil stain.

BOUNCE TEST: Try 'bouncing' each front corner of the car in a rhythmical motion, pressing down as hard as you can. When you let go, the movement should continue for no more than one-and-a-half rebounds. If it does so, BOTH shock absorbers should be replaced.

ANTI-ROLL BAR BUSHES Check the outer mountings, on the suspension, and the body mountings.

JOB 40: STEERING COLUMN, RACK AND TRACK ROD ENDS - *check.*

Get your helper to move the steering wheel, about 100 mm (4 in.) each way while you check for free movement in each track rod end (TRE). Also, look out for a split gaiter. Replace the TRE if the gaiter is split, or it will rapidly fail.

TOP TIP!

• Try placing your hand over the TRE as the steering is moved - feel for signs of wear.

STEERING COLUMN: While your assistant turns the steering wheel, check for movement in the universal joints - one each side of the firewall.
➔ Place your hand over the joint - you can usually feel the movement better than you can see it.
➔ If there is ANY movement at all, play at the steering wheel will be greatly exaggerated - replace the faulty universal joint.

STEERING RACK GAITERS: Check visually for splits or oil leakage. Also, watch the steering rack to see if it is firmly attached. If there is any movement between the rack and its mountings, check the securing bolts for tightness.

JOB 41: POWER STEERING FLUID - *check*.

The reservoir may appear in different places in different models. Apply the parking brake, start the engine and turn the wheels to the straight-ahead position. The oil level should now be between the MAX AND MIN levels on the reservoir.

JOB 42: REAR WHEEL BEARINGS - *check*.

Rear wheel bearings are sealed in their hubs and are usually very long lived. Follow the checking procedures described in *Job 38*.

JOB 43: REAR SUSPENSION - *check*.

ALL MODELS EXCEPT CADDY: Check for tightness:
➔ The rear suspension mountings.
➔ The trailing arm bush pivot bolts.
➔ The shock absorber lower mounting bolts.
➔ The anti-roll bar mounting bolts (when fitted).
➔ Check the condition of each mounting bush by levering with a screwdriver. Replace if excessive movement or bush deterioration are noticed.

GOLF CADDY: As well as the shock absorber mounts, you will need to check the leaf springs, U-bolts and bushes/mountings at each end of the leaf springs.

SHOCK ABSORBERS: Look for signs of leaks. Check the top and bottom rubber mounting bushes. Check that the bump stops are present and correct. Bounce-test the shock absorbers as in *Job 40*.

JOB 44: WHEEL BOLTS FOR TIGHTNESS - *check*.

Remove each wheel bolt in turn and ensure that they all run smoothly. Clean the threads, if necessary. Refit and check that all are tightened to the correct torque.

SAFETY FIRST!

• Be sure to read *Chapter 2, Safety First!*
• Remember that brake fluid is poisonous!
• Do NOT attempt any work on the braking system unless you are fully competent to do so.
• Always start by cleaning the brakes with a proprietary brand of brake cleaner. Never use compressed air to clean off brake dust.
• Always replace brake pads and/or shoes in complete 'axle' sets of four.
• After fitting new brake shoes or pads, the driver should avoid heavy braking for the first 150 to 200 miles (250 to 300 km), except in an emergency.

JOB 45: FRONT AND REAR BRAKES AND PARKING BRAKE - *check*.

Check brake pads, discs, calipers, brake shoe assemblies and parking brake. See *Chapter 12, Brakes*.

JOB 46: BRAKE PIPES - *check*.

FLEXIBLE HOSES: Check the flexible brake pipes. Try bending back on themselves those that are not contained in a protective coil, and look for any signs of cracking. Check for signs of rubbing, splitting, kinks and perishing. Check hoses for 'ballooning' with the brake pedal pressed hard.

RIGID PIPES: Check all rigid pipes for signs of damage or corrosion and check that all of the locating clips are sound and in place.

JOB 47: BRAKE HYDRAULIC FLUID - *change*.

Brake fluid absorbs water from the air. This corrodes brake components and can cause total brake failure. Change the brake fluid at the recommended interval. See *Chapter 12, Brakes*.

JOB 48: HINGES, LOCKS AND CHECK STRAPS - *lubricate*.

Apply a few drops of light oil (from either an aerosol or oil can) to the hinges of the bonnet, doors and tailgate. Dip the door/tailgate key in graphite powder and insert the key to lubricate the lock barrels. Grease the door and tailgate latch mechanism (aerosol grease is handy), the bonnet release, tailgate and fuel filler flap mechanisms.

JOB 49: SLIDING ROOF - *lubricate rails*.

Apply silicone lubricant to the runners and hinges.

JOB 50: SCREEN GLASS - *check*.

Examine for stone chips, cracks and scoring. Some screen chips can be invisibly repaired.

JOB 51: SEAT AND SEAT BELT MOUNTINGS - *check*.

Check the seat backrest adjustment/locking mechanism. Also, check that seat belts: a) retract easily and smoothly, and b) 'hold' when you snatch them, or under sharp braking.

JOB 52: HEADLIGHT ALIGNMENT - *check*.

Headlights can only be properly aligned with the use of a beam setting device.

JOB 53: UNDERBODY - *check*.

Check underbody for damage and corrosion.

JOB 54: SPARE TYRE - *check*.

TOP TIP!

• Put in the maximum recommended pressure for heavy-duty use - it's easy to let air out if necessary.

JOB 55: WIPER BLADES - *check*.

Check to see if the wiper blades need renewing - at least once, and sometimes twice a year is recommended. Try the washers and see if the wipers work okay. Look for the following faults:

❐ **55A: 'SHEETING' -** Causes:
➔ Dirty blade lip. Worn or torn blade lip.

❐ **55B: DROPLETS -** Causes:
➔ Glass and rubbers contaminated by traffic film, oil or grease or wax from washing.
➔ Use panel wipe to clean all traces away.

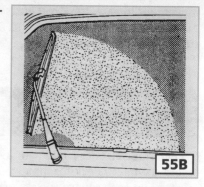

❐ **55C: 'CHATTER' -** Causes:
➔ Deformed or contaminated blade lips - replace.
➔ Glass dirty, contaminated by grease, wax or traffic film or not enough water on screen.

➔ Wiper arms twisted. Bend arm (use a pair of adjustable wrenches) to provide proper blade contact - blade must 'flip' over at the end of each stroke.
➔ Loose or incorrect connection between blade holder and arm. Replace.

JOB 56: AFTER EVERY SERVICE
- *road test and final check*.

If you are not a qualified mechanic, we strongly recommend having someone who is qualified inspect the car before using it on the road.
➔ Before setting out, check lights, indicators, in-car controls, seat belts and seat adjustments.
➔ Run the engine then turn off, check fluid levels and check underneath for leaks.
➔ Check that the steering moves freely in both directions and that the car does not 'pull' one way or the other when driving in a straight line.
➔ Make sure that the brakes work effectively, smoothly and without the need for 'pumping'. There should be no juddering or squealing.
➔ Check that the car does not 'pull' from one side to the other when you brake firmly from around 40 mph. (Don't cause a skid and don't try this if there is any following traffic.)

CHAPTER 6: ENGINE

*Please read **Chapter 2 Safety First** before carrying out any work on your car.*

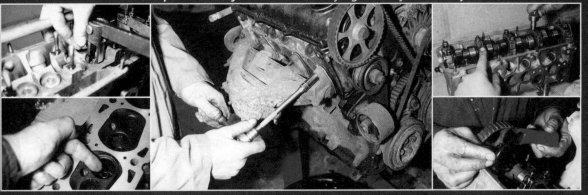

Part A: General Procedures

See **Part B: Which Engine is Which?** for an explanation of the engine types referred to here.

Many of the skills you will use in rebuilding an engine will be common to all engines. So, to save you time and help the job go more smoothly, those skills are shown right here!

JOB 1:   SAFETY FIRST!

Be sure to read and follow the advice in **Chapter 2, Safety First!** before carrying out work on your car. In particular, pay attention to the advice on fuel safety - remember that petrol/gasoline is highly explosive and that there are almost always leaks when disconnecting fuel system components on the engine.

In addition, remember that major components may be heavy enough to cause injury if not lifted correctly. See **Job 11** for further important information.

JOB 2: CYLINDER HEAD BOLTS - *tightening, undoing*.

If you get this wrong, you could easily distort the cylinder head - aluminium heads are more prone to distortion than cast iron ones. NEVER remove the head while there is still heat in the engine.

☐ **STEP 1:** The general rule is to **undo** the outer fixings first, working inwards in a regular, diagonal pattern. And to **tighten** the inner ones first, working evenly and diagonally outwards. HOWEVER - Volkswagen advise different procedures for different engines. MOST IMPORTANT: Don't guess! ALWAYS remove and tighten in the order specified in the relevant section of this manual.

2-1

JOB 3: OVERHEAD-CAMSHAFT ENGINE BEARING CAPS - *removing*.

TOP TIP!

☐ **STEP 1:**
• The camshaft is held down with a number of bearing caps.
• If they aren't numbered, mark them

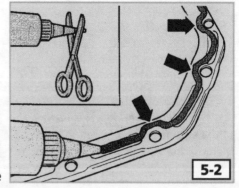
3-1

with a centre punch – it's essential that they aren't mixed up.
• Because of the tension in the valve springs, the caps have to be loosened gradually.
• You can speed things up by leaving two of the caps tight - such as numbers 2 and 4 in a five-cap set-up - while completely removing the other caps.
• Now the two remaining caps can be removed. Loosen each nut a turn at a time to gradually release the pressure from the valve springs.

JOB 4: CYLINDER HEAD GASKETS.

☐ **STEP 1:** NEVER re-use a cylinder head gasket – if you do, it will almost certainly blow. Fit the new one with the word TOP or OBEN (for German-made gaskets), or sometimes the part number facing **upwards**.

☐ **STEP 2: DIESEL ENGINES:** You will have to select the correct gasket thickness because the volume of the combustion chamber is a lot more critical on Diesel engines. The correct procedure for each type of engine is shown in the relevant section of this manual.

JOB 5: GASKET SEALANT.

→ Do NOT use gasket paste on a cylinder head gasket.
→ Neoprene (compressible 'rubber') gaskets do not normally need gasket paste. If necessary use silicone sealant.

☐ **STEP 1:** When a joint has to be sealed, make sure that you clean off all of the old sealant first. On a pressed steel sump, use a wire brush.
You can use a flat scraper on a

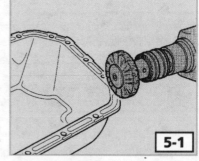
5-1

cylinder block. In the case of aluminium cylinder blocks take great care not to dig the scraper in, and don't use a power tool of any sort.

☐ **STEP 2:** Apply silicone sealing compound as follows:
→ Cut off the nozzle on the sealant tube to give the approximate size of bead

5-2

that you may need. In the case of a sump, it is usually about 3 mm.
→ Apply the bead about 2 to 3 mm thick.
→ Apply the bead in an unbroken line, going around the *inner* sides of the sump bolt holes.

JOB 6: 'STUCK' CYLINDER HEAD - *freeing*.

Even after all the bolts have been removed, it is sometimes difficult to remove a 'stuck' cylinder head. You must NEVER lever between the mating faces of the head and block. Instead:

→ Look for protrusions or strong brackets on both head and block against which you may be able to lever.

→ Try turning the engine over on the starter motor with spark plugs in place but ignition or Diesel injector pump disconnected, so that the engine can't start. The compression created may shift the head.

→ Extra leverage can be applied by leaving the manifolds in place and pulling on them.

→ You can sometimes use a large, soft-faced mallet on a solid protrusion on the head to try to shock it free. Take very great care not to hammer anywhere that can cause damage.

JOB 7: CYLINDER HEAD – *lifting, fitting*.

When the engine is still installed, a cylinder head may (depending on type) be a dangerously heavy component to lift, because of the need to reach into the engine bay. It's best to have someone help you to lift it away.

TOP TIP!

❐ **STEP 1:** • When refitting a cylinder head held down with bolts rather than studs fitted in the block – and if there are no alignment dowels fitted by the manufacturer - you may have difficulty in aligning the bolt holes in the gasket with those in the head. And if they're not aligned, you won't be able to screw the bolts into the block.

7-1

• Make a pair of guides out of two old cylinder head bolts, or two pieces of plain steel bar of a size that will just slide into the threads in the block.

• If using old bolts, cut the heads off with an angle grinder and slot the ends so that you can use a screwdriver to remove them.

• Fit the bolts, or the bars, slide the gasket over them, followed by the cylinder head, so that all holes are aligned.

• You can now fit some of the 'proper' bolts before removing the guides.

JOB 8: CYLINDER HEAD AND COMBUSTION CHAMBERS.

❐ **STEP 1:** The cylinder head can be checked for distortion by use of a straight edge and feeler gauge. At the same time, check for excessive corrosion. If you are in doubt, or if the old gasket has blown, have the cylinder head refaced by your Volkswagen agent or engine specialist.

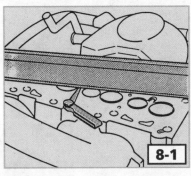

8-1

Clean excessive carbon deposits from the crowns of the pistons without damaging the surface of the aluminium.

TOP TIP!

• If the engine is worn and you don't intend overhauling it at this stage, we strongly advise that you don't scrape the carbon from the piston crowns. It can help preserve compression pressures.

JOB 9: EXHAUST AND INLET VALVES – *removing, replacing*.

VALVE REPLACEMENT

❐ **STEP 1:** Remove the cam followers and valve clearance adjusting shims (not used on finger-tappet

9-1

or hydraulic tappet types), taking care to maintain their original positions for reassembly.

❐ **STEP 2:** With all of these engines, you will need to use a valve-spring compressor with an extension jaw to reach into the recessed valve spring area in the head. (Illustration, courtesy Sykes-Pickavant.)

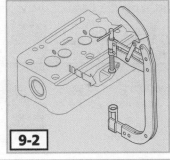

9-2

STEP 3: Give each valve a sharp tap with a hammer to free the top spring plate from the valve. You could place a socket spanner over the plate to avoid striking the end of the valve stem.

9-3

STEP 4: Compressing the valve springs so that you can reach in and remove the collets from around the heads of the valves.

9-4

STEP 5: Slowly and carefully open the spring compressor tool to release the pressure of the valve spring, and remove the upper spring seat...

9-5

9-6

9-7

STEP 6: ...followed by the springs.

STEP 7: Before the valves can be lifted out, the valve seals will have to be removed. This is a Sykes-Pickavant tool - special pliers which grip the seal and lift it off the head of the valve stem.

STEP 8: Slide out the valves, removing the valve seals and discard the old seals; new ones must be used on re-assembly.

9-8

TOP TIP!

• The valves should slide freely out of their guides.
• Any resistance may be caused by a build up of carbon, or a slight burr on the stem where the collets engage.
• This can usually be removed by careful use of fine wet-or-dry paper, allowing you to withdraw the valves without scoring their guides.
• Keep the valves in their correct order by wrapping a numbered piece of masking tape around each stem.

STEP 9: Once all the valves have been removed, clean them up ready for inspection. Remove the carbon deposits with a wire brush and degrease the rest. Exhaust valves are prone to burning at their heads, as are their valve seats in the cylinder head.

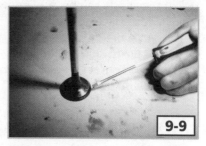

9-9

TOP TIP!

• Check the height of the valve springs against new ones if possible, but if not, compare them with each other.
• If any are shorter than the others, play safe and replace the complete set. They are bound to have suffered fatigue which could cause premature valve failure.

STEP 10: To install valves, start from one end.
→ Lubricate a valve stem with fresh engine oil and slide it in to its guide.
→ Locate a new valve stem seal over the stem of the valve and push down into contact with the guide.
→ Push the seal onto its seat using a suitable metal tube.

9-10

❏ **STEP 11:** • Wrap a short length of insulating tape around the collet grooves at the end of each valve stem.
• This will protect the new valve seals from damage as you slide them over the valve stems.
• When you have pushed the new seal firmly onto the top of the valve guide, remove the tape.

❏ **STEP 12:** Refit the spring seat.

❏ **STEP 13:** Position the inner and outer springs and the spring cap.

❏ **STEP 14:** Re-apply the valve spring compressor and compress the springs enough to allow you to engage the split collets in the stem grooves. Note that the type of collets, the spring caps and the valves must match each other. Unlike the earlier type, the later type has a valve with three grooves, a collet with three single shoulders and a spring cap with an inner chamfer and a wider outer chamfer. Make sure that you buy the correct type of valves, if any have to be replaced.

• Grease the grooves so that the collets will 'stick' in place.
• Collets are easily fitted by 'sticking' the backs of them onto the end of a screwdriver with some grease and feeding them into position.

❏ **STEP 15:** Carefully release the spring compressor and check that the collets are correctly located. Tap the end of each stem with a hammer to bed them all in.

❏ **STEP 16:** Fit the remaining valves.

JOB 10: EXHAUST AND INLET VALVES - grinding in.

• Before grinding-in the valves, clean the tops of the valve heads back to shiny metal.
• Now the sucker on the end of your valve grinding stick won't keep falling off when you grind-in the valves!

❏ **STEP 1:** Check for valve guide wear:
➜ Lift each valve until the end of the stem is level with the top of the valve guide.
➜ Attempt to move the head from side to side.
➜ If you feel any noticeable play then you may need new guides.
➜ This is a job that has to be carried out by your Volkswagen dealer or engine rebuild specialist, who will also have the experience to confirm whether or not wear is acceptable, as well as the special tools needed to replace the valve guides.

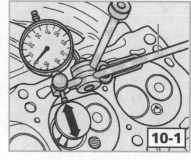
10-1

• Modern engines, with hardened valve seats, are not capable of having valves ground in the traditional way, except to remove the smallest of blemishes. If anything more is needed, take the valves and cylinder head to your dealer and have the valves and seats recut to the correct angle by machine.
• However, Volkswagen state that 16-valve engine valves cannot be reworked but can only be ground in. Valve seats can be reworked within limits by your Volkswagen dealer.

❏ **STEP 2:** A power-operated valve grinder, such as this Wurth tool, attaches to the electric drill and makes valve grinding on engines with hardened valve seats a more practicable proposition.

10-2

❏ **STEP 3:** Apply a small quantity of coarse grinding paste evenly around the valve seat. Use a valve grinding stick tool with a suction cup slightly smaller than the valve face.

10-3

STEP 4: Apply a dab of moisture and press the suction pad firmly onto the valve head. Lower the valve stem into the guide and, holding the grinding stick firmly between the

10-4

palms of your hand, rub back and forth to give rotary grinding action while pressing gently down into the valve seat.

IMPORTANT NOTE:
Absolutely NO paste must find its way into the guide, as this will rapidly wear the guide.

Lift the valve regularly to redistribute the cutting paste around the contact area. When you can feel the paste wearing thin remove the valve, wipe the surfaces clean and check the contact surface on valve and seat. You must aim to achieve a complete, narrow ring of grey around the valve seat and valve face. If there are any blemishes still in the surface then more coarse paste will be needed. Once a complete ring has been obtained, clean off the coarse paste and finish off with fine paste. Finally, thoroughly remove all traces of cutting paste from the valves and head.

TOP TIP!

• A narrow contact band means high pressure on the seat and longer valve life.
• A wide contact band reduces the contact pressure and induces early valve seat burning.

STEP 5: Now repeat this operation on the remaining valves.

10-5

STEP 6: Wash the whole cylinder head again using paraffin (kerosene) and an old brush, making sure that all traces of grinding paste are removed, then dry off. Use compressed air if available.

SAFETY FIRST!

• Treat compressed air with respect. Always wear goggles to protect your eyes.

• Never allow the airline nozzle near any of the body apertures.

JOB 11: ENGINE – *lifting, moving.*

STEP 1: Always use suitable lifting equipment, such as the Clarke Strongarm hydraulic engine hoist we show being used. Hire one from a tool-

11-1

hire specialist if you don't own one. Most ceiling/roof structures are not strong enough to bear the weight of having lifting gear suspended from them, without being suitably reinforced.

The weakest part of the lifting gear used to lift and lower an engine is often the connection to the engine itself. It's best not to use ropes because they can stretch and slip. Ideally, you should make up a solid lifting eye which can be fixed to the engine at one or more cylinder head-to-block bolts. Alternatively, buy a piece of strong steel chain - one with welded links, not open links which could pull apart - and bolt it down to two suitable locations on the engine. The hook on your lifting gear should be of the type that can be snapped closed and can be fitted to the lifting eye or chain on the engine.

If you intend removing the engine while leaving the transmission in place, you will need to make up a suitable bridge, supported on each side of the engine bay and with a vertical chain or rod taking the weight of the otherwise unsupported engine-end of the transmission unit.

When moving major engine and/or transmission components around the workshop, use a sufficiently strong trolley. Make sure that the weight of such components cannot fall on to hands, feet or any other parts of the body.

JOB 12: CRANKSHAFT BEARINGS, CONNECTING ROD BEARINGS – *removing.*

STEP 1: Check that all the connecting rods and their big-end bearing caps are marked with matching numbers, starting from the timing cover end. Make sure that the markings tell you which way round they go. If there are no marks there, use 'dots' of typists' correction fluid on clean metal, or add centre punch marks.

12-1

STEP 2: If you are to refit the same pistons, mark them to show their position and which way round they face. (The arrow points towards the front of the engine.)

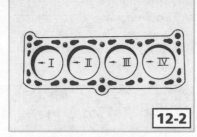
12-2

STEP 3: Undo the securing bolts and remove the caps, keeping them in their correct order.

12-3

TOP TIP!

STEP 4: • Inspect the top of each cylinder bore - there may be a small ring of carbon build-up which can make it

12-4

12-5

difficult to remove the pistons. If so, scrape it carefully away.

• Use a hammer handle to tap the piston/connecting rod assemblies carefully out of the bores.

STEP 5: ...keeping them in the correct order and keep the matching conrods and bearing caps together.

STEP 6: Check that the five crankshaft main bearing caps are correctly marked, starting from the timing cover end. Undo and remove them, keeping them in the correct order.

TOP TIP!

STEP 7: • If any of the caps are difficult to remove, lever the bolt holes with a bar, or a pair of bars - or a pair of fixing bolts, and tap carefully with a hammer.

12-7

• Bearing shells are best removed by sliding them out with your thumbs, pushing the tab-end out first.

• DON'T try to lever them out - it won't work!

STEP 8: Retrieve the thrust washers from each side of the centre main bearing cap.

12-8

STEP 9: When lifting the crankshaft clear of the cylinder block, look out for 'stray' bearing shells or thrust washers falling into the block.

12-9

JOB 13: PISTON RINGS - *fitting*.

STEP 1: Make sure that the bores and pistons are clean, then fit the rings, preferably using a piston ring spreader. Make sure the rings are fitted with the word 'TOP' facing upwards.

13-1

STEP 2: If you don't have access to a piston ring spreader, work the rings down a little at a time, using a feeler gauge or gauges to bridge the gaps. Piston rings are very brittle, very easy to break and are expensive to replace!

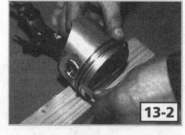
13-2

STEP 3: Fit the piston ring gaps at equal intervals round the pistons circumference and lubricate them well.

13-3

JOB 14: PISTONS – *removing, refitting.*

Pistons may be held to connecting rods by different methods - see relevant section of manual. However, refitting a piston into its cylinder bore is always as described here:

TOP TIP!

• Wrap insulation tape, or push a short piece of plastic tube, over each conrod thread, so that it cannot damage the crank as it goes in.

❑ **STEP 1:** Locate a ring clamp over the piston rings and tighten enough to close the ring gaps, but not too tight! Lubricate the rings so that they compress and slide easily within the clamp.

❑ **STEP 2:** Position the assembly in its correct bore with the connecting rod identification marks facing each other and also so that the complete piston/conrod assemblies face the right way.

14-2

❑ **STEP 3:** With the ring clamp touching the cylinder block, use a hammer shaft to carefully tap the piston through and into the bore.

14-3

TOP TIP!

• Turn the crankshaft so that the journal for the conrod you are working on is at bottom dead-centre. Now the conrod will line up with its crank journal.

❑ **STEP 4:** Locate the upper half of the big end shell bearing in the conrod, making sure that the mating surfaces are clean. Lubricate the crankpin and the big-end shell and draw the conrod down the bore so that the big end locates with the crankpin. Fit

14-4

the other half of the big-end shell to the bearing cap and lubricate. Offer the cap to the connecting rod and make sure that the numbers match. Screw in the fixing bolts and tighten progressively to the correct torque.

JOB 15: ENGINE COMPONENTS – *checking, measuring for wear.*

GENERAL

All parts must be thoroughly cleaned before inspection. Keep them in the right order for reassembly in case they are to be re used. Check each component as follows:

CYLINDER BLOCK

❑ **STEP 1:** Look for any cracks or evidence of gas or water blow-by on both sides of the gasket, on the cylinder head and in the block casting, particularly at bolt holes and between cylinders.

15-1

❑ **STEP 2:** Check the bores as follows:
→ Check for score marks, caused by burned pistons or broken rings.
→ Check for a wear ridge just below the top of the bore where the top piston ring ends its travel.
→ If you have access to a suitable internal micrometer, measure the bores at the points shown. Otherwise, ask your engine specialist to measure the bores for wear if there is any evidence of a wear ridge.

15-2

❑ **STEP 3:** Assuming the bores to be in reasonable condition, it is sometimes possible to 'glaze bust' the bores and fit new piston rings. If not, the cylinders will have to be rebored.

15-3

STEP 4: You can't check for bore ovality like this, but you can gain a good idea of overall wear:
• Push each piston ring squarely into the cylinder until it is about 15 mm from the bottom edge where no wear will have taken place.
• Measure the ring gap with a feeler gauge.
• Now carry out the same check on the most badly worn parts of the bore and see how much wear has taken place.

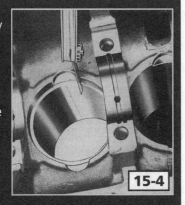

15-4

STEP 5: You will need a suitably large external micrometer to measure the pistons. Check about 15 mm from the bottom of the skirt.

15-5

STEP 6: Check the piston ring clearances with a set of feeler gauges.

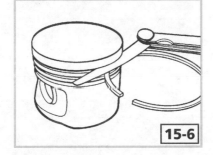

15-6

CRANKSHAFT

STEP 7: Check the main journals and crankpins:
➜ for any signs of wear ridges round the circumference or scoring of the surface.

15-7

➜ for ovality, using a suitable micrometer, although the precision Vernier gauge shown here will give an excellent guide.

STEP 8: Check the shell bearings, which should have an even, dull grey finish, like the ones shown here.

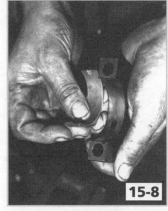

15-8

STEP 9: If the leaded layer is scored or has worn through to the copper coloured backing, or if the crankshaft has any of the previously mentioned faults, the crankshaft should be reground by your specialist who will also supply the new shell bearings and thrust washers.

15-9

STEP 10: Check the crankshaft end float by using a feeler gauge between the thrust washer and the crankshaft.

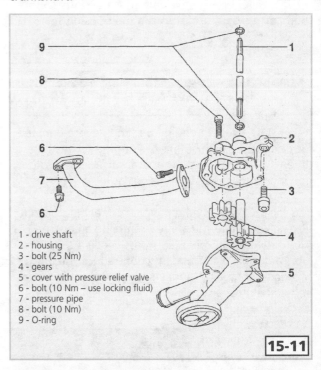

1 - drive shaft
2 - housing
3 - bolt (25 Nm)
4 - gears
5 - cover with pressure relief valve
6 - bolt (10 Nm – use locking fluid)
7 - pressure pipe
8 - bolt (10 Nm)
9 - O-ring

15-11

STEP 11: If an engine is being rebuilt, a new oil pump should be fitted as a matter of course. However, if you are checking a stripped engine to see how badly worn it is, include the oil pump in those checks. This is the VR6 engine's oil pump, and it's internal components are typical of the gear-type oil pump.

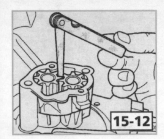

15-12   15-13

STEP 12: Use feeler gauges to measure the backlash between the gears – maximum 0.20 mm.

STEP 13: Use a straight edge and feeler gauges to measure the axial clearance – maximum 0.10 to 0.15 mm. Check that the bearing face of the cover (illustration *15-11, item 5*) is not worn. If in doubt, replace the pump – it's the 'heart' of the engine!

CAMSHAFT

Check the following:

STEP 14: Check each cam lobe for wear, which can be quite rapid once started. If you replace the camshaft, fit new followers as well.

STEP 15: Cam followers (bucket tappets) should also be checked, particularly where they contact the cam lobe.

STEP 16: Check the five camshaft bearings and their corresponding surfaces in the housing for a smooth, shiny surface without wear ridges.

JOB 16:   REASSEMBLING ENGINE COMPONENTS - *lubrication*.

If you start a rebuilt engine up 'dry', severe damage may be caused well before the engine oil has had time to circulate. Metal-to-metal surfaces will 'pick up' and rubber seals will be torn out.

You should keep an oil can with fresh engine oil in it next to you while you are reassembling an engine. Alternatively, you can use purpose-made assembly lubricant. But DON'T use a friction-reducer meant for adding to engine oil. It may prevent the engine from bedding in properly.

STEP 1: Apply copious amounts of lubricant to every rotating, rubbing and oil seal surface as the assembly takes place. You CAN'T over-lubricate!

16-1

STEP 2: If the engine won't be run straight away, wipe grease onto seal surfaces, so that they won't dry out.

16-2

STEP 3: Fill the oil pump housing with as much fresh engine oil as it will take, so that the pump itself is lubricated and so that it delivers fresh oil to the engine as quickly as possible.

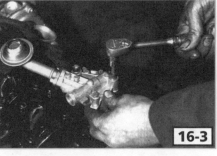

16-3

Before starting the engine, fit a fully charged battery and crank the engine over with spark plugs (or diesel pre-heaters) removed, so that the engine will spin rapidly without starting and without putting strain on the bearings. Turn the engine on the starter for around 30 seconds to circulate oil to the bearings, before starting up.

SAFETY FIRST!

• Make sure that it is safe to spin the engine with HT leads disconnected on your particular engine.

• Some ignition systems may suffer damage if not first completely disconnected.

• Take care not to cause injury from uncontrolled high tension sparks, or from diesel injection spray.

JOB 17:   REASSEMBLING ENGINE COMPONENTS - *clearances*.

Specific assembly details are given in the relevant section of this manual, but it's well worth pointing out some general information, especially with regard to fitting the crankshaft bearings:

IMPORTANT NOTES:
The following points should be regarded as essential and not optional!
• You should change the oil pump when carrying out an engine overhaul.
• All bearings, shells, piston rings and ALL seals that bear on moving parts MUST be copiously lubricated

with fresh engine oil as the engine is being reassembled.

• Work ONLY in clean conditions, with clean components and clean hands.

• Re-assemble in the reverse order of the dismantling procedure and take note of the following steps which will help you carry out a smooth operation.

17-1

❏ **STEP 1:** Make sure you have all the necessary gaskets, before starting work.

TOP TIP!

• If the centre main bearing has separate thrust washers (some have them integral with the main bearing shell), apply grease to the smooth side of the thrust washers and 'stick' them in position each side of the centre main bearing, before lowering the crank into position.

❏ **STEP 2:** Make sure all bearing seats are perfectly clean and locate the shells so that their tabs engage with the slots. Once lubricated, a shell can be placed on a journal and pushed around into its correct position.

17-2

❏ **STEP 3:** Screw bolts in finger tight and check that the crankshaft rotates freely and smoothly.

❏ **STEP 4:** Tighten each bolt evenly and progressively until the specified torque setting is reached. Check after tightening EACH bearing that the crankshaft rotates smoothly. If it doesn't, remove the bearing cap and shells and investigate as follows:

→ Check that there is no dirt or debris under a bearing shell – the most likely cause.

→ The next most likely cause is that there has been a build up of carbon on the rim of a seating and/or cap. Scrape off any that is present.

→ Check that the shells supplied are the right size for any machining that may have been carried out.

❏ **STEP 5:** The checks described in *Step 4* will only tell you if a bearing is too tight; it won't tell you if one is too loose.

Part B: Which Engine is Which?
CONTENTS

JOB 1: UNDERSTAND ENGINE TYPES.

There's no point in talking exclusively about 'Polo', 'Golf' or any other models covered here because very similar engines are used across different models. There are four broad engine types fitted to the vehicles covered here:

'INTERNAL WATER PUMP' ENGINES

❏ **STEP 1:** The (generally) smaller engines from 895cc to 1.6 litres, all with a horizontally-mounted

1-1

distributor on the end of the cylinder head, and (in most cases) a camshaft drive belt adjusted by turning the water pump. A smaller number of these engines have semi-automatic camshaft drive belt adjusters.

'EXTERNAL WATER PUMP' ENGINES

❏ **STEP 2:** All other petrol and diesel - the (generally) larger engines, from 1.5 litres to 2.0 litres, with a cylinder block-mounted distributor (except for 1.8 and 2.0 litre 16V engines) and a camshaft drive belt adjuster located inside the belt cover.

1-2

2.6 LITRE, VR6 ENGINES

❒ **STEP 3:** The VR6 6-cylinder engine - distinctive enough - there are six spark plugs! The cylinders are offset, in a single block.

1-3

ALUMINIUM BLOCK ENGINES

❒ **STEP 4:** These 'new generation' engines were introduced from 1994 to 1998 – and are not all good news for the mechanic! VW say that if the crankshaft main bearing bolts are loosened on any of these engines, the

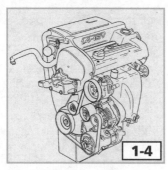
1-4

block and crank assembly will have to be replaced with new. Ouch! The 8-valve cylinder heads are very similar to other 8-valve 4-cylinder OHC Volkswagen engines. The 16-valve 'roller cam' cylinder heads are of a completely different type – see *Part P: 1.4 and 1.6 litre Aluminium Block Engine – Specific info.*

JOB 2: UNDERSTAND CYLINDER HEAD TYPES.

All engines have overhead camshafts (OHC) and can have one of three types of cylinder head:

FINGER ROCKER VALVE OPERATION

(Earlier 'INTERNAL WATER PUMP' engines only). These engines have valves operated by rocker arms. Exhaust and inlet manifolds are on the opposite sides of the head and the distributor is horizontal - fitted on the end of the head. See relevant section for illustration.

8-VALVE ENGINES

These have a belt-driven camshaft, directly operating on the valves, with valve clearances adjusted by changing shims.

16-VALVE ENGINES

The standard 16-valve head has two overhead camshafts. One camshaft operates the exhaust valves; the second camshaft operates the inlet valves. There are three types of 16V head:

2-1

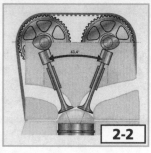
2-2

❒ **ILLUSTRATION 1:** Cast-iron block 1.8 and 2.0 litre 16V engines have the inlet valve camshaft driven by a chain from the belt-driven exhaust valve camshaft.

❒ **ILLUSTRATION 2:** Cast-iron block 1.4 litre 16V engines have both camshafts driven by the same ribbed drive belt.

❒ **ILLUSTRATION 3:** Aluminium block 1.4 and 1.6 litre engines have camshafts which are inserted into the camshaft housing from one end and are driven by two drive belts.

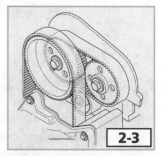
2-3

CYLINDER HEADS – TECHNICAL BACKGROUND INFORMATION

These are diagrams of each of the main cylinder head types featured in this manual. They are referred to in the relevant stripdown sequences.

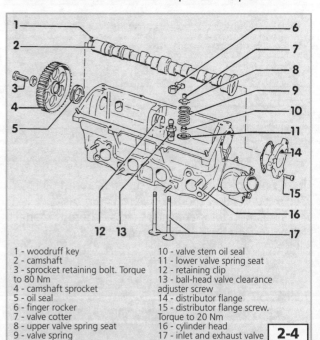

1 - woodruff key
2 - camshaft
3 - sprocket retaining bolt. Torque to 80 Nm
4 - camshaft sprocket
5 - oil seal
6 - finger rocker
7 - valve cotter
8 - upper valve spring seat
9 - valve spring
10 - valve stem oil seal
11 - lower valve spring seat
12 - retaining clip
13 - ball-head valve clearance adjuster screw
14 - distributor flange
15 - distributor flange screw. Torque to 20 Nm
16 - cylinder head
17 - inlet and exhaust valve
2-4

❒ **ILLUSTRATION 4: 'FINGER ROCKER' TYPE:** This was used on all earlier 1.1 and 1.3 litre engines. The camshaft operates the valves indirectly, through the finger rockers (6).

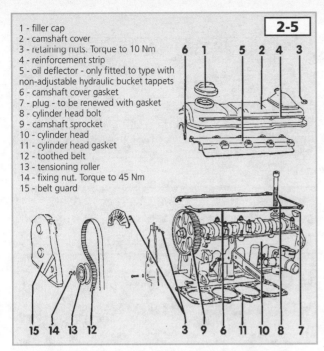

1 - filler cap
2 - camshaft cover
3 - retaining nuts. Torque to 10 Nm
4 - reinforcement strip
5 - oil deflector - only fitted to type with non-adjustable hydraulic bucket tappets
6 - camshaft cover gasket
7 - plug - to be renewed with gasket
8 - cylinder head bolt
9 - camshaft sprocket
10 - cylinder head
11 - cylinder head gasket
12 - toothed belt
13 - tensioning roller
14 - fixing nut. Torque to 45 Nm
15 - belt guard

2-5

□ **ILLUSTRATION 5: 8-VALVE BUCKET TAPPET - PETROL:** This system, where the camshaft operates directly on the valves via bucket tappets, is used on all 8-valve 'EXTERNAL WATER PUMP' petrol and Diesel engines, as well as on later 'INTERNAL WATER PUMP' engines.

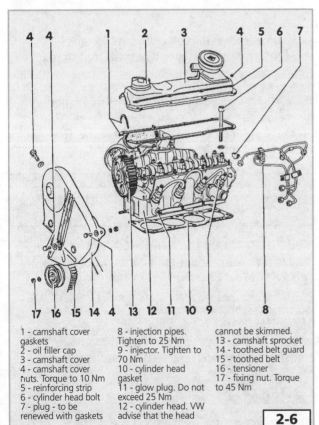

1 - camshaft cover gaskets
2 - oil filler cap
3 - camshaft cover
4 - camshaft cover nuts. Torque to 10 Nm
5 - reinforcing strip
6 - cylinder head bolt
7 - plug - to be renewed with gaskets
8 - injection pipes. Tighten to 25 Nm
9 - injector. Tighten to 70 Nm
10 - cylinder head gasket
11 - glow plug. Do not exceed 25 Nm
12 - cylinder head. VW advise that the head cannot be skimmed.
13 - camshaft sprocket
14 - toothed belt guard
15 - toothed belt
16 - tensioner
17 - fixing nut. Torque to 45 Nm

2-6

□ **ILLUSTRATION 6: 8-VALVE BUCKET TAPPET - DIESEL:** The Diesel engine cylinder head is similar and differences are detailed later in this manual, where appropriate.

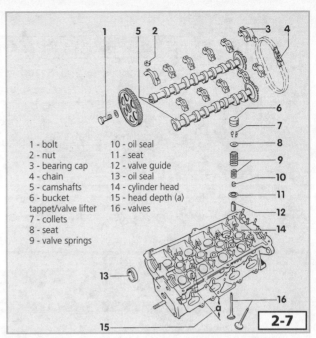

1 - bolt
2 - nut
3 - bearing cap
4 - chain
5 - camshafts
6 - bucket tappet/valve lifter
7 - collets
8 - seat
9 - valve springs
10 - oil seal
11 - seat
12 - valve guide
13 - oil seal
14 - cylinder head
15 - head depth (a)
16 - valves

2-7

□ **ILLUSTRATION 7: 1.8 AND 2.0 LITRE 16-VALVE ENGINES:** The inlet valve camshaft is operated by chain drive from the exhaust valve camshaft.

□ **ILLUSTRATION 8: 1.4 LITRE 16-VALVE ENGINES:** This cylinder head is fitted to Polo 16-valve with iron-block 1390cc engine. Both of the camshafts are operated by belt allowing a wider angle between valves.

2-8

□ **ILLUSTRATION 9: 1.4 and 1.6 LITRE 16-VALVE ALUMINIUM BLOCK ENGINES:** The camshafts are housed within the housing and are inserted from one end.

2-9

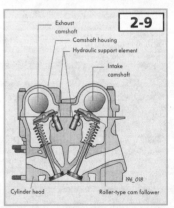

Exhaust camshaft
Camshaft housing
Hydraulic support element
Intake camshaft
Cylinder head
Roller-type cam follower
196_018

TOP TIP!

□ **ILLUSTRATION 10:** • Noisy hydraulic tappets are best checked before a (non-OHV) head is dismantled. Push each tappet down in turn with a wooden or plastic wedge. If free travel of more than 0.1 mm is felt before the valve starts to open, the tappet must be renewed.

2-10

GENERAL CYLINDER HEAD REMOVAL INFORMATION!

- The cylinder head can be removed with the engine in the car.
- Before removing the cylinder head, make sure the engine is stone cold.
- Undo the cylinder head bolts strictly in the order laid out in the relevant section.
- These precautions help to prevent cylinder head distortion.
- The new cylinder head gasket should stay in its packaging until required, to avoid contamination by oil or grease.

SAFETY FIRST!

- Before dismantling, disconnect the battery negative (-) earth/ground terminal. See *Chapter 10, Electrical, Dash, Instruments, Fact File: Disconnecting the Battery* BEFORE doing so!

Part C: Timing Belt or Chain
Inspection, Adjustment, Replacement

CONTENTS

Page No.

Page No.

ENGINE TYPES

We refer to the following broad engine types in this section.

'INTERNAL WATER PUMP' ENGINES

This refers to the (generally) smaller engines from 895cc to 1.6 litres with a horizontally-mounted distributor on the end of the cylinder head, and (in most cases) a camshaft drive belt adjusted by turning the water pump. A smaller number of these engines have semi-automatic adjusters. See *Job 2, Step A9*.

'EXTERNAL WATER PUMP' ENGINES

This refers to all other petrol and diesel (generally) larger engines, from 1.5 litres to 2.0 litres, with a cylinder block-mounted distributor and a camshaft drive belt adjuster located inside the belt cover.

ALL ENGINE TYPES

This sub-heading is for information relevant to all types.

2.6 LITRE, VR6 ENGINES

These engine use timing chains and not timing belts and therefore no regular replacement is necessary. For signs of timing chain wear on stripdown, see the general engine overhaul section. For information on VALVE TIMING see *Part I: 6-Cylinder Engines, Cylinder head - overhaul.*

See *Part B: Which Engine is Which?* for an explanation of the engine types referred to here.

IMPORTANT NOTE:
1.4 AND 1.6 LITRE ALUMINIUM ENGINES: There are several important and completely different features on these engines – see *Part P: 1.4 and 1.6 litre Aluminium Block Engine – Specific info.*

JOB 1:   CAMSHAFT TIMING BELT - *check.*

It is ESSENTIAL that the camshaft drive belt is renewed at the recommended interval. See the *Service Interval Chart* at the start of *Chapter 5, Servicing.* If the belt breaks the valves may collide with the pistons, causing serious engine damage. At the very least, the engine will immediately stop running. *Job 2: Timing belt - replacement and adjustment* explains how to carry out the work.

SAFETY FIRST!

Before dismantling, disconnect the battery negative (-) earth/ground terminal. See *Chapter 10, Electrical, Dash, Instruments, Fact File: Disconnecting the Battery* BEFORE doing so!

☐ **STEP 1: CURSORY INSPECTION:** Unclip or unscrew the top of the camshaft belt outer cover and pull it away. Examine the

belt for wear. This inspection will only show severe damage.

☐ **STEP 2:** In order to examine the belt properly, you will have to remove the cover. If there is any cracking, or if the toothed side appears worn, or any 'teeth' are missing, replace the belt straight away.

☐ **STEP 3:** On some models, the timing belt cover will have a separate upper section which can be removed by itself. On others, the cover passes behind the crankshaft pulley without there being any need to remove the crank pulley. If you have to remove the crank pulley, it may be necessary to disconnect the engine mountings and lower the engine - supporting it on a trolley jack - so that the bottom pulley can be unbolted and removed, after first removing the auxiliary drive belt - V-shaped on some; a flat ribbed belt on others.

☐ **STEP 4:** If the belt is in good condition, it may still need re-tensioning.
➜ EITHER: Check that you can twist the belt through approximately 90 degrees at

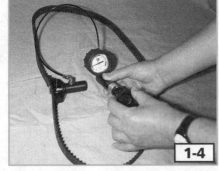

the centre of its longest 'run', using only the strength of fingers and thumb.
➜ OR: Use the correct tool, such as this Sykes-Pickavant tension checking tool – used with the belt *in situ*, of course! If necessary, slacken the adjuster fixing nut and re-adjust as shown in *Job 2*.

'INTERNAL WATER PUMP' ENGINES WITH SEMI-AUTOMATIC ADJUSTER IN PLACE OF ADJUSTMENT AT WATER PUMP

☐ **STEP 5:** This applies to 1.6 litre engines from late 1994-on with engine code AEA. Turn the crankshaft until the timing marks show the engine at TDC. See *Job 3*. Apply firm thumb pressure to the belt at

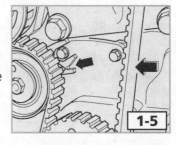

the position of the right-hand arrow. The following two events will take place if the tension is correct - if not adjust until:
➜ The marks on the tensioning roller - see left-hand arrow - should be seen to move apart.
➜ When pressure on the belt is released, the tensioning roller should move back to its initial position.

2.0 LITRE 16-VALVE ENGINES WITH SEMI-AUTOMATIC ADJUSTER

☐ **STEP 6:** Turn the crankshaft two complete turns in the normal direction of rotation. Push against the belt at its longest point with firm thumb pressure. The following two events will take

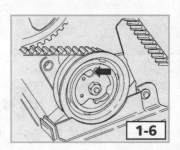

place if the tension is correct - if not adjust until:
➜ The marks on the tensioning roller (arrow) should be seen to move apart.
➜ When pressure on the belt is released, the tensioning roller should move back to its initial position, with marks again aligned.

JOB 2:   **TIMING BELT** – *replacement, adjustment.*

On all engines, the cam belt should be renewed at the recommended interval. If it breaks, the engine will suffer total failure and could be catastrophically damaged.

TOP TIP!

• Volkswagen recommend that, if an engine has been standing for two years or more, you should replace the belt as a matter of course, because it will be prone to early failure.

IMPORTANT NOTE: Avoid potential major problems by following this advice from Volkswagen:
➜ In some engines, the valves will collide with the pistons if the camshaft/s is/are turned while the engine is set to Top Dead Centre (TDC).

➜ To avoid risk of damage, the camshaft/s should NEVER be replaced (or turned if already in place) while the pistons are at TDC.

➜ Volkswagen recommend that you turn the crankshaft/s back from TDC (the *opposite direction* to normal rotation) by a few degrees, moving the pistons safely a little way down the bore.

➜ With the cylinder head fitted to the engine, the camshaft/s must now be turned to their alignment marks for when No. 1 piston is at TDC.

➜ Before the timing belt is refitted, the crankshaft must be moved forward (in the *direction of normal rotation*) to the TDC position again.

Section A: Timing belt replacement and adjustment - WITH ENGINE IN CAR.

POLO AND CADDY FROM 1990-ON

The engine on all of these models has to be lowered on the right-side in order to reach the lower, right hand side of the engine. See *Job 4*.

ALL OTHER MODELS

☐ **STEP A1:** Slacken the alternator and remove the V-belt or belts (ribbed belt/s on later models). Remove the alternator if necessary - certain models. OR: Remove the flat, ribbed belt. See *Part D: Auxiliary Drive Belts*.

☐ **STEP A2:** Set the timing marks (see *Job 3*) to the TDC position.

☐ **STEP A3: ENGINES WITH V-BELT AUXILIARY DRIVES:** To remove the auxiliary belt pulley, grip the crankshaft pulley bolt to prevent it from turning. You can now remove the V-belt pulley retaining bolts and take off the pulley.

☐ **STEP A4: ENGINES WITH RIBBED BELT AUXILIARY DRIVES:** Note that on some later engines, with ribbed auxiliary belt (see illustration), both the crankshaft's **Rib belt pulley** and the **Crankshaft gear wheel** are held to the crankshaft by the same centre **Bolt** instead of the four separate bolts on most engines.

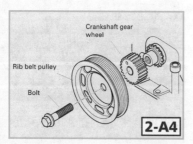

Crankshaft gear wheel

Rib belt pulley

Bolt

• The centre crankshaft pulley nut - *only necessary to remove where the ribbed belt pulley is held on with the crank pulley nut!* - will be difficult to turn.
• If the engine is in the car, engage a gear (or 'Park' in the case of an automatic) and have an assistant hold the footbrake down very firmly. This will stop the engine from turning.
• Alternatively, with the starter motor removed, you can have a helper prevent the flywheel ring gear from turning by using a large screwdriver.

ALL ENGINE TYPES

NOTE: It may be necessary to disconnect the engine mountings and lower the engine - supporting it on a trolley jack - so that the bottom pulley can be unbolted and removed, after first removing the auxiliary drive belt - V-shaped on some; a flat ribbed belt on others.

☐ **STEP A5:** The timing belt cover is held in place with retaining bolts and (on some models) spring clips, and may be one-piece, or in two separate parts.

☐ **STEP A6:** Look out for the recessed screw (**a**) with an Allen key head - other screws are conventional bolt heads - on engines which have a cover that wraps right around the bottom pulley.

IMPORTANT NOTES:
i) To ensure that the replacement belt will be fitted with the valves (and injection pump, on diesel engines) in the correct position - essential to avoid serious engine damage - turn the engine until all the timing marks are aligned. See *Job 3*.
ii) The crankshaft and camshaft must not be turned independently of each other, or the valves may collide with the pistons.

DIESEL ENGINES ONLY

MODELS WITH TWO-PART SPROCKET ON INJECTION PUMP (3 fixing bolts on sprocket): See separate supplement at the end of this Section for the whole process of replacing the camshaft belt on these engines.

MODELS WITH SINGLE-PART SPROCKET ON INJECTION PUMP (ONE CENTRAL FIXING NUT ON SPROCKET):

❑ **STEP A7:** With No. 1 cylinder at TDC (see *Job 3*) prevent the camshaft from turning with a suitably sized bar placed in the slot in the end of the camshaft.

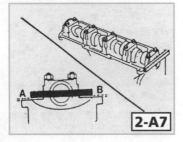

TOP TIP!

The bar will need to be centralised as follows:
• Push one end of the bar down so that it touches the cylinder head.
• Measure the gap at the other end of the bar with a feeler gauge.
• Select two feeler gauges, each one half the gap just measured.
• Push one feeler gauge under each end of the bar to hold it (and thus, the camshaft) central.

❑ **STEP A8:** Lock the injection pump pulley - VW tool 2064 shown.

TOP TIP!

• The location pin for setting the Diesel pump sprocket measures 15.4 mm in diameter.
• The pin is included in the Sykes-Pickavant Diesel Engine Setting/Locking & Fuel Pump Timing Tool Kit, or is available separately, part no. 077006.

IMPORTANT NOTE: DO NOT attempt to replace the timing belt without using these two tools!

'INTERNAL WATER PUMP' ENGINES

❑ **STEP A9: BELT ADJUSTMENT AT WATER PUMP:** On most of these engines, you loosen the water pump retaining bolts and turn the pump body clockwise, which slackens the timing belt.

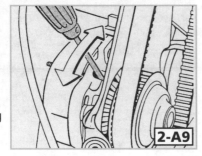

'INTERNAL WATER PUMP' ENGINES WITH SEMI-AUTOMATIC ADJUSTER INSTEAD OF AT WATER PUMP: Slacken the belt by freeing the centre clamp nut, then turning the adjuster anti-clockwise - in the **opposite** direction to the arrow in illustration *2-A15*.

'EXTERNAL WATER PUMP' ENGINES

❑ **STEP A10: TYPE 1:** Slacken the adjuster locknut - prevent the pulley from turning with the (larger) tensioning nut, and turn the adjuster anti-clockwise to take the pressure off the belt.

❑ **STEP A11: TYPE 2:** Prevent the pulley from turning with the adjuster shown in *Step A17* and slacken the tension by loosening the small clamp nut. Turn the adjuster anti-clockwise to remove tension from the belt.

2.0 LITRE 16-VALVE ENGINES WITH SEMI-AUTOMATIC ADJUSTER: Slacken the belt by freeing the centre clamp nut, then turning the adjuster anti-clockwise - in the direction of the arrow in illustration *2-A18*.

ALL ENGINE TYPES

❑ **STEP A12:** Slide the timing belt carefully off the sprockets and take very great care not to rotate any of the toothed pulleys.

❑ **STEP A13:** Check that all of the alignment marks shown in *Job 3* are still correctly lined up. Slide on the new timing belt, again taking very great care not to move any of the sprockets.

'INTERNAL WATER PUMP' ENGINES

❏ **STEP A14:** Tension the belt:

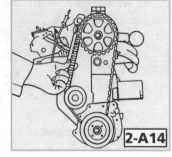

➔ EITHER: until you can just turn the belt through 90 degrees, using thumb and forefinger, at the point shown. Retighten the water pump.
➔ OR: use the correct tool, such as the Sykes-Pickavant tension checking tool (illustration *1-4*) – used with the belt *in situ*, of course! If necessary, slacken the adjuster fixing nut and re-adjust.

❏ **STEP A15:** 'INTERNAL WATER PUMP' ENGINES WITH SEMI-AUTOMATIC ADJUSTER, SEPARATE FROM WATER PUMP: Make sure that the slot in the tensioning roller base plate (**1**) is

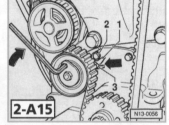

engaged over the securing bolt (**2**). Turn the roller with an Allen key in the direction of the curved arrow until the indicator (**3**) is aligned with the groove in the base plate (straight arrow). Tighten the central clamping nut.

'EXTERNAL WATER PUMP' ENGINES

❏ **STEP A16:** Re-tension the belt by adjusting the tensioner.
➔ EITHER: so that you can just turn the belt through 90 degrees at its longest free length using your thumb and index finger.
➔ OR: use the correct tool, such as this Sykes-Pickavant tension checking tool – used with the belt *in situ*, of course! If necessary, slacken the

adjuster fixing nut and re-adjust. The tensioner locknut should be retightened to 45 Nm.

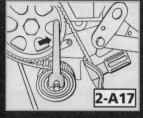
❏ **STEP A18:** 2.0 LITRE 16-VALVE ENGINES WITH SEMI-AUTOMATIC ADJUSTER: With the central clamp nut released, take the tension out of the belt by turning the adjuster in the direction of the

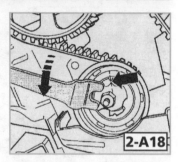

curved arrow as far as the stop. Next, tension the adjuster by turning it clockwise until the pointer on the adjuster part of the pulley lines up with the one on the outer part (straight arrow). Check the adjustment - see *Job 1, Step 6*.

FACT FILE

ALL 16 VALVE AND DIESEL ENGINES

❏ **STEP A19:** Belt tension is particularly important on these engines. It would pay to invest in a

Volkswagen special tool VW210, ordered from your Volkswagen dealer. Tension the belt (arrowed) to the figure indicated on the gauge when applied to the longest belt run.

ALL ENGINE TYPES

❏ **STEP A20:** Check that timing marks (arrowed) are still at (or as close as they will go to) their correct positions before rotating the crank.

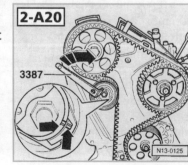

➔ Item 3387 shows the tensioner being released.

STEP A21: To settle the new timing belt into position, rotate the crankshaft through two whole revolutions and recheck/reset the tension.

2-A21

STEP A22: Replace the timing-belt covers and other components removed earlier.

TOP TIP!

• If there is a growling noise which rises and falls with the engine speed, the belt tension may be too tight.

DIESEL ENGINES ONLY

MODELS WITH SINGLE-PART SPROCKET ON INJECTION PUMP - THREE FIXING BOLTS ON SPROCKET

STEP A23: Set the engine to TDC and lock the camshaft - see *Job 3*.

STEP A24:
Remove the drive belt as follows:
→ Use a locking pin (VW tool No. 3359 shown here) to lock the injection pump sprocket.
→ Loosen the sprocket bolts (1).

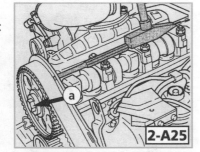
3359   2-A24

→ Loosen the belt tensioner, as shown for petrol engines.
→ Remove the crankshaft pulley and the lower part of the belt guard.
→ Mark the direction of rotation of the belt and remove it.

STEP A25: Fit the new belt as follows:
→ Make sure that the engine is set to TDC and that the camshaft locking bar and injection pump locking pin are both in place.
→ Loosen the bolt
(a) half a turn and use a drift to release the camshaft sprocket from its taper. Fit the toothed belt.
→ Turn the tensioner until the belt is correctly tensioned, as described elsewhere in this Part of the manual.

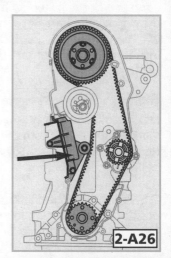
2-A25

→ Make sure that the TDC marks are still aligned.
→ Tighten the camshaft sprocket bolt (a) to 45 Nm.
→ Tighten the injection pump sprocket bolts (2-A24, item 1) to 25 Nm.
→ Remove the camshaft setting bar and injection pump pin.
→ Turn the engine two complete rotations in the normal direction, and re-set to TDC.
→ Check to see if the pin, (2-A24, Part No. 3359) can be fitted. If not, loosen the securing bolts (1) again and turn the hub (behind the sprocket) until the pin fits, then retighten the bolts to 25 Nm.

STEP A26: 1.9 TDI ONLY: On these engines, there is also a hydraulic belt tensioner (arrowed) to keep the belt evenly tensioned and around which the belt passes.

2-A26

Section B: Timing belt replacement and adjustment - DURING ENGINE REBUILD.

The process is similar to the one followed when renewing the cam belt when the engine is in the car, but you will have to establish the sprocket positions from scratch.

FACT FILE

ENGINE REBUILDING DIESEL ENGINES

When rebuilding an engine, and after the pump and camshaft alignment marks have been lost, it is not possible for the Diesel pump to be set without specialist equipment. You can get as far as to fit the camshaft/timing belt, but DO NOT attempt to run the engine without having a specialist set the injection pump timing for you, or serious engine damage can occur.

ALL ENGINES
When fitting a cam belt as part of an engine build, it is MOST IMPORTANT that the camshaft is fitted and the camshaft pulley set to its alignment mark while none of the pistons are at TDC. On some engines, the valves can collide with the pistons if they are at TDC.
→ Once the valve positions are set, the crankshaft position can be aligned.
→ Don't re-use an already used belt. It will be more prone to breakage once removed - replace it!

ALL ENGINES

❏ **STEP B1:** Turn the camshaft so that the camshaft sprocket aligns with the timing mark shown for your engine in **Job 3**.

IMPORTANT NOTE:
If you have followed the IMPORTANT NOTE near the start of **Job 2: Timing belt – replacement, adjustment,** the pistons will all be part-way down the bores. If you are not sure, turn the camshaft with very great care, so that if a valve should come into contact with a piston, you can stop before any damage is done.

❏ **STEP B2: 'VERTICAL DISTRIBUTOR' ENGINES ONLY:** Fit the pulley to the intermediate shaft. Align the mark on the pulley with the edge of the (temporarily fitted) crankshaft V-belt or ribbed-belt pulley. See **Job 3**.

❏ **STEP B3:** Turn the crankshaft so that the TDC position is showing in the inspection hole in the transmission bellhousing. See **Job 3**.

❏ **STEP B4:** Remove the V-belt pulley again, and fit the sprocket to the crankshaft so that the alignment mark is in the position shown in **Job 3**.

❏ **STEP B5:** Fit and tension the belt as described in **Section A: Timing belt replacement and adjustment - WITH ENGINE IN CAR**.

❏ **STEP B6:** Check that the distributor rotor arm is pointing to the No. 1 cylinder mark on the distributor body. If not, turn the distributor or remove and refit it, so that the rotor arm is properly aligned.

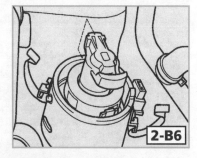
2-B6

❏ **STEP B7:** Note that there are several different distributor types and thus different types of marking to look out for.

2-B7

❏ **STEP B8: PETROL ENGINES:** Check the ignition timing when the work is complete.

JOB 3: VALVE TIMING - *setting timing marks*.

SETTING THE CAMSHAFT PULLEY/S

IMPORTANT NOTE: Avoid potential major problems by following this advice from Volkswagen:
→ On some engines, the valves will collide with the pistons if the camshaft/s is/are turned while the engine is set to Top Dead Centre (TDC).
→ To avoid risk of damage, the camshaft/s should NEVER be replaced (or turned if already in place) while the pistons are at TDC.
→ Volkswagen recommend that the crankshaft is turned back (the *opposite direction* to normal rotation) from TDC, by a few degrees, moving the pistons safely a little way down the bore.
→ With the cylinder head fitted to the engine, the camshaft/s must now be turned to their alignment marks for when No. 1 piston is at TDC.
→ Before the timing belt is refitted, the crankshaft must be moved forward (in the *direction of* normal rotation) to the TDC position again.

'EXTERNAL WATER PUMP' ENGINES

❏ **STEP 1:** The marks on the outside of the camshaft sprocket must align with the mark on the cylinder head cover (**A**); or, if there is no suitable mark there, this mark on the inner

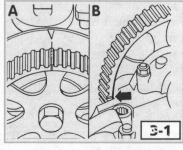
3-1

side of the camshaft sprocket must align with the edge of the cylinder head, adjacent to the camshaft cover (**B,** arrowed). This also applies to 16-Valve engines, because there is only one sprocket and the two camshafts are synchronised with a chain drive. See **Part I and Part J** for correct alignment of camshafts when assembling.

❏ **STEP 2:** Here is an alternative view of the camshaft sprocket marks being aligned with the edge of the cylinder head - pointed to with the end of a screwdriver - with the camshaft cover removed, in this instance.

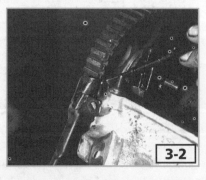
3-2

☐ **STEP 3: SETTING CRANKSHAFT AND INTERMEDIATE SHAFTS TO TDC POSITION:** One way of doing so is to align the mark on the intermediate shaft pulley (the larger pulley) with the mark on the (smaller) crankshaft pulley.

3-3

☐ **STEP 4:** Alternatively, depending on engine type and circumstances, place the toothed belt over the intermediate shaft pulley (out of view in this Volkswagen drawing)

3-4

and turn the pulley by moving the belt in the direction of the arrows, until…

☐ **STEP 5:** …the centre of the end of the rotor arm on the distributor is in line with the TDC mark on the distributor body.

3-5

'INTERNAL WATER PUMP' ENGINES

☐ **STEP 6: SINGLE OVERHEAD CAMSHAFT ENGINES WITH ADJUSTMENT AT WATER PUMP:** The camshaft sprocket timing mark must align with the mark shown (A), and the

3-6

crankshaft sprocket mark must align with the pointer (B) - position 'O', or the single pointer on some engines. But before setting the crankshaft pulley, see *Step 10*.

☐ **STEP 7:** To align the intermediate shaft pulley, temporarily fit the crankshaft V-belt pulley and align the marks on the V-belt pulley and the

intermediate shaft sprocket. Remove the V-belt pulley again so that the rest of the assembly can take place.

☐ **STEP 8: SINGLE OVERHEAD CAMSHAFT ENGINES WITH SEMI-AUTOMATIC ADJUSTER SEPARATE FROM WATER PUMP:** If a piston is at TDC,

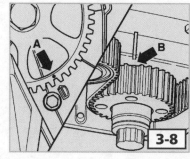

3-8

the valves could strike the piston when turning the camshaft. Set the camshaft sprocket to the mark (A). The crankshaft pulley must align with the marking on the seal flange (B). But before setting the crankshaft pulley, see *Step 10*.

☐ **STEP 9: 1.4 LITRE 16-VALVE ENGINES:** Both camshafts are driven by the toothed belt. Align the marks on the camshafts (a).

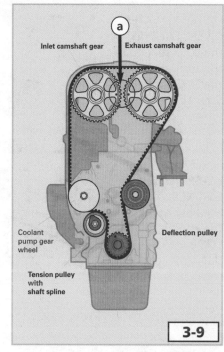

Inlet camshaft gear   Exhaust camshaft gear

Coolant pump gear wheel

Deflection pulley

Tension pulley with shaft spline

3-9

☐ **STEP 10:** The marks that show when No. 1 cylinder is at TDC (Top Dead Centre) are found inside the hole on the top of the bellhousing. Remove the bung, or unscrew the TDC sensor, as appropriate. Appearances differ slightly between models as shown by the examples **A** to **D** here.

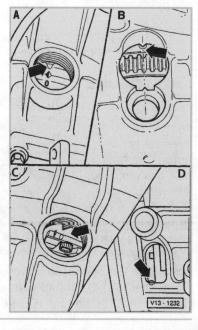

V13 - 1232

DIESEL ENGINES

☐ **STEP 11:** Use a camshaft centralising bar. See **Job 2-A7**.

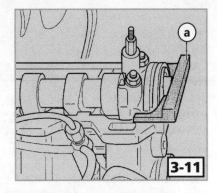

3-11

SETTING THE CRANKSHAFT TO TOP DEAD CENTRE (TDC)

☐ **STEP 12: LATER DIESEL ENGINES:** On these Diesel engines, this is the position of the TDC pointer. See **Step 10** for other types.

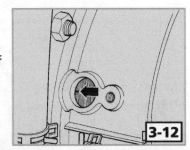

3-12

☐ **STEP 13: LATER DIESEL ENGINES:** It is not easy to set the engine to TDC once it is out of the car.
→ You are advised to use a Vernier gauge (e.g. VW No. 2068A), with the position **A** set to 71 mm.
→ Turn the crankshaft until the pointer on the gauge (B) points to the TDC mark on the flywheel.

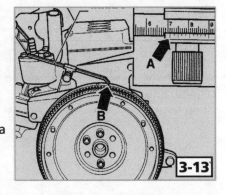

3-13

ALL ENGINES

☐ **STEP 14:** The engine should have been set to TDC before the timing belt was removed. When rebuilding, align the marks on the vibration damper/crankshaft pulley with the pointer on the belt cover. If there is a choice of marks (see **Step 6**), probably labelled 'Z' and 'O', choose the 'O' setting for TDC alignment.

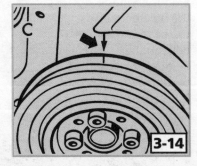

3-14

JOB 4: LOWERING ENGINE - *Polo from 1990-on.*

The lower belt cover and the crankshaft pulley have to be reached from inside the wheel arch. They cannot be removed with the engine in its normal position on these models. Lower the engine as follows:

☐ **STEP 1:** Remove the following items from the engine while it is in its normal position:
→ **a.** The noise insulation tray from the top of the engine.
→ **b.** The connecting hose to the air cleaner and intake pipes.
→ **c.** Cylinder head cover.
→ **d.** Unclip the upper guard to the auxiliary belt.
→ **e.** Remove the three bolts holding the coolant pump pulley and remove the pulley.

☐ **STEP 2:** Support the engine. This is the Volkswagen support bracket. There is a Sykes-Pickavant version of this support, or you could use an engine hoist, or a jack placed beneath the vehicle. NEVER jack directly onto the sump. Spread the load with a piece of wood.

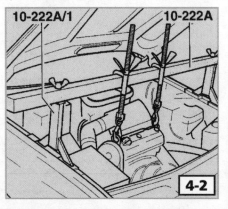

10-222A/1   10-222A

4-2

☐ **STEP 3:** Remove the engine mounting bolts and take off the right hand engine mounting.

DIESEL ENGINES

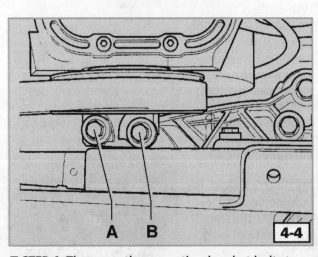

A   B

4-4

☐ **STEP 4:** These are the mounting bracket bolts to be removed (**A**) and (**B**).

STEP 5: Take out the five bolts (arrowed) and remove the engine support bracket from the cylinder block.

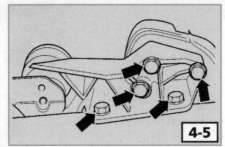

4-5

STEP 6: You can now remove the engine mounting after removing the four engine mounting bolts (arrowed).

4-5

Part D: Auxillary Drive Belts

CONTENTS

See *Part B: Which Engine is Which?* for an explanation of the engine types referred to here.

IMPORTANT NOTE:
1.4 AND 1.6 LITRE ALUMINIUM ENGINES: There are several important and completely different features on these engines – see *Part P: 1.4 and 1.6 litre Aluminium Block Engine – Specific info.*

JOB 1: DRIVE BELT/S - check/adjust.

On all models, the alternator and belt tension adjuster are on the front of the engine. In some cases, they are accessible from inside the engine bay, above the car, but in other cases, access is from beneath. On vehicles from about 1992-on, there may be a plastic undertray that has first to be removed.

Section A: Vee-belts.

IMPORTANT NOTE: • Loosen ALL the alternator fixing and pivot bolts before attempting to adjust the belt tension. Retighten them all after adjustment is complete.
• When installing the belt, ensure that the ribs are correctly seated in the grooves in the pulley. On some models, certain pulleys are wider than the ribbed belt and in those cases, it is MOST IMPORTANT that the belt is seated centrally in the pulley with an equal number of 'spare' grooves on each side of the belt.

CHECK CONDITION OF BELT/S

STEP A1: Check the belt or belts, and if there are any signs of cracking, 'polishing', fraying or severe wear on the inner face/s, replace the belt/s. Each belt should deflect by

1-A1

between 5 and 10 mm (unless shown otherwise, below) when firm thumb pressure is applied to the longest 'run' of each belt between the pulleys (a) in the direction of the arrow. Too little tension and the belt might slip; too much, and belt and bearing wear will increase. A new belt may only require a deflection of 2 mm, however. Try it again later, once it has bedded in.

ADJUST TENSION

IMPORTANT NOTES:
• Belt tension should only be adjusted when the engine is cold.
• After adjustment, run the engine for 15 to 30 seconds, to allow the belt to bed-in, then check again.
• Experienced mechanics claim that belts often go slack when the engine heats up, producing belt squeal.
• If this happens on your vehicle, adjust the belt again when the engine is hot. Wear industrial leather gloves and long-sleeved overalls and take very great care not to burn yourself on the hot engine or exhaust.

VEHICLES WITHOUT AIR CONDITIONING

❒ **STEP A2:** Earlier models have a simple sliding arrangement for the alternator adjustment.

1-A2

❒ **STEP A3:** On earlier models, slacken the fixing bolts and lever the alternator away from the engine until the belt tension is correct. Take very great care not to damage the alternator body. Retighten the bolts.

1-A3

❒ **STEP A4:** On some early engines, the alternator is positioned low down and is accessed from beneath the car. Slacken all the bolts, including the tensioner arm bolts (**1**).

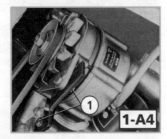

1-A4

TOP TIP!

• Leave a ring spanner on the alternator-to-bracket nut, so that you can tighten it easily and quickly as soon as the belt is properly tensioned.
• Use a piece of wood to lever the alternator.
• Take great care not to apply too much pressure, which could damage the alternator casing.

❒ **STEP A5:** On later models, slacken the bolt on the adjuster rack (**a**) and slacken the locknut on the adjuster pinion (**b**). Turn the cogged adjuster along the rack until the correct tension is applied.

1-A5

❒ **STEP A6:** This is the correct special tool for turning the adjuster. An ordinary spanner works just as well. Loosen the central locknut first; retighten after adjustment is complete.

1-A6

VEHICLES WITH AIR CONDITIONING - GENERAL

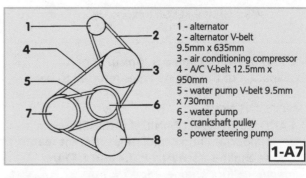

1 - alternator
2 - alternator V-belt 9.5mm x 635mm
3 - air conditioning compressor
4 - A/C V-belt 12.5mm x 950mm
5 - water pump V-belt 9.5mm x 730mm
6 - water pump
7 - crankshaft pulley
8 - power steering pump

1-A7

❒ **STEP A7:** There may be up to four belts to check and adjust, depending on the age of vehicle and systems fitted.

VEHICLES WITH AIR CONDITIONING - UP TO 1977 MODEL YEAR

❒ **STEP A8: ADJUST COMPRESSOR BELT:** Support lever (**A**) on bracket (**C**) and lift bracket (**B**). Tighten bolt (**1-A9, item 1**).
➡ Item (**D**) is the compressor.

1-A8

❒ **STEP A9: ENSURE PULLEYS ARE IN LINE:** by lifting bracket (**1-A8, item B**) again, then tighten bolts (**2, 3** and **4**) if alignment is correct.

1-A9

STEP A10:
ADJUST
ALTERNATOR BELT:

1-A10

→ Only do so after compressor belt has been adjusted.
→ Place screwdriver (F) on bolt in bracket (E).
→ Lift bracket (E) with screwdriver (G) and tighten bolt.

VEHICLES WITH AIR CONDITIONING - FROM 1978 MODEL YEAR

STEP A11:
ADJUSTING
COMPRESSOR BELT:

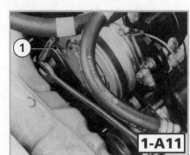

1-A11

→ Turn belt tensioner (1) until a 10 mm external hexagon socket can be inserted through one of the holes in the tensioner into the socket head screw behind it.
→ Loosen socket head screws.
→ Turn tensioner until the belt can only just be deflected 10 mm with firm thumb pressure.
→ Tighten socket head screw.

STEP A12:
ADJUSTING
ALTERNATOR AND
COOLANT PUMP
BELT:

1-A12

→ Loosen adjusting strut on retaining plate (1) and lift strut with screwdriver until the belt can be deflected 10 to 15 mm with firm thumb pressure.
→ Tighten strut again.

DIESEL VEHICLES WITH AIR CONDITIONING - FROM 1979 MODEL YEAR

STEP A13:
ADJUSTING
COOLANT PUMP
AND COMPRESSOR
V-BELTS:

1-A13

→ Remove alternator and toothed belt guard.
→ Screw in bolt (1), push mandrel (2) through compressor lug holes.
→ Loosen off the two M10 nuts on tensioner and

two socket head screws M8 and M10 on compressor bracket.
→ Using VW special tool No. 552, or by some other means, lift compressor until the V-belt can be deflected from above between 5 mm and 10 mm using thumb pressure.
→ Tighten M10 bolts on tensioner and two socket head screws (M8 and M10) on compressor bracket.

NON-DIESEL VEHICLES WITH AIR CONDITIONING -FROM 1979 MODEL YEAR

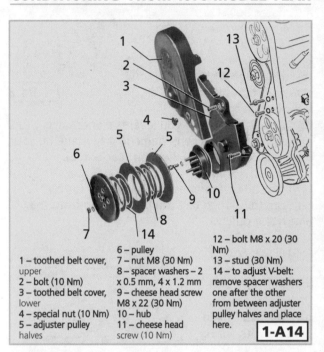

1-A14

1 – toothed belt cover, upper	6 – pulley	12 – bolt M8 x 20 (30 Nm)
2 – bolt (10 Nm)	7 – nut M8 (30 Nm)	13 – stud (30 Nm)
3 – toothed belt cover, lower	8 – spacer washers – 2 x 0.5 mm, 4 x 1.2 mm	14 – to adjust V-belt: remove spacer washers one after the other from between adjuster pulley halves and place here.
4 – special nut (10 Nm)	9 – cheese head screw M8 x 22 (30 Nm)	
5 – adjuster pulley halves	10 – hub	
	11 – cheese head screw (10 Nm)	

STEP A14: V-belt tension is determined by the number of spacer washers used between the two halves of the crankshaft pulley.

Section B: Flat, ribbed belts.

When removing and fitting ribbed belts, bear in mind the following:
→ You do not have to check or manually adjust the tension of ribbed belts, other than as shown here. They should be checked for condition, as for V- belts.
→ Some models have a belt cover which must first be removed.
→ Before removing the ribbed belt, mark the direction of rotation with a felt pen or typists' correction fluid.
→ When installing the belt, ensure that the ribs are correctly seated in the grooves in the pulley. On some models, certain pulleys are wider than the ribbed belt and in those cases, it is MOST IMPORTANT that the belt is seated centrally in the pulley with an equal number of 'spare' grooves on each side of the belt.

One of three different types of adjuster can be fitted to 4-cylinder vehicles, while a different type of adjuster is fitted to the VR6 engine.

4-CYL. ENGINES WITHOUT SEPARATE ADJUSTER ROLLER

☐ **STEP B1:** Loosen the alternator bolts (**1** and **2**) by at least one turn. Press the alternator down in the direction of the arrow so that it swivels against its spring tension. This drawing shows the Volkswagen special tool No. 3297 in use. If you lever the alternator, make sure that you don't damage it or make up your own version of the Volkswagen special tool.

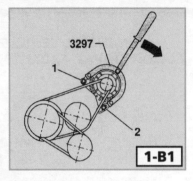

With the alternator pressed against the spring tension, the ribbed belt can be removed from the alternator pulley.

☐ **STEP B2:** For reference, here is another view of the Volkswagen special tool No. 3297 (held in place with spring clips – arrowed), showing how the alternator is levered down, in a clockwise direction in order to free the ribbed belt.

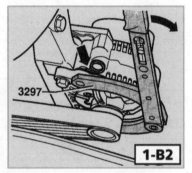

4-CYL. ENGINES WITH ADJUSTER ROLLER

☐ **STEP B3:** On engines with two separate drive belts, the tensioning roller (**a**) has to be moved to take the pressure off the alternator belt. Use an appropriate lever or adjustable wrench (**b**) and turn it in the direction of the arrow before removing the ribbed belt. On this model, the power steering pump (**c**) and the air conditioner compressor (when fitted) are driven by a V-belt.

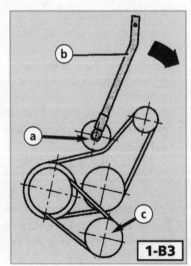

☐ **STEP B4:** On this version, the same ribbed belt drives all of the components (a 'serpentine' belt). By turning the nut on the adjuster in the direction of the lower arrow, the adjuster moves in the direction of the upper arrow enabling removal or installation of the ribbed belt.

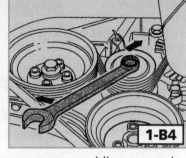

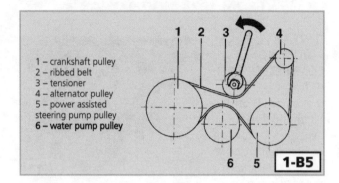

1 – crankshaft pulley
2 – ribbed belt
3 – tensioner
4 – alternator pulley
5 – power assisted steering pump pulley
6 – water pump pulley

☐ **STEP B5:** On this version, typically fitted to Diesel engines from 1997-on, you have to use an open-ended wrench and turn the adjuster in the direction of the arrow in order to release it.

VR6 ENGINES

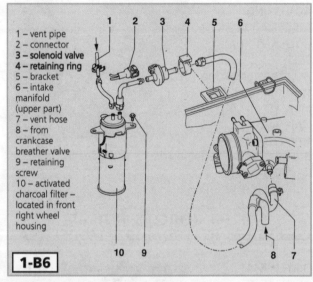

1 – vent pipe
2 – connector
3 – solenoid valve
4 – retaining ring
5 – bracket
6 – intake manifold (upper part)
7 – vent hose
8 – from crankcase breather valve
9 – retaining screw
10 – activated charcoal filter – located in front right wheel housing

☐ **STEP B6:** First, remove the solenoid valve:
➜ The solenoid valve (**3**) is fitted into the retaining ring (**4**), and both can be pulled off the bracket (**5**) on the lower part of the air cleaner.
➜ Now remove the air filter housing complete with the air mass meter.

IMPORTANT NOTE: Engines with air conditioning compressor are fitted with a double ribbed belt.

❏ **STEP B7:** Take an M8 x 80 bolt and screw it into the tensioner threaded hole (**A**) until the ribbed belt is no longer under tension – BUT NO FURTHER otherwise the tensioner housing can be damaged. You can now remove the ribbed belt.

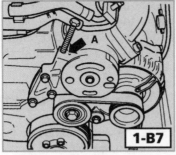

1-B7

❏ **STEP B8:** Before refitting the ribbed belt, make sure that the alternator, air conditioning compressor and power steering pump are all tightly fitted. After making sure that the ribbed belt is central on all of its pulleys, the M8 bolt is removed from the tensioner and the air filter housing, air mass meter and solenoid valve are refitted.

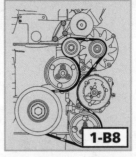

1-B8

Part E: Valve Clearance/Valve Lash
Adjustment
CONTENTS

Page No.

JOB 1: VALVE CLEARANCE – *adjustment*.   6-27

See *Part B: Which Engine is Which?* for an explanation of the engine types referred to here.

IMPORTANT NOTE:
1.4 AND 1.6 LITRE ALUMINIUM ENGINES: There are several important and completely different features on these engines – see *Part P: 1.4 and 1.6 litre Aluminium Block Engine – Specific info.*

TOP TIP!

• You should preferably check the valve clearances with the engine warm. However, if you set the engine cold, such as after a rebuild, you should i) deduct 0.05 mm from the recommended 'warm engine' setting; and ii) check the settings again, with the engine warm, after a further 700 miles (1000 km).

FACT FILE
VALVE OPERATION TYPES

There are three types of valve operation on engines fitted to the models described here:

FINGER ROCKER TYPES
Fitted to earlier-type 'smaller' engines. Two 'fingers' adjust each tappet clearance - see illustration *1-6*.

NON-HYDRAULIC BUCKET TAPPETS
Adjustment by replaceable shims.

HYDRAULIC BUCKET TAPPETS
Non-adjustable and not measurable, except as described in the relevant section.

JOB 1: Valve clearance – *adjustment*.

The valve gear clearances need to be checked at the appropriate intervals, either when the engine is cold, or when warm (above 35 degrees C), as described below and as recommended by **Volkswagen**.

ALL ENGINES

❏ **STEP 1:** Remove the air cleaner assembly (where necessary)...

1-1

❏ **STEP 2:** ...taking care to detach each of the pipes and hoses connected to it.

1-2

❏ **STEP 3:** Detach the top of the cam belt cover, carefully pull it out of the way...

1-3

☐ **STEP 4:** ...and then remove the nuts holding the camshaft cover in place and take it off.

1-4

TOP TIP!

• If the camshaft cover sticks - which it frequently does - DON'T lever the cover or you could easily damage the cover or the gasket, which is sometimes of the re-useable neoprene-type.
• Work the cover free, carefully.

☐ **STEP 5:** The valve clearance is measured directly beneath the cam and must be checked when the high point of the cam (arrowed) is pointing away from the cam follower.

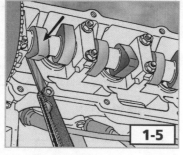

1-5

This is the bucket tappet-type, but the same principle applies to both.

FINGER-ROCKER TYPES

TOP TIP!

• Remember that recommended clearances for inlet and exhaust valves differ. See *Chapter 1, Facts and Figures*.
• Counting from the timing belt end, the EXHAUST valves are: 1, 3, 5, 7, and the INLET valves are 2, 4, 6, 8.
• Run the engine until it reaches its normal operating temperature then turn it off.

☐ **STEP 6:** To adjust the gap, turn the engine until each cam lobe, in turn, faces upwards. Use an Allen key (**a**), inserted between each pair of 'fingers' to adjust each clearance, in turn, to the

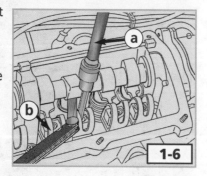

1-6

required figure, while measuring each clearance with a feeler gauge (**b**). The gap will be correct when the feeler gauge can be slid in and out from between the camshaft and finger rocker, with just the smallest amount of 'grip'.

Repeat this action for the rest of the valves and then rotate the engine twice before rechecking the gaps and if necessary readjusting them. Repeat this step until you are happy that all the valve clearances are correctly adjusted.

NON-HYDRAULIC BUCKET TAPPETS

Check the valve clearances. If any are 'out' the relevant shims will have to be changed.

➜ Try different feeler gauge thicknesses until you find one that's a tight sliding fit between cam and follower. See illustration *1-5*.
➜ Make a written note of each clearance, starting with No. 1 at the timing belt end of the engine.
➜ If a clearance is outside the tolerances shown in *Chapter 1, Facts and Figures*, the relevant shim will have to be changed.
➜ New shims are available from your **Volkswagen** dealer.
➜ This work is fully described below.

TOP TIP!

☐ **STEP 7:**
• Remember that recommended clearances for inlet and exhaust valves differ. See

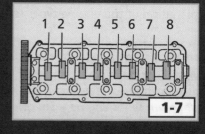

1-7

Chapter 1, Facts and Figures. Counting from the timing belt end, the EXHAUST valves are: 1, 3, 6, 8, and the INLET valves are 2, 4, 5, 7.

☐ **STEP 8:** If the camshaft cover has a replaceable gasket, renew it every time the cover is refitted. Also renew the rubber seal at the camshaft bearing cap (arrow). If the cover is fitted with a

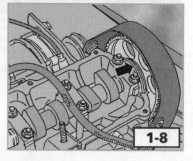

1-8

re-useable neoprene gasket fixed to the face of the cover, examine the gasket before refitting the cover and renew the gasket if it is split or damaged.

☐ **STEP 9:** There is a special tool which can depress the cam follower and which leaves access to insert and remove the shims, without having to remove the camshaft.
➜ You may be better off buying the relevant tool.

1-9

STEP 10: Before using the cam follower depressing tool, the followers must be turned so that the cut-outs (**a**) face position (**b**), which enables the special VW pliers (10 208A) to get a grip on the shim.

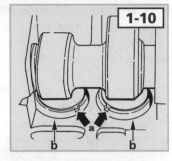

STEP 11: This is a non-Volkswagen version of the special tool for depressing the hydraulic cam follower/lifter.

STEP 12: When inserted between camshaft and lifter, the shim in the top of the lifter can be removed with a pair of screwdrivers.

The alternative is to carry out the procedure described below, bearing in mind that the job will take quite a lot longer without the special tool.

TOP TIP!

• (This *might* make the job slightly easier!) Some manuals suggest that you can make up your own depressing tool and lever the shims out with a pair of small screwdrivers.
• If you want to give it a try, you will find it extremely difficult to a) persuade the lever to stay on the thin edge of the tappet (lifter), and b) just as difficult to free and remove the shim.
• It could be worth a try if there is only one shim to change. However, here is how we recommend that you change the valve clearances, if you wish to do it yourself.

STEP 13: The following assumes that you don't have the luxury of a full set of shims (arrowed) in your garage. But if you follow the following stages, go out and buy

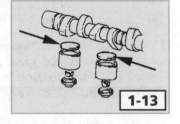

the shims you need from your Volkswagen dealer and fit them yourself, the clearances should be correct:

→ **a.** Make up a table, like the one shown below.
→ **b.** Measure each valve clearance, pushing, or attempting to push in various sizes of feeler gauge until you find the right one.
→ **c.** You can now fill in the first column of the table, writing down all the 'Actual Clearance' figures you measure. You can also fill in the second column, using the information given in *Chapter 1, Facts & Figures* for your particular engine.
→ **d.** Write down the difference you will need to achieve the correct figure. (Go for the 'mid-point' when a 'plus or minus' figure is given. In other words, 45 mm plus or minus 5 mm, means 40 to 50 mm: use 45 as your 'target'.)

STEP 14:
→ **e.** Wait until the engine has gone cold and remove the camshaft. Take out each shim and write down its thickness in the 'Old Shim' column. The thickness should be shown on the shim;

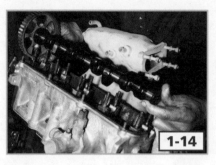

if invisible you will need to measure the shim with a micrometer.
→ **f.** You can now calculate the figure required to reach the recommended figure. If you need to achieve a different clearance, you will have to replace an existing shim.
→ **g.** Reassemble the camshaft and check that the figures are correct. Check, first of all, the 'engine cold' readings (0.05 mm less than the 'engine warm' readings), then check again when the engine has warmed up.

Valve	Actual Clearance	Required Clearance	Difference	Old Shim Size	Required Shim Size	New Clearance
No 1. Exhaust	.38mm	.45mm ±.05mm	.07mm too small			
No 1 Inlet	.26mm	0.25mm ±0.05mm	Within tolerance			
No 2 Exhaust	.48mm					

STEP 15: The thickness of a shim is engraved on it in mm (arrowed). If this is worn away, you will have to measure the thickness with a metric micrometer - or have your Volkswagen dealer do it for you. Be sure to fit the shim with the marking facing down.

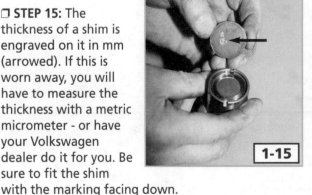

- Where a clearance is too small, even with the thinnest shim in position, the valves should be removed and the stem ground just sufficiently to make the correction.
- The work must be done with the correct engineering equipment, keeping the valve stem end square and retaining a smooth finish.

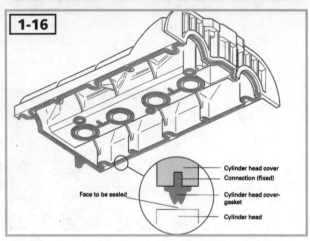

1-16

Cylinder head cover
Connection (fixed)
Face to be sealed
Cylinder head cover-gasket
Cylinder head

☐ **STEP 16:** Be sure to use a new gasket when the camshaft cover is replaced, unless it is of the neoprene type shown here, in which case it will only need replacing if it is damaged.

HYDRAULIC BUCKET TAPPETS

There should be a label on the camshaft cover to identify the type of tappets (lifters) - hydraulic or mechanical - fitted to your engine. Hydraulic tappets can be identified by their plain upper surface, without

the raised shims and without the two opposing cut-outs (a) in illustration *1-10*. If your engine has hydraulic tappets, they cannot be adjusted. When worn out (i.e. noisy) they have to be replaced.

If you suspect that a tappet has become worn check it EITHER as follows:
→ Run the engine until warm - when the radiator fan has turned itself on once.
→ Increase engine speed to 2,500 rpm and hold for about two minutes. If tappet/s are still noisy...
→ ...locate the problem tappet/s after taking off the upper part of the inlet manifold and the camshafts cover.
→ OR, check as recommended by Volkswagen in the following Step...

☐ **STEP 17:** With the cam lobe pointing away from the tappet, press down on the tappet with a wooden or plastic wedge (arrowed). If free travel of more than 0.1 mm

1-17

can be measured (see illustration *1-5*) *before* the valve starts to open, the tappet must be renewed.

FACT FILE
DIESEL ENGINES
- The piston must not be at Top Dead Centre when adjusting valve clearances.
- Turn the crankshaft about 1/4 turn, so that the valves do not touch the piston when the tappet is pressed down.

Part F: 4-Cylinder Engines, Cylinder Head – Removal
CONTENTS

Refer to Part B, Which Engine is Which? for exploded diagrams of each of the cylinder head types covered here.

IMPORTANT NOTE:
1.4 AND 1.6 LITRE ALUMINIUM ENGINES: There are several important and completely different features on these engines – see *Part P: 1.4 and 1.6 litre Aluminium Block Engine – Specific info.*

JOB 1: CYLINDER HEAD – *removal*.

ALL TYPES

☐ **STEP 1:** Before dismantling, disconnect the battery negative (-) earth/ground terminal. See *Chapter 10, Electrical, Dash, Instruments, Fact File: Disconnecting the Battery* BEFORE doing so!

☐ **STEP 2:** Rotate the crankshaft so that No. 1 cylinder is at TDC. (See *Part C: Timing Belt - Inspection, Adjustment, Replacement*.)

STEP 3: If the alternator is top-mounted, remove it.

1-3

STEP 4: Disconnect, drain or remove the following items (refer to the relevant sections of this manual):
→ Drain off the coolant into a suitable container and dispose of responsibly.
→ Remove the air filter and housing and all associated air and vacuum lines, including the air pump fittings and EGR valve and lines, if applicable.
→ **PETROL ENGINES:** Disconnect and remove the HT leads from the spark plugs and also all other connections to the distributor.
→ **DIESEL ENGINES:** Disconnect and remove the glow plugs and the injectors - but ONLY after reading the relevant *Safety First!* notes.
→ Disconnect the fittings to the turbocharger (when fitted) but leave the turbo connected to the exhaust manifold and remove as a unit.
→ Disconnect the fuel line at the engine-end (and plug the line), disconnect the throttle cable, and choke cable if fitted.
→ Remove the carburetor or fuel injection system. See *Chapter 9, Ignition, Fuel & Exhaust*.
→ Remove the coolant hoses to the radiator, heater and choke.
→ Label and detach all remaining electrical connections.
→ Detach the exhaust pipe from the manifold.

STEP 5: Remove the timing belt. See *Part C: Timing Belt - Inspection, Adjustment, Replacement*.

1-5

TOP TIP!

STEP 6: • You may wish to remove the inlet manifold at this stage, because it is a large component and may get in the way.

1-6

TOP TIP!

STEP 7: • If you 'crack' the exhaust manifold nuts at this stage, but leave the manifold in place for now, you will find it easier to lift the head off the block, and easy to undo any stubborn fixing nuts later.

1-7

STEP 8: Remove the camshaft cover, the reinforcing strips (seen here in the mechanic's left hand) and the gasket.

1-8

STEP 9: Make sure that the engine is firmly held, such as in an engine stand, if out of the car. Use an extension on the socket, because of the large amount of force needed...

1-9

STEP 10: ...and loosen the cylinder head bolts by half a turn at a time in the order shown, until all are free, then remove them.

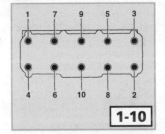
1-10

STEP 11: If the cylinder head has not sealed itself to the gasket, the head can be lifted straight off. It will be far easier to work on if placed onto a cylinder head stand.

1-11

TOP TIP!

• Do not use a wedge to break the seal that often occurs between cylinder head and block.
• Extra leverage can be gained by lifting and rocking carefully on the manifolds.

STEP 12: Remove all traces of the cylinder head gasket from both block and head. Scrape off carbon deposits with a wooden or aluminium scraper, taking care not to gouge the aluminium surface of the head. Stuff rags into all openings in the cylinder head to stop debris dropping into them.

STEP 13: Clean excessive carbon deposits from the crowns of the pistons without damaging the surface of the aluminium.

STEP 14: The cylinder head can be checked for distortion by use of a straight edge and feeler gauge. At the same time, check for excessive corrosion.

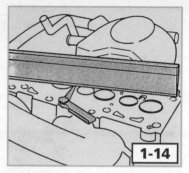

1-14

TOP TIP!

• If the engine is worn and you don't intend overhauling it at this stage, we strongly advise that you leave the piston crowns alone. The carbon on them can actually help preserve compression pressures when the engine is near the point of nearing overhaul.

• An aerosol gasket remover spray will help to remove pieces of stuck-on gasket.

• Always have the cylinder head refaced before refitting to greatly reduce the risk of the cylinder head blowing after being refitted.

• This is not usually applicable to Diesel engines because there is already a high compression with little clearance. If distorted, replace the cylinder head.

Part G: 6–Cylinder Engines, Cylinder Head – Removal

CONTENTS

See *Part B: Which Engine is Which?* for an explanation of the engine types referred to here.

JOB 1: CYLINDER HEAD – *removal*.

STEP 1: Before dismantling, disconnect the battery negative (-) earth/ground terminal. See *Chapter 10, Electrical, Dash, Instruments, Fact File: Disconnecting the Battery* BEFORE doing so!

STEP 2: Remove the HT cable guides (**1** and **2**) from the cylinder head cover (**3**) from above the intake manifold.

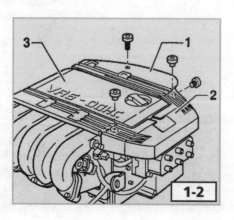

1-2

STEP 3: Undo the clamp and pull the crankcase breather valve from the cylinder head cover.

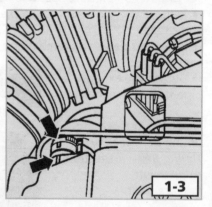

1-3

STEP 4: Undo the clamp and remove the activated charcoal filter breather hose from the upper part of the intake manifold.

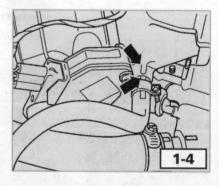

1-4

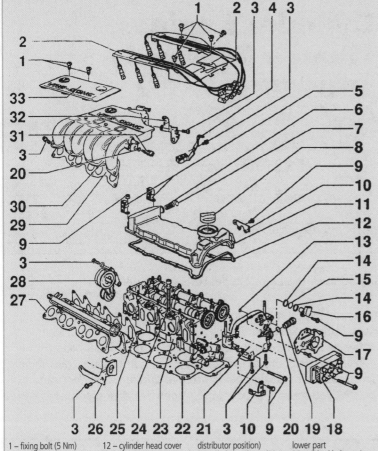

1 – fixing bolt (5 Nm)
2 – HT cable guide
3 – fixing bolts (25 Nm)
4 – rear-right support – fitted between intake manifold upper part and cylinder head
5 – bracket for fuel pipes
6 – flame trap coil
7 – circlip
8 – cap
9 – fixing screw (10 Nm)
10 – bracket for electric cables
11 – cylinder head cover

12 – cylinder head cover gasket
13 – O-ring
14 – spacer ring
15 – O-ring
16 – hall sender unit (distributor fitted to earlier vehicles)
17 – bracket for 42-pin connector and pump for continued coolant circulation
18 – ignition transformer (on vehicles up to December 1992, this is the distributor position)

19 – chain tensioner (30 Nm)
20 – seal
21 – camshaft sprocket cover
22 – cylinder head gasket
23 – cylinder head
24 – cylinder head bolt – to be used once only and then replaced
25 – gasket for intake manifold, lower part
26 – lifting eye
27 – intake manifold, lower part

28 – ribbed belt tensioner
29 – gasket for intake manifold, upper part
30 – intake manifold, upper part
31 – temperature sender unit (10 Nm)
32 – rear left support, fitted between intake manifold upper part and cylinder head, with engine earth/ground connection
33 – cover

1-5

valve and intake manifold temperature sender.
➔ Detach the accelerator cable from the throttle valve housing but do not remove the locating clip.
➔ Drain the cooling system (only when engine cold).
➔ Remove the coolant hose from the throttle valve housing.
➔ Pull the vacuum hose from the fuel pressure regulator.
➔ Take the vacuum hose from the brake servo.
➔ Unclip the fuel pipes from the cylinder head cover
➔ Detach the dipstick guide tubes from the intake manifold.
➔ Remove the upper part of the intake manifold complete with throttle valve housing.
➔ Plug all intake ports with pieces of clean cloth.
➔ Remove the cylinder head cover.
➔ Remove the timing chain. See *Part I, Job 4*.

IMPORTANT NOTES: **i)** When installing an exchange cylinder head with fitted camshaft, the contact surfaces between the bucket tappets and the cam must be thoroughly oiled after installation.
ii) The plastic protectors fitted to protect the open valves must only be removed immediately before fitting the cylinder head.
iii) All of the coolant should be drained and replaced with new.

☐ **STEP 5:** These are the cylinder head components referred to in this and other sections dealing with the 6-cylinder engines' cylinder head. Where appropriate, the correct torque settings for fixing bolts are given after the component name in brackets.

SAFETY FIRST!

• Plug the end of the activated charcoal filter breather hose with an air tight plug so that no fuel fumes can escape.

IMPORTANT NOTE: Never turn the engine without the chain tensioner installed.

☐ **STEP 6:** Now remove the following items in this order:
➔ Remove the intake hose from the throttle valve housing.
➔ Pull the connectors off the throttle valve potentiometer, heater element, idling stabilisation

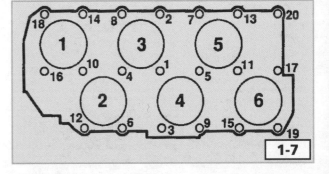

1-7

☐ **STEP 7:** Loosen the cylinder head bolts by half a turn at a time in the order shown here until all are free, then remove them.

IMPORTANT NOTE: When removing the cylinder head, undo the bolts starting with the highest number shown here and working downwards in numerical order.

☐ **STEP 8:** Follow *Part F: 4-Cylinder Engines Cylinder Head - Removal, Job 1, Steps 11-on.*

Part H: 4-Cylinder Engines, Cylinder Head – Overhaul

CONTENTS

See *Part B: Which Engine is Which?* for an explanation of the engine types referred to here.

IMPORTANT NOTE:
1.4 AND 1.6 LITRE ALUMINIUM ENGINES: There are several important and completely different features on these engines – see *Part P: 1.4 and 1.6 litre Aluminium Block Engine – Specific info*.
1. Take a look at *Part A: General Procedures* for further general information on working on the cylinder head.
2. Also, refer to *Part B: Which Engine is Which?* for exploded diagrams of each of the cylinder head types covered here.
3. There are several different camshaft types and specifications capable of being fitted to different cylinder heads. If you need to replace a camshaft, it is most important that you check with your Volkswagen dealer or specialist to ensure that you replace like with like.

JOB 1: WHICH VALVE GEAR?

There are great similarities but detail differences between the various valve gear types fitted to the engines covered here.

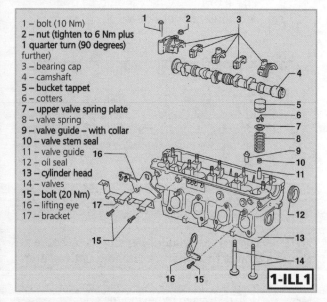

1 – bolt (10 Nm)
2 – nut (tighten to 6 Nm plus 1 quarter turn (90 degrees) further)
3 – bearing cap
4 – camshaft
5 – bucket tappet
6 – cotters
7 – upper valve spring plate
8 – valve spring
9 – valve guide – with collar
10 – oil seal
11 – valve guide
12 – oil seal
13 – cylinder head
14 – valves
15 – bolt (20 Nm)
16 – lifting eye
17 – bracket

1-ILL1

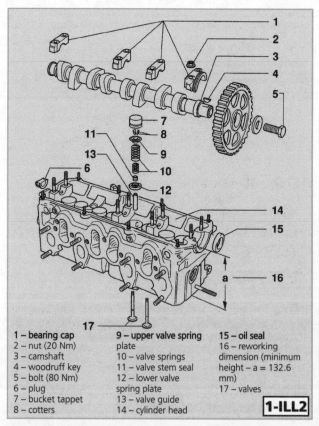

1 – bearing cap	9 – upper valve spring plate	15 – oil seal
2 – nut (20 Nm)	10 – valve springs	16 – reworking dimension (minimum height – a = 132.6 mm)
3 – camshaft	11 – valve stem seal	
4 – woodruff key	12 – lower valve spring plate	
5 – bolt (80 Nm)	13 – valve guide	17 – valves
6 – plug	14 – cylinder head	
7 – bucket tappet		
8 – cotters		

1-ILL2

□ **ILLUSTRATION 1:** This is the valve gear fitted to all of the 'smaller' engines - from 1.0 litre to 1.6, fitted with cylinder head-mounted distributor - fitted from 1992-on. For earlier types, see *Part B, Which Engine is Which?* for exploded diagram of complete cylinder head assembly.

□ **ILLUSTRATION 2:** The valve gear fitted to the 1.8 and 2.0 litre 8-valve engines from 1992-on is very similar to that used on all the earlier engines of a similar type, from 1.5 to 1.8 litres. EXCEPT that No. 4 camshaft bearing cap is no longer used on these engines. VW still refer to the end cap as 'No. 5'.

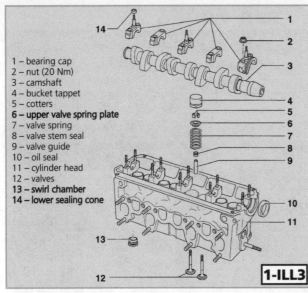

1 – bearing cap
2 – nut (20 Nm)
3 – camshaft
4 – bucket tappet
5 – cotters
6 – upper valve spring plate
7 – valve spring
8 – valve stem seal
9 – valve guide
10 – oil seal
11 – cylinder head
12 – valves
13 – swirl chamber
14 – lower sealing cone

1-ILL3

❏ **ILLUSTRATION 3:** The 1.9 litre Diesel engine's valve gear is essentially very similar to others in the range, but the cylinder head has a swirl chamber.

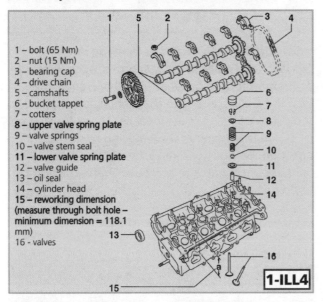

1 – bolt (65 Nm)
2 – nut (15 Nm)
3 – bearing cap
4 – drive chain
5 – camshafts
6 – bucket tappet
7 – cotters
8 – upper valve spring plate
9 – valve springs
10 – valve stem seal
11 – lower valve spring plate
12 – valve guide
13 – oil seal
14 – cylinder head
15 – reworking dimension (measure through bolt hole – minimum dimension = 118.1 mm)
16 - valves

1-ILL4

❏ **ILLUSTRATION 4:** The 16-valve head fitted to 1.8 and 2.0 litre models is similar to the others, apart from the obvious ways in which camshafts are linked and driven.

❏ **ILLUSTRATION 5:** The 16-valve head fitted to 1.4 litre models has detail differences, although valve gear is similar once again.

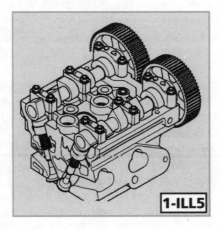

1-ILL5

JOB 2:   CAMSHAFT, 8-VALVE HEAD - *removing.*

PETROL AND DIESEL ENGINES

❏ **STEP 1:** Support the cylinder head on the bench. If you use a cylinder head stand, such as this Sykes-Pickavant stand, it makes the unit easier to work on. On engines with a camshaft-driven distributor, vacuum pump and/or fuel pump, the distributor or pump must be first removed from the end of the cylinder head.

2-1

❏ **STEP 2:** If you need to do it now (such as when replacing a camshaft), remove the cam sprocket. It can be held from turning by passing a bar or screwdriver through the cam sprocket. Remove the Woodruff key for safe keeping and possible later use. See *Step 10.*

2-2

IMPORTANT NOTE: Store hydraulic tappets only with the cam contact surface facing downwards.

❏ **STEP 3:** Before removing the camshaft make a note of the cap numbers and which side they are on. The cam bore is offset and caps will need to be put back correctly. If there are no numbers visible, make your own marks.

2-3

❏ **STEP 4: 1.9 TDI WITH PUMP INJECTION:** Remove the eight fixing bolts (arrowed) and take off the roller-type rocker arm.

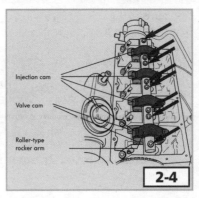

Injection cam

Valve cam

Roller-type rocker arm

2-4

STEP 5: Remove the cam bearings 1, 3 and 5 completely and then slacken each of the four remaining nuts a little at a time, alternately and diagonally, until all the valve springs tension has been released.

2-5

IMPORTANT NOTE: In cases where there is not a No. 4 cap, start by removing Nos. 1 and 3.

STEP 6: Remove the cam shaft for inspection. Look for dull, worn spots at the lobe points and damage to the bearing surfaces. Any problems here could well be due to poor oil circulation. Check the cylinder head oilways and consider replacing the camshaft. If in doubt, consult your Volkswagen dealer.

2-6

STEP 7: If you intend refitting the existing camshaft, it can just as easily be removed with the camshaft sprocket left in position.

2-7

STEP 8: If you need to check the end-float in the camshaft bearings with a dial gauge (arrowed), re-fit the camshaft with just the first and last bearing caps, and with the tappets/lifters removed. The maximum wear limit is 0.15 mm.

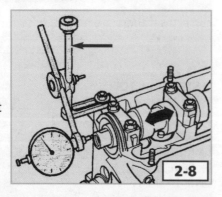

2-8

TOP TIP!

STEP 9: • When refitting the camshaft, use new oil seals.• Hold the seal against its stop inside the cap and head as the end cap is tightened.

STEP 10: • Slightly angle the Woodruff key (arrowed) so that the sprocket slides on easily.

2-9

2-10

JOB 3: CAMSHAFT, 16-VALVE HEAD
– removing.

INSIDE INFORMATION: Before working on the cylinder head make sure that you note the direction of rotation for the camshaft link chain, and refit with the chain running in the same direction, otherwise excessive chain wear could result. Paint an arrow on the chain before removing to show direction. Do not try to mark the chain with a marker punch, notch or any other method which could damage it.

STEP 1: Follow *Job 2, Steps 1 to 3.*

STEP 2: This is how to remove each camshaft. The inlet camshaft is the one *without* a front, toothed belt-driven sprocket.
→ From the inlet camshaft remove

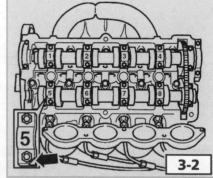

3-2

bearing caps 5, 7 and the rearmost cap, completely.
→ Then slacken off bearing caps 6 and 8 a little at a time until all the valve spring tension has been released.
→ From the exhaust camshaft (with front sprocket) remove bearing caps 1, 3 and the front - and rearmost caps completely.
→ Slacken off bearing caps 2 and 4 a little at a time until all the valve springs tension has been released.

STEP 3: Remove the cam shafts for inspection. Look for dull, worn spots at the lobe points and damage to the bearing surfaces. Any problems here could well be due to poor oil circulation. Check the cylinder head oilways and consider replacing the camshaft. If in doubt, consult your Volkswagen dealer.

JOB 4: CAMSHAFT 'FINGER ROCKER' TYPE – *removing*.

This is the type fitted to very early 'smaller' engines of 900cc to 1.3 litres. See *Part B: Which Engine is Which?* for relevant exploded diagram.

STEP 1: Unscrew the fuel pump from the head, and remove the distributor. See *Chapter 9, Part A*.

STEP 2: Remove the rocker finger retaining clips and mark them individually as each is removed.

STEP 3: You can now remove the rocker fingers. Turn the camshaft so that each cam lobe in turn is pointing away from the rocker finger then lift and pull the finger out with a jerking action in the direction of the arrow.

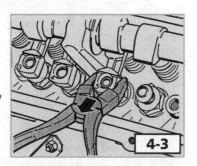
4-3

STEP 4: Earliest versions had this type of spring clip fitted.

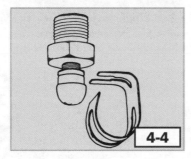
4-4

STEP 5: Remove the camshaft sprocket and Woodruff key. See *Job 2, Step 2*.

STEP 6: Pull the camshaft out (towards the distributor end) taking care that the cam lobes do not damage the bearings.

STEP 7: Look for dull, worn spots at the lobe points and damage to the bearing surfaces. Any problems here could well be due to poor oil circulation. Check the cylinder head oilways and consider replacing the camshaft. If in doubt, consult your Volkswagen dealer and ensure that the correct camshaft-rocker finger combination is purchased - there are different types and must be used in the correct combination.

JOB 5: VALVES - *removing, reworking, refitting*.

Section A: Work on the valves.

STEP A1: See *Job 1* and *Part A: General Procedures* for exploded drawings of the various cylinder head types featured here.

STEP A2: Remove the cam followers and valve clearance adjusting shims (not used on finger-tappet or hydraulic tappet types), taking care to maintain their original positions for reassembly.

5-A2

STEP A3: Give each valve a sharp tap with a hammer to free the top spring plate from the valve. You could place a socket spanner over the plate to avoid striking the end of the valve stem. (Illustration, courtesy Sykes-Pickavant.)

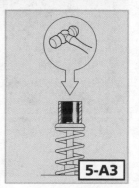
5-A3

STEP A4: You will need to use a valve-spring compressor with an extension jaw to reach into the recessed valve spring area in the head. (Illustration, courtesy Sykes-Pickavant.)

5-A4

STEP A5: Compress the valve springs so that you can reach in and remove the collets from around the heads of the valves.

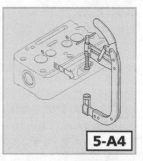
5-A5

STEP A6: Slowly and carefully open the spring compressor tool to release the pressure of the valve spring, and remove the upper spring seat, followed by the springs.

5-A6

☐ **STEP A7:** These are the spring, seat and collets as removed.

5-A7

☐ **STEP A8:** Slide out the valves, removing the valve seals and discard the old seals; new ones must be used on re-assembly.

5-A8

TOP TIP!

• The valves should slide freely out of their guides.
• Any resistance may be caused by a build up of carbon, or a slight burr on the stem where the collets engage.
• This can usually be removed by careful use of fine wet-or-dry paper, allowing you to withdraw the valves without scoring their guides.
• Keep the valves in their correct order by wrapping a numbered piece of masking tape around each stem.

☐ **STEP A9:** Once all the valves have been removed, clean them up ready for inspection. Remove the carbon deposits with a wire brush and degrease the rest.

5-A9

Exhaust valves are prone to burning at their heads, as are their valve seats in the cylinder head.

☐ **STEP A10:** Check for valve guide wear:
➔ Lift each valve until the end of the stem is level with the top of the valve guide.
➔ Attempt to move the head from side to side.
➔ Repeat by inserting valve upside-down into its guide, as shown.
➔ If you feel any noticeably play then you may need new guides. See *Part A, Job 10, Step 1* for the technically correct way to measure valve guide wear.

5-A10

VALVE GUIDE REPLACEMENT: This is a job that is often passed over to a Volkswagen dealer or engine

rebuild specialist, who will also have the experience to confirm whether or not wear is acceptable, as well as the hydraulic press recommended for replacing valve guides. However, it is possible to replace guides without a press, as long as you accept the risk of possibly ruining new guides. See *Job 6* for details.

VALVE GRINDING: Modern engines, with hardened valve seats, are not capable of having valves ground in the traditional way, except to remove the smallest of blemishes. See *Part A: General Procedures, Job 10* for step-by-step details.

If anything more is needed, have the valves and seats re-cut to the correct angle by machine. However, Volkswagen state that 16-valve engine valves cannot be reworked but can only be ground in. Valve seats can be reworked within limits by your Volkswagen dealer.

HEAD REWORKING LIMITS: If too much material is removed from the cylinder head valve seats (and/or from valve heads), the hydraulic tappets may not have sufficient room to work properly and the valves could strike the pistons. Follow the limits shown in **Section B** of this Job.

TOP TIP!

• Check the height of the valve springs against new ones if possible, but if not, compare them with each other. If any are shorter than the others, play safe and replace the complete set. They are bound to have suffered fatigue which could cause premature valve failure.

☐ **STEP A11:** To install the valves, start from one end. Lubricate a valve stem with fresh engine oil or grease and slide it in to its guide.

5-A11

☐ **STEP A12:** Locate the plastic tube supplied (A) on the valve shaft, to prevent damage, and slide a new valve stem seal (B)...

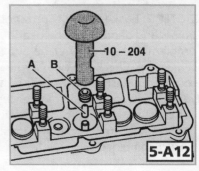
5-A12

STEP A13: ...over the stem of the valve and push down into contact with the guide. Push the seal onto its seat using a suitable metal tube if you don't have the VW special tool shown in **5-A12**.

5-A13

STEP A14: Alternatively, use seal pliers, also useful for removing old seals.

5-A14

TOP TIP!

STEP A15: • If your valves don't come with the plastic tubes, wrap a short length of insulating tape around the collet grooves at the end of each valve stem.
• This will protect the new valve seals from damage as you slide them over the valve stems.
• When you have pushed the new seal firmly onto the top of the valve guide, remove the tape.

STEP A16: Refit the spring seat, the inner and outer springs and the spring cap.

STEP A17: Re-apply the valve spring compressor and compress the springs enough to allow you to engage the split collets in the stem grooves. Note that the type of collets, the spring caps and the valves must match each other. Unlike the earlier type (right), one of the later types has a valve

5-A17

with three grooves, a collet with three single shoulders and a spring cap with an inner chamfer (**A**) and a wider outer chamfer (**B**). Make sure that you buy the correct type of valves, if any have to be replaced.

TOP TIP!

STEP A18: • Grease the grooves so that the collets will 'stick' in place. The collets are easily fitted by 'sticking' the backs of them onto the end of a screwdriver with some grease and feeding them into position.

5-A18

STEP A19: Carefully release the spring compressor and check that the collets are correctly located. Tap the end of each stem with a hammer to bed them in. Fit the remaining valves.

5-A19

STEP A20: Lubricate the bearing surfaces of the valve cam followers with copious quantities of fresh engine oil and place them back in position over their respective valves.

IMPORTANT NOTE: After installing new hydraulic tappets, do not run the engine for at least half an hour, or the valves will strike the pistons.

Section B: Reworking limits.

STEP B1: Push each valve into its guide, slide right down to the face and measure the distance (**a**) between the top of the valve stem and the upper edge of the cylinder head.

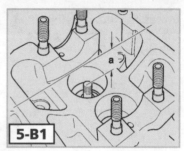

5-B1

STEP B2: Make sure that the measurement is not less than the minimum given in **Step B3**. If it is, but only by a small amount, try a new valve to see if it overcomes the problem. Otherwise, new valve seats will have to be fitted to the head by an engine rebuild specialist.

STEP B3: These are the limits for most major variations of engine code types. See the engine number prefix. It is not possible to give all possible variants - if it is not listed here, check the engine prefix and the minima of the engine you are working on, with your Volkswagen dealer.

Engine Code	Engine Type (litres & valves)	Min. Measurement (mm)	Min. Measurement Exhaust valve (mm)
ABF	2.0, 16V	34.4	34.7
AAM, ABS, 2E, **ADY, ADZ, AGG**	**1.8 & 2.0, 8V**	**33.8**	**34.1**
AEK, AFT	1.6 , 8V	33.8	34.1
AAZ, AEE, AEY, AFN, 1Y, 1Z	1.9, D	35.8	36.1
ABD, ABU, AEA, AEE, AEX, ADX, AEA, AEE, AER, AEV, AEX, ALL	1.0 (Al.) 1.05, 1.3, 1.4, 1.6	35.8	36.1

JOB 6: VALVE GUIDES – *replacement*.

If you accept the risk of damaging and ruining perfectly new valve guides, it is sometimes possible to replace them without the use of specialist equipment.

❏ **STEP 1:** Use a thread tap to make a thread inside each old guide.

6-1

❏ **STEP 2:** Screw a bolt (**a**) into the guide (**b**) and drift the guide (via the end of the bolt) out of the head. This drift is an old threaded stud – anything that slides inside the guide will do.

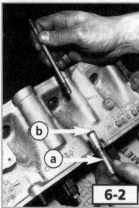

6-2

❏ **STEP 3:** Place another (smaller) bolt in the new guide. Drift down onto the bolt head, protecting the guide.

6-3

❏ **STEP 4:** Make sure all guides are driven in to the correct depth – compare new with old.

6-4

❏ **STEP 5:** Ream out the new guides with the correct size of hand reamer, using plenty of cutting fluid.

JOB 7: SWIRL CHAMBER (LATER DIESEL ENGINES) – *removing, replacement*.

If the swirl chambers are burned or badly carbonated, they will need to be replaced.

❏ **STEP 1:** Take out all of the injectors and glow plugs (to prevent damage to the latter).

❏ **STEP 2:** Insert a drift into the injector opening and drive the swirl chamber out.

❏ **STEP 3:** Clean the swirl chamber housing in the cylinder head, scraping out any carbonated material.

❏ **STEP 4:** Use a mallet to drive each new swirl chamber into position, making sure that the guide lug and groove are correctly located.

❏ **STEP 5:** The swirl chamber must project by no more than 0.07 mm, or it could collide with the piston. Use a dial gauge, as shown here. If projection is greater:

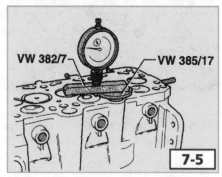

VW 382/7   VW 385/17

7-5

➜ Remove the swirl chamber again and make absolutely certain that the housing is clean.
➜ Alternatively, try fitting different swirl chambers into different positions, in case there are small manufacturing variations.
➜ As a last resort, take the cylinder head to a machine shop and have it machined so that the swirl chamber projection is okay.

JOB 8: CYLINDER HEAD - *re-assembly*.

IMPORTANT NOTE: Avoid potential major problems by following this advice from Volkswagen:
➜ On some engines, the valves will collide with the pistons if the camshaft/s is/are turned while the engine is set to Top Dead Centre (TDC).
➜ To avoid risk of damage, the camshaft/s should NEVER be replaced (or turned if already in place) while the pistons are at TDC.
➜ Volkswagen recommend that the crankshaft is turned back (the *opposite direction* to normal rotation) by a few degrees, moving the pistons safely a little way down the bore.
➜ With the cylinder head fitted to the engine, the camshaft/s must now be turned to their alignment

marks for when No. 1 piston is at TDC.

→ Before the timing belt is refitted, the crankshaft must be moved forward (in the *direction of* normal rotation) to the TDC position again.

→ See *Part C: Timing Belt or Chain - Inspection, Adjustment, Replacement* for information on fitting and aligning sprockets and fitting the cam belt.

❏ **STEP 1:** Change the camshaft oil seal while the assembly is dismantled. Undo the end camshaft cap nuts and carefully lever out the old seal from its seat in the end of the cylinder head.

❏ **STEP 2:** Grease the new seal so that it won't have to run dry on start-up.

❏ **STEP 3:** Fit a new one, ensuring that the new seal is fitted perfectly square, to the end of the head. Tighten the end cap.

❏ **STEP 4: 8-VALVE ENGINES:** Refit the camshaft and sprocket:

→ Carefully lower the camshaft into the head, or in the case of finger-tappet engines, insert the camshaft through the bearings without damaging them.

→ Refit the camshaft sprocket. Note that there is a keyway and key to fix its position on the camshaft.

→ Tighten the bolt to the torque figures shown in *Chapter 1, Facts and Figures*. If the bolt is one of the later type and has to be tightened with an angle gauge, rather than to a fixed torque figure, a new bolt should be fitted.

TOP TIP!

• This only applies to engines with cylinder head-mounted distributor:

• Before tightening camshaft bearing bolts, insert the distributor.

• This centralises the No. 5 bearing cap and ensures that the distributor flange doesn't leak.

❏ **STEP 5:** Make certain that caps are fitted in the correct locations and the right way round. Screw all of the nuts on until they touch the caps without pressing down on them.

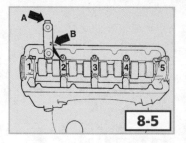

FACT FILE

SPECIFIC VARIATIONS

CROSS-FLOW ENGINES
The wider cast lug (**A**) must be on the intake side of the head and the bearing cap number (**B**) readable from the exhaust side.

1.8 AND 2.0 LITRE ENGINES FROM 1992-ON
These engines do not have a cap where No. 4 would normally be. VW still refer to the end cap as 'No. 5' on these engines.

❏ **STEP 6: 8-VALVE ENGINES:** Refit bearing caps 2 and 4, making sure that they are fitted the right way round!. Tighten each cap nut alternately and diagonally a little

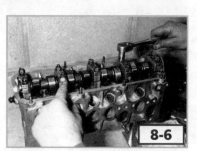

at a time to take up the valve spring tension. Now replace caps 1, 3 and 5 and tighten all of them to the correct torque.

IMPORTANT NOTE: In cases where there is not a No. 4 cap, start by tightening Nos. 2 and 5.

TOP TIP!

❏ **STEP 7:** • Make sure that the seal stays in its correct position as the end cap is tightened.

❏ **STEP 8: 16-VALVE ENGINES:** Fit the sprocket to the camshaft, if it has been removed, and refit the camshafts, complete with the chain, aligning the sprocket markings (arrowed).

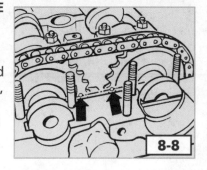

❑ **STEP 9: 16-VALVE ENGINES:** Ensure that the notches on the caps (arrowed) face the intake side of the cylinder head. On the inlet camshaft, replace the bearing caps 6 and 8 and tighten the cap nuts

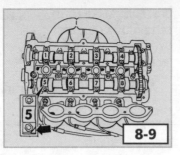

8-9

alternately and diagonally. Finish tightening them to 15 Nm. Replace the remaining inlet cam bearing caps and tighten them all to 15 Nm.

On the exhaust camshaft, position the bearing caps 2 and 4 and tighten the cap nuts alternately and diagonally. Finish tightening them to 15 Nm. Replace the remaining bearing caps and tighten them all to 15 Nm.

❑ **STEP 10: CYLINDER HEAD REMOVED, OR ALL PISTONS HALF-WAY DOWN BORES ONLY:** After fitting all of the caps, and with the cambelt still not fitted, make sure that

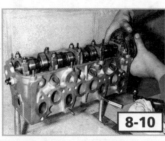

8-10

the camshaft turns. If it doesn't, check to see if any dirt has found its way between journals, shells or caps.

TOP TIP!

• **FINGER ROCKER ENGINES:** Insert the rocking fingers by turning each cam lobe away from its finger, in turn. Replace the rocker clip. If you have difficulty, screw down the adjusting screw to give greater clearance and screw it back out by the same number of turns once the rocker is in position.

❑ **STEP 11: NON-HYDRAULIC VALVE ENGINES:** Check the valve clearances. Note that, when setting the valve clearances after rebuild or repair, the clearances are set cold. Specified clearances for a cold engine are 0.05 mm less than for when the engine is warm. The clearances must be checked (engine warm) and reset if necessary after the vehicle has covered about a further 700 miles (1,000 km).

❑ **STEP 12: ENGINES WITH DISTRIBUTOR ON HEAD:** Refit the distributor and flange, aligning the marks made when they were removed.

Part I: 6-Cylinder Engines, Cylinder Head – Overhaul

CONTENTS

1. *Take a look at* **Part A: General Procedures** *for further general information on working on the cylinder head.*
2. *Also, refer to* **Part B: Which Engine is Which?** *for exploded diagrams of each of the cylinder head types covered here.*
3. *There are several different camshaft types and specifications capable of being fitted to different cylinder heads. If you need to replace a camshaft, it is most important that you check with your Volkswagen dealer or specialist to ensure that you replace like with like.*

JOB 1:   CAMSHAFT – removing, replacing.

IMPORTANT NOTE: Volkswagen advise that cylinder heads which have cracks between the valve seats or between the valve seat inserts and the spark plug thread can continue to be used provided the cracks do not exceed a width of 0.5 mm.

Section A: Camshaft removing.

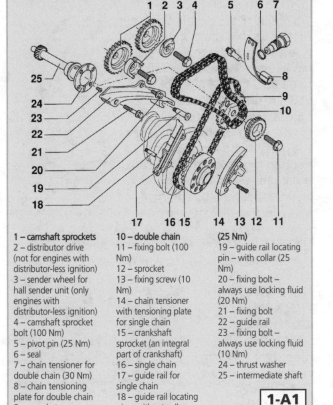

1 – camshaft sprockets
2 – distributor drive
(not for engines with distributor-less ignition)
3 – sender wheel for hall sender unit (only engines with distributor-less ignition)
4 – camshaft sprocket bolt (100 Nm)
5 – pivot pin (25 Nm)
6 – seal
7 – chain tensioner for double chain (30 Nm)
8 – chain tensioning plate for double chain
9 – sprocket

10 – double chain
11 – fixing bolt (100 Nm)
12 – sprocket
13 – fixing screw (10 Nm)
14 – chain tensioner with tensioning plate for single chain
15 – crankshaft sprocket (an integral part of crankshaft)
16 – single chain
17 – guide rail for single chain
18 – guide rail locating pin – without collar

(25 Nm)
19 – guide rail locating pin – with collar (25 Nm)
20 – fixing bolt – always use locking fluid (20 Nm)
21 – fixing bolt
22 – guide rail
23 – fixing bolt – always use locking fluid (10 Nm)
24 – thrust washer
25 – intermediate shaft

1-A1

☐ **STEP A1:** These are the camshaft drive components. Where appropriate, the correct tightening torque is shown after the component name in brackets.

IMPORTANT NOTE: Volkswagen recommend that you should never rotate the engine with either or both of the chain tensioners removed.

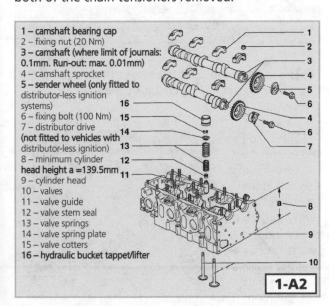

1 – camshaft bearing cap
2 – fixing nut (20 Nm)
3 – camshaft (where limit of journals: 0.1mm. Run-out: max. 0.01mm)
4 – camshaft sprocket
5 – sender wheel (only fitted to distributor-less ignition systems)
6 – fixing bolt (100 Nm)
7 – distributor drive (not fitted to vehicles with distributor-less ignition)
8 – minimum cylinder head height a =139.5mm
9 – cylinder head
10 – valves
11 – valve guide
12 – valve stem seal
13 – valve springs
14 – valve spring plate
15 – valve cotters
16 – hydraulic bucket tappet/lifter

1-A2

☐ **STEP A2:** These are the components of the VR6 cylinders head's valve gear. Where appropriate, the torque bolt tightening figure is given in brackets.

☐ **STEP A3:** If the cylinder head is in the vehicle, set the engine with No. 1 cylinder at Top Dead Centre (TDC).

☐ **STEP A4:** Remove the following components:
→ The cylinder head cover – see *Part G: 6-Cylinder, Cylinder Head - Removal*.
→ Remove the ignition transformer or distributor, according to which type is fitted. See *Chapter 9, Ignition, Fuel & Exhaust*.
→ Remove the double chain tensioner *1-A1, item 7*.
→ Remove the camshaft cover with Hall sender (when fitted).

☐ **STEP A5:** Use white paint or typists' correction fluid to mark the double chain (and the single chain, too, if that is to be removed later) with an arrow. The arrow (see inset) shows the direction of rotation for when the chain is installed again.

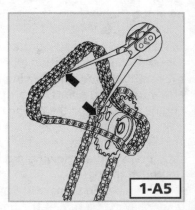

1-A5

IMPORTANT NOTE: Do not mark the chain with a centre punch or any other similar method.

☐ **STEP A6:** Loosen and remove the securing bolt for each camshaft sprocket. As each bolt is being loosened, make sure that the camshaft is prevented from turning with a spanner on the hexagonal section (arrows). Remove the camshaft sprockets.

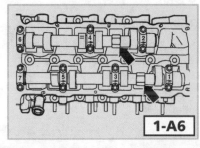

1-A6

☐ **STEP A7:** Remove the camshaft by taking off the bearing caps in the following order:
→ Remove bearing caps Nos. 1 and 7.
→ Slacken off bearing caps Nos. 3 and 5 undoing each nut half a turn at a time, alternately and diagonally.
→ Remove bearing cap No. 4.
→ Slacken off bearing caps Nos. 2 and 6 undoing each nut half a turn at a time, alternately and diagonally.

1-A7

Section B: Camshaft replacing.

❑ **STEP B1:** When refitting the camshafts, the recesses for the camshaft sprockets (arrows) must be at the top.

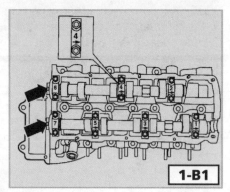

1-B1

❑ **STEP B2:** When refitting the bearing caps, make sure that the identification marks correspond with the positions shown in drawing *1-B1* and that the arrow (see inset) points towards the front of the engine – away from the timing chain.

❑ **STEP B3:** When refitting the camshaft bearing caps, do so in the following order and with all nuts tightened to 20 Nm:
→ Tighten bearing caps Nos. 3 and 5 alternately and diagonally, half a turn at the time.
→ Fit bearing caps Nos. 1 and 7.
→ Tighten bearing caps Nos. 2 and 6 alternately and diagonally, half a turn at the time.
→ Fit bearing cap No. 4.

IMPORTANT NOTE: Add copious amounts of fresh engine oil to all of the camshaft bearings as they are reassembled.

❑ **STEP B4:** Clean the sealing surfaces of the covers for the camshaft sprockets and the cylinder head and remove the old sealant

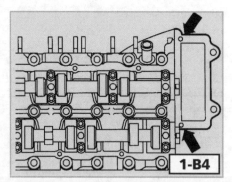

1-B4

from the 3 mm holes in the cylinder head gasket (arrows). Note that with the cylinder head installed, only half of the holes in the cylinder head gasket are visible.

❑ **STEP B5:** Refit the camshaft sprockets and the double chain – see *Job 5*. Be sure to fit the sender wheel (vehicles with distributor-less ignition) or distributor drive in conjunction with the appropriate camshaft sprocket. See illustration *1-A2*.

❑ **STEP B6:** Fill the 3 mm holes in the cylinder head gasket with sealant and coat the sealing surfaces of the cover for the camshafts with silicone sealant.

❑ **STEP B7:** Oil the O-ring (see illustration *Part G, 1-5, item 13*).

❑ **STEP B8:** Refit the camshaft cover.

❑ **STEP B9:** Fit the chain tensioner for the double chain and tighten it to 30 Nm. If the chain tensioner has been pulled apart, it will have to be bled. Push a piece of wire (0.8 mm diameter) through the hole (arrow) in the pressure piston, up to the ball valve. Press the pressure piston and the housing together on to the stop. If the pressure piston moves out again, repeat the bleeding procedure until it stays in place.

1-B9

❑ **STEP B10:** Refit the distributor or ignition transformer, according to which is fitted.

❑ **STEP B11: CHECKING CAMSHAFT END-FLOAT:** The procedure is exactly as described in *Part H: 4-Cylinder, Cylinder Head - Overhaul*. The check

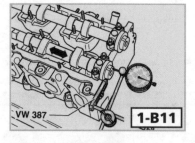

VW 387

1-B11

must be carried out with the hydraulic bucket tappets/lifters removed and with the first and last bearing caps fitted to the appropriate camshaft. The wear limit is a maximum of 0.15 mm.

JOB 2:   VALVES - removing, reworking, refitting.

❑ **STEP 1:** The procedure is almost exactly as described in *Part H: 4-Cylinder, Cylinder Head - Overhaul*.

❑ **STEP 2:** Follow the instructions on determining the maximum permissible working limit on the cylinder heads for the 4-cylinder engine but note that

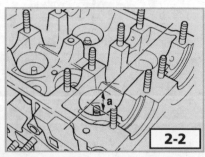

2-2

the minimum dimensions (**a**) are:
→ inlet valve 33.9 mm
→ exhaust valve 34.1 mm

JOB 3: VALVE GUIDES - replacement.

❏ **STEP 1:** The procedure is as described in *Part H: 4-Cylinder, Cylinder Head - Overhaul, Job 6*.

❏ **STEP 2:** Volkswagen recommend pressing out the guide with the drift illustrated – VW Part No. 3121. The worn valve guides should be pressed out from the camshaft side, in the direction of the arrow.

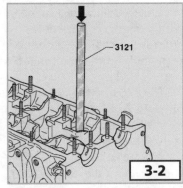

❏ **STEP 3:** New guides should be liberally oiled and pressed in from the same side that the old guides were pressed out – see illustration *3-2*. The cylinder head must be laid flat on a smooth surface and the new guide pressed in until the shoulder makes contact. The pressure must not exceed 1.0 t otherwise the shoulder may break off.

❏ **STEP 4:** Ream the guides with a hand reamer and using plenty of cutting fluid. The Volkswagen Part No. for their reamer is 3120.

JOB 4: VALVE TIMING AND TIMING CHAIN - replacement.

❏ **STEP 1:** If the Top Dead Centre (TDC) No. 1 setting is correct, it is possible to see a notch on the intermediate shaft sprocket (arrow). If No. 1 piston is at TDC but the notch cannot be seen, turn the crankshaft one full turn in the normal direction of rotation.

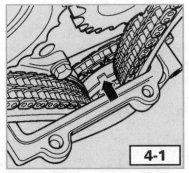

TOP TIP!

• If the crankshaft is turned with the cylinder head removed, an assistant should guide the double chain by hand to prevent it from jamming.

VEHICLES WITH MANUAL TRANSMISSION

❏ **STEP 2: ENGINE INSTALLED:** The TDC mark on the pressure plate – the triangular tooth – must align with the reference point on the clutch housing.

❏ **STEP 3: ENGINE REMOVED:** The TDC mark recessed into the flywheel edge must align with the reference point cast on the flange (arrow).

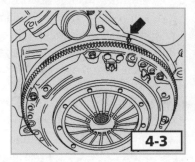

VEHICLES WITH AUTOMATIC TRANSMISSION

❏ **STEP 4: ENGINE INSTALLED:** The torque converter has three TDC marks (arrow) because the hole pattern for fitting the torque converter allows it to be fitted in three different position.

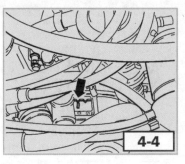

Therefore it is essential that you first turn the engine until one of the torque converter marks (arrow) is aligned with the 'zero' in the torque converter housing access window, and then to check that No. 1 cylinder is actually at the top of its stroke through the spark plug hole. If it is not, turn the engine until the next TDC mark appears and check the piston once again. When both there is a TDC mark showing in the window and the piston it at the top of its stroke, the piston in No. 1 cylinder will be at TDC.

❏ **STEP 5: ENGINE REMOVED:** The mark slotted into the drive plate must align with the reference point cast on the flange (arrow).

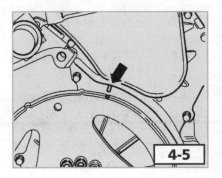

STEP 6: With both camshaft sprockets removed, it can be seen that there is a slot in the end of each camshaft. Both slots must be absolutely horizontal – which only happens every

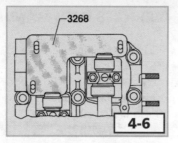

4-6

second TDC position if the engine is rotated with the sprockets fitted. Volkswagen recommend the use of camshaft jig Part No. 3268 in order to ensure that both camshaft grooves are absolutely horizontal.

• If it is necessary to turn the camshafts with the No. 1 piston at TDC, the valves will strike the pistons.

• Before turning the camshafts, turn the engine back against its normal direction of rotation by a few degrees, so that all pistons are a little way down their bores.

• After the camshafts have been correctly aligned, the engine should be turned in its normal direction of rotation so that No. 1 piston is at TDC.

STEP 7: REFITTING TIMING CHAINS: Be sure to follow this procedure precisely:
→ Make sure that No. 1 piston is at TDC.
→ Make sure that the ground-down tooth on the crankshaft sprocket (**B**) aligns with the main bearing joint.

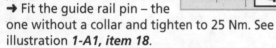

4-7

→ Fit the guide rail pin – the one without a collar and tighten to 25 Nm. See illustration *1-A1, item 18*.
→ Push the guide rail (**2**) on to the pin.
→ Fit the pin with shoulder and tighten to 25 Nm.

→ Slide the single chain (**1**) and both sprockets (**3**) and (**4**) into position. Make sure that the single chain is fitted so that the direction of rotation marking that should have been painted on to it before it was removed is pointing in the correct direction. See illustration *1-A5*. Note that the marking on the single chain sprocket (**4**) must align with either one of the two notches on the thrust washer (**C** or **D**).
→ Release the locking spline in the chain tensioner with a small screwdriver (**A**).
→ Press the chain tensioner against the tensioner plate and tighten the chain tensioner to 10 Nm.

STEP 8: Use three old bolts to fit the flywheel to the crankshaft – or the drive plate to the crankshaft, in the case of automatic transmission. Ensure that all of the TDC settings already aligned are

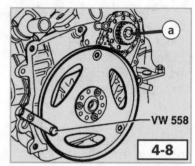

4-8

still precisely in position and lock the flywheel to prevent it from turning. Volkswagen recommend the use of locking tool VW558.

STEP 9: Tighten the intermediate shaft sprockets retaining bolt (illustration *4-8, item a*) to 100 Nm.

STEP 10: Remove the flywheel or drive plate and once again check the position of the TDC markings. Fit the double chain and chain tensioner with tensioning plate – see illustration *1-A1*.

STEP 11: If they are not already installed, fit the camshafts and camshaft sprockets as described in *Job 1*.

Part J: 4-Cylinder Engines, Cylinder Head – Refitting

CONTENTS

See *Part B: Which Engine is Which?* for an explanation of the engine types referred to here.

IMPORTANT NOTE:
1.4 AND 1.6 LITRE ALUMINIUM ENGINES: There are several important and completely different features on these engines – see *Part P: 1.4 and 1.6 litre Aluminium Block Engine – Specific info.*

Have the head skimmed (NOT Diesel engines) by an engine overhaul specialist. Refitting a head that has not been skimmed is likely to lead to a blowing head

gasket. The compression ratio of a Diesel engine will be raised too high if it is skimmed.

JOB 1: CYLINDER HEAD – refitting.

IMPORTANT NOTE:
Ensure that the cylinder head is fitted with none of the pistons at Top Dead Centre, in case yours is of the type where the valves may contact the pistons if

rotated separately:

• On some engines, the valves will collide with the pistons if the camshaft/s is/are turned while the engine is set to Top Dead Centre (TDC).

• To avoid risk of damage, the camshaft/s should NEVER be replaced (or turned if already in place) while the pistons are at TDC.

• Volkswagen recommend that the crankshaft is turned back (the *opposite direction* to normal rotation) by a few degrees, moving the pistons safely a little way down the bore.

• With the cylinder head fitted to the engine, the camshaft/s must now be turned to their alignment marks for when No. 1 piston is at TDC.

• Before the timing belt is refitted, the crankshaft must be moved forward (in the *direction of* normal rotation) to the TDC position again.

FACT FILE

GASKETS AND BOLTS

i) A cylinder head gasket may only be compressed once. After tightening, it loses its resilience and will not seal again properly. So, if you need to remove the head a second time, even if you have just fitted a new gasket and have torqued the head down, you will need to use yet another new gasket.

ii) Use all new gaskets for all applicable items, such as valve cover (early type), manifolds and so on.

iii) The later type of cylinder head bolts may also only be used once. Once-used bolts should not be re-used because the torque settings will be incorrect and a second stretch will weaken them.

iv) When the later type of bolts are used, there is no need to re-tighten the cylinder head bolts after a given period of running the engine.

❒ **STEP 1:** Check the cylinder head for cracks, especially around and between valve seats, and for distortion, using a straight edge and feeler gauges. If any cracking or distortion are found and you are not sure whether or not the head can be re-used, have the head checked by your Volkswagen dealer or engine specialist.

❒ **STEP 2:** Check that all the cylinder head mating surfaces are thoroughly clean. Ensure that the bolt holes in the block are free of debris and that the threads are free running. Check that the pistons are cleaned and that there is no loose debris in the cylinders.

❒ **STEP 3:** On one side of the cylinder head gasket is the part number, or the word "OBEN" or "TOP". This must be placed upwards, facing the cylinder head.

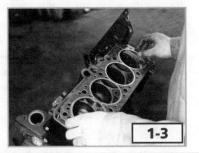

1-3

DIESEL ENGINES

❒ **STEP 4:** Piston protrusion above the block at TDC must be measured. In place of the special Volkswagen tools shown here, you could use a perfectly

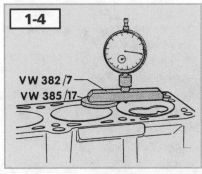

1-4

VW 382/7
VW 385/17

straight steel bar placed over the piston crown, and use a pair of feeler gauge sets to measure the parallel clearances between the block face and each side of the bar.

→ Set No. 1 piston at TDC and measure protrusion.

→ Measure maximum protrusion of each other piston.

→ Take the highest of the four values.

→ If the valves differ greatly, discuss the supply of a better matched set of pistons with your supplier and/or check connecting rods.

❒ **STEP 5:** Select and fit a Diesel engine gasket as follows:

→ The number of notches (white arrow) indicates gasket thickness. See FACT FILE below.

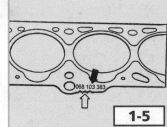

068 103 383

1-5

→ Fit the gasket with the part number (black arrow) uppermost.

→ Gaskets for engines with hydraulic valve tappets/lifters have an extra 16 mm hole between cylinders 1 and 2.

FACT FILE

GASKET - DIESEL ENGINE PISTON PROTRUSION (mm)

No of Notches	1.5 ltr	1.6 & caddy to 08.85 without hydraulic lifters	Caddy 08.85 -on with hydraulic lifters
1	-	0.67-0.80	0.66-0.86
2	0.43-0.63	0.81-0.90	0.87-0.90
3	0.64-0.82	0.91-1.02	0.91-1.02
4	0.83-0.92	-	-
5	0.93-1.02	-	-

IMPORTANT NOTE: Check with your supplier that the gasket you are buying is the correct one!

ALL ENGINE TYPES

TOP TIP!

STEP 6:
• Volkswagen recommend using VW guides 3070 to enable the gasket and head bolt holes to align as the head is lowered into

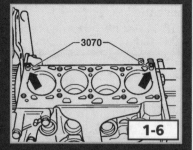

place. Use one of the two alternatives:
→ Two old cylinder head bolts with the heads cut off, OR
→ Two pieces of steel bar about 200 mm (8 in.) long and an easy sliding fit into the threaded cylinder head bolt holes, in the block.
→ They will act as guides when you lower the cylinder head into position and keep the gasket in the correct place at the same time.

STEP 7: Insert the head bolts, but do not tighten them yet. Remove the two bars and insert the last two bolts.

TOP TIP!

STEP 8: • Some models can be fitted with EITHER the 12-point socket head bolt (**a**), OR the older hexagon socket head bolt (**b**). From around 1990, only the later type are generally

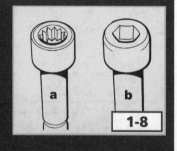

found. Tightening requirements are very different, and the 12-point type should NOT be re-used. Buy new ones every time they are removed.

STEP 9: Cylinder head bolts for 2.0L 16V engines can be one of two different types. The earlier type (**A**) has a smooth head. The later type (**B**) is ONLY for use with the metal cylinder head gasket and has a knurled head.

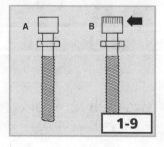

STEP 10: Refer to *Chapter 1, Facts and Figures* for the correct torque stages and settings for your particular model. Tighten the head bolts to their correct settings.

FACT FILE

CYLINDER HEAD BOLT TIGHTENING METHODS

HEXAGON SOCKET HEAD BOLTS
Tighten each bolt in the correct order until it just starts to tighten up. Tighten each bolt in order by half a turn at a time with a torque wrench to the figure shown in *Chapter 1, Facts and Figures*.

12-POINT SOCKET HEAD BOLTS - CAST-IRON BLOCK
1) Pre-tighten all bolts to 30 Nm with a torque wrench. 2) Tighten each bolt in the correct order by a further 1/4 turn (90 degrees). 3) Tighten each bolt again in the correct order by a further 1/4 turn (90 degrees).

12-POINT SOCKET HEAD BOLTS - ALUMINIUM BLOCK (e.g. 999cc AER and ALL engine codes)
1) Pre-tighten all bolts to 40 Nm with a torque wrench. 2) Tighten each bolt in the correct order to 60 Nm. 3) Tighten each bolt in the correct order by a further 1/4 turn (90 degrees). 4) Tighten each bolt again by a further 1/4 turn (90 degrees).

STEP 11: Tighten in the order shown, starting with the LOWEST NUMBER and working upwards.

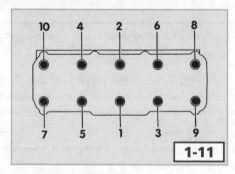

STEP 12: Refit the following:
→ Using new gaskets place the exhaust and inlet manifolds onto their studs and tighten down.
→ The exhaust down pipe can now be reconnected.
→ Replace the carburetor or injection components.
→ Fit a new timing belt. See *Part C: Timing Belt or Chain – Inspection, Adjustment, Replacement, Job 2.*
→ Reconnect all the remaining hoses, cables and wires to the cylinder head.

STEP 13: Apply lots of fresh engine oil to each of the valve tappets, then replace the end seals and camshaft cover, if it is a cork gasket - DON'T re-use the old compressed one!

1-13

STEP 14: For some engines, new camshaft cover screws are provided with the new Volkswagen gasket.

1-14

STEP 15: If the old type are still in place, release each one with a self-grip wrench, remove them and screw in the new ones.

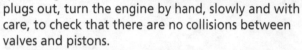
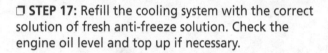

1-15

STEP 16: With spark or glow plugs out, turn the engine by hand, slowly and with care, to check that there are no collisions between valves and pistons.

STEP 17: Refill the cooling system with the correct solution of fresh anti-freeze solution. Check the engine oil level and top up if necessary.

STEP 18: If the earlier type of cylinder head bolts are used (the ones that are tightened to a given torque figure, and not to the multi-stage torque-plus-angular tightening process) the head bolts should be retightened to the correct torque after about 250 miles (400km) of running.

Part K: 6-Cylinder Engines, Cylinder Head – Refitting

CONTENTS

Page No

See *Part B: Which Engine is Which?* for an explanation of the engine types referred to here.

JOB 1: CYLINDER HEAD – refitting.

STEP 1: Make sure that No. 1 piston is at TDC. See *Part C: Timing Belt or Chain – Inspection, Adjustment, Replacement, Job 3.*

STEP 2: Make sure that the slots (arrowed) in the ends of the camshafts are perfectly horizontal. Volkswagen recommend using the crankshaft setting bar Part No. 3268.

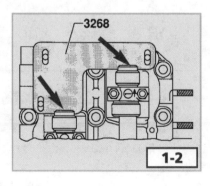

1-2

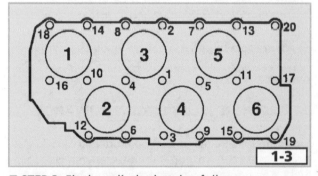

1-3

STEP 3: Fit the cylinder head as follows:
→ Note that the cylinder head stud holes Nos. 12 and 13 have centralising sleeves.
→ Place the cylinder head gasket in position with the work 'TOP' or 'OBEN' or the Part No. uppermost over the two centralising sleeves. Do not use any form of gasket sealant.
→ Put the cylinder head in position on the block, locating it on the centralising sleeves.
→ Insert the new cylinder head bolts (do not reuse the old ones) and tighten by hand.
→ Tighten the cylinder head bolts in the order of the numbers shown here.

CYLINDER HEAD TIGHTENING STAGES

STAGE 1
Tighten each bolt with a torque wrench, in the correct order, to 40 Nm.

STAGE 2
Retighten each bolt in the same order to 60 Nm.

STAGE 3
Use a normal spanner to tighten each bolt, again in the same order by a further quarter of a turn (90 degrees).

STAGE 4
Tighten each bolt in the same order by a further quarter of a turn (90 degrees).
NOTE: There is no need to retighten the cylinder head after a certain distance has been covered.

Part L: Engine and Transmission
– Removal, Separation, Refitting
CONTENTS

Page No.

Page No.

See *Part B: Which Engine is Which?* for an explanation of the engine types referred to here.

IMPORTANT NOTE:
1.4 AND 1.6 LITRE ALUMINIUM ENGINES: There are several important and completely different features on these engines – see *Part P: 1.4 and 1.6 litre Aluminium Block Engine – Specific info.*

There are several different ways in which engines fitted to the vehicles covered by this manual can be removed.

METHOD 1: LIFT ENGINE UPWARDS

This method applies to all Polo models to 1994, plus Golf, Jetta, Scirocco, and Rabbit-based vehicles to 1992. The engine is best removed, complete with the transmission, by lifting it out through the top of the engine bay.

METHOD 2: LOWER ENGINE DOWNWARDS

This method applies to most models. If you prefer, the engine can be lowered to the floor and the vehicle raised by about 1 metre (3 feet) and the engine pulled from beneath. On Golf Mk 2 and 3, and on later Polo models, the engine could be lowered complete with the subframe. (There is no engine subframe on earlier versions of these models.)

METHOD 3: REMOVE ENGINE FORWARDS

This method is recommended by Volkswagen for Golf and Vento from 1992, Polo from 1995, and Corrado from 1989. On these models, the front bodywork can be removed relatively easily (in theory – provided rust hasn't taken a hold!), providing excellent access.

IMPORTANT NOTE: If the vehicle you are working on is fitted with the type of exhaust system which is fixed to the manifold with Volkswagen spring clips, you will need a special tool similar to VW part no. 3049A, available from your auto-parts specialist, if you want to detach the exhaust system in the recommended way. But look out for our TOP TIP! to help you get round the problem - see Step A-32.

JOB 1:   ENGINE AND TRANSMISSION - *removal*

CONTENTS

Section A: Polo up to 1994. Golf and variants up to 1992.
Section B: Golf and variants after 1992. Polo and variants after 1995.

Section A: Polo up to 1994. Golf and variants up to 1992.

TOP TIP!

• Taking stuff off is the easy bit - remembering where it all goes again can be another story - unless you make it easy for yourself!

• Tag each hose, cable, linkage and connection with a piece of masking tape as you take it off.

• Number each tag and write down the place where it connects. If you own a video or digital camera, put it to good use here, taking shots of the engine bay and all the various 'tricky' bits, so producing your instant reference source!

• Alternatively, take photographs with film or using a disposable camera.

☐ **STEP A1:** Before dismantling, disconnect the battery negative (-) earth/ground terminal. See *Chapter 10, Electrical, Dash, Instruments, Fact File: Disconnecting the Battery* BEFORE doing so!

☐ **STEP A2:** You may find the final lift easier if you remove the bonnet now.

☐ **STEP A3:** If your car has twin headlights remove the inner headlight caps.

☐ **STEP A4:** Remove these:

→ If you have a windscreen washer bottle that will be in the way, remove it now.

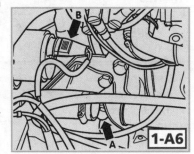

→ You can also remove the alternator, if it is top-mounted, depending on model.

→ The air cleaner body and trunking should also be removed.

→ The bolt holding the exhaust bracket to the rear of the engine, when fitted.

☐ **STEP A5:** Prepare to drain off the coolant by first removing the filler cap and turning the heater control inside the car to HOT. Drain the coolant into a suitable container through the drain plugs, if your vehicle is fitted with them, or in one of the following ways:

☐ **STEP A6:** 'SMALLER' 1.1/1.3 ENGINES: Release the bottom radiator hose (A).

☐ **STEP A7:** 'LARGER' PETROL/GASOLINE 8-VALVE AND DIESEL ENGINES: Remove either of the coolant hoses (1) or disconnect the flange (2), which may prove to be easier if you want to re-use the hoses.

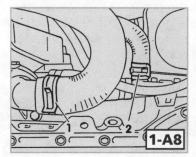

☐ **STEP A8: 16-VALVE ENGINES:** Disconnect the hoses at (1) and (2), using large pliers to unclip the spring clips and pull them out of the way.

☐ **STEP A9:** Disconnect the wiring plug from the thermostat at the fan. See illustration *Job 1-A6, item B*.

☐ **STEP A10:** Disconnect the following:

→ The heater control cables from the engine.

→ The oil cooler (1 - if fitted) from the body but do not remove the hoses. You can place the cooler on the engine. Undo the other radiator hoses and lift out the radiator (2) complete with electric fan.

☐ **STEP A11:** Detach any further electrical connections as required, taking care to check for any missed connections as the radiator is lifted away.

☐ **STEP A12: DIESEL ENGINES:** As well as the radiator (3) and alternator (4) mentioned earlier, the fuel filter (5) must be detached from the body and placed near the windscreen washer bottle, which remains in place.

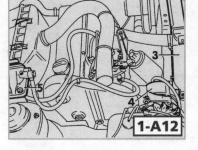

❒ STEP A13: VEHICLES WITH AIR CONDITIONING: Do not, under any circumstances, attempt to separate any air conditioning hoses. If necessary, have this work carried out by your Volkswagen dealer. Start by unscrewing the compressor (**K**) and placing it on one side of the engine bay. The air con. radiator (**C**) can only be removed after the engine cooling radiator has been taken out.

1-A13

❒ STEP A14: VEHICLES WITH AIR CONDITIONING: Remove the condenser and place it along with the compressor on a stand, to one side of the vehicle, without straining hoses.

1-A14

❒ STEP A15: Disconnect any wiring from the engine. There are so many different engines that there are too many variations to list here, so label the connections as you remove them. These are typical 'smaller' engine wiring connections...

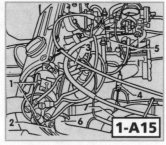

1-A15

❒ STEP A16: ...and these are typical 1.5 and 1.6 engine wiring connections.

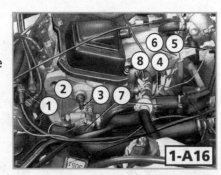

1-A16

❒ STEP A17: FUEL INJECTION ENGINES: Disconnect the warm-up valve (**1**), the cold start valve (**2**), the injectors, and fit protective caps (**3**), but DO NOT disconnect the fuel lines.

1-A17

❒ STEP A18: 16-VALVE ENGINES: The temperature sender wires are: 2 - blue/white; 3 - green/red; 4 - yellow/red; 5 - green/black.

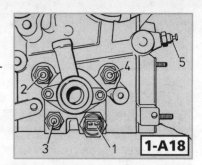

1-A18

❒ STEP A19: DIESEL ENGINES: These electrical connections (**9**) must be disconnected from the Diesel engine: stop control; glow plugs; oil pressure switch; coolant temperature sender; starter; reversing lights switch.

1-A19

❒ STEP A20: Detach or disconnect the following:
→ Any remaining coolant hoses.
→ HT leads and distributor cap, if appropriate.
→ The wiring from the alternator, if still fitted.

❒ STEP A21: CARBURETOR ENGINES:
→ Disconnect the throttle cable at the carburetor by removing the securing clip and disconnect from the bracket without removing the bracket retaining clip.
→ Pull off the fuel return pipe. Seal the end of the pipe.
→ Detach the vacuum reservoir and place it on the engine, leaving the pipework attached.
→ Disconnect the choke cable, when manual choke fitted.
→ Remove the air pre-heater pipe, which runs from the exhaust manifold, when fitted.

❒ STEP A22: AUTOMATIC TRANSMISSION MODELS: Remove the throttle cable bracket, either from the carburetor, or from the cylinder head, but do not alter the adjustment of the cable.

❒ STEP A23: FUEL INJECTION ENGINES: Remove the air intake hose, the crankcase breather hose, the accelerator cable and the vacuum hoses.

❒ STEP A24: DIESEL ENGINES:
→ Disconnect the fuel supply (**6**) and return pipes (**7**) at the injection pump.
→ Disconnect the accelerator cable (**8**) from the injection pump lever and remove it from the pump, complete with bracket (**9**).

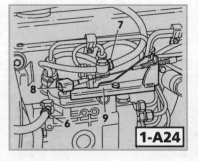

1-A24

STEP A25: DIESEL ENGINES: Disconnect cold start aid operating cable: Loosen the cable clamp screw (**3**), remove the circlip (**2**) and detach the cable from the bracket (**1**).

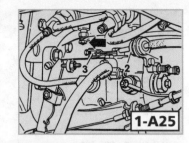

STEP A26: Disconnect the clutch cable (**1**) and the speedometer cable (**2**) and plug the hole in the gearbox with a rag.

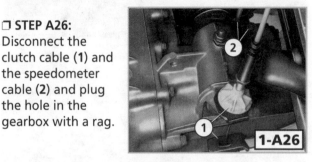

STEP A27: GOLF WITH MANUAL TRANSMISSION: Disengage the gearchange connecting rod mechanism from the gearbox.

STEP A28: EARLY GOLF WITH MANUAL TRANSMISSION, 'SMALLER' ENGINES: Take out the pointed screw from the gear shift rod and take out the gear shift finger.

STEP A29: POLO: Remove the gearchange selector bolt (**a**) and disconnect the shift mechanism.

STEP A30: GOLF WITH AUTOMATIC TRANSMISSION: Place the transmission selector in 'P' (PARK). Disconnect the selector lever cable (**1**), the throttle operating cable (**2**), the cable

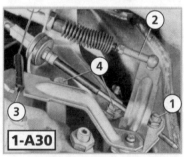

from the accelerator pedal (**3**) and remove the bracket (**4**).

STEP A31: EXHAUST SCREWED OR CLAMPED TO MANIFOLD: Remove the exhaust pipe supports (**16** and **17**) and remove the screws or clamp holding the exhaust downpipe to the manifold (**18**).

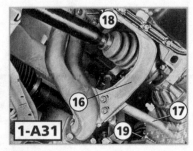

TOP TIP!

STEP A32: EXHAUST CLIPPED TO MANIFOLD - 1: See *Step A33*. Don't confront the problem; go round it!
• EITHER: If you are removing the engine by lowering it to the floor and raising the car over it, leave the exhaust front pipe and manifold in place, disconnect the rear end of the front pipe from the rest of the system and detach the manifold and front pipe later.
• OR: If you are lifting the engine and transmission up and out of the engine bay, leave the front pipe connected to the exhaust manifold, detach the manifold from the engine, tie it out of the way and lift the engine past it. It's tight, but it can be done!

STEP A33: EXHAUST CLIPPED TO MANIFOLD - 2: If you need to remove the clips, it will be almost impossible to do so without causing damage and risk of injury. Purchase special

tool 3049A from your Volkswagen dealer or a non-VW alternative tool from your auto-accessory store.

STEP A34: Use the VW downpipe removing tool as follows:
→ Insert tensioner in clip bores with the adjustable slide (arrowed) facing

down, and pretension with the knurled washers.
→ Use a socket with extension to turn the tensioner in the direction of the arrow on the tensioner, as far as the stop.
→ Push the exhaust pipe in the direction of each clip to be removed, and remove each clip, in turn.
→ When refitting, make certain that the clips are properly inserted in the recesses.

STEP A35: Detach both of the drive shafts from the transmission unit and tie them up out of the way.

STEP A36: Remove the rear transmission support ('engine mounting').

☐ **STEP A37:** Attach a lifting hoist. The one shown is the Clarke Strongarm, but any adequate hoist will be okay, provided that it is securely located at the correct point of balance. Take the weight of the engine on the hoist. Start to detach the engine and transmission mountings.

1-A37

GOLF AND VARIANTS – ENGINE AND TRANSMISSION MOUNTINGS

☐ **STEP A38:** Disconnect the transmission mounting at the right-hand end of the engine and the one at the other end, which is more accurately the

1-A38

transmission mounting – from just underneath the battery carrier. For the variations in engine and transmission mountings used on these models, see *Part O: Engine/Transmission Mountings – Replacement, Job 3*.

TOP TIP!

• You may have to adjust the amount of tension you have on the engine hoist in order to get the pin out.

☐ **STEP A39:** Once the mountings have been disconnected and in order to provide more clearance, they can be unbolted from the engine/transmission...

1-A39

☐ **STEP A40:** ...and removed from the vehicle.

1-A40

☐ **STEP A41:** Between the back of the engine and the transmission, near the gearshift rod, is another engine mounting with three bolts. At the front of the engine, shown here, is a fourth 'mounting' – or more properly, a torque reaction link – which can be removed by unbolting it from the engine and by

1-A41

unbolting the cup in which the rubber bush sits from the front crossmember.

☐ **STEP A42:** From December 1984, the front mounting was changed to this 'hydro' type with damping action. It is removed by undoing the bolts **b**, **e** and **f**.

1-A42

POLO PRE-1995 – ENGINE AND TRANSMISSION MOUNTINGS

☐ **STEP A43:** If you haven't already done so, remove the earth/ground strap (**a**) and remove the engine mounting bolt (**b**) from the mounting on the body side member.

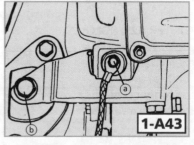

1-A43

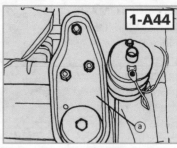

1-A44

☐ **STEP A44:** Take out the three bolts and the through-bolt holding the left-hand transmission mounting (**a**) in place.

☐ **STEP A45:** Detach the transmission rear mounting (illustration *1-A29, item b*) from the transmission and the floorpan.

ALL ENGINE TYPES

☐ **STEP A46: METHOD 1: LIFT ENGINE UPWARDS:** While an assistant helps with the engine hoist, manoeuvre the engine free of all obstacles, while carrying out the

1-A46

final check that nothing remains connected...

☐ **STEP A47:** ...then lift the engine sufficiently high to clear the front of the bodywork. You will probably find that the engine has to be brought out at this sort of angle and then, in order to clear the body, the transmission-end of things will have

1-A47

to be lifted manually while an assistant either trolleys the engine hoist or (preferably) pushes the car back until the engine is clear.

☐ **STEP A48: METHOD 2: LOWER ENGINE DOWNWARDS:** When a Golf engine is to be lowered to the ground rather than lifted out of the engine bay, you can leave the bonnet/hood in place and there is the added advantage that you are

1-A48

less likely to cause damage to the surrounding bodywork. You will still need a hoist, because the engine and transmission unit will have to be lowered to the ground.

☐ **STEP A49:** You will also need some means of lifting the car's bodywork over the engine. Here, a car lift is used to raise the whole vehicle, but you may be able to connect your engine hoist to a couple of engine mounting brackets inside the engine bay and raise the front of the vehicle with your hoist, provided that its lifting capacity is sufficient.

1-A49

☐ **STEP A50:** This technique – of lifting the car from over the engine – needs a minimum lift of around 1 metre (3 ft) and is generally more suitable for the workshop with a hoist.

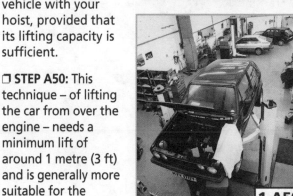
1-A50

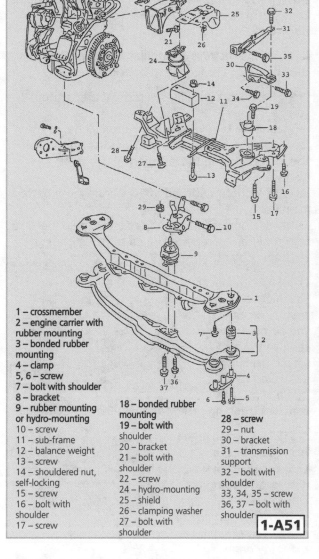

1 – crossmember
2 – engine carrier with rubber mounting
3 – bonded rubber mounting
4 – clamp
5, 6 – screw
7 – bolt with shoulder
8 – bracket
9 – rubber mounting or hydro-mounting
10 – screw
11 – sub-frame
12 – balance weight
13 – screw
14 – shouldered nut, self-locking
15 – screw
16 – bolt with shoulder
17 – screw

18 – bonded rubber mounting
19 – bolt with shoulder
20 – bracket
21 – bolt with shoulder
22 – screw
24 – hydro-mounting
25 – shield
26 – clamping washer
27 – bolt with shoulder

28 – screw
29 – nut
30 – bracket
31 – transmission support
32 – bolt with shoulder
33, 34, 35 – screw
36, 37 – bolt with shoulder

1-A51

☐ **STEP A51:** These are the engine and transmission mountings and subframes as fitted to the Mk 2 Golf with 1.6, 1.8 and 2.0 litre engines. The bracket assembly on the left of the illustration was not used on 1.8 litre models. The set up on 1.05 and 1.3 litre engines is very similar except that the bracket referred to above is not fitted and the transmission mounting has a different appearance.

Section B: Golf and variants after 1992. Polo and variants after 1995.

METHOD 3: REMOVE ENGINE FORWARDS

Volkswagen recommend that the engine is removed forwards, but many mechanics still prefer to remove it upwards (after removing any potential obstructions, such as engine and transmission mountings, complete). If you want to follow the VW approach - and a lot depends on how easily the front panel can be taken from the vehicle - remove the front bumper and front panel - see *Chapter 13,*

Bodywork. The engine is disconnected as described above and then the weight is taken on the hoist. If there is room, push the car back, or draw the engine forward, always taking care not to damage the bodywork.

Detailed instructions are similar to those for earlier cars, but with the following principal stages:

❒ **STEP B1:** Start with these essential preparatory steps:
→ Make sure that you have the radio code, or use a 'code saver' 12v supply to the cigarette lighter, with the ignition key in the 'auxiliary' position, if necessary.
→ With ignition switched off, disconnect the battery terminals.
→ Make a note of where all cable ties are cut off, so that they can be replaced when refitting engine.
→ Drain coolant.

❒ **STEP B2:** Take off the injection system cover, disconnect the air filter and remove the air intake trunking, according to model. This is the complex trunking fitted to some V6-engined models.

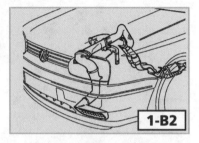

1-B2

❒ **STEP B3:** Remove the front panel – see *Chapter 13, Bodywork*. If air conditioning is fitted:
→ *DO NOT open any of the air conditioner pipes or connections.*
→ Make sure that the compressor is removed from the engine and laid to one side with the front panel.
→ Unbolt the fluid reservoir and allow to hand free.
→ Unbolt the refrigerant hose clamps.
→ Remove the ribbed drive belt.
→ Take great care that hoses and connections are not strained, stretched, kinked or bent.

1-B3

❒ **STEP B4:** If power steering is fitted, remove the pump from the engine and hang it carefully to one side without draining any of the fluid. If this is not possible, remove the reservoir as well. Leave the hoses connected.

❒ **STEP B5:** Disconnect all multi-pin connectors, where fitted. Otherwise, disconnect electrical cables, throttle connections, heater

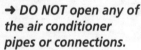

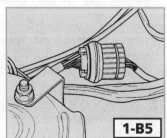

1-B5

cables and pipes, gearchange linkages and all other items as detailed in *SECTION A*. If you remove the engine by LOWERING it, disconnect the drive shafts only at the wheels, not the transmission, to avoid having to drain lubricant or upsetting the differential with driveshafts removed. Otherwise, the driveshafts must be removed from the transmission.

GOLF AND VARIANTS

❒ **STEP B6:** These engine mounting positions are similar to those for the earlier engines already described. The rear right and front mountings shown are disconnected by taking out the top bolts. IMPORTANT NOTE: When refitting the engine, the recesses in the brackets (top arrows) must locate with the lugs in the bonded rubber mountings (lower arrows).

1-B6

POLO AND VARIANTS

❒ **STEP B7:** Where this type of 'pendulum support' is fitted beneath the transmission:
→ Loosen bolt **2**.
→ Remove bolt **1**.
→ Swing the support plate (**3**) free.

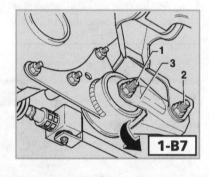

1-B7

❒ **STEP B8:** Where this type is fitted, unbolt the front of the support from the transmission casing (arrowed).

1-B8

❒ **STEP B9:** Where these types of engine and transmission upper mountings are fitted, remove the relevant bolts (arrowed), lower the engine/ transmission until it

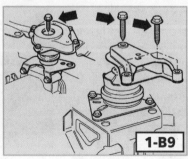

1-B9

is released from the transmission mounting, then remove it by turning and lifting the unit carefully as it is drawn forward, so as not to damage the bodywork.

☐ **STEP B10:** Alternatively (depending on type) disconnect the transmission upper mounting by taking off the nuts (position 2), removing the bolts (**1** and **3**) and taking off the plate (**4**) …

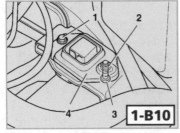

☐ **STEP B11:** …and at the engine-end, remove the mounting bolts (**A** and **B**). The engine can be lowered until free and drawn forwards.

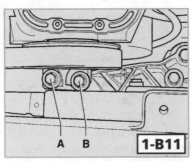

JOB 2: ENGINE AND TRANSMISSION - *separation*

TYPE A - MANUAL TRANSMISSION - EARLY TYPES (TRANSMISSION HELD TO ENGINE WITH FITTED STUDS AND NUTS) – 1.5 LITRE ENGINES AND LARGER ONLY

IMPORTANT NOTES:
i) Do NOT confuse the alignment marks shown with the TDC marks.
ii) The stud-fitted transmission cannot be separated from the engine without aligning these marks.
iii) There is an overlap in the cut-off dates given by Volkswagen for the different alignment systems. This is normal in the production line process. Use whichever is applicable to your engine.

☐ **STEP 1: VEHICLES UP TO DECEMBER 1974:** Remove TDC sender sensor, or screw-in plug (arrowed), to expose TDC marks. Turn the flywheel to the position of the lug - 33 degrees before TDC.

☐ **STEP 2: VEHICLES FROM SEPTEMBER 1974:** There is a depression instead of a lug. Remove TDC sender sensor, or screw-in plug, to expose TDC marks. Turn the flywheel to the position of the depression (arrowed), which is 76 degrees before TDC.

TYPE B - MANUAL TRANSMISSION - LATER TYPE (TRANSMISSION HELD TO ENGINE WITH BOLTS)

☐ **STEP 3:** IMPORTANT NOTES: **i)** When bolts (arrowed) are used in place of fitted studs, the engine and transmission can be turned in relation to each other after the bolts have been removed, until there is sufficient clearance between the flywheel and transmission unit driveshaft. The lug, or recess on the flywheel, is therefore not found on later engines/flywheels.

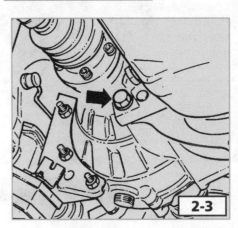

ii) When a later engine or flywheel is used with an earlier transmission, you will have to remove the studs and fit the later-type bolts.

☐ **STEP 4:** Remove the cover flat (arrowed) from over the driveshaft flange.

☐ **STEP 5:** Remove the engine-to-transmission unit bolts and separate them. Take care to pull the transmission from the engine in a straight line, so as not to put any strain on the transmission first motion shaft.

TYPE C - AUTOMATIC TRANSMISSION

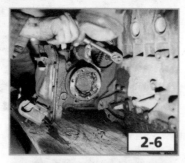

☐ **STEP 6:** Remove the three flywheel-to-torque converter bolts by working through the starter motor aperture.

2-6

☐ **STEP 7:** Draw the transmission off the engine, taking care that the torque converter doesn't fall about.

2-7

☐ **STEP 8:** Wire the torque converter into the bellhousing to keep it secure.

2-8

☐ **STEP 9:** Some 5-speed transmissions (e.g. type 02A) need to have the clutch operating lever pushed towards the housing and located there.
➜ Screw the bolt into the threaded hole in the casing (when one is found there). The threaded hole is later to be sealed by the 3rd cable support bracket (if fitted) or a blanking plug.
➜ Do not tighten any of the engine mounts until all are in place.
➜ Take careful note of the mounting alignments described in *Job 1, Section B*, illustration *1-B6*.

JOB 3: ENGINE - *installation*

☐ **STEP 1:** Installation is generally carried out in the reverse order to removal. However, you must pay particular attention to the following points:
➜ Make sure that the flywheel is correctly aligned on earlier engines. See *Job 2, Type A*.
➜ Make sure that the clutch is properly aligned. See *Chapter 7, Transmission & Clutch*.
➜ Lubricate the release bearing and input spline shaft before assembling the engine and transmission.
➜ If you lower the engine into position from above, guide it carefully and ensure that the drive shafts are clear.
➜ Attach the transmission mounting first, then attach the engine mountings. Align them, then tighten them.

☐ **STEP 2:** Attach and centralise the torque strut (centre-front of engine) or pendulum mounting (centre-rear), according to type fitted.

☐ **STEP 3:** Align the exhaust system so that no undue force is required to push any part of the system towards a mounting point and so that none of the rubber support loops are loaded more than the others.

Part M: 4-Cylinder Engine Block
Dismantling, Rebuilding

CONTENTS

See *Part B: Which Engine is Which?* for an explanation of the engine types referred to here.

IMPORTANT NOTE:
1.4 AND 1.6 LITRE ALUMINIUM ENGINES: There are several important and completely different features on these engines – see *Part P: 1.4 and 1.6 litre Aluminium Block Engine – Specific info.*

JOB 1: 4-CYLINDER ENGINES – *identification.*

'INTERNAL WATER PUMP' ENGINES

The (generally) smaller engines from 895cc to 1.6 litres, all with a horizontally-mounted distributor on the end of the cylinder head, and (in most cases) a camshaft drive belt adjusted by turning the water pump. A smaller number of these engines have semi-automatic camshaft drive belt adjusters.

'EXTERNAL WATER PUMP' ENGINES

All other petrol and diesel - the (generally) larger engines, from 1.5 litres to 2.0 litres, with a cylinder block-mounted distributor (except for 1.8 and 2.0 litre 16V engines) and a camshaft drive belt adjuster located inside the belt cover.

ALUMINIUM BLOCK ENGINES

This 'new generation' engine was introduced in 1998 – and is not good news for the mechanic! VW say that if the crankshaft main bearing bolts are loosened, the block and crank assembly will have to be replaced with new. Ouch! The 8-valve cylinder heads can be worked on in a similar way to other 8-valve 4-cylinder OHC Volkswagen engines. 16-valve cylinder heads are different.

JOB 2: CYLINDER BLOCK – *layouts.*

TYPES OF ENGINE BLOCK ASSEMBLIES

Familiarise yourself with the layout of the engines' bottom ends.

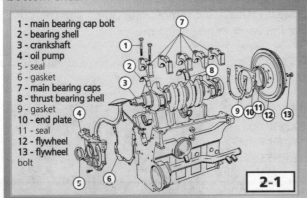

1 - main bearing cap bolt
2 - bearing shell
3 - crankshaft
4 - oil pump
5 - seal
6 - gasket
7 - main bearing caps
8 - thrust bearing shell
9 - gasket
10 - end plate
11 - seal
12 - flywheel
13 - flywheel bolt

2-1

❏ **STEP 1:** This is the layout of the early 'internal water pump' engine block. The 1.05 and later 1.3 litre blocks are almost identical in appearance, although the oil pump housing has a slightly different shape.

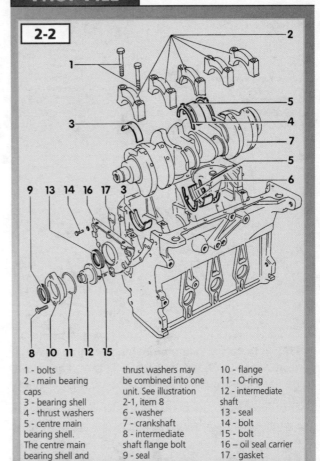

2-2

1 - bolts	thrust washers may be combined into one unit. See illustration 2-1, item 8	10 - flange
2 - main bearing caps		11 - O-ring
3 - bearing shell		12 - intermediate shaft
4 - thrust washers	6 - washer	13 - seal
5 - centre main bearing shell. The centre main bearing shell and	7 - crankshaft	14 - bolt
	8 - intermediate shaft flange bolt	15 - bolt
	9 - seal	16 - oil seal carrier
		17 - gasket

❏ **STEP 2:** These are the block assembly components for the 'external water pump' 1.5 to 2.0 litre engines, with minor visual differences between them.

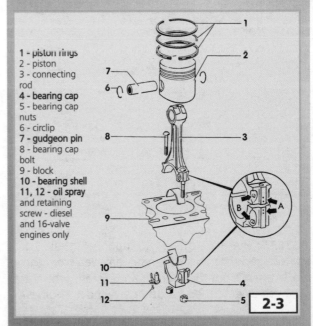

1 - piston rings
2 - piston
3 - connecting rod
4 - bearing cap
5 - bearing cap nuts
6 - circlip
7 - gudgeon pin
8 - bearing cap bolt
9 - block
10 - bearing shell
11, 12 - oil spray and retaining screw - diesel and 16-valve engines only

2-3

❏ **STEP 3:** These are the block and piston components for all engine types, except that only Diesel and 16-Valve engines have a piston oil spray and there are minor differences in conrod bearing cap and bolt arrangements.

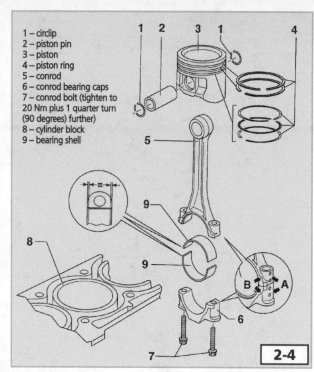

1 – circlip
2 – piston pin
3 – piston
4 – piston ring
5 – conrod
6 – conrod bearing caps
7 – conrod bolt (tighten to 20 Nm plus 1 quarter turn (90 degrees) further)
8 – cylinder block
9 – bearing shell

2-4

❒ **STEP 4:** Note that aluminium block engines have conrod bearings (9) without locating tabs. They have to be fitted, on reassembly, with the bearing shells centralised.

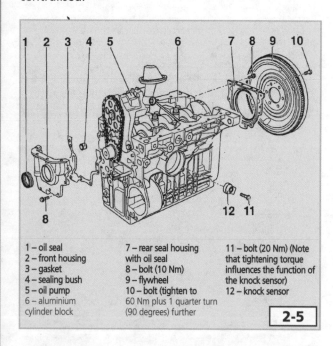

1 – oil seal	7 – rear seal housing with oil seal
2 – front housing	8 – bolt (10 Nm)
3 – gasket	9 – flywheel
4 – sealing bush	10 – bolt (tighten to 60 Nm plus 1 quarter turn (90 degrees) further
5 – oil pump	11 – bolt (20 Nm) (Note that tightening torque influences the function of the knock sensor
6 – aluminium cylinder block	12 – knock sensor

2-5

❒ **STEP 5:** These are the only components that Volkswagen recommend can be removed from the block, apart from the conrods and pistons which are removed as described for other 4-cylinder engines.

> ## WARNING!
>
> • The crankshaft must not be removed. Just loosening the main bearing caps will cause deformation of the cylinder block bearing pedestals. Even if the bearing shells are not renewed bearing damage could occur due to a different bearing clearance.
>
> • If the bearing cap bolts are loosenend, the cylinder block must be replaced complete with the crankshaft.
>
> • Measuring the main bearing clearance is not possible with normal workshop equipment.

JOB 3:   CYLINDER BLOCK – dismantling.

❒ **STEP 1:** Remove all ancillary components and also remove the power steering and air conditioning pumps (if fitted).

3-1

❒ **STEP 2:** Preferably fit the engine to an engine stand and remove the cylinder head.

3-3

3-4

❒ **STEP 3:** Undo and remove the clutch and then the flywheel and shims - if fitted.

❒ **STEP 4:** Turn the engine over on the engine stand and remove the oil sump pan and gasket.

❒ **STEP 5:** 'EXTERNAL WATER PUMP' ENGINES: Take out the two oil pump mounting bolts, noting that one is longer than the other.

3-5

☐ **STEP 6:**
Remove the oil
pump.

3-6

☐ **STEP 7:** Unbolt
the intermediate
shaft sprocket
and tap it
carefully off the
shaft with a soft-
faced hammer.
See *Step 20-on*
for details of
intermediate
shaft removal.

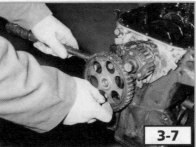
3-7

☐ **STEP 8:** Undo
the crankshaft
sprocket bolt -
lock the
crankshaft with
a piece of wood.

3-8

TOP TIP!

• In the real world, the bolt can be so tight that the
block might have to be removed from the stand
and held down to the floor
• Alternatively, the bolt can be 'shocked' undone
with an impact driver.

☐ **STEP 9:** Undo
and remove the
front crankshaft
seal carrier...

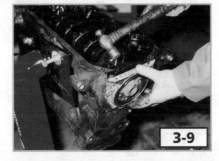
3-9

☐ **STEP 10:** ...and
the rear
crankshaft seal
carrier.

3-10

IMPORTANT NOTE: See *Part A, Job 12* for
illustrations relating to crankshaft removal.

☐ **STEP 11:** Check that all the connecting rods and
their big-end bearing caps are marked with
matching numbers, starting from the timing cover
end. Make sure that the markings tell you which
way round they go - and see illustration *2-3*.

☐ **STEP 12:** If you are to refit the same pistons, mark
them to show their position and which way round
they face. (The arrow points towards the front of
the engine.)

☐ **STEP 13:** Undo the securing bolts (also see
illustration *2-3*) and remove the caps, keeping them
in their correct order.

TOP TIP!

☐ **STEP 14:** Piston removal is as usual:
• Use a hammer handle to tap the piston/
connecting rod assemblies carefully out of the bores.
• Inspect the top of each cylinder bore - there may
be a small ring of carbon build-up which can make
it difficult to remove the pistons. If so, scrape it
carefully away.

☐ **STEP 15:** ...keeping them in the correct order and
the matching conrods and bearing caps together.

☐ **STEP 16:** Check that the five crankshaft main
bearing caps are correctly marked, starting from the
timing cover end. Undo and remove them, keeping
them in the correct order.

TOP TIP!

☐ **STEP 17:** If any of the caps are difficult to remove:
• Lever the bolt holes with a bar, or a pair of bars -
or a pair of fixing bolts, and tap carefully with a
hammer.
• Bearing shells are best removed by sliding them
out with your thumbs, pushing the tab-end out first.

☐ **STEP 18:** Retrieve the thrust washers from each
side of the centre main bearing cap.

☐ **STEP 19:** Lift the crankshaft clear of the cylinder block.

☐ **STEP 20:** The
intermediate shaft
could have been
removed earlier -
in this instance it
was removed now.
The retaining
flange is unbolted
but is always extremely tight.

3-20

☐ **STEP 21:** • Tap the flange around through 90 degrees, so that it protrudes from the side of the block, enabling it to be tapped clear.

3-21

☐ **STEP 22:** The shaft can now be pulled out from the block.

3-22

☐ **STEP 23: DIESEL AND 16-VALVE ENGINES:** Remove the oil spray nozzles from inside the block and check that each is clear before putting it ready for refitting.

JOB 4: ENGINE – *reassembly*.

IMPORTANT NOTES:
• This Job must be read in conjunction with the general fitting notes given in *Part A: General Procedures*.
• All bearings, shells, piston rings and ALL seals that bear on moving parts MUST be copiously lubricated with fresh engine oil as the engine is being reassembled.
• Work ONLY in clean conditions, with clean components and clean hands.

CRANKSHAFT

☐ **STEP 1:** Make sure the bearing seats in the caps and block are perfectly clean and locate the shells so that their tabs

4-1

engage with the slots. Lubricate the shells liberally with fresh engine oil and lower the crankshaft into position.

☐ **STEP 2:** Fit the remaining halves of the shells into the bearing caps:
➜ Lubricate them and position the caps the right way round and in the correct order.
➜ Fit any new seals that may be required in the main bearing end caps.
➜ Cork seals should be soaked in oil, fitted over-length and cut to length once the caps are in place.
➜ Make sure that the block-end of the seal lies flush, but is not trapped by the cap, preventing it from screwing down properly.

4-2

☐ **STEP 3:** Screw the bolts in finger tight and check that the crankshaft rotates freely and smoothly.

☐ **STEP 4:** Tighten the bolts evenly and progressively until the specified torque setting is reached.

4-4

☐ **STEP 5:** Using a suitable screwdriver, lever out the old oil seal (1) from the flywheel end housing (2). Clean the oil seal recess in the housing and push the new seal into position completely evenly all round - the lip of the seal facing in towards

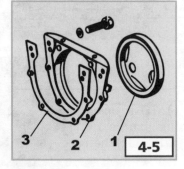

3   2   1   4-5

the block. Lubricate the seal with copious amounts of fresh engine oil.

☐ **STEP 6:** Refit the housing with a new gasket (*4-5, item 3*)and tighten the bolts. Ensure that the seal is flush with the outer face of the housing.

4-6

STEP 7: Take the front oil seal housing (1) and renew the oil seal (2) and fit a new gasket (3). The seal (5) in the intermediate shaft (7) end plate (4) must also be removed, the plate cleaned and a new seal fitted. A new O-ring (6) must be fitted.

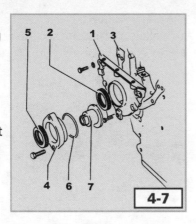

4-7

PISTON/CONNECTING ROD ASSEMBLIES

STEP 8: Make sure that the bores and pistons are clean.
➔ Fit the rings, using a piston ring spreader, if possible.
➔ Fit the piston ring gaps at equal intervals round the pistons circumference and lubricate them well.
➔ Make sure the rings are fitted with the word 'TOP' facing upwards.
➔ Pistons are fitted to connecting rods by pushing in the gudgeon pins...

4-8

STEP 9: ...then fitting the circlips (pointed out here) using circlip pliers.

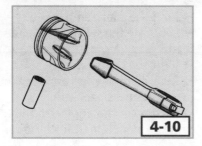

4-9

TOP TIP!

• If the gudgeon pins are too tight to get in, heat the pistons to 60 degrees Celsius (140 degrees Fahrenheit), which is equivalent to hot, but NOT boiling water, and the pin should go straight in.
• DON'T apply direct heat!

STEP 10: These are the trapezoidal piston and conrod fitted to 1.9 TDI engines. Fitting principles are similar.

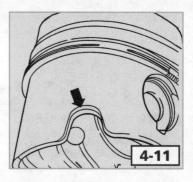

4-11

STEP 11: DIESEL TURBO AND IRON BLOCK 16V ENGINES: Check that the recess (arrowed) for the oil jet in the piston skirt is in the right place.

TOP TIP!

• Wrap insulation tape, or a short piece of plastic tube, over each con. rod thread, so that it cannot damage the crank as it goes in.

STEP 12: Lubricate the piston rings and locate a ring clamp over the piston rings.

STEP 13: Position the assembly in its correct bore with the connecting rod identification marks (arrowed) facing the intermediate shaft.

4-13

STEP 14: With the piston ring clamp touching the cylinder block, use a hammer shaft to carefully tap the piston through and into the bore.

4-14

TOP TIP!

• Turn the crankshaft so that the journal for the con. rod you are working on is at bottom dead-centre.

STEP 15: Locate the upper half of the big end shell bearing in the conrod, making sure that the mating surfaces are clean.
➔ Lubricate the crankpin and the big-end shell and draw the conrod down the bore so that the big end locates with the crankpin.
➔ Fit the other half of the big-end shell to the bearing cap and lubricate.
➔ Offer the cap to the connecting rod and make sure that the numbers match.

STEP 7: Take the front oil seal housing (1) and renew the oil seal (2) and fit a new gasket (3). The seal (5) in the intermediate shaft (7) end plate (4) must also be removed, the plate cleaned and a new seal fitted. A new O-ring (6) must be fitted.

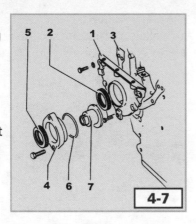

4-7

➜ Screw in the fixing bolts and tighten progressively to the correct torque.

ANTI-FATIGUE BOLTS

❑ **STEP 16:** Bolts should be renewed every time the bearings are changed.
➜ These 'anti-fatigue' bolts have to be tightened to 30 Nm, followed by a further 180 degrees.
➜ DO NOT tighten by the final 180 degrees until you are sure that the crank is finally in place.
➜ Anti-fatigue bolts can be distinguished from rigid bolts as follows.

4-16

	Rigid bolt	Anti-fatigue bolt
A = Thread	M9 x 15 mm long	M8 x 25 mm long
B = Centre	Toothed	Smooth
C = Head shape	Domed	Conical

❑ **STEP 17:** Fit the remaining piston/conrod assemblies and stand the engine upside down on a clean surface.

❑ **STEP 18:** Lubricate the auxiliary shaft bearings and position the shaft in the cylinder block. Fit the auxiliary shaft end plate complete with a new seal and O-ring.

4-18

❑ **STEP 19: 'EXTERNAL WATER PUMP' ENGINES WITH OIL PUMP IN SUMP:**
➜ Lever off the baffle and clean the strainer. Prime the oil pump body with new oil and fit to the block.
➜ Fit the pump, tightening the bolts to their specified torque.
➜ The larger bolts, shown here, locate the pump to the block. The smaller bolts (5) enable you to remove the cover.
➜ Place a new gasket on the cylinder block and fit

4-19

the oil pan sump.
➜ Make sure that the securing bolts have their plates under them and tighten them progressively.

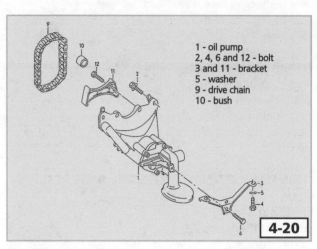

1 - oil pump
2, 4, 6 and 12 - bolt
3 and 11 - bracket
5 - washer
9 - drive chain
10 - bush

4-20

❑ **STEP 20: 'INTERNAL WATER PUMP' ENGINES WITH OIL PUMP IN SUMP:** The later 1.05 and 1.3 litre engines' oil pump has the same function but fit the front of the engine.

❑ **STEP 21: 'INTERNAL WATER PUMP' ENGINES WITH OIL PUMP EXTERNALLY MOUNTED:** Remove and clean the strainer (2) and the relief valve assembly (3). Fit a new seal (4). Refit the pump (1); the V-belt pulley (5) is fitted later.

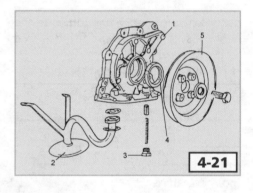
4-21

❑ **STEP 22:** Turn the engine over so that it is now standing on its base. Carry out the following operations, referring to the relevant sections of this manual:
➜ Refit the flywheel.
➜ Refit the cylinder head.
➜ Fit the crankshaft, auxiliary and camshaft sprockets.
➜ Fit the timing belt.
➜ Fit the crankshaft V-belt pulley and tighten the bolt.
➜ Fit the coolant pump.
➜ Refit the clutch.
➜ Refit the fuel pump.
➜ Lubricate the sealing ring and screw on a new oil filter.
➜ Refit the distributor.
➜ Refit all remaining auxiliary components using new gaskets as necessary.
➜ Reconnect the engine to the transmission and refit the complete unit to the car.

❏ **STEP 23:** Start the engine - this might take a few turns more than normal on the initial start up.

❏ **STEP 24:** Allow the engine to warm up on fast idle until it reaches working temperature and then slow it down to its normal speed.

❏ **STEP 25:** Stop the engine and allow it to cool, check the oil and coolant levels and look for any leaks.

❏ **STEP 26:** Avoid over-revving or overloading the engine during its settling down period of 600 miles. We recommend an oil and filter change at this mileage - this will help to extend the life of your new engine.

Part N: 6-Cylinder Engine Block
Dismantling, Rebuilding
CONTENTS

See *Part B: Which Engine is Which?* for an explanation of the engine types referred to here.

JOB 1: CYLINDER BLOCK – *dismantling.*

❏ **STEP 1:** Remove all ancillary components and also remove the power steering and air conditioning pumps (if fitted).

❏ **STEP 2:** Preferably fit the engine to an engine stand and remove the cylinder head.

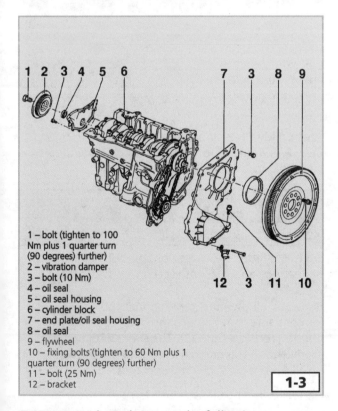

1 – bolt (tighten to 100 Nm plus 1 quarter turn (90 degrees) further)
2 – vibration damper
3 – bolt (10 Nm)
4 – oil seal
5 – oil seal housing
6 – cylinder block
7 – end plate/oil seal housing
8 – oil seal
9 – flywheel
10 – fixing bolts (tighten to 60 Nm plus 1 quarter turn (90 degrees) further)
11 – bolt (25 Nm)
12 – bracket

1-3

❏ **STEP 3:** Undo and remove the following:

→ The clutch ,see *Chapter 7, Transmission & Clutch*.
→ The flywheel or (auto. gearbox driveplate and shims - if fitted – see *Step 5*).
→ The vibration damper.

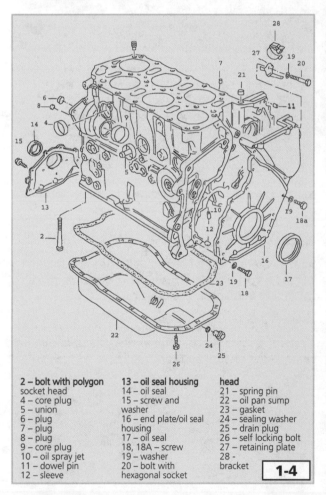

2 – bolt with polygon socket head
4 – core plug
5 – union
6 – plug
7 – plug
8 – plug
9 – core plug
10 – oil spray jet
11 – dowel pin
12 – sleeve
13 – oil seal housing
14 – oil seal
15 – screw and washer
16 – end plate/oil seal housing
17 – oil seal
18, 18A – screw
19 – washer
20 – bolt with hexagonal socket
head
21 – spring pin
22 – oil pan sump
23 – gasket
24 – sealing washer
25 – drain plug
26 – self locking bolt
27 – retaining plate
28 - bracket

1-4

❏ **STEP 4:** You can now take off the following items:
→ The sump and gasket.
→ External brackets and both end plates/oil seal housings. Make a careful note of where the longer bolt **(20)** has to be refitted.

VEHICLES WITH AUTOMATIC TRANSMISSION

❏ **STEP 5:** Use a steel strap bolted in place – similar to the tool VW 558 shown – to lock the driveplate and remove the ring of bolts holding the driveplate to the crankshaft.

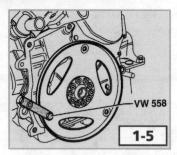

VW 558

1-5

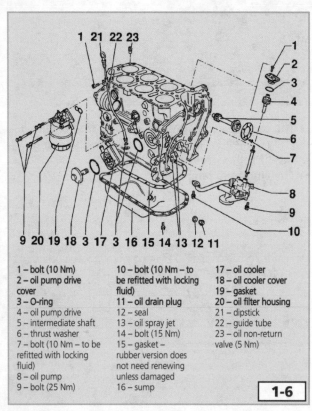

1 21 22 23

9 20 19 18 3 17 3 16 15 14 13 12 11

1 – bolt (10 Nm)
2 – oil pump drive cover
3 – O-ring
4 – oil pump drive
5 – intermediate shaft
6 – thrust washer
7 – bolt (10 Nm – to be refitted with locking fluid)
8 – oil pump
9 – bolt (25 Nm)
10 – bolt (10 Nm – to be refitted with locking fluid)
11 – oil drain plug
12 – seal
13 – oil spray jet
14 – bolt (15 Nm)
15 – gasket – rubber version does not need renewing unless damaged
16 – sump
17 – oil cooler
18 – oil cooler cover
19 – gasket
20 – oil filter housing
21 – dipstick
22 – guide tube
23 – oil non-return valve (5 Nm)

1-6

❏ **STEP 6:** Remove the components shown here. The intermediate shaft (**5**) is removed after first taking off the thrust washer (**6**), while the oil pump drive (**4**) is held in place by the drive cover (**2**).

❏ **STEP 7:** Follow the instructions given in *Part M: 4-Cylinder Engine Block - Dismantling, Rebuilding* and remove the pistons and conrods.

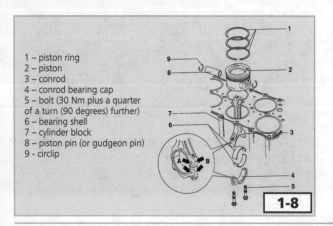

1 – piston ring
2 – piston
3 – conrod
4 – conrod bearing cap
5 – bolt (30 Nm plus a quarter of a turn (90 degrees) further)
6 – bearing shell
7 – cylinder block
8 – piston pin (or gudgeon pin)
9 - circlip

1-8

❏ **STEP 8:** The oil spray jets (also shown in illustration *Job 1-6*) are fitted in main bearings 2 to 7. With the crankshaft removed they can be drifted out with a 4 mm punch and new ones should be installed using a 6 mm punch (arrow).

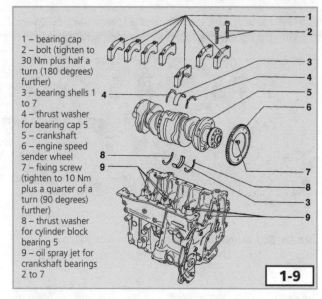

1 – bearing cap
2 – bolt (tighten to 30 Nm plus half a turn (180 degrees) further)
3 – bearing shells 1 to 7
4 – thrust washer for bearing cap 5
5 – crankshaft
6 – engine speed sender wheel
7 – fixing screw (tighten to 10 Nm plus a quarter of a turn (90 degrees) further)
8 – thrust washer for cylinder block bearing 5
9 – oil spray jet for crankshaft bearings 2 to 7

1-9

❏ **STEP 9:** Start by removing the three screws holding the speed sender wheel to the crankshaft and remove the sender wheel.

❏ **STEP 10:** Continue by removing the crankshaft as described in *Part M: 4-Cylinder Engine Block - Dismantling, Rebuilding*.

❏ **STEP 11:** Oil spray jets (arrowed) are installed in main bearings 2 to 7. Remove by drifting out with a 4 mm punch. Fit new ones using a 6 mm punch.

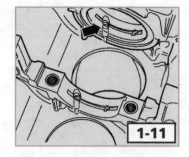

1-11

Reassemble the engine with reference to *Part M: 4-Cylinder Engine Block - Dismantling, Rebuilding*. In addition, note the following:

JOB 2: ENGINE – *reassembly*.

❏ **STEP 1:** Refer to illustration *Job 1-9*.
➜ Bearing cap No. 5 has recesses for the thrust washers.
➜ Renew all the main bearing bolts (**2**).
➜ Make sure that you use the bearing shells 1 to 7 in their correct locations (**3**). The shells with an oil groove go in the cylinder block; the shells without an oil groove go in the bearing caps.

❏ **STEP 2:** Refer to illustration *Job 1-8*.
➜ Refit the conrod bearings with new bolts (**5**).

→ Note the relationship between the marks on the conrods (see inset) and ensure that they are maintained during reassembly.

❏ **STEP 3:** Refer to illustration *Job 1-6*.
→ Oil the O-ring (**3**) before refitting.
→ Note the caption to illustration *Job 1-6* and use locking fluid on bolts where indicated.
→ Coat the oil pressure pipe at the oil pump housing (**8**) and at the cylinder block end with silicon sealant.
→ Coat the reusable sump gasket with non-setting gasket sealant and clean the flange surfaces before installing.
→ Oil the oil filter housing gasket (**19**) before refitting.
→ Make sure that the oil non-return valve (**23**) is fitted in the correct position and clean it if it is badly soiled.

❏ **STEP 4:** When installing the driveplate, fit it temporarily to the crankshaft and hold it in place with at least three oil securing bolts, evenly spaced and tightened to 30 Nm.
→ Check the dimension (**a**) through the three holes for securing the torque converter using a straight

edge and depth gauge and calculate the average.
→ Compare the average with specification (measured distance plus thickness of straight edge). Specification equals 15.7 to 16.5 mm.

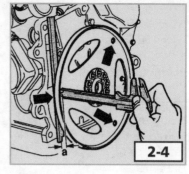

2-4

→ If the distance is not within specification, remove the driveplate and fit a shim of an appropriate thickness, obtainable from your Volkswagen dealer.
→ When the distance is within specification, fit the driveplate using new securing bolts and tighten to 60 Nm then turn a further quarter turn (90 degrees).

❏ **STEP 5:** Refer to illustration *Job 1-3*.
→ Coat the sealing surfaces of the end plates (**5** and **7**) with silicon sealant.

Part O: Engine/Transmission Mountings
– Replacement
CONTENTS

See *Part B: Which Engine is Which?* for an explanation of the engine types referred to here.

IMPORTANT NOTE:
1.4 AND 1.6 LITRE ALUMINIUM ENGINES: There are several important and completely different features on these engines – see *Part P: 1.4 and 1.6 litre Aluminium Block Engine – Specific info.*

JOB 1: MOUNTING TYPES – *overview*

There have been several different engine mounting types, as shown below:

TYPE 1:
POLO TO 1994: Essentially the same type used throughout, with minor variations.

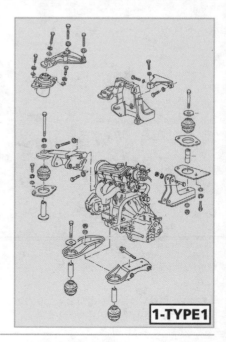

1-TYPE1

TYPE 2: GOLF AND VARIANTS TO 1992: Smaller engines have the right-hand engine mounting bolted to the front face of the block, rather than the end face, as with the larger engine types shown here.

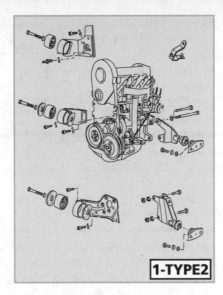

1-TYPE2

TYPE 3: GOLF AND VARIANTS (inc. 6-CYL. ENGINES) FROM 1992. POLO CLASSIC AND CADDY FROM 1996: Generally, the same type of engine mountings are shared right across these ranges, although there is one mounting fitted only to Corrado.

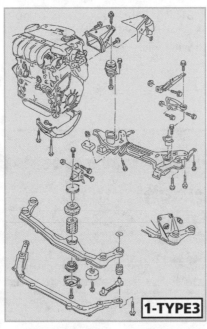

1-TYPE3

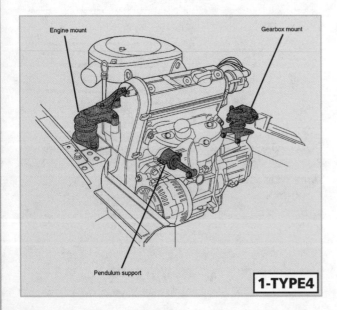

Engine mount

Gearbox mount

Pendulum support

1-TYPE4

TYPE 4: POLO FROM 1994: All other Polos from these years have this type of mounting.

JOB 2: EXISTING ENGINE MOUNTS – *realigning.*

❏ **STEP 1:** Without removing any of them, loosen all the mounting bolts.

❏ **STEP 2:** Shake the whole engine/transmission assembly to settle it into position.

❏ **STEP 3:** Align the mounts and retighten the bolts.

JOB 3: ENGINE MOUNTS – *replacing.*

❏ **STEP 1:** You will need to introduce extra support from above or below to take the weight of the unit while the old mounting is replaced. This can be achieved either by using a jack from below or an engine hoist from above.

❏ **STEP 2:** When fitting new mountings, always ensure than any alignment tabs and recesses (not all mountings have them, but some do) are correctly lined up before tightening.

JOB 4: MOUNTING RUBBERS – *changing.*

❏ **STEP 1:** To replace soft engine mounting rubbers in the later-type of engine mounting:
→ Start

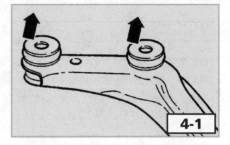

4-1

removing the mounting from the vehicle.
→ Lever the washers from the spacer sleeves (arrows) with pliers.
→ Pull out the spacer sleeves and remove the rubbers.

❏ **STEP 2:** Fit new rubbers and refit the spacer sleeves and washers (or fit new ones, if necessary). This shows VW tools (shaded) for peening the ends of the spacer sleeves over the

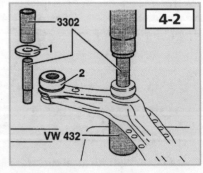

4-2

3302

1

2

VW 432

washers, but this may be carried out with a purpose-made piece of steel.

STEP 3: It helps to use a press when peening the ends of the tube – and you will certainly need one for refitting new rubbers to the large engine mountings used on all Golfs and variants up to 1992.

4-3

STEP 4: To remove the old rubber, place a hacksaw blade through the open part of the bush and cut through the bush. This will remove the tension so that you can drift out the old rubber.

4-4

STEP 5: Start to refit the new rubber by hand, using silicone lubricant (NOT oil or grease!) to start the process off, before pressing the rubber fully home.

4-5

JOB 5:   CORRADO MOUNTING RUBBERS – *changing.*

STEP 1: Remove the front engine mounting, removing the engine mounting/bumper securing bolts.

STEP 2: Dismantle and reassemble the rubbers as follows:

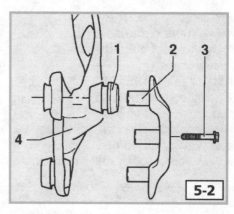

5-2

→ Pull spacer (**2**) out of the mounting by moving it to-and-fro – take careful note of the installed position of the rubber mounting (**1**).

→ Insert a new rubber and press in the spacer – lubricate with silicone lube.

→ Refit the engine carrier (**4**) and tighten the securing bolts (**3**) to 25 Nm.

STEP 3: When refitting the carrier to the car, tighten the securing bolts to 85 Nm.

Part P: 1.4 and 1.6 Litre Aluminium Block Engine – Specific info.

CONTENTS

See *Part B: Which Engine is Which?* for an explanation of the engine types referred to here.

The all-new 1.4 or 1.6 litre aluminium block engines – including those which VW described as 'with roller-type cam follower' - was introduced in 1995. It has a number of features which are so completely different from other VW engines that they are treated separately here. Areas not shown here are covered in the relevant sections of this chapter.

JOB 1: ENGINE – *features.*

❏ **STEP 1:** This engine is very different from the 1.4 and 1.6 litre engines with cast iron blocks. The main differences are:

➔ Crankcase of die-cast aluminium.
➔ Plastic inlet manifold.
➔ Completely different (duocentric) oil pump.
➔ New cylinder head on 'roller cam' versions – several major differences, including...
➔ Valves actuated by roller-type cam followers.

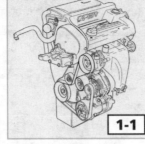

1-1

JOB 2: ENGINE – *removing, installing.*

❏ **STEP 1:** Remove the following:

➔ The battery and battery retainer (bolts, arrowed).
➔ Unclip the cable guide from the battery to the bulkhead.
➔ Disconnect both ends of the positive (+) wire from the battery to the starter motor and remove it together with the assembly.

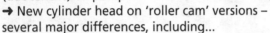

2-1

❏ **STEP 2:** Unclip the accelerator cable from the upper part of the air cleaner. You can now detach the accelerator cable from its support bracket and the throttle valve control but do not remove the locating clip.

SAFETY FIRST!

• Fuel supply pipes are under pressure!
• Start by slackening off the hose retaining clips.
• Wrap a cloth around the connection.
• Release the pressure by carefully pulling the hose off its connection.

❏ **STEP 3:** Remove the fuel supply and return pipes (**1** and **2**).

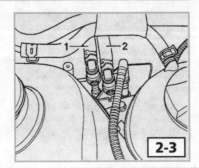

2-3

❏ **STEP 4:** Remove all connections as described for other 4-cylinder engines but note the following positions:

➔ The engine speed sender is below the oil dipstick tube bracket. Pull the connector out from the retainer.
➔ The two pin connector from the knock sensor is at the rear of the cylinder block.
➔ The four pin connector to the intake manifold pressure sender is situated front, right, below the inlet manifold.

JOB 3:   RIBBED (ALTERNATOR) DRIVE BELT – *removing, installing.*

❏ **STEP 1:** This is the layout of the drive belt fitted to vehicles without air conditioning.

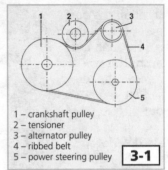

1 – crankshaft pulley
2 – tensioner
3 – alternator pulley
4 – ribbed belt
5 – power steering pulley

3-1

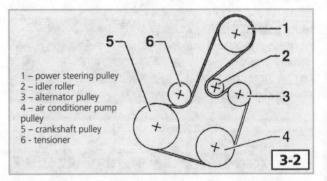

1 – power steering pulley
2 – idler roller
3 – alternator pulley
4 – air conditioner pump pulley
5 – crankshaft pulley
6 - tensioner

3-2

❏ **STEP 2:** This is the drive belt fitted to vehicles with air conditioning.

❏ **STEP 3:** Support the right-hand end of the engine, either from above with a suitable hoist or stand, or from beneath with a trolley jack and protective padding.

➔ Completely remove the right-hand engine mounting from the engine and the body.
➔ Remove the right-hand insulation tray.
➔ Lower the engine until the pulley securing bolt is accessible.

❏ **STEP 4:** After removing the engine cover and – if it is to be replaced – marking the ribbed belt showing the direction of rotation:
➔ Place a spanner on the tensioner roller

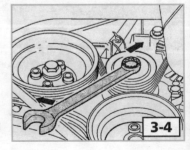

3-4

securing bolt and turn it so that the spanner and the tensioning roller move in the direction of the arrow.

→ Remove the ribbed V-belt.

→ When replacing the V-belt, place it on the crankshaft pulley first and slide it on to the tensioning roller last.

JOB 4:	CAMSHAFT TIMING BELTS – *removing, installing, tensioning.*

❏ **STEP 1:** The main camshaft driving belt also drives the coolant pump while the second camshaft is driven from the first by a connecting drive belt. This smaller belt has its own tensioning pulley.

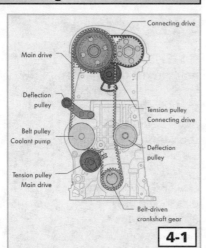

4-1

❏ **STEP 2:** Set the valve timing to TDC – see *Job 5*.

❏ **STEP 3:** Remove the ribbed (alternator) belt as described in *Job 3*.

❏ **STEP 4:** Now remove the following items:
→ The pulley and securing bolt from the crankshaft. Immediately refit the securing bolt with two washers and tighten to secure the toothed belt sprocket.
→ Remove the idler roller on vehicles fitted with air conditioning and the ribbed belt tensioning roller.
→ Remove the lower camshaft belt guard.
→ If they are to be reused, mark the direction of rotation of both camshaft belts.

❏ **STEP 5:** To remove the main camshaft belt:
→ Release the main belt drive tensioner (**1**) and slacken the belt by turning the tensioning roller in the direction of the arrow.
→ Loosen the clamping bolt on the tensioning roller and take off the camshaft belt.

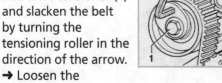

4-5

❏ **STEP 6:** To remove the coupling drive camshaft belt:
→ Loosen the coupling drive tensioner (**1**) and slacken the belt by turning the tensioning

T 10016

4-6

roller in the direction of the arrow.
→ Remove the coupling drive tensioning roller and take off the coupling drive belt.
→ The sprockets are locked with VW tool T10016 or with a made-up steel strap and bolts.

INSTALLING CAMSHAFT DRIVE BELTS

IMPORTANT NOTES:
i) The crankshaft belt sprocket is secured to the crankshaft with a securing bolt and two washers.
ii) The pistons must NOT be positioned at Top Dead Centre (otherwise the valves could strike a piston when turning the camshafts), until AFTER the camshaft sprockets have been locked as described in Step 7.

❏ **STEP 7:** Make sure that both camshaft sprockets are locked in their 'TDC' positions as described earlier. You must now set the crankshaft to TDC for No. 1 cylinder. The drive

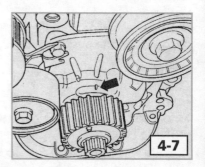

4-7

tooth with one end ground down must align with the mark (arrowed) on the end plate.

❏ **STEP 8:** Fit the coupling drive belt in an anti-clockwise direction, starting at the top of the exhaust camshaft sprocket and then on to the inlet camshaft sprocket. The untensioned section of the toothed belt must be downwards. Make sure that if a belt is being reused, it is fitted in the correct direction of rotation.

❏ **STEP 9:** Fit and tension the coupling drive belt tensioning roller as follows:
→ Use an Allen key (**1**) to turn the tensioner to the untensioned position (arrowed).
→ Push the lower section of the

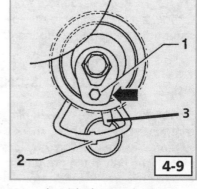

4-9

coupling drive belt upwards with the tensioning roller and fit the tensioning roller's securing bolt.
→ Turn the Allen key in the tensioning roller anti-clockwise until the indicator (**3**) lines up with the lug in the base plate (**2**).
→ You can now tighten the clamping nut on the tensioning roller to 20 Nm.

STEP 10: With both camshaft sprockets still locked in position, start to fit the main drive belt:
→ Fit the belt starting with the water pump and then working in an anti-clockwise direction, fit it to the tensioning

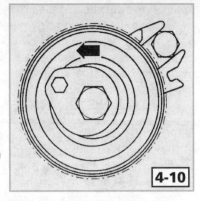

roller, crankshaft pulley, idler roller and the inlet camshaft sprocket. Make sure that a used belt is fitted in the same direction of rotation as before it was removed.
→ Turn the tensioning roller anti-clockwise (arrowed) to the position shown, using an Allen key.

STEP 11: Complete the fitting procedure as follows:
→ Tighten the securing bolt hand tight and note that the base plate cut-out (**1**) must engage over the securing bolt (**2**).
→ Turn the Allen

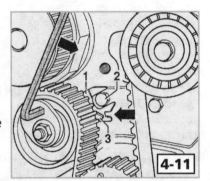

key in the direction of the arrow to tension the toothed belt until the indicator (**3**) aligns with the groove in the base plate (right-hand arrow).
→ Tighten the clamping nut on the tensioning roller to 20 Nm.

STEP 12: Remove the tool from the camshaft sprockets and reassemble the covers, engine mountings and other components removed earlier.

CHECKING SEMI-AUTOMATIC BELT TENSIONER

STEP 13: If, before reassembling the outer engine components, you want to check that the belt tensioner is working correctly, proceed as follows:
→ Push the belt in the position shown using firm thumb pressure. The indicator must be seen to move.
→ Release the tension on the belt and turn the crankshaft two turns in the engines normal direction of rotation.
→ Check the position of the indicator once again. It should have returned to its original position.

STEP 14: If the tensioning roller has returned to its original position, it is working correctly. If it has not done so, it needs replacement.

JOB 5: VALVE TIMING – *checking.*

STEP 1: Remove the belt guard and turn the engine until the marks on the crankshaft pulley are in line with the left-hand edge of the 'O' mark.

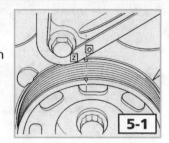

STEP 2: The two holes in the camshaft sprockets (arrowed) should align with the holes behind them in the camshaft housing.

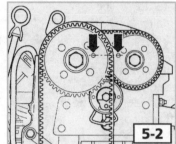

STEP 3: Two locking pins should now be used to lock the camshafts into position. This drawing shows the VW locking tool T10016 with its retainer (**B**) pushed up against the camshaft sprocket (**C**).
→ Locking pinheads (**D**) are shown aligned (**A**).

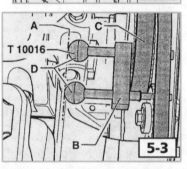

IMPORTANT NOTE: The camshafts must not be turned independently of the rest of the engine – i.e. with the belts removed – unless you are certain that none of the pistons are at TDC. Otherwise, there is a risk of the valves colliding with the tops of a piston or pistons.

JOB 6:   CAMSHAFT HOUSING – *removing, installing.*

STEP 1: After removing the camshaft drive belts as described in **Job 3** continue as follows:
→ Remove the spark plug connectors and HT cables.
→ Pull the four-pin connector off the ignition transformer and the connector off the Hall sender.
→ Remove the securing bolts from the exhaust gas recirculation valve (**1**) as well as the cable retainer (**2**).

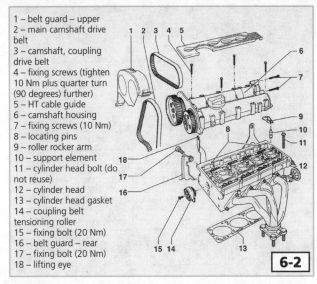

1 – belt guard – upper
2 – main camshaft drive belt
3 – camshaft, coupling drive belt
4 – fixing screws (tighten 10 Nm plus quarter turn (90 degrees) further)
5 – HT cable guide
6 – camshaft housing
7 – fixing screws (10 Nm)
8 – locating pins
9 – roller rocker arm
10 – support element
11 – cylinder head bolt (do not reuse)
12 – cylinder head
13 – cylinder head gasket
14 – coupling belt tensioning roller
15 – fixing bolt (20 Nm)
16 – belt guard – rear
17 – fixing bolt (20 Nm)
18 – lifting eye

6-2

❏ **STEP 2:** Continue by removing the following items:
➔ The rear belt guard.
➔ Loosen the camshaft housing bolts, starting with the centre ones and working outwards in a diagonal fashion.
➔ Lift off the camshaft housing.

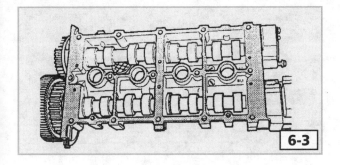

6-3

❏ **STEP 3:** Reinstall the camshaft housing as follows:
➔ Make sure that the pistons are not at TDC.
➔ Clean the sealing surface (shaded) so that it is free of old sealant, oil and grease.
➔ Apply a thin, even coat of sealant to the sealing surfaces.

IMPORTANT NOTE: Do not apply too much sealant otherwise excess material can enter the oil channels and cause damage to the engine.

❏ **STEP 4:**
Make sure that all the roller rocker arms are in contact with the ends of the valve stems (1) and that they are clipped into their

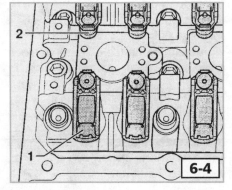

6-4

respective support elements (2).

❏ **STEP 5:**
Complete the installation as follows:
➔ Screw two M60 x 70 studs (arrowed) into the cylinder head to act as guides.
➔ Carefully fit the camshaft housing vertically on to

6-5

the cylinder head and tighten down using new securing bolts and working from the inside bolts, outwards, in a criss-cross diagonal order.

❏ **STEP 6:** Make sure that the sealant has had at least 30 minutes to dry after installing the camshaft housing and before running the engine.

JOB 7: CAMSHAFT AND BEARINGS – *removing, installing.*

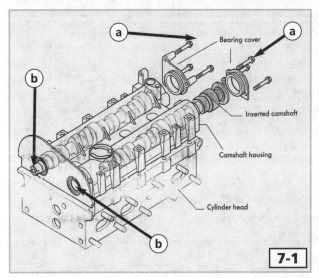

7-1

❏ **STEP 1:** The camshafts themselves are inserted into the camshaft housing and can be removed after taking out the bolts (a) and taking off the relevant bearing cover.

The oil seals (b) can be replaced with the camshafts *in situ* with the correct extractor tool but, in the absence of the tool, the inserted camshafts could be carefully withdrawn a sufficient distance to allow the oil seals to be levered out. New ones should be pressed or carefully drifted in until they reach their stops in the camshaft housing.

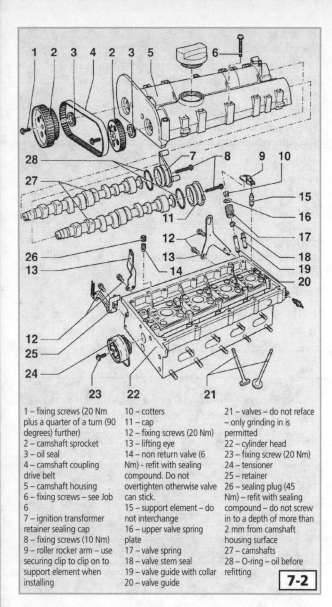

1 – fixing screws (20 Nm plus a quarter of a turn (90 degrees) further)
2 – camshaft sprocket
3 – oil seal
4 – camshaft coupling drive belt
5 – camshaft housing
6 – fixing screws – see Job 6
7 – ignition transformer retainer sealing cap
8 – fixing screws (10 Nm)
9 – roller rocker arm – use securing clip to clip on to support element when installing
10 – cotters
11 – cap
12 – fixing screws (20 Nm)
13 – lifting eye
14 – non return valve (6 Nm) - refit with sealing compound. Do not overtighten otherwise valve can stick.
15 – support element – do not interchange
16 – upper valve spring plate
17 – valve spring
18 – valve stem seal
19 – valve guide with collar
20 – valve guide
21 – valves – do not reface – only grinding in is permitted
22 – cylinder head
23 – fixing screw (20 Nm)
24 – tensioner
25 – retainer
26 – sealing plug (45 Nm) – refit with sealing compound – do not screw in to a depth of more than 2 mm from camshaft housing surface
27 – camshafts
28 – O-ring – oil before refitting

7-2

❏ **STEP 2:** These are the detailed components of the cylinder head and camshaft housing.

JOB 8: ENGINE BLOCK – *dismantling*.

Pistons and conrods can be removed from the block as described for other 4-cylinder engines. The crankshaft main bearing bolts must not under any circumstances be released because otherwise the crankshaft bearing clearances will be irreparably changed. This means that the crankshaft must not be removed from the block.

JOB 9: OIL PUMP – *replacement*.

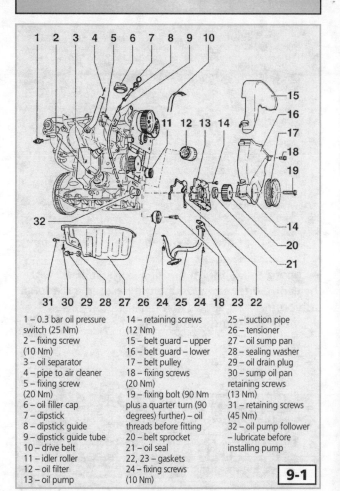

1 – 0.3 bar oil pressure switch (25 Nm)
2 – fixing screw (10 Nm)
3 – oil separator
4 – pipe to air cleaner
5 – fixing screw (20 Nm)
6 – oil filler cap
7 – dipstick
8 – dipstick guide
9 – dipstick guide tube
10 – drive belt
11 – idler roller
12 – oil filter
13 – oil pump
14 – retaining screws (12 Nm)
15 – belt guard – upper
16 – belt guard – lower
17 – belt pulley
18 – fixing screws (20 Nm)
19 – fixing bolt (90 Nm plus a quarter turn (90 degrees) further) – oil threads before fitting
20 – belt sprocket
21 – oil seal
22, 23 – gaskets
24 – fixing screws (10 Nm)
25 – suction pipe
26 – tensioner
27 – oil sump pan
28 – sealing washer
29 – oil drain plug
30 – sump oil pan retaining screws (13 Nm)
31 – retaining screws (45 Nm)
32 – oil pump follower – lubricate before installing pump

9-1

❏ **STEP 1:** This is the layout of the components of the lubrication system and those that you need to remove in order to get at it.

❏ **STEP 2:** With the drive belt removed – see *Job 4* – secure the crankshaft belt sprocket (**1**) to the crankshaft with an old securing screw (**2**). Make sure that the ground-down tooth on the sprocket aligns

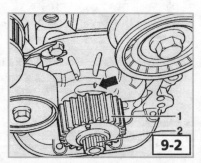

9-2

with the mark on the oil pump (arrow) which positions the crankshaft at TDC, No. 1 cylinder.

❏ **STEP 3:** Now turn the crankshaft so that the ground-down tooth (**A**) moves three teeth anti-clockwise. In other words, the third tooth to the right (arrowed) now aligns with the mark on the oil pump.

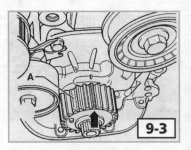

9-3

STEP 4: You can now remove the following items, referring to illustration *Job 9-1*:
→ The belt sprocket.
→ The main camshaft belt drive tensioning roller.
→ The sump (with the engine *in situ*, part of the exhaust will have to be removed).
→ The suction pipe, oil pump and gasket.

STEP 5: Before attempting to fit the new pump, make sure that one of the cams up (arrowed) on the crankshaft is uppermost. Clean any sealant off the mating surfaces on the cylinder block and make sure that the surfaces are free of oil and grease.

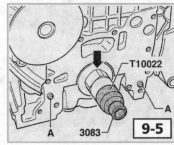

Make up a suitable sized sleeve to support the new oil pump as it is fitted (similar to VW tool T10022) and hold it in place with a suitable sized bolt (similar to VW tool 3083). Now fit a new gasket in place locating it on the guide pins (A).

STEP 6: You can now fit the oil pump as follows:
→ Line up one of the oil pump inner rotor markings (A) on the mark (B) on the oil pump housing cover.
→ Coat the cams on the end of the crankshaft with oil and lightly oil the sealing lip of the oil pump oil seal.

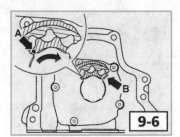

→ Guide the oil pump carefully on to the cams on the crankshaft, turning the inner rotor slightly if necessary so that it lines up, then slide the oil pump carefully on to the guide pins.
→ Use new bolts tightened to 12 Nm to secure the oil pump into position and remove the locating sleeve.
→ Refit the suction pipe, sump and remaining engine components.

JOB 10: CYLINDER HEAD – *removing, installing.*

STEP 1: Remove the battery and battery retainer, see *Job 2, Step 1*.

STEP 2: Remove the air cleaner as follows:
→ Take out the sealing plug (1).
→ Unclip the accelerator cable (2) out of the

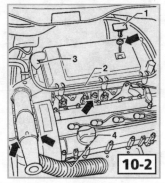

upper part of the air cleaner (3).
→ Pull the crankcase breather hose (3) off the air cleaner.
→ Pull the warm air intake hose (4) off the engine-end.
→ Take out the screws holding the air cleaner in place and remove.

STEP 3: Disconnect the fuel components as described in *Job 2, Step 3*.

STEP 4: Disconnect all remaining hoses and connections, including:
→ The hose from the crankcase breather and the hose from the inlet manifold to the activated charcoal filter.
→ The vacuum hoses from the inlet manifold to the brake servo and from the exhaust gas recirculation valve to the brake servo vacuum hose junction piece.
→ The two-pin connector from the knock sensor (at rear of cylinder block) and the four-pin connector from the inlet manifold pressure sender (front, right, under inlet manifold).
→ Separate the connector from the engine speed sender (below the oil dipstick tube) and pull the connector out from its retainer.
→ Separate the connectors from the ignition transformer, the Hall sender, the throttle valve control, the coolant temperature sender, oil pressure switch and exhaust gas recirculation valve.
→ Disconnect the injector connectors.

STEP 5: Remove the camshaft housing. See *Job 6*.

STEP 6: Cylinder head removal, stripdown and overhaul is as described in *Parts F, H and J* dealing with the cylinder heads for other 4-cylinder engines. Do note, however, that the pipe from coolant pump to thermostat housing can only be removed once the camshaft covers have been taken off.

JOB 11: ENGINE MOUNTINGS.

STEP 1: Follow the instructions for replacing engine mountings as described in *Part O: Engine/Transmission Mountings – Replacement*, but note that some versions with this

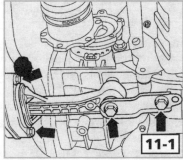

engine were fitted with a pendulum support to the transmission as shown here. The principle is similar on other types but these are the securing bolts (arrowed).

CHAPTER 7: TRANSMISSION, CLUTCH

*PLEASE READ **CHAPTER 2 SAFETY FIRST** BEFORE CARRYING OUT ANY WORK ON YOUR CAR.*

Part A: Clutch Cable and Pedal Box
– Repair, Replacement.

CONTENTS

See *Part B: Which Engine is Which?* for an explanation of the engine types referred to here.

JOB 1: PEDAL BOXES AND CABLES – *types.*

There are very many detailed variations between pedal box and cable components on the vehicles listed in this manual. However, the basic principles can be broken down in to a smaller number of different types.

❏ **TYPE 1:** These are the components for Golfs with 1.5, 1.6 and 1.8 litre engines (including Diesel) up to 1992. The top set of components are for right-hand drive vehicles while the bottom set of components are for left-hand drive.

1 – pedal box – left-hand drive
2 – pedal box – right-hand drive
3, 4, 5, 6 – screws, nuts and washers
8, 8a – pivot pin
9, 9a – brake pedal
10, 10a, 10c, 12 – bush
11, 11a – spring
13, 13a – lock washer
14 – pedal rubber
15 – pin
16 – lock washer
16a, 16b – clutch pedal stop
18 – rubber washer
19, 19a – clutch pedal
21 – clutch cable
22a – cable positioner
22b, c, d – nut, bolt, washer
25a – pin
25b – lock washer
26, 26a – guide
26b – pressure spring
27 – shaft (LHD only)
27a – bush
27b – nut
28 – grommet
29 – clamping washer
30 – sealing washer
32, 33 – plug
42 – brake light switch (LHD only)
43 – washer
44 – lock washer
45 – clutch cable attachment parts – self-adjusting clutch only
46, 47 – bush (LHD only)
48, 49 – tension spring
50 – washer

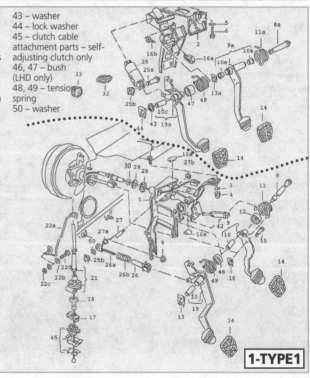

1-TYPE1

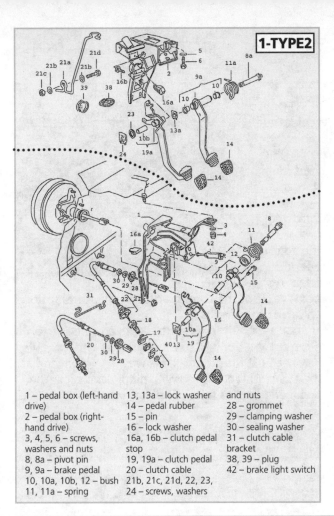

1-TYPE2

← ❏ **TYPE 2:** This, with detailed differences, is the set up used for 1.0 litre to 1.3 Golfs up to 1992 and for Polos up to 1994 although the transmission end of the clutch cable is sometimes different.

1-TYPE4

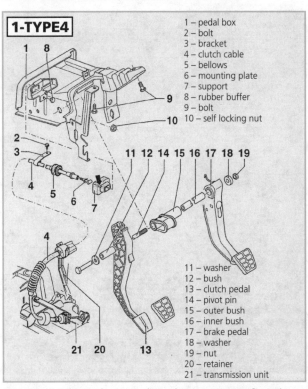

1 – pedal box
2 – bolt
3 – bracket
4 – clutch cable
5 – bellows
6 – mounting plate
7 – support
8 – rubber buffer
9 – bolt
10 – self locking nut

11 – washer
12 – bush
13 – clutch pedal
14 – pivot pin
15 – outer bush
16 – inner bush
17 – brake pedal
18 – washer
19 – nut
20 – retainer
21 – transmission unit

1 – pedal box (left-hand drive)	13, 13a – lock washer	and nuts
2 – pedal box (right-hand drive)	14 – pedal rubber	28 – grommet
	15 – pin	29 – clamping washer
3, 4, 5, 6 – screws, washers and nuts	16 – lock washer	30 – sealing washer
	16a, 16b – clutch pedal stop	31 – clutch cable bracket
8, 8a – pivot pin		
9, 9a – brake pedal	19, 19a – clutch pedal	38, 39 – plug
10, 10a, 10b, 12 – bush	20 – clutch cable	42 – brake light switch
11, 11a – spring	21b, 21c, 21d, 22, 23, 24 – screws, washers	

❏ **TYPE 4:** The Polo introduced in 1995 was fitted with components with this appearance.

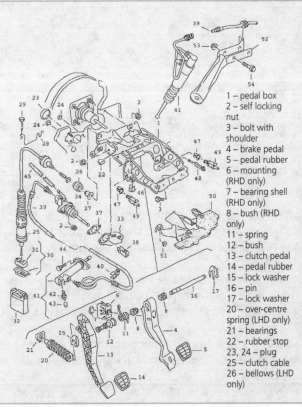

1-TYPE3

1 – pedal box	27 – clutch cable guide tube
2 – self locking nut	28 – bracket for clutch cable
3 – bolt with shoulder	29 – self-tapping screw
4 – brake pedal	30 – clutch cable attachment parts
5 – pedal rubber	31 – buffer
6 – mounting (RHD only)	32 – balance weight (LHD only)
7 – bearing shell (RHD only)	33 – mounting (LHD only)
8 – bush (RHD only)	34 – master cylinder
11 – spring	37 – gasket
12 – bush	38 – mounting
13 – clutch pedal	39 – pressure hose
14 – pedal rubber	40 – bracket
15 – lock washer	41 – slave cylinder
16 – pin	42 – bleeder valve
17 – lock washer	43 – dust cap
20 – over-centre spring (LHD only)	44 – bolt with shoulder
21 – bearings	45 – hose
22 – rubber stop	46 – clamp
23, 24 – plug	47 – clip
25 – clutch cable	48 – brake light switch
26 – bellows (LHD only)	49 – venting valve
	50 – cover
	51 – press stud

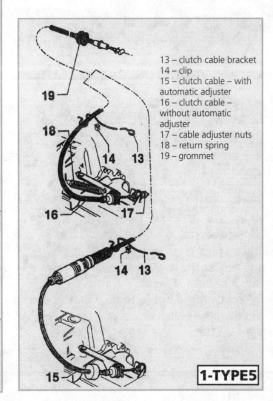

1-TYPE5

13 – clutch cable bracket
14 – clip
15 – clutch cable – with automatic adjuster
16 – clutch cable – without automatic adjuster
17 – cable adjuster nuts
18 – return spring
19 – grommet

❏ **TYPE 3:** These, in essence, are the components used on Golf Mk 3 from 1992-on and also on the 'Polo' Caddy and Polo Classic from 1996-on.

❏ **TYPE 5:** At the transmission end, these are the typical mountings for the adjustable and non-adjustable types of cable.

JOB 2: CLUTCH CABLE – *adjustment.*

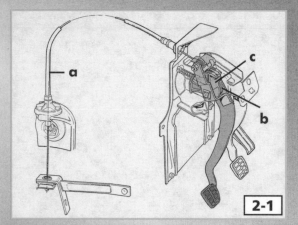

2-1

ADJUSTABLE OR NON-ADJUSTABLE CLUTCH?

❏ **STEP 1:** • You can easily tell which system the car is fitted with. The self-adjusting type looks like this - note the absence of an adjuster screw on the conduit (**a**). The coil spring (**b**) is designed to ensure that the quadrant (**c**) maintains slight tension in the clutch cable.
• The adjustable types - there are two of them - are shown below.
• It pays to keep the operating mechanism well lubricated on all cable-operated clutches, and also to grease the adjuster threads on adjustable clutches.

CABLE OPERATED CLUTCH

❏ **STEP 2:** 'Work' the clutch pedal a few times, then measure the free play at the pedal, which should be between 15 and 20 mm. If not, adjust the clutch pedal free play at the nut (arrowed) on the end of the cable, at the clutch lever on the gearbox...

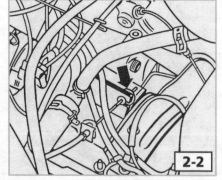

2-2

❏ **STEP 3:** ...or at the end of the clutch cable conduit (outer), on the vertical-type of manual adjuster.

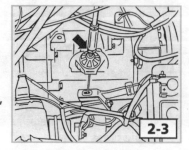

2-3

JOB 3: SMALLER ENGINES' CLUTCH CABLES – *replacement.*

❏ **STEP 1:** To replace the cable:
➔ EITHER: Start by slackening the locknut (arrowed), unscrewing the adjuster nut and releasing the

3-1

pedal cable at the fixed bracket on the transmission and from the lever arm.
➔ OR: Later vehicles are fitted with a cable with a different location system. The adjuster and locknuts are freed off first, in the same way. The cable end at the transmission is fitted with nipple and clips. The pedal end unclips from the pedal - see *Job 1.*

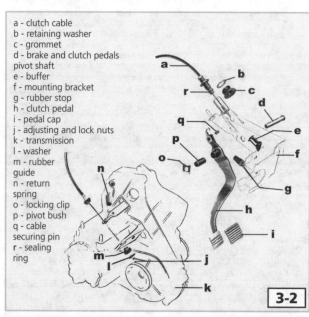

a - clutch cable
b - retaining washer
c - grommet
d - brake and clutch pedals pivot shaft
e - buffer
f - mounting bracket
g - rubber stop
h - clutch pedal
i - pedal cap
j - adjusting and lock nuts
k - transmission
l - washer
m - rubber guide
n - return spring
o - locking clip
p - pivot bush
q - cable securing pin
r - sealing ring

3-2

❏ **STEP 2:** These are the components of the clutch cable operating mechanism and annotations referred to later in this job relate to this drawing.

❏ **STEP 3:** From inside the vehicle, remove panels as necessary to gain access to the clutch pedal. Pull out the pin (**q**) from the top of the clutch pedal.

❏ **STEP 4:** The cable can now be removed and the new one fitted in its place. Check the following points:
➔ The grommet (**c**) and washer (**b**) must be in place in the firewall and the sealing ring (**r**) must be correctly located.
➔ Make sure that the retaining pin (**q**) is correctly located in the centre of the pedal.

JOB 4: LARGER ENGINES' CLUTCH CABLES – *replacement*.

☐ **STEP 1:** The principles of removing and replacing the manually adjusted clutch on these vehicles is virtually identical to that of the types shown in *Job 2* – see also the illustrations in *Job 1*. The adjuster is slackened at the transmission end (**21, 22**) before being unclipped at the pedal-end. The cable sheathing is unclipped from the positioner (**31**). Take note of the positioning of the ancillary components shown here. This drawing also includes brake pedal components.

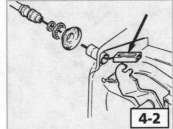

☐ **STEP 2:** The cable end (arrowed) is fitted and removed from the top of the clutch pedal arm as shown.

4-2

JOB 5: AUTOMATICALLY ADJUSTED CLUTCH CABLES, EARLY TYPE – *replacement*.

FACT FILE

SELF-ADJUSTING CLUTCH

• This early type of complex mechanism fitted to the clutch pedal was not used for long.
• It was soon replaced with a cable with integral self-adjuster mechanism at the transmission end.

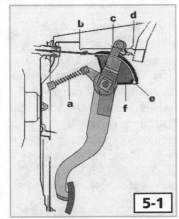

☐ **STEP 1:** Push the quadrant (**f**), hold it in place with the locking pall (**d**) and detach the cable and nipple (**e**) from the quadrant, easing it free.

5-1

☐ **STEP 2:** Lever the guide sleeve (**a**) from the bracket on the transmission and remove the washer. Detach the cable from the clutch operating arm (**b**).

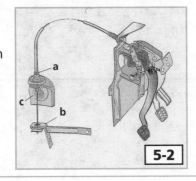

5-2

IMPORTANT NOTE: When refitting the rubber washer on the bracket, make sure that it does not block the gearbox breather (**c**).

☐ **STEP 3:** The cable nipple is released from the operating lever by sliding out the clip (arrowed) and removing the rubber buffer and retaining plate for later use.

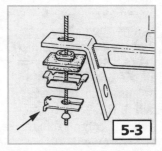

5-3

☐ **STEP 4:** Fit the new cable but before doing so, lightly lubricate the self-adjusting mechanism at the pedal. The cable should adjust itself when the clutch pedal is pressed several times.

JOB 6: AUTOMATICALLY ADJUSTED CLUTCH CABLES, EARLY TYPE – *replacement*.

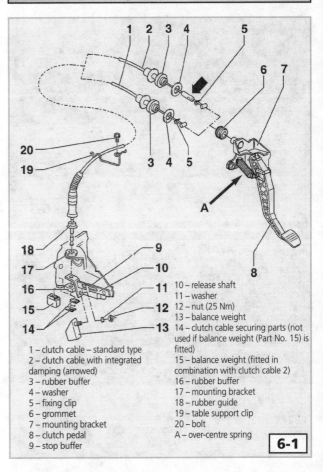

1 – clutch cable – standard type
2 – clutch cable with integrated damping (arrowed)
3 – rubber buffer
4 – washer
5 – fixing clip
6 – grommet
7 – mounting bracket
8 – clutch pedal
9 – stop buffer
10 – release shaft
11 – washer
12 – nut (25 Nm)
13 – balance weight
14 – clutch cable securing parts (not used if balance weight (Part No. 15) is fitted)
15 – balance weight (fitted in combination with clutch cable 2)
16 – rubber buffer
17 – mounting bracket
18 – rubber guide
19 – table support clip
20 – bolt
A – over-centre spring

6-1

☐ **STEP 1:** To release the clutch cable at the pedal end proceed as follows:
➜ Some cable ends are the same as those shown in illustration *4-2*.
➜ Others have a barrel nipple on the end, as shown here.

☐ **STEP 2:** These are typical clutch cable components. The text refers to variations.

STEP 3: On most vehicles, various trim items will have to be removed from around the steering column in order to 'get at' the upper end of the clutch pedal. This Polo stowage compartment is removed by pushing in the tabs (arrowed).

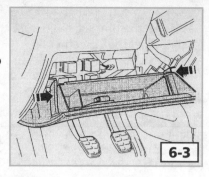

6-3

TOP TIP!

STEP 4: • At first, Volkswagen recommended the use of special tool No. 3151 for compressing the automatic adjuster mechanism. From July 1988, the automatic adjustment housing has been fitted with a sheath (arrowed) and, in spite of what early Volkswagen and other manuals say, tool No. 3151 cannot be used.

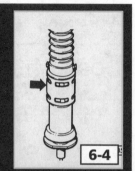

6-4

6-5

STEP 5: Use of this strap is almost essential:
• Volkswagen supply the strap to hold the self-adjuster in its compressed state.
• If you want to use the strap from a new cable to compress the adjuster on an old one before removing it, cut a slot in the strap at the eye (arrowed).
• It can now be removed from the new and used on the old.

STEP 6: Slip the retaining strap in position above the bellows (**1**) and press the adjuster mechanism together. The two eyes of the strap can now be hooked on the two pins (**2**) on the adjuster mechanism.

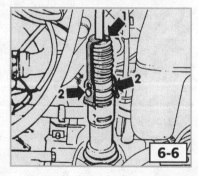

6-6

TOP TIP!

• If the adjuster mechanism cannot be compressed in order to fit the strap as shown, the mechanism is probably faulty and the cable will have to be replaced.
• Cut through the cable between the transmission bracket mounting and the release arm in order to remove it.
• You can sometimes 'rescue' a faulty adjuster. See Steps 9, 10.

STEP 7: Remove the (shaded) clutch pedal cover (when fitted). Unclip (**1**) and remove upwards (**2**).

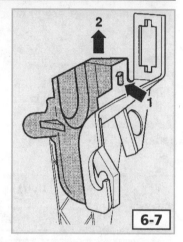

6-7

STEP 8: According to the type used:
➔ EITHER: Unhook the cable end from the recess in the top of the pedal (arrow C), then disconnect and wiring connections. Now remove the over-centre spring. Volkswagen recommend the use of tool 3317. With the spring fully tensioned, the tool is pushed over the spring at both ends (**A** and **B**), the pedal is moved and the spring unclipped and removed.
➔ OR: Detach the cable eye at the pedal lever (see illustration *Job 3-2*)...
➔ ...and remove the cable from the pedal.

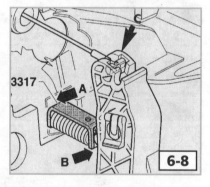

6-8

STEP 9: When fitting a new cable, do so in the following order:
➔ Fit the clutch cable to the pedal.
➔ Fit the strap (**A**)

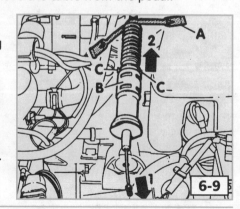

6-9

above the bellows.
→ Pull the end of the cable in the direction of the arrow (**1**) and hold it there.
→ Move the adjuster mechanism (**B**) to-and-fro a few times, until it can be compressed in the direction of the arrow (**2**).
→ Hold the mechanism in this position and attach the strap to the two pins (**C**) - a second pair of hands will be required! Fit the clutch cable to the transmission.
→ Remove the retaining strap (**A**).

☐ **STEP 10:** If you suspect that the self-adjuster mechanism is faulty, test it as follows:
→ Depress the clutch pedal fully for at least five times.
→ Move the

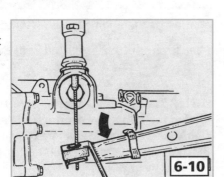

clutch release lever in the direction of the arrow approximately 10 mm. (1/2 in.) - note that this is the opposite of the normal direction of operation.
→ If the release lever is not free to move, the automatic adjustment is faulty and the cable must be renewed.

TOP TIP!

☐ **STEP 11:**
If the self-adjusting mechanism becomes solid you may be able to rescue it as follows:
• Have an assistant push down hard on the clutch pedal while you find some means of fixing the release

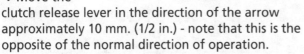

lever (**B**) on the transmission unit in the UP position.
• Inside the vehicle, pull the clutch pedal back to the raised position.
• Pull the cable down in the direction of the large arrow until the adjusting mechanism inside the bellows (**A**) can be pressed together as described earlier.
• Carefully move the release lever on the transmission back to its lowered position.
• Operate the clutch several times and see if the self-adjust mechanism is now working.

JOB 7: CERTAIN TURBO DIESEL MODELS – *notes.*

☐ **STEP 1:** It is important to note the following points:
→ The clutch cable must be routed around the intercooler (**A**) when installing.
→ The cable must also be secured with clips on the air duct (**B**) and on the pressure hose (**C**).
→ In all other respects, removing and fitting the cable is as described earlier.

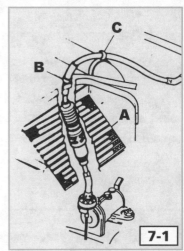

JOB 8: PIVOT PIN FIXING CLIPS – *removal.*

Clips used on earlier vehicles are simply pushed or levered off – as, indeed are later ones, though it might not at first be obvious…

☐ **STEP 1:** To remove the clip on the clutch pedal side, lever the tab in the direction of the arrow (**1**),

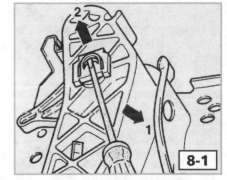

then push the clip off with a screwdriver in an upwards direction (**2**).

☐ **STEP 2:** On the brake pedal side, the clip has a retainer which is lifted allowing the clip to be pushed off in the direction of the arrow. The pivot pin

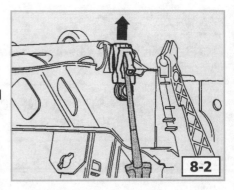

can now be removed. When refitting, align the flats on the pivot pin so that they are in line with the clip.

Part B: Clutch Hydraulic Components
– Replacement
CONTENTS

See **Chapter 6, Part B: Which Engine is Which?** for an explanation of the engine types referred to here.

A very few Mk 2 Golfs, all Corrados and all Mk 3 Golfs and Ventos from 1992 are fitted with the same type of hydraulic clutch.

JOB 1: SYSTEM – *layout.*

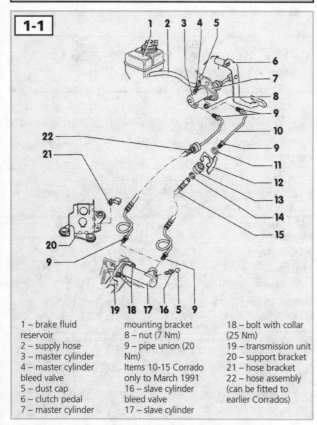

1-1

1 – brake fluid reservoir	mounting bracket	18 – bolt with collar (25 Nm)
2 – supply hose	8 – nut (7 Nm)	19 – transmission unit
3 – master cylinder	9 – pipe union (20 Nm)	20 – support bracket
4 – master cylinder bleed valve	Items 10-15 Corrado only to March 1991	21 – hose bracket
5 – dust cap	16 – slave cylinder bleed valve	22 – hose assembly (can be fitted to earlier Corrados)
6 – clutch pedal	17 – slave cylinder	
7 – master cylinder		

☐ **STEP 1:** This is the layout of the hydraulic components.

JOB 2:   MASTER CYLINDER – *removal, replacement.*

☐ **STEP 1:** Disconnect the supply hose (illustration **1-1, item 2**) and raise the master cylinder end to above the level of the fluid reservoir so that no fluid drains out.

☐ **STEP 2:** Disconnect the pressure hose (**item 9**).

☐ **STEP 3:** Remove the master cylinder by detaching it from the pedal mechanism (see **Part A: Clutch Cable and Pedal Box**) and removing the nuts (**item 8**) to remove the master cylinder from its mounting bracket (**item 7**).

JOB 3: SLAVE CYLINDER – *removal, replacement.*

☐ **STEP 1:** Unscrew the pipe union (**item 9**) from the slave cylinder and plug the end to prevent excessive fluid loss.

☐ **STEP 2:** Take out the two collared bolts (**item 18**) and remove the slave cylinder from the transmission (**item 19**).

JOB 4: HYDRAULIC CLUTCH – *bleeding.*

Refer to illustration **1-1**.

☐ **STEP 1:** Remove the coolant expansion tank (when necessary) and place on one side leaving the pipes connected.

☐ **STEP 2:** Start by bleeding the master cylinder. Use the principles described for brake bleeding in *Chapter 12, Brakes.* Before pushing a pipe on to the bleed valve (**item 4**) remove the dust cap (**item 5**).

☐ **STEP 3:** After the master cylinder has been bled, bleed the slave cylinder via the bleed valve (**item 16**) after removing the dust cap (**item 5**).

☐ **STEP 4:** Depress the clutch pedal several times after the completion of the bleeding process to make sure that no air is still trapped. If the clutch fails to disengage properly, repeat the bleeding process as necessary.

Part C: Gear Lever and Linkage
– Removal, Refitting
CONTENTS

See ***Chapter 6, Part B: Which Engine is Which?*** for an explanation of the engine types referred to here.

JOB 1. GEAR LEVER AND LINKAGE – *removal, refitting*.

Section A:
'Internal Water Pump' engines (including Golf 1.4/1.6 '93-on).

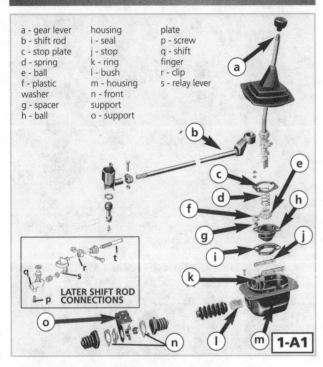

a - gear lever
b - shift rod
c - stop plate
d - spring
e - ball
f - plastic washer
g - spacer
h - ball

housing
i - seal
j - stop
k - ring
l - bush
m - housing
n - front support
o - support

plate
p - screw
q - shift finger
r - clip
s - relay lever

LATER SHIFT ROD CONNECTIONS

1-A1

❒ **STEP A1:** The linkage right through from September 1975 has this appearance.

❒ **STEP A2:** Take note of the way in which the gearchange mechanism from the shift stick works.

❒ **STEP A3:** To adjust the shift linkage:
→ Place the gear lever in neutral.
→ Loosen the nuts on the support plate (1) so that the relay lever can move easily on the shift rod.
→ Move the support plate until there is a distance of 6 mm (a) between the shift finger and the relay plate.
→ Tighten the nuts on the support plate.

1-A3

TOP TIP!
• Measure the gap with a piece of steel bar 6 mm thick.

IMPORTANT NOTE:
Dimension 'a' invariably changes as the nuts are tightened. Check the dimensions again and if 'a' is less than 5 mm, readjust.

The lower arrow (2) enables you to adjust the position of the gear lever but this cannot be done without a special Volkswagen jig (Part No. 2087) which is placed around the gear lever before the nut (2) is retightened. Have a Volkswagen dealer carry out this work for you.

IMPORTANT NOTE:
Locking screws may be held with wire or with threadlock adhesive on the threads. When they are removed, any old threadlock adhesive should be cleaned off the threads and fresh threadlock used when the screw is refitted.

❒ **STEP A4:** When this type of fitting is used:
→ To remove the front selector rod take out the pins (A).
→ And to remove the short gate rod, lever back the clip (B) to remove it from the selector shaft lever.

1-A4

❒ **STEP A5:** At the relay lever:
→ Open the clip (C)…
→ …unhook the long gate rod.

1-A5

❒ **STEP A6:** To remove the gear lever/shift rod unscrew the gear knob, disconnect the bottom of the boot then lift it up, which will probably leave the top of the boot (arrowed) in position until the boot has turned inside out when you can pull it off the gear lever. On later models, there is usually a metal clip on the inside that has to be cut away.

1-A6

STEP A7: Place the gearbox into neutral and disconnect and remove the following:

→ The relay lever and front bearing bracket support plate.

→ The rear bearing plate, pulling it off the shift rod.

→ Remove the nuts holding the guide plates and lift the gear lever out complete with the shift rod and guide plates. You can now take the shift rod off.

→ Bend back the securing tabs on the lower guide plate and take off the upper guide plate, the gear lever, the spring and lower ball shell (early types) or the components shown in illustration *1-A1* (later types).

STEP A8: Adjust the gear lever in front-to-back plane with the gear shift in neutral. Loosen the nuts and slide the plate beneath the nuts so that the lower part of the lever is vertical or very slightly leaning to the rear.

STEP A9: In order to adjust the gear levers side-to-side movement, engage reverse gear then loosen the nuts and move the front bearing plate...

STEP A10: ...until the gear lever is vertical. You can now tighten the front bearing plate nuts.

Section B. 'External Water Pump' engines.

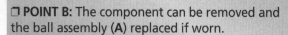

FACT FILE

ENGINES FROM JANUARY 1991

A different type of gearshift lever with adjustable shift mechanism and a replaceable ball was introduced progressively after this date.

Point A

POINT A: To remove the ball, the fixing screw (**B**) is undone after which the upper part can be levered off the lower part (**A**) by using a suitable block (arrowed) across the gearchange aperture.

POINT B: The component can be removed and the ball assembly (**A**) replaced if worn.

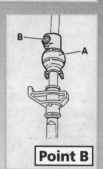

Point B

POINT C: After adjusting the shift mechanism as shown elsewhere in this job:

→ Engage first gear.

→ Press the gear lever lightly to the left to remove any free play.

→ Measure the dimension (a). It should be between 1 and 1.5 mm.

→ If you need to adjust the clearance, slacken off the screw (**B**).

→ Achieve the required dimension by turning the adjustment eccentric (**A**) in whichever direction is necessary, then retighten the screw (**B**).

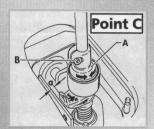

Point C

STEP B1: Take note of the gearchange mechanism as fitted to larger engined vehicles from 1.5 litres-up (except G60

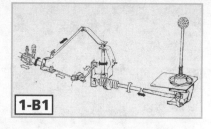

1-B1

supercharged model). The black arrows indicate gearshift movement and the white arrows gear selection movement. This is the gearchange as used on 5-speed transmissions but is essentially the same as that for 4-speed types.

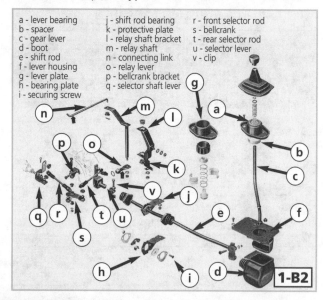

a - lever bearing
b - spacer
c - gear lever
d - boot
e - shift rod
f - lever housing
g - lever plate
h - bearing plate
i - securing screw

j - shift rod bearing
k - protective plate
l - relay shaft bracket
m - relay shaft
n - connecting link
o - relay lever
p - bellcrank bracket
q - selector shaft lever

r - front selector rod
s - bellcrank
t - rear selector rod
u - selector lever
v - clip

1-B2

STEP B2: EARLIER MODELS: Take note of the shift linkage mechanism fitted to these vehicles.

1-B3

STEP B3: To dismantle, start by removing the boot and plate from beneath the vehicle.

1-B4

STEP B4: Unbolt the rear of the linkage.

STEP B5: Remove the trim and unbolt the gearchange lever.

1-B5

STEP B6: The front of the linkage can now be disconnected. The balljoint links can be detached by pressing back the clips on the plastic ends with a screwdriver.

1-B6

The gearchange linkage can only be dismantled after removing other components which may be in the way, such as the console and the exhaust pipe downpipe.

STEP B7: With the engine out, the relay bracket securing bolt can clearly be seen.

1-B7

STEP B8: LATER MODELS: The gear lever mechanism on the later type is considerably different but the shift mechanism is essentially an evolution of the earlier type. The shift rod now passes through an extension to the relay shaft bracket instead of having a separate bearing plate. Note that the relay shaft is fitted at its base with a clip and the relay shaft arm is now separate and held to the relay shaft with a nut.

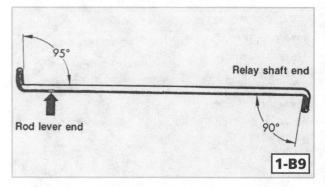

95°

Relay shaft end

Rod lever end

90°

1-B9

STEP B9: IMPORTANT NOTE: **BOTH MECHANISM TYPES:** If the connecting link (illustration **1-B2, item n**) is removed for any reason, the end which fits into the relay shaft lever and the relay shaft lever itself should be marked with a dab of paint. This is because although the connecting link appears to be symmetrical, the angle of the crank at one end is different to that at the other.

1-B8

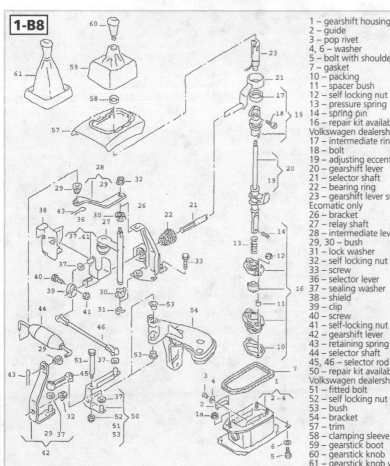

1 – gearshift housing
2 – guide
3 – pop rivet
4, 6 – washer
5 – bolt with shoulder
7 – gasket
10 – packing
11 – spacer bush
12 – self locking nut
13 – pressure spring
14 – spring pin
16 – repair kit available from Volkswagen dealership
17 – intermediate ring
18 – bolt
19 – adjusting eccentric
20 – gearshift lever
21 – selector shaft
22 – bearing ring
23 – gearshift lever switch – Ecomatic only
26 – bracket
27 – relay shaft
28 – intermediate lever
29, 30 – bush
31 – lock washer
32 – self locking nut
33 – screw
36 – selector lever
37 – sealing washer
38 – shield
39 – clip
40 – screw
41 – self-locking nut
42 – gearshift lever
43 – retaining spring
44 – selector shaft
45, 46 – selector rod
50 – repair kit available from Volkswagen dealership
51 – fitted bolt
52 – self locking nut
53 – bush
54 – bracket
57 – trim
58 – clamping sleeve
59 – gearstick boot
60 – gearstick knob
61 – gearstick knob with boot

1-B10

STEP B10: EARLIEST TYPE OF LINKAGE: To adjust the early type of linkage:

→ Place the gear lever in neutral and align the centring holes (arrowed) in the lever plate and the housing cover plate.

→ The tapped holes for the bolts should now be in the centre of the slots (**A**) and if they're not, turn the lever plate through 180 degrees.

→ Screw down the lever bearing.

❒ **STEP B11:** Loosen the clip bolt (arrowed) so that the selector lever can move easily on the shift rod, and pull the cap off the boot.

1-B11

❒ **STEP B12:** Move the shift finger (**1**) so that it is exactly in the centre of the stop plate (**2**), which means that the distances X will be the same.

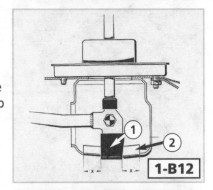

1-B12

❒ **STEP B13:** Use a strip of sheet steel or hardwood 15 mm wide to set the distance (**a**) to 15 mm and tighten the clip.

1-B13

❒ **STEP B14:** To adjust the shift linkage, see **Step A3**.

❒ **STEP B15:** When refitting the gearshift gaiter, screw down the collar until the distance (**a**) is 55 mm (2 in.).

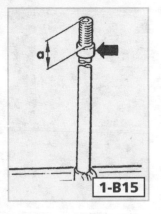

1-B15

❒ **STEP B16:** Turn the gaiter inside out, push it onto the top of the gear stick and pull the gaiter frame down in the direction of the arrows, then insert the lugs on the frame back into the console.

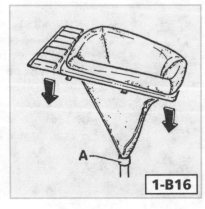

1-B16

Section C: Later-type Golf gearchange mechanism.

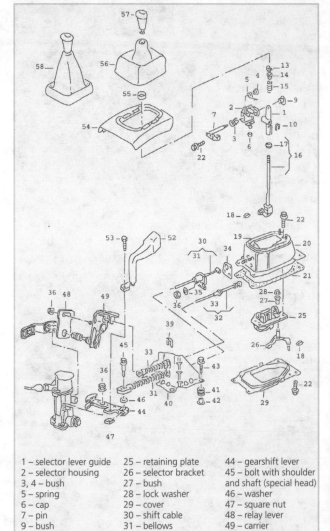

1 – selector lever guide
2 – selector housing
3, 4 – bush
5 – spring
6 – cap
7 – pin
9 – bush
10, 13 – lock washer
14 – bush
15 – pressure spring
16 – gearshift lever
17 – damper
18 – split pin
19 – gasket
20 – housing for shift mechanism
21 – gasket
22 – bolt (special head)
25 – retaining plate
26 – selector bracket
27 – bush
28 – lock washer
29 – cover
30 – shift cable
31 – bellows
32 – selector cable
33 – bellows
34 – gasket
35 – rubber washer
36 – self-locking nut (special head)
39 – lock washer
40 – abutment
41 – grommet
42 – spacer
43 – bolt (special head)
44 – gearshift lever
45 – bolt with shoulder and shaft (special head)
46 – washer
47 – square nut
48 – relay lever
49 – carrier
52 – balance weight
52 – screw
54 – trim for shift mechanism
55 – clamping sleeve
56 – boot for gearstick
57 – gearstick knob
58 – gearstick knob with boot for gearstick lever

1-C1

❒ **STEP C1:** The Golf from the Mk 2 supercharged G60 model through to the 2.0 and 2.8 litre 'performance' models and the 1.9D has a cable-operated mechanism as shown here, for reference. A complex jig – a VW part - is needed to adjust the linkage, so adjusting the mechanism correctly will be a matter for your Volkswagen dealership.

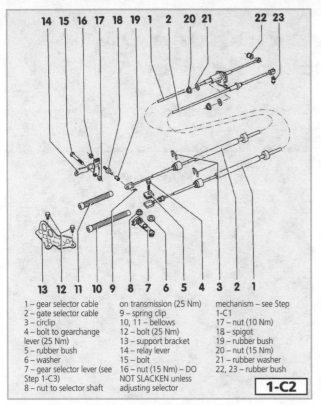

14 15 16 17 18 19 1 2 20 21   22 23

13 12 11 10 9   8 7 6 5 4   3 2 1

1 – gear selector cable
2 – gate selector cable
3 – circlip
4 – bolt to gearchange lever (25 Nm)
5 – rubber bush
6 – washer
7 – gear selector lever (see Step 1-C3)
8 – nut to selector shaft

on transmission (25 Nm)
9 – spring clip
10, 11 – bellows
12 – bolt (25 Nm)
13 – support bracket
14 – relay lever
15 – bolt
16 – nut (15 Nm) – DO NOT SLACKEN unless adjusting selector

mechanism – see Step 1-C1
17 – nut (10 Nm)
18 – spigot
19 – rubber bush
20 – nut (15 Nm)
21 – rubber washer
22, 23 – rubber bush

1-C2

❑ **STEP C2:** Provided that no adjustments are disturbed, it should be possible to change the cables, if necessary.

❑ **STEP C3:** On transmissions with the gear selector cable mounting next to the gear gate selector cable, this is the correct position of the gear selector lever (**1**) and relay lever (**2**). Lubricate with molybdenum grease (arrowed).

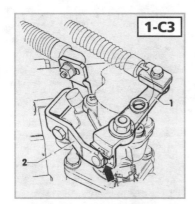

1-C3

Section D: Polo from 1995-on.

❑ **STEP D1:** New mechanisms were fitted to the Polo from 1995-on. This is the mechanism fitted to petrol/gasoline models. A complex jig – a VW part - is needed to adjust the linkage, so adjusting the mechanism correctly will be a matter for your Volkswagen dealership.

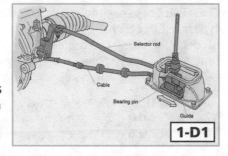

Selector rod
Cable
Bearing pin
Guide

1-D1

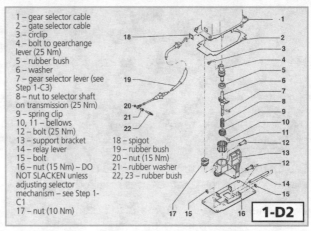

1 – gear selector cable
2 – gate selector cable
3 – circlip
4 – bolt to gearchange lever (25 Nm)
5 – rubber bush
6 – washer
7 – gear selector lever (see Step 1-C3)
8 – nut to selector shaft on transmission (25 Nm)
9 – spring clip
10, 11 – bellows
12 – bolt (25 Nm)
13 – support bracket
14 – relay lever
15 – bolt
16 – nut (15 Nm) – DO NOT SLACKEN unless adjusting selector mechanism – see Step 1-C1
17 – nut (10 Nm)

18 – spigot
19 – rubber bush
20 – nut (15 Nm)
21 – rubber washer
22, 23 – rubber bush

1-D2

❑ **STEP D2:** Items **3** to **16** should not be dismantled without use of the VW jig referred to above.
➜ The cable (**19**) can be replaced.
➜ The cable retainer (**17**) can be difficult to move.
➜ The hook on the new cable must be passed through the seal (**18**) and carefully hooked into place.
➜ Items **20**, **21** and **22** locate the cable at the transmission. Press the bush (**21**) in and out with a drift.

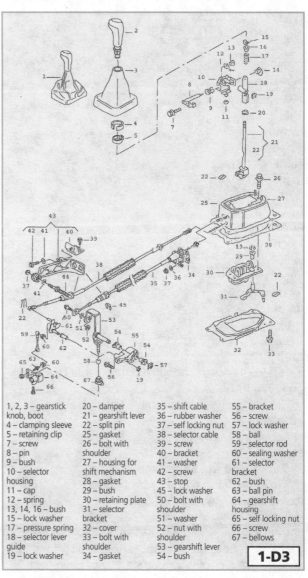

1, 2, 3 – gearstick knob, boot
4 – clamping sleeve
5 – retaining clip
7 – screw
8 – pin
9 – bush
10 – selector housing
11 – cap
12 – spring
13, 14, 16 – bush
15 – lock washer
17 – pressure spring
18 – selector lever guide
19 – lock washer

20 – damper
21 – gearshift lever
22 – split pin
25 – gasket
26 – bolt with shoulder
27 – housing for shift mechanism
28 – gasket
29 – bush
30 – retaining plate
31 – selector bracket
32 – cover
33 – bolt with shoulder
34 – gasket

35 – shift cable
36 – rubber washer
37 – self locking nut
38 – selector cable
39 – screw
40 – bracket
41 – washer
42 – screw
43 – stop
45 – lock washer
50 – bolt with shoulder
51 – washer
52 – nut with shoulder
53 – gearshift lever
54 – bush

55 – bracket
56 – screw
57 – lock washer
58 – ball
59 – selector rod
60 – sealing washer
61 – selector bracket
62 – bush
63 – ball pin
64 – gearshift housing
65 – self locking nut
66 – screw
67 – bellows

1-D3

❑ **STEP D3:** These are the components of the gear-change mechanism used on Diesel Polos from 1995-on.

Part D: Auto. Gear Selector Control Cable – Replacement, Adjustment

CONTENTS

See **Chapter 6, Part B: Which Engine is Which?** for an explanation of the engine types referred to here.

Two general types of automatic shift control have been fitted: both operate on similar principles.

JOB 1:	AUTO. GEAR SELECTOR CONTROL CABLE – *replacement, adjustment.*

TYPE ONE

❑ **STEP 1:** This is the shift control from September 1975 (and is also similar to those fitted earlier). Replace the cable as follows:

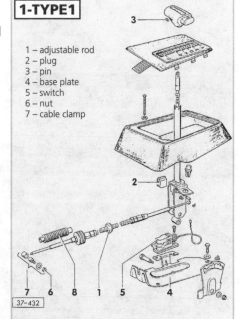

1-TYPE1

1 – adjustable rod
2 – plug
3 – pin
4 – base plate
5 – switch
6 – nut
7 – cable clamp

37–432

→ Attach a piece of wire approx-imately two metres (6 ft.) long to the old cable before removing it so that the new cable can be pulled in its place.
→ Grease the ends of the cable lightly before installing.
→ Remove the console and place the selector lever at 'P'.
→ Slacken the nut on the cable clamp.
→ Move the lever on the transmission to position 'P' (outwards to the stop).
→ Tighten the clamp nut.
→ IMPORTANT NOTE: Adjust the contact plate so that the engine can only be started at positions 'N' and 'P'. If the engine can be started at any other positions, readjust the cable until this can no longer happen.

TYPE TWO

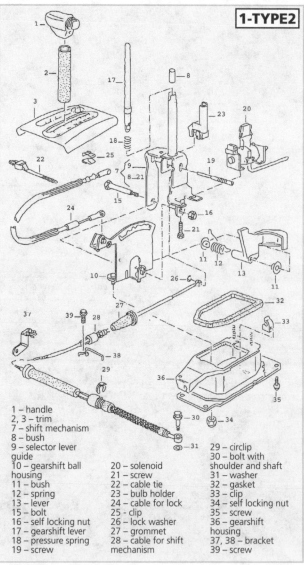

1-TYPE2

1 – handle
2, 3 – trim
7 – shift mechanism
8 – bush
9 – selector lever guide
10 – gearshift ball housing
11 – bush
12 – spring
13 – lever
15 – bolt
16 – self locking nut
17 – gearshift lever
18 – pressure spring
19 – screw
20 – solenoid
21 – screw
22 – cable tie
23 – bulb holder
24 – cable for lock
25 - clip
26 – lock washer
27 – grommet
28 – cable for shift mechanism
29 – circlip
30 – bolt with shoulder and shaft
31 – washer
32 – gasket
33 – clip
34 – self locking nut
35 – screw
36 – gearshift housing
37, 38 – bracket
39 – screw

❑ **STEP 2:** These are the components of all the later types of shift control – fitted to both Golf and Polo models - including the cable run to the transmission unit. Not all models have the locking device attached to the ignition key.

ADJUSTMENT: Follow the instructions given in **Step 1**. Note that the cable clamp referred to is *item 15, 16* in this drawing.

Note that the illustration numbers referred to in the following Steps relate, where necessary, to illustration *1-2*.

STEP 3: The selector lever lock solenoid (*item 20*) can be adjusted by sliding it in the elongated holes after slackening off the fixing screw. Volkswagen recommend removing the fixing screw and applying locking fluid before refitting it. The gap between pressure rod and lever (**a**) should be 0.3 mm.

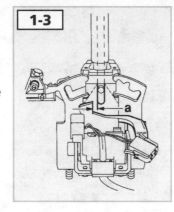

1-3

STEP 4: To remove and replace the selector lever cable:

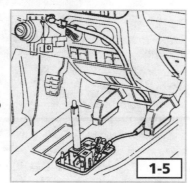

1-4

→ Take off the selector lever handle.
→ Remove the cover and the cover strip.
→ Pull off the electrical switch connector (when fitted).
→ Take the selector lever cable (arrowed) off the selector lever by first removing the circlip. (Always replace with a new circlip.)
→ Remove the lower protective plate and disconnect the exhaust, as necessary – depending on model.
→ Remove the selector lever cable bolt from the lever selector shaft (*item 15*).
→ Take off the circlip (*item 29*) holding the cable to the support bracket (use a new circlip when refitting).
→ Take off the forward selector lever housing bolts and heat shield.
→ Disconnect the selector cable from the transmission (*item 30*).
→ When refitting, make sure that the guide tube (*item 27*) in the gearshift housing (*item 36*) is securely seated.

REMOVING AND INSTALLING LOCKING CABLE FOR VEHICLES WITH IGNITION KEY LOCK

STEP 5: This illustration shows the routing of the locking cable. Strip the gearchange housing as shown. You will also need to remove the steering wheel and the ignition/starter switch trim. See relevant sections of this manual.

1-5

STEP 6: Slacken the cable anchorage screw (**a**), take the locking cable out of the locking lever and pull out of cable anchorage.

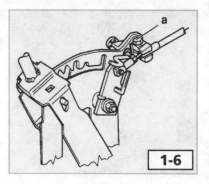

1-6

1-7

STEP 7: Push the cable clip (**a**) out of the switch support bracket (**b**) and remove the ball-end of the cable (**c**).

STEP 8: For reference, this shows the correct routing through the dashboard and the installed appearance of the locking cable.

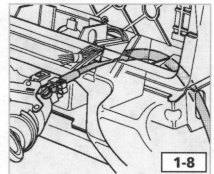

1-8

STEP 9: The locking cable can only be adjusted when correctly installed at both ends:
→ Place the selector lever in to '1' position (1st gear).

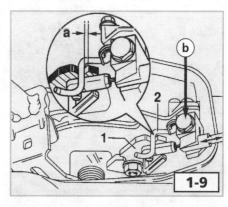

1-9

→ Turn ignition key to the right (starting position) and release.
→ Adjust the clearance (**a**) to 0.7 mm between lever (**1**) and locking pin (**2**) by sliding the locking cable casing (double-ended arrow).
→ Tighten the locking cable anchorage screw (**b**).
→ Check that it is only possible to remove the ignition key with the shift lever in the Park 'P' position and check that with the ignition key removed, the selector lever cannot be shifted out of the 'P' position.

Part E: Driveshafts, Constant Velocity Joints, Gaiters – Removal, Replacement

CONTENTS

See *Chapter 6, Part B: Which Engine is Which?* for an explanation of the engine types referred to here.

JOB 1: DRIVESHAFT – *removal.*

❑ **STEP 1:** Prepare to remove the driveshaft as follows:
→ Raise and support the car on axle stands. Remove the road wheel.
→ Lever off the dust cap and slacken the centre hub nut.
→ The hub nut (illustration *1-2, item 15*) requires a great deal of torque to undo!
→ You will need an extra-long lever to undo the hub nut.

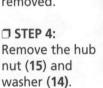

1-1

TOP TIP!

• Undo the hub nut while the car is still on the ground.
• Have an assistant apply the brakes hard while the nut is undone.

The following illustration numbers all apply to illustration *1-2*.

❑ **STEP 2:** Take note of the driveshaft and universal joint components. The top set relate to the left-hand driveshaft and the bottom set relate to the much longer right-hand halfshaft. The vibration damper (2) is only fitted to certain models. To remove the driveshaft from the vehicle:

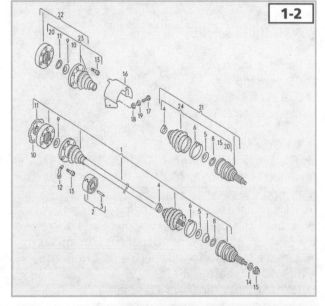

1-2

❑ **STEP 3:** Take out the screws (13) using an Allen key or splined tool, as appropriate. On later vehicles, the shroud (16) will first have to be removed.

1-3

❑ **STEP 4:** Remove the hub nut (15) and washer (14).
→ You may now be able to move the inner end of the driveshaft away from the transmission.
→ Tap the outer end of the driveshaft through the wheel bearing housing.

1-4

1-5

1-6

STEP 5: Alternatively, you can remove the pinch bolt and nut...

STEP 6: ...and detach the balljoint from the wheel bearing housing...

STEP 7: ...which gives more room to tap the halfshaft out of the hub.

1-7

STEP 8: The complete halfshaft can now be lifted away.

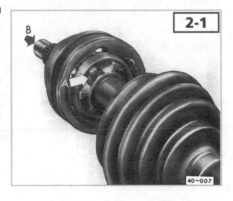

1-8

JOB 2: UNIVERSAL JOINT – removal, replacement.

STEP 1: With the driveshaft gripped in the vice, open out the circlip **(A)** while at the same time an assistant taps the end of the shaft **(B)** until the circlip becomes free.

2-1

40-007

STEP 2: The constant velocity joint can now be hammered smartly to remove it from the shaft.

JOB 3: OUTER CONSTANT VELOCITY JOINT BOOTS – *replacement.*

If the constant velocity joint boots are split or in need of replacement, take off the axle shaft, remove the outer CV joint and fit both new boots.

TOP TIP!

• Note that the outer end of the shaft is smaller than the inner end.
• Therefore the outer CV joint cannot be fitted if only the inner CV joint is removed.

JOB 4: INNER CONSTANT VELOCITY JOINT BOOT – *replacement.*

STEP 1: Remove the circlip...

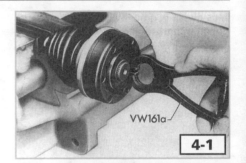

VW161a

4-1

STEP 2: ...drive the protective cap off the CV joint with a drift...

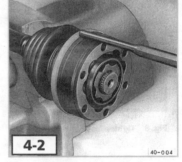

4-2

40-004

STEP 3: ...and push the shaft out of the CV joint. Here a press is shown being used but you may be able to drive the shaft out - taking care not to cause any damage!

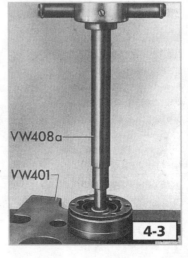

VW408a

VW401

4-3

JOB 5: CV JOINT – *dismantling*.

Although it is possible to dismantle and inspect both constant velocity joints, we recommend that faulty CV joints are replaced as complete units.

JOB 6: OUTER CV JOINT – *replacement*.

☐ **STEP 1:** Start by cleaning the hub and the driveshaft splines and lubricate them with a little molybdenum sulphide based grease. Check also that all flange joint mating surfaces are clean. Use a new gasket on the inner face of the inner CV joint.

☐ **STEP 2: EARLIEST MODELS:** The earliest model has the circlip towards the inner face of the CV joint...

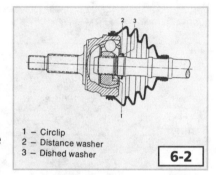

1 – Circlip
2 – Distance washer
3 – Dished washer

6-2

☐ **STEP 3:** ...while later models have the circlip towards the outer end of the driveshaft.

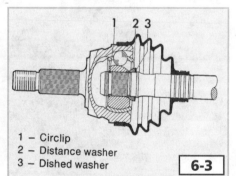

1 – Circlip
2 – Distance washer
3 – Dished washer

6-3

☐ **STEP 4:** After fitting the boot (**b**) to the axle shaft (**h**), fit the dished washer (**c**), the distance washer (**d**), and the circlip (**f**) to the axle shaft (**h**). Note that the dished washer should go with the concave side facing outwards. See **1-2, items 5, 7** (where appropriate) and **8**.
➔ The CV joint (**e**) and clips (**a** and **g**) are the other items here.

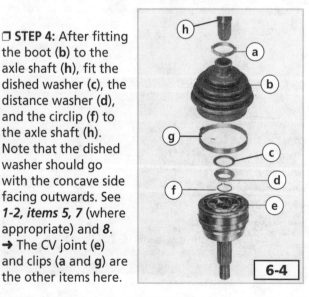

6-4

JOB 7: INNER CV JOINT – *replacement*.

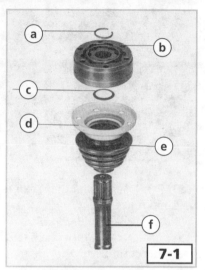

☐ **STEP 1:** Fit the boot (**e**), the protective cap (**d**), the dished washer (**c**). Then have the constant velocity joint (**b**) pressed on to the axle shaft (**f**). Retain it in place with the circlip (**a**).

7-1

VW1275

☐ **STEP 2:** The boots must be held in place with steel clips which are crimped tight.

7-2

TOP TIP!

• Volkswagen supply stainless steel hose clips which are extremely difficult to tighten satisfactorily without the use of much stronger than average pliers.
• You will need access to them in order to use stainless clips.

☐ **STEP 3:** When refitting the driveshaft to the hub, it is essential that the circlip (**A**) is always renewed (vehicles manufactured before July 1987) and it is essential that the circlip on all models is properly seated so that the driveshaft fits properly into the hub.

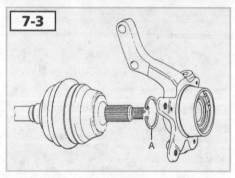

7-3

☐ **STEP 4:** Reassemble the driveshaft as the reverse of the dismantling procedure.

Part F: Transmission
– Removal, Refitting (with engine in the car)

CONTENTS

See *Chapter 6, Part B: Which Engine is Which?* for an explanation of the engine types referred to here.

IMPORTANT NOTES: • Transmission removal can be carried out with the engine remaining in the car.
• If you want to change the clutch, the transmission will have to be removed from the vehicle.
• For further information on removal of several of the components covered here, such as engine and transmission mountings, refer to *Chapter 6, Engine.*

FACT FILE

TRANSMISSION TYPES AND ENGINE REFERENCES

We show the removal and refitting of each of the different transmission types and the following groups of engines:
→ 'INTERNAL WATER PUMP' Engines
→ 'EXTERNAL WATER PUMP' Engines
→ 2.6 LITRE, VR6 Engines
→ ALUMINIUM BLOCK Engines
→ See *Chapter 6, Part B, Which Engine is Which?* for an explanation of these engine types.

JOB 1: GENERAL.

→ Before dismantling, disconnect the battery negative (-) earth/ground terminal. See *Chapter 10, Electrical, Dash, Instruments, Fact File: Disconnecting the Battery* BEFORE doing so!
→ Follow the detailed instructions given in the relevant parts of this manual for information on detaching gearchange mechanism and engine mountings.

→ There are many different types of connectors used on Volkswagen transmission units for items such as electrical connectors, brackets and covers.
→ Most modern units have electrically operated speedometers with a dedicated cable plug, which has to be removed after undoing the retaining clips.
→ Where a separate Automatic Transmission Fluid cooler is fitted, the hoses must be clamped near to where they are removed from the transmission.
→ When a hydraulic clutch is fitted, disconnect the slave cylinder from the transmission and tie to one side. There is no need to disconnect the hydraulic pipes.
→ On vehicles fitted with ABS braking, the transmission mounting may be difficult to get at. If so, remove the coolant system expansion tank, where appropriate.

TIGHTENING TORQUES

When refitting the transmission to an engine with cast-iron block, tighten the engine-to-transmission bolts to the following torque figures:

Bolt diameter	Nm
M 12	80
M 10	60
M 8	20
M 7	10

IMPORTANT NOTE: VW do not appear to supply different torque figures for attachments to engines with aluminium blocks. Check torque figures with your local VW dealer.

JOB 2: FOUR-SPEED TRANSMISSION, FITTED TO 'INTERNAL WATER PUMP' ENGINES
– *removal, installation.*

Section A: Transmission removal.

☐ **STEP A1:** Before starting work, ensure that you can support the car sufficiently high off the ground for the transmission to be removed from beneath. Make sure that the transmission-end

2-A1

of the engine is supported from above the car, or from beneath. We used a Sykes-Pickavant version of this Volkswagen support tool (**2**). Disconnect the battery earth/ground (-) terminal (**1**).

☐ **STEP A2:** Disconnect the following (typically):
→ The clutch cable (**3**) or hydraulic components.
→ Remove the wire from the TDC sensor (**4**).

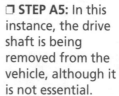

2-A2

→ Detach the torque strut (**5**) from both the transmission and the body.
→ Detach the speedometer cable (**6**).
→ Remove the upper starter bolts (**7**) and bend back the metal tab (arrowed).
→ Detach the transmission mount carrier from both the transmission unit and the body (**8**).
→ Remove the top engine-to-transmission bolts (**9**).

☐ **STEP A3:** Remove:
→ The square headed bolt from the transmission shift relay lever (**10**) and take off the lever.
→ Remove the lower starter bolt (**11**), take out the starter motor and hang it up on a wire hook.
→ Detach the right-hand drive shaft (**12**).
→ Remove the drive shaft mounting screws (**13**) but leave the drive shaft mounting on the engine.

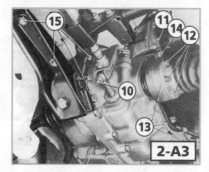

2-A3

Remove the lower-rear engine-to-transmission mounting bolt (**14**).
→ Detach the rear transmission mounting from both the transmission unit and the body (**15**).

☐ **STEP A4:** Remove:
→ The reversing light switch wire (**16**).
→ Take off the earth/ground cable from the transmission (**17**).
→ Take out the front bolt (**19**) from the engine-to-transmission mounting.

2-A4

→ Detach the left-hand drive shaft (**18**) and hang it up out of the way on a wire hook.

☐ **STEP A5:** In this instance, the drive shaft is being removed from the vehicle, although it is not essential.
→ Take the weight of the transmission unit on a trolley jack or other

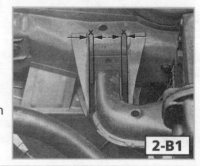

2-A5

suitable support and have two people ready to support the unit as it is removed.
→ Push or lever the transmission off its dowels and remove it downwards.

SAFETY FIRST!

• The unit is heavy and should not be lowered without the use of suitable jacking or lifting equipment and by two people.

Section B: Transmission installation.

When reinstalling the transmission unit to the vehicle, carry out the installation in the reverse of the removal sequence.

IMPORTANT NOTE: When installed, the engine and transmission mountings should be free of strain. Don't tighten any of them up until all are in place.

☐ **STEP B1:** Centralise the engine/transmission unit in the mounting bracket, placing it equidistant between the two outer sides of the bracket.

2-B1

STEP B2: Make sure that the torque strut is centralised, at the front of the engine in most cases.

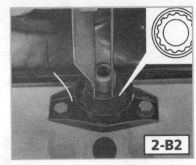

2-B2

IMPORTANT NOTE: When refitting the transmission relay lever (see illustration *2-A3, item 10*) you can reuse the square headed bolt but the hexagon head screw must always be renewed.

STEP B3: On the earliest type of transmission unit the studs (a) which hold the transmission mount carrier (b) to the transmission unit (c) are

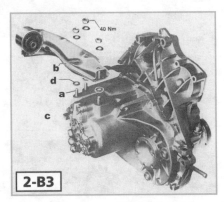

2-B3

plain and have a separate aluminium washer (d) placed between the carrier and the carrier transmission unit.

→ On later assemblies, the stud (a) has an integral shoulder fitted to it and no separate washer should be installed.

IMPORTANT NOTE: Later studs and earlier-type studs cannot be interchanged because the threads in their housings are different.

JOB 3:	FOUR-SPEED TRANSMISSION, FITTED TO 'EXTERNAL WATER PUMP' ENGINES – *removal, installation.*

Section A: Transmission removal.

STEP A1: Support the engine (2) as described in *Job 2, Step A1*, then using a tool like the Sykes-Pickavant engine support (arrowed):

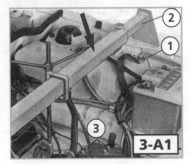

3-A1

→ Disconnect the battery earth/ground terminal (1).
→ Detach the left (end) transmission mounting (3).
STEP A2: Take out:

→ The TDC sender unit (4) with a spark plug spanner.
→ Disconnect the speedo cable retaining screw (5), disconnect the cable and seal the hole with a rag.
→ Remove the upper bolts (6) from transmission-to-engine.

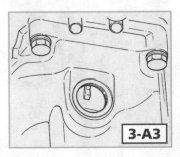

3-A2

→ Take off the reversing light switch cable (7).
→ Disconnect the clutch cable (8).

STEP A3: VEHICLES UP TO AUGUST 1974: Before the transmission can be withdrawn from the engine, you will have to turn the flywheel until the lug, which is 33 degrees before TDC

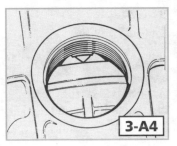

3-A3

appears in the TDC sensor aperture. DO NOT confuse the lug with marks for the TDC sender.

STEP A4: VEHICLES FROM 1974 TO OCTOBER 1978: Before the transmission can be withdrawn from the engine, you will have to turn the flywheel until the indentation shown,

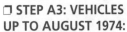

3-A4

which is 76 degrees before TDC, appears in the TDC sender aperture.

> **TOP TIP!**
> • The indentation appears three recesses along the flywheel.

STEP A5: VEHICLES FROM NOVEMBER 1978-ON: On these vehicles, the method of attaching the transmission to the engine has been changed from studs fitted in the

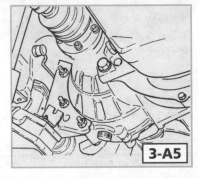

3-A5

transmission unit bellhousing, to bolts which are completely removed, allowing the transmission unit to be turned and making it unnecessary to align the flywheel.

STEP A6:
Disconnect:
→ The gearchange linkage (a) from the selector shaft.
→ Remove the spring clip (b) and disconnect the relay lever.

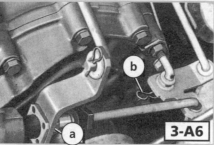

3-A6

STEP A7:
Detach:
→ The earth/ground cable (10) from the transmission unit.
→ Remove the starter motor by taking out the fixing bolts (11).
→ Disconnect the torque strut (12) from the transmission and the body and remove it.

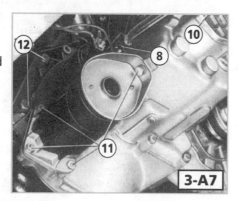

3-A7

STEP A8:
Disconnect and remove:
→The rear transmission mounting (13) from the transmission unit and the body.
→ Detach the left-hand drive shaft (14) and hang it up, out of the way, on a wire hook.

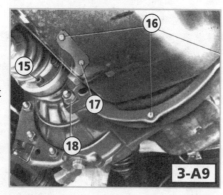

3-A8

STEP A9:
Detach:
→ The right-hand drive shaft (15) and hang it up out of the way on a wire hook.
→ Remove screws (16 and 17) holding the large cover plate but leave the plate on the engine.
→ Support the weight of the transmission unit and note that two people will be required to take it off the engine and remove it from under the vehicle.
→ Remove nut or bolt (18) as appropriate.
→ Push or lever the transmission off the dowel sleeves and take the transmission unit out downwards.

3-A9

Section B: Transmission installation

The transmission unit is installed by reversing the removal sequence. Make sure that the engine and transmission mounts are secured centrally and free of tension.

STEP B1: The
recess in the flywheel must be positioned level with the drive flange (arrowed).

3-B1

JOB 4:	FIVE-SPEED TRANSMISSION, FITTED TO 'EXTERNAL WATER PUMP' ENGINES – *removal, installation*.

Section A: Transmission removal.

STEP A1: See *Job 2, Step A1*.

STEP A2:
Disconnect:
→ The reversing light wires (4).
→ The speedo cable (5) by taking out the securing screw and seal the hole with a rag.
→ The clutch cable (6).
→ Take out the upper bolts attaching the transmission to the engine (7).
→ Remove the starter motor (8).

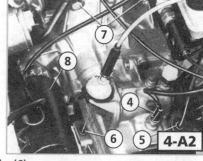

4-A2

STEP A3:
Disconnect:
→ The gearchange connecting link (9).
→ The rear selector rod (10). Remove the front selector rod (11) - see inset and remove it.
→ The earth/ground strap from the transmission and the torque strut from both the transmission unit and the body.

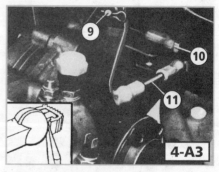

4-A3

STEP A4:
Detach:
→ The exhaust pipe bracket (**12**).
→ The left-hand drive shaft (**14**) and hang it up out of the way with a wire hook.
→ Disconnect the rear transmission mounting (**13**) and remove it from body and transmission unit.

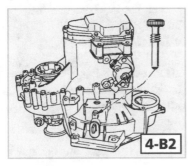

STEP A5: Follow the instructions given for *Job 3, Steps A7-on*.

Section B: Transmission installation

STEP B1: The transmission unit is installed by reversing the removal sequence. Make sure that the engine and transmission mounts are secured centrally and free of tension.

STEP B2: On some later transmission units, the clutch release lever has to be moved and locked into position before the unit is fitted to the engine. Where there is a suitable threaded hole, move the lever and insert an M8 x 35 bolt, or the special VW tool shown. Remove and plug the threaded hole by the cable support bracket securing bolt (or by a blanking plug if no support bracket is fitted).

JOB 5: AUTOMATIC TRANSMISSION – *removal, installation.*

Section A: Transmission removal.

STEP A1: Follow the illustrations for *Job 3, 3-A1* and *3-A2*, where appropriate, and carry out the following:
→ Detach the earth/ground strap and the positive cable from the battery.
→ Detach the speedo cable at the transmission unit.
→ Remove both of the upper engine-to-transmission bolts.
→ Loosen the end transmission mount and place a support in position, such as the one shown here, or a trolley jack beneath the vehicle.

STEP A2:
Detach:
→ The rear transmission mount carrier from both the body and the transmission unit (arrows).
→ Detach both drive shafts.

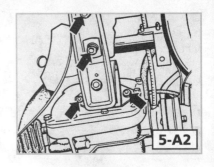

STEP A3: Disconnect and remove the starter motor.

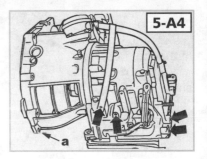

TOP TIP!

• The third bolt holding the starter motor in place is between the engine and starter.

STEP A4:
Remove the transmission protection plate and the cover plate for the torque converter (arrowed).

IMPORTANT NOTE: On earlier units, the protection plate is also fixed to the front of the transmission housing at point (**a**).

STEP A5:
Detach the torque converter from the driveplate, taking out the three bolts – reached through the starter motor aperture.
→ Shift into park ('P') and disconnect the selector lever cable at the transmission unit.
→ Remove the accelerator and carburettor cable brackets from the transmission unit but do not detach the cables or alter the settings.

☐ **STEP A6:** Remove the left-hand side transmission carrier from the transmission and the body.
→ Remove the torque strut from the body and the transmission.

5-A6

→ Support the weight of the transmission unit from beneath and have two people prepared to lift it away.

☐ **STEP A7:** Take out the engine-to-transmission bolts.
→ Lift the transmission unit slightly...
→ ...and swing the left-hand drive shaft out of the way.

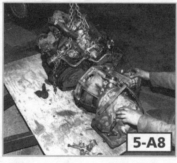

5-A7

☐ **STEP A8:** Pull the transmission unit off the mounting dowels and lower it to the ground. This is being carried out out of the car, but it helps to emphasise the great weight of the unit – it is MUCH heavier than a manual transmission!

5-A8

☐ **STEP A9:** IMPORTANT NOTE: Secure the converter with wire so that it does not fall out.

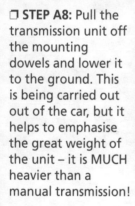

5-A9

TOP TIP!

• Do not tilt the torque converter or fluid will be spilt out of it!

Section B: Transmission installation.

☐ **STEP B1:** Fit the torque converter before installing the gearbox.
→ Ensure that the pump shaft is inserted fully into the splines.
→ Install the converter carefully on the one-way clutch support without tilting it.
→ To engage the splines, turn the converter to-and-fro slightly.

☐ **STEP B2:** Before installing the transmission, check once again that the torque converter is fully home on the one-way clutch support (**b**). The

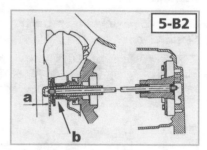

5-B2

converter is located properly when measurement (**a**) is approximately 10 mm (0.4 in.).

☐ **STEP B3:** WATCH OUT FOR THIS!
→ The converter has slipped forward (see left arrow) and has pulled the pump shaft out of the splines in the driving dog (**A**).
→ If the transmission

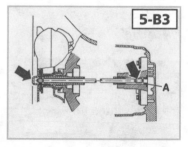

5-B3

is bolted to the engine in this position, the driving dog will be damaged.
→ Before starting to tighten the engine transmission bolts, turn the converter to ensure that it does not slip and become jammed.

☐ **STEP B4:** Centralise the transmission mountings as described in *Steps A5* and *A6* and ensure that they are not stressed when fitted.

JOB 6:   VR6 ENGINES' TRANSMISSION – *removal, installation.*

Section A: Transmission removal.

Follow the instructions given for 4-cylinder engines fitted to 5-speed transmission, with the following variations:

☐ **STEP A1:** Remove the following:
→ The screws (**A**) followed by the radiator cover (**1**).

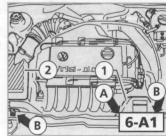

6-A1

→ The screw (**B**) and then the right headlight cover.
→ The upper part of the air cleaner (**2**).

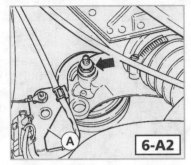

STEP A2: Remove the fixing (arrow) on the engine subframe on the right-hand side, and remove the connector mounting plate (**A**) – if fitted.

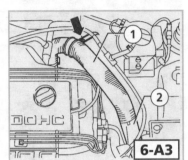

STEP A3: Take off the upper air ducting for cooling the front exhaust pipe as follows:
→ Loosen the hose clamp on the cooling air hose (**1**) at the heat shield.
→ Remove the securing screw (arrow, but not visible here) from hose retainer.
→ Pull cooling air hose off the air ducting (**2**).

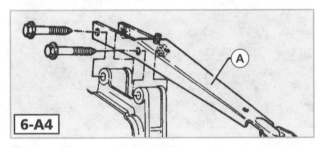

STEP A4: Remove the transmission support (**A**) from the transmission unit.

STEP A5: Remove the following:
→ Unclip the HT cables from their retainers and pull the three upper HT cables out of the distributor cap.
→ Take out the three securing bolts (arrows) and remove the trim (**1**).

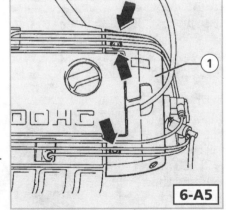

STEP A6: Remove the air ducting cover for both disc brakes, right and left.

STEP A7: Remove the cover in front of the toothed belt guard on the engine.

STEP A8: Remove the lower air ducting for cooling the front exhaust pipe as follows:
→ Remove the bolt (arrow **A**) separating the air ducting (**1**) from air ducting (**2**).

→ Lift air ducting (**2**) upwards out of the retainer on the body and then remove downwards.
→ Remove the retaining bracket for the power steering pipe (**3**) by removing the bolts (arrow **B**).

STEP A9: Separate the exhaust system at the joint in front of the catalyst.

STEP A10: Disconnect the drive shafts and turn the steering to full left lock. Tie up the drive shaft as high as possible.

STEP A11: Push the engine/transmission assembly as far to the right as possible.

STEP A12: Remove the transmission mounting (**A**) from the transmission as follows:
→ Lift the engine/transmission assembly until the exhaust contacts the heat shield but

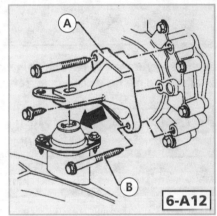

take care not to damage the selector cable support bracket.
→ Remove the transmission mounting bolt (**B**) from below the mounting plate (arrowed).
→ Push the front engine/transmission mounting sideways and turn it so that the mounting retaining lugs face to left or right.

STEP A13: Lower the engine/transmission assembly to its original position and then lower the transmission end sufficiently so that you can remove the clutch cover plate.

STEP A14: Remove the engine to transmission to securing bolts, slide the transmission off its dowels and lower to the ground.

IMPORTANT NOTE: In order to remove the transmission, you will need to press the engine forwards until it just touches the engine carrier. Take care when lowering the transmission not to damage the power assisted steering pipe.

Section B: Transmission installation.

❑ **STEP B1:** In order to make the transmission mounting bracket holes align with the left-hand mounting position, VW recommend using Tool 3300 A to push the transmission into position. It may well be necessary to make up your own version of this tool.

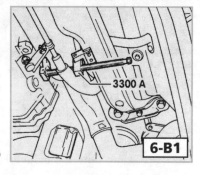

3300 A

6-B1

JOB 7: POLO WITH DIESEL ENGINE FROM 1995-ON.

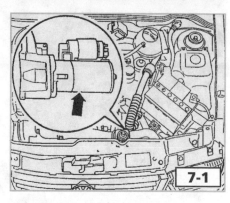

❑ **STEP 1:** Install the starter motor before refitting the transmission.

7-1

Part G: Clutch – Replacement

CONTENTS

See *Chapter 6, Part B: Which Engine is Which?* for an explanation of the engine types referred to here.

JOB 1: SMALLER ENGINE CLUTCH – *dismantling, inspection, fitting.*

Section A: Clutch dismantling, inspection.

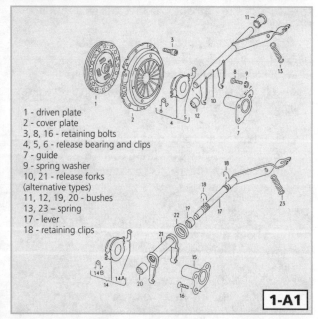

1 - driven plate
2 - cover plate
3, 8, 16 - retaining bolts
4, 5, 6 - release bearing and clips
7 - guide
9 - spring washer
10, 21 - release forks
(alternative types)
11, 12, 19, 20 - bushes
13, 23 – spring
17 - lever
18 - retaining clips

1-A1

❑ **STEP A1:** Items **1**, **2** and **4** are the parts you will need to obtain when you renew the clutch.

CLUTCH WEAR

• We strongly recommend that all three main components: clutch cover, driven plate and release bearing are replaced after a high mileage, ensuring longer life and smoother operation.
• If one is worn, they are all likely to be, so save yourself another big stripdown in the near future!
• The release bearing can be checked for wear: look for signs of escaping grease from the sealed component, and spin the bearing for signs of roughness, indicating worn ball bearings.

❑ **STEP A2:** Remove the transmission. See *Part F: Transmission*.

❑ **STEP A3:** Remove the clutch as follows:
➜ If you intend refitting the same clutch, make alignment marks between cover plate and flywheel.

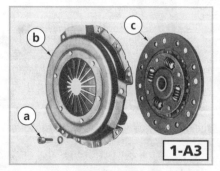

1-A3

➜ Unscrew the clutch cover bolts (**a**) progressively, half a turn at a time, until the spring pressure is released, then remove the bolts.

→ Ease the cover (**b**) off its dowels and catch the driven plate (**c**) as it falls.

TOP TIP!

❏ **STEP A4:** • Check the inside of the transmission bell housing for contamination by oil. This indicates a leak from either the crankshaft rear seal or the gearbox input shaft seal. Oil can cause judder and slip. Replace the transmission seal by prising out the old and fitting a new seal (**b**). See *Chapter 6, Part A.* for the replacement of the rear crankshaft seal.

❏ **STEP A5:** Check the surface of the flywheel that mates with the clutch for distortion (check with a straightedge and feeler gauges), for scoring, and for significant

1-A5

micro cracking caused by excessive heat generated by clutch slip. Replace the flywheel if in doubt.

❏ **STEP A6:** Check the ends of the diaphragm spring for grooves. Anything more than barely visible (up to 0.3 mm) means the plate needs replacing.

1-A6

❏ **STEP A7:** Check the release fork pivots, inside the bellhousing, for wear and check the release bearing (**d**) and runner (**b**). Remove the pairs of

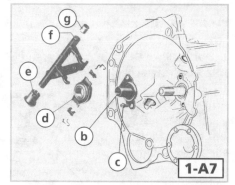
1-A7

spring clips, carefully noting how they are fitted, and take the release bearing off the fork mechanism (**f**).
→ Two bolts (**c**) hold the release bearing runner to the transmission.

❏ **STEP A8: TYPE 1:** (See illustration *1-A1, item 10* and *1-A7*). Replace the bushes if necessary:
→ lever the outer bush (**1-A7, item**

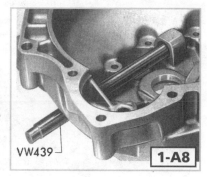
VW439
1-A8

e) from the casing
→ manoeuvring out the fork (*1-A7, item f*)
→ tap out the inner bush (*1-A7, item g*) and fit the new inner bush with a suitable drift, similar to VW439, shown here
→ lubricate with a small quantity of molybdenum disulphide grease.

❏ **STEP A9: TYPE 2:** (See illustration *1-A1, items 17* and *21*). Replace the bushes if necessary:
→ lever off the spring clips (**18**)
→ slide out the lever (**17**) and remove the fork (**21**)
→ push out and replace the bushes (**19** and **20**)
→ lubricate with a small quantity of molybdenum disulphide grease.

Section B: Clutch fitting.

❏ **STEP B1:** Clean any oil (or protective film) from the clutch cover and flywheel faces.

❏ **STEP B2:** Offer the driven plate to the flywheel.

❏ **STEP B3:** Locate the clutch cover on the flywheel dowels and screw in the fixing bolts finger tight.

❏ **STEP B4:** Use an aligning tool (VW part 10-213 shown, but an auto-accessory store version is as good) pushed through the

10-213
10-201
1-B4

clutch and into the end of the crankshaft to make sure that the clutch is centralised, otherwise the gearbox will not relocate on the engine and damage can be caused to the centre plate. Re-align any alignment marks (arrowed).

❏ **STEP B5:** Tighten the cover bolts evenly to the correct torque. See *Chapter 1, Facts and Figures*.

TOP TIP!

• Illustration *1-B4, item 10-201* shows a Volkswagen special tool used to lock the engine.
• You could make up your own lock plate, or insert a bolt into the rear of the engine and have a helper jam the flywheel with a large screwdriver.

❏ **STEP B6:** Smear a little 'copper' grease on the release bearing guide and the gearbox input shaft.

❏ **STEP B7:** Refit the transmission.

JOB 2: LARGER ENGINE CLUTCH – *dismantling, inspection, fitting.*

Section A: Clutch dismantling, inspection.

FACT FILE
LARGER ENGINE CLUTCH MECHANISM

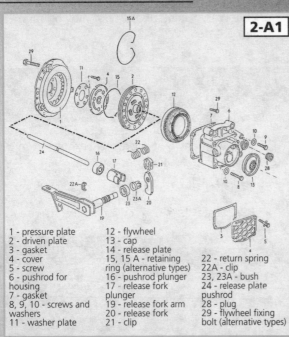

2-A1

1 - pressure plate
2 - driven plate
3 - gasket
4 - cover
5 - screw
6 - pushrod for housing
7 - gasket
8, 9, 10 - screws and washers
11 - washer plate

12 - flywheel
13 - cap
14 - release plate
15, 15 A - retaining ring (alternative types)
16 - pushrod plunger
17 - release fork plunger
19 - release fork arm
20 - release fork
21 - clip

22 - return spring
22A - clip
23, 23A - bush
24 - release plate pushrod
28 - plug
29 - flywheel fixing bolt (alternative types)

❏ **STEP A1:** It helps to understand how this clutch works! It is quite unusual for a car - more like some motorbike clutches:
→ First, the pressure plate (**1**) is bolted to the flange on the end of the crankshaft with six bolts and a multi-hole washer (**11**).
→ Next, the release plate (**14**) is held to the pressure plate with a spring clip (**15** or **15A**, depending on type).
→ The clutch friction plate (**2**) has to be centred inside the flywheel (**12**) which is fitted last, and bolted to the pressure plate (**1**) with a ring of bolts or studs and nuts (**29**) - the exact opposite of the great majority of car clutches!

The release mechanism works as follows:
→ The lever on the end of the release mechanism shaft (**19**) is operated by the clutch cable, from the pedal.
→ The shaft turns in the housing (**6**), the lever (**20**) pushes on the plungers (**16** and **17**), which push on the pushrod (**24**).
→ The pushrod passes down the middle of the flywheel and clutch friction plate, and pushes against the release plate (**14**), which is then forced against the springs in the pressure plate (**1**). With the friction plate no longer held against the flywheel (**12**), drive is disengaged.
→ The hydraulically operated system can be seen in *Section C*.

TOP TIP!

❏ **STEP A2:** • Pull out the pushrod (see 2-A1, item 24) if it is still in place. Lock the flywheel to prevent it from turning. Here, a Volkswagen special tool is being used to lock the engine. You could make up your own lock plate, or insert a bolt into the rear of the engine and have a helper jam the flywheel with a large screwdriver.

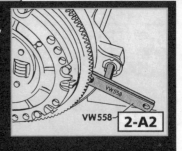

VW558   **2-A2**

IMPORTANT NOTE: The following illustration numbers, in brackets, all refer to illustration **2-A1**.

❏ **STEP A3:** Unbolt the flywheel (**12**), remove it, and remove the driven plate (**2**).

❏ **STEP A4:** Take out the bolts half a turn at a time, in the order shown, until all are loose, then remove them.

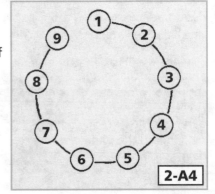

2-A4

❏ **STEP A5:** Use a screwdriver to unhook the retaining ring at the position arrowed. There are three types but the principle for all is the same. Remove the release plate (**14**).

2-A5

❏ **STEP A6:** Take out the six bolts, take off the washer plate (**11**) and remove the pressure plate (**1**).

TOP TIP!

• The bolts will be extremely difficult to shift, because they are fitted with strong thread locker and tightened to a high torque. Use an extension arm on your socket.

Section B: Clutch flywheel fitting.

☐ **STEP B1:** When fitting either the (smaller engine's) flywheel or the (larger engine's) pressure plate, use locking fluid on the bolts so that they don't come undone.

2-B1

☐ **STEP B2:** With the larger engine's clutch, the next item to fit is the release plate and the retaining clip.

2-B2

☐ **STEP B3:** Make sure that the clip is fitted as shown here, with the ends of the clip pushed into the retaining holes in the release plate. There are two types of retaining clip (release plates and retaining clip types are not interchangeable) but both fit in essentially the same way.

2-B3

☐ **STEP B4:** Next, on the larger engine's clutch, the driven plate is fitted followed by the flywheel.

2-B4

☐ **STEP B5:** Note that these pins on the inside of the flywheel locate in holes in the clutch pressure plate.

2-B5

☐ **STEP B6:** As with any other clutch, the driven plate is held in place under spring loading, except that on the smaller engines the 'cover' is the pressure plate whereas on these engines, it's the flywheel. Put the bolts in but don't tighten them. Use this Sykes-Pickavant VW clutch centring tool, to make sure that the driven plate is centred inside the flywheel.

2-B6

☐ **STEP B7:** Refit the transmission.

JOB 3: HYDRAULICALLY OPERATED CLUTCH.

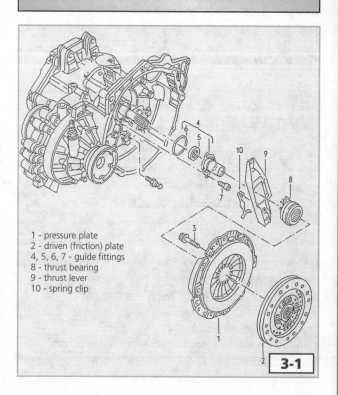

1 - pressure plate
2 - driven (friction) plate
4, 5, 6, 7 - guide fittings
8 - thrust bearing
9 - thrust lever
10 - spring clip

3-1

☐ **STEP 1:** Remove and refit the clutch in a similar fashion to that described in *Section A:* or *Section B*, as appropriate.

CHAPTER 8: COOLING SYSTEMS

*Please read **Chapter 2 Safety First** before carrying out any work on your car.*

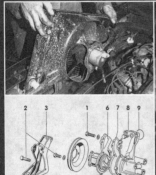
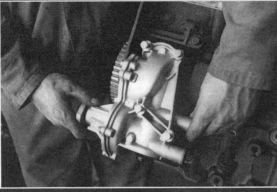
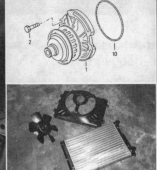

CONTENTS

IMPORTANT NOTE: See **Chapter 5, Servicing** for information on refilling the cooling system with coolant.

The cooling systems on all the vehicles in the vehicles covered here have a great deal in common, at the body-end, although higher-powered vehicles may have twin cooling fans mounted on the radiator.

At the engine-end, there are four types of system in use:

➜**'INTERNAL WATER PUMP' ENGINES**
➜**'EXTERNAL WATER PUMP' ENGINES**
➜**2.6 LITRE, VR6 ENGINES**
➜**1.0 LITRE ALUMINIUM BLOCK ENGINES**

IMPORTANT NOTES: For a general description of these engine types, see **Chapter 6, Part B: Which Engine is Which?**
➜ The 1.4 and 1.6 aluminium block engines come under the 'Internal Water Pump' Engines category from the point of view of the cooling system.
➜ The 1.0 litre engine is different.

JOB 1:   COOLING SYSTEMS
- the systems explained.

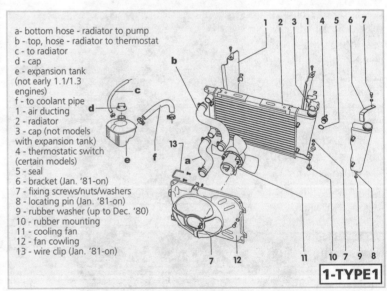

a- bottom hose - radiator to pump
b - top, hose - radiator to thermostat
c - to radiator
d - cap
e - expansion tank (not early 1.1/1.3 engines)
f - to coolant pipe
1 - air ducting
2 - radiator
3 - cap (not models with expansion tank)
4 - thermostatic switch (certain models)
5 - seal
6 - bracket (Jan. '81-on)
7 - fixing screws/nuts/washers
8 - locating pin (Jan. '81-on)
9 - rubber washer (up to Dec. '80)
10 - rubber mounting
11 - cooling fan
12 - fan cowling
13 - wire clip (Jan. '81-on)

1-TYPE1

❐ **TYPE 1:** These are the radiator components and fixings as applicable to all earlier vehicles, with some minor differences. Note that if a new radiator is fitted to a vehicle produced before January 1981, the rubber mounting system will have to be replaced with the locating system used on later radiators.

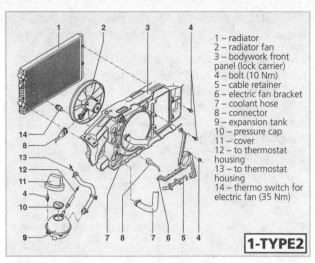

1 – radiator
2 – radiator fan
3 – bodywork front panel (lock carrier)
4 – bolt (10 Nm)
5 – cable retainer
6 – electric fan bracket
7 – coolant hose
8 – connector
9 – expansion tank
10 – pressure cap
11 – cover
12 – to thermostat housing
13 – to thermostat housing
14 – thermo switch for electric fan (35 Nm)

1-TYPE2

❏ **TYPE 2:** This, in essence, is the layout of the 'body-side' of the cooling system fitted to all later vehicles.

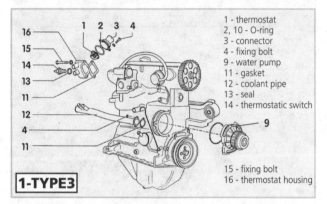

1 - thermostat
2, 10 - O-ring
3 - connector
4 - fixing bolt
9 - water pump
11 - gasket
12 - coolant pipe
13 - seal
14 - thermostatic switch

15 - fixing bolt
16 - thermostat housing

1-TYPE3

❏ **TYPE 3: 'INTERNAL WATER PUMP' ENGINES:** The layout of all these engines is similar. The water pump is driven off the cambelt and is mounted in the end of the block.

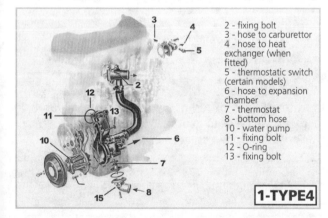

2 - fixing bolt
3 - hose to carburettor
4 - hose to heat exchanger (when fitted)
5 - thermostatic switch (certain models)
6 - hose to expansion chamber
7 - thermostat
8 - bottom hose
10 - water pump
11 - fixing bolt
12 - O-ring
13 - fixing bolt

1-TYPE4

❏ **TYPE 4: 'EXTERNAL WATER PUMP' ENGINES:** The water pump is mounted on the side of the block and is driven by the crankshaft pulley V-belt. The thermostat is housed beneath the water pump.

> **TOP TIP!**
> • Whenever you have drained and disconnected any part of the cooling system, always run the engine, after reassembly, to normal working temperature and check for leaks.

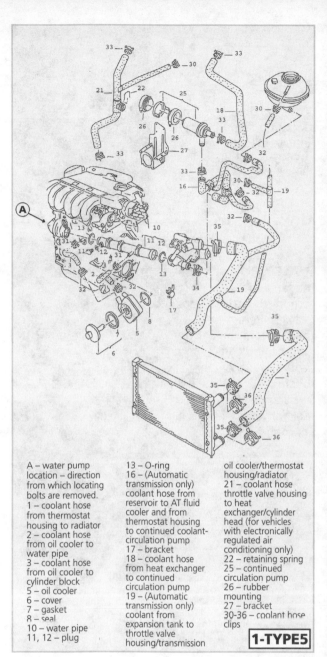

A – water pump location – direction from which locating bolts are removed.
1 – coolant hose from thermostat housing to radiator
2 – coolant hose from oil cooler to water pipe
3 – coolant hose from oil cooler to cylinder block
5 – oil cooler
6 – cover
7 – gasket
8 – seal
10 – water pipe
11, 12 – plug
13 – O-ring
16 – (Automatic transmission only) coolant hose from reservoir to AT fluid cooler and from thermostat housing to continued coolant-circulation pump
17 – bracket
18 – coolant hose from heat exchanger to continued circulation pump
19 – (Automatic transmission only) coolant from expansion tank to throttle valve housing/transmission
oil cooler/thermostat housing/radiator
21 – coolant hose throttle valve housing to heat exchanger/cylinder head (for vehicles with electronically regulated air conditioning only)
22 – retaining spring
25 – continued circulation pump
26 – rubber mounting
27 – bracket
30-36 – coolant hose clips

1-TYPE5

❏ **TYPE 5: VR6 ENGINES:** This is the general layout of this complex system.

JOB 2: RADIATOR AND COOLING FAN – *replacement*.

❏ **STEP 1:** Unplug the electrical connections from the fan motor and thermostatic switch.

> **TOP TIP!**
> • Pre-1986 vehicles do not have the connector which will be fitted to the new fan. The old connector must be replaced with a new connector, available from your Volkswagen dealership.

STEP 2: Undo the fan mounting fixing bolts and remove the complete radiator assembly.

2-2

STEP 3: Remove the fan and shroud from the radiator. Remove the fan from the motor spindle by drifting out the rollpin, or levering off the shakeproof washer, as appropriate.

2-3

STEP 4: Refit in reverse order. Where anti-vibration rubber mounting pads have been fitted, be sure to replace or renew them, as necessary.

2-4

| JOB 3: | RADIATOR FAN THERMOSWITCH – *remove, check*. |

STEP 1: The thermostatic switch which controls the fan is located in one of the positions shown in *Job 1: Cooling systems - the systems explained*.

STEP 2: To remove, drain the cooling system, disconnect the switch and unscrew it from its fitting point.

STEP 3: Test the switch using a test bulb and three wires:
→ Connect one wire from a 12V battery terminal to the bulb.
→ Connect another from the bulb to one of the switch terminals.
→ Connect the third wire between the remaining switch and battery terminal.
→ Switches for 2-stage motors will have to be connected with reference to the relevant wiring diagram.

STEP 4: Lower the switch into water until the thread is just covered and the terminals remain dry.

STEP 5: Heat the water slowly.
→ **SINGLE STAGE MOTORS:** The bulb should light just below boiling point (90 to 94 degrees Celsius) and go out when the temperature falls below 85 to 89 degrees Celsius.
→ **2-STAGE MOTORS:**
Stage 1:   ON = 92 degrees to 97 degrees Celsius.
            OFF = 84 degrees to 91 degrees Celsius.
Stage 2:   ON = 99 degrees to 105 degrees Celsius.
            OFF = 91 degrees to 98 degrees Celsius.

STEP 6: Refit with a new O-ring or gasket but do not over tighten.

| JOB 4: | RUN-ON THERMOSWITCH – *testing*. |

STEP 1: Switch on the ignition then switch off again.

STEP 2: Pull the connector off the thermoswitch as shown and hold it to earth/ground. The radiator fan should now run. If it doesn't, investigate:

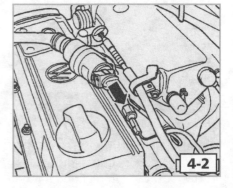

4-2

→ The quality of the earth/ground (-) connection.
→ The wiring.
→ The switch.

IMPORTANT NOTE: The illustration relating to all 'External Water Pump' Engines can be found in *Job 1: Cooling systems – the systems explained* except that the slightly different layouts of certain Diesel engines can be seen in *Step 7* of this Job, and in *Job 7: Coolant pump - replacement.*

| JOB 5: | THERMOSTAT – *replacement*. |

STEP 1: Drain the cooling system.

STEP 2: Disconnect the hoses from the thermostat housing. See relevant illustrations. Undo the bolts and remove the housing/thermostat assembly.

STEP 3: Clean the mating surfaces, fit the new unit with a new gasket.

STEP 4: Reconnect the hoses and refill the cooling system with the correct 50/50 anti-freeze coolant mixture. See *Chapter 5, Servicing*.

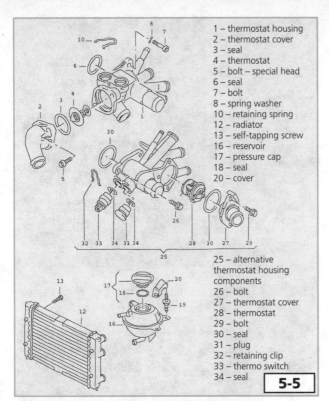

1 – thermostat housing
2 – thermostat cover
3 – seal
4 – thermostat
5 – bolt – special head
6 – seal
7 – bolt
8 – spring washer
10 – retaining spring
12 – radiator
13 – self-tapping screw
16 – reservoir
17 – pressure cap
18 – seal
20 – cover
25 – alternative
thermostat housing
components
26 – bolt
27 – thermostat cover
28 – thermostat
29 – bolt
30 – seal
31 – plug
32 – retaining clip
33 – thermo switch
34 – seal

5-5

❏ **STEP 5:** These are two alternative sets of components for the 'Internal Water Pump' Engines.

IMPORTANT NOTE: For 'External Water Pump' Engines, see *Job 1: Cooling systems - the systems explained*.

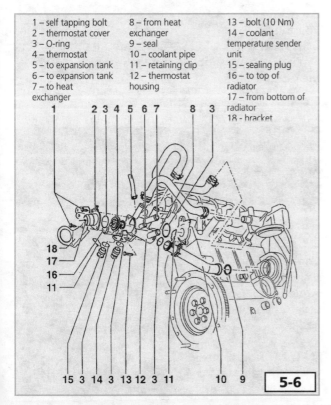

1 – self tapping bolt
2 – thermostat cover
3 – O-ring
4 – thermostat
5 – to expansion tank
6 – to expansion tank
7 – to heat exchanger
8 – from heat exchanger
9 – seal
10 – coolant pipe
11 – retaining clip
12 – thermostat housing
13 – bolt (10 Nm)
14 – coolant temperature sender unit
15 – sealing plug
16 – to top of radiator
17 – from bottom of radiator
18 – bracket

5-6

❏ **STEP 6: INTERNAL WATER PUMP ENGINES:** Although the housing arrangements are more complex than on earlier engines of this type, the layout is similar and this is the arrangement of the components.

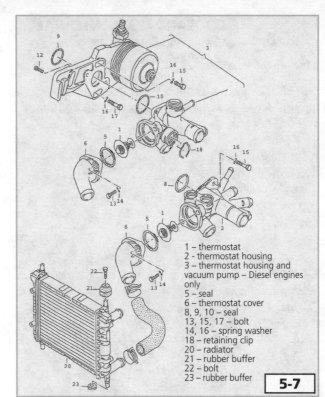

1 – thermostat
2 – thermostat housing
3 – thermostat housing and vacuum pump – Diesel engines only
5 – seal
6 – thermostat cover
8, 9, 10 – seal
13, 15, 17 – bolt
14, 16 – spring washer
18 – retaining clip
20 – radiator
21 – rubber buffer
22 – bolt
23 – rubber buffer

5-7

❏ **STEP 7: CERTAIN DIESEL ENGINES:** This is the arrangement of the thermostat housing and vacuum pump – which shares the same mounting – on Diesel engines where the thermostat is mounted in this position. Note that the non-Diesel thermostat housing (**2**) is the same as that shown in *Step 5*.

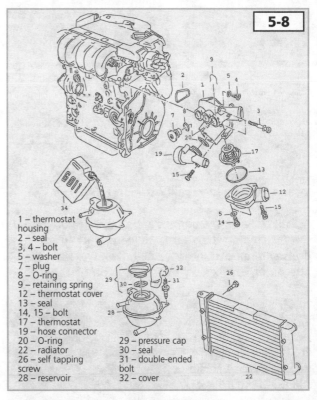

5-8

1 – thermostat housing
2 – seal
3, 4 – bolt
5 – washer
7 – plug
8 – O-ring
9 – retaining spring
12 – thermostat cover
13 – seal
14, 15 – bolt
17 – thermostat
19 – hose connector
20 – O-ring
22 – radiator
26 – self tapping screw
28 – reservoir
29 – pressure cap
30 – seal
31 – double-ended bolt
32 – cover

❏ **STEP 8: 2.6 LITRE, VR6 ENGINES:** This is the layout and components of the thermostat on the 6-cylinder engines.

JOB 6: COOLANT PUMP 'INTERNAL WATER PUMP' ENGINES – *replacement*.

❏ **STEP 1:** Drain the cooling system. Remove the timing belt as described in *Chapter 6, Part C: Timing Belt or Chain*.

❏ **STEP 2:** Remove the two bolts (**2**) holding the pump (**1**) in place and remove the O-ring (**10**).

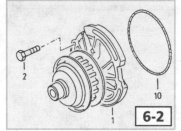

6-2

❏ **STEP 3:** Refit in the reverse order, using a new O-ring, and following the detailed instructions in *Chapter 6, Part A: Engine* on refitting the camshaft timing belt.

JOB 7: COOLANT PUMP 'EXTERNAL WATER PUMP' ENGINES – *replacement*.

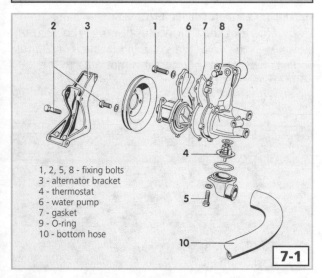

1, 2, 5, 8 - fixing bolts
3 - alternator bracket
4 - thermostat
6 - water pump
7 - gasket
9 - O-ring
10 - bottom hose

7-1

❏ **STEP 1:** Take note of the water pump fittings. The location can be seen in illustration *1-1-Type 4*.

❏ **STEP 2:** Raise the bonnet and drain the cooling system. Unplug the alternator leads, slacken the bolts and remove the drive belt. Remove the alternator, if necessary - depending on type.

❏ **STEP 3: VEHICLES WITH POWER STEERING, AIR CONDITIONING:** Slacken the adjuster and remove the drive belt/s.

7-3

7-4

❏ **STEP 4:** Take off the power steering pump bracket.

❏ **STEP 5:** Remove the alternator bracket, if necessary, and the crankshaft and water pump belt pulleys.

❏ **STEP 6:** Undo the securing bolts and remove the coolant pump, but you DO NOT need to remove the main housing bolts shown here UNLESS the replacement pump and housing are supplied complete, which is often the case.

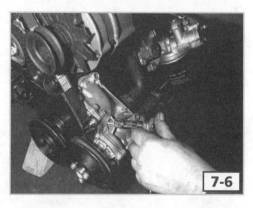

7-6

TOP TIP!

• Leave the hoses on the pump until it has been removed.
• If the hoses are being replaced, there will be no need to pick a fight with their connections to the pump!

❏ **STEP 7:** Discard the old gasket and clean off the mating surfaces. Refit the pump in reverse order using a new gasket.

❏ **STEP 8:** Adjust the drive belt tension.

❏ **STEP 9:** Fill the cooling system with the correct 50/50 solution of anti-freeze solution.

7-7

TOP TIP!

STEP 10: VW sell just the pump without the housing. Most non-original pumps come complete with housing.

7-10

• The six 10mm bolts holding the pump into the housing always seem to shear off when you unscrew them.

• Buying a pump complete with housing (almost!) overcomes this problem – just remove the complete housing, and change the pulley and thermostat.

• The thermostat housing bolts will also be prone to shearing. Apply releasing fluid, gently heat the housing and remove them carefully, with housing off engine.

STEP 11: 1.7 AND 1.9 LITRE DIESEL ENGINES: The location of the thermostat and water pump on these engines is almost the same as other 'External Water Pump Engines' but the component layout is as shown here.

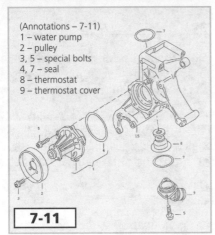

(Annotations – 7-11)
1 – water pump
2 – pulley
3, 5 – special bolts
4, 7 – seal
8 – thermostat
9 – thermostat cover

7-11

JOB 8: ENGINE-DRIVEN COOLANT PUMP – *replacement*.

2.6 LITRE, VR6 ENGINES

STEP 1: For the layout of the components for the 6-cylinder engine see illustration *1-1-Type 5*.

STEP 2: Removing and installing the water pump is an extremely complex business and is described here. For relevant illustrations and detailed instructions of component removal refer to the relevant sections of this manual.

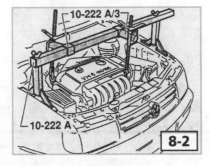

10-222 A/3
10-222 A
8-2

➜ Disconnect the battery and drain the coolant.

➜ Prepare the engine as if for removal.
➜ Support the engine and detach all of the engine and transmission mountings.
➜ Carefully lift the engine so that you can get at the coolant pump.

TOP TIP!

STEP 3: • VW recommend the use of this special spanner to grip the pulley bolts while removing them.

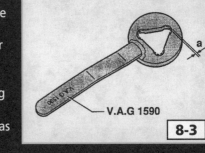

V.A.G 1590
a
8-3

• It works just as well if you can grip the two bolts which you are not removing with a pipe wrench while slackening the third.

STEP 4: To remove and install the coolant pump, you will have to push the engine slightly to the left to gain clearance.

STEP 5: Reassembly is the reverse of the removal process.

JOB 9: ELECTRIC COOLANT PUMP – *replacement*.

STEP 1: The continued coolant circulation pump is designed to circulate coolant for a time after the engine has stopped running, if the coolant temperature requires it. See illustration *1-1-Type 5* The pump is fitted to a mounting bracket on the camshaft sprocket cover on the top of the engine.

STEP 2: To check the operation of the pump switch, located in the thermostat housing:
➜ Take off the thermostat housing cover.
➜ Switch the ignition ON then OFF again.

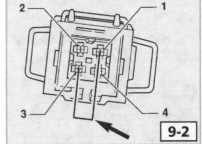

2 1
3 4
9-2

➜ Take the 4-pin connector off the run-on thermo. switch (F87), with yellow coolant temperature gauge sender (G2).
➜ BEWARE COOLING FAN/S WHICH SHOULD NOW RUN.
➜ Use cable (arrowed) to bridge contacts (1) - brown/red cable, and (3) - brown cable (NOT contacts 2 and 4!). If switch works, radiator fan and electric coolant pump should both run.

CHAPTER 9: IGNITION, FUEL, EXHAUST

*Please read **Chapter 2 Safety First** before carrying out any work on your car.*

We have placed both **Ignition** and **Fuel** systems in this, the same chapter. In the old days, the two areas could be treated separately, but that is no longer the case, and with today's electronic devices, ignition and fuel systems are inter-related.

SAFETY FIRST!

• Disconnect the battery before carrying out any work on the ignition or fuel systems. (Make sure that you first have the radio code, or use a backup power supply as described in *Chapter 10, Electrical, Dash, Instruments, page 10-1*.

• Take very great care when working on a vehicle equipped with electronic ignition.

• ELECTRONIC IGNITION SYSTEMS MAY INVOLVE VERY HIGH VOLTAGES! All manufacturers recommend that only trained personnel should go near the high-tension circuit (coil, distributor and HT wiring) and it is ESSENTIAL that anyone wearing a medical pacemaker device does not go near the ignition system.

• Only connect or disconnect electrical leads on the ignition system - including HT leads and testing units leads - when the ignition is switched off.

• If the engine has to be turned over on the starter but without starting, for example when checking compressions, disconnect all the cables from the distributor and also removed the HT lead from the coil.

• Never connect a condenser to terminal 1 (negative).

• Refer to *Chapter 2, Safety First!* and also to the *Safety First!* notes in this chapter.

Part A: Petrol / Gasoline Engines
CONTENTS

• When working on engines with electronic ignition systems, note the following, to avoid personal injury or damage to the ignition system.

• Make sure the ignition is switched off before removing any wires from the ignition system.

• If the engine is to be turned on the starter without starting:

EITHER - NON-ELECTRONIC IGNITION: Pull the centre HT lead from the distributor and connect it firmly to earth/ground.

OR - ELECTRONIC IGNITION: Disconnect the multi-pin plug from the distributor or ignition transformer (i.e. whichever one has the HT spark plug leads connected to it.)

PLUS - Where fuel injectors are fitted with electrical plugs (e.g. 16-valve, 1.6 litre 'roller rocker arm' engine from '98-on - engine code AJV and/or 4AV injection/ignition system), disconnect the plug from each of the four injectors. • Do not connect a capacitor/condenser to the coil terminals.

• Do not replace the rotor arm with a non-standard one, even to reduce radio interference.

• When suppressing interference, only resistors with 1 kohm and spark plug connectors with 5 kohms may be used on HT leads.

• If the car has to be towed with the ignition turned on, after the system has developed a fault, disconnect the wiring from the *TCI-H* switch unit.

• The ignition should be turned off when washing the engine or engine bay.

• A starting boost with a quick starter should be limited to no more than 60 seconds at 16.5 volts max.

• If electric arc, MIG or spot welding is carried out on the car, BOTH battery terminals must be disconnected.

JOB 1: SYSTEMS – *explained*.

In general, the earlier the vehicle, the more easily-serviceable parts are fitted to the ignition/fuel intake side, while the later the vehicle, the more complex the electronics become. See the relevant PART of this chapter for detailed illustrations and information.

Section A: Ignition.

There are three types of system fitted, although changes take place piecemeal and some vehicles will have elements of different systems:

EARLIEST VEHICLES

Whether carburettor of fuel injection, these vehicles have a single coil mounted in the engine bay, and a distributor with contact breaker points.

LATER VEHICLES

Later, the points set-up gave way to an electronic distributor without points. Increasingly, the coil was replaced with an ignition transformer. In some cases, this is capable of producing a higher power output and multiple-sparks. These vehicles have ignition timing which can still be adjusted by turning the distributor body in the traditional way.

NEWEST VEHICLES

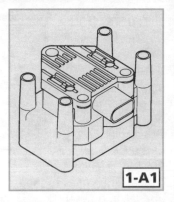

1-A1

❏ **ILLUSTRATION A1:** Later again, distributors that were not adjustable for ignition timing were fitted and the rotating distributor itself was done away with on some types. In these cases, a sensor or sensors measure engine speed and crankshaft position (via a TDC sensor). Engine load sensors combine with this data to constantly assess and if necessary change the ignition timing according to engine requirements. No adjustment is necessary or possible. See relevant part of *Job 4* for identification of relevant engines.

Section B: Fuel intake/injection.

Here, the evolutionary process passes through:
➔ Carburetors (with increasing amounts of sophistication)...
➔ Single-point injection systems, which more or less fit onto inlet manifolds as a replacement for carburetors...
➔ The more sophisticated multi-point injection systems. Many different injection types have been fitted.

❏ **ILLUSTRATION B1:** Latest diesel engines have injectors individually controlled by their own solenoid valves.

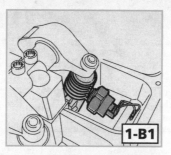

1-B1

Section C: Fuel supply.

The passage of time sees a simple piped supply from the tank supplanted by flow-and-return pipes, the addition of breathers to the tank/filler area and other evaporative control systems (such as a charcoal canister) to prevent the escape of fumes to the atmosphere. One of two basic types of fuel pump are fitted: an electric pump at the tank, or a mechanical pump at the engine.

Section D: Exhaust systems.

❏ **ILLUSTRATION D1:** The largest changes to exhaust systems came about when emission control equipment was fitted, mandatory in the UK from 1992. A catalytic converter is fitted to the front end of the exhaust, and a Lambda sensor is bolted into the exhaust upstream of the 'cat'.

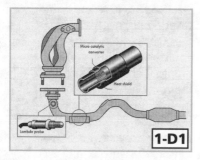

1-D1

Section E: Engine management.

❏ **ILLUSTRATION E1:** In order to control the newer equipment and take advantage of the greater precision in settings and faster operation, all modern engines have a computer-based ECU, or Electronic Control Unit.

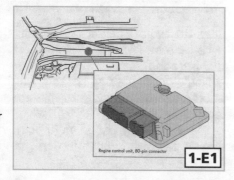

1-E1

❏ **ILLUSTRATION E2:** The ECU requires extra data so that it can control the major ignition and fuel supply components with greater efficiency. Newer engines have a whole range of sensors, including those to measure throttle, and sometimes brake and clutch pedal positions.

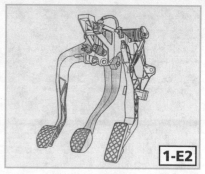

1-E2

JOB 2: DIAGNOSTICS - *carry out checks.*

Section A: Background.

Vehicles are becoming increasingly dependent on electronics. When things are going well, this has great advantages for the driver, including:
➔ Greater efficiency.
➔ Better reliability.
➔ Less maintenance.

Of course, almost everything has its downside, and vehicle electronics are no exception. Features often seen as 'problems' include:
➔ The need for special tools - mainly electronic diagnostic stuff.
➔ The need for knowledge and information not found in traditional manuals.
➔ The fact that it's impossible to see faults with electronic systems.

However, the problems presented by vehicle electronics are 'overcome-able' - and indeed, such problems can be turned on their heads. Then, instead of appearing as problems, they can be seen as a set of extra advantages for the mechanic, such as:
➔ Rapid fault diagnosis.
➔ Less guesswork.
➔ Fewer 'grey' areas caused by wear - electronics tend to work or not-work, and they don't usually wear out in a mechanical sense.

Turning the minuses into pluses is a matter of knowing where to obtain information and how to use it. It is not possible to fault-find many areas affected by electronics on an old-fashioned common-sense basis. But fortunately, the information is not too difficult to put to use - and it's even easier to find, if you know where to look!

• It's a myth that only the manufacturers' own diagnostics gear can do the job! But you will need a plug-in diagnostics tester to interrogate electronic-based systems.
• There are several makes of tester on the market. We feature the pro-oriented Sykes-Pickavant ACR System Tester. It's typical of the best of the testers available.

❏ **STEP A1:** It is not possible - even in a manual of this size - to cover diagnostics in specific detail; there's no room, and no need. We will describe how to use diagnostic test equipment and the equipment itself will do the rest. Or at least, that's the theory! What diagnostic test equipment,

such as the Sykes-Pickavant ACR System Tester, is good at is identifying specific fault areas:
→ If a component such as the engine knock sensor, the hall sender unit, or the Lambda sensor is failing to give a reading, the tester can tell you, almost instantly.
→ If you want to fool a component into working without the engine running, an advanced unit such as this one can simulate a signal to the component, so that you listen and feel for a solenoid clicking, a flap opening and closing, or the buzz of an EGR valve working.

What it can't always tell you is the source of the fault. Before fitting an expensive replacement, you will want to know:
→ Is the wiring to or from the component at fault?
→ Is it a corroded plug or socket?
→ Has someone else connected it up incorrectly?

• Check the basics before assuming that anything more complex is at fault.
• See *Chapter 4, Workshop Notes* and in particular Workshop Top Tips! and Pic 28 in that Chapter.

To analyse the results, you will need to go a step further. You will still need a wiring diagram, to check circuits and connections. And you will need extra diagnostics information to know how to check out potential faults. Most of the information you will need is in this manual - but if all of it had been printed here, the book would have been too thick to carry!

❏ **STEP A2:** Detailed diagnostic information is available from a number of sources:
→ You can order the manufacturer's own data, although some of it may be restricted information and not widely available. Try your local Volkswagen dealer's parts department.

→ There are several companies who specialise in producing detailed data of this sort. The one shown here is produced by CAPS (Computer Aided Problem Solving). It covers, as do all of them, a very wide range of manufacturers and models. All of these data compilations are expensive, typically costing many times the price of this manual!

❏ **STEP A3:** CAPS lists an immense amount of data on each disk, including:
→ ECU pin settings.
→ Values expected for various test readings using, for instance, a standard test meter.

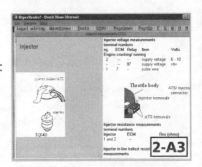

→ Waveforms for oscilloscope component testing.
→ Virtually everything you may need in order to carry out extensive diagnostic testing, in conjunction with a fault code reader.

❏ **STEP A4:** A good quality multi-meter will be an essential tool for the diagnosis of the more basic faults, such as continuity and correct connections. This Sykes-Pickavant multi-meter comes complete with full instructions for use and is both versatile and

accurate. We have come across cheaper tools that are most inaccurate, which makes them next to useless. How can you tell if there is a fault with the level of current (for instance) if the meter reads inaccurately?

❏ **STEP A5:** We look later at a more comprehensive and complete diagnostic tool from Sykes-Pickavant, but this sensor simulator and tester is an extremely useful piece of kit in its

own right. Although it is not designed to actually drive solenoids and actuators (it will test them both to see if they are receiving a control signal), it will test the following: Camshaft sensor; Crankshaft sensor; Mass Air Flow Meter; Manifold absolute pressure sensors; Oxygen sensor; Power steering pressure switch; Temperature sensors; Throttle position sensor.

STEP A6: An efficient Lambda sensor is essential for protecting the catalytic converter, allowing the vehicle to run efficiently and enabling the engine to pass the emissions laws. The Sykes-Pickavant tester can be used to check the sensor while it is in situ.

2-A6

FACT FILE

DIAGNOSTIC TESTING

BACKGROUND INFORMATION FROM SYKES-PICKAVANT

Electronic fuel injection and ignition systems on modern vehicles have a computer (called an ECU) to provide the proper control of the fuel-air mixture. The ECU works by measuring many different characteristics of the car then, using this information, it calculates the correct quantity of fuel, the time of the fuel injection and the time for the ignition spark.

The ECU is a computer, like any other you could buy from a High Street shop, but instead of a keyboard it has SENSORS as inputs, and instead of a TV screen, it has ACTUATORS. These are the output of the computer; for example the ECU controls the fuel injectors by opening and closing them for a few thousandths of a second. During this time fuel is sprayed into the inlet manifold (near the inlet valves) in the exact proportions required for efficient combustion. The ECU also controls the engine's idle speed with the "idle speed control valve".

Sensors are prone to failure, mainly due to being exposed to the harsh engine environment where harness connections can easily deteriorate over a few years. When this kind of fault occurs the ECU can be misled by the information being sent from the sensor, this results in the wrong quantity of fuel or timing for the sparks. Soon, the car allows too much of the wrong exhaust gases to escape, becomes difficult to drive or even does not start at all.

ECUs are able to detect faults in sensor signals by comparing the value with a range of values which are programmed by the designer of the ECU. If a signal is outside the expected range then something is wrong. The ECU does not "know" what exactly is wrong but it can sense that the signal is not in the range it expects to receive. This detected fault is stored as a code number in the memory of the ECU and it is this code which is known as a "fault-code". ECU designers have built-in limited number of such fault-codes into most modern systems. Each manufacturer has a different coding system and a different way of reading the codes, but they have some basic similarities.

Somewhere on the car's harness is a diagnostic socket which connects directly to the ECU. By connecting a second computer (the ACR Systems Tester, in this instance) to this socket we can send messages back and forth between the two computers and read the stored codes.

A simple code reader will show only the two or three digit code numbers which you then need to look up in a book to find out what they mean. The Sykes-Pickavant ACR Systems Tester does much more, by READING, CLEARING, ACTUATOR TESTS, and COMPONENT TESTS.

READ CODES

The ACR System Tester is able to read codes and display the meaning of each code. For example if the coolant temperature sensor is faulty then on some Bosch ECU's the fault-code stored is "15". The ACR System Tester shows the following on its two line display:

15 COOLANT SENS - VOLTAGE LOW
CLEAR CODES

When this problem has been corrected (perhaps by replacing the sensor) the stored fault code (15) must be removed from the ECU, otherwise the ECU will still think something is wrong. This is what the Clear Codes function is for. After clearing codes, the engine should be started and a final check for any stored fault codes made, just to be certain that nothing else has occurred.

ACTUATOR TEST

This feature is a method of testing the ECU outputs when the engine is turned off. For example to test the injectors involves sending a signal from the ACR System Tester to trigger a special program in the ECU which, in turn, causes the injectors to open and close every second. The injectors can be heard quite clearly "ticking" like a clock every second. With this we have clear proof that a signal is able to reach the injectors, we DO NOT KNOW if the injectors are blocked or gummed, so we do not know if any fuel can get into the engine...there are other ways of testing for that.

The final group of tests are components, (this is another way of saying sensors) where we can show the voltage, time or angle of various sensors which provide input to the ECU.

IMPORTANT NOTES:

• The ECU can only measure what is happening to the car using the sensors it is connected to. If there is no sensor it cannot be measured. This may seem obvious but some people seem to think computers are all-powerful.

• The ECU calculates the value that the ACR System Tester displays; the Tester is NOT connected directly to the sensor. The display you see is what the ECU "thinks" is the correct value. So if you see "Coolant Temperature 79 degrees Celsius" and the engine is stone-cold, you know something is wrong, but the ECU doesn't. This is a vital point to understand about code-readers which connect to the diagnostic socket; they can only display what the ECU is programmed to show and what the ECU calculates from its input.

Section B: The ACR tester – using.

STEP B1: The first job is to identify what you will need to use on the car you are testing. Look up the cable number in the handbook entitled "ACR System Tester Applications", supplied with the kit. Out of the Sykes-Pickavant case, you will need to take:

2-B1

→ The main ACR unit.
→ The correct plug-in pod, containing the ROM of data relevant to the vehicle you are testing.
→ The correct interface cable for connecting the ACR unit to the vehicle.

STEP B2: Find the location of the diagnostic plugs or sockets (as appropriate) on the vehicle you are working on. The plug-in pod's mini-manual will show you where to look. On all Golfs and derivatives, the socket is beneath the centre of the dash…

STEP B3: …and this is the area on Polos, under the glovebox under-tray. Originally, the plugs were stuck to the surface of the underside of the glovebox undertray, but often they are just left floating around.

2-B3

STEP B4: With the ignition OFF, push the plug/s into the relevant socket/s. Volkswagens have different numbers of sockets, depending on model – follow the instructions with the ACR kit.

2-B4

STEP B5: Each ROM pod (and there are several - each one covering a range of makes and models) comes with its own small manual which 'walks' you through the setting up and running procedure.
→ When the unit comes to life, you select the type of system (e.g. Motronic or

2-B5

Simos) on the menu offered on the read-out. The ACR then communicates with the vehicle's ECU.
→ You then select from the menu which type of test you want to carry out, such as 'Read Errors', 'Clear Errors' or 'Test Actuators'.
→ If you selected 'Test Actuators' for instance, the next menu allows you to choose which one - say, 'Fuel Injector'.
→ The ACR then interrogates the system for errors.
→ If an error is found, the error code number appears AND (unlike many testers) an abbreviated description of the error, such as **"0522: COOLANT TEMP SENSOR"** appears on the screen.
→ Pressing the **'OK'** button on the ACR applications can expand abbreviations. **"INJ P/W"**, for example, becomes **"INJECTOR PULSE WIDTH"** - useful until you are able to memorise the abbreviations.

STEP B6: A similar approach is followed - a walk-through by the manual, combined with step-by-step on-screen prompts and menus - allows the user to carry out most of the other functions that

2-B6

would normally only be carried out by the main dealer. Depending on the system, the SP ACR has the following capabilities:
→ Identifying ECU number and type.
→ Reads and clears fault codes.
→ Drives actuators e.g. coil, injectors etc..
→ Shows 'live engine data' e.g. throttle potentiometer, Lambda switching etc..
→ CO timing and base idle adjustment.
→ Service light reset.
→ Instrument panel codes and actuators (gauges, warning lights) on some Volkswagen vehicles.

IMPORTANT NOTES:
• Fault code readers that only display code numbers can be misleading. 'Live engine data' is far more useful.
• A fault code will only be logged by a system if the component has failed open circuit or short to ground. If the component is working but incorrectly, like the hot engine showing a coolant reading of 20 degrees Celsius, this would only be seen using the component 'live data' option.
• Also it is highly recommended that any fault code is read, then deleted. The car should then be driven and re-tested to see if the code has returned, if it does then treat is as real.

TOP TIP!

• Many fault codes are introduced by people simply unplugging components – double-check before assuming a component fault!

We have dealt in outline with the type of ACR pods and cables used for the vehicles covered by this manual. Other vehicles and other manufacturer's vehicle groups require their own modules and their own specific setting-up approaches. In each case, the set-up is described in the Sykes-Pickavant manual supplied with the relevant ROM pod.

JOB 3: CONTACT BREAKER POINTS (early vehicles only) - *check/replace*.

See *Chapter 5, Servicing*.

JOB 4: IGNITION TIMING - *check/set*.

See *Chapter 6, Part B: Which Engine is Which?* for an explanation of the engine types referred to here.

IMPORTANT NOTE:
1.4 AND 1.6 LITRE ALUMINIUM ENGINES: There are several important and completely different features on these engines – see *Chapter 6, Part P: 1.4 and 1.6 litre Aluminium Block Engine – Specific info.*

Section A: Background information.

FACT FILE

ENGINES WITH KNOCK SENSORS

The ignition timing on these engines is constantly monitored and is set automatically as the engine is running. In the majority of cases, no ignition timing adjustments are either necessary or possible, except:
• Some 1.4 and 1.6 engines, such as those with engine codes AEE and AEX, are designed to have their ignition timing set with a VW test module fitted to the TDC indicator in the bellhousing.
• It might be possible to set the ignition timing on these engines by traditional means, but we cannot be sure that it will be so for all engines of this type.
• The timing figures quoted by VW are: **WHEN CHECKING:** 3 degrees to 8 degrees BTDC; **WHEN ADJUSTING:** 5 degrees to 7 degrees BTDC, both with engine speed at 1150 to 1400 rpm.
• IMPORTANT NOTE:
If there are no timing marks on the flywheel, or they are not accessible as described in the following section, the timing can only be tested with specialist test equipment.

□ **STEP A1:** The knock sensor is a device for detecting when the ignition is too far advanced (leading to 'engine knock') and retarding the ignition timing accordingly. On many 4-cylinder and all 6-cylinder engines, the knock sensor is bolted to the front of the engine block, towards the centre and quite low down…

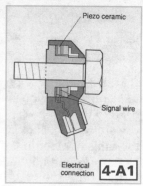

□ **STEP A2:** …while on other engines, the knock sensor is on the opposite side of the engine, at the rear of the block.

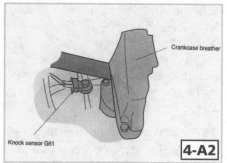

□ **STEP A3:** This is a typical layout of the type of ignition system where no adjustment of any sort is possible. Note the transformer (2) which combines some of the role of distributor and coil, while engine speed and position are taken care of by the Hall sender unit (9) fitted to the top-end of the engine. The knock sensor here is item (6). Other main items are connectors (3, 5 and 8), HT lead (1) and cable guide (12).

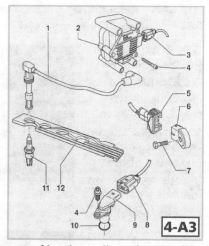

□ **STEP A4:** Ignition timing is taken care of by the Hall sender unit which scans the three teeth on the sender wheel.

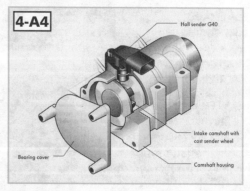

IMPORTANT NOTES:
OLDER ENGINES NOT ORIGINALLY SPECIFIED FOR UNLEADED FUEL:

- If the ignition timing has been changed to allow an engine to run on unleaded fuel, the timing marks on the flywheel, referred to below, will not apply.
- It will then be necessary to adjust the timing using a relatively sophisticated stroboscopic timing light - one which is capable of being adjusted to give different readings from the TDC mark on the flywheel.

ALL ENGINE TYPES:
- There are very many different ignition and associated carburation/injection systems fitted to the vehicles covered here.
- We believe, after exhaustive research, that the following data is correct. However, it has not been possible to confirm that this is so in every specific case, especially since much of the published data is contradictory or appears to be incomplete.
- If in doubt, consult your local Volkswagen dealership.

FACT FILE

DISTRIBUTORS WITH VACUUM ADVANCE

☐ **STEP A5:** Check to see if the distributor has a vacuum advance unit - see illustrations in *Chapter 5, Servicing*.
- On all the following models with a vacuum advance unit...
→ ALL MK 1 AND MK 2, 1.1 AND 1.3 ENGINES WITH VACUUM CONTROL.
→ 1.5, 1.6 AND 1.8 ENGINES WITH CONTACT BREAKER POINTS AND *SINGLE* VACUUM UNIT ON DISTRIBUTOR.
→ MK 1, 1.6 AND 1.8 ENGINES WITH BOSCH K-JETRONIC INJECTION.
-disconnect and plug the ends of the vacuum advance pipes, at the distributor.
- On all the following models with *dual* vacuum advance units...
→ OTHER TYPES, INCLUDING 1.5, 1.6 AND 1.8 ENGINES - the vacuum pipes should be left connected.

☐ **STEP A6:** Before checking the ignition timing:
→ The engine must be at its normal operating temperature.
→ The idle speed adjustment must be correct - see *Job 8*.

Section B: Timing marks – locating.

'INTERNAL WATER PUMP' ENGINES

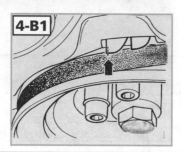
4-B1

☐ **STEP B1:** This is the position on early 1.1 engines with contact breakers.

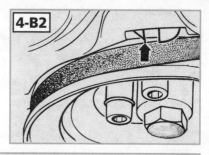
4-B2

☐ **STEP B2:** This is the position on early 1.3 engines with contact breakers.

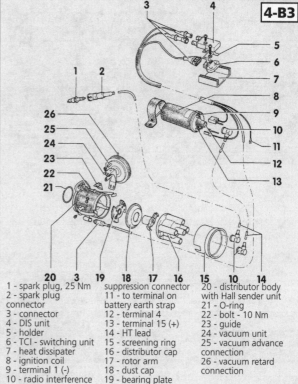
4-B3

1 - spark plug, 25 Nm	suppression connector	20 - distributor body
2 - spark plug connector	11 - to terminal on battery earth strap	with Hall sender unit
3 - connector	12 - terminal 4	21 - O-ring
4 - DIS unit	13 - terminal 15 (+)	22 - bolt - 10 Nm
5 - holder	14 - HT lead	23 - guide
6 - TCI - switching unit	15 - screening ring	24 - vacuum unit
7 - heat dissipater	16 - distributor cap	25 - vacuum advance connection
8 - ignition coil	17 - rotor arm	26 - vacuum retard connection
9 - terminal 1 (-)	18 - dust cap	
10 - radio interference	19 - bearing plate	

☐ **STEP B3:** This, for identification, is the TCI-H ignition system fitted to some 1.1 and 1.3 litre engines...

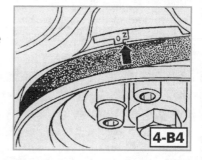
4-B4

☐ **STEP B4:** ...and this is the position of the timing marks.

'EXTERNAL WATER PUMP' ENGINES

☐ **STEP B5:** Locate the timing mark opening in the transmission bellhousing. Note that the '0' mark stands for TDC (or zero advance). Look for another mark - this indicates the correct timing for the engine you are working on.

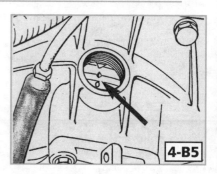
4-B5

TOP-DEAD-CENTRE MARKS IN TRANSMISSION OPENING

• On earliest vehicles with a TDC sensor (including USA cars) with manual transmission, remove the cable from the TDC sensor on the bellhousing. Using a 'male' hexagonal wrench, unscrew and remove the sensor. The TDC marks will now be visible.

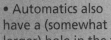

☐ **STEP B6:** On later cars with manual transmissions, remove the plastic plug from the TDC sensor hole.
• Automatics also have a (somewhat larger) hole in the transmission bellhousing.

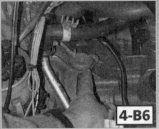

4-B6

2.6 LITRE, VR6 ENGINES

No manual adjustments are required - or possible - on any of these engines.

OHC AND OHV ALUMINIUM BLOCK ENGINES

Section C: Timing - checking and adjusting.

No manual adjustments are required - or possible - on any of these engines.

IMPORTANT NOTE: Some engines have extra requirements. Check *FACT FILE: SPECIAL PROCEDURES* at the end of this sequence.

☐ **STEP C1:** Connect a stroboscopic lamp with integral rev. counter, in accordance with the manufacturer's instructions. The timing light should always be connected to No. 1 spark plug lead - the one nearest the timing belt end of the engine.

4-C1

☐ **STEP C2:** Start the engine and run it at the engines regular tick-over speed - see *Chapter 1, Facts and Figures*.

☐ **STEP C3:** Point the timing light at the timing point and ensure that the relevant marks line up on the flywheel or crankshaft pulley.

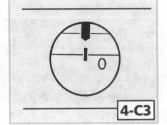

4-C3

☐ **STEP C4:** If the reading is 'out' stop the engine and slacken the clamp nut/s on the distributor so that the distributor can just be turned with firm hand pressure.

4-C4

→ Turn the distributor a very small amount, restart the engine and check again.
→ Repeat the procedure until, with the engine running, the relevant timing marks line up.
→ Retighten the nut/s securing the distributor to the engine block.

SPECIAL PROCEDURES

ENGINES WITH ELECTRONIC IGNITION
• Connecting a tachometer (rev. counter) to some engines with electronic ignition can damage the ignition system. Check with the equipment instructions that the tachometer you will be using will be suitable for your engine.
• Never use a test bulb instead of a stroboscopic timing light. It might damage the ignition system.
1.8 ENGINES WITH *TCI-H* (TRANSISTORISED) ELECTRONIC IGNITION
• Observe the *SAFETY FIRST!* precautions shown earlier.
• On engines with engine code DX, JH, JJ and KT: disconnect the vacuum hose from the vacuum unit.

☐ **STEP C5:** On engines with DIS idle speed control (the DIS unit is fitted above the control unit on the firewall), pull the two plugs off the unit and join them together, as shown.

4-C5

1.8 ENGINES WITH *DIGIFANT* ELECTRONIC IGNITION
• Raise the engine idle speed to a minimum of 2,100 rpm four times, to cancel the computer controlled hot start idle speed function, then allow the engine to idle normally.

☐ **STEP C6. 1.8 ENGINES WITH *DIGIFANT* ELECTRONIC IGNITION:** Unplug the coolant temperature connector (usually blue, and connected

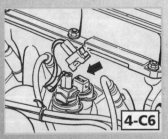

4-C6

to the temperature sensor connector.
→ Set the timing at 2,000 to 2,5000 rpm.
→ Re-attach the plug to the coolant temperature sender, give three bursts on the throttle, then check the idle speed again.

FACT FILE

STEP C7: VEHICLES FROM LATE 1975-ON: From late 1975, a TDC sensor is fitted over the flywheel and may be used with Volkswagen's own test equipment to give TDC and

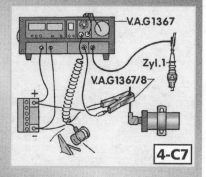

4-C7

advance setting readings. Those without access to the Volkswagen equipment will have to use a stroboscopic timing light.

STEP C8: CHECK THE MECHANICAL AND VACUUM ADVANCE SYSTEMS (when fitted):
→ Disconnect the vacuum advance pipe and, with the timing light connected, check the position of the timing marks at tick-over.
→ Increase the engine speed to approximately 2,000 rpm, with the timing light still pointed at the timing marks. If the position is no further advanced than it was, the mechanical advance system inside the distributor is probably seized.
→ Stop the engine, reconnect the vacuum advance pipe and repeat the procedure.
→ You should see a further amount of advance taking place and if not, the diaphragm inside the vacuum advance mechanism is probably punctured.

STEP C9: If either or both of these faults have occurred, your engine will run uneconomically and inefficiently and it will pay you to fit a new or exchange distributor.

4-C9

JOB 5: IGNITION COIL - *replacement*.

STEP 1: Locate the coil (when fitted - see *Job 1: Systems - explained*) usually at the rear of the engine bay.

5-1

STEP 2: Make sure the ignition is switched off and disconnect all LT (the smaller, low tension) wires from the coil, making note of their locations for refitting.

STEP 3: Unplug the HT (the thicker, high tension) lead to the distributor at the coil end. Undo the mountings and remove the coil.

STEP 4: Mount the new coil, remake all connections correctly and firmly.

JOB 6: DISTRIBUTOR – *removal, refitting*.

See *Chapter 6, Part B: Which Engine is Which?* for an explanation of the engine types referred to here.

IMPORTANT NOTE:
1.4 AND 1.6 LITRE ALUMINIUM ENGINES: There are several important and completely different features on these engines – see *Chapter 6, Part P: 1.4 and 1.6 litre Aluminium Block Engine – Specific info.*

Section A: All-electronic ignition.

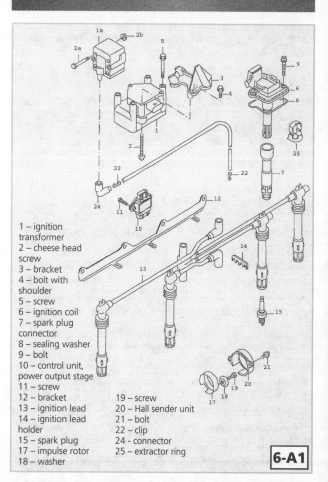

1 – ignition transformer
2 – cheese head screw
3 – bracket
4 – bolt with shoulder
5 – screw
6 – ignition coil
7 – spark plug connector
8 – sealing washer
9 – bolt
10 – control unit, power output stage
11 – screw
12 – bracket
13 – ignition lead
14 – ignition lead holder
15 – spark plug
17 – impulse rotor
18 – washer
19 – screw
20 – Hall sender unit
21 – bolt
22 – clip
24 – connector
25 – extractor ring

6-A1

STEP A1: Some later models are not fitted with a rotating distributor - see *Job 1: Systems - explained*. This section does not apply to those engines.

Section B: 'Internal water pump' engines.

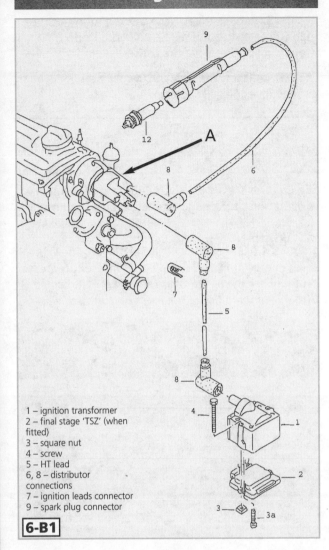

1 – ignition transformer
2 – final stage 'TSZ' (when fitted)
3 – square nut
4 – screw
5 – HT lead
6, 8 – distributor connections
7 – ignition leads connector
9 – spark plug connector

6-B1

☐ **STEP B1:** IMPORTANT NOTE:

• Earlier engines do not have the electronic components shown here. The distributor body (**A**) is bolted to the end of the cylinder head. The distributor can only be fitted in one position; the camshaft/ distributor shaft mating components are offset. Replace the plates fitted beneath the unit, when fitted and replace the O-ring when refitting.

Parts that can easily be tested and replaced (see *Chapter 5, Servicing* for checks) are:
→ screening ring connections.
→ distributor rotor arm, if burned or cracked.
→ distributor cap.
→ vacuum advance unit (when fitted) if sucking on connections fails to make unit work. Unscrew unit from distributor body.
→ contact breaker unit and capacitor.

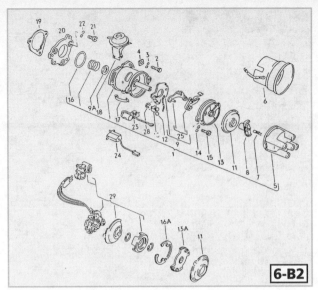

6-B2

☐ **STEP B2: 1.05 AND (LATER) 1.3 LITRE ENGINES:** The top set of parts are for the contact-breaker distributor, and the bottom set are for the fully electronic-type. They consist of:
→ screening ring (**6**) connections.
→ distributor rotor arm (**8**), if burned or cracked.
→ distributor cap (**5**).
→ vacuum advance unit (**18**) if sucking on connections fails to make unit work. Unscrew unit from distributor body.
→ contact breaker unit (**25**) and capacitor (**23**). The electronic type requires no maintenance and rarely goes wrong. It cannot be diagnosed without specialised equipment and should NOT be stripped down for repair. See *SAFETY FIRST!* below.

SAFETY FIRST!

• **FURTHER PRECAUTIONS** - To be taken when a vehicle has electronic ignition:

→ **Never attempt to start the car with poor battery connections.**

→ **Do not use a fast charger to start the engine.**

→ **Don't disconnect the battery while the engine is running.**

→ **Before fast charging - disconnect the battery.**

→ **Remove the ECU (electronic control unit) before putting the car in a bodyshop paint oven over 80 degrees Celsius.**

→ **Make sure the ignition is OFF before plugging in or unplugging the ECU multi-plug.**

→ **When electric welding - disconnect the battery.**

Section C: 'External water pump' engines.

Read the instructions for *Section B: 'Internal water pump' engines*, especially with regard to *SAFETY FIRST!* and regarding the types of repair work can that can and cannot be carried out on mechanical and electronic distributors.

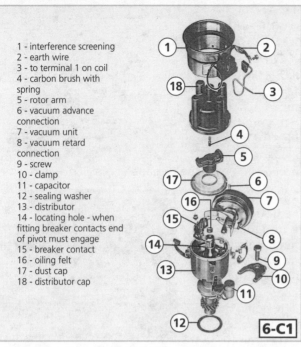

1 - interference screening
2 - earth wire
3 - to terminal 1 on coil
4 - carbon brush with spring
5 - rotor arm
6 - vacuum advance connection
7 - vacuum unit
8 - vacuum retard connection
9 - screw
10 - clamp
11 - capacitor
12 - sealing washer
13 - distributor
14 - locating hole - when fitting breaker contacts end of pivot must engage
15 - breaker contact
16 - oiling felt
17 - dust cap
18 - distributor cap

6-C1

❏ **STEP C1:** These are the components of the basic, non-electronic contact breaker distributor fitted to 'Internal water pump' engines.

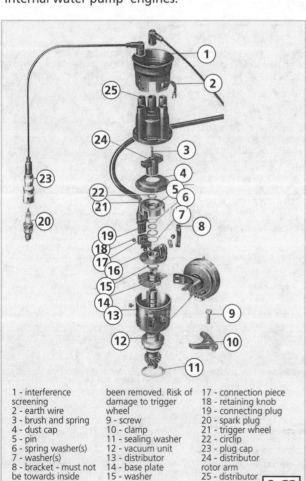

1 - interference screening
2 - earth wire
3 - brush and spring
4 - dust cap
5 - pin
6 - spring washer(s)
7 - washer(s)
8 - bracket - must not be towards inside when dust cap has

been removed. Risk of damage to trigger wheel
9 - screw
10 - clamp
11 - sealing washer
12 - vacuum unit
13 - distributor
14 - base plate
15 - washer
16 - Hall sender

17 - connection piece
18 - retaining knob
19 - connecting plug
20 - spark plug
21 - trigger wheel
22 - circlip
23 - plug cap
24 - distributor rotor arm
25 - distributor cap

6-C2

❏ **STEP C2:** These are the components of the semi-electronic system. The electronic components are NOT repairable and should not be broken down.

❏ **STEP C3:** These are the fully electronic system distributor unit, still with vacuum advance unit (**14A**) and fitted to the engine block via the screw, washer and plate (**11, 10** and **9**) seen on earlier types. The electronic components are NOT repairable and should not be broken down.

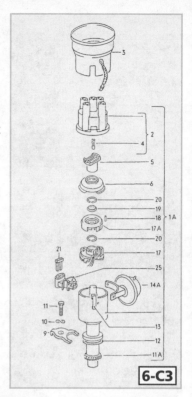

6-C3

❏ **STEP C4:** Distributor removal is easily carried out by taking out the fixing screw, lifting off the plate and pulling out the distributor.

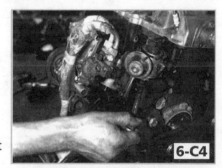

6-C4

❏ **STEP C5: TO REPLACE THE DISTRIBUTOR:** Set the flywheel to TDC on No. 1 cylinder. See *Chapter 6, Engine* for the relevant information. If the engine is out, and the flywheel is off, use the TDC mark on the front crank pulley and align it with the mark on the timing belt cover.

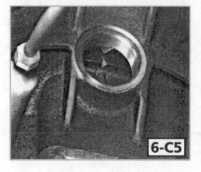

6-C5

☐ **STEP C6:** Align the mark on the camshaft sprocket with the cylinder head.

6-C6

TOP TIP!

• The oldest vehicles do not have a mark on the camshaft sprocket.
• In this case, turn the engine until the cams for No. 1 cylinder both point upwards, evenly.

☐ **STEP C7:** Make sure the distributor engagement lug on the oil pump shaft, inside the block, is correctly aligned. There will be one of two locations, depending on where the threaded hole for the clamp plate is situated.

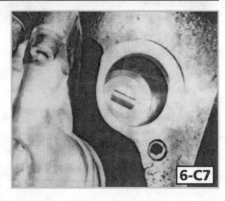
6-C7

☐ **STEP C8: ENGINES WITH CLAMP PLATE HOLE AWAY FROM BLOCK:** When the clamp plate threaded hole (a) is in this position, the drive shaft on the oil pump (b) should lie *parallel* with the crankshaft.

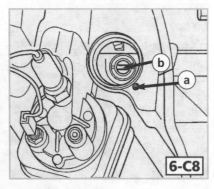
6-C8

☐ **STEP C9: DISTRIBUTORS WITH ALIGNING PINS:** Some distributors have two aligning pins, as shown here. When fitted, the pins should lie each side of the threaded hole (arrowed).

6-C9

☐ **STEP C10: ENGINES WITH CLAMP PLATE HOLE NEAR THE BLOCK:** When the clamp plate threaded hole (c) is in this position, the drive shaft on the oil pump (d) should align with the threaded hole.

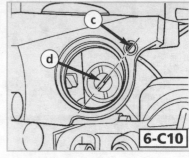
6-C10

☐ **STEP C11:** To fit the distributor:
➜ Turn the rotor so that it is pointing to the mark on the distributor or Hall sender body (depending on age and type of distributor).
➜ Insert the distributor
➜ Adjust the dwell angle and ignition timing - see *Job 4*.

6-C11

TOP TIP!

• Before inserting the distributor, turn the rotor arm slightly to the right of the distributor marking shown in *Step C11*.
• As the distributor is inserted, the rotor arm will turn back towards the marking.
• If the markings shown in *Step C11* are not properly aligned, remove the distributor and reinsert it, changing the rotor arm starting position slightly - do NOT change the oil pump drive shaft position shown in *Step C10*.

JOB 7: LAMBDA SENSOR (engines with cat.) - *testing, replacement*.

Section A: Removing, replacing.

☐ **STEP A1:** The Lambda sensor is:
➜ EITHER screwed into the exhaust manifold (b)
➜ OR the exhaust system (a).

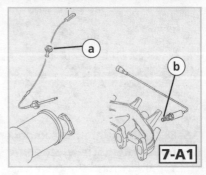
7-A1

STEP A2: Trace the wiring back from the sensor and disconnect the plug. Unscrew the sensor from the manifold or exhaust system.

7-A2

FACT FILE

LAMBDA SENSOR

• The Lambda sensor is very fragile and should not be knocked or dropped.
• No cleaners should be used on the sensor.

STEP A3: Before refitting, check that the sensor sealing ring is in good condition, and lubricate the thread of the sensor with a high-temperature anti-seize compound.

Section B: Testing.

SAFETY FIRST!

• Beware of hot exhaust components, which can burn badly - wear suitable industrial gloves.

• Work only with the vehicle passing its exhaust gases directly to outdoors, never in an enclosed space.

STEP B1: You will need a Lambda sensor tester, such as this Sykes-Pickavant unit which is simply connected up to the sensor wiring as described in the tester manual.

7-B1

STEP B2: Prepare for the test as follows:
→ Run engine to normal full running temperature (fan turns on and off twice).
→ If engine already hot, run for 30 seconds at 3,000

rpm to heat Lambda sensor and ensure exhaust gas at correct temperature.
→ Allow engine to slow to normal tick-over. If testing is prolonged, run engine up to 3,000 rpm for 30 seconds at intervals.

STEP B3: Check the voltage at the sensor. The average should be about 0.45 to 0.5 volts but it's okay if it fluctuates between 0.2 and 0.8 volts. (Illustration, courtesy Sykes-Pickavant.)

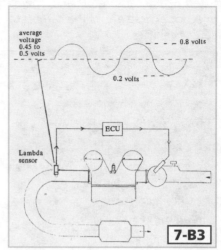
7-B3

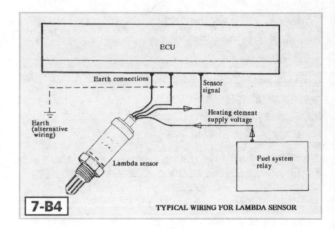
7-B4   TYPICAL WIRING FOR LAMBDA SENSOR

STEP B4: If readings are outside these limits:
→ If the reading is consistently too high (mixture too strong), snap the throttle open several times and see if the level readjusts itself to within the acceptable range.
→ If the reading is too low (mixture too weak), weaken the mixture - try running without air cleaner - and see if the level readjusts itself to within the acceptable range.
→ If not, the Lambda sensor is probably faulty. (Illustration, courtesy Sykes-Pickavant.)

STEP B5: Some Lambda sensors also have a heating element. Typically, the supply is from the fuel system relay - check wiring diagrams - and the earth/ground will be via a separate cable, either to the ECU, or direct to an earth/ground point. To check the heating element, disconnect the plug and check the resistance across the heating element wires. A typical resistance is 5 to 10 ohms. A faulty element usually gives no reading (short circuit) or a very high reading (open circuit).

JOB 8: CARBURETOR - *adjustment*.

From around 1990, none of these vehicles has been fitted with a carburetor, all of them using fuel injection. These are all the carburetor types fitted to earlier vehicles.

		Page No
Type A:	PICT - 1.1 litre engines.	9-16
Type B:	PIC - 1.3 litre engines.	9-16
Type C:	TLA - 1.1 litre engines.	9-17
Type D:	2E3 - 1.3 litre engines.	9-18
Type E:	1B3 - 1.1 and 1.5 litre engines.	9-19
Type F:	31/34 PICT -1.1, 1.3 ,1.5 and 1.6 litre engines.	9-19
Type G:	2B2 and 2B5 - 1.5 and 1.6 litre engines.	9-20
Type H:	Keihin - 1.6 litre engines (Sweden, Austria and low-octane engines only).	9-21
Type I:	2E2 - 1.6 and 1.8 litre engines.	9-22
Type J:	2EE (Not adjustable) - 1.6 and 1.8 litre engines.	9-23

FACT FILE
TAMPER PROOFING

• Many carburetors originally had a tamper-proof seal placed over the mixture adjustment screw.
• These seals are to prevent anyone unauthorised from altering the mixture and exhaust emissions.
• In certain countries these seals must be retained by law.
• If the seal is a plastic cap placed over the adjuster screw, it can be broken off with pliers.
• If it is a plug within the screw recess, force it out with a sharp object.

USA MODELS AND THOSE IN SOME OTHER STATES
• It may be illegal for an unauthorised person to remove tamperproof plugs on carburetors or fuel injection systems.

GENERAL

Setting the idle speed and mixture is not just a matter of making the car run smoothly and economically; it's also a question of allowing it to run within the legal hydrocarbon (HC), Nitrous Oxide (NO) and carbon monoxide (CO) emission limits for the territory in which you live. However, a worn engine will fail even if the carburetor or injection system is set up correctly.

CARBURETOR SYSTEMS

Volkswagen seem to have had a liking for varying the types of carburetors fitted to their vehicles over the years. All are shown here, even though several are clearly close relatives of one another!

FACT FILE
ESSENTIAL PREPARATIONS

• When tuning the engine you should adjust the carburetor (when fitted) last of all, as their settings will be affected by the state of tune of the rest of the engine.
• Ignition dwell angle and timing must be correct, the air filter should be clean, there should be no air leaks on the induction system, and all electrical consumers and the air conditioning (if fitted) should be switched off (unless stated otherwise in the instructions given below.
• Run the engine up to full operating temperature before checking and adjusting.
• If you warm the engine on tick-over (instead of on a journey), it won't be hot enough until you have heard the electric cooling fan cut in at least twice.
• Make sure there are no holes or leaks in the exhaust system.

TOP TIP!

• These Jobs require the use of a tachometer (rev-counter) and an exhaust gas analyser to carry out the work successfully. If you don't own them - and relatively inexpensive tools are now available - you may wish to have the work carried out by your local **Volkswagen** dealer.

FACT FILE
CARBURETTOR TYPES AND ADJUSTER SCREWS

• There is a variety of 'correct' terms for adjustment screws.
• In **Volkswagen** parlance, the terms 'idle speed' refers to the tick-over speed, and 'CO' refers to the richness of the mixture, usually at tick-over.

IDLE SPEED ADJUSTMENT
• Connect a rev-counter according to the maker's instructions, and check the idle speed. Turning the screw clockwise increases the idle speed, anti-clockwise reduces it. Set the idle speed in accordance with *Chapter 1, Facts and Figures* or the figures given in the following sequences.
• *ROUGH GUIDE: Turn the screw until the engine is running at the slowest speed at which it runs smoothly and evenly.*

Continued over page

FACT FILE *Continued*

CO ADJUSTMENT

• Check that the idle speed is correct and make sure that the engine is at full operating temperature. Connect an exhaust gas analyser as instructed by the maker. If the CO reading is outside the range shown in the following sequence, or the legal limits for your territory, adjustment is required.

• Use a narrow-blade screwdriver and turn the adjuster screw clockwise to weaken (reduce) or anti-clockwise to richen (increase) the reading.

• *ROUGH GUIDE: As you turn the mixture screw inwards (clockwise), the tick-over speed will increase, until the point comes where the engine starts to run 'lumpily'. Back off the screw until the engine runs smoothly again, and then some more until the speed just starts to drop. At this point, screw the adjuster back in by a quarter-turn and you'll be somewhere near the optimum setting for smooth running.*

• IMPORTANT NOTE:
After setting the mixture adjustment, re-check and, if necessary, re-adjust the idle speed.

• If there is a very large deviation when checking the CO figure (of over 1%), **Volkswagen** recommend that the CO adjustment screw is removed and cleaned (as well as the housing, with the 2E2 carburetor) before trying to set the carburetor. Clean the point of the adjustment screw and the drillings in the 2E2 carburetor's housing.

TOP TIP!

• In every case where the crankcase breather hose has been disconnected in order to adjust the carburetor, the CO level will probably rise after the hose is reconnected. This is because stopping and starting the engine introduces fuel into the crankcase. After a long, fast drive, CO levels will return to normal.

Type A: PICT - 1.1 litre engines.and Type B: PIC - 1.3 litre engines.

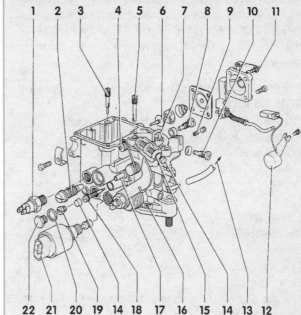

Engine codes - GF, GG, GS
Note: Take note of different arrangement of idling and auxiliary fuel jets on versions '1', '2' and '3'.
1 - thermostatic switch for partial throttle channel heating
2 - idling speed adjusting screw - check O-ring for damage
3 - auxiliary fuel/air jet
4 - roller catch for smooth running notch - approx. 08/81-on
5 - air correction jet and emulsion tube
6 - mushroom valve
7 - injection pipe
8 - auxiliary fuel jet (version '1') - pilot jet (version '2')
9 - auxiliary fuel jet - (versions '2')
10 - pilot jet (versions '1' and '3')
11 - stop screw
12 - partial throttle channel heater - contact surface must be in contact with carburetor body (earth connection)
13 - to carburetor upper body
14 - sealing cap
15 - stop screw
16 - modification number
17 - connection for 'advance' vacuum pipe from distributor
18 - CO adjusting screw - check O-ring for damage
19 - main jet
20 - sealing washer
21 - bypass cut-off valve, 5 Nm - should click when ignition is switched on; with the valve removed, the pin must first be pushed in 3 to 4 mm
22 - main jet plug

8-B1

❏ **STEP B1:** And this is the main body of the **PIC** carburetor.

ADJUSTING IDLE AND CO SETTINGS - BOTH TYPES:

➔ Disconnect hose from air cleaner and seal the end of the hose.
➔ Ensure choke is fully open (turned OFF).

Engine codes - FA, FJ
1 - air correction jet and emulsion tube
2 - injection pipe
3 - auxiliary fuel jet
4 - pilot jet
5 - adjusting nut
6 - partial throttle channel heater
7 - sealing cap
8 - from carburetor upper body
9 - stop screw - cold idling speed
10 - stop screw - basic throttle adjustment
11 - connection for 'advance' vacuum hose from distributor vacuum unit
12 - CO adjusting screw
13 - bypass cut-off valve, 5 Nm - must click when the ignition is switched on; with the valve removed, the pin must first be pushed in 3 to 4 mm
14 - sealing washer
15 - main jet plug
16 - main jet
17 - idling speed adjusting screw - check O-ring for damage

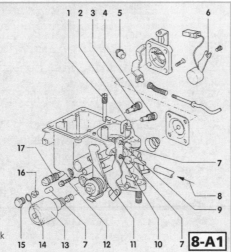

8-A1

❏ **STEP A1:** This, for reference is the main body of the **PICT** carburetor.

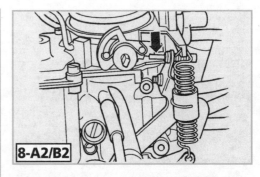

8-A2/B2

❏ **STEP A2/B2:** Check that the cold-idle device is not operating when the engine is idling at normal running temperature. Adjust if necessary (arrowed).
➔ All electrical components must be turned OFF and the cooling fan must not be running.

AIR CLEANERS WITH SUMMER/WINTER POSITION:
Set to Summer position while carrying out work.
ENGINE CODE *GS* WITH EXHAUST AFTERBURNING:
Disconnect hoses from non-return valves and seal valve connections.

❑ **STEP A/B3: SCIROCCO WITH *DIS* IDLE SPED REGULATION:**
Disconnect both connectors from the **DIS** unit and connect them together (arrowed).

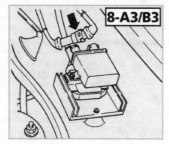

8-A3/B3

❑ **STEP A4/B4:** Turn the idle speed adjustment screw (**1**) if necessary to adjust the speed. Turn the CO adjusting screw (**2**). then readjust the idle speed, if necessary. Fit a new anti-tamper cap to the CO adjustment screw.

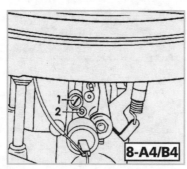

8-A4/B4

FACT FILE

VOLKSWAGEN RECOMMENDED SETTINGS (TYPES A and B)

Engine Code	Carburettor Type	Idling speed(rpm)	CO content (% by vol.)
FA and FJ (08/74-on)	34 PICT-5	950 ± 50	1.5 ± 0.5
FA and FJ (12/74-on)	34 PICT-5	950 ± 50	1.5 ± 0.5
FA and FJ (05/75-on)	31 PICT-5	950 ± 50	1.5 ± 0.5
FA (08/78-on)	31 PICT-5	950 ± 50	1.5 ± 0.5
GF (08/79-on)	34 PIC-5	950 ± 50*	1.0 ± 0.5
GF (10/81-on)	34 PIC-6	950 ± 50*	1.0 ± 0.5
GF (01/82-on)	34 PIC-6	950 ± 50*	1.0 ± 0.5
GG (08/79-on)	31 PIC-6	950 ± 50	1.0 ± 0.5
GG to 799 900 (08/81-on)	31 PIC-7	950 ± 50	1.0 ± 0.5
GG (Formule E) - 800 000-on (01/81-on)	31 PIC-6	950 ± 50	1.0 ± 0.5
GG (Formule E) - 800 000-on (08/81-on)	31 PIC-7	950 ± 50	1.0 ± 0.5
GS	34 PIC-6	950 ± 50	1.5 ± 0.5

Continued...

FACT FILE *Continued...*

* Scirocco with **TCI-H** ignition system and **DIS**. Testing level: 850 to 950 rpm, setting level: 850 ± 50 rpm

IMPORTANT NOTE: On vehicles not originally fitted with a catalytic converter but which have had one fitted at a later date, the CO level measured in the tailpipe can drop to 0% even though the carburetor is correctly adjusted. Adjustment is only necessary if the maximum level is exceeded or the engine runs unevenly at idling speed.

Type C: TLA - 1.1 litre engines.

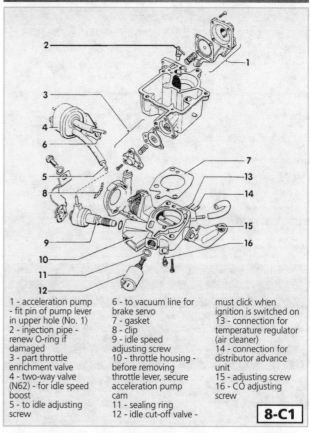

1 - acceleration pump - fit pin of pump lever in upper hole (No. 1)
2 - injection pipe - renew O-ring if damaged
3 - part throttle enrichment valve
4 - two-way valve (N62) - for idle speed boost
5 - to idle adjusting screw
6 - to vacuum line for brake servo
7 - gasket
8 - clip
9 - idle speed adjusting screw
10 - throttle housing - before removing throttle lever, secure acceleration pump cam
11 - sealing ring
12 - idle cut-off valve -
must click when ignition is switched on
13 - connection for temperature regulator (air cleaner)
14 - connection for distributor advance unit
15 - adjusting screw
16 - CO adjusting screw

8-C1

❑ **STEP C1:** This, for reference is the main body of the **Weber 32 TLA** carburetor.

ADJUSTING IDLE AND CO SCREWS:
➜ Disconnect hose from air cleaner and seal the end of the hose.
➜ Ensure choke is fully open (turned OFF).

❑ **STEP C2:** Check that the cold-idle device is not operating when the engine is idling at normal running temperature. Adjust screw (**1**) on cam (**2**) if necessary.
➜ All electrical components must be turned OFF and the cooling fan must not be running.

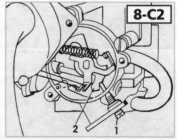

8-C2

STEP C3: ENGINES FROM JULY 1985-ON: Pull connector (a) from 2-way valve (b). (Here, the valve is being examined with a diode test lamp (VAG 1527 shown). Below 700 rpm, LED should light up; above 1,100 rpm, LED should go out.)

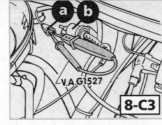

8-C3

STEP C4. Turn the idle speed adjustment screw (arrowed) if necessary to adjust the speed. A = up to June 1985. B = July 1985-on.

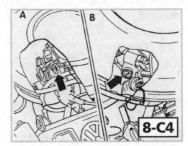

8-C4

STEP C5: Turn the CO adjusting screw (arrowed) then readjust the idle speed, if necessary. Fit a new anti-tamper cap to the CO adjustment screw.

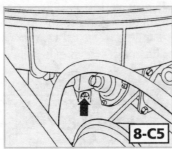

8-C5

FACT FILE

VOLKSWAGEN RECOMMENDED SETTINGS (TYPE C)

Idle speed - 750 to 850 rpm.
CO content - 1.5 to 2.5% by vol.

Type D: 2E3 - 1.3 litre engines.

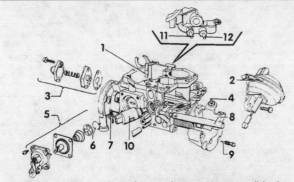

1 - injection pipe	6 - mushroom valve	Nm - must click when
2 - vacuum unit, stage II	7 - full throttle stop screw	ignition is switched on
3 - partial throttle enrichment valve - do not re-use valve after removal (replace)	8 - idling speed adjusting screw	11 – hose connector to temperature regulator
4 - adjusting screw - cold idling speed	9 - CO adjusting screw - replace O-ring if damaged	12 – hose connector to vacuum advance
5 - accelerator pump	10 - idle jet cut-off valve, tightened to 6	

8-D1

STEP D1: This, for reference is the main body of the 2E3 carburetor.

ADJUSTING IDLE AND CO SETTINGS:
→ Disconnect hose from air cleaner and seal the end of the hose.
→ Ensure choke is fully open (turned OFF).

STEP D2: Check that the cold-idle device is not operating when the engine is idling at normal running temperature. Adjust if necessary (2). If adjustment is out...

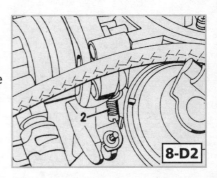

8-D2

STEP D3: ADJUSTING FAST (COLD ENGINE) IDLE: a) Set idle speed. **b)** Remove air cleaner and seal temp. regulator connection. **c)** Run engine to normal operating temp.,

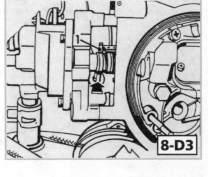

8-D3

open throttle to 2,500 rpm. Press down stepped cam plate (1) to its stop (arrowed) and release throttle. **d)** Ensure that the adjusting screw (see 8-D2) is on the second-highest step on the cam plate. Turn screw until engine speed is from 1,900 to 2,100 rpm.
→ The cooling fan must not be running and all electrical components must be turned OFF, EXCEPT...
→ ...main beam headlights must be turned ON.

STEP D4: Turn the idle speed adjustment screw (A), if necessary, to adjust the speed. To reach CO adjustment screw, remove sealing cap from cam plate guide hole. Turn the CO adjusting

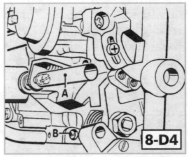

8-D4

screw (B). then readjust the idle speed, if necessary. Fit a new anti-tamper cap to the CO adjustment screw.

FACT FILE

VOLKSWAGEN RECOMMENDED SETTINGS (TYPE D)

Idle speed - 750 to 850 rpm.
CO content - 2.5 to 3.5% by vol.

Type E: 1B3 - 1.1 and 1.5 litre engines.

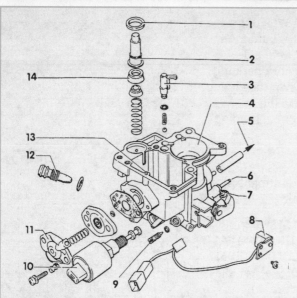

1 - bearing ring
2 - pump plunger
3 - injection tube
4 - bottom part of carburetor
5 - to pull-down unit
6 - connection for temperature regulator of air cleaner
7 - cold-idle adjusting screw
8 - part throttle channel heating
9 - CO adjusting screw - remove and clean adjusting screw and

connection if necessary before adjusting CO content
10 - bypass air cut-off valve, 5 Nm - must click when ignition is switched on
11 - part-load enrichment valve
12 - idle adjusting screw
13 - part-load enrichment nozzle
14 - collar

8-E1

☐ STEP E1: This, for reference is the main body of the PICT carburetor.

ADJUSTING IDLE AND CO SETTINGS - BOTH TYPES:
➔ Disconnect hose from air cleaner and seal the end of the hose.
➔ Ensure choke is fully open (turned OFF).

☐ STEP E2: Check that the cold-idle adjusting screw (**B**) is not making contact with the cam (**A**) when the engine is idling at normal running temperature. Adjust if necessary.
➔ All electrical components, inc. air conditioning, must be turned OFF and the cooling fan must not be running.

8-E2

☐ STEP E3: IDLE SPEED - ALL VEHICLES WITH *DIS* AUTOMATIC IDLE SPEED REGULATION: Disconnect both connectors from the **DIS** unit and connect them

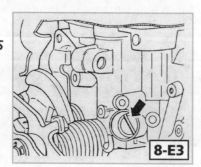

8-E3

together. See illustration **8-A3/B3**. Adjust the idling speed screw (arrowed).

☐ STEP E4: CO CONTENT SETTING - VEHICLES WITH *DIS* AUTOMATIC IDLE SPEED REGULATION BUT NOT WITH TCI-H IGNITION: With **DIS** unit connections still in their temporary positions, adjust the CO level screw (arrowed). Fit a new anti-tamper cap to the CO adjustment screw.

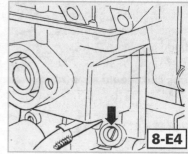

8-E4

CO CONTENT SETTING - VEHICLES WITH *DIS* AUTOMATIC IDLE SPEED REGULATION AND ALSO WITH TCI-H IGNITION: Stop engine, reconnect the **DIS** unit, restart engine and rev the engine with three bursts on the throttle. Adjust the CO level - see **8-E4**. Fit a new anti-tamper cap to the CO adjustment screw.

FACT FILE

VOLKSWAGEN RECOMMENDED SETTINGS (TYPE E)

Without DIS: Idle speed - 900 to 1,000 rpm. CO content - 0.5 to 1.5% by vol.
With DIS: Idle speed - 750 to 850 rpm. CO content - 0.5 to 1.5% by vol.

Type F: 31/34 PICT -1.1, 1.3 ,1.5 and 1.6 litre engines.

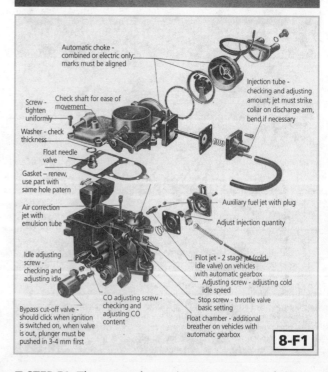

Automatic choke - combined or electric only; marks must be aligned

Injection tube - checking and adjusting amount; jet must strike collar on discharge arm, bend if necessary

Screw - tighten uniformly

Check shaft for ease of movement

Washer - check thickness

Float needle valve

Gasket – renew, use part with same hole patern

Air correction jet with emulsion tube

Auxiliary fuel jet with plug

Adjust injection quantity

Idle adjusting screw - checking and adjusting idle

Pilot jet - 2 stage jet (cold idle valve) on vehicles with automatic gearbox

Adjusting screw - adjusting cold idle speed

Stop screw - throttle valve basic setting

CO adjusting screw - checking and adjusting CO content

Bypass cut-off valve - should click when ignition is switched on, when valve is out, plunger must be pushed in 3-4 mm first

Float chamber - additional breather on vehicles with automatic gearbox

8-F1

☐ STEP F1: These are the main components of the earlier **34 PICT** carburetor.

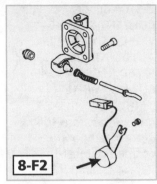

8-F2

☐ **STEP F2:** And this is an addition to the later **34 PIC** carburetor - a part-throttle channel heater (arrowed), whose contact surface must be earthed/grounded against the carb. body.

ADJUSTING IDLE AND CO SETTINGS - BOTH TYPES:
➜ Disconnect hose from air cleaner and seal the end of the hose.
➜ Ensure choke is fully open (turned OFF).

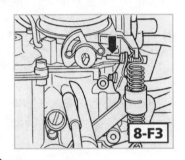

8-F3

☐ **STEP F3:** Check that the engine cold, fast-idle device is not operating when the engine is idling at normal running temperature. Adjust if necessary (arrowed). Should be 2,350 to 2,450 rpm after start-up.
➜ All electrical components must be turned OFF and the cooling fan must not be running.

AIR CLEANERS WITH SUMMER/WINTER POSITION:
Set to Summer position while carrying out work.

☐ **STEP F4: ENGINES WITH EXHAUST AFTERBURNING:**
Disconnect hoses from check valve (arrowed) and seal the valve opening.

VEHICLES WITH AUTO. TRANSMISSION:
Throttle cable setting must be correct.

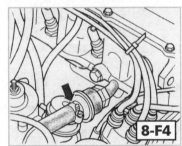

8-F4

To adjust the carburetor, refer to illustration **8-F1**. Turn the idle speed adjustment screw if necessary to adjust the speed. Turn the CO adjusting screw, then readjust the idle speed, if necessary. Fit a new anti-tamper cap to the CO adjustment screw.

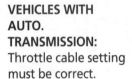

FACT FILE

VOLKSWAGEN RECOMMENDED SETTINGS (TYPE F)

1.5 litre engine: Idle speed - 900 to 1,000 rpm. CO content - 1.0 to 2.0% by vol.

1.6 litre engine: Idle speed - 900 to 1,000 rpm. CO content - 0.5 to 1.5% by vol.

1.6 (Sweden, Australia): Idle speed - 850 to 1,000 rpm. CO - 0.8 to 2.2% by vol.

Type G: 2B2 and 2B5 - 1.5 and 1.6 litre engines.

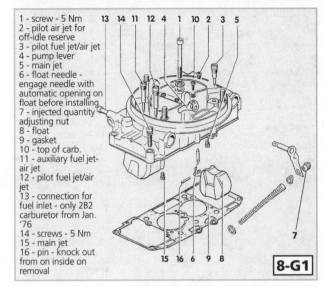

1 - screw - 5 Nm
2 - pilot air jet for off-idle reserve
3 - pilot fuel jet/air jet
4 - pump lever
5 - main jet
6 - float needle - engage needle with automatic opening on float before installing
7 - injected quantity adjusting nut
8 - float
9 - gasket
10 - top of carb.
11 - auxiliary fuel jet-air jet
12 - pilot fuel jet/air jet
13 - connection for fuel inlet - only 2B2 carburetor from Jan. '76
14 - screws - 5 Nm
15 - main jet
16 - pin - knock out from on inside on removal

8-G1

☐ **STEP G1:** This is both types of **2B** carburetor.

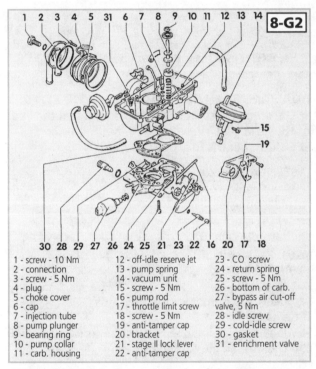

8-G2

1 - screw - 10 Nm	12 - off-idle reserve jet	23 - CO screw
2 - connection	13 - pump spring	24 - return spring
3 - screw - 5 Nm	14 - vacuum unit	25 - screw - 5 Nm
4 - plug	15 - screw - 5 Nm	26 - bottom of carb.
5 - choke cover	16 - pump rod	27 - bypass air cut-off valve, 5 Nm
6 - cap	17 - throttle limit screw	28 - idle screw
7 - injection tube	18 - screw - 5 Nm	29 - cold-idle screw
8 - pump plunger	19 - anti-tamper cap	30 - gasket
9 - bearing ring	20 - bracket	31 - enrichment valve
10 - pump collar	21 - stage II lock lever	
11 - carb. housing	22 - anti-tamper cap	

☐ **STEP G2:** This is the main body of the **2B2** carburetor to Dec. 1975, and the **2B5** carburetor.

FACT FILE

VOLKSWAGEN RECOMMENDED SETTINGS (TYPE G)

1.5: Idle speed - 900 to 1,000 rpm. CO content - 1.0 to 2.0% by vol.

1.6 without DIS: Idle speed - 900 to 1,000 rpm. CO content - 0.5 to 1.5% by vol.

1.6 with DIS: Idle speed - 750 to 850 rpm. CO content - 0.5 to 1.5% by vol.

CHAPTER 9 Part A Job 8

9-20

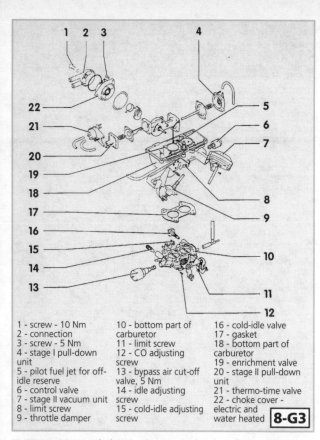

1 - screw - 10 Nm	10 - bottom part of carburetor	16 - cold-idle valve
2 - connection	11 - limit screw	17 - gasket
3 - screw - 5 Nm	12 - CO adjusting screw	18 - bottom part of carburetor
4 - stage I pull-down unit	13 - bypass air cut-off valve, 5 Nm	19 - enrichment valve
5 - pilot fuel jet for off-idle reserve	14 - idle adjusting screw	20 - stage II pull-down unit
6 - control valve	15 - cold-idle adjusting screw	21 - thermo-time valve
7 - stage II vacuum unit		22 - choke cover - electric and water heated
8 - limit screw		
9 - throttle damper		**8-G3**

❒ **STEP G3:** And this is the main body of the **2B2** carburetor from January 1976-on.

ADJUSTING IDLE AND CO SETTINGS - BOTH TYPES:
➔ Disconnect hose from air cleaner and seal the end of the hose.
➔ Ensure choke is fully open (turned OFF).

❒ **STEP G4:** Check that the engine cold, fast-idle adjuster screw (**A**) is not on the fast-idle cam (**B**) when the engine is idling at normal running temperature. Adjust if necessary.

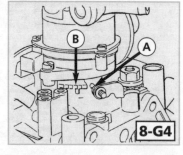

➔ All electrical components must be turned OFF and the cooling fan must not be running.

VEHICLES WITH AUTO. TRANSMISSION: Throttle cable setting must be correct.

VEHICLES WITH *DIS* AUTOMATIC IDLE SPEED REGULATION: Disconnect both connectors from the **DIS** unit and connect them together. See illustration *8-A3/B3*.

❒ **STEP G5:** Turn the idle speed adjustment screw (arrowed) if necessary to adjust the speed.

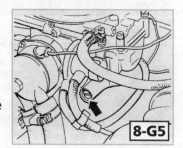

❒ **STEP G6: CO CONTENT SETTING - VEHICLES WITH *DIS* AUTOMATIC IDLE SPEED REGULATION BUT NOT WITH *TCI-H* IGNITION:** With **DIS** unit connections still in their temporary positions, adjust the CO level screw (arrowed). Fit a new anti-tamper cap to the CO adjustment screw.

CO CONTENT SETTING - VEHICLES WITH *DIS* AUTOMATIC IDLE SPEED REGULATION AND ALSO WITH *TCI-H* IGNITION: Stop engine, reconnect the **DIS** unit, restart engine and rev the engine with a burst on the throttle. (The idle speed should settle to 800 to 900 rpm. If it does not, the DIS unit is probably faulty - seek advice from your **Volkswagen** dealer.) You can now adjust the CO level - see *8-G6*. Fit a new anti-tamper cap to the CO adjustment screw.

Type H: Keihin - 1.6 litre engines (Sweden, Austria and low-octane engines only).

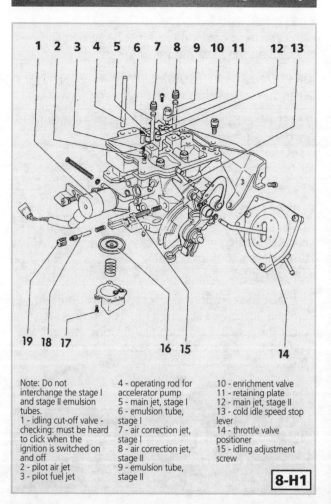

Note: Do not interchange the stage I and stage II emulsion tubes.	4 - operating rod for accelerator pump	10 - enrichment valve
1 - idling cut-off valve - checking: must be heard to click when the ignition is switched on and off	5 - main jet, stage I	11 - retaining plate
	6 - emulsion tube, stage I	12 - main jet, stage II
	7 - air correction jet, stage I	13 - cold idle speed stop lever
2 - pilot air jet	8 - air correction jet, stage II	14 - throttle valve positioner
3 - pilot fuel jet	9 - emulsion tube, stage II	15 - idling adjustment screw
		8-H1

❒ **STEP H1:** This, for reference is the main body of the **Keihin** carburetor to July 1978.

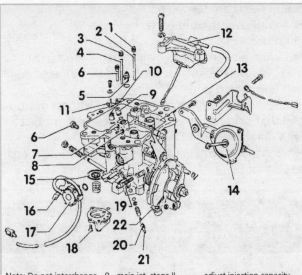

Note: Do not interchange the stage I and stage II emulsion tubes.
1 - air correction jet, stage II
2 - emulsion tube, stage II - holes at bottom
3 - air correction jet, stage I
4 - emulsion tube, stage I - holes at top
5 - enrichment valve
6 - plug
7 - pilot fuel jet
8 - pilot air jet
9 - main jet, stage II
10 - main jet, stage I
11 - retaining plate
12 - vacuum unit, stage II
13 - lower part of carburetor
14 - throttle valve positioner - for overrun boost (only manual gearbox 08/84-on); for idling speed boost (only automatic gearbox)
15 - diaphragm - for acceleration pump
16 - stop – bend to
adjust injection capacity
17 - idling cut-off valve
18 - screw
19 - idling adjustment screw
20 - CO adjustment screw
21 - anti-tamper cap
22 - adjusting screw - for overrun boost (only for manual gearbox 08/84-on); for idling speed boost (only for automatic gearbox)

8-H2

❒ **STEP H2:** And this is the main body of the **Keihin** carburetor from August 1978-on.

ADJUSTING IDLE AND CO SETTINGS - BOTH TYPES:
➔ **EARLY CARB:** Disconnect hose from cam cover and seal the end of the hose.
➔ **LATER CARB:** Disconnect hose from cam cover and route away from engine, so that only fresh air can be drawn into hose.
➔ Ensure choke is fully open (turned OFF).

❒ **STEP H3:** Check that the cold-idle device is not operating when the engine is idling at normal running temperature. Adjust the stop lever if necessary (arrowed).
➔ All electrical

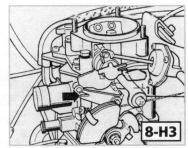

8-H3

components must be turned OFF and the cooling fan must not be running, EXCEPT...

EARLY CARB. ONLY: Headlight main beam must be ON.

AIR CLEANERS WITH SUMMER/WINTER POSITION: Set to
Summer position while carrying out work.

❒ **STEP H4: EARLY CARB:** Turn the idle speed adjustment

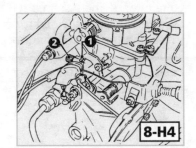

8-H4

screw (**1**) if necessary to adjust the speed. Turn the CO adjusting screw (**2**). then readjust the idle speed, if necessary. Fit a new anti-tamper cap to the CO adjustment screw.

❒ **STEP H5: LATER CARB.:** This is a later type of adjuster screw layout.

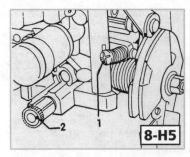

8-H5

❒ **STEP H6: LATEST CARB.:** These are the positions of the idle speed screw (**A**) and the CO adjustment screw (**B**) on latest engines.

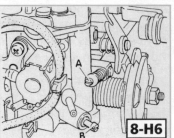

8-H6

FACT FILE

VOLKSWAGEN RECOMMENDED SETTINGS (TYPE H)

Keihin to July 1978: Idle speed - 850 to 1,000 rpm. CO - 1.1 to 2.5% by vol.
Keihin from Aug. 1978: Idle speed - 900 to 1,000 rpm. CO - 0.5 to 1.5% by vol.

Type I: 2E2 - 1.6 and 1.8 litre engines.

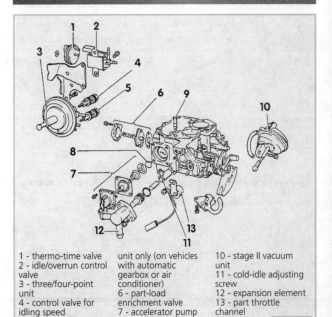

1 - thermo-time valve
2 - idle/overrun control valve
3 - three/four-point unit
4 - control valve for idling speed
5 - control valve for idling boost - 4-point
unit only (on vehicles with automatic gearbox or air conditioner)
6 - part-load enrichment valve
7 - accelerator pump
8 - poppet valve
9 - injection tube
10 - stage II vacuum unit
11 - cold-idle adjusting screw
12 - expansion element
13 - part throttle channel heating

8-I1

❒ **STEP I1:** This, for reference is the main body of the **2E2** carburetor

ADJUSTING IDLE AND CO SETTINGS:

➔ Disconnect hose from cam cover and route away from engine, so that only fresh air can be drawn into hose.

➔ Ensure choke is fully open (turned OFF).

❑ **STEP I2:** Check that the cold-idle device is not operating when the engine is idling at normal running temperature. Adjust the diaphragm rod (**A**) in the idle position and the adjusting

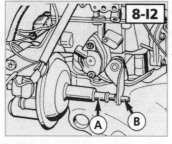

screw (**B**) is in contact with the diaphragm rod.

➔ All electrical components must be turned OFF and the cooling fan must not be running.

❑ **STEP I3:** Turn the idle speed adjustment screw (**A**) if necessary to adjust the speed. Turn the CO adjusting screw (**B**). Then readjust the idle speed, if necessary. Fit a new anti-tamper cap to the CO adjustment screw.

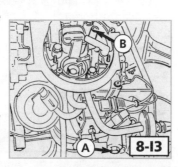

FACT FILE

VOLKSWAGEN RECOMMENDED SETTINGS (TYPE I)

1.6 litre (Austria - cat. + TCI): Idle speed - 700 to 800 rpm. CO - 0.5 to 1.5% by vol.

1.6 litre (Austria - cat, no TCI): Idle - 700 to 800 rpm. CO - 0.5 to 1.5% by vol.

1.6 litre (Austria - no cat.): Idle - 700 to 800 rpm. CO - 0.5 to 1.5% by vol.

1.6 litre (Low emission/cat): Idle speed - 700 to 800 rpm. CO - 0.5 to 1.5% by vol.

1.8 litre - cat.: Idle speed - 700 to 800 rpm. CO - 0 to 1.5% by vol.

1.8 litre - no cat.: Idle speed - 700 to 800 rpm. CO - 0 to 1.5% by vol.

ADJUST IDLE SPEED BOOST - AUTO AND AIR CON. MODELS ONLY:

❑ **STEP I4:** These are the components of the system that makes sure that the engine does not stall when extra load is placed on it, as a number of

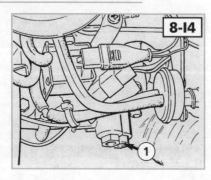

components are turned on. To adjust:

➔ Set idle adjustment correctly.

➔ Ensure air con. condenser is clean.

➔ Switch air con. ON to max. cooling and fan to max. 'blow'. The idle speed should be between 900 to 1,000 rpm. If not:

➔ Check that diaphragm rod is in idle boost position and that cold idle speed adjust screw is in contact with diaphragm rod.

➔ Turn the control valve (**1**) to adjust the idle speed to 950 rpm.

Type J: 2EE - 1.6 and 1.8 litre engines (not adjustable).

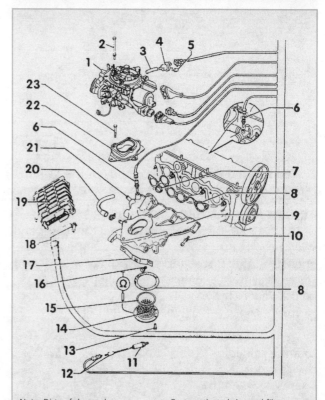

Note: Dirty of damp plug connections can cause the Ecotronics to malfunction. If necessary, clean plugs and contacts - including on control unit - with ethanol and moisten slightly with contact spray.
1 - 2EE carburetor
2 - bolt - 10 Nm
3 - to intake manifold
4 - activated charcoal filter system solenoid valve I - N80
5 - to activated charcoal filter
6 - temperature sender
7 - sealing ring
8 - gasket
9 - intake manifold - with connection to solenoid valve for activated charcoal filter system
10 - bolt - 25 Nm
11 - Lambda probe - G39
12 - Lambda probe connector
13 - screw - 10 Nm

8-J1

❑ **STEP J1:** These, for reference, are the components of the **2EE** carburetor and ancillary electronic components. The system is self-regulating and no adjustments are provided for or possible. In the event of a fault with idling speeds or CO output, the vehicle will have to be taken to your **Volkswagen** dealer who will be able to correctly diagnose faulty components.

JOB 9: CARBURETOR - *removal, replacement*.

9-1

❏ **STEP 1:** Disconnect the battery negative (-) terminal, then remove the air cleaner.

> **TOP TIP!**
>
> • Check for any vacuum hoses fitted in 'odd' places, such as the underside of the air filter housing.
> • Disconnect and carefully lift the filter housing, then check the underside before lifting away.

❏ **STEP 2:** Disconnect any coolant hoses from the carburetor body, and plug them.

❏ **STEP 3:** Disconnect the throttle and choke controls.

❏ **STEP 4:** Disconnect the fuel lines from the carburetor and plug the ends.

> **TOP TIP!**
>
> • Ensure that, when two fuel lines are fitted, fuel delivery and return lines are identified for refitting in their correct positions.

❏ **STEP 5:**
There are two different methods of holding the carburettor to the manifold:
➜ EITHER: Remove the long through-bolts, from above,

9-5

➜ OR:Unscrew the carburetor mounting nuts and remove the unit from the intake manifold.

❏ **STEP 6:** Clean the mating flanges, fit a new carburetor base gasket and refit/reconnect in the reverse order.

JOB 10: FUEL INJECTION SYSTEMS - *adjustment*.

	Page No.
Type A: Digijet - 1.3 litre engines	9-25
Type B: K-Jetronic - 1.6 and 1.8 litre engines.	9-26
Type C: KE-Jetronic - 1.8 litre engines.	9-29
Type D: Mono-Jetronic - 1.8 litre engines.	9-30
Type E: Digifant - 1984-89 1.8 litre engines.	9-30
Type F: Digifant - 1990-on.	9-31
Type G: KE-Motronic - 2.0 litre 16V Corrado '89-on.	9-31
Type H: Simos - 2.0 litre engines 1994/5-on.	9-32
Type I: Bosch Motronic (MP 9.0), Magneti Marelli 1AV - 1995-on.	9-34
Type J: 4AV System.	9-35

INJECTION SYSTEM NAMES

➜ Volkswagen use many different names for their injection systems - sometimes different names for what are virtually the same systems! - but these are the types of systems they use.
➜ If you don't know the name of the system fitted to the vehicle you are working on, identify it from the illustrations used here.
➜ VW also move components around a lot! These illustrations show the main component locations, but there may be differences. If you can't find one of the components you need, go to - or telephone - your nearest Volkswagen dealer, with the VIN number of your vehicle, and they should be able to locate it for you.

> **FACT FILE**
>
> ### LEGAL RESTRICTIONS
>
> • It may be illegal in some territories for an unauthorised person to remove tamperproof plugs on carburetors or fuel injection systems

GENERAL

➜ Setting the idle speed and mixture is not just a matter of making the car run smoothly and economically; it's also a question of allowing it to run within the legal hydrocarbon (HC), Nitrous Oxide (NO) and carbon monoxide (CO) emission limits for the territory in which the vehicle is used.
➜ However, a worn engine will fail even if the carburetor or injection system is set up correctly.
➜ Some injection systems cannot be adjusted. Their elements can be tested as described here, or by a fully equipped injection specialist or VW main dealer.

SAFETY FIRST!

• Never work on the fuel system unless the engine is completely cool.

• Some fuel injection systems inject fuel at extremely high pressure.

• Pressure must be released in a controlled fashion to avoid any risk of a pressurised spray of fuel being produced.

• Residual pressure can remain in the fuel system for some considerable time, even if the engine has been switched off.

• IMPORTANT NOTE: Removing pressure from the fuel lines, as described below, will not necessarily remove pressure from each of the components - they may still be pressurised.

• Before working on any part of the system it is necessary to relieve the pressure, as follows:

1. Disconnect the battery negative terminal. (See Chapter 10, page 10-1.)

2. Work out of doors and away from any sources of flame or ignition. Wear rubber or plastic gloves and goggles. Have a large rag ready.

3. Place a container beneath the filter to catch the fuel that is likely to be spilt.

4. Place your spanner on the first connection to be undone. Before undoing it, wrap the rag, folded to give several thicknesses, over the joint.

5. Undo the connection very slowly and carefully, allowing the pressure within the pipework to be let out without causing a dangerous jet of fuel.

6. Release the pressure from each of the pipes in the same way.

7. Mop up all traces of fuel and allow to dry thoroughly before reconnecting the battery, starting the car or taking it back indoors.

• Do NOT touch ignition wires while engine is running or being turned on the starter.

• Switch the ignition OFF before disconnecting any components or wires.

• If the engine is to be turned on the starter without starting, disconnect the centre HT lead from the distributor and fix it securely to a good earth/ground connection on the car.

IMPORTANT NOTES:
• The accelerator linkage must be adjusted and lubricated if the fuel injection system is to operate smoothly and correctly.
• Never attempt to adjust any fuel injection system without appropriate CO content measuring equipment.
• NEVER try turning adjustment screws at random: the chances of making things better are remote; the chances of making things much worse are very high!

• Use an automotive fuel injection specialist or your local Volkswagen dealer if you do not possess the appropriate measuring equipment.
• In every case, you will need to use a small screwdriver to lever off the anti-tamper cap from the CO adjuster screw, if adjustments need to be carried out. Replace with a new cap when you have finished making adjustments.
• If you use a starting booster, use it at a maximum of 16.5 volts, for no more than 60 seconds.
• If the vehicle is heated to 80 degrees C (such as in the paint booth), wait for it to cool before attempting to start it.
• Make sure ignition is switched OFF before washing engine.

Type A: Digijet - 1.3 litre engines Code NX, (not UK).

FACT FILE

VOLKSWAGEN RECOMMENDED SETTINGS (TYPE A)

• Up to June '89 - Idle speed: 750 to 850 rpm.
• From June '89-on - Idle speed: 880 to 980 rpm.

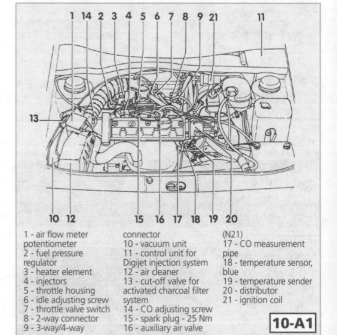

1 - air flow meter potentiometer
2 - fuel pressure regulator
3 - heater element
4 - injectors
5 - throttle housing
6 - idle adjusting screw
7 - throttle valve switch
8 - 2-way connector
9 - 3-way/4-way connector
10 - vacuum unit
11 - control unit for Digijet injection system
12 - air cleaner
13 - cut-off valve for activated charcoal filter system
14 - CO adjusting screw
15 - spark plug - 25 Nm
16 - auxiliary air valve
(N21)
17 - CO measurement pipe
18 - temperature sensor, blue
19 - temperature sender
20 - distributor
21 - ignition coil

10-A1

❏ STEP A1: This, for reference, is the layout of a typical **Digijet**-equipped engine bay.

❏ STEP A2: You will need a CO tester capable of being connected to the CO measuring pipe, at the engine.

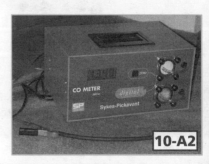

10-A2

STEP A3:

Volkswagen recommend the use of special tools no. VAG 1630 and the adapter VAG 1721, shown. (VAG 1630 is set to 1.8 kohms.) Alternatively, use a tester such as the

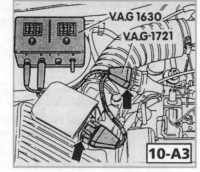

Sykes-Pickavant unit shown in **Job 2**, which is capable of being used with adaptors for various vehicles. The plug is pulled off the air flow meter and the meter and the plug are connected as shown.

ADJUSTING IDLE AND CO SETTINGS

Disconnect crankcase breather hose from the top of the pressure regulator and seal the end of the hose.

STEP A4: Check that the throttle valve switch is not operating when the engine is idling at normal running temperature. Adjust if necessary, as follows:

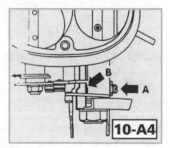

→ Place a thin piece of paper between the stop screw (**A**) and the throttle lever (**B**).
→ Screw in the stop screw until the paper can just be withdrawn.
→ Take out the paper and turn the screw in a further half-turn.

IMPORTANT NOTE: All electrical components must be turned OFF and the cooling fan must not be running while taking readings.

STEP A5: Ensure ignition is OFF. Separate Lambda probe connector (**a**).

STEP A6: ENGINES WITHOUT CONTROL UNIT WITH COPPER BROWN STICKER ONLY: - (see below):
→ Turn the idle speed adjustment screw (**A**) if necessary to adjust the speed.
→ Turn the CO adjusting screw (**B**), then readjust the idle speed, if necessary.
→ Refer to the RECOMMENDED SETTINGS in the following FACT FILE.

Reconnect the plug for the Lambda probe. CO reading should now be in range 0.3 to 1.2% by vol. If so, fit a new anti-tamper cap to the CO adjustment screw.

FACT FILE

ENGINES WITHOUT CONTROL UNIT - VOLKSWAGEN RECOMMENDED SETTINGS (TYPE A)

• Up to June '89 - Idle speed: 750 to 850 rpm. CO content - 0.3 to 1.1% by vol.
• From July '89-on - Idle speed: 900 to 1000 rpm. CO content - 1.0 to 1.4% by vol.

ENGINES *WITH* CONTROL UNIT PART NO. 030 906 021-/A (with copper brown sticker) - VOLKSWAGEN RECOMMENDED SETTINGS:
→ Adjust settings as described in paragraph **8-A6**.
→ Let engine idle for about 2 mins. CO should settle to approx. 1.5%.
→ Set the idle speed:

Up to June '89 - Idle speed: 750 to 850 rpm.
From July '89-on - Idle speed: 880 to 980 rpm
→ Increase speed to about 2,000 rpm and note CO reading.

STEP A7: Pull vacuum pipe (**1**) off fuel pressure regulator (**2**) and seal the pipe:
→ The CO reading should briefly increase, then drop again.
→ If not, the Lambda probe or control systems are probably faulty.

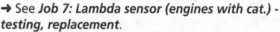

→ See **Job 7: Lambda sensor (engines with cat.) - testing, replacement**.
→ Alternatively, have your Volkswagen dealer or specialist, with the necessary test equipment, check them out.
→ Fit new anti-tamper plug to CO adjustment screw.

Type B: K-Jetronic or CIS - 1.6 and 1.8 litre engines.

IMPORTANT NOTE:
These are two alternative names for the same system. 'CIS' stands for 'Continuous Injection System'. The system is a non-electronic fuel injection system, although it is often used with electronic ignition and other controls.

VOLKSWAGEN RECOMMENDED SETTINGS (TYPE B)

ENGINES WITHOUT CATALYST
- Idle speed - 950 to 1,050 rpm.
- CO content - 0.5 to 1.5% by vol.

ENGINES WITH CATALYST
- With idle speed boost- Idle: 800 to 1,000 rpm. CO content - 0.5 to 1.5% by vol.
- Without idle speed boost- Idle: 900 to 1,000 rpm. CO content - 0.5 to 1.5% by vol.
- With DIS* - Idle: 900 to 1000 rpm. CO content - 1.0 to 2.0% by vol.
- Without DIS - Idle: 750 to 850 rpm. CO content - 1.5 to 2.0% by vol.
- *With DIS reconnected, idle speed = 850 to 950 rpm.

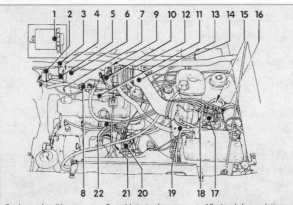

Engine code - JH
1 - Lambda regulation control unit - Location: usually behind the lower glovebox trim, or in plenum chamber (ahead of bulkhead/firewall).
2 - two-way valve for idling speed boost
3 - test connection for measuring duty cycle - on the Scirocco near the coil on wiring loom
4 - auxiliary air valve
5 - cold start valve
6 - intake manifold
7 - CO measuring pipe
8 - vacuum switch for cold running enrichment
9 - idling speed adjustment screw
10 - full throttle switch
11 - injection pipe to injector
12 - coil
13 - intake hose
14 - TCI-H ignition switch unit
15 - Lambda regulation frequency valve
16 - fuel filter
17 - fuel metering distributor
18 - CO adjustment screw
19 - air flow meter
20 - distributor
21 - Lambda regulation thermo switch
22 - thermo time switch

10-B1

❒ **STEP B1:** This, for reference, is the layout of a typical **K-Jetronic** installation in a vehicle equipped with non-electronic ignition.

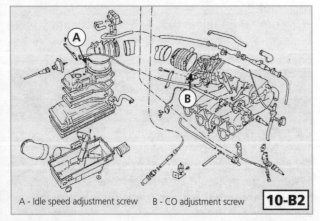

A - Idle speed adjustment screw   B - CO adjustment screw   **10-B2**

❒ **STEP B2:** This, for reference, is the typical layout of the **K-Jetronic** installation in vehicles with **TCI-H** and **FEI** ignition systems.

IMPORTANT NOTE: You will need a CO tester capable of accurately measuring CO emissions.

PREPARATIONS - CARRY OUT FIRST!

The following preparations apply to most vehicles with K-Jetronic/CIS fuel injection, and should be followed *unless* shown differently in the specific model-type information given in the following sequences.

ENGINES WITH IDLE SPEED BOOST

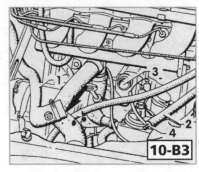

❒ **STEP B3:** Preparation:
→ Disconnect crankcase breather hose or hoses (sometimes there are two - items **1** and **2**) from the breather housing (**3**).
→ Route the main hose so that the opening (arrowed) is away from the engine and can only draw in fresh air.
→ If the second hose has a calibrated drilling (**4**) it must not be removed from the hose.

10-B3

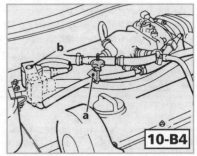

❒ **STEP B4:** 1) Turn OFF all electrical components and ensure the cooling fan is not running while taking readings.2) Place a clamp (**a**) on the hose from the idling speed boost valve (**b**) to the intake manifold.

10-B4

ENGINES FROM AUG. '84-ON, WITHOUT IDLE SPEED BOOST

Turn ON headlight main beams. Turn OFF all other electrical components and ensure the cooling fan is not running while taking readings.

ENGINES WITH CATALYTIC CONVERTER

Turn OFF all electrical components and ensure the cooling fan is not running while taking readings.

16V ENGINES WITHOUT CATALYTIC CONVERTER

1). Turn off all electrical equipment. 2). Ensure that idling stabilisation valve, alongside manifold, at transmission-end, buzzes when ignition switched on. (If not, there is a fault which must first be put right.)

VEHICLES WITH TWO EXHAUST PIPES

Seal second exhaust pipe. Use CO tester in first pipe, unless stated otherwise in following instructions.

ENGINES WITH DIGITAL IDLE SPEED MAINTENANCE

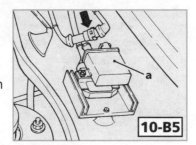

10-B5

❑ **STEP B5:** Remove both connectors from the switch unit (**a**) and connect them together (arrowed).

ALL ENGINES

If injector pipes have been disturbed, rev the engine to 3,000 rpm several times, then allow to idle for 2 minutes, before continuing.

IMPORTANT NOTES:
• When adjusting the CO setting, do not press down or lift up the adjusting key.
• Do not accelerate engine with adjusting key in place.
• After each idle speed or CO adjustment, remove the key, accelerate the engine and return to idle, before taking a fresh reading.

ADJUSTING IDLE AND CO SETTINGS - 8 VALVE ENGINES WITHOUT CATALYST

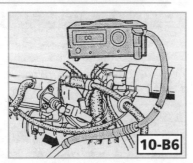

10-B6

❑ **STEP B6: ENGINE CODE RG:** Test CO level at engine measuring pipe (arrowed).

VEHICLES UP TO AUGUST 84

Turn headlight main beams ON; turn OFF all other electrical components.

VEHICLES FROM SEPTEMBER 84

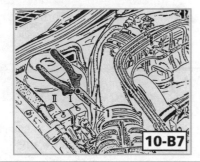

10-B7

❑ **STEP B7:** Preparation:
➜ Turn OFF all electrical components.
➜ Clamp shut the hose (**1**) from the two-way valve for idling speed boost.

➜ Pull off and re-route the crankcase breather hose - see illustration **10-B8,** items **A** and **B**.

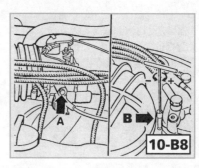

10-B8

❑ **STEP B8:** To adjust:
➜ Turn the idle speed adjustment screw (**A**) if necessary to adjust the speed.
➜ Turn the CO adjusting screw (**B**). then readjust the idle speed, if necessary.
➜ Fit a new anti-tamper cap to the CO adjustment screw.

ADJUSTING IDLE SETTING - 8 VALVE ENGINES *WITH* CATALYST

IMPORTANT NOTE: The CO tester has to be connected to the CO measuring pipe (illustration **10-B6, arrowed**) at the engine, not at the exhaust. (Thus, no need to blank off 2nd pipe of twin exhaust pipe systems.)

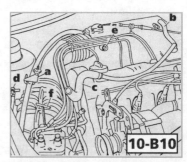

10-B9

❑ **STEP B9:** Preparation:
➜ Clamp the hose (**a**) from the idle speed boost valve.
➜ Pull the crankcase breather hoses (**b** and **c**) off the inlet manifold and air cleaner and direct both ends away from the engine, so only fresh air can enter.
➜ Disconnect the hose (**f**) from the activated charcoal filter at the connector (**d**).

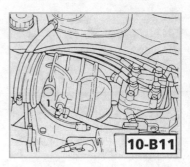

10-B10

❑ **STEP B10: ENGINE CODE GX ONLY:** As above, but there is no need to disconnect a hose from the activated charcoal filter. Also, note the different layout of components.

❑ **STEP B11:** Change over the angled connector (**1**) so that the free connection with the restrictor is in the intake elbow. However, if there is no restrictor fitted, pull the hose off the angled connector.

10-B11

9-28

CHECK IDLE SPEED and adjust, if necessary, to between 800 to 1,000 rpm, at *point e*, on illustration *10-B9* or *10-B10*.

☐ **STEP B12: CHECK CO CONTENT:** Should be from 0.3 to 1.2% by vol. If necessary, use an appropriate adjuster key (**A**). (Alternatively, for code GX engines, see illustration *10-B10, point f*)

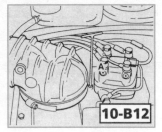

10-B12

IMPORTANT NOTE:
You will first have to remove the anti-tamper plug over the adjustment screw:
• Drill a 2.5 mm hole in the plug.
• Screw a 3 mm self-tapping screw into the plug.
• Pull out the plug with pliers.
• After adjusting the CO level, readjust idle speed, if necessary.

ADJUST IDLE AND CO - 16V ENGINES

☐ **STEP B13:** Ensure ignition is OFF.
→ Separate Lambda probe connector (**1**), near to ignition coil.
→ Start engine and run it at idling speed.

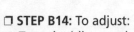

10-B13

☐ **STEP B14:** To adjust:
→ Turn the idle speed adjustment screw (**A**) if necessary to adjust the speed.
→ Turn the CO adjusting screw (**B**). then readjust the idle speed, if necessary.

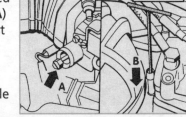

10-B14

→ Fit a new anti-tamper cap to the CO adjustment screw.

Type C: KE-Jetronic - 1.8 litre engines.

FACT FILE

VOLKSWAGEN RECOMMENDED SETTINGS (PART C)

GX ENGINES: Idle speed test figure - 800-1,000 rpm. Idle speed setting figure - 870-930 rpm.
HT AND RD ENGINES: Duty cycle test figure - 26%-30%. Duty cycle setting figure - 28%-30%. Idling speed - 800-900 rpm.
ALL TYPES WITHOUT CATALYST: Control current - 10 mA (constant). CO content - 0.5-1.5% by volume.
ALL TYPES WITH CATALYST: Control current test figure - 4-16 mA fluctuating. Setting figure - 10 mA average fluctuating. CO content - 0.3-1.2% by volume.

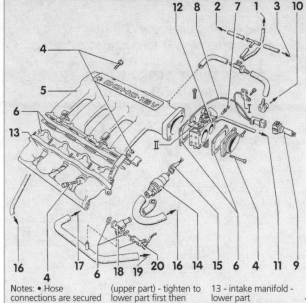

Notes: • Hose connections are secured either with screw type or spring type clips.
• Always renew hose clips.
1 - to FEI control unit
2 - to air conditioner
3 - to temperature regulator (in air intake elbow)
4 - 20 Nm
5 - intake manifold
(upper part) - tighten to lower part first then secure to rear bracket
6 - gasket
7 - idling adjustment screw
8 - throttle valve switch I and II
9 - connector, black
10 - to brake servo unit
11 - to vacuum switch
12 - throttle valve housing
13 - intake manifold - lower part
14 - idling stabilization control valve
15 - connector, white
16 - to intake air elbow
17 - to crankshaft breather
18 - 10 Nm
19 - to air cleaner
20 - cold start valve

10-C1

☐ **STEP C1:** This is the general layout of the **KE-Jetronic** system.

FACT FILE

TESTING AND SETTING NOTES

• When carrying out the following checks and test, make sure that:
→ Minimum engine oil temperature is 80 degrees Celsius.
→ All electrical components, including radiator fan and air conditioning switched off.
→ Pressure gauge not connected.
→ Exhaust system free from leaks.
→ Lambda control okay and connected and ignition firing point okay.
→ If injector pipes have been detached or renewed, rev engine to 3,000 rpm several times and idle for at least two minutes before adjusting.

IMPORTANT NOTE:
The following information relates to engine code letters GX, HT and RD engines, unless specified.

When setting the idling speed, the following three areas should all be checked at the same time:
→ Ignition timing.
→ CO content, via control current setting of differential pressure regulator.
→ Idling speed (HT and RD engines: via duty cycle setting of control valve for idle stabilisation).

WITH THE IGNITION SWITCHED OFF

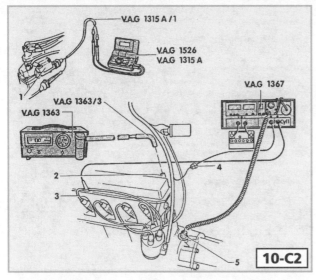

V.A.G 1315 A /1
V.A.G 1526
V.A.G 1315 A
V.A.G 1367
V.A.G 1363/3
V.A.G 1363

10-C2

☐ **STEP C2:** Connect the VAG equipment as follows:
Connecting point for differential pressure regulator, to measure the control current. (If the system is capable of being set correctly, it may be assumed that this is operating correctly and does not need checking.)

CO measuring pipe.

No. 1 cylinder HT lead.

Connector from ignition coil terminal 1 (if connector is not available, connect directly to terminal 1 on coil - green wire).

HT AND RD ENGINES ONLY: Connector for measuring duty cycle (yellow connector on blue/white lead, or white, round, two-pin female connector on blue/white lead).

HT AND RD ENGINES ONLY: Connector for checking FEI system. (White connector on blue/brown lead.)

TDC sender pick-up (green).

In order to check and, if necessary, adjust the idling speed and control current (CO content) refer to illustration *10-B10*:

→ Pinch off hose (**a**) from two-way valves for idling boost valve.

→ Disconnect hoses for crankcase ventilation and position so that only fresh air is sucked in.

→ Remove hose (**b**) from intake manifold (do not plug connections) and hose (**c**) from air cleaner.

VEHICLES WITH ACTIVATED CHARCOAL FILTER

Reconnect angled connection (**d**) and insert free connection with throttle bore into air intake.

ALL TYPES

→ Check idling speed and if necessary adjust with adjusting screw (**e**).

→ Check control current and CO content and if necessary adjust with key (**f**).

Type D: Mono-Jetronic - 1.8 litre engines.

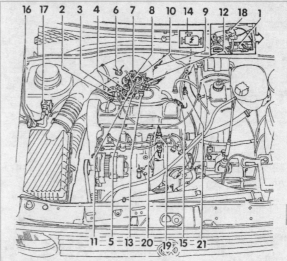

16 17 2 3 4 6 7 8 10 14 9 12 18 1

11 5 13 20 19 15 21

10-D1

1 - mono-jetronic injection system control unit
2 - connector for throttle valve positioner and idling switch
3 - throttle damper (only with manual gearbox)
4 - connector for injector and intake air temperature sender
5 - throttle valve positioner with idling switch
6 - intake air preheating temperature regulator
7 - injector and intake air temperature sender
8 - regulator for fuel

pressure
9 - connector for intake manifold preheater (hedgehog)
10 - control valve for ignition timing vacuum control
11 - injection unit
12 - throttle valve potentiometer
13 - water separator for throttle valve potentiometer
14 - fault warning lamp for self-diagnosis
15 - connector for Lambda probe
16 - activated charcoal

filter solenoid - valve 1 (grey), pulsed
17 - activated charcoal filter solenoid - valve II (black), cut-off valve
18 - series resistor for injector
19 - thermoswitch - red - for intake manifold preheater - hedgehog
20 - sender for coolant temperature - to July 88, as shown - August 88-on: (blue) next to the thermoswitch
21 - plug for self-diagnosis

☐ **STEP D1:** This, for identification, is the layout of a typical **Mono-Jetronic**-equipped engine bay. As you can see, there are no adjustment points. Any faults will be have to be analysed with the appropriate equipment.

Type E: Digifant 1984-89 - 1.8 litre engines.

FACT FILE

VOLKSWAGEN RECOMMENDED SETTINGS (TYPE E)

• **IDLE SPEED:** If not from 900 to 1000 rpm, (sender unit disconnected), adjust the idle speed at the screw - see illustration *E1*. With sender unit reconnected, idle speed should be from 750 to 850 rpm.

• **CHECK CO CONTENT:** Should be: WITH CAT: 0.3 to 1.1% by vol. WITHOUT CAT: 0.5 to 1.5% by vol. If necessary, use an appropriate adjuster key to bring CO within tolerances.

• Reconnect sender unit, give three bursts on the throttle, as before, and let engine idle. With sender unit reconnected, idle speed should be from 750 to 850 rpm. CO readings should remain within tolerances.

• After adjusting the CO level, readjust idle speed, if necessary.

• Replace anti-tamper cap, if fitted.

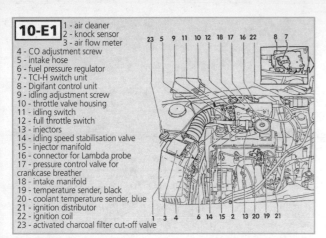

10-E1
1 - air cleaner
2 - knock sensor
3 - air flow meter
4 - CO adjustment screw
5 - intake hose
6 - fuel pressure regulator
7 - TCI-H switch unit
8 - Digifant control unit
9 - idling adjustment screw
10 - throttle valve housing
11 - idling switch
12 - full throttle switch
13 - injectors
14 - idling speed stabilisation valve
15 - injector manifold
16 - connector for Lambda probe
17 - pressure control valve for crankcase breather
18 - intake manifold
19 - temperature sender, black
20 - coolant temperature sender, blue
21 - ignition distributor
22 - ignition coil
23 - activated charcoal filter cut-off valve

❏ **STEP E1:** This is the general layout of the **Digifant** system used from 1984-89.

❏ **STEP E2:** Measure the CO level:

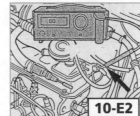
10-E2

➡ **ENGINES WITH CATALYST:** The CO tester has to be connected to the CO measuring pipe (arrowed) at the engine.

➡ **ENGINES WITHOUT CATALYST:** Take reading at exhaust pipe. Blank off 2nd pipe of twin exhaust pipe system and take CO reading at first exhaust pipe.

❏ **STEP E3:** Pull crankcase breather hose (**a**) from breather housing stub and plug the hose (**b**).

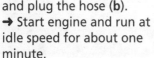
10-E3

➡ Start engine and run at idle speed for about one minute.
➡ Remove the blue plug from the coolant temperature sender (see illustration **10-E3, item c**) and rev the engine three times to just over 3,000 rpm.
➡ Let engine idle.

Type F: Digifant 1990-on.

FACT FILE

VOLKSWAGEN RECOMMENDED SETTINGS (TYPE F)

• **IDLE SPEED:** If not from 900 to 1000 rpm, (sender unit disconnected), adjust the idle speed at the screw (see illustration **10-F2, point A**).
• **CHECK CO CONTENT:** Should be 0.3 to 1.1% by vol. If necessary, adjust (see illustration **10-F2, item B**) to bring CO within tolerances.
• Reconnect sender unit, give three bursts on the throttle, as before, and let engine idle. With sender unit reconnected, idle speed should be from 750 to 850 rpm. CO readings should remain within tolerances.
• After adjusting the CO level, readjust idle speed, if necessary.
• Replace anti-tamper cap, if fitted.

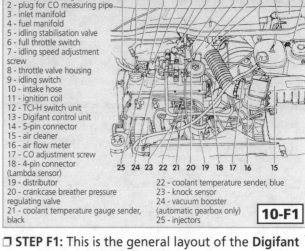

1 - fuel pressure regulator
2 - plug for CO measuring pipe
3 - inlet manifold
4 - fuel manifold
5 - idling stabilisation valve
6 - full throttle switch
7 - idling speed adjustment screw
8 - throttle valve housing
9 - idling switch
10 - intake hose
11 - ignition coil
12 - TCI-H switch unit
13 - Digifant control unit
14 - 5-pin connector
15 - air cleaner
16 - air flow meter
17 - CO adjustment screw
18 - 4-pin connector (Lambda sensor)
19 - distributor
20 - crankcase breather pressure regulating valve
21 - coolant temperature gauge sender, black
22 - coolant temperature sender, blue
23 - knock sensor
24 - vacuum booster (automatic gearbox only)
25 - injectors

10-F1

❏ **STEP F1:** This is the general layout of the **Digifant** system used from 1990-on.

➡ Turn ignition on. Check that idle speed control valve buzzes. If not, there is a fault with the system which must be put right before continuing.
➡ The CO tester has to be connected to the CO measuring pipe (see illustration **10-E2**, arrowed) at the engine.

❏ **STEP F2:** Pull crankcase breather hose (**1**) from pressure regulating valve and plug the hose.

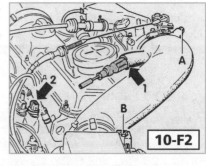
10-F2

➡ Start engine and run at idle speed for about one minute.
➡ Remove the blue plug from the coolant temperature sender (**2**) and rev the engine three times to just over 3,000 rpm.
➡ Let engine idle.

Type G: KE-Motronic - 2.0 litre 16V Corrado '89-on.

FACT FILE

VOLKSWAGEN RECOMMENDED SETTINGS (TYPE G)

• Idle speed - 800 to 1,000 rpm.
• CO content - 0.2 to 1.2% by vol.
• Ignition timing - 4 to 8 degrees BTDC

The CO level can be checked via the CO level checking pipe (**10-G1, item 5**) and the idling speed can be checked. No adjustments can be made to these two areas - the system is self adjusting. If the figures fall outside the recommended levels:
➡ Check the vacuum pipes.
➡ Check all electrical connections.

➜ Interrogate the in-built fault code system.
➜ Check other components for faults as described in *Job 2, Diagnostics - carry out checks.*

This system is similar to other Bosch multi-point fuel injection systems but its layout is very different because of the type of engine to which it is fitted.

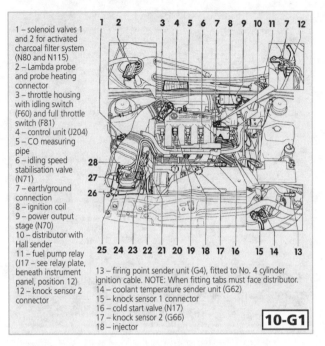

1 – solenoid valves 1 and 2 for activated charcoal filter system (N80 and N115)
2 – Lambda probe and probe heating connector
3 – throttle housing with idling switch (F60) and full throttle switch (F81)
4 – control unit (J204)
5 – CO measuring pipe
6 – idling speed stabilisation valve (N71)
7 – earth/ground connection
8 – ignition coil
9 – power output stage (N70)
10 – distributor with Hall sender
11 – fuel pump relay (J17 – see relay plate, beneath instrument panel, position 12)
12 – knock sensor 2 connector

13 – firing point sender unit (G4), fitted to No. 4 cylinder ignition cable. NOTE: When fitting tabs must face distributor.
14 – coolant temperature sender unit (G62)
15 – knock sensor 1 connector
16 – cold start valve (N17)
17 – knock sensor 2 (G66)
18 – injector

10-G1

❑ **STEP G1:** These are the locations of the fuel injection and ignition system components.

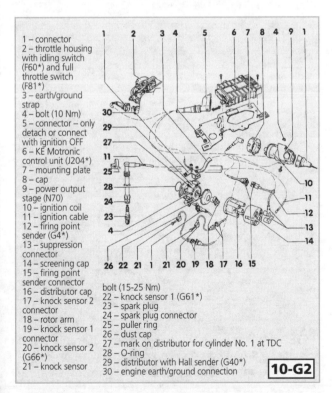

1 – connector
2 – throttle housing with idling switch (F60*) and full throttle switch (F81*)
3 – earth/ground strap
4 – bolt (10 Nm)
5 – connector – only detach or connect with ignition OFF
6 – KE Motronic control unit (J204*)
7 – mounting plate
8 – cap
9 – power output stage (N70)
10 – ignition coil
11 – ignition cable
12 – firing point sender (G4*)
13 – suppression connector
14 – screening cap
15 – firing point sender connector
16 – distributor cap
17 – knock sensor 2 connector
18 – rotor arm
19 – knock sensor 1 connector
20 – knock sensor 2 (G66*)
21 – knock sensor

bolt (15-25 Nm)
22 – knock sensor 1 (G61*)
23 – spark plug
24 – spark plug connector
25 – puller ring
26 – dust cap
27 – mark on distributor for cylinder No. 1 at TDC
28 – O-ring
29 – distributor with Hall sender (G40*)
30 – engine earth/ground connection

10-G2

❑ **STEP G2:** This is a breakdown of the components of the fuel injection and ignition system. Components with an * are checked by the vehicles own self-diagnosis system. See *Job 2: Diagnostics –*

carry out checks for information on interrogating the fault memory.

IMPORTANT NOTES:
• Before looking for faults in the fuel injection system, interrogate the fault memory to see if there are any reported faults on the system and also check all of the vacuum hoses (see *Step G3*) to make sure that there are no air leaks. In particular, check any rubber connectors which do deteriorate over a period of time and are a likely source of leaks and thus problems.
• It is essential that the knock sensor bolts (**21**) are both tightened to between 15 and 25 Nm. Their tightness has an effect on the effective operation of the knock sensors.

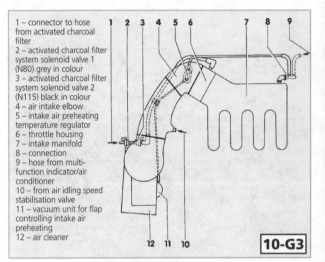

1 – connector to hose from activated charcoal filter
2 – activated charcoal filter system solenoid valve 1 (N80) grey in colour
3 – activated charcoal filter system solenoid valve 2 (N115) black in colour
4 – air intake elbow
5 – intake air preheating temperature regulator
6 – throttle housing
7 – intake manifold
8 – connection
9 – hose from multi-function indicator/air conditioner
10 – from air idling speed stabilisation valve
11 – vacuum unit for flap controlling intake air preheating
12 – air cleaner

10-G3

❑ **STEP G3:** These are the components operated by vacuum connections. Before suspecting any faults with the injection/ignition system, check that all of the vacuum hoses are sound and secure, with no splits or leaks.

Type H: Simos - 2.0 litre engines 1994/5-on

This system was fitted to 2.0 litre Golf, Vento and Corrado from 10/94 for a period of 12 to 15 months, depending on model.

FACT FILE

VOLKSWAGEN RECOMMENDED SETTINGS (TYPE H)

• No settings are provided by Volkswagen, except for the set-up described in *Step 1*.
• The system is self adjusting.

❑ **STEP H1:** Volkswagen do not issue settings for this system. If you suspect a fault:
➜ Check all electrical connections.
➜ Interrogate the in-built fault code system.
➜ Check other components for faults as described in *Job 2: Diagnostics - carry out checks.*

SETTING UP

The only setting up required is to ensure that all of the following marks are at TDC, as described in *Job 6: Distributor – removal*.

➜ The flywheel (manual transmission) or drive plate (auto. transmission).

➜ The distributor fitted so that the drive shaft is correctly aligned.

➜ The mark on the distributor rotor arm must line up with the mark on the distributor or Hall sender cover.

AND, IF ANY ENGINE DISMANTLING HAS TAKEN PLACE:

➜ The crankshaft V-belt pulley to the mark for No. 1 cylinder at TDC.

➜ The mark on the camshaft sprocket must line up with the arrow on the cylinder head.

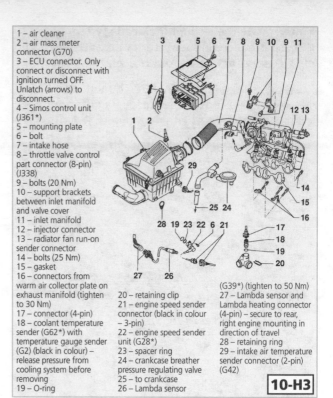

1 – air cleaner
2 – air mass meter connector (G70)
3 – ECU connector. Only connect or disconnect with ignition turned OFF. Unlatch (arrows) to disconnect.
4 – Simos control unit (J361*)
5 – mounting plate
6 – bolt
7 – intake hose
8 – throttle valve control part connector (8-pin) (J338)
9 – bolts (20 Nm)
10 – support brackets between inlet manifold and valve cover
11 – inlet manifold
12 – injector connector
13 – radiator fan run-on sender connector
14 – bolts (25 Nm)
15 – gasket
16 – connectors from warm air collector plate on exhaust manifold (tighten to 30 Nm)
17 – connector (4-pin)
18 – coolant temperature sender (G62*) with temperature gauge sender (G2) (black in colour) – release pressure from cooling system before removing
19 – O-ring
20 – retaining clip
21 – engine speed sender connector (black in colour – 3-pin)
22 – engine speed sender unit (G28*)
23 – spacer ring
24 – crankcase breather pressure regulating valve
25 – to crankcase
26 – Lambda sensor
(G39*) (tighten to 50 Nm)
27 – Lambda sensor and Lambda heating connector (4-pin) – secure to rear, right engine mounting in direction of travel
28 – retaining ring
29 – intake air temperature sender connector (2-pin) (G42)

10-H3

□ **STEP H3:** This is the injection part of the Simos system. Components with an * are checked by the vehicles own self-diagnosis system. See *Job 2: Diagnostics – carry out checks* for information on interrogating the fault memory.

ECU VOLTAGE SUPPLY: Currently supplied from the relay (J361) and terminal 15.

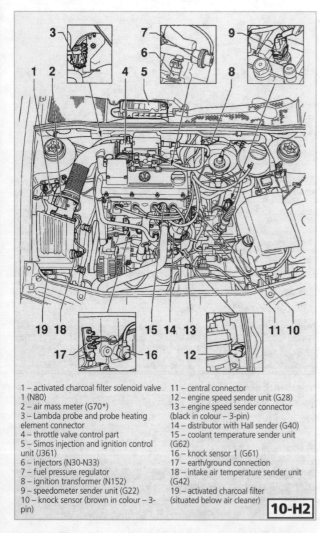

1 – activated charcoal filter solenoid valve 1 (N80)
2 – air mass meter (G70*)
3 – Lambda probe and probe heating element connector
4 – throttle valve control part
5 – Simos injection and ignition control unit (J361)
6 – injectors (N30-N33)
7 – fuel pressure regulator
8 – ignition transformer (N152)
9 – speedometer sender unit (G22)
10 – knock sensor (brown in colour – 3-pin)
11 – central connector
12 – engine speed sender unit (G28)
13 – engine speed sender connector (black in colour – 3-pin)
14 – distributor with Hall sender (G40)
15 – coolant temperature sender unit (G62)
16 – knock sensor 1 (G61)
17 – earth/ground connection
18 – intake air temperature sender unit (G42)
19 – activated charcoal filter (situated below air cleaner)

10-H2

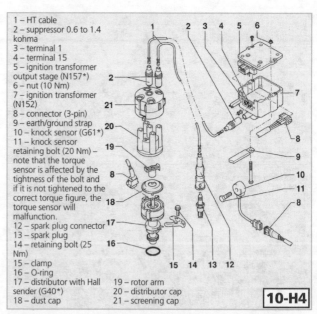

1 – HT cable
2 – suppressor 0.6 to 1.4 kohma
3 – terminal 1
4 – terminal 15
5 – ignition transformer output stage (N157*)
6 – nut (10 Nm)
7 – ignition transformer (N152)
8 – connector (3-pin)
9 – earth/ground strap
10 – knock sensor (G61*)
11 – knock sensor retaining bolt (20 Nm) – note that the torque sensor is affected by the tightness of the bolt and if it is not tightened to the correct torque figure, the torque sensor will malfunction.
12 – spark plug connector
13 – spark plug
14 – retaining bolt (25 Nm)
15 – clamp
16 – O-ring
17 – distributor with Hall sender (G40*)
18 – dust cap
19 – rotor arm
20 – distributor cap
21 – screening cap

10-H4

□ **STEP H2:** This is the layout of the components fitted to the Simos injection and ignition system. Components with an * are checked by the vehicles own self-diagnosis system. See *Job 2: Diagnostics – carry out checks* for information on interrogating the fault memory.

□ **STEP H4:** These are the components of the ignition side of the Simos system. Components with an * are checked by the vehicles own self-diagnosis system. See *Job 2: Diagnostics – carry out checks* for information on interrogating the fault memory.

IMPORTANT NOTE: After carrying out some of the fault code checks, it is possible that the control unit will detect and store a fault. After completing the checks, it will be necessary to interrogate the fault memory and erase any faults shown if necessary.

Type I: Bosch Motronic (MP 9.0), Magneti Marelli 1AV - 1995-on.

FACT FILE

VOLKSWAGEN RECOMMENDED SETTINGS (TYPE I)

4-CYLINDER ENGINES

• Engine speed for setting ignition - 1,100 to 1,500 rpm.
• Ignition timing test figure - 3 to 8 degrees BTDC.
• Ignition timing setting figure - 5 to 7 degrees BTDC.

6-CYLINDER ENGINES

• Engine speed for setting ignition - 650-750.
• Ignition timing test figure - 6 degrees BTDC.
• Ignition timing setting figure - ECM controlled.

4-CYLINDER 'EXTERNAL WATER PUMP' ENGINES

Components with an * are checked by the vehicles own self-diagnosis system.

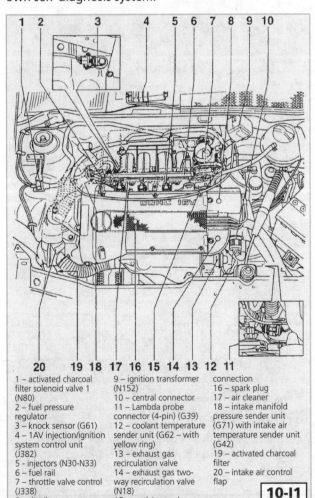

1 – activated charcoal filter solenoid valve 1 (N80)
2 – fuel pressure regulator
3 – knock sensor (G61)
4 – 1AV injection/ignition system control unit (J382)
5 - injectors (N30-N33)
6 – fuel rail
7 – throttle valve control (J338)
8 – distributor
9 – ignition transformer (N152)
10 – central connector
11 – Lambda probe connector (4-pin) (G39)
12 – coolant temperature sender unit (G62 - with yellow ring)
13 – exhaust gas recirculation valve
14 – exhaust gas two-way recirculation valve (N18)
15 – earth/ground
16 – spark plug
17 – air cleaner
18 – intake manifold pressure sender unit (G71) with intake air temperature sender unit (G42)
19 – activated charcoal filter
20 – intake air control flap
10-I1

☐ **STEP I1: 16-VALVE ENGINES:** This is the layout of the components fitted to 4-cylinder engines. See *Job 2: Diagnostics – carry out checks* for information on interrogating the fault memory.

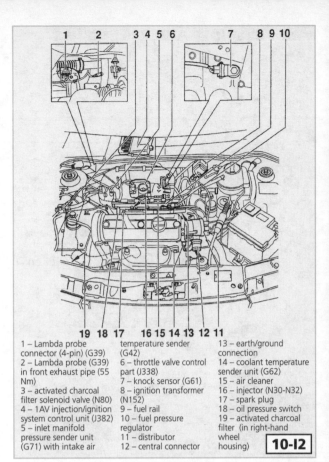

1 – Lambda probe connector (4-pin) (G39)
2 – Lambda probe (G39) in front exhaust pipe (55 Nm)
3 – activated charcoal filter solenoid valve (N80)
4 – 1AV injection/ignition system control unit (J382)
5 – inlet manifold pressure sender unit (G71) with intake air
6 – throttle valve control part (J338)
7 – knock sensor (G61)
8 – ignition transformer (N152)
9 – fuel rail
10 – fuel pressure regulator
11 – distributor
12 – central connector
temperature sender (G42)
13 – earth/ground connection
14 – coolant temperature sender unit (G62)
15 – air cleaner
16 – injector (N30-N32)
17 – spark plug
18 – oil pressure switch
19 – activated charcoal filter (in right-hand wheel housing)
10-I2

☐ **STEP I2: 8-VALVE ENGINES:** This is the layout of the components fitted to 4-cylinder engines.

2.6 LITRE, VR6 ENGINES

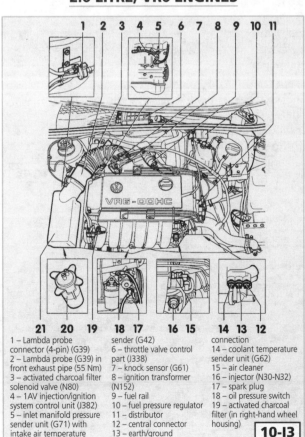

1 – Lambda probe connector (4-pin) (G39)
2 – Lambda probe (G39) in front exhaust pipe (55 Nm)
3 – activated charcoal filter solenoid valve (N80)
4 – 1AV injection/ignition system control unit (J382)
5 – inlet manifold pressure sender unit (G71) with intake air temperature
6 – throttle valve control part (J338)
7 – knock sensor (G61)
8 – ignition transformer (N152)
9 – fuel rail
10 – fuel pressure regulator
11 – distributor
12 – central connector
13 – earth/ground
sender (G42)
connection
14 – coolant temperature sender unit (G62)
15 – air cleaner
16 – injector (N30-N32)
17 – spark plug
18 – oil pressure switch
19 – activated charcoal filter (in right-hand wheel housing)
10-I3

☐ **STEP I3: 6-CYL ENGINES:** Component layout.

4-CYLINDER AND VR6 ENGINES

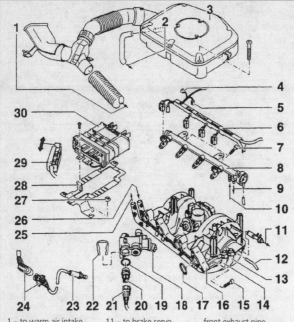

1 – to warm air intake
2 – to oil separator
3 – air cleaner
4 – inlet manifold pressure and air temperature sender connector
5 – throttle valve control part connector (8-pin)
6 – cable guide
7 – fixing bolt (10 Nm)
8 – fuel rail with injectors
9 – return connection
10 – supply connection
11 – to brake servo
12 – vacuum hose
13 – supply hose
14 – return hose
15 – fixing bolt
16 – inlet manifold
17, 19 – O-ring
18 – thermostat housing
20 – coolant temperature sender unit (G62*)
21 – connector
22 – retaining clip
23 – Lambda probe in front exhaust pipe
24 – Lambda probe and heating connector
25 – to fuel tank
26 – from fuel supply unit
27 – nut (10 Nm)
28 – mounting plate
29 – connector. Only remove or fit with ignition turned OFF.
30 – 1AV control unit

10-I4

❒ **STEP I4:**
These are typical fuel injection components.

❒ **STEP I5:**
These are components of the fuel rail and injectors.

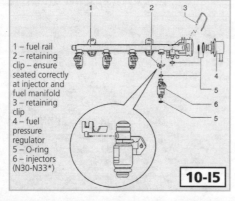

1 – fuel rail
2 – retaining clip – ensure seated correctly at injector and fuel manifold
3 – retaining clip
4 – fuel pressure regulator
5 – O-ring
6 – injectors (N30-N33*)

10-I5

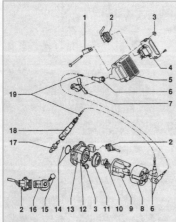

1 – earth strap
2 – connector
3 – nut (10 Nm)
4 – ignition transformer output stage (N157)
5 – ignition transformer (N152)
6 – suppressor (0.6 to 1.4 kohms)
7 – rotating latch
8 – screening cap
9 – distributor cap
10 – rotor arm
11 – dust cap
12 – marking for No. 1 cylinder at TDC
13 – distributor
with Hall sender unit (G40*)
14 – O-ring
15 – knock sensor fixing bolt – note that the torque sensor is affected by the tightness of the bolt and if it is not tightened to the correct torque figure, the torque sensor will malfunction.
16 – knock sensor (G61*)
17 – spark plug
18 – spark plug connector
19 – HT cable

10-I6

❒ **STEP I6:** These are the ignition components.

FACT FILE

VOLKSWAGEN RECOMMENDED SETTINGS (TYPE J)

• No settings are provided by Volkswagen - none are required or possible.
• The system is self adjusting

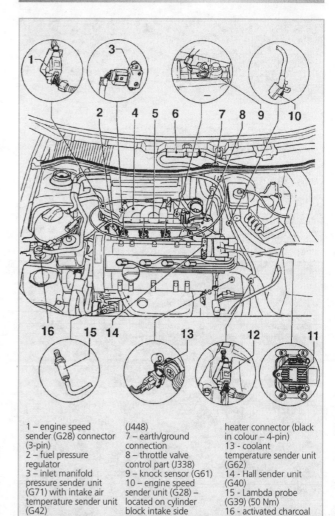

1 – engine speed sender (G28) connector (3-pin)
2 – fuel pressure regulator
3 – inlet manifold pressure sender unit (G71) with intake air temperature sender unit (G42)
4 – inlet manifold
5 – injectors (N30-N33)
6 – 4AV control unit
7 – earth/ground connection
8 – throttle valve control part (J338)
9 – knock sensor (G61)
10 – engine speed sender unit (G28) – located on cylinder block intake side
11 – ignition transformer (N152)
12 – Lambda probe and (J448)
heater connector (black in colour – 4-pin)
13 - coolant temperature sender unit (G62)
14 - Hall sender unit (G40)
15 - Lambda probe (G39) (50 Nm)
16 - activated charcoal filter solenoid valve (N80)

10-J1

❒ **STEP J1:** Although there are no adjustments needed or possible, this is the layout of the injection system for reference.

IMPORTANT NOTE:
The fuel hoses in the engine bay must only be secured with spring clips, not with clamp- or screw-type clips.

❒ **STEP J2:** The injector assembly and injector rails are very similar to those for *TYPE I: Bosch Motronic (MP 9.0), Magneti Marelli 1AV* systems.

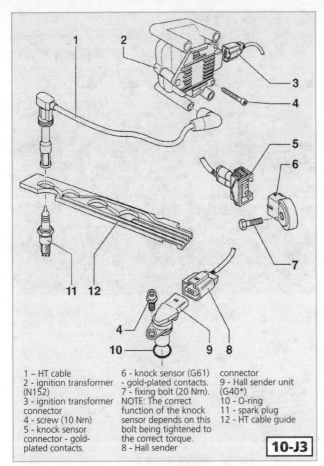

1 – HT cable
2 - ignition transformer (N152)
3 - ignition transformer connector
4 - screw (10 Nm)
5 - knock sensor connector - gold-plated contacts.
6 - knock sensor (G61) - gold-plated contacts.
7 - fixing bolt (20 Nm).
NOTE: The correct function of the knock sensor depends on this bolt being tightened to the correct torque.
8 - Hall sender

connector
9 - Hall sender unit (G40*)
10 - O-ring
11 - spark plug
12 - HT cable guide

10-J3

❏ **STEP J3:** These are the components for the ignition side of the system - note the absence of a conventional rotating distributor.

JOB 11: FUEL INJECTION UNITS - *removal, replacement.*

SAFETY FIRST!

• Read and act upon the *Safety First!* notes at the start of *Job 10.*

IMPORTANT NOTES:
• There should be no major problem in working on fuel injection systems, provided that you follow the correct *Safety First!* procedures, and use a methodical, informed approach.
• No adjustment or fault diagnosis of the fuel injection system is possible without the correct diagnostic equipment. You may wish to replace components yourself, but we **strongly recommend** that you do not change components at random and without proper diagnosis of faults.
• There are two broad types of fuel injection unit: Single Point, which injects fuel into the inlet manifold in place of the carburetor, and Multi-Point, which injects fuel (more efficiently) directly into each cylinder.

Section A: Single point injection.

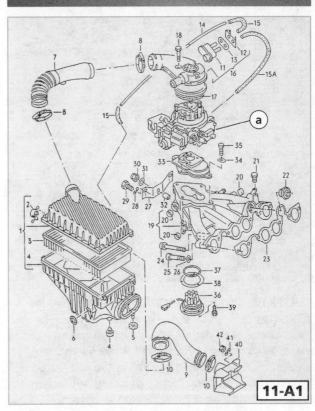

11-A1

❏ **STEP A1:** The Mono-Jetronic single-point injection unit, on the inlet manifold.

❏ **STEP A2:** Disconnect the battery negative (-) terminal. Disconnect/remove the following:
➜ The air cleaner connector bolt (**18**), hose (**7**) and clip (**8**) and the rubber sealing ring (**17**) from the top of the injection unit (**a**).
➜ Disconnect all electrical connections.
➜ The fuel supply and return hoses (**15** and **15A**).
➜ Detach the throttle link rod from the injection unit throttle lever.
➜ The injection unit and base gasket from the flange (**33**).
➜ The 'hedgehog' (**36**) can be unbolted (**39**) from the bottom of the manifold. Renew the gasket (**38**) and, if necessary, the O-ring (**37**) when refitting.

❏ **STEP A3:** Refit in the reverse order.

Section B: Multi-point systems.

You will need to use the following two sections in connection with this Job:
➜ Refer to the illustrations and instructions in *Job 10: Fuel injection systems - adjustment* for specific information on the system fitted to the vehicle you are working on.
➜ Refer to *Job 2: Diagnostics - carry out checks.* This should help you to decide which, if any, components are faulty.

CHAPTER 9 Part A Job 11

9-36

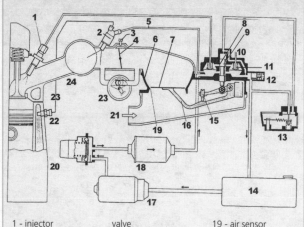

1 - injector
2 - cold start valve
3 - bypass screw
4 - throttle valve
5 - injection line
6 - venturi
7 - sensor plate
8 - metering port
9 - control plunger
10 - fuel distributor
11 - pressure regulating

valve
12 - pressure relief valve
13 - control pressure regulator/warm running compensation
14 - fuel tank
15 - idle mixture control screw
16 - lever
17 - electric fuel pump
18 - fuel filter

19 - air sensor
20 - fuel accumulator
21 - air inlet
22 - thermo-time switch
23 - auxiliary air regulator
24 - intake air distributor

11-B1

☐ **STEP B1: CIS FUEL INJECTION SYSTEM:** The diagnosis of faults is something that can only be carried out with the necessary test equipment and data. Injectors can be removed, checked and replaced, after first depressurising the system. See *Part B: Job 4. Fuel injectors - checking, replacement.* Before starting work, disconnect the battery negative (-) terminal.

☐ **STEP B2:** On all systems, it is *essential* that the control unit is only unplugged or reconnected with the ignition turned OFF. On most vehicles, the control unit is situated in the plenum chamber between the windscreen and engine bay. This K-Jetronic unit is partly concealed beneath a mounting plate.

11-B2

☐ **STEP B3:** It is essential, of course, that all connections can be remade in exactly the same position from which they came.

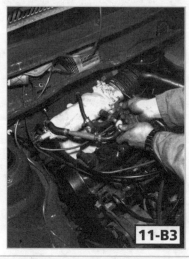

11-B3

TOP TIP!

• Tag both parts of each connection with a piece of masking tape and write a number on it to identify its location.
• Check all connection plugs for bent or corroded connectors inside the plugs and sockets.
• ALWAYS pull on the connectors themselves NEVER on the cable, when pulling them undone.
• Many electrical connectors have some kind of 'latch' to hold them in place. Disconnect any such latch before attempting to separate connectors.
• Check vacuum pipes and connectors for deterioration, splits and air-tight connections.
• VERY MANY PROBLEMS ARE CAUSED BY POOR ELECTRICAL OR HOSE CONNECTIONS - don't assume straight away that expensive electronic components are at fault!

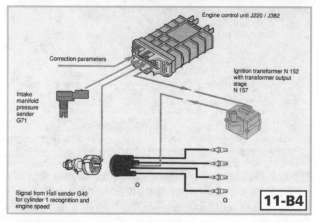

11-B4

☐ **STEP B4:** These are the ignition system components of the 1AV ignition. Two levels of signal cause the ignition to readjust itself as necessary.

MAIN PARAMETERS:
→ Engine speed
→ Intake manifold pressure (a measurement of engine load)

SECONDARY PARAMETERS:
→ Intake air temperature
→ Coolant temperature
→ Engine knock sensor
→ Throttle valve potentiometer

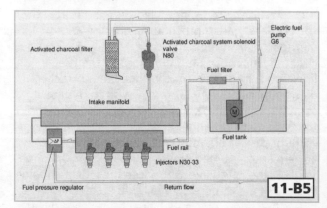

11-B5

☐ **STEP B5:** These are the fuel injection components of the 1AV system. The fuel injection side is also connected to and affected by the ECU, although not shown here:

→ All the injectors (on this system - not on most) operate simultaneously as Cylinder 1 TDC is 'recognised'.

→ The solenoid valve on the activated charcoal filter is open when power ON; closed when power OFF.

→ Two levels of signal cause the injection system to readjust its injection points and richness or weakness of mixture, as necessary.

MAIN PARAMETERS:

→ Engine speed

→ Intake manifold pressure (a measurement of engine load)

SECONDARY PARAMETERS:

→ Lambda sensor readings
→ Intake air temperature
→ Coolant temperature
→ Battery voltage
→ Throttle valve potentiometer
→ Activated charcoal filter condition

FURTHER FUNCTIONS OF THE INJECTION SYSTEM:

→ Fuel shut-off on over-run
→ Engine speed limiter

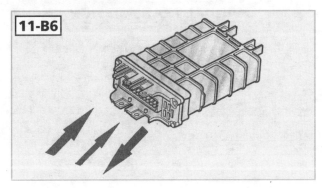

11-B6

□ STEP B6: The Electronic Control Unit (ECU) also has the following functions on the 1AV set-up. (It has some but not necessarily all on other systems):

→ Engine speed for the rev. counter and for the gearbox control unit if automatic transmission is fitted.

→ The current vehicle speed is indicated to the ECU so that a) the ignition dwell angle is altered at stationary idling speeds to give a smoother tick-over, and b) at speeds less than 10 mph (15 km/h) the air conditioner is switched off for a short time.

→ Data arrives from the automatic transmission control unit so that if the transmission selector is placed in 'Drive' the throttle valve is open slightly by the throttle valve positioner.

→ Gearshift points are signalled to the ECU so that the ignition is temporarily retarded, reducing engine torque and producing smoother gearshifts.

→ Throttle valve data passes from the ECU to the gearbox control unit as a load signal from which to calculate the correct timing for gearshifts.

→ If the air conditioner is switched on (when fitted), data is received by the ECU and idling speed is increased.

→ When high throttle loadings are required, the ECU temporarily switches off the air conditioner to preserve power for the engine.

□ STEP B7: The distributor is in many ways conventional except that its role is perhaps even

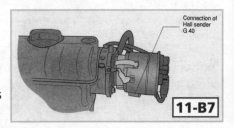

11-B7

more important in that its ability to detect accurately the position of No. 1 cylinder at TDC is crucial to the operation of the rest of the system. The distributor must be installed with precision. In addition, a distributor with worn bearings will provide false readings and thus false parameters on which the ECU bases its information. This is unlikely to prevent the vehicle from running but will introduce greater inefficiency with potential emissions problems.

□ STEP B8: This shows how the knock sensor is bolted directly to the cylinder block and the position of the knock sensor on these particular engines.

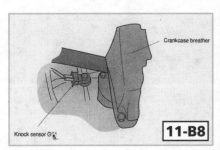

11-B8

□ STEP B9: If the knock sensor securing bolt is not tightened to the correct torque, the ability of the knock sensor to recognise vibration and noise signals will be affected and this will cause the ignition to be mis-timed. The ignition system tries to provide the maximum amount of ignition advance

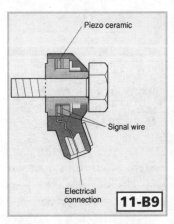

11-B9

consistent with the engine not showing signs of pre-ignition. This pre-ignition produces vibrations in the crankcase well before the pinking/pinging or pre-ignition knock can be detected aurally.

□ STEP B10: In addition to the air intake air temperature sender, this

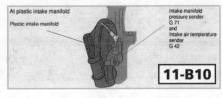

11-B10

system also has its inlet manifold pressure sender built in to the same housing. The ECU is programmed so that if the inlet manifold pressure sender fails, the signal from the throttle valve potentiometer is used as a substitute signal for detecting engine load.

☐ **STEP B11:**
This is the throttle valve control unit, which could equally well be called the idling speed control unit.

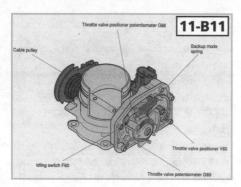

☐ **STEP B12:** This is the fuel distribution/injection system fitted to vehicles with 2.0 litre engines and Digifant fuel injection system from 1991-94.

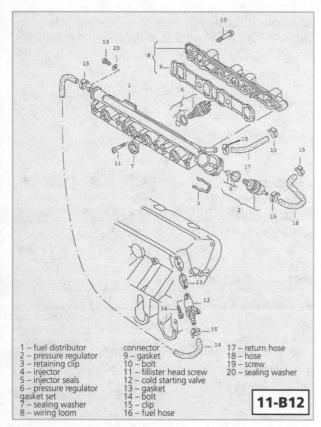

1 – fuel distributor	connector	17 – return hose
2 – pressure regulator	9 – gasket	18 – hose
3 – retaining clip	10 – bolt	19 – screw
4 – injector	11 – fillister head screw	20 – sealing washer
5 – injector seals	12 – cold starting valve	
6 – pressure regulator	13 – gasket	
gasket set	14 – bolt	
7 – sealing washer	15 – clip	
8 – wiring loom	16 – fuel hose	**11-B12**

JOB 12: THROTTLE CABLE – *adjustment, replacement.*

TOP TIP!

• To check the cable adjustment, have a helper press down the throttle pedal as far as it will go.
• The throttle lever at the carburetor or fuel injection unit must NOT be hard against the end stop-
• The clearance MUST be less than 1.0 mm (0.04 in.)

There are several different types of fitting at the carburetor, as shown in the following illustrations.

☐ **STEP 1:** Disconnect the battery negative (-) terminal. Inside the engine bay, release the outer cable from its bracket - pull out the cable clip (arrowed) and release the cable from the quadrant...

☐ **STEP 2:** ...or undo the adjuster/locknuts and release the cable from the quadrant...

☐ **STEP 3:** ...or disconnect the cable clamp screw at the quadrant and detach the cable.

MANUAL TRANSMISSION

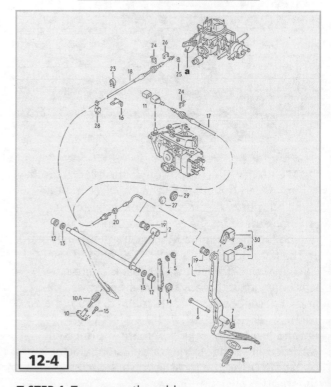

☐ **STEP 4:** To remove the cable:
→ **CARBURETTOR PETROL/ GASOLINE ENGINES:** Disconnect the cable nipple from the top of the pedal arm (**19, 30, 31**), or the cross-shaft lever arm (**2, 19**) (right-hand drive vehicles).
→ **INJECTION PETROL/ GASOLINE ENGINES:** Remove the clip and unhook the cable (see **3-3, items 22, 33, 35**).
→ Pull out the firewall grommet and release the cable.

AUTO. TRANSMISSION

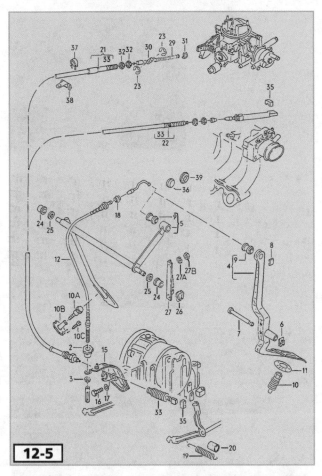

12-5

☐ **STEP 5:** Throttle cables fitted to automatic transmission cars are similar but also have to take in the kick-down mechanism, as shown here. See *Chapter 6, Engine* for adjustment details.

☐ **STEP 6:** Refit in the reverse order.

JOB 13: CHOKE CABLE – *adjustment, replacement.*

☐ **STEP 1:** Disconnect the battery negative (-) terminal. Remove the air cleaner. Release the inner and outer cables from the carburetor.

☐ **STEP 2:** From inside the vehicle:
→ Remove spring clip (**4**), loosen locknut (**5**), unscrew handle (**6**).

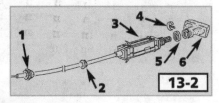

13-2

→ From behind dash, remove cable mechanism. Unplug the warning light lead.
→ Pull cable through bulkhead, grommets (**1 and 2**).

☐ **STEP 3:** Fit the new cable in reverse order.
→ Pull out choke knob car by about 2 mm before securing inner cable at carburetor.

JOB 14: MECHANICAL FUEL PUMP - *replacement.*

☐ **STEP 1:** Disconnect the battery negative (-) terminal.

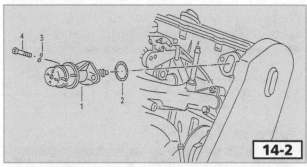

14-2

☐ **STEP 2:** Disconnect the two fuel lines, labelling them for correct refitting, and plug the ends.
→ Undo the two mounting bolts (**4**) and remove the pump (**1**) and spacer block, if fitted.
→ Clean off any old gasket residue (early models) or check the O-ring (**2** - later models) and refit in reverse order using new gaskets.

TOP TIP!

☐ **STEP 3:**
Check the pump's oil seal:
• If engine oil seeps from the vent hole, shown here, an internal seal has failed

14-3

and the pump must be replaced.
• **EARLY MODELS ONLY:** Before assuming that the pump has failed, undo the nut and take off the cover to check the internal filter.

☐ **STEP 4:** On all models with an O-ring, replace the O-ring **before** refitting the pump.

14-4

JOB 15: ELECTRIC FUEL PUMP - *replacement.*

On early fuel-injected engines, the lift pump assembly is located next to the fuel tank. On all other systems, the pump is inside the tank, combined with the fuel gauge sender unit.

SAFETY FIRST!

• Depressurise the fuel system before starting work - this is important because fuel can remain under pressure in the system long after the engine has been switched off.

• Depressurise the fuel system by unplugging the electrical leads to the fuel pump (or remove the fuse) and run the engine until it stops.

• Switch off the ignition and disconnect the battery leads, starting with the negative (-) terminal.

TOP TIP!

• Before starting work, find a screwdriver or bolt which you can push into the flexible hose from the tank and retighten the clamp.
• This will plug the hose and prevent the tank from draining dangerous and harmful fuel.

Section A: External fuel pump.

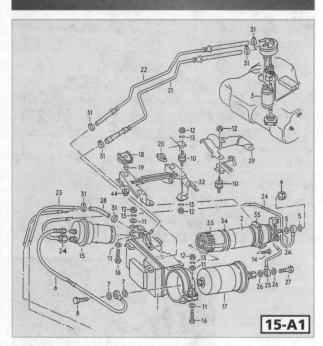

15-A1

❒ **STEP A1:** There are several different types of external fuel pump but the principles are all the same. These are the K-Jetronic injection system pump components.
➜ Remove the filler cap, to release pressure and remove the rear wheel to improve access.
➜ Remove the electrical connections, the soundproofing box (when necessary), and the fuel connections, after thoroughly cleaning them to prevent dirt ingress.
➜ Immediately plug the hoses (**21** and **22**) from the tank (**3**).
➜ Take out the fixings (**14**) and remove the pump

(**2**), and/or the filter (**17**) or pressure accumulator (**15**), as necessary.

15-A2

❒ **STEP A2:** The pump itself is enclosed in a soundproofing casing. Its support brackets are likely to be well corroded - they unbolt from the body.

15-A3

❒ **STEP A3:** The pressure accumulator is similarly bracketed and bolted into place. It regulates the fuel flow and must not be confused with a fuel filter!

Section B: Internal fuel pump.

15-B1

15-B2

❒ **STEP B1:** On all models, a cover plate has first to be removed - take out or lift the rear seat base first.

❒ **STEP B2:** Pull off the electrical connector.

TOP TIP!

• Take care when pulling Off the plug!
• The terminals inside the plug are very small and may pull right through if you tug on the cable.

❒ **STEP B3:** The Volkswagen pipe connectors have to be cut off with side-cutters and disposed of. Mark the hoses so that they will be refitted to the correct outlet stubs.

15-B3

TOP TIP!

☐ **STEP B4:** • There isn't room to pull the pipes off, but you can push them off their stubs with the end of a drift or screwdriver.

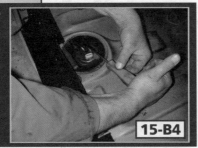

15-B4

☐ **STEP B5:** Use a drift to push the sealing ring in an anti-clockwise direction, releasing it from the tank top.

IMPORTANT NOTE: Some versions have a plastic sealing ring. Undo with extreme care - if you hammer the drift, the lugs will almost certainly break off.

15-B5

☐ **STEP B6:** Lift the sender unit and pump out of the top of the tank quite a fiddly operation!

15-B6

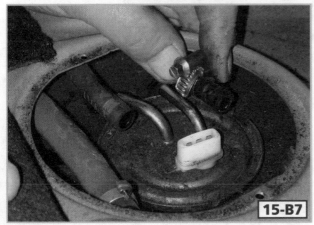

15-B7

☐ **STEP B7:** Use new clips - screw-type clips are fine - to hold the flexible fuel pipes in place.

JOB 16: FUEL EVAPORATIVE SYSTEM.

☐ **STEP 1:** A complex control system exists to control fuel tank pressure under different temperature conditions...

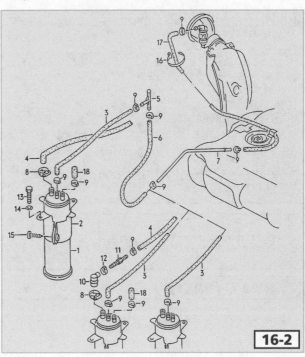

16-2

☐ **STEP 2:** ... and to prevent evaporative loss of fuel vapour to the atmosphere. The system comprises a charcoal canister (1 - different fitting types also shown) which absorbs fuel vapour from the fuel tank at the filler neck (17), mostly while the vehicle is standing, then re-injects it when the engine is running.

☐ **STEP 3:** Other than occasional replacement of the charcoal canister, no component maintenance is needed. However, a fault with the system can lead to running problems. See *Job 2: Diagnostics - carry out checks*.

☐ **STEP 4:** Obvious points to check are the network of pipes and especially those at the filler neck, inside the bodywork.

16-4

Part B: Diesel Engines

CONTENTS

FURTHER INFORMATION

1. **DIESEL ENGINE FAULT FINDER MANUAL**, produced in association with **Perkins Engines**, is the definitive guide to Diesel engine diagnostics, fault finding, tune-up and overhaul. All Diesel engine types covered.

In case of difficulty, please contact **Porter Manuals** at the address/'phone number shown near the start of this book.

JOB 1: SYSTEMS - *explained*.

IMPORTANT NOTE: GLOW PLUGS - checking, replacement, see *Chapter 10, Job 12*.

SAFETY FIRST!

• Never work on the fuel system unless the engine is completely cool.

• All Diesel fuel injection systems inject fuel at extremely high pressure.

• Pressure must be released in a controlled fashion to avoid any risk of a pressurised spray of fuel being produced.

• If spray from injectors or partly detached pipes penetrates the skin or hits the eyes, severe injury can result.

• Residual pressure can remain in the fuel system for some considerable time, even if the engine has been switched off.

• IMPORTANT NOTE: Removing pressure from the fuel lines, as described below, will not necessarily remove pressure from each of the components - they may still be pressurised.

• Before working on any part of the system it is necessary to relieve the pressure, as follows:

1. Disconnect the battery negative terminal. (See *Chapter 10, page 10-1*.)

2. Work out of doors and away from any sources of flame or ignition. Wear rubber or plastic gloves and goggles. Have a large cloth ready.

3. Place a container beneath the filter to catch the fuel that is likely to be spilt.

4. Place your spanner on the first connection to be undone. Before undoing it, wrap the cloth, folded to give several thicknesses, over the joint.

5. Undo the connection very slowly and carefully, allowing the pressure within the pipework to be let out without causing a dangerous jet of fuel.

6. Release the pressure from each of the pipes in the same way.

7. Mop up all traces of fuel and allow to dry thoroughly before reconnecting the battery, starting the car or taking it back indoors.

JOB 2: DIAGNOSTIC - *carry out checks*.

The process of carrying out diagnostic electronic tests on Diesel versions of these cars is exactly the same as for petrol/gasoline versions - see *Part A, Job 2: Diagnostic - carry out checks*.

Where the ACR test module described in *Part A* allows you to choose which fuel injection system to interrogate with the ACR tester, the option "MOTRONIC" applies to Diesel as well as all other versions of the Motronic injection system that are relevant to this manual.

JOB 3:   DIESEL INJECTION PUMP - *removal, refitting, timing.*

Section A: Pump removal, refitting.

Section B: Check injection timing
- older engines.

Section C: Check injection timing
- newer engines.

Section D: Speed adjustments.

Section E: Engine Code AEF.

Section F: Polo from 1995-on.

IMPORTANT NOTE:
For the 1.9 TDI system with 'pump injectors', see *Job 8*.

SAFETY FIRST!

• Read and follow the *Safety First!* information at the start of this chapter, as well as *Chapter 2, Safety First!*.

Section A: Pump removal, refitting.

❑ **STEP A1:** Read this Job in connection with *Chapter 6, Part C: Timing Belt or Chain*. Be sure to set and retain all the TDC settings mentioned there.

IMPORTANT NOTES:
i. POLO FROM 1995-ON: A large amount of dismantling is necessary in order to get at the injection pump. See *Section E: Polo from 1995-on* for further information.
ii. When working on the injection system:
→ Go to great lengths to ensure that not even the smallest particles of dirt can get in.
→ Wipe pipe unions clean before dismantling.

❑ **STEP A2:** Disconnect and remove the fuel feed and return lines (plug the ends), the accelerator cable and the fast idle control cable. (See also, *Jobs 6 and 7*.)

❑ **STEP A3:** Undo the fuel supply pipes from the injectors and from the pump. Remove them from the vehicle, as a unit.

❑ **STEP A4:** Unplug the cable from the engine cut out solenoid plug.

❑ **STEP A5:** Undo the bolts and remove the timing cover. Turn the engine to No. 1 cylinder at TDC and lock the camshaft in position. Remove the timing belt. See *Chapter 6, Part C: Timing Belt or Chain*.

❑ **STEP A6:** Loosen - but do not remove - the nut holding the injection pump sprocket in place. Using a puller, (Volkswagen special tool VW203b illustrated), loosen the sprocket from the pump shaft. Remove the puller, and take off the sprocket.

3-A6

❑ **STEP A7:** BEFORE starting to remove the pump:
→ Make a precise mark to indicate the position of the pump on its mounting bracket.
→ The mounting holes are slotted and the pump swivels when the mounting bolts are loose, allowing the injection timing to be altered.
→ Many pumps have an extra mounting bolt at the rear (arrowed).
→ Remove the bolts holding the pump to its mounting bracket and remove the pump. See *Section E: Polo from 1995-on, Step 3* for bolt positions on later pumps.

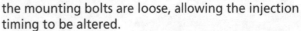
3-A7

❑ **STEP A8:** To install the pump, align the marks on the pump body and the mounting plate, as shown, before tightening the fixing bolts.

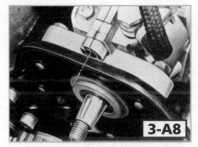
3-A8

❑ **STEP A9:** Refit the pump sprocket. Align the mark on the sprocket with the mark on the mounting plate (**a**), lock the sprocket position with a locating pin, and refit the belt (provided that crank and camshaft are correctly aligned. See *Chapter 6, Part C: Timing Belt or Chain*.

3-A9

TOP TIP!

• The location pin for setting the Diesel pump sprocket measures 15.4 mm in diameter.
• The pin is included in the Sykes-Pickavant Diesel Engine Setting/Locking & Fuel Pump Timing Tool Kit, or is available separately, part no. 077006.

PUMPS WITH REAR SUPPORT BOLT: See illustration, *3-A7*. Tighten the securing bolt with the conical nut, on the rear support, first.

TOP TIP!

• If you don't have access to the special tool for locking the pump sprocket, double-check that the marks on mounting plate and sprocket are aligned before, during and after fitting the belt.

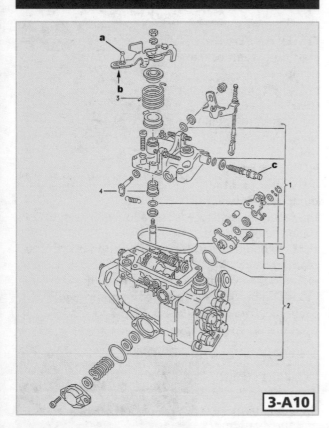

3-A10

❐ **STEP A10:** Reconnect the pump:
➜ Note that the ball pin (**a**) must be positioned on the accelerator lever in the centre of the slot, next to the mark on the arm (**b**).
➜ Bleed fuel from the bleed screw (**c**) - see *Job 7*.

Section B: Check injection timing - older engines.

Older systems have no mounting bolt at the rear of the pump and have a plug on the rear of the pump body.

❐ **STEP B1:** The timing is checked with a dial gauge (range 0 to 3.0 mm) and special adapter or other means of supporting the dial gauge (arrowed) on the rear of the pump.
➜ Rotate the crankshaft slowly in the opposite direction of normal engine rotation until

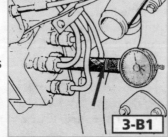

3-B1

the dial gauge needle no longer moves.
➜ 'Zero' the dial gauge with approximately 1 mm preload.
➜ Rotate crankshaft in normal direction of engine rotation until the TDC mark on the flywheel is in line with the TDC position. See *Chapter 6, Part C: Timing Belt or Chain*.
➜ **TEST VALUE:** 0.98-1.12 mm. If the amount of stoke shown on the pump is between these limits with the engine at TDC, no adjustment is necessary.
➜ If the pump timing has to be reset, it should be set to 1.03-1.07 mm.
➜ The pump timing can be altered by slackening the bolt holding the pump to its mounting bracket and turning the pump until the correct value is shown on the dial gauge.

Section C: Check injection timing - newer engines (not Engine Code AEF).

Newer engines have an ECU-controlled pump and no manual adjustments are possible other than with Volkswagen's own electronic test equipment.

Section D: Speed adjustments.

To accurately check and adjust the diesel's idle speed you need a diesel-specific rev-counter. If you're happy with the idle speed, leave well alone. But if you wish to adjust the speed:
➜ Run the engine to normal operating temperature.
➜ Check that there is some free play in the accelerator cable before proceeding.
➜ Turn OFF all electrical components.
➜ Ensure knob of cold-start is not pulled.
➜ **MAXIMUM SPEED SETTINGS:** Do not attempt to set the maximum speed unless you are sure that the general engine condition, and in particular the condition of the timing belt, are in sufficiently good condition. Otherwise, running the engine at maximum speed may cause a catastrophic breakdown!

BOSCH INJECTION PUMP

❐ **STEP D1: IDLE SPEED:** Slacken the lock-nut of the adjuster screw (arrowed), then turn the screw inwards to increase the speed - or outwards to

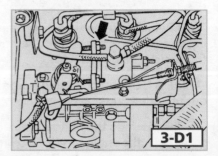

3-D1

decrease. Retighten the lock-nut when the speed is correct - 850 to 1,000 rpm.

□ **STEP D2:**
MAXIMUM SPEED:
Slacken the lock-nut of the adjuster screw (arrowed), then turn the screw inwards to increase the speed - or outwards to decrease. Retighten

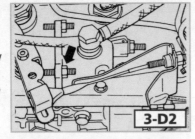

the lock-nut when the speed is correct. Engines code JP, ME: 5,300 to 5,400 rpm. Engines code JAR: 5,050 to 5,150 rpm. Engines code RA, SB: 5,000 to 5,200 rpm. Engines code 1V: 5,250 to 5,450.

CAV INJECTION PUMP

□ **STEP D3:** Adjust the idle speed, which should be from 850 to 950 rpm, by slackening the lock-nut of the adjuster screw (1) and turning the screw to give the desired speed. Retighten the lock-nut. IMPORTANT

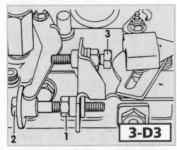

NOTE: Do NOT turn the governor stop (3). This has been factory set and must not be altered.

□ **STEP D4: MAXIMUM SPEED:** Slacken the lock-nut of the adjuster screw (arrowed), then turn the screw inwards to increase the speed - or outwards to decrease. Retighten the lock-nut when the

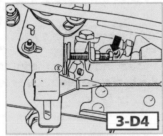

speed is correct - 5,300 to 5,400 rpm.

PUMP WITH IDLE SPEED BOOST

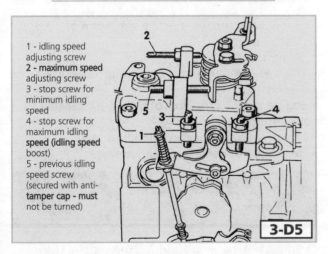

1 - idling speed adjusting screw
2 - maximum speed adjusting screw
3 - stop screw for minimum idling speed
4 - stop screw for maximum idling **speed (idling speed** boost)
5 - previous idling speed screw (secured with anti-**tamper cap - must** not be turned)

□ **STEP D5:** To increase the idle speed, turn the adjuster (1) to the right to increase speed; to the left to decrease speed.

IMPORTANT NOTE: On earlier models, the idle speed screw (5) is in a different position and should be used where the idle speed screw at position (1) does not exist. Where the later-type of screw is fitted, the 'old' screw is capped and must not be turned. Engines code JP, JR, 1V, ME: 820 to 880 rpm. Engines code RA, SB: 870 to 930 rpm.

LIMITING SCREW ADJUSTMENT: If the limiting screw (3) prevents the adjusting screw from lowering the revs below 900 rpm:
→ Slacken the locknut of screw (3) and turn screw well back.
→ Set idling speed as described above.
→ Turn stop screw (3) until it is just touching the minimum idle speed stop and tighten the locknut.

COLD START SPEED ADJUSTMENT: Fully pull out the cold start knob. If engine speed is not from 1,000 to 1,100, slacken stop screw (4) locknut and adjust speed with the stop screw, to 1,050 rpm. Retighten locknut.

Section E: Engine Code AEF.

This engine was fitted to a number of models, including Caddy from 1997-on. No adjustment can be carried out, only checking and aligning the factory pre-set position. The timing position can be checked as follows:

> **FACT FILE**
> ## NEW INJECTION PUMPS
> • VW-supplied replacement pumps for these engines are not fitted with multi-pin connectors.
> • The connections on the plug must be remade exactly as removed.

□ **STEP E1:** Turn the camshaft, flywheel and all other settings to the TDC position. See *Chapter 6, Part C: Timing Belt or Chain*. When the pump timing is correctly aligned, a pin (VW locking pin 3359 illustrated) can be inserted

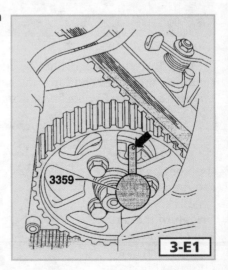

into the hole behind the hub (onto which the pulley is bolted) with a 3 mm gap.

☐ **STEP E2:** If, with all TDC positions aligned, the pin cannot be inserted. Loosen the three bolts (arrowed) holding the sprocket to the hub by half a turn.

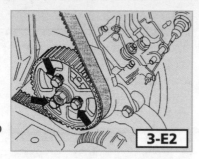

3-E2

☐ **STEP E3:** Use a drift to tap the sprocket loose on the camshaft taper.

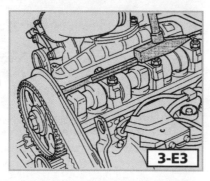

3-E3

☐ **STEP E4:** Turn the hub (behind the sprocket) until the pin fits correctly and retighten the bolts to 45 Nm.

☐ **STEP E5:** IMPORTANT NOTE: DO NOT loosen the nut (**1**) under any circumstances, otherwise the basic timing settings will be lost. It will then be necessary for a Volkswagen dealer to have the pump reset - probably by VW themselves.

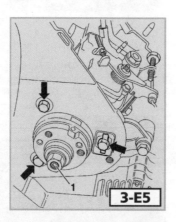

3-E5

Section F: Polo From 1995-on.

☐ **STEP F1:** Start by supporting the engine and removing the right-hand top engine mounting. See *Chapter 6, Part O: Engine/Transmission Mountings*.

☐ **STEP F2:** Unbolt the front panel and rest it on the front 'chassis' member on the left of the car and on a suitable support such as an upturned bucket on the right-hand side of the vehicle.

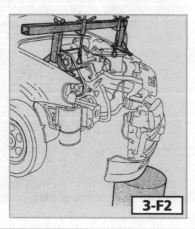

3-F2

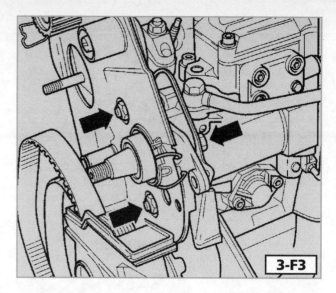

3-F3

☐ **STEP F3:** The pump can be removed as described in *Section A: Pump removal, refitting*. These are the three bolts (arrowed) at the front of the pump and there is one more at the rear – see *Step A7*.

JOB 4:   FUEL INJECTORS – *checking, replacement*.

IMPORTANT NOTE:
For the 1.9 TDI system with 'pump injectors', see *Job 8*.

SAFETY FIRST!

• Read and follow the information given in *Job 1: Systems - explained*, as well as in *Chapter 2, Safety First!*.

Section A: Injector faults.

The following are some of the symptoms of defective injectors:
• Misfiring.
• Knocking on one or more cylinders (difficult to discern!).
• Engine overheating, loss of power, higher fuel consumption.
• Excessive blue smoke, starting from cold.
• Excessive black smoke when running.

Section B: Injector removal.

☐ **STEP B1:** After depressurising the system, clean thoroughly around each injector to prevent dirt from entering the cylinders when removing the injectors.

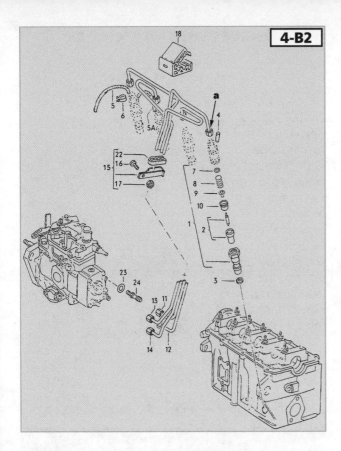

4-B2

❏ **STEP B4:** Thoroughly clean the injector body before refitting, as dirt here can cause cylinder leakage, as can the re-use of a sealing washer - always use new.

❏ **STEP B5:** Refit the injector, tightening it to the specified tightening torque. See *Chapter 1, Facts and Figures.* Always fit a new heat shield (when fitted) between cylinder head and injectors.

❏ **STEP B6:** Reconnect all parts in the reverse order and bleed the system.

TOP TIP!

• Run the engine at a fast idle initially to clear air from the high pressure side of the fuel system.

Section C: Injector servicing.

❏ **STEP B2: SINGLE-STAGE INJECTORS:** Remove as follows:
➜ Unscrew each fuel pipe union (**a**) at the injector, using a flare nut wrench (split ring spanner).
➜ Loosen each union at the injection-pump-end of each injector pipe (**11, 12, 13, 14**).
➜ Disconnect the fuel-return unions at each injector (**5 and 5A**) and move the return pipes away.
➜ Take very great care not to distort the shape of the pipes.
➜ Unscrew the injector (**1**) using a deep 27 mm A/F socket, or, preferably, a purpose-made injector socket. Collect the injector and its base washer. All seals should be renewed every time the injector is replaced.

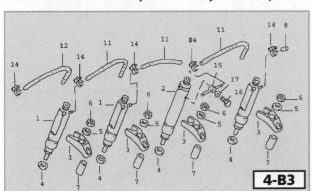

4-B3

❏ **STEP B3: TWO-STAGE INJECTORS:** The process is similar to that for single-stage injectors, except that the injectors (**1**) are held to the cylinder head by clamp plates, nuts and washers (items **3, 5, 6**). In addition, injectors are linked via hose (**12**) and clips (**14**). Seals are items (**4**).

❏ **STEP C1:** It is possible to dismantle the injectors by clamping the upper part of the injector in the vice and loosening the screw connection. Loosen, but do not yet dismantle.

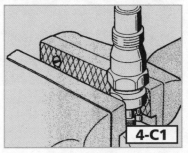

4-C1

❏ **STEP C2:** Turn the injector over and clamp the lower part in the vice to prevent the components falling out while you dismantle the injector. The item most prone to wear is the nozzle needle (**6**) and nozzle body (**7**). To test the injector, you need specialist equipment.

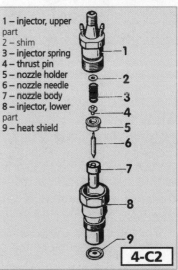

1 – injector, upper part
2 – shim
3 – injector spring
4 – thrust pin
5 – nozzle holder
6 – nozzle needle
7 – nozzle body
8 – injector, lower part
9 – heat shield

4-C2

Replacement shims are available and a thinner shim reduces the opening pressure and a thicker increases the opening pressure. Increasing the pre-load by 0.05 mm increases the opening pressure by approximately 5 bar. Shims are available in thicknesses from 1.0 to 1.95 mm in graduations of 0.05 mm from a Volkswagen dealership.

When pressure testing equipment is available, new injectors should start with an opening pressure of 130 to 138 bar and the wear limit is 120 bar.

JOB 5: TURBOCHARGER (DIESEL ENGINE) - *replacement*

IMPORTANT NOTES:
• For the 1.9 TDI system with 'pump injectors', see *Job 8*.
• On all types, always start by disconnecting the battery negative (-) terminal.

Section A: Pre-1992 models.

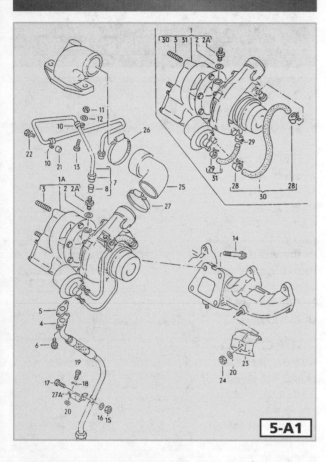

5-A1

❏ **STEP A1:** Disconnect the following:
➜ Undo the two clips (**26** and **27**) and remove the compressed air supply pipe (**25**), from turbo to inlet manifold. Disconnect the air intake pipe
➜ Disconnect and remove all the coolant pipes, oil pipes and breather pipes and unplug all wiring.
➜ Remove any heat shields or other bracketry.

❏ **STEP A2:** Undo the exhaust manifold nuts, then remove the turbocharger complete with the exhaust manifold.

❏ **STEP A3:** Undo the bolts (**14**). The two units can easily be separated once they are off the vehicle.

❏ **STEP A4:** Refitting is the reverse of removal.

ENGINES WITH INTERCOOLER

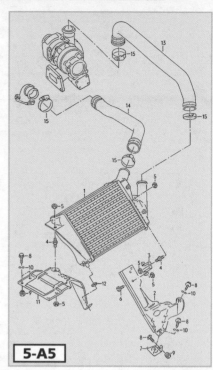

5-A5

❏ **STEP A5:** Removal of the turbocharger with intercooler is similar, except the compressed air pipe (**13**) runs from the turbocharger to the intercooler (**1**) and then, via a second pipe (**14**) to the inlet.

Section B: Vehicles from 1992-on.

ENGINE CODE 1Z

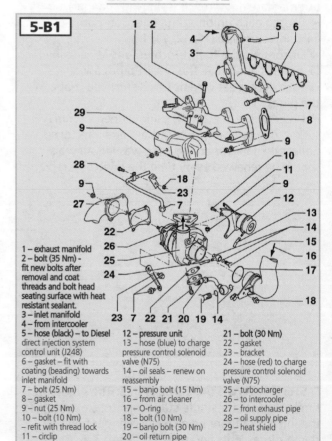

5-B1

1 – exhaust manifold
2 – bolt (35 Nm) - fit new bolts after removal and coat threads and bolt head seating surface with heat resistant sealant.
3 – inlet manifold
4 – from intercooler
5 – hose (black) – to Diesel direct injection system control unit (J248)
6 – gasket – fit with coating (beading) towards inlet manifold
7 – bolt (25 Nm)
8 – gasket
9 – nut (25 Nm)
10 – bolt (10 Nm) – refit with thread lock
11 – circlip

12 – pressure unit
13 – hose (blue) to charge pressure control solenoid valve (N75)
14 – oil seals – renew on reassembly
15 – banjo bolt (15 Nm)
16 – from air cleaner
17 – O-ring
18 – bolt (10 Nm)
19 – banjo bolt (30 Nm)
20 – oil return pipe

21 – bolt (30 Nm)
22 – gasket
23 – bracket
24 – hose (red) to charge pressure control solenoid valve (N75)
25 – turbocharger
26 – to intercooler
27 – front exhaust pipe
28 – oil supply pipe
29 – heat shield

❏ **STEP B1:** The intercooled 1.9 turbo D engine fitted to engines with engine code 1Z. This engine was fitted to Golf and Vento from late 1993-96 and Polo Classic from late 1995-on.

☐ **STEP B2:** This shows the turbocharger pipework connections on vehicles with engine code 1Z.

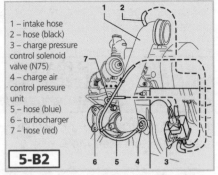

1 – intake hose
2 – hose (black)
3 – charge pressure control solenoid valve (N75)
4 – charge air control pressure unit
5 – hose (blue)
6 – turbocharger
7 – hose (red)

5-B2

ENGINE CODE AFN

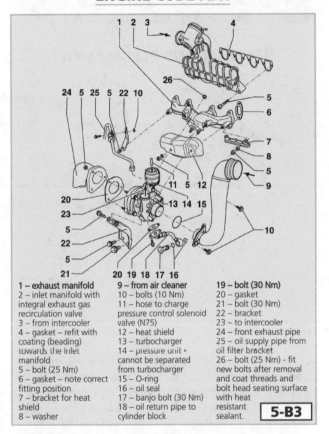

1 – exhaust manifold
2 – inlet manifold with integral exhaust gas recirculation valve
3 – from intercooler
4 – gasket – refit with coating (beading) towards the inlet manifold
5 – bolt (25 Nm)
6 – gasket – note correct fitting position
7 – bracket for heat shield
8 – washer
9 – from air cleaner
10 – bolts (10 Nm)
11 – hose to charge pressure control solenoid valve (N75)
12 – heat shield
13 – turbocharger
14 – pressure unit - cannot be separated from turbocharger
15 – O-ring
16 – oil seal
17 – banjo bolt (30 Nm)
18 – oil return pipe to cylinder block
19 – bolt (30 Nm)
20 – gasket
21 – bolt (30 Nm)
22 – bracket
23 – to intercooler
24 – front exhaust pipe
25 – oil supply pipe from oil filter bracket
26 – bolt (25 Nm) - fit new bolts after removal and coat threads and bolt head seating surface with heat resistant sealant.

5-B3

☐ **STEP B3:** These are the components of the turbo system used on engines with code AFN. This was fitted to Golf TDI models from 1996.

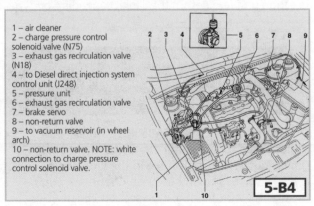

1 – air cleaner
2 – charge pressure control solenoid valve (N75)
3 – exhaust gas recirculation valve (N18)
4 – to Diesel direct injection system control unit (J248)
5 – pressure unit
6 – exhaust gas recirculation valve
7 – brake servo
8 – non-return valve
9 – to vacuum reservoir (in wheel arch)
10 – non-return valve. NOTE: white connection to charge pressure control solenoid valve.

5-B4

☐ **STEP B4:** These are the pipework connections for

the engine code AFN with turbocharger and intercooler.

ENGINE CODE AAZ

☐ **STEP B5:** These are the components of the engine code AA7 turbo-charged Diesel engine without intercooler. Note that the charge pressure control is switched off during part throttle openings by the glow plug timer control unit, via the exhaust gas recirculation two-way valve.

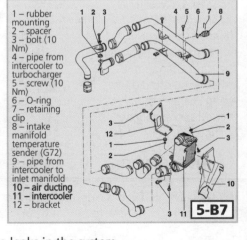

1 – gasket – place the coating (beading) towards inlet manifold
2 – inlet manifold
3 – bolt (45 Nm) - fit new bolts after removal and coat threads and bolt head seating surface with heat resistant sealant.
4 – gasket - note correct fitting position
5 – exhaust manifold
6 – nuts (25 Nm)
7 – to crankcase breather
8 – from air cleaner
9 – turbocharger
10 – waste gate - cannot be replaced separately from turbocharger
11 – oil return pipe to cylinder block
12 – sealing washers - renew on reassembly
13 – banjo bolt (50 Nm)
14 – pipe union (40 Nm)
15 – gasket
16 – exhaust pipe
17 – pipe union (25 Nm)
18 – oil supply pipe from oil filter bracket
19 – air hose

5-B5

☐ **STEP B6:** These are the hose connections to either the KKK or Garrett-type turbo-charger, either of which may be fitted to engines with code AA7.

1 – two-way valve
2 – to vacuum pump
3 – KKK turbocharger
4 – charge pressure control valve
5 – Garrett turbocharger
6 – charge pressure control valve

5-B6

☐ **STEP B7:** INTER-COOLER PARTS – ENGINE CODE 1Z AND AFN: Check that the intercooler hoses are correctly secured with clips and that there are no leaks in the system.

1 – rubber mounting
2 – spacer
3 – bolt (10 Nm)
4 – pipe from intercooler to turbocharger
5 – screw (10 Nm)
6 – O-ring
7 – retaining clip
8 – intake manifold temperature sender (G72)
9 – pipe from intercooler to inlet manifold
10 – air ducting
11 – intercooler
12 – bracket

5-B7

Section C: Vehicles from 1992-on: turbocharger - removal, replacement.

☐ **STEP C1:** ENGINES (CODES 1Z AND AFN) WITH INTERCOOLER: There are detailed differences between the two engines but both are similar to the illustration here. Remove the hoses

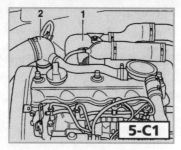

5-C1

between the inlet manifold and turbocharger (1) and between turbocharger and air cleaner (2). Continue by removing the following:

→ Oil supply and oil return pipes.
→ Smaller diameter hoses for control valves.
→ Exhaust pipe from turbocharger.
→ Turbocharger to cylinder block support bracket.

☐ **STEP C2:** ENGINE CODE 1Z ONLY: Remove the following:
→ Securing nut (1) from below.
→ Securing bolts (2) from above.
→ Lift turbocharger unit out, upwards.

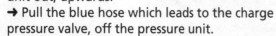

5-C2

→ Pull the blue hose which leads to the charge pressure valve, off the pressure unit.

☐ **STEP C3:** ENGINE CODE AFN ONLY: Disconnect the following:
→ Remove the securing nuts (1) from below.
→ Remove the securing nut (2) from above.
→ Lift the turbocharger unit out, upwards.

5-C3

☐ **STEP C4:** ENGINE CODE AAZ ONLY: Remove the securing bolts (arrowed) between the turbocharger and exhaust manifold using a ring spanner or a jointed socket spanner as shown.

5-C4

INSTALLATION – ALL ENGINE TYPES

IMPORTANT NOTE: It is essential that the turbocharger is not started up and run 'dry'.

1. Before refitting the oil supply pipe to the turbocharger, fill the turbocharger with fresh engine oil through the connection point.

2. After installation, run the engine for approximately one minute at idling speed. DO NOT rev. the engine until the turbocharger has been properly lubricated and all air locks removed.

JOB 6: **ACCELERATOR, COLD START CABLE AND PEDAL –** *adjustment, replacement.*

IMPORTANT NOTE: For the 1.9 TDI system with 'pump injectors', see *Job 8*.

Section A: Accelerator cable and pedal.

REMOVAL AND REPLACEMENT

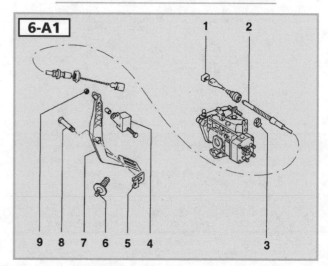

6-A1

☐ **STEP A1:** Disconnect the battery negative (-) terminal. Inside the engine bay, release the outer cable from its bracket - pull out the cable clip and release the washers and outer cable at the bracket. **EITHER:** Clip off the cover (1) and lift the cable end off the ball. To remove the cable, take the nut (9) off the cable clamp. Withdraw through the firewall, after first loosening the grommet.
OR: Disconnect the cable clamp screw at the fuel injection unit and detach the cable, depending on type.

TOP TIP!

• There are several different cables, so take the old cable as a pattern when buying a replacement to make sure the new one is exactly the same.

☐ **STEP A2:** AUTO. TRANSMISSION: Accelerator cables fitted to automatic transmission cars are similar but also have to take in the kick-down mechanism, as shown here. See *Chapter 6, Engine* for the relevant transmission section which gives adjustment details.

STEP A3: Refit in the reverse order - not forgetting the grommet in the bulkhead!

ADJUSTMENT

STEP A4: There are two different ways of adjusting cables, depending on age of vehicle:
LATER MODELS *WITHOUT* ECU: →
Hold the accelerator cable in the full throttle position (engine not running).

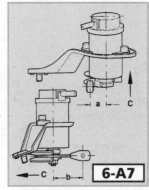

6-A4

→ Remove the positioning clip (arrowed, and also illustration *6-A1, item 3*).
→ Slide the cable (*item 2*) until the lever on the injection pump is lightly touching the full-throttle stop.
LATER MODELS *WITH* ECU: Adjustment is at the accelerator pedal (see *6-A6, item 8*). Volkswagen recommend the use of the VW code reader for setting this device, without which settings are likely to be hit-and-miss.
EARLY MODELS: On early models, there may be a cable clamp on the fuel injection unit and a screw holding the end of the inner cable. Slacken and adjust as described for all later models.

PEDAL REMOVAL

STEP A5: Take off the clip holding the end of the pivot rod onto the bracket and remove. This is the early type. A later type can be seen in illustration *6-A1, items 4 to 9*. In addition, *item 4* is the balance weight, and *item 6* is the throttle pedal stop.

6-A5

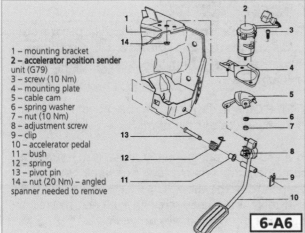

1 – mounting bracket
2 – accelerator position sender unit (G79)
3 – screw (10 Nm)
4 – mounting plate
5 – cable cam
6 – spring washer
7 – nut (10 Nm)
8 – adjustment screw
9 – clip
10 – accelerator pedal
11 – bush
12 – spring
13 – pivot pin
14 – nut (20 Nm) – angled spanner needed to remove

6-A6

STEP A6: This type of throttle pedal system relates

to vehicles with electronic control units. Details vary between models but general principles are the same.

STEP A7: The accelerator position sender unit can only be checked with a fault code reader. If it needs to be replaced, you will need to refit the cable cam to the sender unit so that it aligns with the dimensions shown when facing forwards:
a = 22 mm
b = 41 mm
C = Forwards

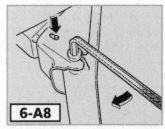

6-A7

STEP A8: To remove the accelerator pedal:
→ Press the accelerator pedal shaft locking device carefully out of its drilling (top arrow).
→ Turn the shaft with a 6 mm hexagonal Allen key (lower arrow) until it can be pulled out.

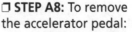

6-A8

Section B: Cold start cable and handle.

This section applies to earlier vehicles, without electronic control systems, only.

CABLE REMOVAL

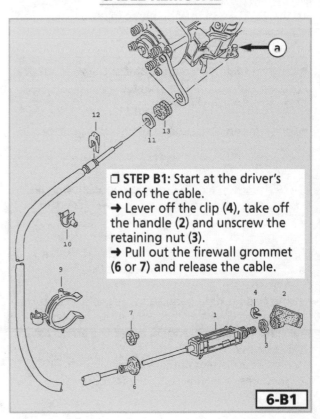

STEP B1: Start at the driver's end of the cable.
→ Lever off the clip (4), take off the handle (2) and unscrew the retaining nut (3).
→ Pull out the firewall grommet (6 or 7) and release the cable.

6-B1

CABLE ADJUSTMENT

❏ STEP B2:
After slackening the locking screw (3), this is a three-stage process:
→ Slide the washer (1) on the cold start operating cable, and secure the cable with the securing clip (2).

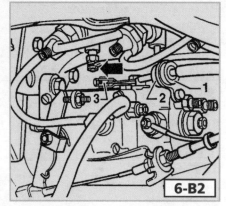

6-B2

→ Push the cold start lever in the direction of the arrow until in the fully OFF position.
→ Pull the inner cable reasonably taut with a pair of pliers and tighten the locking screw (3).

JOB 7:   FUEL SYSTEM AND FILTERS - bleeding, changing filters.

Section A: CAV system.
Section B: Early Bosch system.
Section C: Later Bosch system.
Section D: Drain water from Diesel fuel filter.
Section E: Change Diesel fuel filter.

IMPORTANT NOTE:
For the 1.9 TDI system with 'pump injectors', see *Job 8*.

SAFETY FIRST!

• Read and follow the information given in *Safety First!* at the start of this chapter, as well as *Chapter 2, Safety First!*.

• Do not allow Diesel fuel onto your skin. Wear impermeable gloves.

IMPORTANT NOTES:
• NEVER slacken a high pressure connection unless great care is taken to first wrap several layers of cloth around the connection so that no jet of fuel under high-pressure can be produced. Fuel under high pressure is capable of penetrating the skin with, potentially, extremely dangerous consequences.
• If the engine stalls because of lack of fuel or if fuel low pressure lines have been disconnected or the fuel filter has been changed, bleed the pump as shown below.
• Many later systems are self-bleeding and will purge themselves of air as the starter motor is turned over.

• If you need to 'spill' Diesel fuel, make sure that you have plenty of rags and/or containers to catch fuel and keep it from polluting the ground or drains.
• Do not let Diesel fuel get onto rubber components, such as hoses or mountings. If you do, wipe it off.

TOP TIP!

• If the self-bleeding system, or the procedures described in *Sections A* or *B* don't work, try the one described in *Section C*.

Section A: CAV system.

❏ STEP A1: Operate the fuel lift pump by hand until you can see fuel, free of air bubbles, in the inlet pipe.

❏ STEP A2: Loosen the bleed screw by one or two turns.

❏ STEP A3: Turn the engine on the starter for 15 seconds:
→ If the engine starts within 15 seconds, turn it off.
→ Tighten the bleed screw and start, or restart the engine.

Section B: Early Bosch system.

❏ STEP B1: Place a suitable container beneath the filter:
→ Loosen the vent screw at the top of the filter (1).
→ Operate the pump primer (2) with your thumb until fuel free of air bubbles appears.
→ Start the engine in the normal way.

7-B1

Section C: Later Bosch system.

SAFETY FIRST!

Follow the *Safety First!* approach at the start of *Job 1: Systems - explained,* to avoid the very harmful effects of high pressure spray penetrating skin or eyes.

❏ STEP C1: Bleed the fuel injection pump:
→ Push a piece of clear plastic tube over the bleed screw.
→ Bleed fuel from the bleed screw, into a suitable container, until you see fuel, free of air bubbles coming from the tube.
→ If there is no bleed screw in evidence, slacken the fuel inlet pipe to the injection pump.
→ Crank the engine on the starter until fuel without air bubbles begins to appear from the union.
→ Tighten the union as the engine is being cranked.

☐ **STEP C2:** Unscrew the unions fastening the delivery lines to the four injectors. Start the engine and run until fuel emerges from the loose injector fittings. If the engine will not start, crank it on the starter motor.

☐ **STEP C3:** Keep the engine running and tighten the four injector fittings.

TOP TIP!

If the engine will not start, and before assuming anything worse:
➔ Check all fuel inlet pipe union points and also the pipe fittings.
➔ Replace seal washers to eliminate the possibility of air leaks.

Section D: Drain water from Diesel fuel filter.

IMPORTANT NOTES:
• Some models are fitted with a water-in-fuel sensor. Drain the filter when the warning light comes on. Unplug the sensor from the base of the filter, first.
• Do not let Diesel fuel get onto rubber components, such as hoses or mountings. If it does, wipe it off.
• Do not allow Diesel fuel onto your skin. Wear impermeable gloves.

The fuel filter is located in the rear of the engine compartment. Water carried in the fuel accumulates in the bottom of the filter, and should not be allowed to build up.

☐ **STEP D1: FILTER WITHOUT DIESEL FUEL PRE-HEATING:** Loosen the vent screw (**A**). Place a receptacle under the filter, then unscrew the knurled tap at the bottom of the filter (**B**) by a couple of turns and drain out about 100 cc (approx. a cupful) of fuel. Tighten the drain screw and the vent screw.

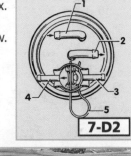

7-D1

7-D2

☐ **STEP D2: FILTER WITH DIESEL FUEL PRE-HEATING:** Pull off the retaining clip (**5**).

☐ **STEP D3:** With the clip removed, the control valve (arrowed) is now removed, but the two pipes are left connected to the valve.

7-D3

7-D4

☐ **STEP D4:** Unscrew the knurled tap at the bottom of the filter by a couple of turns and drain out about 100 cc (approx. a cupful) of fuel. Tighten the drain screw and refit the control valve.

TOP TIP!

• Avoid fuel spills by pushing a piece of plastic tube on to the stub (arrowed) on the base of the drain tap.

BOTH TYPES: Check for leaks. Accelerate the engine several times, then check that the fuel flowing through the transparent hose is free of bubbles with the engine idling.

Section E: Change Diesel fuel filter.

IMPORTANT NOTE:
• Some models are fitted with a water-in-fuel sensor.
• Before draining the filter, unplug the sensor from the base of the filter.

DIESEL MODELS WITHOUT FUEL PREHEATING

☐ **STEP E1: CLAMP-ON FILTERS:** Drain the filter. Disconnect the hose from the fuel tank (**A**) and the hose to the injection pump (**B**). Undo the clamp and remove. Fill the new filter with Diesel fuel and fit the hoses in their correct positions.

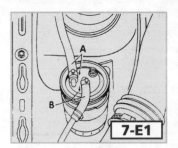

7-E1

DIESEL MODELS WITH FUEL PREHEATING

This text refers to the illustration *7-D2*.
• If a water-in-fuel light is fitted, unclip the sensor plug (if fitted) from the base of the unit.
• Empty the fuel filter, into a container, through the drain tap.
• Pull off the spring clip (**5**) and detach the control valve but leave the return pipes connected to the stubs (*items 3* and *4*).
• Detach the return pipes from the stubs on the filter (*item 1* - from fuel tank, and *item 2* - to injection pump).
• Fit a new O-ring to the control valve when fitting the new filter.
• Fill the new filter with fuel, fit it, refitting the control

valve and locking clip and refit the return pipes to the stubs on the filter - in their CORRECT locations!

JOB 8: 1.9 TDI WITH PUMP INJECTORS.

A new Diesel fuel injection system was fitted to the 1.9 TDI from about 1998. Instead of the traditional single injection pump mounted on the side of the block and four injectors in the cylinder head, the new engine has injectors which have their own solenoid-operated pumps combined within them. The feed to the injectors is therefore at not such a high pressure as it is with a conventional Diesel injection system. The Bosch pump injector system fitted to these vehicles is electronically controlled and faults should be identified through interrogating the fault code system.

❒ **STEP 1:** The fuel pump is combined with the vacuum pump on these engines and fitted to the end of the cylinder head. The fuel supply

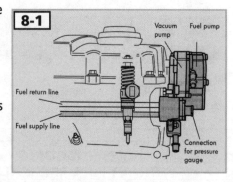

and return lines pass down the cylinder head and are connected to each injector in turn.

FUEL COOLING SYSTEM

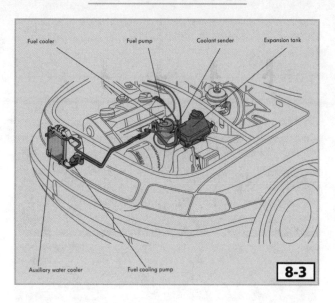

❒ **STEP 3:** The pump injector system heats the fuel to such an extent that it has to be cooled down before it flows back into the fuel tank. The fuel cooling circuit is separate from the engine cooling circuit. Note that both circuits share the same expansion tank.

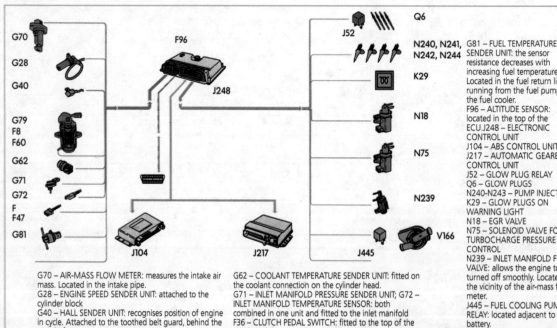

G70 – AIR-MASS FLOW METER: measures the intake air mass. Located in the intake pipe.
G28 – ENGINE SPEED SENDER UNIT: attached to the cylinder block
G40 – HALL SENDER UNIT: recognises position of engine in cycle. Attached to the toothed belt guard, behind the camshaft gear.
G79 – ACCELERATOR POSITION SENDER UNIT; F8 – KICKDOWN SWITCH; F60 – IDLING SPEED SWITCH: attached to the throttle pedal.

G62 – COOLANT TEMPERATURE SENDER UNIT: fitted on the coolant connection on the cylinder head.
G71 – INLET MANIFOLD PRESSURE SENDER UNIT; G72 – INLET MANIFOLD TEMPERATURE SENSOR: both combined in one unit and fitted to the inlet manifold
F36 – CLUTCH PEDAL SWITCH: fitted to the top of the clutch pedal.
F – BRAKE LIGHT SWITCH; F47 – BRAKE PEDAL SWITCH: fitted to the top of the brake pedal unit.

G81 – FUEL TEMPERATURE SENDER UNIT: the sensor resistance decreases with increasing fuel temperature. Located in the fuel return line running from the fuel pump to the fuel cooler.
F96 – ALTITUDE SENSOR: located in the top of the ECU.J248 – ELECTRONIC CONTROL UNIT
J104 – ABS CONTROL UNIT
J217 – AUTOMATIC GEARBOX CONTROL UNIT
J52 – GLOW PLUG RELAY
Q6 – GLOW PLUGS
N240-N243 – PUMP INJECTORS
K29 – GLOW PLUGS ON WARNING LIGHT
N18 – EGR VALVE
N75 – SOLENOID VALVE FOR TURBOCHARGE PRESSURE CONTROL
N239 – INLET MANIFOLD FLAP VALVE: allows the engine to be turned off smoothly. Located in the vicinity of the air-mass flow meter.
J445 – FUEL COOLING PUMP RELAY: located adjacent to the battery.
V166 – FUEL COOLING PUMP: mounted on the end of the cylinder head.

❒ **STEP 2:** These are the components of the engine management system.

Part C: Both Engine Types

JOB 1: FUEL TANK – *removal, refitting.*

SAFETY FIRST!

• We strongly recommend that you carry out all of this work out of doors.

• Read *Chapter 2, Safety First!* before carrying out this work!

• Always work away from all sources of heat or ignition.

• Do not smoke.

• Make sure that you have a container which is large enough to take all of the fuel in the tank.

• Store the drained fuel in an approved, safe container or containers.

• Wear gloves and goggles – petrol can be harmful to the skin and is always harmful to the eyes.

❏ **STEP 1:** Disconnect the battery negative (-) terminal.

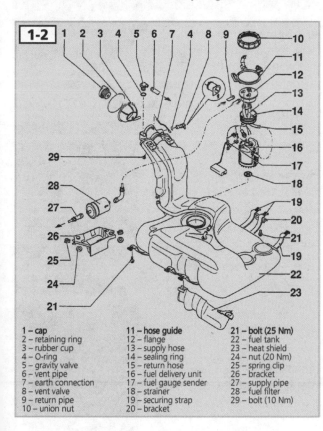

1-2

1 – cap
2 – retaining ring
3 – rubber cup
4 – O-ring
5 – gravity valve
6 – vent pipe
7 – earth connection
8 – vent valve
9 – return pipe
10 – union nut
11 – hose guide
12 – flange
13 – supply hose
14 – sealing ring
15 – return hose
16 – fuel delivery unit
17 – fuel gauge sender
18 – strainer
19 – securing strap
20 – bracket
21 – bolt (25 Nm)
22 – fuel tank
23 – heat shield
24 – nut (20 Nm)
25 – spring clip
26 – bracket
27 – supply pipe
28 – fuel filter
29 – bolt (10 Nm)

❏ **STEP 2:** These are typical tank assembly components. As described here, you will have to:

→ Disconnect from the fuel sender/fuel pump (**13**) the wiring and fuel hoses.

→ Disconnect the filler and breather hoses from the tank. (Earliest models are less complex than the later model shown here.)

→ Note in particular the tank strap securing bolts and fixing plates (where fitted) at rear of the tank (*items 19, 20* and *21*).

1-3

❏ **STEP 3:** To get at the fuel filler pipework, you will have to remove the cover from beneath the wheelarch.

❏ **STEP 4:** Drain the remaining fuel from the tank.

1-4

SAFETY FIRST!

• Find out how much fuel is in the tank and make sure you have enough safe storage capacity before draining it.

❏ **STEP 5:** Disconnect the plethora or small pipes and electrical connections at the tank. Because the tank lives in such a hostile environment, you may find that some of the clips are unwilling to shift. DO NOT use heat or anything that could create a spark while undoing them. If necessary, cut through the rubber pipework with a knife, and then cut through metal clips after the tank has been removed and all fumes have been cleaned out of it.

1-5

❏ **STEP 6:** Remove the external fuel pump and pressure regulator - early models only. Filters come in all shapes and sizes, and models from later Mk 2-on may have external charcoal canisters which must also be removed.

1-6

STEP 7: On the great majority of Golfs and Jettas, the tank is held in place with a number of straps, hooked to the underbody at one end and bolted at the other.

1-7

STEP 8: On 'Mk 1' Cabriolet models, the tank is bolted directly to the underfloor.

1-8

STEP 9: With everything unbolted, the tank can be carefully lowered but take great care that there are no pockets of fuel to spill out onto your clothes or into your face. Lower the tank a very small amount at a time, enough to check whether any hoses remain attached, then lower it fully to the ground.

1-9

STEP 10: Fuel tanks are somewhat prone to corrosion especially on the upper face.

1-10

SAFETY FIRST!

• You must NEVER simply leave the fuel tank at this stage!

• If you are only planning to store it for a very short time, all of the apertures must be thoroughly sealed off.

• The biggest danger in a fuel tank comes from the fumes within it. Petrol/gasoline fumes are highly flammable (as opposed to the liquid fuel which, ironically, is not particularly so) and a tank full of fumes is a bomb waiting to go off if any sparks or cigarette ends should get near it.

• If the tank is to be stored for more than a couple of days, it should be steam cleaned internally to remove all traces of fuel.

STEP 11: EARLIER MODELS ONLY: To remove the filler neck from the vehicle, three screws have to be taken from around the filler neck opening. They are frequently

1-11

rusted solid in place and it may be necessary to drill them out. This is why you should carry out this part of the work once the fuel tank has been removed and taken away for safe storage, as described earlier. **LATER MODELS:** Remove the retaining ring (illustrations *1-2, item 2*) and the neck, which is integral with the tank itself, becomes free.

STEP 12: The later the model, the more complex the filler neck gear, with fuel evaporation systems and recirculation systems being fitted. In each case, removal is a relatively simple and straightforward process.

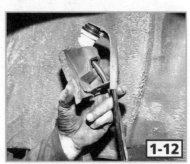
1-12

STEP 13: On earlier models with steel pipes, rusty fuel filler necks are very common on Golfs and Jettas but fortunately, replacements are available.

1-13

STEP 14: With the tank held tightly in place, the two straps (on this model) are hooked into place at the rear...

1-14

STEP 15: ...then new zinc-plated nuts and washers are fitted hand tight...

1-15

STEP 16: ...after which the straps are tightened and all the tank connections remade in the reverse order, making sure all connections are sound. Reconnect the battery leads.

`1-16`

JOB 2: FUEL GAUGE SENDER UNIT - *replacement.*

See *Part A, Job 15. Electric Fuel Pump - replacement. Section B: Internal Fuel Pump.* This shows how to remove and replace the type of unit where the pump and sender unit are combined. The process for the type without an integral fuel pump is exactly the same, except that there are no fuel hoses to disconnect.

JOB 3: EXHAUST SYSTEM - *replacement.*

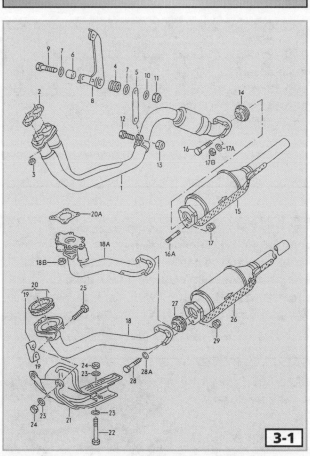

`3-1`

STEP 1: Exhaust systems are similar in principle - and mostly in appearance, except that:
→ Some have a Lambda sensor and a catalytic converter. These are typical systems with bolt-on downpipes (**3** and **18B**) and clip-on pipes (**19**)

→ There are two different methods of holding the downpipe to the engine - one that you can disconnect yourself, and one that you can't without the use of a special tool.
→ See *Chapter 6, Part L: Engine and Transmission Removal, Separation, Refitting* for information on fitting the exhaust.
• Use all new gaskets (**2, 20, 20A, 14, 27**).

`3-2`

STEP 2: Fit the exhaust system components into place starting at the manifold.

`3-3`

STEP 3: Apply exhaust jointing paste, assemble the components and fit the pipe clamps loosely.

`3-4`

STEP 4: Ensure that the exhaust is mounted evenly, with adequate clearances and only then tighten the exhaust pipe clamps.

STEP 5: Fit new rubber straps. Ensure no straps are under more tension than others by realigning the pipe joints as necessary. Only then should the pipe clamps be tightened.

`3-5`

CHAPTER 10: ELECTRICAL, DASH, INSTRUMENTS

*Please read **Chapter 2 Safety First** before carrying out any work on your car.*

CONTENTS

SAFETY FIRST!

• Never smoke, use a naked flame or allow a spark near the battery.

• Never disconnect the battery with battery caps removed - or with engine running, which will damage electronic components.

• BATTERY TERMINALS: ALWAYS disconnect earth/ground FIRST and reconnect LAST.

• If battery acid comes into contact with skin or eyes, flood with cold water and seek medical advice.

• Don't top up the battery within half an hour of charging it - electrolyte may flood out.

FACT FILE

DISCONNECTING THE BATTERY

• If you disconnect the battery, you might find the car alarm goes off, the ECU loses its 'memory', or the radio needs its security code.

• You can ensure a constant supply with a separate battery, protected with a 1 amp fuse.

• In some cases, you might need to disconnect the battery completely. For instance, if you need to disable the air bag/s.

• When the battery DOES need to be disconnected, you

MUST make sure that you've got the radio security code before disconnecting it.

• This is the Sykes-Pickavant Computer Saver. Clip the cables to your spare battery and plug into the cigar lighter before disconnecting the car battery.

JOB 1:   ALTERNATOR - *removal, refitting.*

IMPORTANT NOTES: **i)** For details of the different drive belts and mountings, see *Chapter 6, Part D: Auxiliary drive belts.*
ii) On engines with power steering and/or air conditioning, the alternator is mounted on a bracket.

❑ **STEP 1:** Before dismantling, disconnect the battery negative (-) earth/ground terminal. See *Chapter 10, Electrical, Dash, Instruments, Fact File: Disconnecting the Battery* BEFORE doing so!

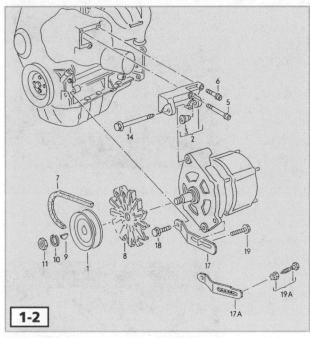

1-2

❑ **STEP 2:** Disconnect the wiring plug or plugs from the back of the alternator. Slacken the bolt (**14**) securing the pivot mounting (**2**), slacken the adjustment arm bolt (**18**) and the adjuster at the alternator (**19** or **19A**). Slacken the drivebelt and remove it.

❑ **STEP 3:**
Where the alternator is fitted to a bracket, there may be two long through-bolts, on one of which the unit pivots. Note the tensioner spring (**10**) fitted to this type, where the engine has power steering but not air conditioning.

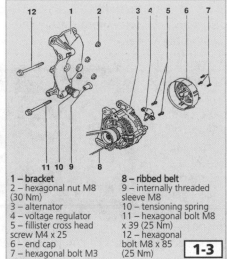

1 – bracket
2 – hexagonal nut M8 (30 Nm)
3 – alternator
4 – voltage regulator
5 – fillister cross head screw M4 x 25
6 – end cap
7 – hexagonal bolt M3
8 – ribbed belt
9 – internally threaded sleeve M8
10 – tensioning spring
11 – hexagonal bolt M8 x 39 (25 Nm)
12 – hexagonal bolt M8 x 85 (25 Nm)

1-3

❑ **STEP 4:** When the alternator is fitted in this position, the pivot bolt can only be reached by first removing this plug from the camshaft belt cover.

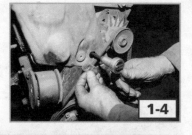

1-4

❑ **STEP 5:** On many models, to adjust the tension on the belt, you slacken the centre bolt (arrowed) then turn the outer hexagon, moving the alternator adjuster along the rack

1-5

❑ **STEP 6:** Undo the nut from the long through bolt and note the position of the washers. Support the alternator and remove the bolt, then withdraw the alternator from the car.

❑ **STEP 7:** Refit in reverse order and make sure your electrical connections are sound. Adjust the drivebelt tension. See *Chapter 6, Part D: Auxiliary drive belts.*

JOB 2.   STARTER MOTOR – *removal, refitting.*

❑ **STEP 1:** Before dismantling, disconnect the battery negative (-) earth/ground terminal. See *Chapter 10, Electrical, Dash, Instruments, Fact File: Disconnecting the Battery* BEFORE doing so!

❑ **STEP 2:** Undo and remove all the electrical connections from the starter and solenoid.

❑ **STEP 3:** Undo the two or three mounting bolts (depending on version) and remove the starter motor.

❑ **STEP 4:** If the motor is being exchanged, it's a wise precaution to change the bush in which the motor shaft runs. Take a suitable-sized thread tap and run it into the bush, accessed through the starter motor mounting position. The bush will be pulled out by the action of the thread.

2-4

❑ **STEP 5:** To fit the new bush, slide it onto the end of the pinion shaft and insert it with the starter motor. Take care not to damage the bush.

2-5

STEP 6: Refit in reverse order, ensuring that all connections are sound.

JOB 3:   DASHBOARD AND INSTRUMENT PANEL – *removal, refitting.*

FACT FILE
DASHBOARD TYPES

• Several different types have been used, with detail fixing differences.

• You often have to remove trim or finishers (especially near the outer sides) to get at fixings, and a number of screws are concealed behind trim plugs, which have to be carefully levered out.

• If some screws cannot be found, try removing all the screws you can find, then very carefully twist and moving the component. Look for points of non-movement as likely locations for hidden screws.

• In all cases, the steering wheel and indicator switch housing has first to be removed.

• In some cases, the indicator switch itself has to be removed – take out the two securing screws.

• The Volkswagen drawings shown here are mainly of left-hand drive vehicles. Right-hand drive fittings are transposed.

STEP 1: Before dismantling, disconnect the battery negative (-) earth/ground terminal. See *Chapter 10, Electrical, Dash, Instruments, Fact File: Disconnecting the Battery* BEFORE doing so! See Chapter 11, Part B, Job 1.

SAFETY FIRST!
MODELS WITH AIR BAGS:

• It will be necessary to remove the relevant air bags before the dash can be removed.

• Do not remove or dismantle the air bags without carefully following the instructions in *Chapter 11, Part B, Job 1*

Section A: Dash insert, speedo head – removal.

 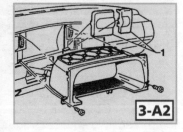

STEP A1: EARLY MODEL GOLF: This fixing screw is cunningly concealed behind a cover plate which first has to be carefully levered off.

STEP A2: GOLF 1992-ON: Unclip the covers (1) and the lighting switch. Remove two screws and pull out the instrument cluster trim.

STEP A3: POLO, LATER GOLFS: On this model Polo, two screws (arrowed) hold the dash insert trim panel in place. On

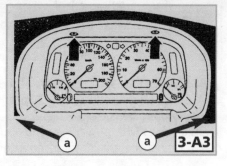

later Golfs, the insert screw positions are approximately at points (**a**) or, in some cases, a little higher. The insert trim can be removed by pulling out of its location, although it is sometimes difficult to move.

STEP A4: EARLY MODEL GOLF: The heater knobs are pulled off and the heater fascia plate removed, followed by

the radio. You will need special U-shaped clips, two of them, which are pushed into two holes on each end of the radio, releasing the concealed clips and allowing you to pull the radio free.

STEP A5: With the radio out of the way, the larger dash fascia plate upper screw can now be removed. The larger dash panel fascia

plate can now be removed, remembering to disconnect the wiring plugs from the switches on the back of the panel.

STEP A6: ALL MODELS: The speedo head can be pulled free, disconnecting all of the wiring plugs once again, and also disconnecting

the speedo cable. On the majority of vehicles, the speedo cable is disconnected by squeezing together the two wings but on a few models, the cable is unscrewed.

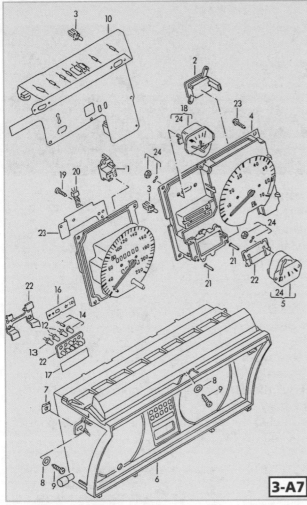

3-A7

☐ **STEP A7:** Individual instrument layout components can be changed, as shown here:
➜ The greatest care must be taken with the delicate connectors and with the printed circuit board itself (**10**).
➜ If you experience faults with instruments, check connections first (especially in the engine bay) and don't forget to check any vacuum connections.

☐ **STEP A8:** The LED warning lights (**13** and **14**) can be changed by pulling out the old one and pushing in the new, but note that the polarity MUST be the right way round.

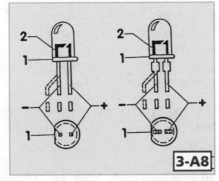

3-A8

INSIDE INFORMATION: The negative (-) terminal is identified by:
➜ a chamfer on the diode housing (**1**)
➜ a larger pole inside the housing (**2**)
➜ an angled 'leg' (see broken line) on some versions.

Section B: Dashboard – removal.

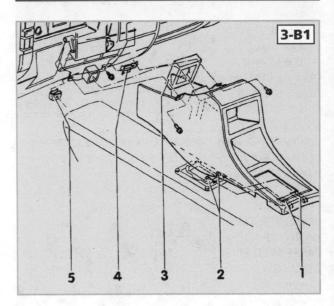

3-B1

☐ **STEP B1:** When a centre console is fitted, it will have to be removed first. After removing the gearstick gaiter:
➜ Pull console carefully upwards until guides (**1**) unclip from pins (**2**).
➜ Push or swing console to one side.
➜ Remove the retaining plate (**4**) by taking out the screw from the spring nut (**5**).
➜ Refit the seal (**3**) when reassembling.

☐ **STEP B2:** On automatic models, there is no gearstick gaiter, of course, but there is a screw holding the end of the console in place.

3-B2

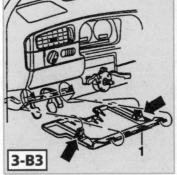

3-B3

3-B4

☐ **STEP B3:** Where a clip-on undertray is fitted, unclip it – press the locking buttons (arrows) and remove.

☐ **STEP B4:** Several different types of dash undertray have been fitted. Whichever one is fitted must now be unscrewed and removed.

STEP B5: An alternative system is the one shown here, with a knee-bar (**A**) running across the full width of the dashboard. Once

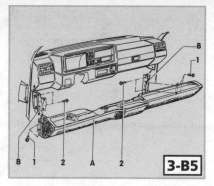

3-B5

again, this is a left-hand drive model. The retaining brackets are shown here (**B**) along with the retaining screws (**1** and **2**).

STEP B6: LATER VEHICLES WITHOUT PASSENGER-SIDE AIR BAGS: Remove the screws and lower the undertray downwards, noting the

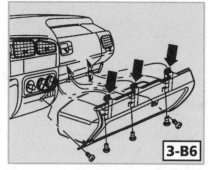

3-B6

positions of the locating pins (arrowed).

STEP B7: Lever off the cover (**1**), remove the four screws and push the heater control panel (**2**) out of the way, under the dash.

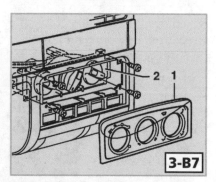

3-B7

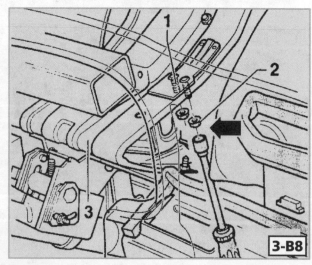

3-B8

STEP B8: GOLF 1992-ON: Unscrew nuts (**2**), as follows:

TOP TIP!

• Find the nuts on the inside of the steering column bracket.
• They are difficult to see and can only be unscrewed with a 10 mm socket (as shown) reached from beneath (arrowed), from between the steering column bracket (**3**) and the bulkhead/firewall.
• Unscrew them from the threaded studs (**1**).

STEP B9: GOLF 1992-ON: Remove the following:
→ The nut (**1**).
→ The earth/ground cable (**2**).
→ Disconnect the aerial/antenna connection (**3**).

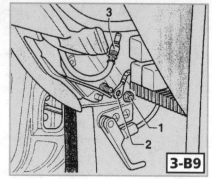

3-B9

→ Pull the dash panel wiring loom connectors off the relay plate.
→ Unplug the connectors at the immobiliser control unit and the heater fan.

STEP B10: On some models, you need to lever away the trim surrounding the heater controls, and remove the screws (arrowed)

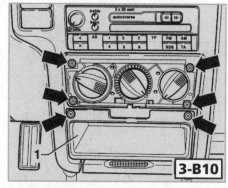

3-B10

found beneath. Also, remove:
→ **EITHER:** The tray (**1**),
→ **OR:** The switches for seat heating and window lifters, whichever is fitted.

STEP B11A: POLO MODELS: Depending on model, there will be a number of (not concealed) screws still holding the

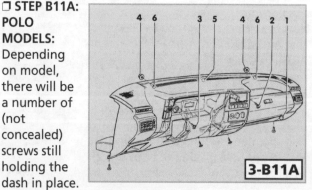

3-B11A

dash in place. Find them out and remove.

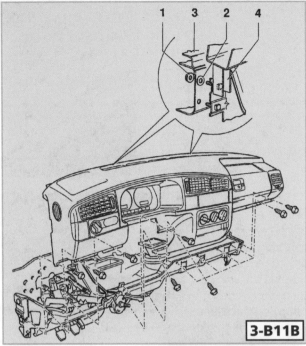

3-B11B

❒ **STEP B11B: GOLF MODELS:** These are typical fixings for the Golf equivalents.

❒ **STEP B12:** Start to work on the screws holding the ends of the dash in place.

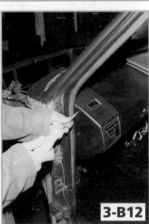

3-B12

❒ **STEP B13:** This is a view of the screw (1) and cap (2). On later models, you must also:
➜ Disconnect the multi-pin plug (4).
➜ Pull grommet (3) out of A-post and unplug connectors inside.
➜ Take off the nut (5) and the earth/ground cable (6).

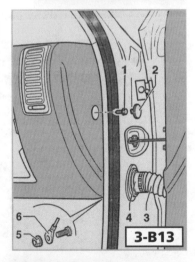

3-B13

❒ **STEP B14:** You can now lift the dash out of the vehicle.

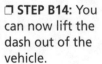

3-B14

❒ **STEP B15:** If you need to, now is the time to remove the heater unit.

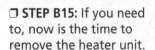

3-B15

Section C: Refitting.

Generally, refitting is the reverse of removal, but take note of the following:

SAFETY FIRST!

• Take extreme care not to short out any electrical connections, or to pinch any cables when reconnecting.

• Have a fire extinguisher ready when you reconnect the battery and stand by to disconnect the battery instantly if necessary.

• An electrical fire can easily be caused by careless re-assembly!

EARLY MODELS

❒ **STEP C1:** Refit the spring nuts or fit new ones.

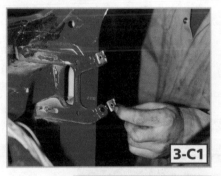

3-C1

❒ **STEP C2:** A pair of spring clips fit to the front underside of the dash on some models. The dash is pushed down until it clips into place.

3-C2

❏ **STEP C3:** The Scirocco's dash top trim has to be refitted beneath the screen rubber.

3-C3

JOB 4: SPEEDOMETER CABLE - *replacement.*

This work is fully described in *Chapter 9: Ignition, Fuel, Exhaust, Job 12: Throttle cable – adjustment, replacement*.

JOB 5: WINDSCREEN WIPER MOTOR - *replacement.*

TOP TIP!

• Remove the trim or cover panels in order to expose the wiper motor/mechanism.
• The cover material used is often very thin and brittle – take great care when levering off thr tri, clip material holding it in place not to cause damage.

❏ **STEP 1:** Before dismantling, disconnect the battery negative (-) earth/ground terminal. See *Chapter 10, Electrical, Dash, Instruments, Fact File: Disconnecting the Battery* BEFORE doing so!

❏ **STEP 2:** Note the position of the wiper blades on the screen. Remove the two windscreen wiper arms. Mark the position of the crank arm so that if it is removed at any stage, it can be replaced in exactly the same position. See **Section B: Crank Arm -** *positioning.*

Section A: Motor – removal.

Although details differ, the principles of removal are the same for all types – there is a motor attached to a frame which is removed with the wiper arm spindles.

EARLY GOLF/RABBIT

❏ **STEP A1:** It is probably simplest to remove the nuts from the wiper spindles...

5-A1

❏ **STEP A2:** ... disconnect the wiring from the plug-and-socket (a), take out the retaining bolt...

5-A2

❏ **STEP A3:** ...and lift the entire assembly away, although it is possible to remove the motor without removing the frame, and leave the crank arm (c) in place.

5-A3

SCIROCCO

❏ **STEP A4:** Some have a single wiper arm and spindle (a), while others have two. Do not remove the frame (20). DO NOT remove the crank from twin-arm systems; DO remove the crank (b) from single-arm systems.

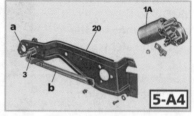

5-A4

POLO TO 1994, MK 2 GOLF, JETTA TO 1992

❏ **STEP A5:** The motor should only be installed in conjunction with the frame.

POLO FROM 1994, POLO CLASSIC, CADDY FROM 1996

❏ **STEP A6:** Before the motor can be removed, the entire assembly must first be removed, by taking out the three retaining bolts (b).

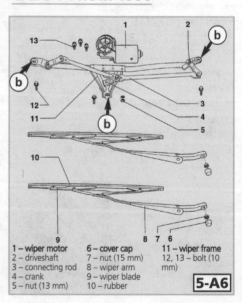

1 – wiper motor	6 – cover cap	11 – wiper frame
2 – driveshaft	7 – nut (15 mm)	12, 13 – bolt (10 mm)
3 – connecting rod	8 – wiper arm	
4 – crank	9 – wiper blade	
5 – nut (13 mm)	10 – rubber	

5-A6

**CORRADO, MK 3 GOLF,
VENTO, FROM 1992**

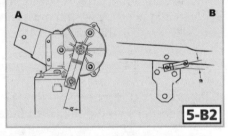

❏ **STEP A7:**
Although
the motor is
mounted
from above
the frame,
the entire
frame may
well have to
be removed
in order to
reach the
mounting
bolts.

1 – cap	rod	17 – bolt
2 – nut	10 – connecting	18 – snap ring
3 – washer	lever	19 – washer
4 – wiper arm	11 – nut	20 – cap
5 – wiper motor	12 – bolt	21 – wiper blade
6 – wiper frame	13 – spring	rubber
assembly	washer	22 – wiper blade
7 – nut	14 – washer	23 – retaining
8 – crank	15 – rubber ring	clip
9 – connecting	16 – O-ring	**5-A7**

Section B: Crank Arm - positioning.

❏ **STEP B1:** In all cases, after refitting the motor, let
it rest at its normal PARK position.

❏ **STEP B2:**
Fit the crank
so that it is in
the position
relevant to
the vehicle
you are
working on:
• **MK 1**

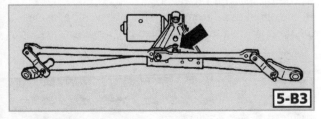

GOLF/RABBIT AND SCIROCCO TWIN-ARM (A): the
crank angle (**a**) is at 20 degrees to the vertical.
RIGHT-HAND DRIVE: the angle of slope is opposite to
the one shown here.
• **MK 2 GOLF (B):** the crank angle (**a**) is at 4 degrees
to the horizontal. • **RIGHT-HAND DRIVE:** the angle of
slope is opposite to the one shown here.
• **SCIROCCO SINGLE-ARM WIPERS:** the crank position
must be horizontal.

❏ **STEP B3: LATER POLO:** When installing the crank,
align it with the arrow.

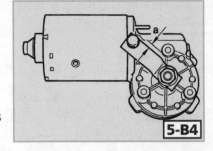

❏ **STEP B4: GOLF,
VENTO MK 3
FROM 1992:** The
crank must be
located so that
the distance (**a**) is
10 mm.

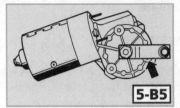

❏ **STEP B5: CORRADO:**
Align the crank so
that it just covers the
hole (arrowed).

JOB 6:   **TAILGATE WIPER, MOTOR
- *replacement*.**

❏ **STEP 1:** Before dismantling, disconnect the battery
negative (-) earth/ground terminal. See ***Chapter 10,
Electrical, Dash, Instruments, Fact File:
Disconnecting the Battery*** BEFORE doing so!

❏ **STEP 2:** Remove the trim covering the motor assembly.

❏ **STEP 3:** Mark the position of the crank arm (when
the system has a separate one) so that if it is
removed at any stage, it can be replaced in exactly
the same position.

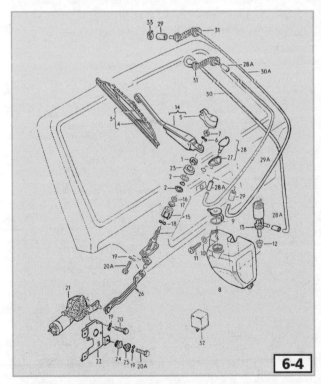

❏ **STEP 4: EARLIER MODELS:** Disconnect the motor
(**21**) from the mechanism (**26**) and the mounting
bracket (**22**). Early systems on Polo, Golf/Rabbit and
Scirocco are similar though simpler in layout.

STEP 5: LATER MODELS: This is a typical layout fitted to later vehicles. The layout is self-explanatory, except that the washer jet (11) squirts water through the cover (10), and is located in the

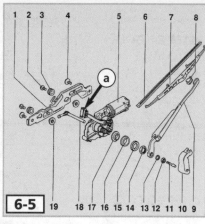

6-5

end of the pipe (18), which is pushed through the centre of the wiper motor shaft. The wiring is disconnected at the wiring plug (a).

JOB 7: SCREEN AND HEADLIGHT WASHER PUMPS - *replacement*.

STEP 1: Before dismantling, disconnect the battery negative (-) earth/ground terminal. See *Chapter 10, Electrical, Dash, Instruments, Fact File: Disconnecting the Battery* BEFORE doing so!

STEP 2: Locate the pump and disconnect the water tubing and the electrical plug:
→ On earliest models, the pump is mounted externally but adjacent to the reservoir, and is unscrewed from its bracket
→ On later models (see illustrations *6-4, item 13*), the pump is a push fit in the washer fluid reservoir. Always ensure that the sealing washer (12) is in place, when refitting.

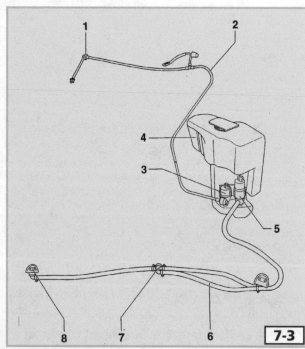

7-3

STEP 3: SHARED RESERVOIR: On some models, the reservoir (4) houses both screenwash pump (3) and

headlight or rear wash pump (5). On this version, the hoses (2, 6) run to the jets (1, 8) via a non-return valve (7).

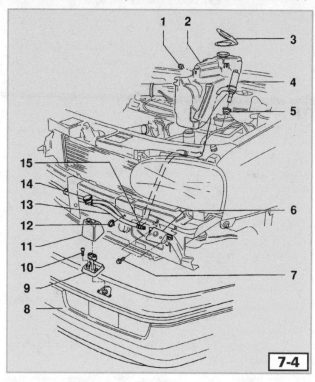

7-4

STEP 4: This Mk 3 Golf headlight wash system is similar in principle to the screen wash systems referred to above.
→ The pump (4) and seal (5) are pushed into (and pulled out of) the side of the reservoir body (2).
→ The washer jet assembly (9) is unscrewed (10) from the bumper (8) after removing the cap (11).
→ When removing pipes, you must FIRST remove the jets, THEN remove the bumper.
→ With the bumper removed, the jet mounting bracket (6) can be seen separately mounted to the body.
→ Take care to disconnect the clips (12) and note the pipe connections on the fluid distributor (14).

JOB 8: RADIO AERIAL/ANTENNA - *replacement*.

STEP 1: Before dismantling, disconnect the battery negative (-) earth/ground terminal. See *Chapter 10, Electrical, Dash, Instruments, Fact File: Disconnecting the Battery* BEFORE doing so!
Remove the following:
→ The radio from the dash.
→ The aerial cable from the foam plastic tube inside the dash, and detach from the dash panel wiring loom.

TOP TIP!
• On later models, there will be an aerial connector quite near to the aerial (and inside the grommet, when fitted) so there will be no need to remove the entire cable from aerial to radio.

❏ **STEP 2: FRONT BODY-MOUNTED AERIAL/ANTENNAS:** From inside the engine bay, pull the aerial cable and grommet from the firewall and remove any clips, depending on model.

❏ **STEP 3:** Remove the wheel arch liner. See *Chapter 13, Bodywork.*

❏ **STEP 4:** Remove the nut (arrowed)...

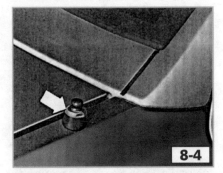

8-4

❏ **STEP 5:** ...pull the aerial (**1**) down, into the wheel arch, and remove it from its bracket (**2**).

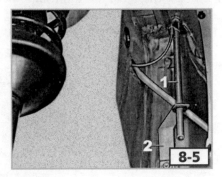

8-5

❏ **STEP 6:** Reverse the process to refit but ensure that:
→ the seal is good between the aerial and the bodywork to prevent water ingress.
→ the earth/ground connection between aerial and body is good.
→ the grommets are put back in place.

❏ **STEP 7: ROOF-MOUNTED AERIAL/ ANTENNAS:** The rear of the roof liner will need to be lowered.
→ Some models have two cables (**3**); others have one.
→ The cable passes through the left, lower A-pillar on its way to the radio.
→ The serrated washer (**5**) is attached to the fixing nut with a plastic ring – make sure it is fitted the right way up!
→ Apply copper grease to the roof in the area of the washer when refitting.

8-7

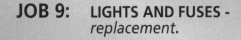

JOB 9: LIGHTS AND FUSES - *replacement.*

Section A: Headlight bulbs – replacement.

Section B: Headlight units – replacement.

Section C: Front and side direction indicator bulbs – replacement.

Section D: Front foglight bulbs – replacement.

Section E: Rear lights – replacement.

Section F: Fusebox and relay plate – replacement.

Section G: Number plate light.

Section H: Interior and (Jetta) luggage compartment lights.

Section I: Dashboard bulbs.

TOP TIP!

• Whenever a light fails to work, check its fuse before replacing the bulb.
• A blown bulb often causes a fuse to blow in sympathy.
• See *Section F: FACT FILE: FUSES AND RELAYS.*

There are very many detail differences between the light units fitted to the various models and variants covered in this manual, but the principles of removing and replacing are the same for all of them.

IMPORTANT NOTE: After removing and replacing any of the headlight components, have the headlights adjusted with a beam adjuster before using the vehicle at night.

SAFETY FIRST!

• Before dismantling, disconnect the battery negative (-) earth/ground terminal. See *Chapter 10, Electrical, Dash, Instruments, Fact File: Disconnecting the Battery* BEFORE doing so!

• Beware! A bulb that has recently been ON may be extremely hot and cause a burn.

Section A: Headlight bulbs – replacement.

CORRADO MODELS: To replace the headlight bulb, the headlight has first to be removed from the body. See *Section B*.

❑ **STEP A1:** Pull off the headlight electrical multi-plug connector.

9-A1

EARLY MODELS, WITHOUT HALOGEN BULBS

❑ **STEP A2:** IMPORTANT NOTE: Most vehicles will have been converted to halogen by now.
➜ Peel the rubber cover (1) from the back of the headlight.
➜ Press ring (2) in slightly, turn it to the left and take it off.
➜ Take the bulb (3) out of the reflector (4).
➜ When fitting the new bulb, make sure the locating lug on the bulb fits in the recess in the reflector.
➜ Item (5) is the sidelight.

9-A2

ALL VEHICLES WITH HALOGEN BULBS

❑ **STEP A3:** The operation is similar, but:
➜ Pull off the headlight multi-plug and peel the rubber cover (1) from the back of the headlight.
➜ **GOLF/VENTO FROM 1992-ON:** Turn the round plastic cover on the rear of the headlight by a part-turn to release it, then remove.
➜ Unhook the bulb securing springs (7) from the retention clip by squeezing inwards, fold it clear and

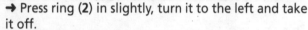

9-A3

withdraw the bulb (6).
➜ Without touching the bulb glass, fit the new bulb. A locating tag ensures it only goes in the correct position. Refit and reconnect in the reverse order.
➜ Item (5) is the sidelight.

ADDITIONAL HEADLIGHTS IN GRILLE

❑ **STEP A4:** Follow the instructions for the regular halogen headlights (see illustration *9-A3*), but note that there is no connector to remove (as in illustration *9-A1*).
Instead, the cable is fed through the cap, as shown, until the bulb can easily be reached. The connector is then pulled off the bulb, before removing the bulb.

9-A4

❑ **STEP A5: JETTA MODELS ONLY:**
➜ Before removing the right-hand headlight, it may be necessary to remove the cover shown here, first.
➜ Press both clips in the direction of the arrow and remove the cover, upwards.

9-A5

TOP TIP!

• If you touch a halogen headlight (or driving light) bulb with bare fingers you will shorten its life, so handle with a piece of tissue paper.
• If the bulb is accidentally touched, wipe it carefully with methylated (mineralised) spirit.

Section B: Headlight units – replacement.

TOP TIP!

• When refitting items such as headlights, where small screws have to be fitted into recessed places, use a screwdriver with a magnetic tip.
• The screw is easily held in place on the end of the screwdriver until it reaches its target.

❑ **STEP B1:** Remove the radiator grille – see *Chapter 13, Bodywork*. On some models, with wrap-around light units, the direction indicator light units have to be removed first – see *Section C*.

STEP B2: Disconnect the wiring both to the headlight bulb and the sidelight, when fitted in the headlight unit. See *Section A*.

STEP B3: On all models, the headlight units are held to the bodywork with Philips-head screws. Later models also have screws that are removed

vertically, from the top face of the front panel.

ELECTRIC HEIGHT ADJUSTERS

IMPORTANT NOTE: On most models, the headlight unit must be removed before the height adjuster can be removed.

STEP B4: On round headlight units, the motor is detached from the frame by twisting it to the right (clockwise) and refitted by twisting it to the left. On most rectangular headlight

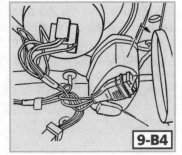

units, the motor on the right-hand side is disconnected by turning it to the left; on the left-hand side, the motor must be turned to the right.

STEP B5: This is one of the systems fitted (to the Corrado, in this instance). This particular motor is removed by being carefully eased out with a screwdriver.

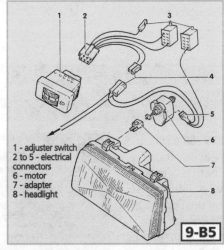

1 - adjuster switch
2 to 5 - electrical connectors
6 - motor
7 - adapter
8 - headlight

Section C: Front and side direction indicator bulbs – replacement.

STEP C1: Establish which type of front indicator lights are fitted. Some are accessed from inside the engine compartment; the majority require the indicator lens and unit to be removed first.

EARLY GOLF AND POLO

STEP C2: Early Golf and Polo models are identical:
➜ Remove the lens by undoing the two fixing screws.
➜ Remove the bulb - push in a little and twist to the left.
➜ Make sure that the gasket seals correctly when the lens is replaced.

JETTA

STEP C3: This is the access for Jetta models, inside the engine bay:
➜ Pull off the rubber cap.
➜ Press the lug (arrowed) on the bulb holder, towards the bulb.
➜ Pull the bulb holder out.

GOLF AND VENTO, 1992-ON

STEP C4: Remove the following:
➜ The towing eye cover.
➜ Lever out the reflector next to the direction indicator by levering carefully with a screwdriver.
➜ Release the catch (arrowed) and pull the direction indicator outwards.
➜ Remove the bulbholder by turning it anti-clockwise and take out the bulb.

POLO 1990-1994

STEP C5: The bulb holder and bulb are removed from inside the engine bay.

POLO 1994-ON

STEP C6: 'REGULAR' POLO MODELS: The light unit is removed after first taking out the screw (position a).
POLO CLASSIC AND

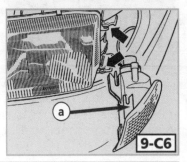

CADDY, 1996-ON: Remove the bulb from inside the engine bay, see illustration *9-C7, item a*. When refitting the light unit (not necessary when just replacing the bulb), make sure the pegs (arrowed) locate in their slots (illustration *9-C7, items b*).

❒ **STEP C7:** To remove the light unit, press the tab (arrowed).

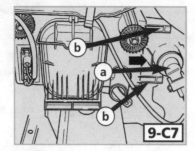

9-C7

CORRADO

❒ **STEP C8:** The direction indicator light is carefully levered out from the front of the vehicle with a screwdriver.

TOP TIP!

• The screw in the top-inner corner of the lens does NOT hold the lens in place – it is in fact the adjuster for the adjacent fog light and should not be turned.

SIDE MARKER LIGHTS

❒ **STEP C9:** On all models, the lens and light assembly are carefully levered off. Variations include:
➔ **POLO:** Push to the rear and lever out at the front.
➔ **GOLF/VENTO FROM 1992-ON:** Carefully lever against the top edge.

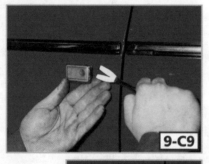

9-C9

❒ **STEP C10:** Inside the light unit, the bulb is removed after first twisting and removing the bulb holder.

9-C10

Section D: Front foglight bulbs – replacement.

EARLY MODELS

➔ Remove the screw on the lower-front of the fog light.
➔ Take out the insert and disconnect cable connector.

➔ Unhook the spring clip, fold it back, take out and replace the bulb.

LATER POLO AND GOLF/VENTO

❒ **STEP D1:** Reach behind the light unit, twist the cover anti-clockwise and remove it.
➔ Take off the connector (**1**) from the bulb.
➔ Press the legs of the spring clip (**2**) over the lugs and swing out.
➔ Remove bulb from housing.

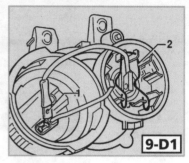

9-D1

CORRADO

❒ **STEP D2:** Take off the direction indicator lens (see *Section C, Step C7*) and beneath the lens two foglight securing screws will be found. Remove the light unit and replace the bulb.

POLO CADDY AND CLASSIC, 1996-ON

❒ **STEP D3:** Remove the three screws (positions a) from the rear of the unit and take off the cover. Undo the connector (1), disconnect the spring clip (2) and remove the bulb from the housing.

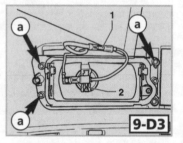

9-D3

Section E: Rear lights – replacement.

❒ **STEP E1:** In a few instances, there is a cover which must first be unclipped. In the great majority of cases, the bulbholder is unclipped by pressing the tabs and removing the bulbholder from inside the vehicle. There are several different shapes and sizes.

9-E1

IMPORTANT NOTE:
On early models, the wiring clip beneath the lamp must be undone, and the rear screen wash water container (when fitted) must be removed from the right-side of the vehicle.

STEP E2: The bulbholder is connected to a wiring plug which can be detached if necessary.

9-E2

STEP E3: The lens is held to the rear panel with a series of studs (on the lens unit) and nuts, removed from inside the vehicle, except on Golf Caddy models, whose lenses are held on with external screws.

9-E3

Section F: Fusebox and relay plate – replacement.

TOP TIP!

• On older vehicles, a fusebox can be a source of problems.
• Because of the location of the fusebox, a leaking windscreen surround can allow water onto the fusebox, corroding terminals.
• The only way to check properly is to remove it and inspect both front and rear connections.

STEP F1: The fuse box, as you would expect, has an enormous number of cable connections but as you can see from the plugs in the background, each one is different from all the others, so it's simply a matter of patiently refitting them in a systematic order.

9-F1

Section G: Number plate light.

STEP G1: Undo the screws and remove the lens.
➔ Press the bulb in a little, turn to the left and remove. Install a replacement.
➔ When refitting the lens, make sure that the gasket seals properly.

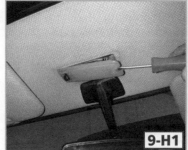

9-G1

➔ Make certain that the lug on the lens locates in its recess, otherwise the number plate will not be illuminated properly.

Section H: Interior and (Jetta) luggage compartment lights.

INTERIOR LIGHT

STEP H1: To remove the interior light lens:
➔ Press in the retaining spring (at the opposite end to the switch) and take out the light unit. Replace the bulb.

9-H1

➔ When refitting, insert the switch-end first, then clip the spring-end into place.

LUGGAGE COMPARTMENT LIGHT

➔ Insert a screwdriver into the front opening and carefully press the light unit out. Replace the bulb.
➔ When refitting the light unit, insert the wire-connection side first.

FACT FILE

FUSES AND RELAYS

• Although the precise location varies slightly, the fuse box on most models is found to the left of the front footwell, behind a trim panel or cover.
• **STEP F2:** On some models, the fuse box is in a similar location, but on the engine bay side of the firewall/bulkhead.
• Numbers on the fuse box lid tells you which

9-F2

circuit each fuse protects. Spare fuses can be located in the fuse box lid.
• Remove and renew a 'blown' fuse, using the plastic clip supplied to pull the fuse body.
• **ELECTRIC WINDOW LIFTERS** and **ELECTRIC SEAT HEIGHT ADJUSTER** motors each have thermal overload cut-outs, which reset themselves, instead of conventional fuses.
• Fuse colour codes are as follows: RED = 10 Amp; BLUE = 15 Amp; YELLOW = 20 Amp; GREEN = 30 Amp.
• On many vehicles, there are additional fuses, in separate holders, above the relays, often covering systems such as air conditioner and ABS relays.

Section I: Dashboard bulbs.

See *Job 3: Dashboard and instrument panel - removal and refitting* for details of instrument panel removal for access to the light bulbs.

JOB 10: FUEL GAUGE SENDER UNIT – *removal, refitting.*

This work is the same as that for removing or replacing the fuel pump mounted in the tank. See *Chapter 9, Part A, Job 15: Electric fuel pump - replacement. Section B: Internal Fuel Pump*.

For gaining access to the fuel gauge, see *Job 3: Dashboard and instrument panel – removal, refitting*.

JOB 11: CENTRAL LOCKING - *replacement of components.*

IMPORTANT NOTES:

i) The drawing used here shows a left-hand drive car. The driver's door switch will, of course, be on the other side on RHD cars, with a pneumatically-operated door lock on the left-hand side.

ii) The pump is found beneath the luggage bay side-trim, but not on the same side on all models. For instance:

GOLF, POLO: Right-hand side of luggage bay.
VENTO: Left-hand side of luggage bay.

FACT FILE

TESTING THE SYSTEM

• The pump runs both ways to provide vacuum or pressure, as required. It normally runs for up to two seconds.
• If the pump does not work, check the fuse, the wiring and the pump itself.
• If the pump runs for more than five seconds, there is a leak somewhere in the system. After 35 seconds, the pump automatically shuts off.
• Find the position of a leak by clamping the first pipe from the pump (**4A**), and operate the door lock, which will cause the pump to operate and then stop after two seconds - unless the leak is at the pump, or the pump cut-off switch is faulty.
• Then, remove the clamp and clamp the next pipe (either **7** or **11**) from the branch (**3**) and so on, in a logical fashion, until each part of the circuit has been tested and the leak discovered.

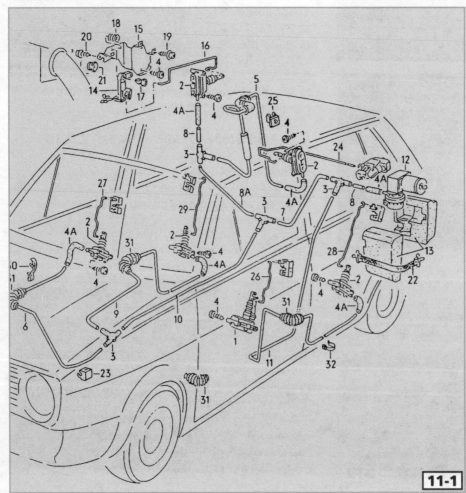

❏ **STEP 1:** Take note of the following description and components.
➜ The central locking system comprises a master switch at the driver's door (**1**), which operates the driver's door and is also wired to the pump (**12**) in the luggage compartment.
➜ The pump operates pneumatic valves (**2**), which operate the door, tailgate and fuel flap (**14**) locks via steel rods (items **16, 24, 27, 28, 29**)
➜ The pump is encased in soundproofing (**13**), held together with a strap (**22**).
➜ Whenever pipework is removed from a door opening, make sure that the flexible channel (**31**) is correctly fitted to both door and pillar when replacing it.

11-1

JOB 12: DIESEL ENGINES' GLOW PLUGS – *checking, replacement.*

☐ **STEP 1:** Before dismantling, disconnect the battery negative (-) earth/ground terminal. See *Chapter 10, Electrical, Dash, Instruments, Fact File: Disconnecting the Battery*

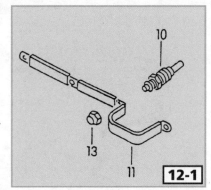

12-1

BEFORE doing so! Undo the retaining nut (**13**) at each plug top (**10**) and remove the bridging strip (**11**) from between the glow plugs.

☐ **STEP 2:** With the wire or connecting strap removed, proceed as follows:
→ Clean away dirt from around the plugs, then fully unscrew and remove them.
→ Examine the condition of each plug by wiping soot away and examining for erosion of the element sheath.
→ Check the internal resistance of each glow plug with a resistance meter. If the reading is much higher than 5 ohms, or is infinity, the plug must be renewed.
→ Fit a complete set of new plugs if any one plug is in poor condition.
→ Refit as the reverse of the above, but note that over tightening a glow plug can damage it!

JOB 13: AIR CONDITIONING EQUIPMENT.

SAFETY FIRST!

• The air conditioning system must not be opened under any circumstances – this applies also to the control switches on Climatronic auto. air conditioning units.

• The substance contained in the system is dangerous. It can cause asphyxiation in an enclosed area, damages the skin and is extremely harmful to the environment.

• If the system needs to be drained for any reason, or if you suspect a leak, take the vehicle to a Volkswagen dealer or air conditioning specialist.

• When moving air conditioning components with the pipework still attached, such as when removing the engine, take very great care not to strain or twist the pipes or to cause a leak.

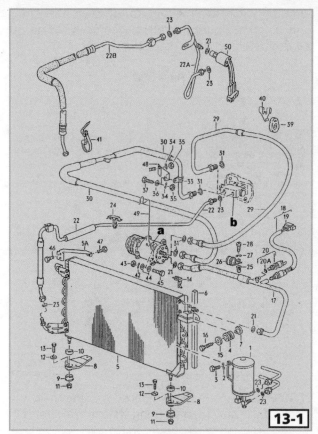

13-1

☐ **STEP 1:** So that you can identify the parts of the air conditioning system and differentiate them from the cooling or heater system pipes, for instance, here they are!
→ Item (**5**) is the air conditioning system radiator (the condenser)
→ Item (**a**) is the compressor pump
→ Item (**b**) connects to the evaporator, which transfers cold air to the vehicle interior.
→ Item (**1**) is the receiver.
→ None of these components must be detached from their pipes. If the condenser (**5**) has to be moved in order to change the coolant radiator, support it carefully out of the way while the work is carried out, taking care not to damage the tubes or fins.

☐ **STEP 2:** If the compressor has to be taken from its bracket, do not disconnect any of the pipes. There are several different types of compressor and bracket. Make a careful note of the way in which the compressor is mounted and take equally careful note of the system of bushes, shims and bolts which are used on the mounting and adjusting system.

JOB 14: ANTI-THEFT EQUIPMENT – *servicing.*

IMPORTANT NOTE: Several elements within the anti-theft system require programming with Volkswagen special equipment. This includes the settings of the key-based transponder and the receiving coil, at the ignition switch, and the fuel cut-off valve. This can only be carried out by a Volkswagen dealer or an appropriately equipped specialist.

ALARM

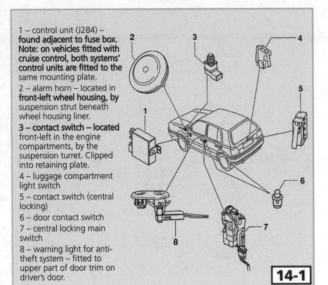

1 – control unit (J284) – **found adjacent to fuse box. Note: on vehicles fitted with cruise control, both systems' control units are fitted to the** same mounting plate.
2 – alarm horn – located in **front-left wheel housing, by** suspension strut beneath wheel housing liner.
3 – contact switch – located front-left in the engine compartments, by the suspension turret. Clipped into retaining plate.
4 – luggage compartment light switch
5 – contact switch (central locking)
6 – door contact switch
7 – central locking main switch
8 – warning light for anti-theft system – fitted to upper part of door trim on driver's door.

14-1

❏ **STEP 1:** These are the components of the main items of the anti-theft warning system, with notes on replacement where appropriate.

IMMOBILISER

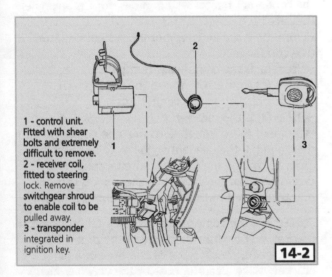

1 - control unit. **Fitted with shear bolts and extremely difficult to remove.**
2 - receiver coil, **fitted to steering** lock. Remove switchgear shroud to enable coil to be pulled away.
3 - transponder integrated in ignition key.

14-2

❏ **STEP 2:** These are the components of the main items of the immobiliser system, with notes on replacement where appropriate.

❏ **STEP 3:** Problems with the immobiliser and alarm system may be identified by interrogation with a fault code reader, such as the Sykes-Pickavant unit described in *Chapter 9: Part A, Job 2: Diagnostics - carry out checks*. Alternatively, the work will have to be carried out by a Volkswagen dealer.

JOB 15: CRUISE CONTROL SYSTEM.

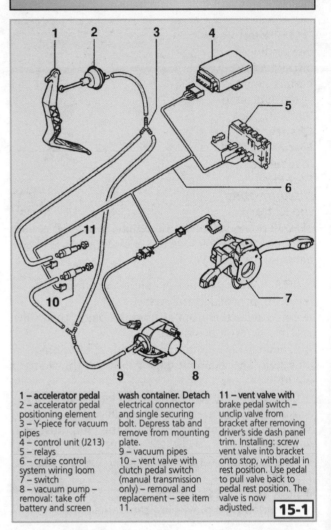

1 – accelerator pedal
2 – accelerator pedal positioning element
3 – Y-piece for vacuum pipes
4 – control unit (J213)
5 – relays
6 – cruise control system wiring loom
7 – switch
8 – vacuum pump – removal: take off battery and screen
wash container. Detach electrical connector and single securing bolt. Depress tab and remove from mounting plate.
9 – vacuum pipes
10 – vent valve with clutch pedal switch (manual transmission only) – removal and replacement – see item 11.
11 – vent valve with brake pedal switch – unclip valve from bracket after removing driver's side dash panel trim. Installing: screw vent valve into bracket onto stop, with pedal in rest position. Use pedal to pull valve back to pedal rest position. The valve is now adjusted.

15-1

❏ **STEP 1:** These are the components of the cruise control system and removal instructions, where appropriate.

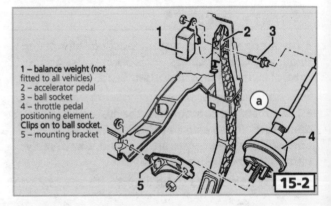

1 – balance weight (not fitted to all vehicles)
2 – accelerator pedal
3 – ball socket
4 – throttle pedal positioning element. **Clips on to ball socket.**
5 – mounting bracket

15-2

❏ **STEP 2:** To adjust the throttle pedal positioning element, remove the adjusting sleeve (a) on the positioning element (4) and push fully forwards. Adjust the accelerator cable – pull adjusting sleeve (a) to rear until there is a maximum of 1 mm play and lock by turning clockwise on to stop.

CHAPTER 11: STEERING, SUSPENSION

*Please read **Chapter 2 Safety First** before carrying out any work on your car.*

Part A: Systems Explained

JOB 1: THE SYSTEMS - explained.

EARLY GOLF TYPE, COVERING:
Golf/Rabbit/Jetta Mk 1, Scirocco, Golf Caddy and Cabriolet To 1994

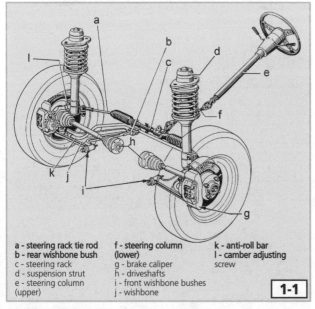

a - steering rack tie rod
b - rear wishbone bush
c - steering rack
d - suspension strut
e - steering column (upper)
f - steering column (lower)
g - brake caliper
h - driveshafts
i - front wishbone bushes
j - wishbone
k - anti-roll bar
l - camber adjusting screw

1-1

☐ **POINT 1:** This is the Mk 1 TYPE front suspension and steering layout.

➜ It was also used for models that continued unchanged, such as Scirocco, Caddy and Golf Cabriolet.

LATER GOLF TYPE, COVERING:
Golf/Jetta Mk 2, 1984-on, Golf/Vento Mk 3, 1992-on, Polo Classic, 1996-on, Polo Caddy, 1996-1997

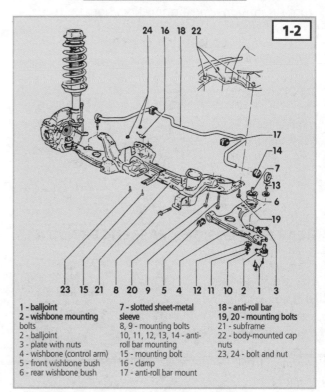

1-2

1 - balljoint
2 - wishbone mounting bolts
2 - balljoint
3 - plate with nuts
4 - wishbone (control arm)
5 - front wishbone bush
6 - rear wishbone bush
7 - slotted sheet-metal sleeve
8, 9 - mounting bolts
10, 11, 12, 13, 14 - anti-roll bar mounting
15 - mounting bolt
16 - clamp
17 - anti-roll bar mount
18 - anti-roll bar
19, 20 - mounting bolts
21 - subframe
22 - body-mounted cap nuts
23, 24 - bolt and nut

☐ **POINT 2: GOLF MK 2 FROM 1994 ON:**
➜ It was continued with only detail changes on Golf and Vento Mk 3 models, from 1992-on. The same

system was used for Corrado as well as for the later Polo Classic and Caddy models.

A cross-member, carrying the engine mountings, bolts to the front-end of the side rails; a rear cross-member, known as a subframe by Volkswagen, carries the suspension, anti-roll bar mounting points, when fitted, and steering rack.

EARLIER POLO TYPE, COVERING:
All models to 1994

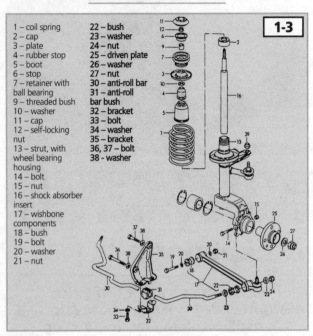

1 – coil spring
2 – cap
3 – plate
4 – rubber stop
5 – boot
6 – stop
7 – retainer with ball bearing
9 – threaded bush
10 – washer
11 – cap
12 – self-locking nut
13 – strut, with wheel bearing housing
14 – bolt
15 – nut
16 – shock absorber insert
17 – wishbone components
18 – bush
19 – bolt
20 – washer
21 – nut
22 – bush
23 – washer
24 – nut
25 – driven plate
26 – washer
27 – nut
30 – anti-roll bar
31 – anti-roll bar bush
32 – bracket
33 – bolt
34 – washer
35 – bracket
36, 37 – bolt
38 - washer

1-3

❏ **POINT 3:** These are the components of the Polo front suspension from introduction, right up to 1994.

LATER POLO TYPE

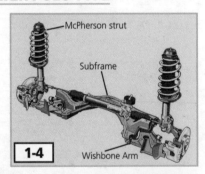

❏ **POINT 4:** This type covers all models from 1994-on, except Polo Classic and Caddy '96-'97,

McPherson strut
Subframe
Wishbone Arm

1-4

REAR SUSPENSION – PASSENGER MODELS

❏ **POINT 5:** The principle of the rear suspension design shown here is common to all passenger models (although components

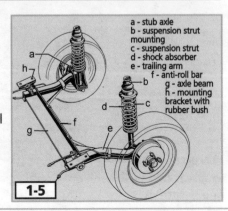

a - stub axle
b - suspension strut mounting
c - suspension strut
d - shock absorber
e - trailing arm
f - anti-roll bar
g - axle beam
h - mounting bracket with rubber bush

1-5

are different). Caddy models all have different rear suspension.

REAR SUSPENSION – CADDY (COMMERCIAL) MODELS

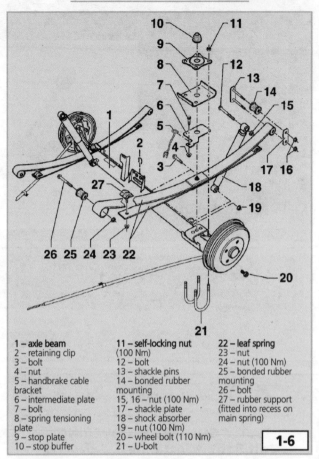

1 – axle beam
2 – retaining clip
3 – bolt
4 – nut
5 – handbrake cable bracket
6 – intermediate plate
7 – bolt
8 – spring tensioning plate
9 – stop plate
10 – stop buffer
11 – self-locking nut (100 Nm)
12 – bolt
13 – shackle pins
14 – bonded rubber mounting
15, 16 – nut (100 Nm)
17 – shackle plate
18 – shock absorber
19 – nut (100 Nm)
20 – wheel bolt (110 Nm)
21 – U-bolt
22 – leaf spring
23 – nut
24 – nut (100 Nm)
25 – bonded rubber mounting
26 – bolt
27 – rubber support (fitted into recess on main spring)

1-6

❏ **POINT 6:** These are the rear suspension components for all Caddy models up to 1996.

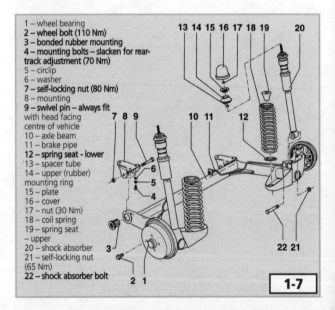

1 – wheel bearing
2 – wheel bolt (110 Nm)
3 – bonded rubber mounting
4 – mounting bolts – slacken for rear-track adjustment (70 Nm)
5 – circlip
6 – washer
7 – self-locking nut (80 Nm)
8 – mounting
9 – swivel pin – always fit with head facing centre of vehicle
10 – axle beam
11 – brake pipe
12 – spring seat - lower
13 – spacer tube
14 – upper (rubber) mounting ring
15 – plate
16 – cover
17 – nut (30 Nm)
18 – coil spring
19 – spring seat – upper
20 – shock absorber
21 – self-locking nut (65 Nm)
22 – shock absorber bolt

1-7

❏ **POINT 7:** From 1997-on, the Caddy was fitted with its own coil spring rear suspension.

Part B: Steering

CONTENTS

JOB 1: STEERING WHEEL – *removal, refitting*.

Section A: Vehicles without airbag.

☐ **STEP A1:** Before dismantling, disconnect the battery negative (-) earth/ground terminal. See *Chapter 10, Electrical, Dash, Instruments, Fact File: Disconnecting the Battery* BEFORE doing so!

☐ **STEP A2:**
Remove the wheel:
➜ Pull off the cover - different styles on different vehicles.

1-A2

☐ **STEP A3:** Use a socket spanner and support the wheel with the other hand:
➜ Undo the centre fixing nut, remove the nut and washer...
➜ ...disconnect the wiring inside the wheel and remove the steering wheel.

1-A3

TOP TIP!

• Don't let the wheel hit you in the face as it suddenly comes off the splines!
• Leave the nut on by a full turn, hit the wheel towards you until it comes free, then remove the nut.
• Never use the steering column lock to stop the wheel turning when removing and refitting the centre nut - this could cause expensive damage!

☐ **STEP A4:** Refit in reverse order, tightening the fixing nut to its specified torque. See *Chapter 1, Facts and Figures*. Also see *Chapter 14, Job 12: Air bags.*

Section B: Vehicles with airbag.

SAFETY FIRST!

• Before dismantling, disconnect the battery negative (-) earth/ground terminal. See *Chapter 10, Electrical, Dash, Instruments, Fact File: Disconnecting the Battery* BEFORE doing so!

• When reconnecting the battery, after reinstalling the air bag, make sure that NO ONE IS IN THE VEHICLE!

• Rear *Safety First!* at the start of *Chapter 14, Job 12* before carrying out any of this work.

☐ **STEP B1:** Make sure that the steering wheel is centralised, with the wheels facing straight-ahead.
➜ Remove both socket head bolts from the air bag unit.
➜ Remove the air bag unit from the steering wheel and pull the connector off the air bag unit.

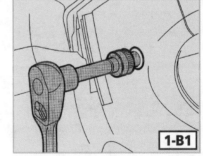
1-B1

☐ **STEP B2:** Before removing the steering wheel:
➜ Remove the trim from below the steering column switch.
➜ Separate the electrical connector (arrowed) and pull the foam rubber sleeve off the connector if fitted.
➜ Remove the steering wheel as shown in *Section A*.

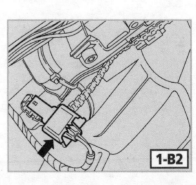
1-B2

STEP B3: With the wheel removed:
→ Hold the steering wheel in the position it would be when in the vehicle.
→ Turn the centring ring slightly so that the wire (arrowed) faces downwards.
→ The centring ring is now located and is prevented from turning.

IMPORTANT NOTE:
If this Step is not carried out or if the centring ring is turned unnecessarily, it can lead to the coil connector in the centring ring being over-stressed when the steering wheel is turned in normal usage, causing irreparable damage.

REFITTING

Refitting is the reversal of removal with the following important points:
→ Use new hexagon socket head bolts for the air bag unit.
→ After completing the installation, first switch on the ignition.
→ Then MAKE SURE THAT NO ONE IS INSIDE THE VEHICLE, and…
→ …reconnect the battery, connecting the positive (+) terminal first.
→ If the air bag has not accidentally gone off you can now get in the vehicle and turn the ignition off.

JOB 2: **TRACK ROD END (TRE) BALLJOINT** – *replacement*.

Section A: Golf and later Polo with conventional tie rod.

FACT FILE

FIXED AND ADJUSTABLE TIE RODS

STEP A1: There is an important feature you need to know about when changing the TREs on some low-mileage Volkswagens.
• When they leave the factory, these vehicles have one adjustable tie- rod (**a**) and one fixed tie rod (**b**).
• The fixed, left-side tie rod, fitted to new vehicles, has to be removed and scrapped when the left-side TRE is worn.
• New, fixed tie rods are not supplied by Volkswagen. The replacement will be adjustable, like the right-side tie rod.
• If the left-side TRE has been previously replaced on your vehicle, you have to change the TRE in the conventional way. See *Section B: Fixed tie rod*.
• EARLY POWER STEERING RACK: See *Section C* for important information.

STEP A2: Slacken the road wheel nuts on the side to be worked on. Jack up and support the car on axle stands and remove the road wheel.

STEP A3: Slacken the lock nut (**c**) on the track rod by just enough to free the TRE on the steering arm (**d**), but no more.
• Leave the nut where it is so that when the new TRE is fitted, its location will be about the same.

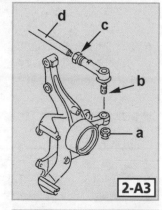

2-A3

STEP A4: Straighten and pull out the split pin on the TRE. Undo the balljoint to steering arm locknut (*2-A3, item a*) until the bottom of the nut is level with the end of the thread (*2-A3, item b*).

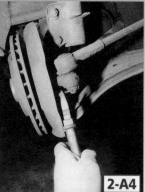

2-A4

STEP A5: Use a suitable splitter tool to break the grip of the taper, remove the securing nut and withdraw the balljoint from the steering arm.

2-A5

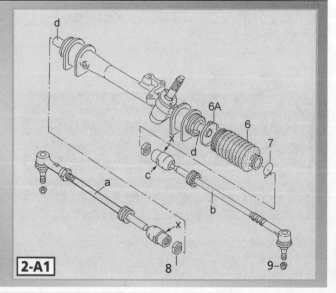

2-A1

❐ **STEP A6:** • If the balljoint taper proves stubborn, a sharp blow with a hammer to the side of the eye momentarily distorts the eye and releases the taper.

2-A6

❐ **STEP A7:** Unscrew the balljoint from the trackrod. You will probably have to grip the steering arm (illustration **2-A3, item d**) with a self-grip wrench to stop it from turning.

❐ **STEP A8:** Clean and grease the tie bar threads before fitting the new balljoint to prevent them from rusting together in future. Fit the new balljoint in reverse order and tighten the nuts. Always fit a NEW split-pin, and bend the ends over in opposite directions.

2-A8

IMPORTANT NOTE: Before using the vehicle again, have the front wheel alignment set as soon as possible to avoid severe tyre wear and dangerous braking and steering!

❐ **STEP A9:** Refit and tighten the road wheel, and lower the car to the ground.

Section B: Golf and later Polo with fixed tie rod.

❐ **STEP B1:** Remove both sets of bellows. Carefully measure the distance (a) from the centre-line of the TRE to the shoulder on the fixed rod inner balljoint.

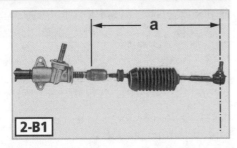

2-B1

❐ **STEP B2:** Centralise the rack by making the distance the same on both sides from

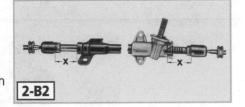

2-B2

the shoulders on the inner ball joints (**x**) to the shoulder on the steering rack.

→ Slacken the locknut (**2-A1, item 8**) and unscrew the inner end of the left-hand (fixed) tie rod using the flats (**c**). Remove the tie rod.

❐ **STEP B3: FIT TIE ROD:** To fit the new tie rod, screw the locknut onto the threaded shaft at the end of the rack.

❐ **STEP B4:** Screw the new, adjustable tie rod onto the rack so that the distance between the shoulder on the rack and the shoulder on the tie rod is the same as the other side.

❐ **STEP B5:** Fit the new TRE as shown in **Section A**...

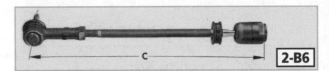

c

2-B6

❐ **STEP B6:** ...and make sure that the distance between the centre line of the TRE and the shoulder on the steering rack (**c**) is the same as it was when measured before dismantling.

• If you lose the correct measurement, obtain it from your Volkswagen dealer – there are many different dimensions given for different models.

• If you drive the vehicle with the settings misaligned, the track will be 'out' and the vehicle could be dangerous to drive.

POWER STEERING RACK WITH FIXED TIE ROD

IMPORTANT NOTE: This next Step DOES NOT apply to power steering racks with the usual removable-type of left-hand TRE.

❐ **STEP B7:** Volkswagen recommend that the rack has to be removed. See **Job 4**. This is because:

→ The tie rod has a male thread which screws into a female thread in the steering rack shaft.

→ The threads are held with thread lock, instead of a locknut.

→ The old threadlock has to be cleaned out with a thread tap, while the end of the rack is packed with a rag to prevent any stray matter from getting in.

→ The thread on the tie rod must also be cleaned if it is to be re-used.

→ Both threads must be cleaned with a proprietary brand of (pre-threadlock) thread cleaner, then dried off completely.

→ Only ONE drop of thread lock should be applied, to the second thread-down of the female thread in the steering rack shaft. If you apply too much, it might be impossible to remove the tie rod in future.

→ The tie rod should be fitted to align as for a manual rack – see **Steps 1 to 6**, and tightened into the rack shaft to 70 Nm, with a torque wrench.

Section C: Polo to 1994.

☐ STEP C1: This process is very similar to that described in earlier sections, but this is the location of the TRE, high up on the strut. See also *Part C: Suspension, Job 3, Step B2.*

2-C1

JOB 3: STEERING RACK GAITER - *replacement.*

☐ STEP 1: Note the location of the steering rack gaiters under the car. ONLY carry out this work when the exhaust system is cold. Remove the Track Rod End (TRE) balljoint. See *Job 2.*

☐ STEP 2: Undo the securing clip from each end of the gaiter and pull the gaiter off the tie rod.

☐ STEP 3: Wipe away contaminated grease and replace with new (lithium-based molybdenum disulphide) grease. Secure the new gaiter in position at both ends with new bands or screw-type clips.

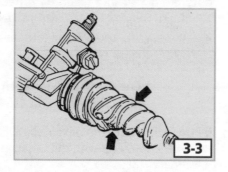

3-3

TOP TIP!

Avoid the following faults:
• If the gaiter is not seated correctly in its correct location (check when removing) it may not seal and the life of the rack will be severely reduced.
• If the gaiter is twisted (3-3, arrowed) when fitting, it will partly collapse, as shown.
• If the gaiter concaves-in, try opening up the large end to let air in and restore its correct shape.

☐ STEP 4: Refit the TRE balljoint. See *Job 2.*

JOB 4: STEERING RACK – *replacement.*

FACT FILE

WHAT TO REMOVE FIRST

To provide enough clearance for the rack to be removed, it will be necessary on some models to move or remove certain key components.

POLO TO 1994
• No major dismantling required.

GOLF/RABBIT/JETTA TO 1984
• It will be necessary to remove the gearchange linkage (manual shift models) and front-end of exhaust system.

POLO FROM 1994-ON
• Dismantle as follows *in addition to* the removal information given in the main text:
Large grommet on engine-side: Release it and push it forward over the lower joint.
Disconnect support cable from transmission housing (manual transmission only).
Remove front-end of exhaust system.
Remove bolt from engine/transmission rear mounting.
Support subframe from below, loosen support bolts and lower (after undoing steering column-to-rack pinion bolt) to disengage column from rack.

GOLF/VENTO FROM 1992-ON, CORRADO
• Dismantle as follows *in addition to* the removal information given in the main text:
After undoing steering column-to-rack pinion bolt, to disengage column from rack (see main section).
Support the engine – hoist from above or jack from beneath.
Remove the left-hand subframe bolt. Loosen, but do not remove the right-hand subframe bolt.
Remove the gearchange pivot (manual shift models) from the lower end of the steering column – lower the subframe slightly, to give clearance.
At the appropriate stage, lower the engine/transmission unit enough to allow the steering rack to be removed.

☐ STEP 1: Raise the front of the car and support securely on axle stands. Remove the road wheels.

☐ STEP 2: Disconnect the trackrod ends from the steering arms. See *Job 2.*

☐ STEP 3: Unscrew the electrical earth/ground cable (arrowed) connection from the body of the steering rack, when fitted.

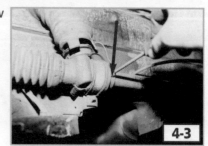

4-3

STEP 4: Remove – or lift the lower end of - the boot/s covering the bottom of the steering column, where it enters the rack. Use a pair of spanners to undo, then remove the pinch bolt securing the steering column to the rack pinion. Make a mark on the column and the shaft so that the components can be refitted in the same position.

4-4

STEP 5: LATER MODELS, WITH POWER STEERING: These (arrowed) are the universal joint clamping bolts

➜ The two parts are separated when the engine/transmission assembly is lowered.

➜ It takes two people to re-assemble this type –

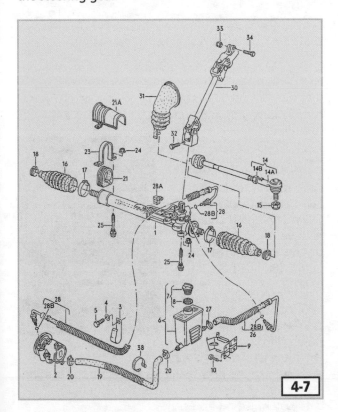

4-5

one to guide the UJ parts together while another lifts the engine/transmission assembly.

STEP 6: Where necessary (dependant on model) disconnect the gear change mounting bracket from the steering gear.

4-7

STEP 7: POWER STEERING: Disconnect hydraulic pipe unions (**26** and **28**) and drain the fluid, before removing the rack.

VR6-ENGINED MODELS WITH SUPERCHARGER: These vehicles are also fitted with additional cooling pipes to the low-pressure supply pipe.

STEP 8: Remove the rack as follows:
➜ Take out the bolts holding the rack to body or subframe.
➜ With a lever, separate the steering column pinch-joint from the rack pinion.

4-8

➜ Pull the rack assembly away from the body or subframe.

> **TOP TIP!**
>
> • If it helps, disconnect the steering column - try doing so just at the upper universal joint clamp - so that there is room for the steering rack pinion to clear the steering column clamp.

STEP 9: Remove the rack from beneath the driver's-side wheel arch. Slide it as far as possible so that the pinion (arrowed) is up against the passenger side, then lower it and remove it on the driver's side.

4-9

RACK REPLACEMENT

STEP 10: Place the steering wheel in the straight ahead position and engage the rack pinion splines with the column coupling. Make sure that the groove in the

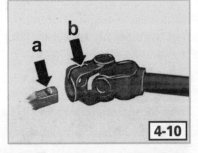

4-10

pinion (**a**) lines up exactly with the clamp bolt hole (**b**).

> **TOP TIP!**
>
> **STEP 11:** • The replacement rack should be centred before installation.
>
> • Measure the total travel of a TRE when moved from lock to lock. Go back half this distance and your rack is centred.

STEP 12: Before using the vehicle again, have the front wheel alignment set as soon as possible to avoid severe tyre wear and dangerous braking and steering!

MANUAL STEERING RACK FREE PLAY ADJUSTMENT

☐ **STEP 13:** IMPORTANT NOTES:

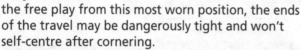

4-13

• The steering rack tends to wear most around the straight-ahead position.

• If you remove all the free play from this most worn position, the ends of the travel may be dangerously tight and won't self-centre after cornering.

• If the rack is more than very slightly worn, renew it.

• The following DOES NOT apply to power steering racks.

If there is too much free play at the steering wheel adjust the steering rack free play as shown below:

➜ Check, first, that free play is not caused by wear or looseness anywhere else in the system - the most common reason by far. If not:

➜ With front wheels off ground, and in the straight-ahead position:

➜ Carefully screw in the self-locking adjuster screw (arrowed) by about 20 degrees - no more than 1/3rd of a flat on the hexagon.

➜ Check that the steering does not feel tight when turned from lock-to-lock. If it does, back off the adjuster and ask your Volkswagen dealer for advice. Otherwise:

➜ Road test the vehicle: IMPORTANT SAFETY NOTE! If the steering does not return to straight-ahead on its own after cornering, loosen the adjuster screw again. Check especially that the steering does not tighten up at the ends of the travel of the rack, and that the steering self-centres from those positions.

➜ If there is still play, tighten by the smallest possible amount.

TOP TIP!

• On Polo models from 1994, and others where access is difficult use a socket extension with universal joint attachment to reach the rack adjustment nut.

JOB 5: POWER STEERING PUMP – *removal, refitting.*

There are two main types of mounting, although there are several different pump types and detail differences. Because no repairs to the pump are possible, we only cover removal and replacement procedures.

Section A: Adjustable-type pump.

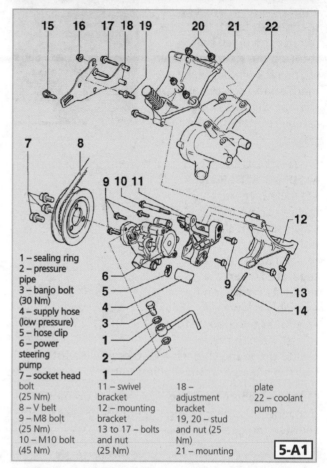

1 – sealing ring
2 – pressure pipe
3 – banjo bolt (30 Nm)
4 – supply hose (low pressure)
5 – hose clip
6 – power steering pump
7 – socket head bolt (25 Nm)
8 – V belt
9 – M8 bolt (25 Nm)
10 – M10 bolt (45 Nm)
11 – swivel bracket
12 – mounting bracket
13 to 17 – bolts and nut (25 Nm)
18 – adjustment bracket
19, 20 – stud and nut (25 Nm)
21 – mounting plate
22 – coolant pump

5-A1

☐ **STEP A1:** This is a typical pump mounting.

☐ **STEP A2:** Remove the fluid pipes from the pump and remove the sealing washer. Drain the fluid into a suitable container. Seal the open ends of pipes and connections with masking tape to keep out any contamination.

☐ **STEP A3:** Slacken the power steering pump pivot/attachment bolts, swivel the pump and remove the drivebelt. Unbolt and remove the pump. (Engine here on bench.)

5-A3

☐ **STEP A4:**
When refitting:
➜ Follow illustration *5-A1*
➜ Be sure to use new sealing washers on the unions.
➜ Top up the pump with power steering fluid before connecting hoses.
➜ Fit mounting bracket (**12**) together with pump (**6**) to the mounting plate (**21**) and engine block. Fit bolts loosely at first, then tighten to the correct torque.

STEP A5: Continue as follows:

→ Fit the adjuster bracket (**18**) using bolts (**17**), to cylinder block.

5-A5

→ The adjuster mechanism is now fitted to both brackets. The bolt which passes through the mechanism applies pressure through the fork at the bottom of the adjuster bracket and the stud passes through the slotted hole in the adjuster bracket and the plane hole in the pump bracket. It is MOST IMPORTANT that when you adjust the power steering belt, the locknut on the inside of the brackets is released before the adjuster bolt is turned, and the locknut is then retightened after adjustment.

→ Finally, tighten bolts and adjust the belt correctly.

→ Bleed the system - see *Job 6*.

Section B: Fixed-type pump.

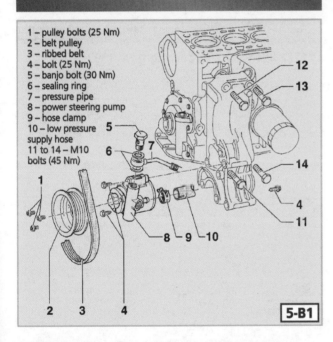

1 – pulley bolts (25 Nm)
2 – belt pulley
3 – ribbed belt
4 – bolt (25 Nm)
5 – banjo bolt (30 Nm)
6 – sealing ring
7 – pressure pipe
8 – power steering pump
9 – hose clamp
10 – low pressure supply hose
11 to 14 – M10 bolts (45 Nm)

5-B1

STEP B1: The pump fitted to smaller-engined vehicles is driven by a flat belt and is held in a fixed position. The belt has a separate adjuster.

STEP B2: The dismantling procedure is almost exactly the same, except that there is less complexity because of the absence of the belt adjustment assembly.

STEP B3: In addition, when reassembling:

→ Follow illustration *Section B, Step 1*.

→ Top up the pump with power steering fluid before connecting hoses.

→ First tighten bolt (**12**), then bolt (**11**).

→ Finally, tighten bolts (**13**, **14**).

STEP B4: Bleed the system - see *Job 6*.

JOB 6: BLEEDING THE POWER STEERING.

The power assisted steering system is self-bleeding. This operation should be carried out each time the connecting pipes are removed or refitted:

→ Top up the reservoir, and the pump (remove hose/s) before starting.

→ You should slowly apply full lock alternately to the right and left with the car stationary and the engine running, while an assistant tops up the reservoir.

→ DO NOT allow the reservoir to run out of fluid, or air will be introduced.

→ On initial start-up, run the engine for only a few seconds at a time until the system is full of fluid.

→ DO NOT leave the steering at full lock - risk of damage.

JOB 7: STEERING COLUMN – *removal, refitting.*

STEP 1: Before dismantling, disconnect the battery negative (-) earth/ground terminal. See *Chapter 10, Electrical, Dash, Instruments, Fact File: Disconnecting the Battery* BEFORE doing so!

→ The steering wheel (see *Job 1*) and air bag, when fitted (see *Chapter 14, Interior and Trim*.)

→ The shrouds, column switchgear and wiring plugs.

→ Immobiliser components, when fitted.

→ Trim and/or grommets at the base of the steering column.

STEP 2:
The top of the steering column is held to the bottom of the scuttle with a pair of shear bolts. These

7-2

are cunningly designed to shear off when they are tightened up to the correct torque, leaving the potential thief without a bolt head to grip if he wants to take the locking steering column off the car.

→ You may be able to grip the shear bolt with a pair of self-grip wrenches and turn it in the normal way.

→ Alternatively, you may be able to tap the head of the shear screw round with a small chisel until it comes loose.

→ If all else fails, the heads must be drilled off.

TOP TIP!

• Use a heat gun or hair dryer to heat the metal into which the shear bolts are screwed.
• This should make it easier for them to come free.

❏ **STEP 3:** The column is also bolted further down, nearer the end of the column on earlier Golf and Polo models.

7-3

❏ **STEP 4:** Bearing in mind that the end of the column has already been detached from the steering rack (see *Job 3: Steering rack - replacement*) and noting that the clutch and brake pedals are attached to this column and must also be detached, the steering column can now be lifted away.

7-4

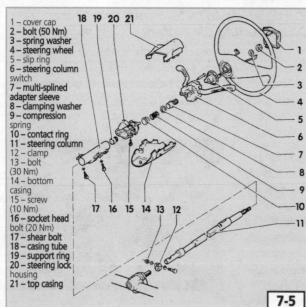

1 – cover cap
2 – bolt (50 Nm)
3 – spring washer
4 – steering wheel
5 – slip ring
6 – steering column switch
7 – multi-splined adapter sleeve
8 – clamping washer
9 – compression spring
10 – contact ring
11 – steering column
12 – clamp
13 – bolt (30 Nm)
14 – bottom casing
15 – screw (10 Nm)
16 – socket head bolt (20 Nm)
17 – shear bolt
18 – casing tube
19 – support ring
20 – steering lock housing
21 – top casing

7-5

❏ **STEP 5:** These are the components of the Polo steering column up to 1994.

❏ **STEP 6:** Before the end of 1986, the Polo's column (**A**) was split, unlike the later (**B**) one-piece column.

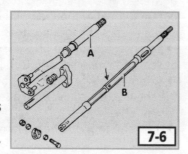

7-6

❏ **STEP 7: ALL RELEVANT GOLF AND POLO MODELS:** See illustration **7-6**. The small metal lug on the lower section must be visible in the hole (arrowed) in the upper section. If necessary, manipulate the two halves until the lug is in position.

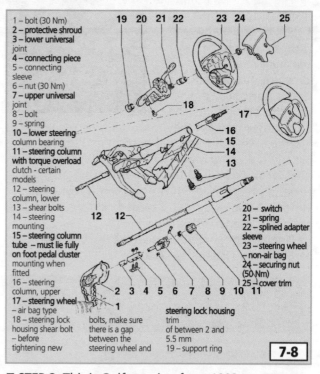

1 – bolt (30 Nm)
2 – protective shroud
3 – lower universal joint
4 – connecting piece
5 – connecting sleeve
6 – nut (30 Nm)
7 – upper universal joint
8 – bolt
9 – spring
10 – lower steering column bearing
11 – steering column with torque overload clutch - certain models
12 – steering column, lower
13 – shear bolts
14 – steering mounting
15 – steering column tube – must lie fully on foot pedal cluster mounting when fitted
16 – steering column, upper
17 – steering wheel – air bag type
18 – steering lock housing shear bolt – before tightening new bolts, make sure there is a gap between the steering wheel and steering lock housing trim of between 2 and 5.5 mm
19 – support ring
20 – switch
21 – spring
22 – splined adapter sleeve
23 – steering wheel – non-air bag
24 – securing nut (50 Nm)
25 – cover trim

7-8

❏ **STEP 8:** This is Golf steering from 1992.

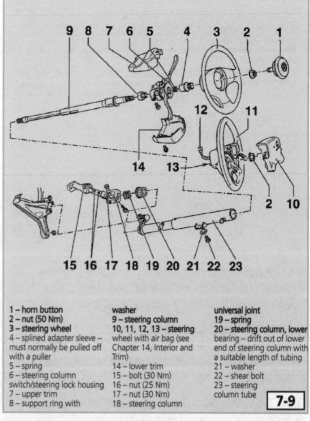

1 – horn button
2 – nut (50 Nm)
3 – steering wheel
4 – splined adapter sleeve – must normally be pulled off with a puller
5 – spring
6 – steering column switch/steering lock housing
7 – upper trim
8 – support ring with washer
9 – steering column
10, 11, 12, 13 – steering wheel with air bag (see Chapter 14, Interior and Trim)
14 – lower trim
15 – bolt (30 Nm)
16 – nut (25 Nm)
17 – nut (30 Nm)
18 – steering column
universal joint
19 – spring
20 – steering column, lower bearing – drift out of lower end of steering column with a suitable length of tubing
21 – washer
22 – shear bolt
23 – steering column tube

7-9

❏ **STEP 9: CORRADO AND POLO CADDY/CLASSIC:** (Caddy Pick-up from 1997 continued with early Golf-type steering.)

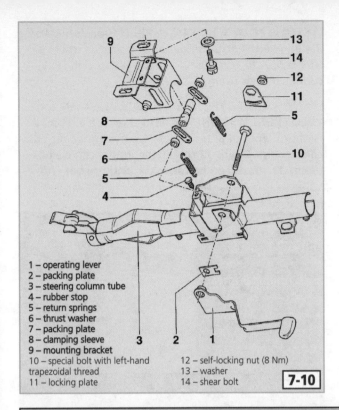

1 – operating lever
2 – packing plate
3 – steering column tube
4 – rubber stop
5 – return springs
6 – thrust washer
7 – packing plate
8 – clamping sleeve
9 – mounting bracket
10 – special bolt with left-hand trapezoidal thread
11 – locking plate
12 – self-locking nut (8 Nm)
13 – washer
14 – shear bolt

7-10

❑ **STEP 10:** Corrado and Polo Caddy/Classic models (not Pick-up) height adjuster mechanism.

❑ **STEP 11: POLO FROM 1994-ON:** The red arrows indicate the directions in which the column will collapse in the event of a crash. The shear bolts fixing the column to the dash (a) are removed as described in *Step 2*. The UJ is unbolted (b) on models up to 1998 and the whole assembly unclipped from the mounting (c) as it is pulled out.

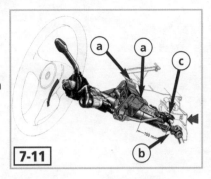

7-11

IMPORTANT NOTE:
On Polos from 98, the top UJ is an integral part of the column and cannot be unbolted at point (b).

Part C: Suspension

CONTENTS

JOB 1: GOLF, POLO FRONT SUSP. - *types.*

❑ **POINT 1:** These are the components of the Golf-type front strut.

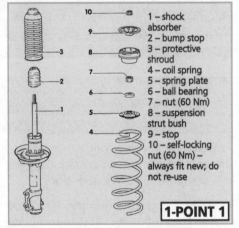

1 – shock absorber
2 – bump stop
3 – protective shroud
4 – coil spring
5 – spring plate
6 – ball bearing
7 – nut (60 Nm)
8 – suspension strut bush
9 – stop
10 – self-locking nut (60 Nm) – always fit new; do not re-use

1-POINT 1

❑ **POINT 2:** ...and these are the components of the suspension fitted to all later Golf variants.

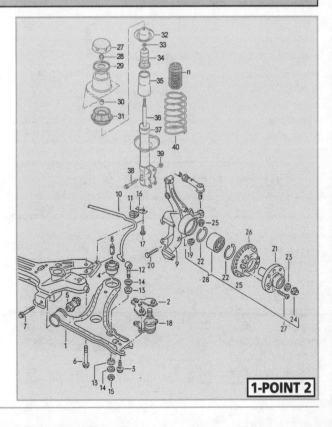

1-POINT 2

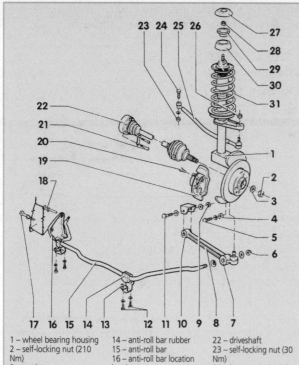

1 – wheel bearing housing	14 – anti-roll bar rubber	22 – driveshaft
2 – self-locking nut (210 Nm)	15 – anti-roll bar	23 – self-locking nut (30 Nm)
3 – washer	16 – anti-roll bar location bracket	24 – hexagon bolt M 8 x 60
4 – self-locking nut (50 Nm)	17 – hexagon bolt M 12 x 80 (120 Nm)	25 – tie rod
5 – hexagon bolt		26 – self-locking nut (35 Nm)
6 – self-locking nut (75 Nm)	18 – hexagon bolt M 12 x 1.5 x 50 (120 Nm)	27 – cap
7, 10 – lower arm bush (in lower arm)		28 – self-locking hexagon nut (60 Nm)
8 – lower arm	19 – brake caliper	29 – bump stop
9 – self-locking nut (55 Nm)	20 – socket head bolt (70 Nm)	30 – shock absorber ring
11 – hexagon bolt M 10 x 70	21 – socket head bolt (45 Nm)	31 – suspension strut
12 – bolts (30 Nm)		
13 – anti-roll bar bracket		**1-POINT 3**

❑ **POINT 3:** The early Polo system – used until 1994 – has a lower arm instead of a wishbone. The anti-roll bar locates the outer end of the arm and prevents it from having too much longitudinal movement.

❑ **POINT 4:**
From 1995, the Polo's front suspension is much stronger and more Golf-like, with a separate subframe.

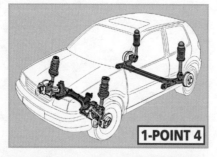

1-POINT 4

JOB 2:   FRONT ANTI-ROLL BAR – remove, refit.

❑ **STEP 1: MK 1 GOLF-TYPE MODELS:** Remove the clamp nuts (**d**), clamp (**b**) and outer bush, and the similar fittings holding the two inner bushes (**a**) and remove the anti-roll bar.

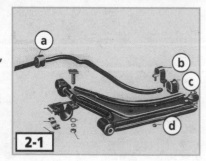

2-1

❑ **STEP 2: POLO TO 1994:** See illustration *Job 1, Point 3*. Remove the anti-roll bar ends from the lower arm (*items 6, 7, 8*) and the two clamp plates and split rubber bushes (*items 12, 13, 14*).

❑ **STEP 3: GOLF-TYPE MODELS FROM 1984-ON and POLO FROM 1994-ON:** See illustration *Job 1, Point 2* for both types of anti-roll bar. Remove the outer bush components (*items 12 to 15*), the inner bush clamps (*items 11, 16, 17*) and remove the anti-roll bar (*10*).

TOP TIP!

❑ **STEP 4:** • It can be difficult to attach the brackets when new rubber bushes have been fitted.
• Try using a clamp of some sort to hold the brackets in place while the bolts are inserted.

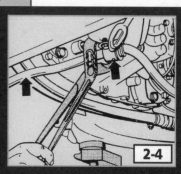

2-4

• When replacing, lubricate tight bushes with a small quantity of brake fluid. Ordinary oil and grease rots rubber.

JOB 3:   FRONT STRUT, TOP BEARING, SPRING AND SHOCK ABSORBER - *replacement.*

The strut assembly can be removed as a unit and the compression taken out of the coil spring with the strut off the vehicle.

TOP TIP!

• **ALL MODELS:** If both rear struts are removed at the same time, be sure to support the suspension on axle stands or jacks.
• If you don't the suspension will hang down on the brake hoses!

Section A: Golf - and later Polo-type repairs.

The two systems are fundamentally similar, but there are detail differences between Golf and early Polo in the area of the front suspension.

❑ **STEP A1:** Before lifting the vehicle off the ground, loosen the stub axle nut. (See *Job 5, Wheel Bearing, Front and Rear - replacement*). Raise the front of the vehicle and support it on axle stands. Start by removing the brake caliper and suspending it so that there is no tension on the brake hose. Disconnect the track-rod end. See *Part B, Job 2.*

IMPORTANT NOTE:
A few Mk 1 Golf-type vehicles will have a bracing bar bolted across the engine bay, using the two studs which hold the strut to the body.

➜ The Caddy from 1997-on has them as standard and others are fitted as accessories.

➜ Remove the bracing bar from both sides before removing a strut.

❐ **STEP A2: MK 1 GOLF-TYPE SUSPENSION:** Remove the two sets of nuts and washers (**a**) from the strut tops, inside the engine bay. DO NOT, under any circumstances, remove nut (**b**) at this stage!

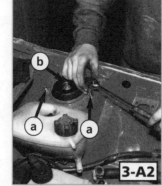

❐ **STEP A3: ALL OTHER SUSPENSION TYPES:** Remove the nut from the top of the strut, inside the engine bay. You will need to use a large ring spanner to undo the nut, while stopping the rod at the top of the strut from turning.

➜ Some models have an Allen-key socket on the rod.

➜ Others have a small hexagon on the end of the rod. Use a ring spanner.

➜ Others again have a pair of flats – use an open-ended or adjustable wrench.

❐ **STEP A4:** After disconnecting the brake caliper and hanging it up with a cable tie (so that there is no strain on the hose)...

❐ **STEP A5:** ...and on Golf-type models, remove the two sets of nuts, bolts and washers (arrowed) from the bottom of the strut.

❐ **STEP A6:** Fully remove the already loosened hub nut (see *Job 5, Wheel bearing, front and rear - replacement*)...

❐ **STEP A7:** ...and lever the strut away from the wheel bearing housing.

❐ **STEP A8:** Take the strut away from the vehicle.

❐ **STEP A9:** New struts, springs, or strut inserts must always be fitted in pairs, NEVER singly.

❐ **STEP A10:** Refit all components in reverse order.

Section B: Early Polo-type - repairs.

The two systems are fundamentally similar, but there are detail differences between Golf and early Polo in the area of the front suspension.

❑ **STEP B1:** Before lifting the vehicle off the ground, loosen the stub axle nut. (See *Job 5, Wheel Bearing, Front and Rear - replacement).* Raise the front of the vehicle and support it on axle stands.

TOP TIP!

❑ **STEP B2:** • When disconnecting the track-rod end from the strut, the pin in the TRE tends to turn instead of the nut.

• Use a ball-joint splitter 'in reverse', as shown, to press the taper pin into the arm, preventing it from turning.

• Don't apply too much pressure on the TRE; you'll push the ball out!

❑ **STEP B3:** Undo the bottom suspension ball joint...

❑ **STEP B4:** ...and use a large lever to lever against the anti-roll bar, so that the ball comes free.

❑ **STEP B5:** Pull the hub at the bottom of the strut off the drive shaft.

❑ **STEP B6:** Disconnect the strut top. See *Section A: Step A3.*

❑ **STEP B7:** Remove the strut and proceed as described in *Section A, Steps 5 to 8.* New struts, springs, or strut inserts must always be fitted in pairs, NEVER singly.

Section C: Coil springs - replacement.

Remove the strut as described in *Sections A* and *B.*

FACT FILE

COIL SPRINGS

• If a coil spring is cracked, sagged or heavily rusted, replace the front springs AS A PAIR.
• VOLKSWAGEN springs are colour- and paint stripe-coded. Use only a matching pair.
• New struts, springs, or strut inserts must always be fitted in pairs, NEVER singly.

FRONT SPRINGS

❑ **STEP C1:** Using two coil spring compressors, spread over as many spring coils as possible, compress the spring, tightening each compressor a little at a time,

in turn, until the spring ends are free of their seats. If a regular type of locknut is used to hold the spring retaining plate in position, remove them.

❑ **STEP C2:** If a slotted nut is fitted, you will have to use a special tool such as the Sykes-Pickavant tool shown here. Remove the various components carefully, saving them for later use, or replacing them as necessary.

❑ **STEP C3:** Where a regular nut is fitted, use a ring spanner. In both cases, grip the rod to stop it turning.
➜ Some models have an Allen-key socket on the rod.
➜ Others have a small hexagon on the end of the rod. Use a ring spanner.
➜ Others again have a pair of flats – use an open-ended or adjustable wrench.

STEP C4: Take off the top bush and the roller bearing within it...

3-C4

STEP C5: ...and the spring top seat and spring (with spring compressors) can be lifted away. Release the spring compressors evenly, each one a little at a time, until the tension is out of the springs.

3-C5

STEP C6: Make sure the coil spring is properly seated in the spring seats. Tighten top nuts to the specified tightening torques.

3-C6

Section D: Strut inserts – replacement.

STEP D1: After removing the strut and coil spring, take off spacers and shroud from the top of the strut.

STEP D2: Undo the cap on the top of the insert housing on the strut.
➜ Often, there is oil inside the strut.
➜ Prepare for spills; drain out the old oil.

3-D2

TOP TIP!

• The cap can be difficult to remove.
• Try using a chain wrench, used mainly for oil filter removal.
• If all else fails, try a large stilson wrench.

STEP D3: Take out the old strut insert and fit the new one as a direct replacement. Some owners prefer to fit uprated strut inserts at this stage. The performance trade-off means that the vehicle will, of course, be marginally less comfortable.

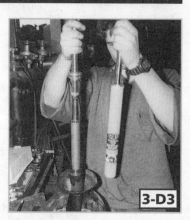

3-D3

JOB 4: LOWER ARM, BUSHES AND BALLJOINT – *replacement/ camber adjustment*.

SAFETY FIRST!

• Lower suspension arms ('wishbones' on Golfs and later Polos) are prone to damage.

• A bent or kinked wishbone will affect the steering geometry.

• A rusty or damaged wishbone should be scrapped and replaced with a new one.

Section A: Ball joints – all models.

STEP A1: Raise the front of the vehicle off the ground with the road wheel or road wheels removed. Place a jack beneath the wheel bearing housing in such a way that the jack supports it, but does not lift it to any noticeable extent.

STEP A2: Refer to *Job 1, Point 1-2* for the illustration numbers shown here. Before removing the balljoint, its position must be marked precisely on the wishbone. The bolts (3) which hold the balljoint (18) in place pass through slotted holes in the ends of the wishbone and screw into weld nuts on a plate (2). If the position of the balljoint is changed, the vehicle's handling, steering and tyre wear characteristics will change and the wheel camber angle will have to be checked with a camber setting gauge.

STEP A3: Remove the anti-roll bar, where applicable. See *Job 2*.

STEP A4: Disconnect the balljoint from the wheel bearing housing by undoing the nut and tapping out the bolt (arrowed) without damaging its thread. The top of the balljoint can now be drifted downwards and out of the bottom of the wheel bearing housing.

4-A4

STEP A5: The balljoint can now be unbolted from the outer end of the wishbone.

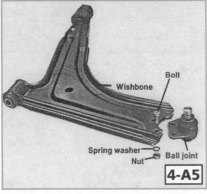

Wishbone

Bolt

Spring washer
Nut
Ball joint

4-A5

STEP A6: Reassemble as the reverse of removal, applying grease to the assembled components to help prevent corrosion.
• Lubricate all threads before refitting and make sure that bolts run smoothly into their welded nuts.
• If bolts show any signs of corrosion, replace them with new ones.
• Fit all of the bolts loosely before tightening any of them.
• Note that the pinch bolt head faces forwards.

AUTOMATIC TRANSMISSION MODELS

If the front pivot bolt on the left-hand side is not accessible:
• Support the engine either from above with a hoist or from below with a jack.
• Remove the front left mounting and disconnect but do not remove the rear mounting and the engine steady strut (front mounting).
• Raise the engine until the front wishbone bolt can be removed.

Section B – Wishbone and bushes - Golf and variants, Mk 1-type*.

*The Mk 1-type suspension was used on several variants after 1984, when Golf Mk 1 finished, including Cabriolet, Golf Caddy and Scirocco.

The part numbers referred to in the following Steps relate to the illustration in *Job 1, Point 2*.

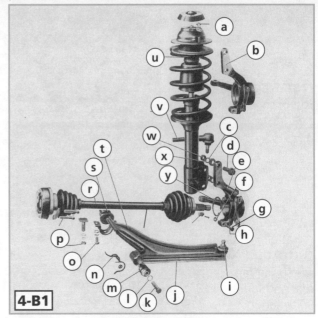

4-B1

STEP B1: Remove the bolt (k) and washer (l) which are screwed through the bush (m) and into the welded nut (n) on the vehicle bodywork.

STEP B2: The bolts (o) - nuts fitted to bolts on captive plates on very earliest models - are removed and the wishbone (j) is removed.

TOP TIP!

STEP B3: Make up a puller to remove the front bush with a bolt, washer small enough to pass through the bush eye, socket large enough for the bush to be pulled into it and a washer and nut to go over the end of the socket. Tighten the nut until the bush is pulled out.

STEP B4: • When fitting new bushes, use silicone lubricant.

4-B4

Section C: Wishbone and bushes - Golf and variants 1984-on, all models*.

*The Mk 1-type suspension was used on several variants after 1984, including Cabriolet, Golf Caddy and Scirocco. See *Section B.*

The part numbers referred to in the following Steps relate to the illustration in *Job 1 Point 2* and *Section B, illustration 4-B1* of this Job.

IMPORTANT NOTE:
At about the time that the Mk 2 Golf/Jetta appeared, Volkswagen started calling the 'wishbone', the 'track control arm' – can be confusing, depending on who you're buying parts from, but they're the same thing!

STEP C1: If a new wishbone is being fitted, fit the balljoint mounting nuts to the centre of the slotted holes. Slacken the strut mounting bolts (**items d** and **38**) connecting the strut to the wheel bearing housing, adjusting the position of the two components relative to one another...

STEP C2: ...before checking the camber angle with a camber setting gauge.

STEP C3: Apply copious amounts of releasing fluid to the mounting bolts and remove the front pivot bolt (**7**).

STEP C4: Remove the bolt (**6**) which holds the rear of the wishbone in place. Remove the bush (**4**) and the split sleeve (**8**) with pliers.

STEP C5: Lever the wishbone away from the subframe and remove it.

STEP C6: Replace the front and rear bushes. Make sure that the kidney-shaped opening in the rear bush (**A**) points towards the centre of the vehicle, and that one of the embossed arrows points towards the recess in the wishbone.

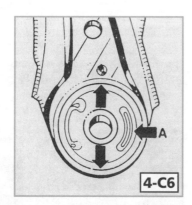

TOP TIP!

• For front bush replacement, see *Step B3*.
• If the rear bush is severely corroded into place, pass a hacksaw blade through the curved slot in the bush, reattach the hacksaw frame and cut through the rubber and steel sections of the bush, which will help you to drive it out. Take great care not to damage the wishbone.

Section D: Lower arm and bushes – Polo to 1994.

Refer to the illustrations *Job 1, Point 3* in connection with the component numbers shown here.

STEP D1: Raise the vehicle and detach the anti-roll bar, as described in *Job 2: Front anti-roll bar – removal, refitting*.

STEP D2: Disconnect the ball joint as described in *Section A: Ball joints*.

STEP D3: Remove the lower arm as follows:
→ Take off the nut (**9**) and washers.
→ Drift out the pivot bolt (**11**) and remove the lower arm (**8**).
→ Replace the bushes (**7, 10**) as necessary. See *Section B: Wishbone and bushes - Golf and variants, Mk 1-Type, Step B3 and B4*.

Section E: Wishbone and bushes – Polo from 1994-on.

STEP E1: CADDY PICK-UP FROM 1997-ON: This is almost identical to the type shown in *Section B: Wishbone and bushes - Golf and variants, Mk 1-Type*.

STEP E2: ALL OTHER POLO MODELS, INCLUDING EARLIER POLO CADDY: This is almost identical to the type shown in *Section C: Wishbone and bushes - Golf and variants 1984-on, all models*.

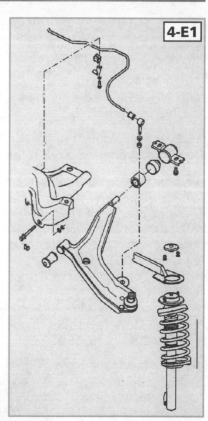

JOB 5: WHEEL BEARING, FRONT AND REAR – *replacement*.

STEP 1: Take note of the exploded drawings that relate to this Job. Unless stated otherwise, the illustration numbers shown here refer to the illustrations in *Job 1*, of Golf (and variants) components.

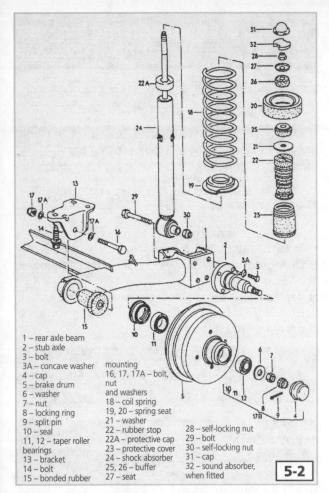

1 – rear axle beam
2 – stub axle
3 – bolt
3A – concave washer
4 – cap
5 – brake drum
6 – washer
7 – nut
8 – locking ring
9 – split pin
10 – seal
11, 12 – taper roller
bearings
13 – bracket
14 – bolt
15 – bonded rubber

mounting
16, 17, 17A – bolt,
nut
and washers
18 – coil spring
19, 20 – spring seat
21 – washer
22 – rubber stop
22A – protective cap
23 – protective cover
24 – shock absorber
25, 26 – buffer
27 – seat

28 – self-locking nut
29 – bolt
30 – self-locking nut
31 – cap
32 – sound absorber,
when fitted

5-2

☐ **STEP 2:** These are the pre-1994 Polo components. Post-1994 cars are similar.

☐ **STEP 3:** For Polo front suspension items, see *Job 3: Front strut, spring and shock absorber - replacement.*

☐ **STEP 4:** Remove the following components from the wheel bearing housing and take it off the vehicle, complete with hub (*item 21*):
→ The disc brake calliper (hang it carefully on a piece of wire) and disc, or the drum brake assembly. See *Chapter 12, Brakes.*
→ The TRE balljoint (*item 25*) from the steering arm. See *Part B, Job 2.*
→ The suspension balljoint (*item 18*). See *Job 4.*
→ The strut lower-end bolts (*items 13, 14*), and lever off the bottom of the strut.

☐ **STEP 5:** See *Chapter 12, Brakes* for information on how to remove the rear brake drum.

5-6

☐ **STEP 6:** The inner bearing race tends to stay on the hub and be difficult to remove. This is a front hub, but the principle is the same at both ends.

☐ **STEP 7:** Where the bearing races also decide to stay in place inside the rear brake drum/hub (which they do!) you will have to take a hammer and punch and carefully drift them out.

5-7

TOP TIP!

☐ **STEP 8:** • When drifting or pressing a bearing in or out, only ever apply force to the outer race:
→ There are three indents - more easily visible inside this new hub - which allow you to drift the outer race of the bearing.
→ If the hub is still covered in grease, locate these indents with the end of the drift.

5-8

5-9

5-10

☐ **STEP 9:** These are the bearing races and seal ready to fit to the brake drums.

☐ **STEP 10:** Drift in the new outer race. An old socket makes a perfectly acceptable drift. A press would be better.

5-11

5-12

☐ **STEP 11:** Grease the inside of the hub, then work more in to the bearing race, spinning the bearings to make sure that the grease is present around each roller.

☐ **STEP 12:** The seal is tapped in last – it must go in evenly – and more grease is applied to the seal so that it won't be running dry.

STEP 13: Finally, it's a matter of refitting the components removed earlier. After the hub nut has been tightened to the correct torque

5-13

setting, a new split pin should be used, before fitting the grease cap back in to place.

STEP 14: Press the bearing from the wheel bearing housing in the following order:
→ Press the hub (*item 21*) from the bearing, after removing the screw (*item 27*). The bearing race will almost certainly be destroyed as the inner race remains fixed to the hub.
→ Use a puller or drift to remove the inner race from the hub.
→ Remove the circlips (*item 22*).
→ Press or drift the bearing outer race from the wheel bearing housing.

STEP 15: When fitting the new bearing, press the bearing into the carrier using pressure on the outer track ONLY. Fit the circlips.

STEP 16: Press the hub into the bearing, pushing ONLY on the inner track with a suitable piece of strong tube.

STEP 17: Tighten the hub nut (arrowed) correctly.
→ Note the torque figure required for front and rear disk brake hubs.
→ See the *TOP TIP!* below for the

5-17

correct way of tightening the rear hub nut on rear drum-brake vehicles.

TOP TIP!

• This is the method recommended by VW for ensuring that the hub nut is torqued up correctly on rear drum-brake vehicles.
• The washer behind the nut has an oversized hole which allows it to move behind the nut.
• The nut is correctly tightened when the washer can *just* be slid when pushed (not levered) with a screwdriver.

STEP 18: Reassemble the front suspension and brakes in the reverse order of removal. See relevant Jobs for detailed information. Use a NEW hub nut.

JOB 6: REAR SHOCK ABSORBERS, COIL SPRINGS - *replacement*.

COIL SPRUNG REAR SUSPENSION

STEP 1: ALL EXCEPT CADDY: There is very much less tension in rear coil springs (except on Syncro or possibly some modified vehicles) and it is not necessary to use spring compressors to remove or replace them PROVIDED THAT you take great care when removing the top nut, holding the spring seating plate in place. There MAY BE enough pressure to make the nut fly off as it is undone. Press down hard on the top of the spring until the nut is undone. If in doubt, apply a pair of spring compressors, as for the front springs.

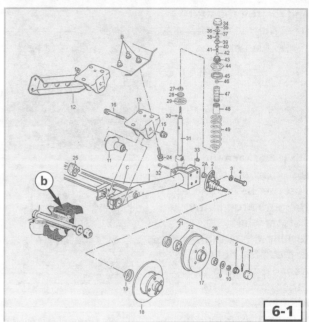

6-1

STEP 1: The illustration numbers given in the following Steps refer to this drawing.
→ See *Illustration 5-2* for an illustration of Polo components.
→ Take the weight of the suspension with a jack under the stub-axle end of the trailing arm (**1**) but don't compress the spring.

STEP 2: Take the cap (**34**) off the top of the strut (**31**), from inside the vehicle. Undo the nuts and fittings (**35 to 40**) that retain the shock absorber to the body. Grip the flats at the top of the shock absorber shaft to prevent it from turning.

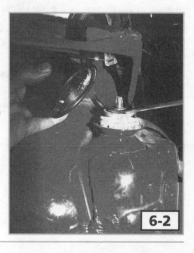

6-2

STEP 3: Take off the locknut (**33**), remove the bolt (**32**)...

STEP 4: ...and detach the bottom of the strut from the trailing arm.

6-3

STEP 5: Lower the jack and remove the strut from the vehicle.

6-5

STEP 6: Take the spring off the shock absorber by holding the centre rod at the flats (**a**) while turning the nut (**b**). Remove the nut (**6-1, item 41**) and the other components (**42 to 48**) and remove the spring (**49**).

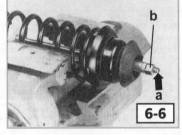

6-6

Refit in reverse order making sure that the components are in good condition and assembled in the correct order, and that the retaining nuts are tightened to the correct torque.

STEP 7: MK 1 GTI: Make sure that the cut-off part off the upper spring seat (arrowed) is in the outer position, to give sufficient type clearance.

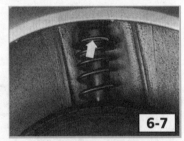

6-7

STEP 8: ALL OTHER GOLF AND POLO MODELS: Locate the end of the spring (arrowed) in the top mounting plate, as shown...

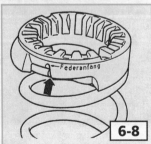

6-8

STEP 9: ...and the lower mounting plate (**1**) must be fitted so that – when this type are fitted - the holes (**a**) are parallel with the bush (**2**) in the shock absorber eye.

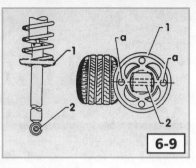

6-9

CADDY MODELS

The principles of spring and shock absorber replacement are very similar for the coil sprung models, from 1997-on. The spring is separate from the shock absorber, so it is necessary to remove the shock absorbers before removing thesprings.

Leaf sprung models are completely different.

See *Job 9: Rear Axle Assembly and Bushes - removal and replacement* for details of the two Caddy systems.

JOB 7:	REAR ANTI-ROLL BAR (when fitted) – *remove, replace*.

A rear anti-roll bar was fitted to some Golf and later Polo and derivative models.

GOLF MK 1-TYPE SUSPENSION

STEP 1: The rear anti-roll bar is bolted to the rear suspension frame.

7-1

STEP 2: Retrieve the brackets and fixings for later use. Check the rubbers and fit new ones if they are at all soft or worn.

7-2

STEP 3: At its outer ends, the anti-roll bar is held to the trailing arms by these metal clips. Bend up one end of the metal clip with a lever...

7-3

STEP 4: ... use a drift to slide the clip off, noting that it has a narrow end and a wider end.

7-4

STEP 5: You can now remove the clip, bush and anti-roll bar from the trailing arm.

7-5

GOLF (AND DERIVATIVES) FROM 1984-ON AND LATER POLO

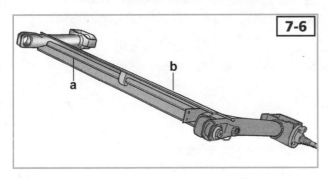

7-6

STEP 6: The anti-roll bar (**a**), when fitted, is permanently welded into the triangular section of the Mk 2 Golf-type rear axle beam (**b**).

JOB 8:	REAR AXLE ASSEMBLY AND BUSHES – *remove, replace*.

Section A: Rear suspension – with coil springs (not Caddy).

The illustration numbers given in the following Steps refer to illustration *Job 6* unless stated otherwise.

IMPORTANT NOTE:
From 1988, the rear suspension mounting bracket bolts have a shoulder, and the tightening torque is reduced from 85 Nm (63 lbf ft) to 70 Nm (52 lbf ft). On some models, the bracket is welded to the body and cannot be removed.

STEP A1:
Disconnect the following:
→ Unclip the handbrake cables at the support clips, adjacent to the pivot bolts (**15, 16**).
→ Disconnect the rear brakes (see *Chapter 12, Brakes*) and remove the rear brake compensator, where necessary.
→ Remove the springs and shock absorbers – see *Job 6*.
→ Support the weight of the axle while the vehicle rear body is supported on a pair of axle stands.
→ Take out the pivot bolts (**15, 16**) - or remove the bracket from the body, as shown here - and prepare to lower the axle assembly.

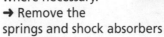

8-A1

TOP TIP!

• Don't remove the mounting brackets (**13**) unless you have to!
• If necessary, and to reduce the risk of shearing the bolts (**24**), soak them with releasing fluid several times over the days before carrying out this work.
• 'Work' each bolt backwards and forwards, a little at a time, adding more releasing fluid, if it tightens up as it is removed.
• If necessary, remove the fuel tank and apply heat to each threaded insert (**B**).

STEP A2: Rubber bushes have to be pressed out and then new ones pressed into position - remove any corrosion first. Use a puller and soapy water to help the rubber to slip into place. Do NOT use oil or grease!

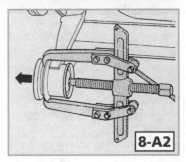

8-A2

STEP A3: GOLF MK 1-TYPE SUSPENSION: When refitting the axle to the mounting bracket, before tightening the bolts, raise the angle of the trailing arm so that the angle

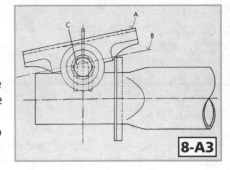

8-A3

of line B is parallel with the top face of the bracket (**A**), then tighten the pivot pin nut (**C**).

❏ **STEP A4: OTHER MODELS - TYPE 1:** The protruding section of the rubber mount must point towards the front of the vehicle.

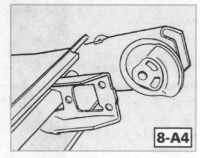

8-A4

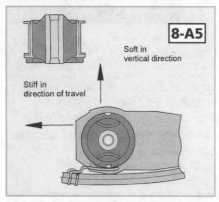

8-A5

Soft in vertical direction

Stiff in direction of travel

❏ **STEP A5: OTHER MODELS - TYPE 2:** Make sure the bush is fitted the right way up.

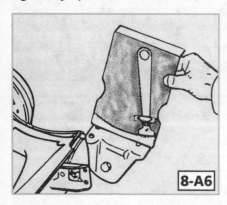

8-A6

❏ **STEP A6:** The angle of the mounting bracket to the axle beam must be 12 degrees, plus or minus 2 degrees.

❏ **STEP A7: ALL OTHER MODELS EXCEPT GOLF MK 1-TYPE:** With all mounting bolts fitted but still loose, arrange the left-hand side of the axle beam so that the bush is centred in the mounting. On the right-hand side, lever the mounting with a pair of tyre levers (**a**) and (**b**) so that there is only a very small gap at point (**c**).

Have an assistant tighten the bolts.

MODELS WITH BOLT-ON MOUNTING BRACKETS

SAFETY FIRST!

• The location of the brackets on the body affects the rear track.

• It is essential that the brackets are located so that the rear wheels track symmetrically.

• After refitting brackets, check the rear track and adjust if necessary.

Section B: Rear suspension - Caddy with leaf springs.

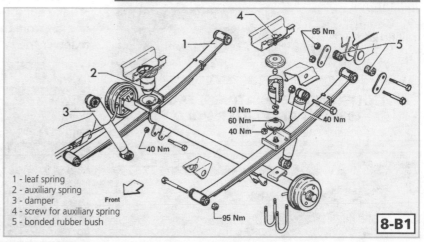

1 - leaf spring
2 - auxiliary spring
3 - damper
4 - screw for auxiliary spring
5 - bonded rubber bush

Front

65 Nm
40 Nm
60 Nm
40 Nm
40 Nm
40 Nm
95 Nm

8-B1

❏ **STEP B1:** The Caddy rear suspension is a very straightforward, very traditional type of leaf-spring suspension. On later models, the auxiliary leaf spring is replaced by a buffer and other minor changes occurred during production. Do not mix parts on left-hand and right-hand sides.

Section C: Rear suspension - Caddy with coil springs.

❏ **STEP C1:** The Caddy coil sprung rear suspension is similar in everything except the spring arrangement. See the illustration *Part A, Job 1, Point 7*.

CHAPTER 12: BRAKES

Please read Chapter 2 Safety First before carrying out any work on your car.

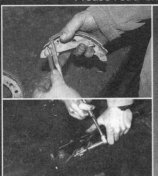
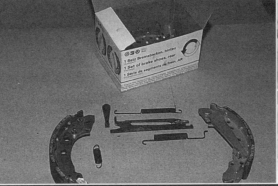

CONTENTS

SAFETY FIRST!

• We advise you not to rebuild hydraulic components. If faulty, buy new or exchange replacements.

• When replacing brake shoes, pads, discs or drums, always do so on both wheels at the same end of the car - as complete 'axle' sets.

• The hydraulic system on an ABS (anti-lock brake) equipped vehicle contains fluid at extremely high pressure. DO NOT open the system without depressurising it first. See *Job 15. ABS systems - essential notes.*

• Read *Chapter 2, Safety First!* in connection with the risks associated with brake fluid.

• In summary, brake fluid is poisonous, may be flammable, attacks paint and plastics, and should only be used out of a previously unopened container.

FACT FILE

BRAKE FLUID

When disconnecting brake pipes or hoses you can minimise brake fluid loss by:

• Unscrewing the master cylinder reservoir cap, and...

• ...laying a sheet of plastic across the opening.

• Refit the cap.

• This will help prevent atmospheric pressure from pushing the fluid out of opened lines.

JOB 1: IDENTIFY FRONT BRAKE TYPE.

FRONT BRAKE TYPES

• Several types of front brakes have been fitted to the Golf range of vehicles. The 'TYPE' letters shown here are ours, not Volkswagens!

TYPE A-a

• TYPE A: *VW II* BRAKES (known earlier as *VW 'MK II'* or *KELSEY-HAYES*), not necessarily related to Mk 2 vehicles! Type (**a**) is the 'EARLY' style of brake caliper, fitted initially only to US-built vehicles, and type (**b**) is the 'LATER' style - although there are cosmetic differences within them - see later in this Job.

TYPE A-b

• TYPE B: *GIRLING (LATER-TYPE)* have this appearance.
• TYPE C: *GIRLING (EARLY-TYPE)* front brakes have this appearance. 12 mm and 10 mm disc types are very similar, although the 12 mm disc has a groove around its outer edge.

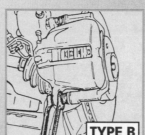

TYPE B

• TYPE D: *TEEVES* front disc brakes look like this. There are different variations for different disc sizes and types.

TYPE C

• TYPE E: Early base-model Golfs not sold in the UK or North America were produced with **front drum brakes**, with finned drums.

TYPE D

TYPE E

JOB 2: GENERAL NOTES.

Section A: All brakes types – READ THIS FIRST!

❑ **POINT A1:** Start by raising the wheel to be worked on and supporting it on an axle stand. Remove the road wheel - see *Chapter 2, Safety First!* Work on firm, level ground, make sure the parking brake is fully on, and that the rear wheels are firmly chocked, in front and behind.

❑ **POINT A2:** Spray proprietary brake cleaner over the caliper assembly both before dismantling and again, once dismantled, over the exposed assembly, to wash off brake dust.

2-A2

We use Wurth Brake Cleaner in an aerosol can.

❑ **POINT A3:** After fitting the pads or shoes, and before using the vehicle, apply the brakes firmly, several times to adjust them.

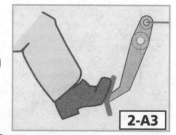

2-A3

❑ **POINT A4:** • Remember that new brake pads will not reach their maximum efficiency until they have 'bedded in', especially if the brake disc/rotor is worn and grooved.

• Allow for the fact that the brakes may be a little below par when you first drive the car and drive accordingly.

❑ **POINT A5:** The ideal place to work on brakes is on the wheel-free type of Tecalemit hoist that we use. The wheels are 'free' to be worked on and can be raised to a perfect, safe work height.

Section B: Disc brakes – READ THIS FIRST!

❑ **POINT B1:** At the full service interval, you are STRONGLY RECOMMENDED to remove the caliper and examine both pads and the caliper piston seal, as shown here, and to clean out accumulated brake dust.

❑ **POINT B2:** IMPORTANT NOTE: After removing the

caliper (where appropriate), DO NOT allow the weight of the caliper to hang from the flexible hose – position it to rest on the driveshaft, or support it from the road spring using a length of wire.

❏ **POINT B3:** Scrape rust and hard deposits from the lips of the caliper housing and any other places where deposits build up. These last two operations help to reduce the risk of brake squeal.

2-B4

❏ **POINT B4:** With the discs removed, now is a good time to check the thickness of the brake disc.

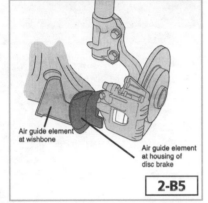

❏ **POINT B5:** If air ducting was fitted as standard, it is ESSENTIAL that it is all present and correct.

Air guide element at wishbone

Air guide element at housing of disc brake

2-B5

BRAKE DISC WEAR SYMPTOMS

❏ **POINT B6:** • Look for any obvious grooves worn into the disc. Slight undulations are acceptable, but anything worse and the disc should be replaced.
• Look and feel for any wear-ridge on the outer edges of the disc. The depth will give an indication of wear.
• Check for corrosion of the disc surface. If any is found, the brake caliper is probably faulty, and needs checking.
• If any surface flaking is found on either side of the disc, replace them both.
• Check the disc thickness at its thinnest point, with a micrometer.

❏ **POINT B7:** Check the caliper piston seal for damage and look for rust on the piston itself.

❏ **POINT B8:** • In order to fit new pads, the caliper piston must be pushed back into the bore.
• Use an old (but perfectly clean) battery hydrometer to draw about half of the fluid from the master cylinder.

2- B8

• EITHER: Push the piston back into the caliper, using a G-clamp, or other suitable tool, as shown.
• OR: Some VW brakes have a screw to pull each piston in. Use them, if fitted – reset them later.
• Make sure that fluid doesn't overflow the master cylinder!

❏ **POINT B9: PAD WEAR INDICATORS:** Some early US vehicles have mechanical, audible pad

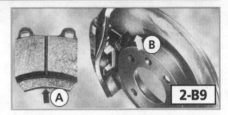

2-B9

wear indicators. There is an extended area of friction material (**A**) on each pad, and a lug, or projection (**B**) on the brake rotor. When the main part of the pad wears down to the level of the extended friction material area, the 'extra' material catches on the lug, making a noise, and warning the driver that the brake pads need changing.

❏ **POINT B10:** Some brakes are fitted with electrical pad wear indicators. If so, disconnect the wiring when removing the pad; be sure to purchase the correct pad type (so that the

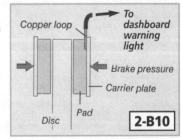

To dashboard warning light

Copper loop

Brake pressure

Carrier plate

Disc

Pad

2-B10

indicator light on the dash will work) and check and refit the wiring when fitting new pads.

Section C: Drum brakes - READ THIS FIRST!

The following applies to the inspection of all of the types of drum brakes covered here.

❏ **POINT C1:** Even though there are inspection holes in the brake backplates, you are STRONGLY RECOMMENDED, at the full service interval, to remove the drums and examine the shoes and the wheel cylinder piston seal and to clean out accumulated brake dust.

FACT FILE

DRUM BRAKE WEAR SYMPTOMS

❒ **POINT C2:** There are certain essential checks you should carry out for yourself, with the drum removed:

• Look for any obvious grooves worn into the braking surface of the drum. Slight undulations are acceptable, but anything worse and the drum should be replaced.

• Look and feel for any wear-ridge on the outer edges of the drum. The depth will give an indication of wear.

• With the drums removed, now is a good time to check their thickness – there should not be a significant wear ridge around the edge of the drum.

• Hang the drum up on a piece of string or wire. Lightly tap it with a piece of metal - not a hammer. The drum should produce a clear ringing sound. If not, it is cracked and MUST NOT be re-used.

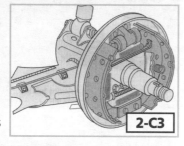

2-C3

❒ **POINT C3:** Examine the brake shoes for wear or oil contamination. If the latter, the wheel cylinder is probably leaking and the shoes will have to be scrapped. We recommend a **minimum** 2.5 mm shoe lining (friction material) thickness.

❒ **POINT C4:** Fold back the two rubbers on the wheel cylinders. Any fluid found inside requires a new cylinder. However, new-ish cylinders may have a little brake grease still in there.

❒ **POINT C5:** Take special care to wash all the brake dust away from the adjuster mechanism. Make sure that it is not seized but if it is, you will have to strip down the assembly and free off or replace. Add brake grease (NOT ordinary grease) very sparingly to the mechanism.

❒ **POINT C6:** Replace missing or damaged springs, rear brake shoes or wheel cylinders.

JOB 3: FRONT DISC BRAKE – *check, replace pads.*

Section A: Type A - VW II brakes (known earlier as VW 'MK II' or Kelsey-Hayes.)

❒ **STEP A1:** This is the earliest-type, without a 'window' in the caliper. To check for pad thickness (**a**), look for the distance between the inner-face of the pad backing plates (**b**) and the outer edges of the disc/rotor (**c**). When the distance comes down to 2 mm (3/32 in.), replace the pads.

❒ **STEP A2:** Very early

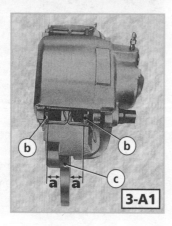

3-A1

on in production, a modified caliper was introduced, with a small inspection opening.

3-A2

TOP TIP!

• Unless you are familiar with these brakes, it can be difficult to be sure of the amount of friction material left on the pads.

• You may find it easier to remove the piston housing and pads.

❒ **STEP A3:** Later still, the opening became larger again. You can now examine the thickness of the inner pad through the opening in the caliper (arrowed).

3-A3

❒ **STEP A4:** On this later type (same as in *3-A3*), **Volkswagen** recommend that pad and backing plate thicknesses together (**a**) should be 7 mm or more. If not, replace the pads. Only the inner pad can be seen through the opening. The outer has to be viewed from the front of the caliper, as shown here.

3-A4

❒ **STEP A5:** The type illustrated here is the earlier-type.

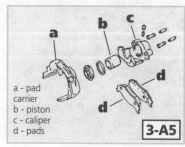

a - pad carrier
b - piston
c - caliper
d - pads

3-A5

1 - brake discs
2 - bolt - 10 Nm
3 - guard
4 - wheel bearing housing
5 - pad spring clip
6 - brake pads
7 - brake caliper
8 - upper sleeve
9 - lower sleeve
10 - upper bush
11 - lower bush
12 - upper spacer
13 - lower spacer
14 - upper securing bolt - 25 Nm
15 - lower securing bolt - 25 Nm
16 - wheel bolt torque: 110 Nm
17 - rotor for speed sensor (only for vehicles with ABS)
18 - speed sensor (only for vehicles with ABS) - clean and coat all around
with solid lubricating paste before installing)
19 - bolt - 10 Nm
20 - wheel hub
21 - phillips screw

3-A6

☐ **STEP A6:** This drawing illustrates the various components of the later-type front brake assembly.

3-A7

3-A8

☐ **STEP A7:** Slacken the securing bolts...

☐ **STEP A8:** ...swivel the caliper up and away, bottom first.

3-A9

3-A10

☐ **STEP A9:** Lift the pads away...

☐ **STEP A10:** ...and remove the brake pad springs.

☐ **STEP A11:** When fitting the new pads, fit NEW retaining springs. Parts (a) are the earlier type of spring (b) the later type.

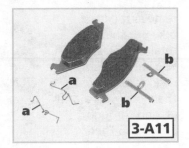

3-A11

Before fitting the pads:
→ fit the spring clips, with the spring tangs towards the inner pad (later type)
→ put a light smear of proprietary brake grease (NOT ordinary grease) on the pads' metal backplates where they bear on the piston, the caliper and the caliper housing lips
→ IMPORTANT NOTE: Be very sparing or grease could migrate to the friction linings!

☐ **STEP A12:** Install the brake caliper, top first, then refit the bolts - the longer bolt at the top. Fit NEW locking bolts and tighten them to the correct torque.

IMPORTANT NOTE:
Only press the brake caliper far enough in for the securing bolts to be installed. Pressing the caliper in too far can deform the spring clips and cause noise when braking.

SAFETY FIRST!

☐ **STEP A13:** • If the calipers are still fitted with the old-type non-locking bolts (pre-1981-type – item 2), they should be replaced with the newer, safer, locking type (1). The bolt holes in the calipers (arrowed) should be given a 45 degree chamfer, to a width of 1 mm, by a machine shop.

3-A13

Section B: Type B - Girling (later-type) brakes.

Visually inspect the thickness of the brake pads through the window in the caliper (see illustration **3-B1**, arrowed). Pad and backing plate thicknesses together should be 7 mm or more. If not, replace the pads.

☐ **STEP B1:** Use an open-ended spanner (a) to prevent the guide pin from turning, while undoing the lower securing bolt (b). The upper securing bolt (c) is left in place.

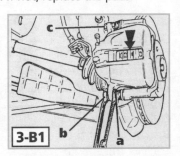

3-B1

☐ **STEP B2:** Swing the caliper (a) up and out of the way. Remove the pads (b) and if their thickness is 7 mm or less (friction material plus backing pad), replace, following the instructions at the start of this Job.

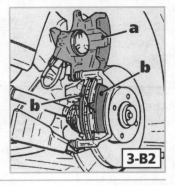

3-B2

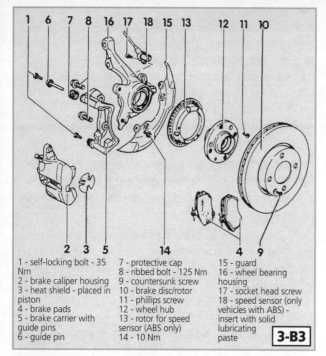

1 - self-locking bolt - 35 Nm
2 - brake caliper housing
3 - heat shield - placed in piston
4 - brake pads
5 - brake carrier with guide pins
6 - guide pin
7 - protective cap
8 - ribbed bolt - 125 Nm
9 - countersunk screw
10 - brake disc/rotor
11 - phillips screw
12 - wheel hub
13 - rotor for speed sensor (ABS only)
14 - 10 Nm
15 - guard
16 - wheel bearing housing
17 - socket head screw
18 - speed sensor (only vehicles with ABS) - insert with solid lubricating paste

3-B3

❏ **STEP B3:** These are the components of the caliper, disc/rotor and pad assembly.

➜ Fit new self-locking bolts (*item 1*) every time they are removed.

Section C: Type C – Girling (early-type) brakes.

❏ **STEP C1:** Remove the pad spring from the back of the caliper, providing a good view of the thicknesses of the pads.

3-C1

❏ **STEP C2:** If their thickness is 7 mm or less (friction material plus backing pad), replace them, following the instructions at the start of this Job. In addition, remove the retainer screw (arrowed)...

3-C2

❏ **STEP C3:** ...pull out the retainer pins and remove the pad.

3-C3

❏ **STEP C4:** Before refitting the pad retainer and spring, check them for wear and renew them if necessary. Fit the spring with the arrow facing down.

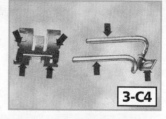

3-C4

IMPORTANT NOTE:
Reduce the risk of brake squeal. In addition to the steps mentioned at the start of this Job:
i) Clean the edges of the pads with emery cloth.
ii) Apply a proprietary brand of brake grease to the edges of the pads (the *smallest* amount!) and to the spring and retainer where shown (arrows)
iii) Be sure to refit any anti-squeal shims, if originally fitted behind the brake pad backing plates.

Section D: Type D – Teeves brakes.

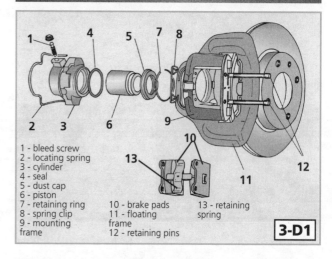

1 - bleed screw
2 - locating spring
3 - cylinder
4 - seal
5 - dust cap
6 - piston
7 - retaining ring
8 - spring clip
9 - mounting frame
10 - brake pads
11 - floating frame
12 - retaining pins
13 - retaining spring

3-D1

❏ **STEP D1:** This is an exploded view of the Teeves (ATE) brake assembly. Note that springs and retaining pins may be different on some models.

❏ **STEP D2:** Inspect the brake pads through the rear of the caliper assembly. Pad (a) and backing plate thicknesses together should be 7 mm or more. If not, replace the pads.

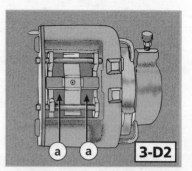

3-D2

❏ **STEP D3:** To remove the pads, take out the retaining pins (a). You will probably need to hammer them out with a drift at, and through, points (b). Then

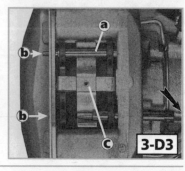

3-D3

remove the cross-shaped retaining spring (**c**).

☐ **STEP D4:** You may need to push the pads in slightly to relieve the pressure on scored discs/rotors. Start by removing the inner pad. Then remove the outer pad (illustrated). The

3-D4

floating frame has to be pressed inwards to disengage the pad from the notch (arrowed).

☐ **STEP D5:** Before fitting the pads, check the recess in the face of each piston (arrowed). Here, a **Volkswagen** gauge is being used to ensure that the recess is at the required 20 degree angle. Turn the piston, if

3-D5

necessary. But TAKE VERY GREAT CARE NOT TO DAMAGE THE PISTON OR PISTON SEAL AS YOU DO SO!

☐ **STEP D6:** If refitting the original pads, it is essential that they are fitted to their original locations. Clean the edges of the

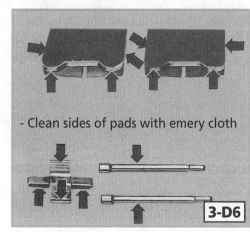

- Clean sides of pads with emery cloth

3-D6

backing plates and apply a very thin smear of proprietary brake grease (NOT ordinary grease) at the points indicated. Refit the anti-squeal shims, if originally fitted.

Fit two new retaining pins per caliper. Install by:
➜ Fitting the pads, followed by ONE of the pins.
➜ Fit the retaining spring...
➜ ...and then the other pin.

☐ **STEP D7:** Always fit the pin retaining clips in the correct location (arrowed).

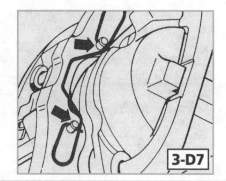

3-D7

JOB 4: DISC REAR BRAKES
– *check, replace*.

REPLACEMENT

☐ **STEP 1:** The procedure is similar to that described in *Job 3*, depending on type. Read this in conjunction with the inspection, dismantling notes and safety warnings in *Job 3*.

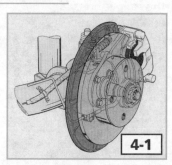

4-1

VEHICLES UP TO JULY 87

☐ **STEP 2:** Remove the handbrake cable (arrowed) from the caliper.

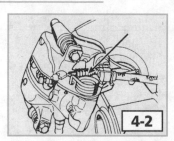

4-2

☐ **STEP 3:** Unscrew the upper caliper bolt (**a**), swing the caliper (**b**) towards the rear of the vehicle and remove the pads (**c**).

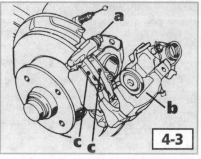

4-3

☐ **STEP 4:** Before replacing the brake pads, adjust the piston ONLY by turning with a socket wrench (arrowed), until there is 1 mm clearance between the caliper and the outer brake pad, when fitted.

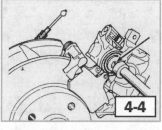

4-4

☐ **STEP 5:** The gaps can be measured with a feeler gauge.

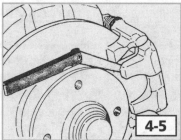

4-5

IMPORTANT NOTE: Do not operate the brake pedal. Otherwise the auto. brake adjustment will be destroyed.

The brakes can now be reassembled.

ADJUST PARKING BRAKE: See *Job 6*.

12-7

VEHICLES FROM AUGUST 87

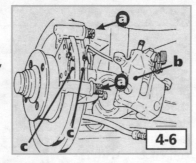

❑ **STEP 6:** Unscrew the caliper bolts (**a**), remove the caliper (**b**) and remove the brake pads (**c**).

`4-6`

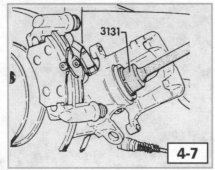

❑ **STEP 7:** Before replacing the brake pads, adjust the piston ONLY by turning with the special tool illustrated or with an a suitable adapter on a socket wrench.

`3131`

`4-7`

IMPORTANT NOTE: Do not under any circumstances adjust the piston with a clamp, and do not operate the brake pedal. Otherwise the auto. brake adjustment will bw destroyed.

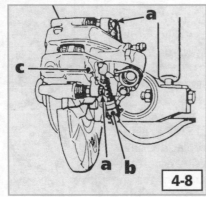

❑ **STEP 8:** Fit the brake caliper with NEW self-locking bolts (**a**) and refit the parking brake cable (**b**) to the caliper housing (**c**).

`4-8`

ADJUST HANDBRAKE: SEE *JOB 6.*

REPLACEMENT

Checking the brake pads and changing them are virtually identical jobs. Please read the notes at the start of *Job 2* and see *Job 3* for information on how to carry out the work.

JOB 5: DRUM BRAKES – *check, replace.*

Section A: Type E – Front drum brakes (not-UK or US vehicles).

CHECKING

❑ **STEP A1:** The adjuster hole in the backplate is seen here, just ahead of the drive shaft line. The drum can be removed without removing the wheel bearing. The wheel is left attached to the drum, the screw (see *5-A2, item L*) is removed

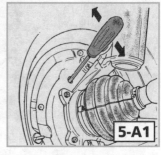

`5-A1`

and, once the brakes have been backed off, the drum can be pulled off, with the wheel.

REPLACEMENT

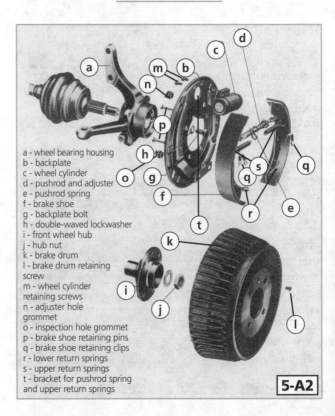

a - wheel bearing housing
b - backplate
c - wheel cylinder
d - pushrod and adjuster
e - pushrod spring
f - brake shoe
g - backplate bolt
h - double-waved lockwasher
i - front wheel hub
j - hub nut
k - brake drum
l - brake drum retaining screw
m - wheel cylinder retaining screws
n - adjuster hole grommet
o - inspection hole grommet
p - brake shoe retaining pins
q - brake shoe retaining clips
r - lower return springs
s - upper return springs
t - bracket for pushrod spring and upper return springs

`5-A2`

❑ **STEP A2:** Take note of the brake drum and shoe components.

❑ **STEP A3:** Insert a screwdriver through the hole in the backplate (**b**) and turn the adjuster (**d**) until the brakes are backed right off.

❑ **STEP A4:** Remove the clips (**q**), take out the pins (**p**) and unhook the lower return spring (**r**).

❑ **STEP A5:** Pull the bottom of the shoes over the wheel hub (**i**) and disengage them from the pushrod (**d**) and top return springs (**s**).

`5-A5`

STEP A6: Clean the backplate and adjuster with a proprietary brand of brake cleaner, such as Wurth Brake Cleaner. Check the adjuster for smooth operation and lubricate it.

STEP A7: Hook the upper return springs (**s**) to the bracket (**t**). Fit the pushrod (**d**), in the backed-off position (to the backplate) making sure that, as in this drawing, the pushrod (**A**) has the pushrod spring (**B**) around it and hooked into the backplate (**C**).

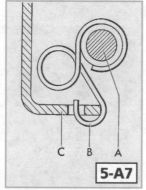

Complete the installation as the reverse of the removal process. Adjust the brakes as shown in **Section B**.

Section B: Rear drum brakes.

SAFETY FIRST!

• Read **Chapter 2, Safety First!** before proceeding!

CHECKING DRUM REMOVAL

STEP B1: MANUALLY ADJUSTED (180 mm drum) AND EARLY AUTO. ADJUSTED (200 mm drum) SHOES: Push a screwdriver through the hole (**a**) in the backplate and turn the adjuster star wheel (**b**) to free the brakes.

STEP B2: When you lever the screwdriver upwards, the shoes will be moved away from the drum.

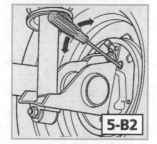

STEP B3: LATER AUTO. ADJUSTED SHOES, 'LEVER' SYSTEM (180 mm drum): Turn the drum so that one of the wheel bolt holes is at '2 O'clock' on the right-side of the vehicle; '10 O'clock' on the left-side of the vehicle. Insert a narrow-bladed screwdriver through the hole...

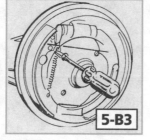

STEP B4: ...and aim for this hole, in the lever. Push it upwards (lever down with the screwdriver) to release the tension on the brake shoes.

STEP B5: Remove the grease cap...

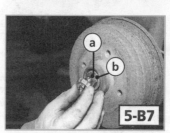

STEP B6: ...straighten out the split pin, pull it out and discard it.

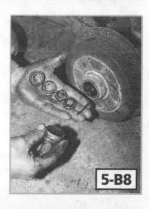

STEP B7: Take off the lock ring and unscrew the hub nut (**a**) from behind it. Pull off the thrust washer (**b**).

STEP B8: These are the components to remove from left to right: wheel bearing; tab washer; hub nut; locking plate; split pin; grease cap.

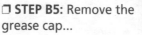

STEP B9: You can now take off the drum. Take care not to catch the grease seal or bearing races on the stub axle threads as you remove it. You can now carry out the inspections and checks referred to earlier.

1 - grease cap
2 - split pin
3 - lock ring
4 - hub nut
5 - thrust washer
6 - outer wheel bearing
7 - brake drum
8 - bolt - 60 Nm
9 - dished washer (large contact surface points towards brake carrier)
10 - brake carrier with brake shoes
11 - stub axle

5-B10

☐ **STEP B10:** Before refitting the drum, clean the stub axle and coat it in a thin layer of grease. When refitting, follow the correct sequence of components shown here. Take care not to damage the grease seal or bearing race.

☐ **STEP B11:** Turn the hub nut until the thrust washer can *just* be moved with a screwdriver. Spin the hub and check again.

5-B11

☐ **STEP B12:** Fit the lock ring so that its projections do not cover the split pin hole, then fit a new split pin, bending the ends over as shown.

5-B12

You can now adjust the brakes:
1. Turn the starred wheel in the opposite direction to that shown in illustration *5-B2*.
2. As soon as the shoes begin to touch the drums, apply the brakes firmly, several times, to centralise the shoes. You may have to do this several times during the adjustment process.
3. Turn the adjuster until the road wheel cannot be turned by hand.
4. Back off until the brake shoes *just* stop rubbing - a lightly rubbing high-spot will be acceptable.
The brakes can only be finally adjusted with brake efficiency testing equipment. Have them checked before using the car on the road.

REPLACEMENT

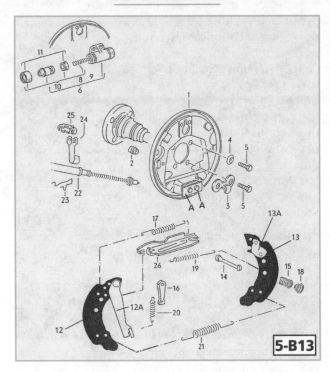

5-B13

☐ **STEP B13:** These are the most common rear drum brake components. The part numbers shown here are referred to in the text.

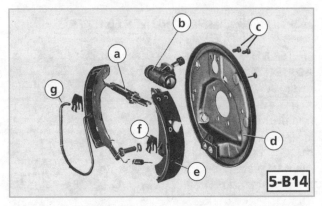

5-B14

☐ **STEP B14:** These are the early rear brakes, manually adjusted, fitted to 180 mm brake drums. The shoes (**e**) are removed after slackening the adjuster (**a**), removing the pins and clips (**f**) - see *Steps B18 and B19*, removing the spring (**g**) with pliers, then proceeding as shown below. The wheel cylinder (**b**) is held to the backplate (**d**) by the bolts (**c**).

☐ **STEP B15:** These are the early rear brakes, automatically adjusted, fitted to 200 mm brake drums. See *Step B14* for details, EXCEPT that

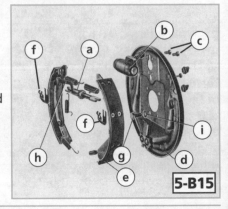

5-B15

the tension is taken off the adjuster (**h**) before removing the brake drum by feeling through a wheel bolt hole in the front of the drum, with a piece of wire with a hook on the end, while the adjuster wheel is turned back. The backplate is held to the stub axle with the bolts (**g**) and washers (**i**).

❏ **STEP B16:** Remove the road wheel and brake drum, check the wheel cylinder and use aerosol brake cleaner.

❏ **STEP B17:** • Complete all the work on one side of the car at a time, so that you can use the other side as a reference.

5-B17

❏ **STEP B18:** Push in each of the two slotted washers (**18**) against their springs (**15**), while holding the pins (**14**) at the back of the brake drum, and turn each washer through 90 degrees. Take off the washer...

5-B18

❏ **STEP B19:** ...and the spring, and pull the pin out through the back of the backplate.

5-B19

❏ **STEP B20:** Take the pressure off the lower spring (**21**) before you try to remove it.
➜ Lever the shoes (**12, 13**) away from their lower mounting point (**a**), pull them a little way forwards, so that

5-B20

they slide over the front of the mounting point and carefully release the tension.
➜ Unhook and remove the lower return spring (**21**) and the self adjuster return spring (**20**) followed by the upper return spring (**19**).
➜ Remove the brake shoes and retrieve the return springs.

➜ Check the springs carefully. If any are stretched, or the ends are damaged, fit new replacements.

❏ **STEP B21:** Put wire or a cable tie around the wheel cylinder to stop the piston from coming out.

5-B21

❏ **STEP B22:** Turn the set of shoes head-over-heels and disconnect the handbrake cable (**22**) from the operating lever on the shoes.

5-B22

❏ **STEP B23:** Release the self adjuster return spring from the self-adjuster wedge (**16**) and separate.

5-B23

❏ **STEP B24:** • Hold one shoe in the vice; pull on the other shoe while pushing the wedge up with your thumb...

5-B24

❏ **STEP B25:** ...and remove the wedge.

5-B25

❏ **STEP B26:** Pull off the push rod...

5-B26

STEP B27: ...and the pushrod spring (17), and pull the pushrod off the brake shoe.

5-B27

STEP B28: These are the new brake shoes, assembled with the springs and plates from the old brake shoes.

5-B28

STEP B29: Prepare the assembly as follows:
➜ Clean and lubricate the adjuster assembly sparingly with a brand of brake grease - not regular lubricating grease!
➜ Smear a little proprietary brake grease very sparingly on all the shoe contact points on the backplate and the springs.

STEP B30: Fit the pushrod spring (17) to the bracket (13A) and place the shoe (13) on the pushrod (26). Insert the wedge (16) - the lug goes towards the backplate.

5-B30

STEP B31: Fit the brake lever (12A) to the pushrod (26), then continue to re-assemble as follows:
➜ Connect the upper return spring.
➜ Hook the handbrake cable on the lever.
➜ Place the shoes on the cylinder pistons.
➜ Connect the lower return spring and lift the shoes onto the lower support.
➜ Connect the wedge spring.
➜ Install the shoe retaining springs and washers.
➜ Install drums and adjust wheel bearings.
➜ Depress brake pedal firmly once to set the rear brake shoes.

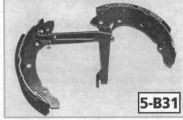

5-B31

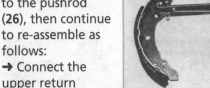
SAFETY FIRST!

• NEVER change the brake shoes only on one wheel.
• ALWAYS change them as a complete 'axle' set.

Refer to *Job 6* for handbrake cable adjustment.

JOB 6: PARKING BRAKE – *check, adjust.*

DRUM BRAKES

When a vehicle is fitted with automatic adjusters at the rear brakes, parking brake adjustment is not necessary, although it is necessary to check periodically that the self-adjuster mechanism is working. See *Job 5, Section B* for descriptions of both brake types. You will need to do so, however, after fitting parking brake cables or replacement brake shoes. To do so:
➜ Work on firm, level ground. Raise the rear of the vehicle off the ground on axle stands, chock the front wheels in front and behind.
➜ Release the parking brake and firmly depress the brake pedal once.
➜ **VEHICLES WITHOUT AUTOMATIC ADJUSTER:** Pull the parking brake lever up TWO or THREE notches.
➜ **VEHICLES WITH AUTOMATIC ADJUSTERS:** Pull the parking brake lever up FOUR notches.

STEP 1A: GOLF-BASE MODELS, POLO FROM 1994-ON: Remove the cover, if fitted. Tighten each of the adjuster nuts, beneath the parking brake lever, a little at a time until both wheels can *just* be turned by hand.

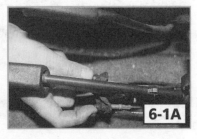

6-1A

➜ Release the parking brake and check that each wheel turns freely. If, not slacken nut until wheel turns when brake is off; but can just be turned when the lever is up TWO/FOUR notches, depending on year.

STEP 1B: EARLIEST POLO: A nut on the adjuster thread (b) – which passes through the compensator (c) beneath the car is where the cable is adjusted.

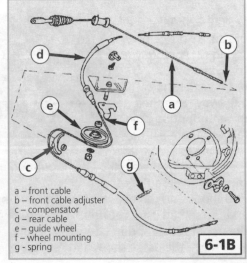

a – front cable
b – front cable adjuster
c – compensator
d – rear cable
e – guide wheel
f – wheel mounting
g - spring

6-1B

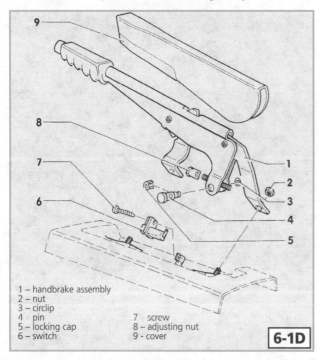

1 – adjusting nut (beneath car)
2 – compensator
3 – bush
4, a – handbrake cable, front
5 – bellows

6 – retaining ring
7 – ratchet segment
8 – ratchet pawl
9 – rod
10 – spring
11 – button
12 – lever

13 – pins
14 – spring clips
15 – bush
16 – bolt
17 – nut

6-1C

❐ **STEP 1C:** These are the earliest Polo's handbrake mechanism components. Grease regularly.

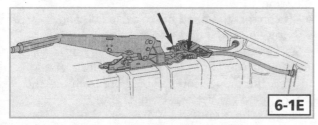

1 – handbrake assembly
2 – nut
3 – circlip
4 – pin
5 – locking cap
6 – switch

7 – screw
8 – adjusting nut
9 – cover

6-1D

❐ **STEP 1D: LATER POLO (UP TO 1994):** These are the later-type Polo's handbrake, with single adjuster nut (8).

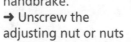

6-1E

❐ **STEP 1E: POLO FROM 1994:** There are two separate cables and two adjusters (arrowed) similar to Golf models.

DISC BRAKES

There are auto. adjusters and adjustment is only normally needed after renewing hand brake cables, calipers, pads or discs/rotors. In both cases, apply the brakes after adjustment and make sure that the road wheel turns freely when the brake is released.

❐ **STEP 2: VEHICLES TO JULY 87:** With the parking brake in the released position, tighten the adjusting nuts so that the lever (arrowed) on the brake caliper just lifts off the stop. Max. permissible distance from stop - 1 mm.

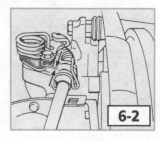

6-2

❐ **STEP 3: VEHICLES FROM AUGUST 87:** The procedure is the same as for earlier models (*Step 2*). The lever on this model is arrowed. From JANUARY 1988, the maximum permissible distance to the stop is 1.5 mm.

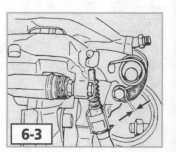

6-3

| JOB 7: | PARKING/HANDBRAKE CABLES, LEVER AND SWITCH – *replacement*. |

See *Job 6* for handbrake types not shown here, and illustration *Step 5, Handbrake Lever*.

❐ **STEP 1:** Jack up and support the rear of the car on axle stands.

❐ **STEP 2:** From inside the car, remove the handbrake lever cover or covers and fully release the handbrake.
→ Unscrew the adjusting nut or nuts from the end of the compensator or cable bracket.

7-2

❐ **STEP 3:** Release the front ends of the rear cables from the compensator, then pull the front cable through the floor aperture.
→ Refit in the reverse order and adjust the cable.

7-3

❐ **STEP 4:** The cable outer is push-fit at both ends. It also clips to the suspension arm. See *Job 5* for details of connections to brake shoes.

7-4

PARKING BRAKE LEVER

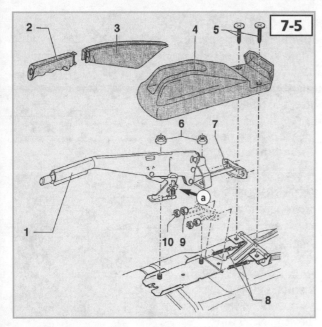

7-5

☐ **STEP 5:** After removing the trim (items **2** – press down lug with small screwdriver, **3, 4, 5**), remove the handbrake lever (**1**) by removing the circlip and removing the pivot (early models) or the fixings nuts (**6**) - later models.

JOB 8: **PARKING BRAKE SWITCH –** *replacement.*

☐ **STEP 1:** On all models, the switch (illustration **7-5, item a**) is screwed to the assembly. The exact location varies between models.

JOB 9: BRAKE CALIPER – *replacement.*

SAFETY FIRST!

• The hydraulic system on an ABS (anti-lock brake) equipped vehicle contains fluid at extremely high pressure.

• DO NOT open the system without depressurising it first.

• See *Job 15. ABS systems - essential notes.*

FRONT BRAKES

☐ **STEP 1:** Slacken the front road wheels, jack up the car and support on axle stands. Remove the wheels.

☐ **STEP 2:** Unplug the brake pad wear sensor, if fitted and remove the fluid pipe/hose from the bracket/s.

☐ **STEP 3:** Undo the brake fluid pipe union from the caliper body and plug the end to prevent too much fluid loss.

9-4

9-5

☐ **STEP 4:** Undo the bolts and remove the caliper.

☐ **STEP 5:** Refit in reverse order and bleed the brakes, see *Job 19*.

REAR BRAKES

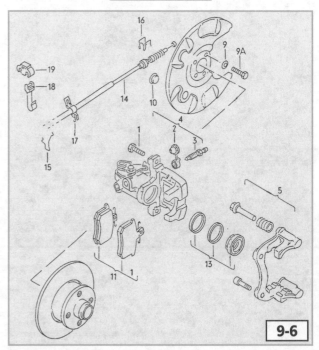
9-6

☐ **STEP 6:** This job is carried out in the same way as for FRONT BRAKES with the addition of the following:

➜ Dis-connect the hand-brake cable (**14**) and withdraw from the brake assembly.

➜ Slacken the brake hose at the caliper end, undo the caliper fixing bolts (**1**), remove the caliper and unscrew the caliper and flexible hose from the end of the previously slackened rigid hose.

➜ Plug the hose ends.

TOP TIP!

• If you prime the new caliper before fitting it, brake bleeding will be easier! Connect a tube to the opened bleed screw (**3**) and pour brake fluid through it until it comes out of the hole where the brake hose fits. Then lock up the bleed screw.

☐ **STEP 7:** Refit the caliper using NEW self locking bolts.

JOB 10: FRONT BRAKE DISC – *replacement*.

FRONT BRAKES

❑ **STEP 1:** Carry out *Steps 1 to 4* in *Job 9*. The hydraulic system on an ABS (anti-lock brake) equipped vehicle contains fluid at extremely high pressure. DO NOT open the system without depressurising it first. See *Job 15. ABS systems - essential notes*.

❑ **STEP 2:** Undo the securing bolts and remove the caliper support bracket (brake carrier).

❑ **STEP 3:** Undo the hub bolts and withdraw the brake disc.

10-3

> ### TOP TIP!
>
> • Before refitting the disc, ensure that the mating surfaces - hub to disc, are clean and undamaged.
> • Spin the disc to be sure there is no 'run out' before proceeding further.

❑ **STEP 4:** Refit the remaining parts in reverse order of removal.

REAR BRAKES

❑ **STEP 5:** Remove the brake pads and caliper as described in *Jobs 2* and *3*. The hydraulic system on an ABS (anti-lock brake) equipped vehicle contains fluid at extremely high pressure. DO NOT open the system without depressurising it first. See *Job 15. ABS systems - essential notes*.

❑ **STEP 6:** The rear disc is also the rear bearing carrier. See *Chapter 11, Steering and Suspension* for how to remove the disc/wheel bearing assembly.

JOB 11: WHEEL CYLINDER – *replacement*.

The part numbers in this Job relate to illustrations *5-A2* (front brakes - lower case letters) or *5-B13* (rear brakes - numbers)

❑ **STEP 1:** Refer to *Job 5* and remove the brake shoes.

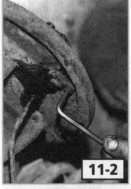

11-2

❑ **STEP 2:** Undo the brake pipe union at the back of the wheel cylinder (**c** and **6**) and plug the end. Unscrew the two fixing bolts (**m** and **7**) and take off the cylinder.

❑ **STEP 3:** Refit in the reverse order of removal. Refer to *Job 19* for brake bleeding.

11-3

JOB 12: MASTER CYLINDER – *replacement*.

ABS (ANTI-LOCK BRAKE) SYSTEMS

The ABS master cylinder is not covered here. See *Job 15* and *Job 16* for an illustration and further details. The hydraulic system on an ABS (anti-lock brake) equipped vehicle contains fluid at extremely high pressure. DO NOT open the system without depressurising it first. See *Job 15. ABS systems - essential notes*.

NON-ABS (ANTI-LOCK BRAKE) SYSTEMS

IMPORTANT NOTES:
• Protect all paint surfaces from possible brake fluid spillage before starting work.
• You might have to move ancillary items, such as air filter before starting on the hydraulic items.

❑ **STEP 1:** These are the components of a typical master cylinder fitted to cars without a servo...

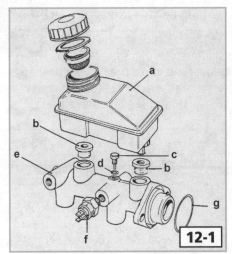

12-1

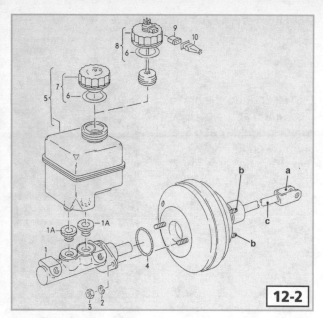

12-2

☐ **STEP 2:** ...and this is a typical servo-assisted layout.

☐ **STEP 3:** Siphon off as much brake fluid as possible or bleed it out through one of the front brakes (see *Job 19*) until the master cylinder makes 'sucking' noises.

☐ **STEP 4:** Remove the reservoir (*12-1, item a*) from the master cylinder by pulling it out of the grommets (*12-1, item b* or *12-2 item 1A*) – easier to do at this stage but not essential.

☐ **STEP 5:** Use a spanner - preferably a purpose-made split ring spanner - to undo all the pipe unions from the master cylinder.

12-5

☐ **STEP 6:** Undo the nuts (**3**) securing the master cylinder to the servo (if fitted) or firewall and remove it. Remove and refit any ancillary items, such as warning light switch/es (**f**).

☐ **STEP 7:** Lubricate the grommets with a smear of brake fluid, push them in to the master cylinder and refit the reservoir. Refit in the reverse order and refer to *Job 19* for bleeding the brakes.

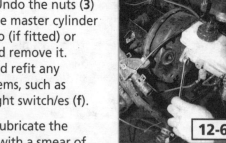

12-6

JOB 13: SERVO – *check, remove, refit*.

ABS (ANTI-LOCK BRAKE) SYSTEMS

The ABS servo is not covered here. See *Job 15* and *Job 16* for illustrations and further details. The hydraulic system on an ABS (anti-lock brake) equipped vehicle contains fluid at extremely high pressure. DO NOT open the system without depressurising it first. See *Job 15. ABS systems - essential notes*.

NON-ABS (ANTI-LOCK BRAKE) SYSTEMS

FACT FILE

SERVO FAULT CHECKS

• Before condemning the servo for lack of efficiency, check the condition of the one-way valve and vacuum pipe connecting it to the inlet manifold.
• Ease the valve out of the front of the servo and disconnect the pipe from the inlet manifold.
• Check that you can only blow one way through the valve - from the servo end towards the inlet manifold (or the brake vacuum pump - Diesel models).
• The vacuum pipe can suffer failure in many ways. Age can harden it until it cracks, causing an air leak which sometimes results in a whistling noise and rough slow-running.
• Loose connections could also produce the same result.
• The other type of vacuum hose failure is an implosion (where the hose is sucked flat by the vacuum) often because oil has softened the hose.
• This is not so easily detected, as it rarely upsets the engine performance and resumes its normal shape shortly after the engine is stopped.
• The inner lining can also deteriorate, causing a blockage.

☐ **STEP 1:** Follow *Job 12* to remove the master cylinder. The part numbers shown here refer to the illustration *12-2*.

☐ **STEP 2:** From inside the car, take out the split pin and clevis pin fixing the accelerator pedal to the pushrod clevis (**a**). You will

13-2

have to remove the lower trim from the driver's side to get at it. (Passenger side on Mk 2 Golfs, as shown here.)

☐ **STEP 3:** Undo the three fixing nuts from the set screws (**b**). The nuts are self-locking and new ones should be used when refitting. (On Mk 1 models, disconnect the cross-linkage to the brake pedal.)

STEP 4: From inside the engine bay, remove the servo.

13-4

STEP 5: If the servo has an adjustable pushrod, there will be a locknut at the position (c) - none fitted to this version. When the locknut has been slackened, the clevis fork can be screwed in or out to adjust its position. Free play at the brake pedal should be between 2 mm and 4 mm.

The pressure regulating valve reduces the amount of pressure applied to the back brakes when the vehicle is unladen, reducing the risk of rear wheel lock-up.

JOB 14: PRESSURE REGULATING VALVE – *replacement, adjustment*.

The hydraulic system on an ABS (anti-lock brake) equipped vehicle contains fluid at extremely high pressure. DO NOT open the system without depressurising it first. See *Job 15. ABS systems - essential notes*.

SEMI-MECHANICAL SYSTEM

STEP 1: This is one of the semi-mechanical systems fitted to the majority of vehicles. Another type has a hydraulic residual pressure valve mounted adjacent to the regulator.

14-1

Without specialist equipment, the regulator and valve can only be checked for obvious mechanical faults, although it can easily be replaced, after which the brakes must be bled. See *Job 19*. ALWAYS press the lever firmly to the rear of the vehicle (in the direction of the arrow) when bleeding the rear brakes.

STEP 2: If brake pressure gauges are available:
→ The vehicle must be at kerbside weight: no load; with driver; with full fuel tank.
→ Connect them to the left-front brake caliper/cylinder and the rear-right brake caliper/cylinder and bleed them.
→ Apply pressure to the brake pedal to give the following combination of pressures:

FRONT 50 bar - REAR 31 to 35 bar
FRONT 100 bar - REAR 53 to 67 bar

→ If rear pressures are too low, increase the regulator spring tension.
→ If rear pressures are too high, decrease the regulator spring tension.

ALL-HYDRAULIC SYSTEMS

STEP 3: This is the pressure-dependent regulator fitted to Scirocco models from 1981.

14-3

STEP 4: This is the retardation sensitive regulator fitted to some Caddy models. It is fitted beneath the vehicle, just ahead of the rear axle.

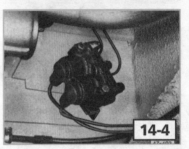

14-4

STEP 5: Both regulators can be tested in exactly the same way as in *Step 2* and if the pressures are not in the range shown, the regulator must be replaced and the brakes bled. See *Job 19*.

JOB 15: ABS SYSTEMS – *essential notes*.

SAFETY FIRST!

• The hydraulic system in an ABS (anti-lock brake system) equipped vehicle contains brake fluid at extremely high pressure.

• The pressure is created whenever the ignition is turned on, and stays there even after the ignition has been turned off.

• Opening the hydraulic system can cause a jet of hydraulic fluid to be ejected that could maim or kill.

• The ABS pressure modulator is capable of creating up to 21,000 kpa (3,045 pounds per square inch) of pressure.

• Before opening an ABS-equipped hydraulic system:

→ Turn OFF the ignition key switch.

→ Remove the battery negative (-) terminal.

• Pump the brake pedal fully for at least 20 times, to dissipate the pressure.

SPECIAL NOTES!

➜ Unplug the electronic control unit (ECU) from the left-side A-pillar before any electric welding is carried out.

➜ When oven drying paint, the ECU cannot withstand 95 degrees Celsius (203 degrees Fahrenheit) for more than a few minutes or 85 degrees Celsius for more than 2 hours.

➜ Disconnect the battery earth before removing any of the controls.

JOB 16: ABS SYSTEMS AND RPM SENSORS – *repair limits*.

TOP TIP!

• Don't immediately assume the worst if the ABS warning light comes on! A build up of dirt, sand, grass or a combination of dirt and water, on a wet day, at the wheel sensors, will cause the ABS system to shut down. Check the rotors and wheel sensors for cleanliness and physical damage.

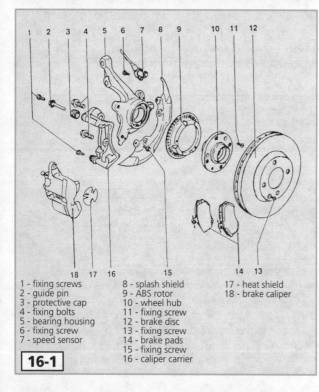

1 - fixing screws
2 - guide pin
3 - protective cap
4 - fixing bolts
5 - bearing housing
6 - fixing screw
7 - speed sensor
8 - splash shield
9 - ABS rotor
10 - wheel hub
11 - fixing screw
12 - brake disc
13 - fixing screw
14 - brake pads
15 - fixing screw
16 - caliper carrier
17 - heat shield
18 - brake caliper

16-1

❏ **STEP 1:** The RPM sensors align with the rotors, which look like toothed rings. The sensors' signals are sent to the ECU to prevent the brakes from locking up.

Check that the gap between the end of each sensor and rotor is clear and not contaminated in any way. No adjustments can be made.

❏ **STEP 2:** To remove the sensor:
➜ Undo the fixing screw, withdraw the sensor and unplug the electrical connector.

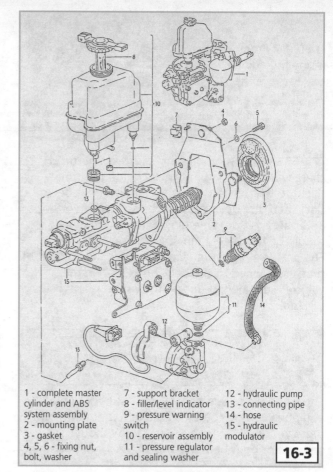

1 - complete master cylinder and ABS system assembly
2 - mounting plate
3 - gasket
4, 5, 6 - fixing nut, bolt, washer
7 - support bracket
8 - filler/level indicator
9 - pressure warning switch
10 - reservoir assembly
11 - pressure regulator and sealing washer
12 - hydraulic pump
13 - connecting pipe
14 - hose
15 - hydraulic modulator

16-3

➜ Clean round the housing and fit the new sensor, ensuring that it is properly seated.

➜ Secure the wire along its route to the connector and plug in.

❏ **STEP 3:** These, for information, are the components of the ABS master cylinder, pump (modulator) and other components. Almost none of these components can be diagnosed as faulty without highly specialised test equipment. At the last count, there were almost 50 pages in a special Volkswagen check list, of potential checks to be carried out with special test equipment - a job for your Volkswagen dealer. Non-dealership checks should be restricted to a physical examination of the exterior components.

JOB 17: FLEXIBLE HOSES – check, *replace*.

Check the flexible brake pipes that connect the calipers to the metal pipes on the body. Try bending back on themselves those that are not contained in a protective coil, and look for any signs of cracking, particularly at the bends. Check them all for signs of rubbing, splitting, kinks and perishing of the rubber. Check hoses for 'ballooning' with the brake pedal pressed.

The hydraulic system on an ABS (anti-lock brake) equipped vehicle contains fluid at extremely high pressure. DO NOT open the system without depressurising it first. See *Job 15. ABS systems - essential notes*.

❐ **STEP 1:** This is a typical set of hose components.

➜ To disconnect a flexible hose (15), unscrew and remove the rigid hose (14) from one end of it, pull off the clip (1) to free it from the bracket and unscrew the flexible hose from its other end.

➜ Refit in reverse order and replace any washers with new. Clip the hose at its anchorage point, so as to prevent chafing on the body when suspension and steering movement take place.

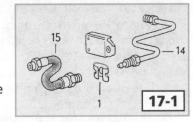

17-1

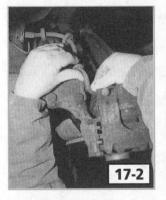

17-2

17-3

❐ **STEP 2:** The correct flexible hoses have buffer built into them in many cases. When this is so, position the buffers to stop the pipes from rubbing on steering or suspension components.

❐ **STEP 3:** When tightening each union, make sure you haven't put a twist in the hose!

❐ **STEP 4:** Bleed the brakes - see *Job 19*.

JOB 18: METAL PIPES – check, *replace*.

Check all rigid pipes for signs of damage or corrosion and check that all of the locating clips are sound and in place.

The hydraulic system on an ABS (anti-lock brake) equipped vehicle contains fluid at extremely high pressure. DO NOT open the system without depressurising it first. See *Job 15. ABS systems - essential notes*.

TOP TIP!

• When disconnecting brake pipes or hoses, it is essential to minimise brake fluid loss. This can be done by unscrewing the master cylinder reservoir cap, laying a sheet of plastic across the opening, and refitting the cap. This will prevent atmospheric pressure from pushing the fluid out of opened lines. A pipe spanner make the job much easier!

❐ **STEP 1:** Undo the unions at each end of a pipe length. Patience is often required because of the union seizing both in its threads and on the pipe. Use penetrating oil to help free seized unions, and use a split-ring spanner rather than an open-ended one, to reduce the risk of rounding off the union nuts.

TOP TIP!

• If a rigid pipe starts to twist as its union is undone, grip the pipe as lightly as possible without damaging it with a self-grip wrench and see if you can stop it from turning.
• If not, or if the pipe becomes damaged, cut through it with a junior hacksaw and replace the length of rigid pipe.

❐ **STEP 2:** Detach the pipe length from its securing clips and remove it.

❐ **STEP 3:** Cut brake pipe with a perfectly square end. Be sure to remove any burr and ALL traces of swarf or filings. Fit the correct end coupling...

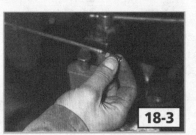

18-3

❐ **STEP 4:** ...use the Sykes-Pickavant flaring tool to put the correct flare on the end of the pipe...

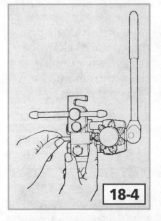

18-4

❐ **STEP 5:** ...before connecting the rigid pipe and clip to the flexible pipe and bracket. (Courtesy Sykes-Pickavant)

18-5

TOP TIP!

❐ **STEP 6:** • Where possible, use the old pipe as a pattern to shape the new one prior to fitting.

STEP 7: • Copper brake pipe is much easier to bend than steel, but nevertheless, forming a sharp bend or a bend near the end of a piece of pipe can be particularly difficult. This simple and inexpensive Sykes-Pickavant bending tool is a great help for fitting pipework into tight corners.

18-7

STEP 8: As the brass connector is tightened on to the end of the flexible pipe, the clip holds everything tightly in position. Note that you will have to use a second spanner to prevent the flexible pipe from turning while you tighten the rigid pipe.

18-8

STEP 9: Follow the original route and secure the pipe in the body clips.

STEP 10: Connect the unions and bleed the system. See **Job 19**. The hydraulic system on an ABS (anti-lock brake) equipped vehicle contains fluid at extremely high pressure. DO NOT open the system without depressurising it first. See **Job 15. ABS systems - essential notes**.

18-10

JOB 19: BRAKE BLEEDING.

TOP TIP!

• Unless the master cylinder or pressure regulating valve has been disturbed, it will only be necessary to bleed the end of the braking system which has been opened. If bleeding the whole system, bleed in the following order: Rear right; Rear left, Front right; Front left.
• When bleeding the rear brakes, keep the normal weight on the rear wheels to prevent the pressure limiting valve from inhibiting the brake fluid flow.

STEP 1: Push a tight fitting length of plastic or rubber tubing (**a**) onto the first bleed screw (**b**) and immerse the other end in a small quantity of brake fluid (**c**) contained in a glass jar in such a way that no air can accidentally be pulled up the tube.

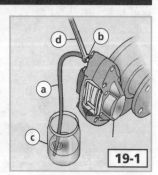

19-1

STEP 2: With a ring spanner (illustrations **19-1, item d**), undo the brake bleed screw by half a turn. This is the position of the screw, at the drum brake backplate or on the disc caliper body on disk brake models. Have your helper push the brake pedal to the floor and hold it there while you lock up the bleed valve. Then release the pedal slowly. Repeat several times.

19-2

IMPORTANT NOTE:
Take great care not to let the master cylinder run out of brake fluid. Otherwise you will introduce fresh air into the system and have to start again. Use ONLY fresh brake fluid from a previously unopened container.

STEP 3: Top up the fluid reservoir frequently while repeating the bleeding operation until all air is expelled from the brake line (no bubbles appear in the tube or jar). Bleed each remaining brake in the same way.

SAFETY FIRST!

• After completing the bleeding operation, and with your helper's foot firmly on the brake pedal, check all connections for leaks.
• Remember to top up the fluid, replace the master cylinder cap and reconnect the wires to it.

JOB 20: BRAKE HYDRAULIC FLUID – *change.*

IMPORTANT NOTE:
• Brake fluid absorbs water from the air.
• This corrodes brake components and can cause total brake failure.
• With brakes applied heavily, the fluid can heat to above 100 degrees Celsius, the water vaporises, and the pedal goes to the floor!
• Change the brake fluid at the recommended intervals.

STEP 1: Fit a brake bleeding tube to one of the rear wheel bleed nipples and lead the open end to a suitable container. Open the bleed nipple and pump the brake pedal until all of the fluid in the reservoir has been pumped out.

STEP 2: Bleed the brakes as described in **Job 19**. Make sure all of the old fluid is pumped out of each of the brake lines.

CHAPTER 13: BODYWORK

Please read Chapter 2 Safety First before carrying out any work on your car.

CONTENTS

JOB 1: RADIATOR GRILLE
- *removal, replacement.*

❏ **STEP 1:** There are several different styles of grille fitted as standard to the models covered in this

1-1

manual and there are also several different models of accessory or aftermarket grille available. The good news is that most fit in a similar way! This Mk 1 Jetta, for instance, has four clips (**1**) across the top of the upper grille, and six screws (**2**).

❏ **STEP 2:** These (**1**) are typical screw locations on many Polo models. Note the retaining brackets (**3**). Not all vehicles have the same number of fixings; GT and GTI grilles and those with extra headlights sometimes have more than the 'standard' fixings shown here.

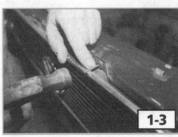

1-2

❏ **STEP 3:** Most of the fixings are self-tapping screws into nylon inserts. On many models, the centre two fixings consist of push-out pegs which are driven out with a piece of thin rod, as shown here.

1-3

STEP 4: On other models, the upper edge of the grille is held in place with plastic clips.
→ Use a screwdriver, inserted as shown, to push down the tag on the clip, while easing the grille panel forward. The clip is attached to the grille.

1-4

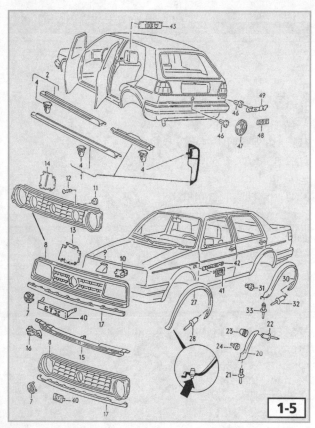

1-5

STEP 5: These are typical grille (and other trim) fixing arrangements:
→ On models with a trim moulding (**17**), the moulding is eased off its clips, as is the lower grille (**15**).
→ Make sure that all wiring is disconnected from models with lights mounted in the grille.
→ The (front) grille badge (**7**) is a push in-ease out fit, and the rear badges (**47, 48, 49**) also push into/pull out of plastic sockets (**46**).

IMPORTANT NOTE: On Golf models from 1992-on:
• The grille includes the painted section that runs beneath the black grille, and extends beneath the headlights.
• The lower clips are beneath this panel.

JOB 2: BONNET/HOOD - *refit*

STEP 1: These are typical components.

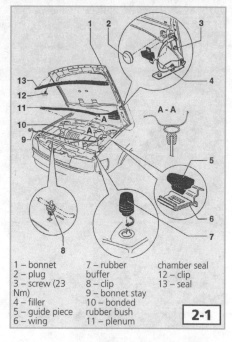

1 – bonnet	7 – rubber
2 – plug	buffer
3 – screw (23 Nm)	8 – clip
4 – filler	9 – bonnet stay
5 – guide piece	10 – bonded
6 – wing	rubber bush
	11 – plenum

chamber seal
12 – clip
13 – seal

2-1

STEP 2: The screen washer pipe is often difficult to remove and it's all too easy to break the bottom off the jet.

2-2

TOP TIP!

• Cut through the pipe with a craft knife level with the bottom of the jet.
• Then carefully cut through the stub of pipe remaining on the jet in order to remove it.

2-3

2-4

STEP 3: Draw around each hinge with a felt pen before taking out the two screws from each side. This radio interference protection strap is fitted to some models.

STEP 4: Two people can now lift the panel away.

☐ STEP 5: REPLACEMENT: Note the following:
→ There is adjustment at the hinge bolts.
→ Note the adjusting buffers at the corners - screw them in and out as necessary.
→ The front of the bonnet should be level with the surrounding panels and all gaps even.

JOB 3:	BONNET/HOOD RELEASE CABLE, MECHANISM - *removal, replacement*.

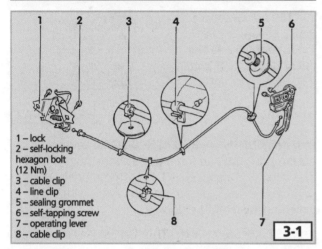

1 – lock
2 – self-locking hexagon bolt (12 Nm)
3 – cable clip
4 – line clip
5 – sealing grommet
6 – self-tapping screw
7 – operating lever
8 – cable clip

3-1

☐ STEP 1: Principle differences between models relate to such items as cable clips, some of which are screwed in, while others are a push-fit.

☐ STEP 2: On many North American vehicles, the bonnet closing panel and latches are different to European models. Two versions were fitted, only one of them with an interior cable pull. For this, the Deluxe version, the cable is fitted via a cable clip (**A**).
The arrow shows the access hole for the cable clip.

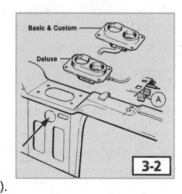

Basic & Custom
Deluxe
A
3-2

☐ STEP 3: Take note of the method holding the release mechanism to the front panel:
→ On early Golf/Rabbit models, the mechanism is removed by drilling the heads off the four large pop rivets holding the latch to the front panel.
→ On all other models, the mechanism is screwed to the front panel.

3-3

→ On Golf and late Polo models, the screws are found beneath the grille and face the rear of the car.
→ On early Polo models, the mechanism is on the inside of the front panel - the screws face the front of the vehicle - see illustration **3-1**.

☐ STEP 4: On European models, the interior cable pull is disconnected from the underside of the latch by loosening the fixing screw which grips the cable inner.

3-4

☐ STEP 5: Inside the car, the cable is held to the left-hand footwell panel with two more cross-head screws. The cable, now disconnected from the bonnet latch, can be fed back through the bulkhead grommet.

3-5

TOP TIP!

• Where the cable is difficult to reach (usually because of the extra equipment fitted to later vehicles), it can be difficult to replace.
• After detaching both ends of the cable, disconnect all of the cable clips.
• Tie the end of the new cable to the end of the old one being removed (make sure the new one will be the right way round!).
• As the old one is withdrawn, the new one will follow the same route as the old.

JOB 4: GAS STRUT – *replacement*.

Most gas struts are held on with a spring clip:
→ There are several different shapes and size of clip, but all are levered off with a small screwdriver.
→ Take care not to lose the clip if it flies off!
→ On the type shown in **Step 1**, the spring clip should NOT be removed completely, or it will be damaged.

SAFETY FIRST!

• If the spring clip flies off, it could hit you in the eye!

• Support the clip as it is removed to prevent it from 'springing' away.

☐ **STEP 1:** This type of strut is fitted to many different types of vehicle, not just the Polo Classic shown here:
➔ Lift retaining clip (**2**) with a screwdriver.
➔ Pull the strut (**3**) off the ball stud (**1**) at each end.

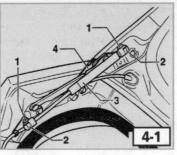

4-1

☐ **STEP 2:** On some older models:
➔ The spring clip is a piece of spring wire (**8**).
➔ The pin at the upper end of the strut (**7**) may be held with a clip (**6**) or a self-locking nut.

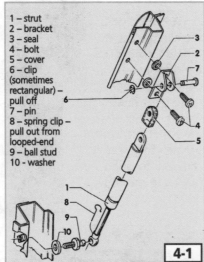

1 – strut
2 – bracket
3 – seal
4 – bolt
5 – cover
6 – clip (sometimes rectangular) – pull off
7 – pin
8 – spring clip – pull out from looped-end
9 – ball stud
10 - washer

4-1

☐ **STEP 3:** On Mk 1 Golf, the lower end is bolted to the bodywork.

4-3

JOB 5: DOORS, DOOR GEAR - *removal, stripdown.*

IMPORTANT NOTE:
CORRADO: See *Section C: Corrado door glass and mechanism*.

Section A: Door (earlier type) - removal.

IMPORTANT NOTE:
In all cases, other items will also have to be disconnected:
• Door check straps have to be removed.
• Electrical connections and central locking tubing (when fitted) will first have to be disconnected.
• Wiring grommets with corrugated sleeve wiring coverings should also be disconnected, at least at one end.

☐ **STEP A1:** The first job is to disconnect the check strap. Depending on type:
➔ **EITHER:** Use a punch to drift the pin upwards and out of the strap then replace it in the strap for safe keeping.

5-A1

☐ **STEP A2: OR:** Use a pair of spanners to undo and remove the pivot nut (**4**) and bolt (**3**).

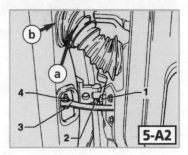

5-A2

WIRING CONNECTORS, LATER DOORS: Unscrew the locking ring (**b**) and unplug the connector (**a**) from the door. See also *Step A3*. On other models, there is a simpler sheath containing the wiring which is levered free from the door.

HINGE FIXINGS, ALTERNATIVE TYPES: (See also, *Step A5*).
EITHER (WITH GRUB SCREW ON HINGE): Unscrew the grub screw (**2**) from each hinge and lift the door with hinge pins up and away.
OR (*WITHOUT* GRUB SCREW ON HINGE): Remove the bolts (**1**) holding each hinge to the door. Use an Allen key.

☐ **STEP A3:** This is another view of the wiring connector referred to in *Step 2*. The locating ring (**b**) is unscrewed, allowing the connector (**7**) to be pulled free. Note the

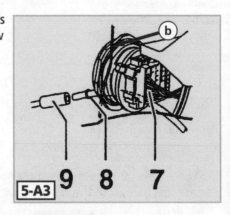

5-A3

position of the central locking hose connector (**9**) on models with central locking. The connector has to be pushed up to the coloured mark (**8**) on the hose when reconnecting.

☐ **STEP A4:** On some models, the central locking couplings are of this type. Release by pressing the ring sides (arrowed) together, then pulling the separate sections (**1** and **2**) apart.

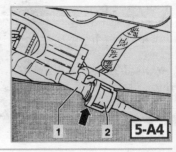

5-A4

□ **STEP A5:** IMPORTANT NOTE: As the door hinges are disconnected from the door, it is ESSENTIAL that an assistant takes the weight of the door.

`5-A5`

Section B: Front doors - stripdown, refitting.

IMPORTANT NOTES: • CORRADO: See *Section C: Corrado door glass and mechanism.*
• For information on door trim removal, see *Chapter 14, Interior and Trim, Job 2*.

STRIPDOWN - DOOR COMPONENTS

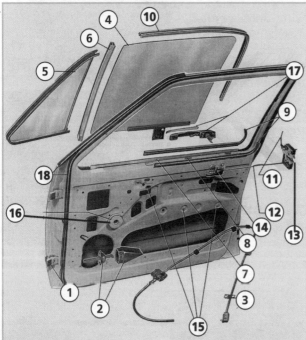

1 - bolt-on door - tightening torque: 45 ± 5 Nm
2 - door check strap with protective sleeve (2 hexagon bolts - 2 washers - 1 pin - 1 lock washer)
3 - window lifter (4 hexagon bolts with dished washer - 2 x standard and 2 x oversized, standard washers on drive)
4 - door window (2 hexagon bolts with dished washers)
5 - corner window with seal
6 - guide rail with window channel (1 Phillips screw at the top - 1 hollow rivet at the bottom)
7 - clips (six clips for window slot seals)
8 - clips (3 clips for door trim)
9 - internal and external window slot seals (press into clips for window slot seals)
10 - window channel (install starting from corner window)

11 - fastening rod with securing sleeve (insert fastening rod with securing sleeve from outside through recess and bring into position until plastic lugs on sleeve contact)
12 - tie rod (attach tie rod to operating lever)
13 - door lock (2 hexagon socket head screws)
14 - inner door operating mechanism with tie rod (2 hexagon bolts with dished washers)
15 - expanding nuts and clips for armrest
16 - window crank seal
17 - door handle (2 fillister head screws - 2 washers - 2 packing elements for door handle - 1 trim piece)
18 - door seals

`5-B1`

□ **STEP B1:** The principle of stripping each of the doors is similar. The door check strap is removed by taking out the bolts through an aperture in the door, next to the hinge. Remove other components in the numerical order shown here. This is the layout used on earlier Golfs and Polos.

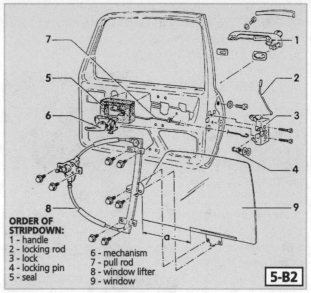

ORDER OF STRIPDOWN:
1 - handle
2 - locking rod
3 - lock
4 - locking pin
5 - seal
6 - mechanism
7 - pull rod
8 - window lifter
9 - window

`5-B2`

□ **STEP B2:** Front door, from around August 1987-on. The dimension (**a**), is 310 mm from the front of the glass.

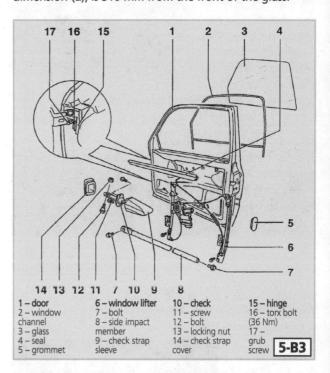

1 – door	6 – window lifter	10 – check	15 – hinge
2 – window channel	7 – bolt	11 – screw	16 – torx bolt (36 Nm)
3 – glass	8 – side impact member	12 – bolt	17 – grub screw
4 – seal	9 – check strap sleeve	13 – locking nut	
5 – grommet		14 – check strap cover	

`5-B3`

□ **STEP B3:** This is the later type of front door.

□ **STEP B4:** These are the side airbag components.

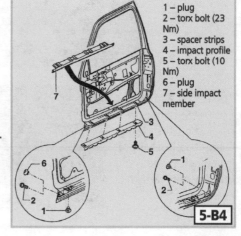

1 – plug
2 – torx bolt (23 Nm)
3 – spacer strips
4 – impact profile
5 – torx bolt (10 Nm)
6 – plug
7 – side impact member

`5-B4`

IMPORTANT NOTE: See *Chapter 14, Interior and Trim* for relevant information before attempting to work on a door fitted with an airbag.

STRIPDOWN PROCEDURE

❏ **STEP B5:** The glass seals are held with concealed spring clips and have to be carefully levered off.

5-B5

❏ **STEP B6:** A plastic or foam sealing membrane should be glued in place on the inside of the door. If you peel it off with care and store away from dirt and dust, you should be able to re-use the membrane. If not, replacements can be purchased and the material can be bought off the roll - produced by Wurth (among others).

5-B6

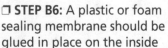
TOP TIP!

• The foam membrane is (even more!) prone to tearing than the plastic type.
• Try cutting through the sealant mastic, between the membrane and door frame.

GLASS AND WINDER GEAR

IMPORTANT NOTE: **CORRADO:** See *Section C: Corrado door glass and mechanism*.

❏ **STEP B7:** Start by temporarily refitting the winder handle and winding the glass down.

5-B7

❏**STEP B8: EARLIER MODELS:** Lower the glass until the clamp fixing the bottom of the glass to the winder mechanism can be accessed, then remove the fixing bolts.

5-B8

❏ **STEP B9: LATER MODELS:** The mechanism has to be lowered until the two clamping jaw bolts can be reached through the access holes (a). The mechanism itself is unbolted from the door frame at the positions shown (1).

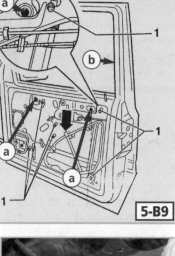

5-B9

❏ **STEP B10:** On non-Cabriolet models, with cable-operated mechanism, the cable tube also has to be unbolted from the door shell...

5-B10

❏ **STEP B11:** ...and the mechanism – slightly more trickily – can be manoeuvred free.

❏ **STEP B12:** Remove the glass, tilting it towards the front as it is lifted out. Also see *Step B15*.

5-B11

TOP TIP!

❏ **STEP B13:** • Along the edge of each door is a rubber seal.
• They are held with hidden clips or screws.
• Just pulling the seal off will destroy it - and it's expensive!

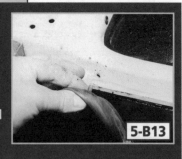

5-B13

GOLF CABRIOLET MODELS

❏ **STEP B14:** The clamp plate holding the glass to the runner is removed.

5-B14

5-B15

5-B16

QUARTER LIGHTS (EARLY VEHICLES ONLY) AND/OR FRONT GLASS RUNNERS

5-B21

5-B22

❑ **STEP B15:** The Cabriolet glass can now be slid up and out of the door frame. The non-Cabriolet's glass is removed in the same way except that it has to be turned at an angle so that it misses the door frame as it comes out.

❑ **STEP B16:** Remove the trim capping and disconnect the top of the glass runner...

❑ **STEP B21: GOLF CABRIOLET:** Start by taking out the screw holding the sealing trim in place...

❑ **STEP B22:** ...before carefully removing the seal and runner channel.

5-B17

5-B18

❑ **STEP B23: FIXED-TOP MODELS:** The screw holding the top of the quarter light is cunningly concealed beneath the glass runner channel. Ease it out before accessing the screw.

5-B23

❑ **STEP B17:** ...the bottom of the glass runner from underneath the door...

❑ **STEP B18:** ...and the runner can now be extracted from the Cabriolet's door frame.

❑ **STEP B24:** This is the screw on the Cabriolet model, in a similar location but much more easily seen, of course.

5-B24

5-B19

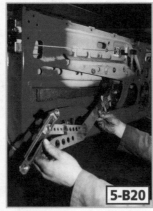

5-B20

❑ **STEP B25:** Lift out the Cabriolet's quarter light and glass runner, after first unbolting the runner from the door shell.

5-B25

❑ **STEP B19:** The winder mechanism can now be disconnected from the door...

❑ **STEP B20:** ...and angled out of the door shell.

❑ **STEP B26:** There are two fixings holding the glass channel in place.

5-B26

STEP B27: GOLF MK 1: Things are not quite so simple on the Golf Mk 1 fixed top's door. The top fixing, for reasons best known to the manufacturer, is a large pop rivet whose head has to be drilled off.

5-B27

STEP B28: You can now carefully ease the channel to one side while the quarter light and surrounding rubber are eased out of the door frame.

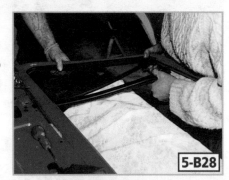
5-B28

STEP B29: With the quarter light safely out of the way, extract the channel from the door shell.

5-B29

STEP B30: EARLIER MODELS: These are the locations of the fixings for an electrically operated window regulator. To remove, follow the previous instructions but:

→ Note that the motor is connected via a plug and socket (1).
→ The motor itself is connected to the door frame with three bolts (2).
→ The guide rails are connected by three bolts (3), similar to other models.

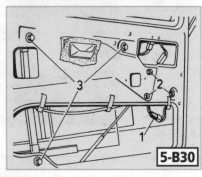
5-B30

STEP B31: LATER MODELS:
→ Unclip the bowden cable clip (arrowed).
→ Remove the lower bolts (2) and loosen the upper bolts (1).
→ Raise the window

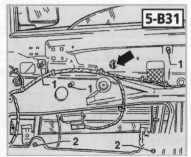
5-B31

lifter slightly and remove the upper screws (1).
→ Remove the window lifter assembly downwards through the aperture in the door.

LOCK AND LATCH MECHANISMS - EXTERNAL-LOCK VERSIONS

On earlier models, the door lock was fitted on the outside of the door frame.

STEP B32: The buffer for the door check strap is fitted inside the door and is unbolted from the door frame.

5-B32

STEP B33: Before starting to remove the lock, set it in the locked position by pressing down on the interior knob. To remove the door lock, use an Allen key to take out the two screws holding it to the door frame.

5-B33

STEP B34: Pull the lock a little way away from the door so that you can push a screwdriver into the hole in the bottom of the lock, as shown.

5-B34

STEP B35: The screwdriver is pushed through the hole (E) and is used to make sure that the operating lever (A) remains in the extended position.

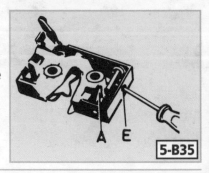
5-B35

☐ **STEP B36:** You will now be able to:

→ Unhook the end of the operating rod (**2**) from the operating lever (**1**) and pull the body of the lock (**7**) away from the door frame (**3**).

→ For reference, the two fixing screws go in the positions shown by (**6**), while the control lever (**4**) slots into the sleeve (**5**).

→ The screwdriver referred to earlier is shown here by the black arrow.

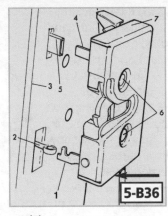

5-B36

5-B37

☐ **STEP B37:** The operating lever can easily now be removed from inside the vehicle…

5-B38

☐ **STEP B38:** …and all of the assemblies and operating rods taken from the door. Note that the locking knob is detached from the operating rod by simply unscrewing the knob.

☐ **STEP B39:** To remove the exterior door handle, take out this screw from the end of the door…

5-B39

☐ **STEP B40:** …then slide the handle forwards to release the hook at the end of the handle. On some models, there may be a cover strip beneath which is another screw at the front end of the handle – see illustration *5-B45.*

LOCK AND LATCH MECHANISM - INTERNAL-LOCK VERSIONS

Later doors have the lock fitted inside the door casing. Some of the above applies, but the procedure for this type is as follows:

☐ **STEP B41:** These are the components of a typical later-type of lock mechanism. To release the interior release handle (**11**), you insert the end of a screwdriver in the recess at the base of the handle so

as to press the securing clip out of the hole in the door inner panel. You can now push the interior release handle in the direction of the arrow and out of its securing holes.

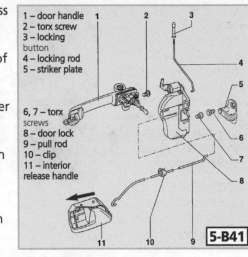

1 – door handle
2 – torx screw
3 – locking button
4 – locking rod
5 – striker plate

6, 7 – torx screws
8 – door lock
9 – pull rod
10 – clip
11 – interior release handle

5-B41

☐ **STEP B42:** To remove the door lock:

→ Close the door window.

→ **DRIVER'S DOOR ONLY:** Place the key into the lock cylinder (**a**).

→ Turn the key through 90 degrees in a clockwise direction.

a – lock cylinder
1 – door handle
2 – key - inserted into lock cylinder
3 – seal
4 – socket-head screw with collar
5 – door handle spring
6 – coupling plate
7 – coupling plate spring
8 – connecting rod spring
9 – connecting rod - attached in the inner end of the lock cylinder (a)
10, 11 – backing plates
12 – leaf spring

5-B42

→ **ALL DOORS:** Take out the fixing screw (**4**).

→ Slide the handle forwards so as to free the locating lug (**b**).

→ **DRIVER'S DOOR ONLY:**

→ Pivot the exterior handle assembly out from the door, key-end first.

→ In order to remove the lock cylinder, unhook and remove the connecting rod (**9**), the connecting rod spring (**8**) and the coupling plate spring (**7**).

→ With the key in the lock cylinder (**2** and **a**) the lock cylinder can be withdrawn from the lock.

REFITTING

LOCK AND LATCH MECHANISMS - EXTERNAL-LOCK VERSIONS

☐ **STEP B43:** Before fitting the door lock, lift the lever (**A**) as shown, push a screwdriver into the hole (**E**) and hold the shaft in this position.

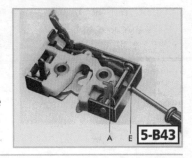

A E 5-B43

STEP B44: Insert fastening rod with securing sleeve (**1**) from the outside. The plastic lugs on the securing sleeve must make contact. Attach tie rod (**2**) to operating lever and take the screwdriver out of the door lock. Screw door lock into place (arrows).

5-B44

STEP B45: To fit the outside door handle, push the handle and packing pieces into position and slide in the direction of the arrow. Fit the screws and refit the trim strip.

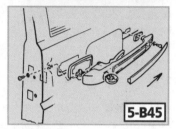

5-B45

STEP B46: To fit the type of inside mechanism with finger plate:
→ Pull the retaining tab (**1**) out of the hole in the door inner panel.
→ Push finger plate and door mechanism (**2**) out, in direction of arrow.

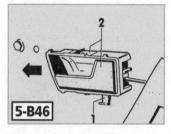

5-B46

LOCK AND LATCH MECHANISM - INTERNAL-LOCK VERSIONS

STEP B47: To re-install:
→ If necessary, renew the spring clip (**1**).
→ Pivot the door handle in, at arrow position first.
→ Slide handle back and refit screw (**2**).

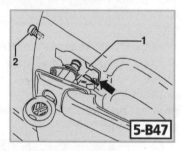

5-B47

GLASS AND WINDER GEAR - EARLIER MODELS

IMPORTANT NOTE: **CORRADO:** See *Section C: Corrado door glass and mechanism*.

STEP B48: Fit the door glass and window lifter (**3**) next, making sure that the correct dished washers are used on the drive (**4**) when fitted:
→ Insert door glass from above.
→ Attach glass loosely to window lifter.
→ Wind glass up fully.

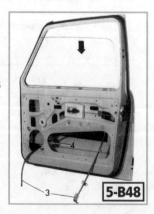

5-B48

STEP B49: → Slide the quarter light and glass guide rail into place and fit it with Phillips screws at points **a** and **b**.
→ Wind the window down slightly and fix it tightly to the window lifter through the fitting holes.
→ Fit the window seal clips to the points (**7**).
→ Push the window channel (**8**) into position, starting from the top corner (**9**).

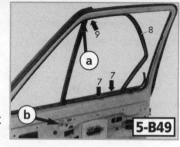

5-B49

DOOR GLASS - LATER MODELS

IMPORTANT NOTE: **CORRADO:** See *Section C: Corrado door glass and mechanism*.

STEP B50: Make sure that the glass is fitted to the clamps located as in *Step B9, position a*.
→ Loosen the clamp screws.
→ Push the glass so that it is lying in its runner at the back of the door frame (**b**).
→ Retighten the clamp screws (**a**).

Section C: Corrado door glass and mechanism.

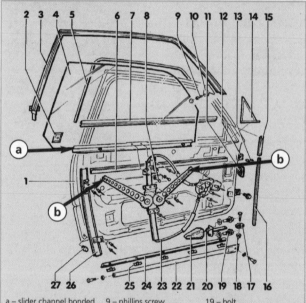

a – slider channel bonded to bottom of glass
b – mounting points for door window sliding block
1 – door
2 – door window sliding block
3 – surround – self-adhesive, buttoned into window frame
4 – door glass
5 – door frame edge protector
6 – inner window slot seal
7 – outer window slot seal
8 – bolt
9 – phillips screw
10 – bracket
11 – door check strap cover – self-adhesive
12 – door hinge
13 – bolt (55 Nm)
14 – cover – clipped in and screwed at the front
15 – window guide, upper – buttoned into guide channel
16 – window guide, lower – buttoned into guide channel
17 – clip
18 – self-locking nut
19 – bolt
20 – door check strap
21 – sleeve
22 – side impact bar (when fitted)
23 – window lifter
24 – door seal – self-adhesive
25 – retaining clips – pressed on to door T-bolts
26 – guide channel – riveted in place
27 – door stop – adjust so it is slightly compressed

5-C1

STEP C1: These are the components of the Corrado's door gear.

STEP C2: To remove glass:
→ Wind window down fully.
→ Pull guide arms (**b**) off window channel (**a**) and detach window glass and channel.
→ Remove inner window slot seal (**6**).
→ Tilt front corner forwards, pull the glass out, rear-corner first, through inner side of glass aperture.

STEP C3:
To remove the lifter mechanism, drill out the rivets (arrowed).
→ Use a 5 mm drill to drill the head off each rivet.

5-C3

→ Remove window lifter through lower opening.
→ When refitting, use new blind rivets.

Section D: Rear side doors and rear side windows - stripdown, refitting.

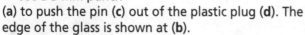

For information on Cabriolet side windows, see *Chapter 14, Job 11*.

STEP D1: There are very few differences between the principles of front and rear doors, when fitted. The main difference is:
→ **POLO FROM 1994-ON:** The glass is attached to the regulator in a completely different way. After undoing the guide channel bolts:

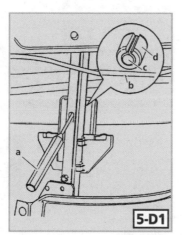

5-D1

→ Use a 3 mm punch (**a**) to push the pin (**c**) out of the plastic plug (**d**). The edge of the glass is shown at (**b**).
→ Push out the plug with a screwdriver and retrieve both from the inside of the door.
→ Raise the window glass to release it from the regulator, then lower it so that the guide channels can be removed.

STEP D2: Where side windows are fixed in position, we strongly recommend that you use a professional windscreen fitting company. The principles are similar to those for front screens, and all side glass requires fitting with adhesive - and it can be difficult to remove the old without breaking the glass.

Section E: Cabriolet door glass - adjustment.

CABRIOLET TO 1994

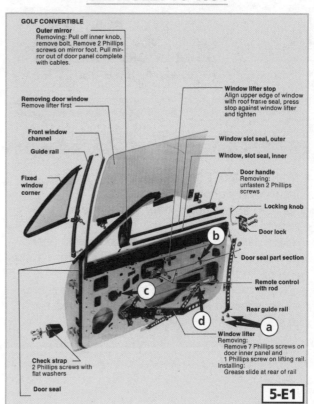

GOLF CONVERTIBLE

Outer mirror
Removing: Pull off inner knob, remove bolt. Remove 2 Phillips screws on mirror foot. Pull mirror out of door panel complete with cables.

Removing door window
Remove lifter first

Front window channel

Guide rail

Fixed window corner

Check strap
2 Phillips screws with flat washers

Door seal

Window lifter stop
Align upper edge of window with roof frame seal, press stop against window lifter and tighten

Window slot seal, outer

Window, slot seal, inner

Door handle
Removing: unfasten 2 Phillips screws

Locking knob

Door lock

Door seal part section

Remote control with rod

Rear guide rail

Window lifter
Removing: Remove 7 Phillips screws on door inner panel and 1 Phillips screw on lifting rail.
Installing: Grease slide at rear of rail

5-E1

STEP E1: Cabriolet door gear, produced up to 1994:
→ Adjust rear guide rail by slackening bolts (**a**).
→ Inside the aperture (**b**) is a bolt which is slackened to adjust the height of the rear of the window.
→ Inside the aperture (**c**) is a bolt which is slackened to adjust the height of the front of the window.
→ At the end of the arm (**d**) is a bolt which allows adjustment of the front-to-rear positioning.

CABRIOLET 1994-ON

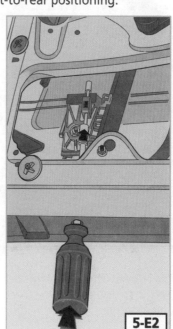

STEP E2: To adjust:
→ The door glass inclination is adjusted by the wedges on the lowering/raising mechanism.
→ The height setting can (theoretically!) be adjusted through holes in the bottom of the door with the trim in place using a Torx end.
→ Insert the tool through the relevant hole/s in the bottom

5-E2

of the door and turn the height adjuster/s (arrowed) which are on the front and rear height stops on the adjuster mechanism.

→ In practice, it's going to be far easier to remove the door trim first!

JOB 6: HATCHBACK, BOOT/TRUNK AND CADDY TAILBOARD /REAR DOORS AND LOCKS - *removal, replacement.*

Section A: Doors - removing.

IMPORTANT NOTE: In all cases, other items will also have to be disconnected. For example:

→ On Caddy rear doors, door stops have to be removed.

→ Electrical connections and central locking pipes and washer tubing (when fitted) will first have to be disconnected.

→ Wiring grommets with corrugated sleeve wiring coverings should also be disconnected, at least at one end.

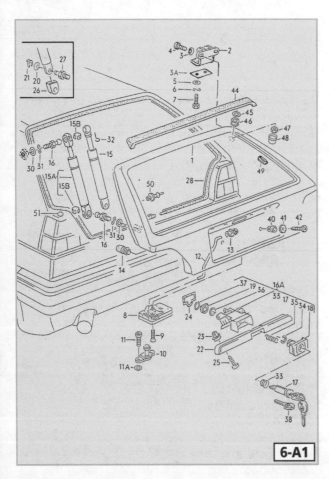

6-A1

❏ **STEP A1:** These are typical tailgate components. The gas filled strut is removed as described in *Job 4*.

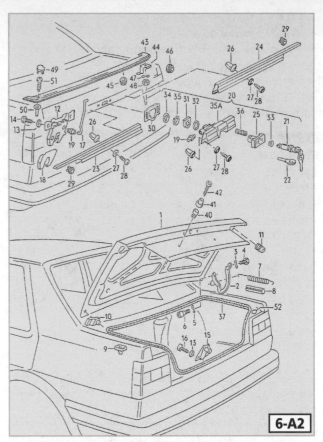

6-A2

❏ **STEP A2:** These are the Mk 2 Jetta's components. The part numbers in these illustrations are referred to later in this Job.

TOP TIP!

• The tailgate/flap/boot/trunk lid will only close properly when the mechanisms are perfectly aligned.

• Don't force it, or you may get it stuck shut!

❏ **STEP A3:** Before removing a tailgate or boot/trunk lid:

→ Mark the hinge positions with a felt pen so that exact realignment can be carried out.

→ If a replacement panel is being fitted, the panel position should be adjusted in the opening before setting the lock/catch mechanism.

6-A3

→ With the mounting bolts slack, move the panel as required and retighten.

→ Two people are needed to lift all doors and opening panels (except Cabrio. rear hatch) because they are both heavy and unwieldy.

❏ **STEP A4: GOLF CADDY VAN REAR DOORS:** The hinge retaining screws are behind trim caps which have to be levered out from the body side.

Section B: Tailgate lock.

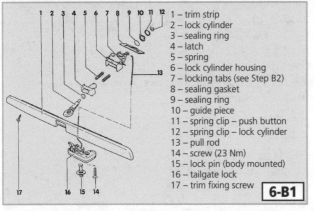

1 – trim strip
2 – lock cylinder
3 – sealing ring
4 – latch
5 – spring
6 – lock cylinder housing
7 – locking tabs (see Step B2)
8 – sealing gasket
9 – sealing ring
10 – guide piece
11 – spring clip – push button
12 – spring clip – lock cylinder
13 – pull rod
14 – screw (23 Nm)
15 – lock pin (body mounted)
16 – tailgate lock
17 – trim fixing screw

6-B1

❏ **STEP B1:** These are typical tailgate lock components.

❏ **STEP B2: PUSH BUTTON HANDLE REMOVAL:**
→ **MK 2 GOLF:** Remove the Phillips screws from the outside.
→ **MK 2 GOLF:** Squeeze the tabs (arrowed) together and remove the handle.

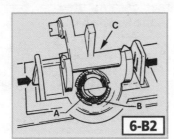

6-B2

→ **ALL MODELS:** Put key in lock, key in vertical position (or tumblers will fall out!), remove circlip (**A**) and take out the lock cylinder.
→ Remove the retaining ring (**B**) and take the lock housing out of the handle.

❏ **STEP B3: PUSH BUTTON HANDLE REPLACEMENT:** If fitting a new handle, and with the handle turned the right way up, refer to illustration **6-B1**:
→ The slide (position **C**) has to be pushed to the LEFT for vehicles WITH central locking; to the RIGHT for vehicles WITHOUT central locking.

Section C: Cabriolet 'rear flap' lock.

❏ **STEP C1:** The Cabriolet 'rear flap' as Volkswagen call it, has a very similar mechanism to the Mk 1 Golf/Rabbit and Scirocco hatchback mechanisms. The push-button/lock (**a**) is almost the same, although the operating rod (**b**) is longer, and the relay lever (**c**) is built in to the lock (**d**) on non-Cabrio. models.

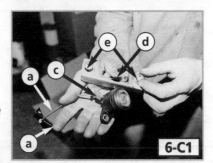

6-C1

On all models, when refitting:
→ Fit the seal behind the push-button/lock.
→ Fit the striker plate to the body.
→ Fit the lock so that the screws (**e**) just grip.
→ Lower the tailgate or flap and check alignment as you go. Tighten when satisfactory. Adjust stop rubbers.

Section D: Caddy rear doors locks.

❏ **STEP D1: GOLF CADDY PICK-UP TAILBOARD:** To remove the lock mechanism:
→ Open the tailboard slightly, and press the retaining tab (arrowed) on the clip (**1**) to free the release rod (**2**).

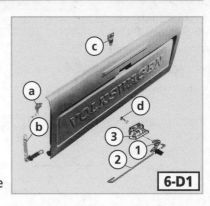

6-D1

Pull the rod out of the circlip on the handle (**3**).
→ Take out the three screws (**d**) to remove the handle (**3**).
→ The latches (**a**) - one at each end - are held with three screws, one of which also holds the folding stay (**b**). The latches are pulled out of the tailboard complete with the rods (**2**).
→ The striker plate bracket (**c**) is only fitted with a hardtop.

❏ **STEP D2: CADDY VAN (1996-on) REAR LEFT-HAND DOOR:** To remove the lock mechanism:
→ Take out the two bolts (**2**) and remove the door handle (**1**).
→ Remove the door trim panel and the right-hand licence plate light.
→ Detach cables (**7** and **8**).
→ Remove the bolt (**4**) and take out the door lock (**3**).

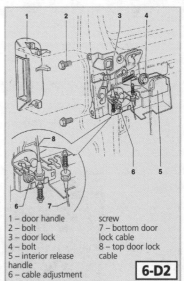

1 – door handle
2 – bolt
3 – door lock
4 – bolt
5 – interior release handle
6 – cable adjustment
screw
7 – bottom door lock cable
8 – top door lock cable

6-D2

❏ **STEP D3:** To adjust the door pull cables:
→ Loosen the adjuster screw (**6**).
→ Pull the interior release handle (**5**) until a resistance is felt and retighten the screw (**6**).

❏ **STEP D4: REAR RIGHT-HAND DOOR:** Although the shape of the release lever is different, the principle and layout of the release cables and adjustment are as shown in **Step D2**.

Section E: Corrado power rear spoiler – removing.

☐ STEP E1: To remove the spoiler:
➔ Raise the spoiler.
➔ Remove socket-head screws (**2**).
➔ Remove rear spoiler (**1**) from locating pins (**3**).
➔ Remove Phillips screws (arrowed).

6-E1

☐ STEP E2: This is the spoiler lifting mechanism.
➔ Remove the tailgate inner trim panel.
➔ If necessary raise the spoiler manually by pulling out

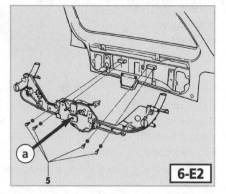

6-E2

knob (**a**), turning anti-clockwise to raise (clockwise to lower) then push back in again.
➔ Four socket-head bolts (**5**) hold the mechanism to the tailgate. Unplug the electrical socket first.

JOB 7: BUMPERS - *removal, replacement*.

Section A: Front bumpers - Golf to 1992 (inc. Caddy); Polo to 1982.

☐ STEP A1: Remove the front lower grille, when fitted, by taking out the fixing screws.

☐ STEP A2: Most types of front and rear bumpers are bolted on.
➔ On Golf Mk 1 models,

7-A2

both front and rear bumpers are unbolted from the inner face of the chassis legs.
➔ The front bumpers on Mk 1s are unbolted from inside the engine bay – see *Section C, Step 1*.
➔ Polo bolts are beneath bumper and body.

☐ STEP A3: Some **NORTH AMERICAN GOLF MK 1 MODELS** have this energy-absorbing bumper which bolts sideways to the side-

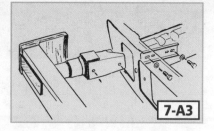

7-A3

members. SCIROCCO bumpers, front and rear, are fitted in a similar way.

☐ STEP A4: A number of different types of bumper guides are used.
➔ Some models have a pin with shoulders (**A**) fitted to the body which slides into guides (**B**) in the bumper.
➔ Some, such as

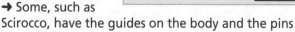

7-A4

Scirocco, have the guides on the body and the pins on the bumper.
➔ Some have a taller, rectangular plate on the body and guides on the bumper.
➔ In all cases, the bumper is pulled off the guides (or pins) by sliding it forwards and free.

☐ STEP A5: CADDY MODELS: These are the bumper components:
• The bumper support brackets (**D**) bolt to the body (**A, B**).
• The bumper (**J**) bolts to the bracket

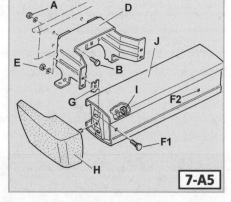

7-A5

with special square-shank bumper bolts (**F1**) to fit the square holes (**F2**). When refitting, be sure to use the spacers (**G**).
• The end caps (**H**) are bolted on through the inside of the bumper, with nuts and washers (**I**).

TOP TIP!

• If the nuts (**E**) rust themselves to the bumper bolts (**F1**), the bolts will turn in their square holes. Remove the brackets (**D**) complete with bumper, place the assembly face down on a large cloth (to avoid damage), and use a small, sharp chisel to cut through the nuts (**E**).

Section B: Front bumpers - Golf from 1992-on; Polo from 1982.

❒ **STEP B1:** Remove the grille - see *Job 1*. Take out the screws and/or clips holding the wheelarch liners to the wheelarches.

❒ **STEP B2:** Remove the bumper as follows:
➜ **GOLF MODELS:** Take out the five lower bolts (**8**) and the three upper bolts (**5**).
➜ **POLO MODELS:** Take out lower and upper bolts.
➜ Disconnect the wiring connectors from the indicators and from any other lights that may be fitted. Make sure the wiring is disconnected from any wiring clips on the bumper.
➜ Disconnect the headlight washer supply tubing.
➜ Carefully release the ends of the bumper from the guides (**7**) and pull the bumper away from the vehicle.

IMPORTANT NOTE: Polo: Lower screws are accessed after removing the lower grille.

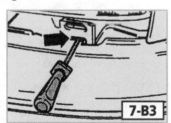

1 – bumper cover
2 – spreader rivet – connects to wheel arch liner
3 – buffer
4 – cross-member
5 – upper bolts
6 – plastic washer
7 – guide
8 – lower bolts
9 – spoiler
10 – cover

7-B2

❒ **STEP B3:** This is how to disconnect the cover retaining clips on this type of bumper.

7-B3

❒ **STEP B4: POLO CLASSIC** models are fitted with front bumper guides similar to those shown for the rear bumper. See *Section C, Step C2*.

❒ **STEP B5: CORRADO:** The front bumper forms part of the structure, DO NOT USE CAR with bumper detached.

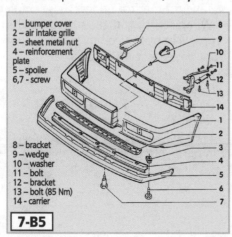

1 – bumper cover
2 – air intake grille
3 – sheet metal nut
4 – reinforcement plate
5 – spoiler
6,7 - screw
8 – bracket
9 – wedge
10 – washer
11 – bolt
12 – bracket
13 – bolt (85 Nm)
14 - carrier

7-B5

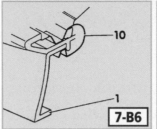

7-B6

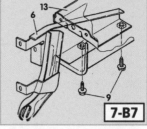

7-B7

❒ **STEP B6:** In order to remove the bumper, you first have to unclip the sheet metal clamps (**10**) between the bumper cover (**1**) and the engine carrier.

❒ **STEP B7:** The bolts (**9**) have to be removed from the bracket (**6**) and engine carrier (**13**).

❒ **STEP B8:** The bumper can now be removed in a forwards direction.

❒ **STEP B9:** When refitting, the gap between the bumper and each wing/fender panel should be 8 mm.

Section C: Back bumpers.

Back bumpers are removed and replaced as for the front bumpers, apart from the differences shown here:

❒ **STEP C1:** The fixing bolts on Mk 1 models are found inside the rear luggage compartment.

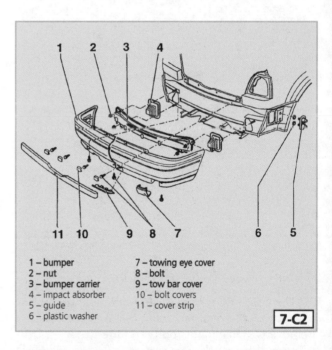

1 – bumper
2 – nut
3 – bumper carrier
4 – impact absorber
5 – guide
6 – plastic washer
7 – towing eye cover
8 – bolt
9 – tow bar cover
10 – bolt covers
11 – cover strip

7-C2

❒ **STEP C2:** These are the components of the Golf back bumper from 1992-on.

ESTATE MODELS: In addition to guides (**5**) there are also clips on forward ends of bumper to be disconnected before removing bumper.

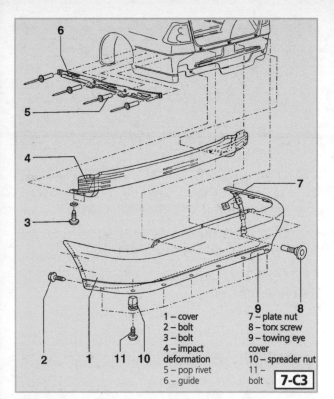

1 – cover
2 – bolt
3 – bolt
4 – impact deformation
5 – pop rivet
6 – guide
7 – plate nut
8 – torx screw
9 – towing eye cover
10 – spreader nut
11 – bolt

7-C3

☐ **STEP C3:** Polo Classic from 1996-on.

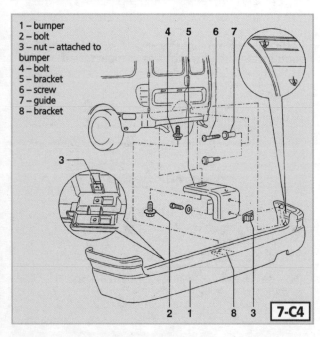

1 – bumper
2 – bolt
3 – nut – attached to bumper
4 – bolt
5 – bracket
6 – screw
7 – guide
8 – bracket

7-C4

☐ **STEP C4:** Caddy van from 1996-on.

☐ **STEP C5: CADDY PICKUP, 1997-ON:** Rear mudflaps are attached to rear panel and rear bumper edges. Remove two fixing nuts/bolts and the two lever-off clips per side.
→ The two bumper side trims are bolted in place at their top edges. Take off side panels inside loadbay.

☐ **STEP C6: CORRADO:** They are bolted from beneath.
→ Attached to body with a line of wedges (see illustration **7-B6, item 9**). Carefully lever bumper off with a screwdriver. Pull bumper forwards.

JOB 8: FRONT PANEL - *removal*.

GOLF FROM 1992; POLO FROM 1995:
→ The new, removable front panel is made lighter by use of plastics.
→ Removal improves access immeasurably when carrying out major engine work.
→ VW call the front panel the 'lock carrier'.

☐ **STEP 1:** To remove front panel, take of:
→ Coolant hoses and connectors.
→ Disconnect the cable at the bonnet lock.
→ Disconnect the air conditioning pipes (when fitted) from their pipe clips. DO NOT open the hoses themselves!
→ Remove air ducting pipes (when fitted).

GOLF/VENTO MODELS

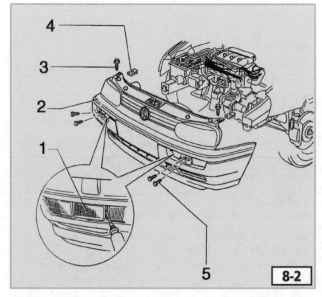

8-2

☐ **STEP 2:** Dismantle and remove the front panel (2) in the following order:
→ Lever the towing eye/cover (1) towards the front and pull out of holder.
→ Take out the screws (3) and (5).
→ Take off the front panel as a complete unit.
→ When refitting, make sure the speed nuts (4) are properly in place. Do not induce any stress into the front panel as it is fitted.

POLO MODELS

☐ **STEP 3:** Remove the front bumper. See *Job 7: Bumpers - removal, replacement.*

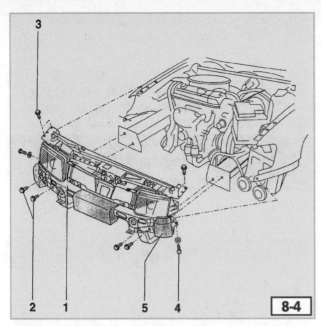

8-4

STEP 4: Dismantle and remove the front panel in the following order:

→ Remove the bolts (**1, 2, 3** and **4**).

→ If bolts (**2**) are partly concealed by the deformable sections (**5**), pull them away, as necessary.

→ Take off the front panel as a complete unit.

→ When refitting, use suitable body adhesive to glue the deformable sections (**5**) back in place, if necessary. Do not induce any stress into the front panel as it is fitted.

JOB 9: FRONT WINGS/FENDERS - *replacement*.

STEP 1: Start by removing the following (in each case, when fitted to the particular model you are working on):

→ The wheelarch 'eyebrow' trim - either screws, or self-adhesive.

→ The wheelarch liner. Either screws or plastic rivets - push out the centres of the rivets so that the 'spread' legs are released and the rivet can be removed.

→ The front bumper. See *Job 7*.

→ Direction indicator repeater light, headlight unit.

→ Trim and badges - usually self-adhesive but sometimes bolted through - check inside of panel.

TOP TIP!

• It is easy to damage self-adhesive trim as it is being removed - and it can be expensive - and sometimes unobtainable!

• Carefully heat the self-adhesive backing with a heat gun or hair dryer to soften it.

• Use a thin-bladed spatula to push through the adhesive - don't try to lever the trim off.

9-2

9-3

STEP 2: If a radio aerial/antenna is fitted, remove the special nut holding it to the car but leave the cable in place – there's no need to remove it.

→ Reassemble the nut, seals and washers on the top of the antenna (that's it shown here, having been pushed down into the wheel arch) so that you don't lose the separate parts or forget their correct order.

→ On some models, the radio antenna steady bar is fitted to one of the mounting bolts.

STEP 3: You can now undo the bolts from under the wheel arch.

STEP 4: You'll find this bolt at the bottom, just ahead of the door. If it won't come undone, try:

→ Releasing fluid.

→ Locally applied heat.

9-4

→ Working the bolt steadily to-and-fro.

→ If it shears, resign yourself to having to drill out the stud and re-tap the hole.

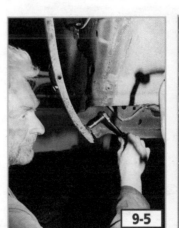

9-5

9-6

STEP 5: The same applies to the bolt holding the bottom of the wing/fender to the front apron.

STEP 6: Leaving the easiest until last, you can now take out the bolts from adjacent to the engine bay.

☐ **STEP 7:** Volkswagen apply copious amounts of sealer/adhesive and so you have to ease the front end away from the front panel, starting at the bottom, as shown.

9-7

TOP TIP!

• This adhesive is **very** difficult to move!
• You will certainly benefit from using a heat gun to soften it and then a spatula to push through the adhesive that you can see.
• DO NOT use a blow lamp or other exposed flame, because of the risk of fire!

☐ **STEP 8:** The front can now be eased away but the back will be found to be very securely stuck. To some extent, the adhesive can be weakened by pulling the front of the wing/fender out a little way but you'll be very fortunate not to distort the rear of the panel.

9-8

After lifting away, be sure to retrieve any small fixtures and fittings that you may wish to reuse, such as stops which may be glued to the rebated area, where it bolts down to the engine bay panel, the front mounting bracket and the bumper mounting bracket.

☐ **STEP 9:**
REFITTING: The first job is always to offer up a new panel to make sure that it fits correctly – and also to make sure that you have been supplied with the version that it exactly right for your model of car!

9-9

☐ **STEP 10:** The first fit should always be a trial fit without using any sealer/adhesive.
→ Start off by fitting two new bolts to the centre fixings, just to hold the panel in place, then add more bolts and check the fit with adjacent panels.

9-10

→ If necessary, use card packing pieces to allow for the thickness of panel adhesive to be used later.

JOB 10: DOOR MIRRORS - *removal, replacement*.

Section A: Mirror assembly replacement.

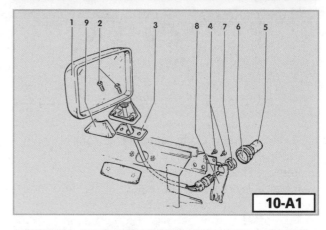
10-A1

☐ **TYPE A1: DOOR MOUNTING, NON-REPLACEABLE GLASS (e.g. early Polo, Golf):**
→ **NOT SCIROCCO:** To remove the mirror from the door, lever off the trim cover (**9**) and remove the screws (**2**).
→ **SCIROCCO:** Take off the interior door trim and remove the three screws which pass through the door frame.
→ **INTERNALLY ADJUSTABLE MIRRORS:** Pull off the lever cap (**5**), the bellows (**6**), remove the door trim and disconnect the adjuster from the bracket (**8**) by removing the nut (**7**) or ring.

☐ **TYPE A2: DOOR MOUNTING, REPLACEABLE GLASS (e.g. Corrado):**
→ Remove the two fixing screws (**8**) holding the mirror base to the door.
→ Turn the mirror head (**7**) first one way, then the other, to gain access to the screws.
→ Glass replacement - see *Section B: Glass replacement*.

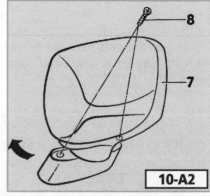
10-A2

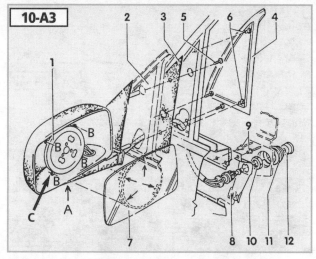

10-A3

□ **TYPE A3: LATER MOUNTING (e.g. Mk 2 Golf to 1992, later Polo.):** There are variations, but the principles of removal are the same.

→ Remove the trim from inside the door (**4**) - lever it off the clips (**6**). There is another insulating trim piece behind the outer trim on later models.

→ Disconnect the adjuster mechanism (items **8** to **12**) as described in *Type A1*.

→ Remove the screws (**5**) and take off the mirror.

→ Glass replacement - see *Section B: Glass replacement*.

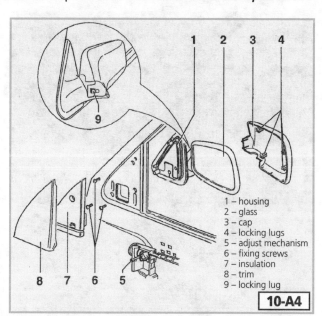

1 – housing
2 – glass
3 – cap
4 – locking lugs
5 – adjust mechanism
6 – fixing screws
7 – insulation
8 – trim
9 – locking lug

10-A4

□ **TYPE A4: LATER MOUNTING (e.g. Mk 3 Golf, from 1992.):** See *Type A3*.

→ The housing (**3**) can be replaced. Remove the glass, fold the mirror towards the door, then squeeze the locking lugs (**4**) together while pressing lug (**9**). Pull off the housing.

→ Glass replacement - see *Section B: Glass replacement*.

□ **TYPE A5: LATER MOUNTING (e.g. Polo Caddy and Classic.):**

→ Pull off the button (**1**) and carefully lever the trim (**2**) off the fixing clips (**3**).

→ Remove the adjuster nut (**5**), take out the screws (**4**) and remove the mirror assembly.

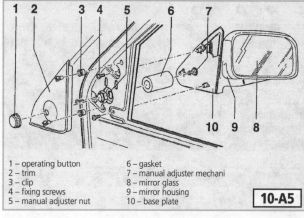

1 – operating button
2 – trim
3 – clip
4 – fixing screws
5 – manual adjuster nut
6 – gasket
7 – manual adjuster mechani
8 – mirror glass
9 – mirror housing
10 – base plate

10-A5

→ Glass replacement - see *Section B: Glass replacement*.

□ **TYPE A6: ELECTRICALLY OPERATED MIRRORS:** To remove the mechanism, remove glass (see *Section B: Glass replacement*) and taking out screws inside glass mounting plate (see *10-3, item C*).

Section B: Glass replacement.

□ **TYPE B1: SCREW-FIXING:**
Look for a hole in base of mirror-back (see illustration *10-Type A3, position A*).

→ Insert a narrow screwdriver and turn wheel (**1**), to release glass (**7**).

→ Fit a new one in reverse order.

10-B2

□ **TYPE B2: PUSH-ON FIXING:** If there is no hole in the base of the mirror (see *Type B1*), it is safe to assume that the mirror has push-on replaceable glass.

SAFETY FIRST!

• There is a strong chance of breaking the mirror glass as it is removed. Wear goggles and industrial leather gloves.

→ Rock the glass back at the top as far as it will go.

→ Insert a thin lever and lever the glass off its lower sockets. (See *10-Type A3, items B*.)

→ Rock the glass forward at the top as far as it will go and lever the glass free at the top.

→ Push the new glass on so that the lugs on the back of the glass push into the sockets.

JOB 11: SUN ROOF.

If you can avoid dismantling the sunroof, do so! The refitting and adjustment of the two main types of sunroof is always complex and difficult. The following information is supplied for reference.

TOP TIP!

• If removal or adjustment of the sunroof involves the removal of headlining, have a trimmer carry out the work.
• The Volkswagen sunroofs are designed to be fitted as complete 'cassette' assemblies. A severely damaged sunroof may be best replaced with a new or good second-hand one.

Section A: Early type.

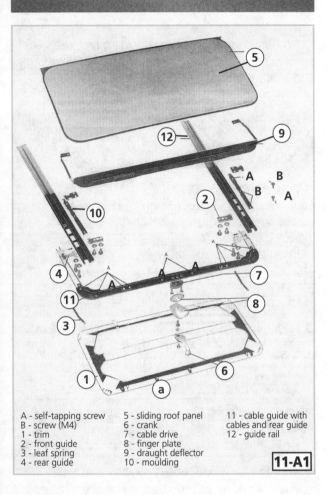

A - self-tapping screw
B - screw (M4)
1 - trim
2 - front guide
3 - leaf spring
4 - rear guide
5 - sliding roof panel
6 - crank
7 - cable drive
8 - finger plate
9 - draught deflector
10 - moulding
11 - cable guide with cables and rear guide
12 - guide rail

11-A1

❑ **STEP A1:** These are the main components of a typical earlier-type sliding sunroof. To remove the roof, do so in the numerical order shown; refitting is in the opposite order. The following notes relate to the part numbers shown.

→ Half open roof. Lever front edge of trim (1) so clips (a) come free. Open roof fully. Push trim forward as far as possible, bend upwards and remove from guide rails (12).
→ To remove the cable guide (11), mask front corners of roof opening. Pull cable guide with cable forward to remove from guide rails (4). Oil cables and grease guide rails before refitting.
→ Disengage leaf spring from rear guides (4) by moving in direction of arrow.

❑ **STEP A2:** Adjust the roof so that the clearances are as shown, to avoid wind noise. (The front of the car is the left of this illustration.)

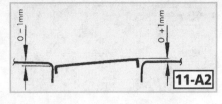

0 – 1mm   0 +1mm   11-A2

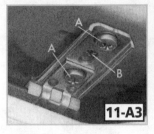

11-A3

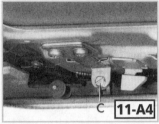

C   11-A4

❑ **STEP A3: FRONT:**
Unclip trim panel and push to rear. Slacken mounting screws (A). Turn height adjustment screw (B) and retighten (A) when correct.

❑ **STEP A4: REAR:** Disengage leaf spring. Slacken slotted screw (C) and move plate manually. Retighten screw.

TOP TIP!

BOTH SUNROOF TYPES
• Clean out all four water drain pipes with flexible wire at least 2,300 mm long - old speedo. cable is perfect!
• Look out for the ends of the pipes, inside the A-pillars (open front doors and look between doors and pillars) and just beneath car, at end of sills/body rockers - bumper removed.

Section B: Later type.

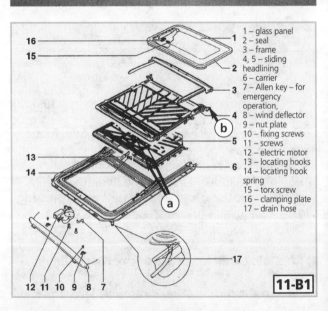

1 – glass panel
2 – seal
3 – frame
4, 5 – sliding headlining
6 – carrier
7 – Allen key – for emergency operation,
8 – wind deflector
9 – nut plate
10 – fixing screws
11 – screws
12 – electric motor
13 – locating hooks
14 – locating hook spring
15 – torx screw
16 – clamping plate
17 – drain hose

11-B1

❑ **STEP B1:** These are the main components of a typical later-type sliding sunroof.

GLASS PANEL – REMOVING, INSTALLING, HEIGHT ADJUSTMENT

☐ **STEP B2:** To remove and install the glass panel:
➜ Tilt the back of the roof open.
➜ Slide the headlining (1) to the rear.
➜ Slide the trim frame (2)

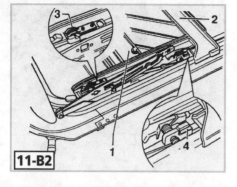

to the rear (it is clipped on in the area of the front guide (3) and guided at the rear by lugs (4).

☐ **STEP B3:** Remove the torx screws (a) and take off the adjusting plates (b). The glass panel can now be lifted out.

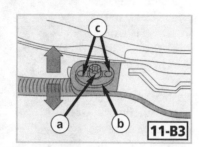

ADJUSTMENT: With the glass sliding panel in the closed position:
➜ If replacing the panel, make sure that the centralising pins (c) on the reverse of the clamping plates (b) locate correctly.
➜ Adjust the sun roof height front and rear so that it matches that shown in *Section A, Step A2*.
➜ Retighten the securing screws (a).

☐ **STEP B4: ADJUST PANEL SEAL:** It should just be possible to pull a piece of thin card about 0.3 mm thick between the glass panel seal and the bodywork all the way around.

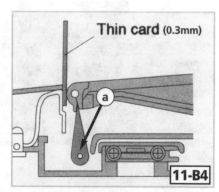

Thin card (0.3mm)

➜ The effective seal thickness can be adjusted by removing the glass and opening the seal with a wedge (a) or pushing it shut, as necessary.

☐ **STEP B5: CHECKING AND ADJUSTING PARALLEL RUNNING:**
➜ Have the glass panel in the closed position and the

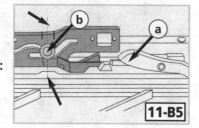

sliding headlining pushed fully back.
➜ Push trim frame to rear (clipped on in area of front guide).
➜ Make sure that the locating hooks with rollers (a) are engaged in the guide rails.
➜ Pin (b) should be within the marks shown (arrows). If they are in the correct position, no adjustment is necessary. If you need to adjust the parallel running:

☐ **STEP B6:** Disconnect the battery earth (-) terminal. Push off the cover in the direction of the arrow and remove the electric drive mechanism.
➜ Now make sure that the pins (b) are in

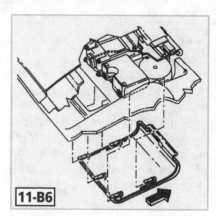

their correct locations, as shown in *Step B5*.
➜ Make sure that the electric drive mechanism is in the '0' (closed) position.
➜ Use new screws (illustration *11-B1, items 11*) – don't re-use the old ones.

☐ **STEP B7: REMOVING SLIDING HEADLINING UP TO AUGUST 1994:** Refer to the illustration *11-B1*.
➜ Remove the screw securing the slide (a) to the sliding headlining on one side only and pull out of the carrier unit guide channels.
➜ Release the spring at point (b) – not visible when installed – and pull sliding headlining forwards out of the roof cutout. Note that the sliding headlining must be angled when being pulled out.
➜ Reinstall as a reverse of the removal procedure but Volkswagen recommend that new screws are fitted each time.

☐ **STEP B8: REMOVING SLIDING HEADLINING SEPTEMBER 1994-ON:**
➜ Unclip the stop (2) on one side and press the

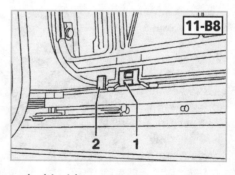

headlining towards this side.
➜ Lever the slide (1) out of the guide channel on the opposite side, levering from front to rear with a screwdriver.
➜ Swing the headlining out of the assembly unit.
➜ Reinstall as the reverse of the removal procedure.

STEP B9: REMOVING AND INSTALLING CARRIER UNIT:

→ Pull the beading off the moulded headlining cutout.

11-B9

→ Remove the electric drive unit.

→ Remove the headlining complete.

→ Pull the water drain hoses (arrowed) off the carrier unit.

→ Either remove the carrier unit complete or remove the sliding roof panel first, according to preference.

→ Take out the bolts shown and lift out the carrier unit – at least two people required.

→ When reinstalling, place the carrier unit on the rear mountings and swing upwards, making sure that the three fixing pins are located in the mounting holes.

JOB 12: SCREEN GLASS – *replacement*.

Section A: Screen held in with rubbers.

It is possible to fit a new windscreen yourself where an early Golf or Polo has its screen held in place with windscreen rubbers. However, we don't recommend it! A company such as Autoglass will be able to supply and fit a screen for little more than the cost of buying one. The risk of breaking a screen when you fit it yourself is quite high.

☐ **STEP A1:** Mel from Autoglass removed the old screen from the vehicle and cleaned off any adhesive from the aperture.

12-A1

→ Allow time for de-rusting and painting any affected areas.

→ The new rubber has been fitted to the glass.

→ Fitting string into the groove on the rubber which will fit over the lip in the windscreen aperture.

→ The loose ends seen here have simply been tucked in to the upper edge of the rubber so that they are out of the way as the glass is being fitted.

→ Soapy lubricant is applied to the rubber to help it slip in to place.

☐ **STEP A2:** If you are doing this yourself, it's best to have two people offer up the new glass with rubber. The

12-A2

rubber must be seated evenly in to the aperture all the way around.

☐ **STEP A3:** As the fitting string is pulled out of the rubber, the inner lip is eased over the windscreen aperture. Particularly on an older, brittle rubber, you have to take great care not to pull the string through the rubber.

12-A3

☐ **STEP A4:** There is always a little tidying up of rubber flanges to carry out, to make sure that they are all sitting evenly. If

12-A4

the screen is pushed in too far, the rubbers will start to recess in to the seating around the windscreen aperture. The outer lip should lie more or less flush with the bodywork.

Section B: Bonded glass.

It is best to have a windscreen specialist replace a bonded windscreen because of the equipment required. Once again, Autoglass demonstrated how they replaced a typical type of bonded windscreen.

❐ **STEP B1:** • Mel from Autoglass recommends putting masking tape over the screen vent outlets to prevent debris from falling into the vents.

12-B1

• If debris – or worse still, shards of broken glass – fall into the vent, it could be thrown into the eyes of the car's occupants next time the screen vent fan is turned on.

❐ **STEP B2:** There will inevitably be interior trim to remove from around the screen. In this case, the trim is partly screwed and partly clipped into place.

➜ Use an upholstery lever for freeing the trim clips.

➜ Take special care where, as in this case, an alarm sensor is fitted on the trim. Be sure not to disturb the wiring.

12-B2

❐ **STEP B3:** In cases where a trim cover is fitted at the base of the screen, remove the wipers and unscrew or clip off the trim cover.

12-B3

❐ **STEP B4:** Mel wears protective goggles and gloves for this stage of the work.

➜ The bonded glass has to be cut from the screen aperture.

➜ This special tool has a blade which reaches behind the glass and cuts through the sealant as Mel pulls it around the perimeter of the screen.

12-B4

12-B5

❐ **STEP B5:** The old glass can now be lifted away.

❐ **STEP B6:** Mel spends quite a considerable amount of time cleaning up the screen aperture before applying the adhesive hardener to the aperture frame.

12-B6

➜ On anything more than a few years old, there will almost inevitably be rust found behind the glass or glass trim.

➜ In worst cases, some welding may be necessary; in almost all cases it will be necessary to clean off the rust, apply a product such as Wurth Rust Killer and then prime and paint the metal.

12-B7

❐ **STEP B7:** As with the screen frame, Mel uses a panel wipe to clean all traces off the surface of the glass (where it will touch the screen frame) before wiping hardener on to the surface of the glass.

STEP B8: The glass seals are now fitted in place around the edge of the glass – only applicable to certain types of screen.

12-B8

12-B9

STEP B9: A very thick bead of bonding filler is now applied by Mel all the way around the screen frame.

STEP B10: Note the special suction lifting pads that Mel uses to grip the glass so that he can lower it accurately in to

12-B10

position on the screen frame. Note also the tabs of masking tape fitted ready in place on top of the screen...

STEP B11: ...so that they can be used to hold the screen at the correct height while the bonding filler goes off.

12-B11

12-B12

STEP B12: Where the rear view mirror is fitted to the glass, use special double-sided mirror fixing tape but be sure to clean both the mounting pad on the mirror and the area of the glass to which it is fitted with panel wipe so that there are no traces of grease on either.

TOP TIP!

- The screen that Mel took from this vehicle was cracked right down the middle, starting from the rear view mirror mounting position.
- The crack was caused by someone having previously fitted the mirror using Superglue or epoxy resin.
- Either of them will cause differential expansion to take place in the glass and will, in every case, cause it to crack.

12-B13

STEP B13: A properly fitted screen will be free from leaks and also free from crack-inducing stresses.

TOP TIP!

- Be sure to clean the windscreen wiper blades and, if necessary, replace them so that the new screen is not instantly marked with disfiguring scratches.

CHAPTER 14: INTERIOR, TRIM

Please read **Chapter 2 Safety First** before carrying out any work on your car.

CONTENTS

SAFETY FIRST!

ALL INTERIOR TRIM AREAS:

• Before carrying out any work on any part of the interior, read *Job 13: Airbags and Pre-Tensioners - essential Safety First!*

• There are very important safety hazards attached to working on, OR IN THE VICINITY OF these components.

JOB 1: TRIM FIXINGS.

INTERIOR STRIPOUT

At first sight, it may look as though interior trim was never designed to be removed! But with a little thought and the certain knowledge that all the fixings *can* be found once you know where to start looking for clues, you'll find yourself able to work through the whole proceedings, step-by-step.

➔ Start with the outer fixings first. Work patiently and methodically.

➔ Pull carefully on plastic trim - you'll be able to see where it flexes and this often tells you where fixings are located and whether panels are separate, with a concealed join, or all-in-one.

➔ If you are certain that there are no fixings that can be unscrewed, try pulling - the trim may be held with concealed clips.

❐ **STEP 1:** In some cases, self-tapping screws are used to hold trim in place. Whenever you see a cap or other type of finisher, you can assume that it's there to cover something up. In this case, the cap is levered off, exposing the screwhead beneath.

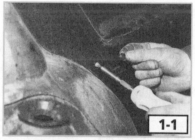

1-1

❐ **STEP 2:** Similar at first sight, but in fact much flatter, is this type of plastic clip. To remove it, all you need to do is carefully lever under the head of the clip.

1-2

STEP 3: Some similar looking clips (**1**) have a peg under the head, rather like a plastic nail, which pushes into a plastic socket mounted in the bodywork. The peg is pulled

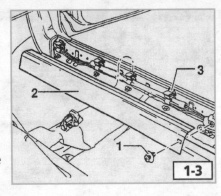

1-3

out first and then the socket (sometimes still attached to the peg; sometimes not) pulls out after it. On these later-type door aperture trims (**2**), the cover is also clipped down to spring clips (**3**) on the body.

1-4

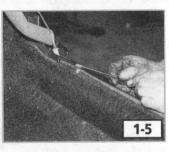

1-5

STEP 4: Door seals are simply pushed on to the edge of the door and tread plates are either clipped or screwed down. Replacement door seals are remarkably expensive so, if yours are in good condition, do your best to save them.

STEP 5: On this (earlier) model, the tread plates were held in place with metal clips which have stayed on the body seam and need to be levered off.

STEP 6: Door trim and rear side trim is often fitted with concealed spring clips which push into the bodywork. If there is no evidence of any other type of clip, try easing the trim carefully back and see if it springs away.

1-6

STEP 7: Two fixing types shown here:
→ Another version of the hidden clip (**3**) may pull out of the trim panel (this is a Golf 1992-on A-pillar trim panel), or might stay in the

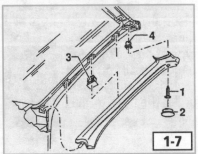

1-7

body. Whichever - before refitting, make sure it's first properly clipped into the trim panel.
→ The threaded screw (**1**) is covered by a cap (**2**) which has to be carefully levered out with a flat-bladed screwdriver. The screw goes into an expanding plastic plug (**4**) which is pushed into a square hole in the body. On some versions, the cap is a softer material and is flush-fitting to the trim.

STEP 8: Some sections of plastic trim and, more often, carpet are glued down. Take the very greatest care when pulling them off because the carpet is shaped and will be impossible to replicate from a flat piece.

1-8

JOB 2: DOOR, TAILGATE, SIDE TRIM - *removal, replacement.*

SAFETY FIRST!

• Before carrying out any work on any part of the interior, read *Job 13: Airbags and Pre-Tensioners - essential Safety First!*

• There are very importnat safety hazards attached to working on, OR IN THE VICINITY OF these components.

See *Chapter 13, Bodywork, Job 5* for information on removing some types of door handles.

Refer to *Job 1: Trim fixings* for general information on releasing trim parts.

DOOR LATCH AND WINDER HANDLES

STEP 1: This type of internal door latch appears to be impossible to remove until you realise that the cup-shaped cover (right) has to be levered out which exposes the fixing screw or screws (depending on model) beneath.

2-1

STEP 2: On later models, the cover (1) exposes two screws. The screw (a) is also removed to allow the main handle trim piece (2) to be removed.

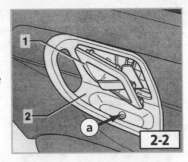

`2-2`

STEP 3A: WINDOW WINDER HANDLES, EARLY TYPE: The window winder handles (right) are removed after carefully levering the trim finisher off the

`2-3A`

centre of the handle - it stays attached at the outer-end - and taking out the screw from beneath it. When the doors are fitted with manual mirror adjusters, the adjuster knobs and the bellows beneath them simply pull off.

STEP 3B: WINDOW WINDER HANDLES, CORRADO-TYPE: Remove as follows:
➜ Push in screwdriver blade (1) and lever it (2).
➜ Pull the cover off the handle (3).

`2-3B`

STEP 3C: WINDOW WINDER HANDLES, GOLF FROM '92, POLO FROM '94: Behind the centre of the winder handle is a spacer (1). Slide it in the

`2-3C`

direction of the arrow - the handle now pulls off the shaft.

WINDOW WINDER HANDLES, CADDY PICK-UP FROM '97: Slide off the end cap, remove the screw and take off the handle. See illustration *2-4B, item 18*.

STEP 4A: DOOR PULL, EARLY (CRANKED-SHAPE) TYPE: To get this angled type of door pull off:
➜ Take out the two screws that you can clearly

`2-4A`

see in the bottom of the arm rest...
➜ ... and then *pivot* the whole arm rest/door pull round to the angle shown here, around the top mounting point (arrowed).
➜ Pull top of door pull from its clip on the door.

EARLY POLO AND CORRADO:
➜ The door pull is held on with two screws into the door frame.
➜ Lever off the cover strip to expose the screws.

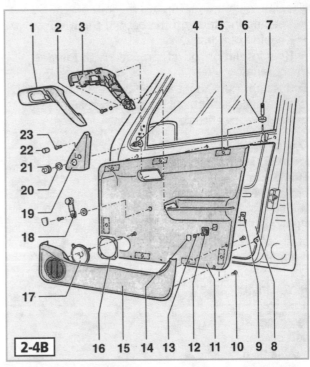

`2-4B`

STEP 4B: DOOR PULL, GOLF FROM '92, POLO FROM '94: Various shapes and sizes, but in general:
➜ Lever off the trim cover (1).
➜ On some models, the mirror adjustment mechanism (4) operating knob has to be pulled off first.
➜ Take out retaining screws, and take off handle.
➜ On some versions, the retaining screws are reached after taking off the door trim panel.

STEP 5: DOOR LOCK OPERATING KNOB: The knob unscrews from the operating lever inside door.

STEP 6: STORAGE TRAY, SPEAKER POD: If either has to be removed before taking off door trim, lever off trim pieces off the screw heads or recessed holes. If so, take out the screws and, if necessary disconnect the speakers. If not, try taking off the door trim

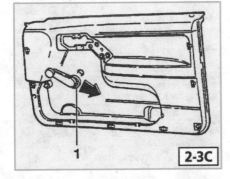

complete with tray/pod. It/they may be screwed on from behind trim panel.

❐ **STEP 7: DOOR TRIM:** When all fixings have been removed, ease the trim away as shown in *Job 1, Step 6.*

2-7

CABRIOLET TO 1994: IMPORTANT NOTE: The waist rail finisher strips on the insides of Cabriolet doors are glued on.
• They can only be removed by careful levering.
• Luckily, they are reasonably flexible but beware – they are also prone to cracking!

❐ **STEP 8:** Behind door and side trim should be a sealing membrane. This has the jobs of:
➜ Keeping moisture off the back of the trim.
➜ Keeping out drafts.
➜ Heat insulation, on later models with foam membranes.
➜ It is important that the membrane is not ripped as it is removed, and that it is stuck down all the way around when refitted.

❐ **STEP 9: PILLARS, SIDE TRIMS:** On all but earliest vehicles, these are plastic mouldings (2).
➜ You might have to remove seat belt or grab handle (5, 6 and 7) before taking off the moulding.

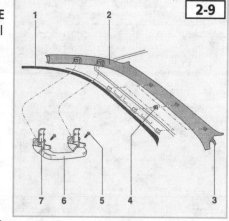

2-9

➜ Take out any fixing screws, levering off any trim cover first.
➜ Lever the trim off its concealed fixings (4).
➜ Many pillar trims have a lug or lugs (3) inserted into the next piece of trim down.
➜ Reposition any seals (1) when refitting.

JOB 3: CENTRE CONSOLE.

See *Chapter 10, Job 3.*

JOB 4: DASHBOARD.

SAFETY FIRST!

• Before carrying out any work on any part of the interior, read *Job 13: Airbags and Pre-Tensioners - essential Safety First!*

• There are very importnat safety hazards attached to working on, OR IN THE VICINITY OF these components.

See *Chapter 10, Job 3.*

JOB 5: INTERIOR MIRROR.

❐ **TYPE 1: BODY MOUNTED:** Remove the trim cover or screw covers, take out the screws and remove the mirror.

❐ **TYPE 2: SCREEN MOUNTED MIRRORS:** This type of mirror is fitted to a base that is glued into place. There are several types.

TOP TIP!

• Only use a proprietary brand of metal-to-glass adhesive for sticking mirror or mirror base to screen.
• It is tempting to use 'superglue' or epoxy glue, but both types will cause the screen to crack over a period of time.

❐ **TYPE 2A: SCREEN MOUNTED, REMOVABLE - ROUND BASE - TYPE B:** This type is rotated 90 degrees in the direction of the arrow (anti-clockwise) and removed from the base plate.

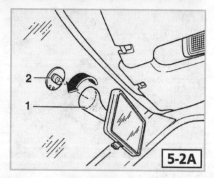

5-2A

❐ **TYPE 2B: SCREEN MOUNTED, REMOVABLE - ROUND BASE - TYPE A:** This type is rotated 15 to 20 degrees in the direction of the arrow (clockwise), and removed from the base plate.

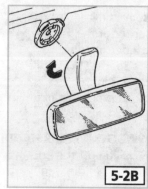

5-2B

TYPE 2C: SCREEN MOUNTED - RECTANGULAR BASE: The non-removable type is glued direct to the screen. When such a mirror needs fitting, see *Type 2D*.

TYPE 2D: To fit a mirror or base plate to a screen:
→ Clean all old adhesive from the baseplate with abrasive paper.
→ Clean all old adhesive from the screen with a window scraper (a razor-blade in a holder, in effect).
→ Use a fresh, clean cloth and panel wipe, or surgical spirit (mineralised spirit) to clean all residual grease off both surfaces - don't touch surfaces with fingers.
→ Use fabric-type of proprietary mirror adhesive - cut to shape of base, press into place. *Wear hand protection and follow maker's instructions*.
→ Mirror can usually be fitted to base after about 15 minutes (when working at room temperature).

JOB 6: HEADLINING.

Section A: Suspended headlining.

STEP A1: This traditional-type of headlining is best fitted only by a professional trimmer. It is suspended on steel rails...

6-A1

STEP A2: ...which are sprung into place between the roof side-members. All glass is removed, the headlining material is wrapped and glued around the window apertures and glass refitted.

6-A2

Section B: Moulded headlining.

STEP B1: Later vehicles have a one-piece moulded headlining (1). Replacing is still fairly complex. Battery must be

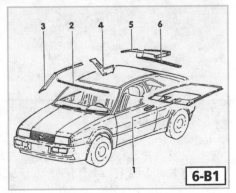
6-B1

disconnected and interior light removed. On Corrado, for instance:
→ Front frame trim (2) is levered off the roof frame.
→ Pillar trim and roof trim pieces (3, 4, 5 and 6) are removed - see *Job 2: Door, tailgate, side trim - removal, replacement*.

STEP B2: On all models, items such as sun visors, grab handles and all other fittings must be detached. They will also help to

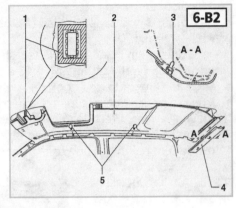
6-B2

hold the headlining in place. On Polo Classic:
→ Note the position of the clips (3) holding the headlining (2) to the roof.
→ Trims (4) have to be removed.
→ The spacer (1) must be properly stuck to the upper surface of the headliner.

STEP B3: MODELS WITH SUNROOF: The winding handle and trim will have to be removed, and the finishing trim from around the inner edges of the sunroof. It is not normally necessary to remove the factory-fitted sunroof in order to remove the moulded-type headlining.

JOB 7: SEAT BELTS.

SAFETY FIRST!

• Before carrying out any work on any part of the interior, read *Job 13: Airbags and Pre-Tensioners - essential Safety First!*

• There are very importnat safety hazards attached to working on, OR IN THE VICINITY OF these components.

Section A: Seat belts without pretensioners.

STEP A1: On some Mk 1 two-door models, the lower seat belt mounting is spring loaded so that the belt is held out of the

7-A1

way for when rear passengers want to get in and out. On other models, the lower belt slides along a rail bolted and hooked to the body side. In the case of the sprung lever-type:

→ Lever off the hinged cap over the spring.

→ The spring is clipped to a hook at the 3 o'clock position and is best released with a pair of long-nosed pliers.

→ The spring is now simply pulled off the bolt on which it is placed.

→ Note that when being refitted, you should start with the hook on the spring at the 12 o'clock position and then turn the hook through three quarters of a turn before clipping it back in to place. This will give the correct degree of tension.

→ The bolt head beneath the spring is the one that holds the seat belt mounting to the bodywork.

❒ **STEP A2:** The inertia reel unit is held to the B-post underneath a plastic trim plate which is first eased away.

7-A2

→ The inertia mechanism retaining bolt, being pointed to here, can be removed and once the bolt holding the belt to the top of the B-pillar has been removed, the whole belt and mechanism can be lifted away.

→ Rear seat belts are simple to remove.

→ There is a trim capping over the top bolt and the belt passes through the side section of the rear parcel shelf.

❒ **STEP A3:** On later models, there is often a separate belt mounting, fitted to the sill beneath the level of the inertia reel assembly.

→ From behind the sill trim, remove the mounting bolt and washer.

→ When refitting, make sure the mounting plate slots on to the locating pin for refitting the bolt.

❒ **STEP A4:** On some models, height-adjustable seat belts are fitted, as

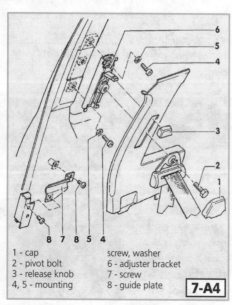

1 - cap
2 - pivot bolt
3 - release knob
4, 5 - mounting
screw, washer
6 - adjuster bracket
7 - screw
8 - guide plate

7-A4

shown here (earlier models). Later models are less complex - remove the pillar trim to unbolt.

❒ **STEP A5:** On some models, the front seat has to be removed before the belt lock (1) can be removed, by taking the bolt (2) from the inner guide rail (3).

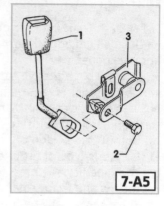

7-A5

❒ **STEP A6:** Rear belts are simply removed after taking off any covering trim panels. Inertia reel assemblies are usually found in the luggage bay. Lower mountings are usually removed after taking out the rear seat base.

Section B: Seat belts with pretensioners.

SAFETY FIRST!

• Before carrying out any work on any part of the interior, read *Job 13: Airbags and Pre-Tensioners - essential Safety First!*

• There are very importnat safety hazards attached to working on, OR IN THE VICINITY OF these components.

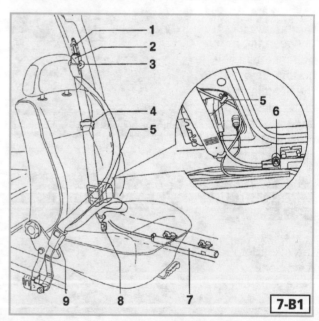

7-B1

❒ **STEP B1:** A seat belt with tensioner can be removed as follows:

→ Remove the sill panel and lower B-panel trim.

→ LOOSEN THE LOCKNUT (6). THIS DETACHES THE TENSIONING UNIT (7) AND MAKES IT SAFE. The locknut is always towards the cable-end of the tensioning unit.

→ Remove the belt guide (**4**), relay (**3**) and front anchor (**8**).
→ Unbolt the belt reel (**5**) and the upper mountings (**1, 2** and **3**).
→ To remove the front belt lock (**9**), unbolt it from the base of the seat support. If necessary, see **Section A, Step A5.**

JOB 8: FRONT SEATS - *removal.*

SAFETY FIRST!

• Before carrying out any work on any part of the interior, read *Job 13: Airbags and Pre-Tensioners - essential Safety First!*

• There are very importnat safety hazards attached to working on, OR IN THE VICINITY OF these components.

IMPORTANT NOTES: **i)** This 'earlier type' continued to be used on some vehicles, such as Polo Classic, 'Mk 1' Cabriolet and Caddy, and well into the 1990s.
ii) Later Polo Caddy (from '97) used an even simpler system - the runners are bolted down to the floor - one at the front of each runner; two towards the rear.

Section A: Seat removal.

IMPORTANT NOTES: VEHICLE WITH SIDE-AIRBAGS: Before the seat can be removed:
→ Disarm airbag and seat belt pre-tensioners (**See Job 13**).
→ Disconnect the electrical connector to the seat-mounted airbag before lifting the seat out.

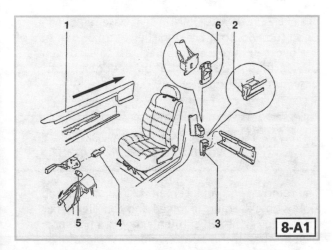

8-A1

❏ **STEP A1:** The basic principles of seat removal are the same for all types (other than Caddy from 1997, described above).
→ Start by removing the front seat runner cover. It is

---

unclipped and removed in the direction of the arrow.
→ Slide seat rearwards. Remove stop from end of runner. **TYPE SHOWN HERE:** Pull out the locking wedge (**2**) on back of cap (**3**) with flat-bladed pliers and remove cap from outer guide rail. **OTHER TYPES:** Remove screw and take out stop from guide rail.
→ Slide seat forwards. **TYPE SHOWN HERE:** Press clip (**4**) together and pull out.

❏ **STEP A2: EARLIER TYPE:** Remove bolt, nut and washer.

❏ **STEP A3: ALL TYPES:**
→ Disconnect the seat heater cable connector (if fitted).
→ Fully lift the adjuster mechanism lever and slide seat back and off.
→ Recoonect airbag electrical connectors and battery - **See Job 13.**

8-A2

8-A3

❏ **STEP A4:** Before refitting the seats, check, and if necessary, replace the single front slides (illustration **8-A1, item 5**) and the two rear slides (**6**).

Section B: Backrest removal - later models.

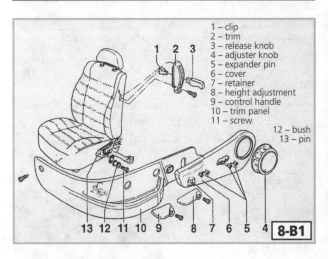

1 – clip
2 – trim
3 – release knob
4 – adjuster knob
5 – expander pin
6 – cover
7 – retainer
8 – height adjustment
9 – control handle
10 – trim panel
11 – screw
12 – bush
13 – pin

8-B1

❏ **STEP B1:** To remove the back rest from the seat base (necessary on models with side air bag, if a side air bag unit is to be replaced):
→ Carefully lever off the adjusting knob (**4**).
→ Use a drift to drive out the expander pins (**5**) towards the inside of the seat.

→ Pull the cover (6) off the backrest frame.
→ Take out the screw (11) and take off the left and right retainers (7).
→ Pull the back rest frame off its mounting pin (13).

TOP TIP!

• The front expander pin will contact the seat frame before it becomes free.
• After drifting it in as far as it will go, push it downwards with a screwdriver to release it.

INSTALLATION

→ If necessary, renew the left and right-hand bushes (12).
→ When replacing the screw (11) a new one should be used, obtainable from a Volkswagen dealership.
→ Before fitting a new screw (11) use a thread tap to remove residual locking fluid from the nut threads and coat the new screw threads with fresh locking fluid.

JOB 9: REAR SEAT – *removal*.

SEAT BASE

❏ **TYPE 1A: FOLDING SEAT BASE:** The seat base is tipped forwards and the hinge mounting screws removed from the body.

❏ **TYPE 1B: FIXED SEAT BASE:** Depending on type:
→ **EITHER:** The base is pushed back against the detente (direction of arrow), which releases the seat base, so that it can be lifted up and removed forwards...

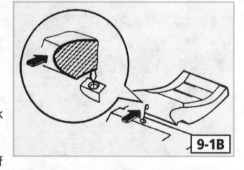

9-1B

→ **OR:** The seat base screws (if fitted) are taken out and the base lifted away.

SEAT BACKREST

❏ **TYPE 2A: EARLY VEHICLES:**
→ **MK 1 GOLF:** Take off the spring clip which holds the support bracket to the body. The seat base and backrest are hinged against each other and come out of-a-piece.

9-2A

→ **EARLY POLO:** The seat retaining bolts can clearly be seen. Remove bolts and lift out seat base.

❏ **TYPE 2B: MK 2 GOLF '84-'92:** The rear seat back rest is held by two retaining hooks (a), which are released while an assistant pushes the back rest

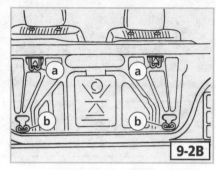

9-2B

downwards. On Jetta and some Golf Convertible models, the retaining hooks are at the base of the seat – see positions (b).

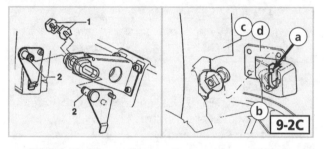

9-2C

❏ **TYPE 2C: GOLF 1992-ON, POLO 1995-ON, POLO CLASSIC:**
→ Fold both backrests down.
→ On the backrest centre pivot, pull out the clips (1) and release the clip (2).
→ On the outer sides of the backrests, use a screwdriver through the opening (a) to push the hooks (b) to one side. Lift the backrests (c) out of the mountings (d).

❏ **TYPE 2D: CABRIOLET:**
→ The seat backs are screwed in to place.
→ **LATER MODELS:** Open the soft-top, and fold the seat base forwards. Unclip the fixing at the left- and right-ends. See illustration *Type 9-2C, items a to d.* Then take out the seat belt anchor bolt.

❏ **TYPE 2E: CORRADO:** With seat base removed, undo the two bolts holding the centre of one side of the backrest in place. Push backrest towards centre of vehicle to release pivot at outer edge of seat base. Repeat with other side.

JOB 10: SOFT TOP - *removal, adjustment, replacement*.

The removal and replacement of the soft-top on any Golf is an extremely involved and complex affair. There are certain adjustments that can be made but, beyond that, if the hood skin need replacing, or if the mechanism becomes damaged, you are strongly recommended to have the work carried out by a trimmer with experience of Volkswagen soft-tops. There are two distinct versions:

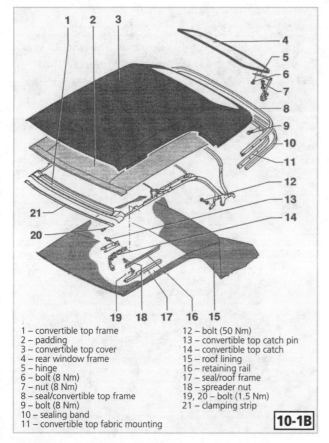

10-1A

be adjusted after releasing the Torx screw.

→ On the earlier version, the hook on the catch is screwed in or out, after slackening the locknut.

→ On earlier versions, the front of the hood frame should be an even fit on the top of the screen frame. The sealing rubber should be lightly compressed. DO NOT overtighten the adjusters.

→ On later versions, the front edge of the convertible top should be 5 mm below the top of the screen frame when closed.

❏ **STEP 1A: CABRIOLET TO 1994:** Based on the Mk 1 Golf bodyshell.

10-1B

1 – convertible top frame
2 – padding
3 – convertible top cover
4 – rear window frame
5 – hinge
6 – bolt (8 Nm)
7 – nut (8 Nm)
8 – seal/convertible top frame
9 – bolt (8 Nm)
10 – sealing band
11 – convertible top fabric mounting
12 – bolt (50 Nm)
13 – convertible top catch pin
14 – convertible top catch
15 – roof lining
16 – retaining rail
17 – seal/roof frame
18 – spreader nut
19, 20 – bolt (1.5 Nm)
21 – clamping strip

❏ **STEP 1B: CABRIOLET FROM 1994-ON:** Based on the Mk 3 ('92-on) Golf bodyshell.

❏ **STEP 2: ADJUSTMENT:** The only adjustment is at the windscreen rail clips, on both versions of Cabriolet, EXCEPT:

→ For door and rear side window glass adjustment, see *Chapter 13, Bodywork, Job 11*.

→ For Mk 1 models the contact between the top and roll-over bar are adjusted at the 'eccentrics' (see illustration *10-1A*).

→ On the later model, the convertible top catch can

JOB 11: CENTRAL LOCKING.

❏ **STEP 1: MK 1-TYPE TO 1994:** To adjust the position of the rear glass:

→ Slacken bolt (**a**) to move the glass backwards or forwards.

11-1

→ Slacken bolt (**b**) to adjust the glass up or down.

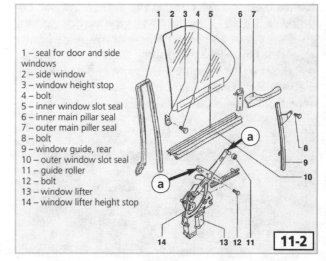

11-2

1 – seal for door and side windows
2 – side window
3 – window height stop
4 – bolt
5 – inner window slot seal
6 – inner main pillar seal
7 – outer main piller seal
8 – bolt
9 – window guide, rear
10 – outer window slot seal
11 – guide roller
12 – bolt
13 – window lifter
14 – window lifter height stop

❏ **STEP 2: MK 3-TYPE 1994-ON:** These are the components of the later Mk 3-based Cabriolet's rear side windows.

❏ **STEP 3: REMOVING SIDE WINDOW:**
→ Take off the interior trim and remove the window

slot inner seal.

➜ Loosen the main pillar inner seal.

➜ Lower the side window and unclip the glass runner from the window lifter – (see illustration *11-2, items a.*)

❏ STEP 4: REMOVING AND INSTALLING ELECTRIC WINDOW LIFTERS:

➜ Disconnect the window lifter from the window channel. (See illustration *11-2, items a.*)

➜ Push the side window upwards and secure it with strong tape.

➜ Completely lower the window lifter and unscrew its fixing bolts.

➜ Separate the plug from motor and take out the window lifter in a downwards direction.

➜ After refitting, check the side window adjustment.

❏ STEP 5: ADJUSTING SIDE WINDOW TO CHANNELS:

➜ Loosen the window rear guide bolts (**1** and **2**) and the bolts (**3** and **4**).

➜ Raise the side window so that it is about 50 mm (2 in.) below its fully raised position.

➜ Press the side window into the window guide (illustration *11-2, item 1*).

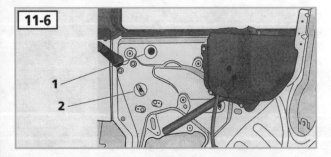

11-5

➜ Press rear window guide (*11-2, item 9*) lightly against the window at its top and tighten the bolt (**1**).

➜ Lower the side window part of the way down and press the lower end of the rear window guide lightly against the window and tighten the bolt (**2**).

➜ Raise the side window once more and make sure that it is aligned parallel to the B-pillar seal (*11-2, item 1*). Tighten bolts (**3**) and (**4**).

11-6

❏ STEP 6: SIDE WINDOW HEIGHT ADJUST-MENT:

➜ Loosen the height stop bolt (**1**).

➜ Loosen the window lifter height stop bolt (**2**).

➜ Raise the side window.

❏ STEP 7: When the side window is correctly raised, it will just compress the roof frame seal as shown, with the lip shaped sealing edge folded over the outer edge of the glass. When the glass is in the correct position:

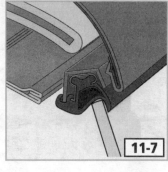

11-7

➜ Retighten the height adjustment bolt (*11-6, item 2*).

➜ Slide the height stop (*11-6, item 1*) down against the side window and tighten the height stop bolt.

JOB 12: AIR BAGS.

SAFETY FIRST!

• Before carrying out any work on any part of the interior, read *Job 13: Airbags and Pre-Tensioners - essential Safety First!*

• There are very importnat safety hazards attached to working on, OR IN THE VICINITY OF these components.

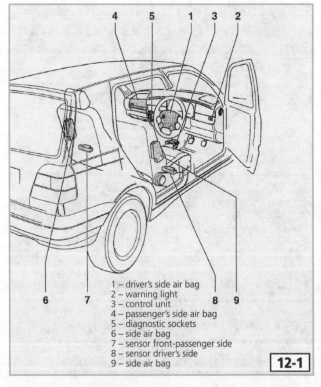

1 – driver's side air bag
2 – warning light
3 – control unit
4 – passenger's side air bag
5 – diagnostic sockets
6 – side air bag
7 – sensor front-passenger side
8 – sensor driver's side
9 – side air bag

12-1

❏ STEP 1: GOLF/VENTO MODELS: Depending on the model and the year, all, some or none of these air bag components may be fitted to the vehicle you are working on.

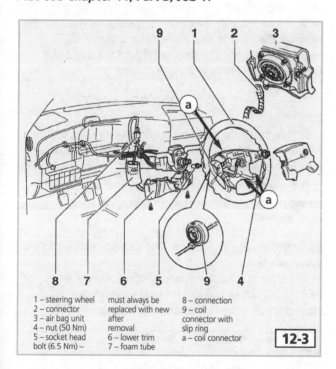

1 – driver's side air bag
2 – passenger's side air bag
3 – diagnostic sockets
4 – air bag control unit
5 – air bag warning light
6 – junction box
7 – earth/ground strip

12-2

❒ **STEP 2: POLO CLASSIC, CADDY MODELS:** The relative positions of major components can be found on the opposite side of the vehicle on right-hand drive vehicles.

IMPORTANT NOTE:
Also see *Chapter 11, Part B, Job 1.*

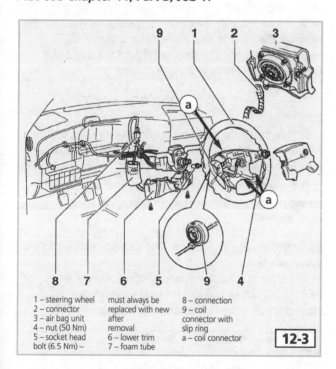

1 – steering wheel
2 – connector
3 – air bag unit
4 – nut (50 Nm)
5 – socket head bolt (6.5 Nm) –

must always be replaced with new after removal
6 – lower trim
7 – foam tube

8 – connection
9 – coil connector with slip ring
a – coil connector

12-3

❒ **STEP 3:** To remove the steering wheel air bag:
→ Place the steering wheel (1) in the centre position with the wheels facing straight-ahead.
→ Unscrew the socket head bolts (5).
→ Lift the air bag unit (3) off the steering wheel and pull the red connector (2) off the air bag unit.

If the coil connector with slip ring needs to be replaced:
→ With the driver's side air bag unit removed, take off the trim (6), the foam tube (7) off the connector (8) and separate the connector. Take off the nut (4) and pull the steering wheel off the column. See *Chapter 11, Job 1.*

→ Take off the horn connector on the steering wheel.
→ Take out the three phillips screws (**a**) and pull the coil connector with slip ring (**9**) off the steering wheel.
→ IMPORTANT NOTE: If the steering wheel is not in the centre position with wheels facing straight-ahead when the coil connector and slip ring are removed and when they are reinstalled, damage can occur when the steering wheel is turned.
→ The coil connector with slip ring are fitted as new parts in the centre position using a cable tie.

GOLF AND VENTO MODELS

❒ **STEP 4:** To remove and install the front passenger's air bag:
→ Before dismantling, disconnect the battery negative (-) earth/ground terminal. See

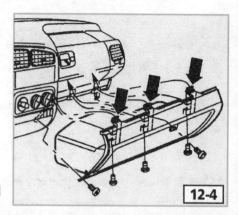

12-4

Chapter 10, Electrical, Dash, Instruments, Fact File: Disconnecting the Battery BEFORE doing so! See *Safety First!* at the start of this job before reconnecting the battery.
→ Take out the phillips head screws shown and take out the tray downwards, at an angle, paying attention to the locating pins (arrowed).

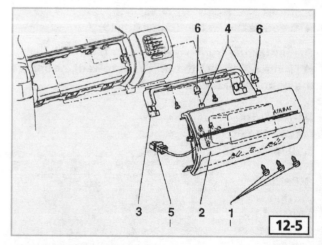

12-5

❒ **STEP 5:** Remove:
→ The three bolts (**1**), pull the bottom part of the air bag unit (**2**) off the dash panel and take it out of its retaining frame (**3**), paying attention to the tabs (**4**) at the top of the air bag unit.
→ Disconnect the air bag unit connector (**5**).
→ Release the locking lugs and press the guide clips (**6**) out of the mounting frame (**3**).

POLO CLASSIC AND CADDY MODELS

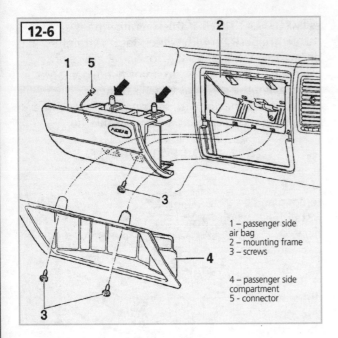

12-6

1 – passenger side air bag
2 – mounting frame
3 – screws

4 – passenger side compartment
5 - connector

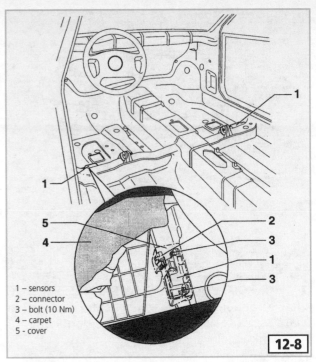

1 – sensors
2 – connector
3 – bolt (10 Nm)
4 – carpet
5 - cover

12-8

❏ **STEP 6:** To remove and install the front passenger's air bag unit:

➔ Before dismantling, disconnect the battery negative (-) earth/ground terminal. See *Chapter 10, Electrical, Dash, Instruments, Fact File: Disconnecting the Battery* BEFORE doing so! See *Safety First!* at the start of this job before reconnecting the battery.

➔ Take out the three screws (**3**).

➔ Loosen the lower part of the air bag unit (**1**) and pull it out of its retaining frame (**2**), noting the positions of the pins (arrowed).

➔ Separate the air bag connection (**5**).

To reinstall the front passenger's air bag unit:

➔ Fit the guide clips to the tabs (arrowed), noting the positions of the relevant chamfers.

❏ **STEP 7:** To remove the side air bag from the seat:

➔ Before starting work, carry out the safety step in *Job 13*.

➔ Remove the back rest (see *Job 8: Front seats*).

➔ Remove the bolt (**2**) and the similar top bolt and pull the connector (**3**) off the air bag unit (**1**).

➔ Take the air bag unit off the back rest frame (**4**).

➔ Loosen the back rest cover in the area of the air bag.

1 – side air bag
2 – earth/ground (-) wire securing bolt
3 – connector
4 – back rest frame

12-7

❏ **STEP 8:** ➔ Remove the seat on the side for which the sensor is to be removed.

➔ Pull away the carpet (**4**) and insulation mat in the area of the sensor and lever off the cover (**5**).

➔ Disconnect the connector (**2**) and take out the bolts (**3**), the sensor is now released.

AIR BAG CONTROL UNIT

• Before carrying out any work on any part of the interior, read *Job 13: Airbags and Pre-Tensioners - essential Safety First!*

• There are very importnat safety hazards attached to working on, OR IN THE VICINITY OF these components.

Before the air bag control unit can be removed you will have to:

➔ Remove the centre console and footwell vent.

➔ Make a cut in the carpet and soundproofing if necessary in order to reach the fixing screws.

❏ **STEP 9: VEHICLES UP TO AUGUST 1994:**

➔ Move the bar (**2**) in the opposite direction of the arrow on the unit and pull the connector (**3**) out of the control unit (**1**).

➔ Take off the nuts (**4**) and remove the control unit, with its bracket, off the mounting studs.

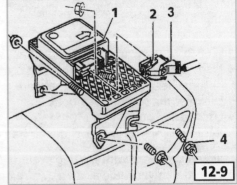

12-9

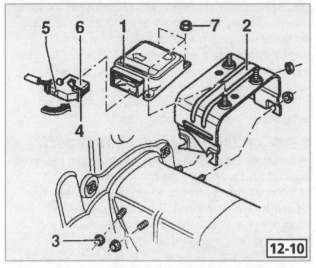

12-10

☐ **STEP 10: VEHICLES FROM SEPTEMBER 1994-ON:**
→ Press the locking tab (5), swivel the bar (4) in the direction of the arrow and pull the connector (6) out of the control unit (1).
→ Take off the three nuts (3) and remove the control unit (1) complete with its bracket (2) from the mounting studs.
→ The control unit can be taken off its bracket by taking off the nuts (7).
For detailed information on removal/replacement of the following components..

JOB 13: AIRBAGS AND PRE-TENSIONERS - *essential Safety First!*

→ **SEAT BELT PRE-TENSIONERS** - see *Job 6.*
STEERING WHEEL and PASSENGER-SIDE AIRBAGS - see *Job 12.*

FACT FILE

ESSENTIAL SAFETY PREPARATION

WHENEVER YOU WORK ON ANY OF THE DEVICES DESCRIBED HERE, YOU MUST CARRY OUT THE FOLLOWING WORK IN THE SEQUENCE SHOWN HERE:
a. Turn off the ignition, disconnect the battery and remove it from the vehicle so that there is no possibility of the battery leads accidentally contacting the terminals.
b. Leave the vehicle for 30 minutes to ensure that any stored electrical energy in the airbag/pre-tensioner has been dispersed.
c. Carry out the remainder of the work for replacing the unit, as described in the relevant Job.
d. As the battery is reconnected, there is a small risk that the airbag will deploy. Before reconnecting the battery, close the vehicle's doors and leave the front side windows open by a small amount. Park the vehicle out of doors and make sure that no-one is standing closer than 10 metres from the vehicle. Reconnect the battery.

SAFETY FIRST!
• THE WHOLE OF THIS JOB IS 'SAFETY FIRST!'
• Read ALL of the information in this Job before working ON OR NEAR air bags and seat belt pre-tensioners.

Section A: Essential safety notes.

A seat belt pre-tensioner is a device which is designed to pull the seat belt tight in the event of a frontal crash.
→ Air bags and seat belt pre-tensioners all normally contain a pyrotechnic (explosive) charge.
→ It is MOST IMPORTANT that the whole of this Job is read and understood before you consider how to deal with air bags and seat belt pre-tensioners and the components surrounding them.
→ The risks of harm from these items are not extreme, but they are real and must be acted upon in an appropriate way.
→ IF THERE ARE REGULATIONS IN THE TERRITORY IN WHICH YOU ARE WORKING WHICH MEAN THAT YOU SHOULD NOT DO ANYTHING DESCRIBED HERE, YOU MUST FOLLOW THOSE REGULATIONS.

☐ **STEP A1:** Note the location of all airbags and seat belt pre-tensioners before starting work.
→ **AIR BAGS:** These may be fitted, for example, in the steering wheel, in front of the passenger seat, in the door or in the side of the seat. There is normally an embossed label at the position of an air bag.
→ **SEAT BELT PRE-TENSIONERS:** These may not easily be visible until the seat is partly dismantled. See the vehicle's handbook and also see *Jobs 4 and 5* relating to front seats and *Job 7: Seat belts* in this Chapter.
→ If you are not sure whether or not a vehicle is fitted with air bags or pre-tensioners, or which type you are dealing with, or you are not fully competent to carry out any of the work described here, consult with, or take the vehicle to the vehicle manufacturer's dealership.

☐ **STEP A2:** All manufacturers recommend that air bags and seat belt pre-tensioners are worked on only by their own, trained personnel.
→ IF FOR ANY REASON, YOU ARE UNABLE TO COMPLY EXACTLY WITH THE INSTRUCTIONS AND WARNINGS GIVEN HERE, DO NOT HANDLE OR WORK ON THE AIR BAG OR SEAT BELT PRE-TENSIONER COMPONENTS - leave it to the vehicle manufacturer's dealership.

☐ **STEP A3:** You may choose to have a dealer carry out the removal and replacement of air bag and/or pre-tensioner components so that you can carry out other work on the vehicle.
→ If you choose to drive the vehicle to or from a main dealer with any of the pyrotechnic safety devices removed or disarmed, you will be taking a risk. In the event of a crash, you and/or your passengers will not

be able to benefit from the normal function of the safety devices.

→ Take care not to commit an offence or illegal act. Do not contravene any laws or regulations by using the vehicle with safety devices disabled.

❏ **STEP A4:** If a pre-tensioner or airbag needs to be renewed:

→ Remember that levering these units or shorting across their terminals can cause them to be triggered.

→ Make sure the new unit is supplied in its correct safety packaging. It must be kept in its packaging at all times until fitted to the vehicle.

→ Place the old unit in the safety packaging after removing and fitting the new one.

→ Immediately take the old unit to the vehicle's main dealer and have them dispose of it.

→ Make sure that you carry out the work when you have access to the main dealer's premises - do not store new or old pyrotechnic safety devices.

→ If air bags or pre-tensioners have to be moved in a motor vehicle, they should be placed in the (closed) luggage compartment and EMPHATICALLY NOT in the passenger compartment.

❏ **STEP A5:** It must not be assumed that a replaced air bag or seat belt pre-tensioner will work properly.

→ Take the vehicle to the vehicle's main dealer to have the unit checked and, if necessary, re-programmed.

→ Take note of the warning in *Step A3*.

❏ **STEP A6: IMPORTANT GENERAL NOTES:** The following notes apply to all seat belt pre-tensioners and air bags, where relevant.

→ **Both air bags and pre-tensioners are referred to as 'safety devices' in these notes**.

→ Where a safety device has a safety locking mechanism, the safety device should not be removed from a vehicle or handled unless the locking mechanism is used, activated or fitted, as described in the relevant part of this manual.

→ A safety device which has been dropped on the floor, or dented or damaged in any way must not be used.

→ On some vehicles, a seat belt on which the tensioner has been 'fired' is not safe to use. On those vehicles, the seat belt cannot be checked for locking once 'fired'.

→ Do not subject safety devices to blows, drilling, mechanical working or heating.

→ DO NOT drop safety devices or subject them to impacts. If one is accidentally dropped, it should not be used but returned to the main dealership.

→ If the safety devices has been activated, ALWAYS wait for at least 30 minutes after the activation before carrying out any operations to it - it may be hot enough to burn skin.

→ If a safety devices which has been activated has to be handled, use protective gloves and goggles.

→ Wash your hands with soap and water after handling a safety device.

→ Safety devices have been designed to be fitted only on the type and model of vehicle for which they are intended. They cannot be adapted, reused or fitted on other vehicles, but only on those for which they were designed and produced. Any attempts to reuse, adapt or fit safety devices on different types of vehicles could cause serious or fatal injuries to the occupants of the vehicle, either in the case of an accident or in normal usage.

❏ **STEP A7: WHEN WORKING ON THE VEHICLE:**
→ **Both air bags and pre-tensioners are referred to as 'safety devices' in these notes.**

→ Do not subject an area surrounding the safety device to strong impacts. When, during bodywork repairs, for example, the use of a hammer is necessary, remove the complete unit.

→ If it is necessary to heat the area surrounding any of the safety devices or to carry out welding or brazing, then the complete safety devices in that area MUST be removed.

→ Before carrying out electric welding, disconnect and remove the vehicle battery.

→ Never use an electrical or electronic test meter on any part of an air bag or pre-tensioner circuit.

❏ **STEP A8: IN THE DEPLOYMENT AREA OF AN AIRBAG...**
→ NEVER fit accessories or store objects.
→ Use ONLY seat covers approved by the vehicle's manufacturer.

Section B: Airbags and seat belt pre-tensioners - handling and storage.

This Section is taken from general information on how to handle and store airbags and seat belt pre-tensioners aimed originally at garages and workshops which handle and store only limited numbers, i.e. up to three or four, at any one time.

→ *Anyone working in domestic premises is strongly advised to follow the guidelines laid down here.*

→ This information is reproduced from the leaflet INDG280 10/98 C400 produced by the British Health & Safety Executive (HSE), and contains notes on good practice which are not at the time of publication compulsory in the UK but which you may find helpful in considering what you need to do.

→ Users in other territories must act upon laws and regulations which may apply to them.

→ This information is current at August 1998 and is reproduced with thanks to HSE.

More and more vehicles are being fitted with a range of airbags and seat belt pre-tensioners. There is therefore an increasing likelihood that you will come across these devices at work. Even though these devices are designed to save lives, there is the possibility of: i) physical injury; and ii) poisoning; if they are not handled correctly. While the likelihood of an accident involving an airbag or seat belt pre-tensioner is low, a few simple precautions can be taken to reduce the risks further.

❒ STEP B1: WHAT TO DO:

→ Find out from your supplier the UN hazard classification of the airbags and seatbelt pre-tensioners that you may handle.

→ **If any are classed as UN Hazard Class 1 (the explosives class) and you want to keep them on the premises**, you will need to register for a **Mode B Registered Premises** with your local authority under the Explosives Act 1875. The department dealing with registration varies from region to region, but it is usually: the fire brigade; trading standards; or environmental health.

❒ STEP B2: REGISTRATION:

The HSE recommend that, as a garage or workshop, you should register even if you don't plan to keep these devices, as delays in fitting them to the vehicle may mean they need to be kept on the premises, overnight, for example.

TOP TIP!

• **For airbags or seat belt pre-tensioners which are classed as UN Hazard Class 2 or UN Hazard Class 9,** the HSE recommend that you keep them under similar conditions to those required for Mode B registration.

❒ STEP B3: STORING AIRBAGS AND SEAT BELT PRE-TENSIONERS:

→ You can buy cabinets or containers which meet the requirements for Mode B registration. In general terms, these requirements are for a substantial container which: i) has no exposed steel; ii) is easy to keep clean; and iii) can be closed and locked.

→ You should keep the container away from: i) oils, paints and other flammable material; ii) areas where hot work, such as welding or brazing, is taking place; and iii) electricity cables, sockets, distribution boards etc.

→ Also make sure the container is: i) secured to the wall or floor if possible; and ii) kept dry at all times.

❒ STEP B4: HANDLING:

→ IT IS ESSENTIAL that the manufacturer's or supplier's information is checked before starting work on vehicles containing airbags, as procedural differences will occur from make to make.

→ Never place your head or body close to the front of an undeployed airbag, especially when fitting it, or removing it from a vehicle.

→ Always carry the airbag module with the trim cover facing away from you.

→ Never place an airbag module, or steering wheel assembly fitted with an airbag, face (trim side) down or with the trim against a hard surface.

→ Never attempt to repair or modify airbag modules.

→ Never expose airbag modules to excessive heat (over 90 ^{0}c), impact, electrical current (including static electricity) or radio transmitters.

→ Always use new components. Return any modules which are damaged or appear suspect to your supplier, **except** where the damage has resulted in the contents of the inflator cartridge being exposed or spilt, in which case obtain specialist advice from your supplier.

→ Return undeployed airbags to your supplier using the packaging the replacement device is supplied in. If for any reason this packaging is not available, contact your supplier and ask them to provide you with it.

→ Airbags should only be deployed by appropriately trained personnel working to the manufacturer's procedures.

→ Seek the advice of your supplier before disposing of any deployed airbags and seat belt pre-tensioners. Some manufacturers advise that their deployed airbags or seat belt pre-tensioners can be disposed of, or recycled, as normal waste; others recommend that they are treated as hazardous waste.

→ It is illegal to dispose of explosives as normal waste and domestic/commercial waste bins **must not** be used for disposing of **undeployed** airbags or seat belt pre-tensioners in Class 1.

❒ STEP B5: MORE INFORMATION:

→ Comprehensive guidance for those handling, storing or transporting larger numbers of these devices is provided in: ***The handling, storage and transport of airbags and seat belt pre-tensioners: HSE Books 1998 ISBN 0 7176 1598 7.***

→ HSE publications are available mail order: HSE Books, PO Box 1999, Sudbury, CO10 6FS. Tel: 01787 881165 Fax: 313995.

→ Other enquiries - HSE InfoLine: 0541 545500 or HSE's Information Centre, Broad Lane, Sheffield S3 7HQ.

CHAPTER 15: WIRING DIAGRAMS

→ If the model you need is not here, try another, similar diagram. There are many common areas.
→ To show all the wiring diagrams relating to the Volkswagen models covered in this manual would take literally thousands of pages!

→ The selection of wiring diagrams here is intended to cover the majority of jobs that may be carried out on the majority of models.
→ If you need further information, you may need to consult your nearest Volkswagen dealership.

FACT FILE

VOLKSWAGEN CABLE ABBREVIATIONS

bl = blue   gn = green   ro = red
br = brown   gr = grey   sw = black
ge = yellow   li = lilac   ws = white

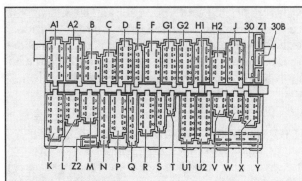

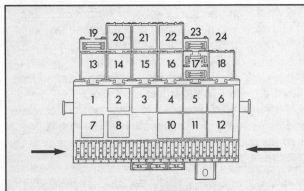

FUSE AND RELAY IDENTIFICATION

→ Fuse and relay positions and numbers vary between models, years and countries.
→ Fuse numbers are shown on the inside of the fusebox lid.
→ Fuse and relay numbers are also shown on the relevant wiring diagrams and in the owner's handbook for the vehicle.

Fuse colours (fuse positions arrowed):

Green = 30 Amp   Yellow = 20 Amp   Red = 10 Amp
White = 25 Amp   Blue = 15 Amp

Numbers 1-12 are typical relay positions, while connections 13-24 are fitted above the relay plate.

FUSE/RELAY PANEL

These are typical connection positions on the fuse/relay panel:

A1 Connector (yellow), 8-pin, headlight wiring loom
A2 Connector (yellow), 8-pin, headlight wiring loom
B Connector (green), 6-pin, for headlight washer system
C Connector (yellow), 8-pin, headlight wiring loom
D Connector (green), 12-pin, for optional extras
E Connector (green), 5-pin, instrument wiring loom
F Connector (white), 9-pin, engine compartment wiring loom, right
G1 Connector (white), 12-pin, engine compartment wiring loom, right
G2 Connector (white), 12-pin, engine compartment wiring loom, right
H1 Connector (red), 10-pin, steering column switch wiring loom
H2 Connector (red), 8-pin, steering column switch wiring loom
J Connector (red), 10-pin, steering column switch wiring loom
K Connector (black), 12-pin, rear wiring loom
L Connector (black), 7-pin, rear wiring loom
M Connector (black), 6-pin, rear wiring loom
N Connector (green), 6-pin, A/C wiring loom
P Connector (blue), 9-pin, rear window and fog light wiring loom
Q Connector (blue), 6-pin, instrument wiring loom
R Connector (blue), 10-pin, headlight wiring loom
S Connector (white), 5-pin, engine compartment wiring loom, right
T Connector (green), 2-pin
U1 Connector (blue), 14-pin, dash panel insert wiring loom
U2 Connector (blue), 14-pin, dash panel insert wiring loom
V Connector (green), 14-pin, multi-function indicator wiring loom
W Connector (green), 6-pin, for optional extras
X Connector (green), 8-pin, warning light wiring loom (trailer towing, anti-locking brake system)
Y Connector, single, Terminal 30

MULTI-PIN CONNECTORS

These are typical multi-pin connector positions:

A Plug (blue) 28-pin, for dash panel wiring loom
B Plug (red) 28-pin, for dash panel wiring loom
C Plug (yellow) 22-pin, for wiring loom, engine compartment, left
D Plug (white) 28-pin, for wiring loom, engine compartment, right
E Plug (black) 18-pin, for rear wiring loom
G Single-pin plug
H Plug (brown) 6-pin, for air conditioner wiring loom

K Plug (transparent) 5-pin, for seat belt warning system wiring loom
L Plug (grey) 4-pin, connections for dual tone horn
M Plug (black) 2-pin, connector for lighting switch terminal 56 and dip and flasher switch terminal 56 b
N Single-pin plug, connection for single fuse (heater element for intake manifold heating)
P Single-pin plug - terminal 30
R Plug (green) 2-pin, electronic control unit current supply

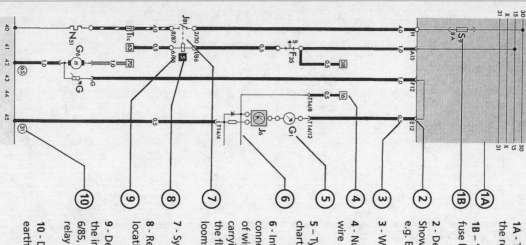

Here is what each part of a Volkswagen wiring diagram stands for.

1A – The top area represents the connections at the relay unit and fuse box.

1B – 'S' = fuse. This, fuse number 9 (8 amps) on fuse box.

2 – Designation of connectors on relay plate: Shows wiring of multi-pin or single connectors. e.g. E 12 = multi-pin connector E, contact 12.

3 – Wire cross sections in mm² and wire colour.

4 – Numbers in square: Shows in which track the wire is continued.

5 – Type of component - see Component Locations chart on each diagram.

6 – Internal connections (thin lines): These connection are **not** always to be found in the form of wires. Internal connections are however current-carrying connections. They make it possible to trace the flow of current inside components and wiring looms.

7 – Symbol for a component: e.g. Relay.

8 – Relay location number: Indicates the relay location on the relay plate or on the relay carrier.

9 – Designation of connectors on relay plate: Shows the individual contacts in a multi-pin connector e.g. 6/85, 6 = contact 6, at location 5, on relay plate or relay carrier. 85 = contact 85 on relay/control unit.

10 – Designation of earth/ground: Location of earth/ground points in the vehicle are indicated.

CARBURETOR – 1.1 AND 1.3 LITRE ENGINES

EARTH/GROUND: 10 = Fuse box bracket, **20** = Cylinder head, cam cover.

F12

F26 Thermo switch for choke

F35 Thermoswitch for intake manifold preheating

F80

J81 Intake manifold preheating relay

K15

N1 Automatic choke

N3

N51 Heater element for intake manifold preheating

N52 Heater element (part throttle channel heating/carburettor)

T1

T1a Connector single, behind dash panel, centre

T1b Connector single, behind relay plate

T1c Connector single, behind dash panel, right

T2 Connector 2-pin, in plenum chamber, left

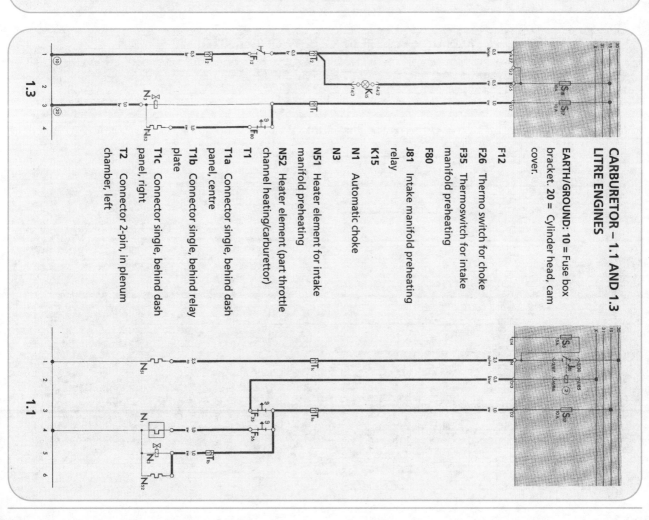

DIESEL GLOW PLUG SYSTEM (Golf Mk2)

EARTH/GROUND: 85 = Connection
(1), in engine compartment
wiring loom.

G27 Sensor for engine temperature
J52 Glow plug relay
Q6 Glow plug
S39 Strip fuse for glow plugs

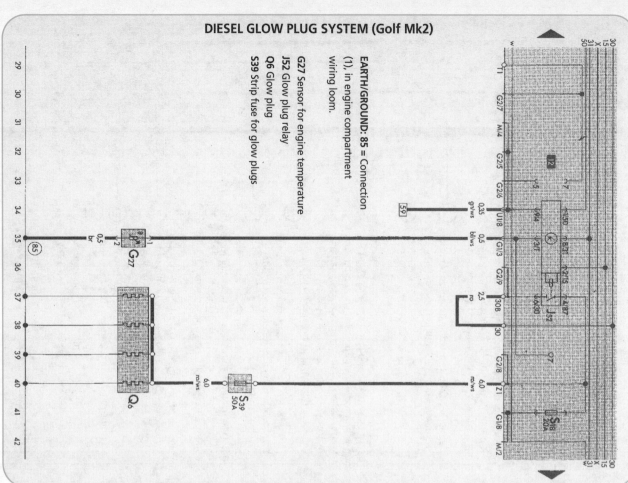

RADIATOR FAN, FRESH AIR BLOWER (Golf Mk2)

EARTH/GROUND: 119 =
Connection (1), in headlight
wiring loom.
C3 = Positive (+) connection
(30), in headlight wiring
loom.
E9 Fresh air blower switch
F18 Radiator cooling fan
thermostat
F87 Radiator cooling fan
thermoswitch
J138 Radiator cooling fan
after run control unit
L16 Fresh air control lever
light
N23 Fresh air blower series
resistance
S24 Overheat fuse
T2a Connector 2-pin, near
headlight, left
V2 Fresh air blower
V7 Radiator cooling fan

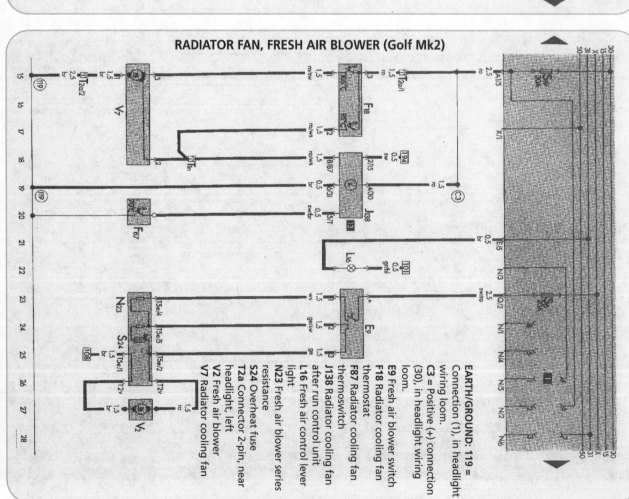

AUTOMATIC CHOKE (CARB.), INTAKE MANIFOLD PREHEATING (Golf Mk2)

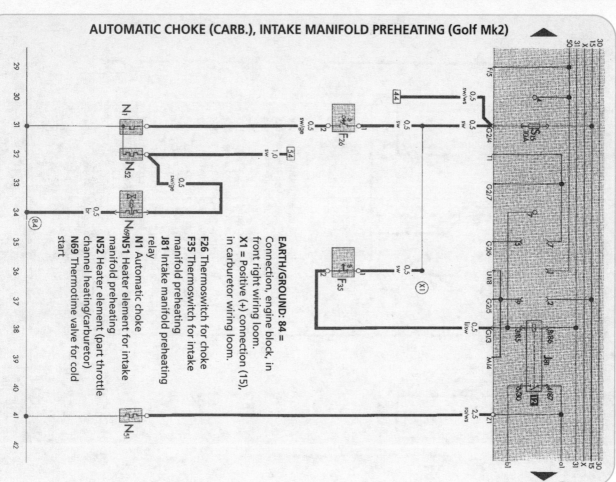

EARTH/GROUND: 84 =
Connection, engine block, in
front right wiring loom.
X1 = Positive (+) connection (15),
in carburetor wiring loom.

F26 Thermoswitch for choke
F35 Thermoswitch for intake
manifold preheating
J81 Intake manifold preheating
relay
N1 Automatic choke
N51 Heater element for intake
manifold preheating
N52 Heater element (part throttle
channel heating/carburetor)
N69 Thermotime valve for cold
start

HANDBRAKE AND BRAKE FLUID LEVEL WARNING (Golf Mk2)

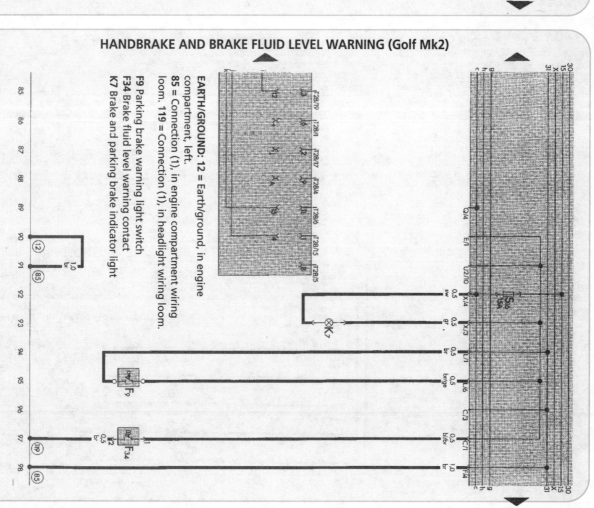

EARTH/GROUND: 12 = Earth/ground, in engine
compartment, left.
85 = Connection (1), in engine compartment wiring
loom. 119 = Connection (1), in headlight wiring loom.

F9 Parking brake warning light switch
F34 Brake fluid level warning contact
K7 Brake and parking brake indicator light

INTERIOR LIGHT, BOOT LIGHT, NUMBER PLATE LIGHT (Golf Mk2)

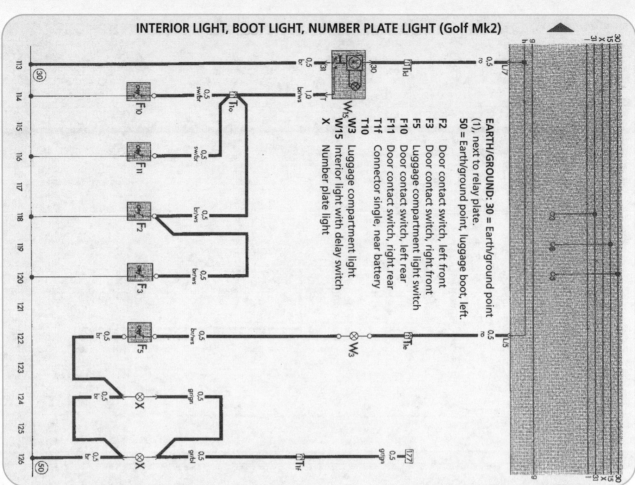

EARTH/GROUND: 30 = Earth/ground point
(1), next to relay plate.
50 = Earth/ground point, luggage boot, left.

F2	Door contact switch, left front
F3	Door contact switch, right front
F5	Luggage compartment light switch
F10	Door contact switch, left rear
F11	Door contact switch, right rear
T1f	Connector single, near battery
T10	
W15 W3	Luggage compartment light
W15	Interior light with delay switch
X	Number plate light

TURN SIGNALS AND EMERGENCY LIGHTS, PARKING LIGHT SWITCH (Golf Mk2)

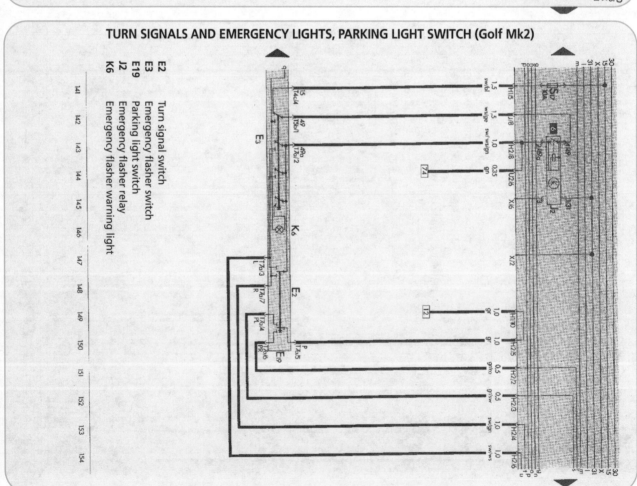

E2	Turn signal switch
E3	Emergency flasher switch
E19	Parking light switch
J2	Emergency flasher relay
K6	Emergency flasher warning light

TURN SIGNALS, TAIL-LIGHTS (Golf Mk2)

LIGHTING SWITCH, BRAKE LIGHTS (Golf Mk2)

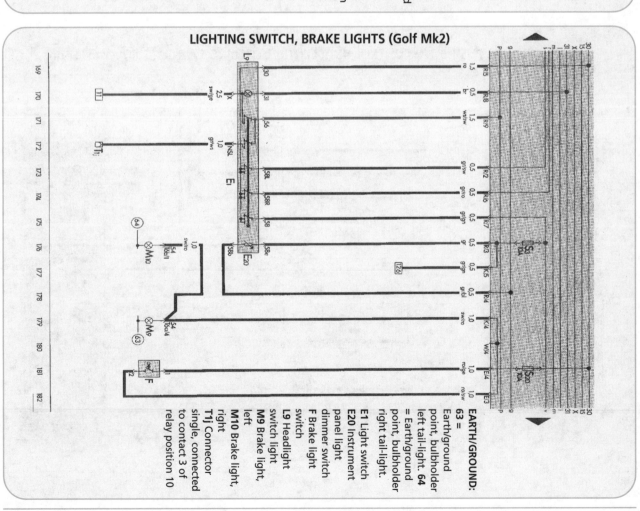

EARTH/GROUND: 54 = Earth/ground point, on rear cross panel. **63 =** Earth/ground point, bulbholder left tail-light. **64 =** Earth/ground point, bulbholder right tail-light. **119 =** Connection (1), in headlight wiring loom. **120 =** Connection (2), in headlight wiring loom.

M2 Tail-light bulb, right
M4 Tail-light bulb, left
M5 Turn signal light, left front
M6 Turn signal light, left rear
M7 Turn signal light, right front
M8 Turn signal light, right rear
M18 Side turn signal bulb, left
M19 Side turn signal bulb, right

EARTH/GROUND: 63 = Earth/ground point, bulbholder left tail-light. **64 =** Earth/ground point, bulbholder right tail-light.

E1 Light switch
E20 Instrument panel light dimmer switch
F Brake light switch
L9 Headlight switch light
M9 Brake light, left
M10 Brake light, right
T1j Connector single, connected to contact 3 of relay position 10

CENTRAL LOCKING ACTUATORS (Golf/Vento '91-on)

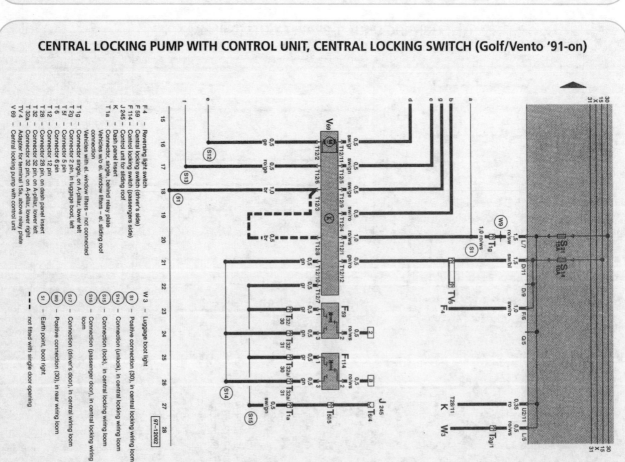

CENTRAL LOCKING PUMP WITH CONTROL UNIT, CENTRAL LOCKING SWITCH (Golf/Vento '91-on)

BATTERY, IGNITION/STARTER SWITCH (Golf/Vento '96-on)

A — Battery
B — Starter
D — Ignition/starter switch
J 59 — Relief relay for X contact

1 — Earthing strap, battery – body
2 — Earthing strap, gearbox – body
119 — Earth connection – 1 –, in headlight loom

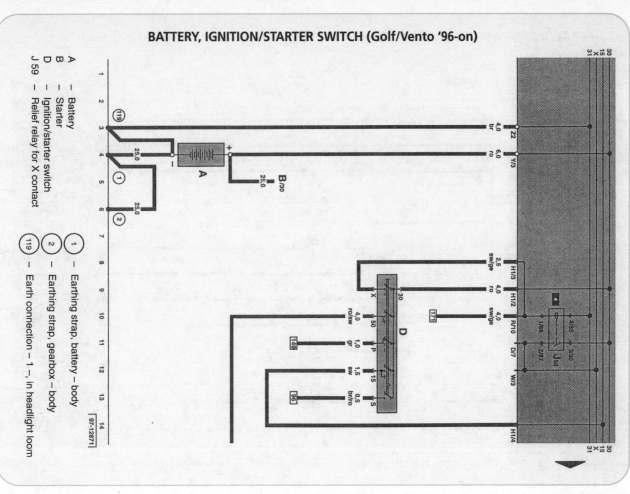

FRESH AIR BLOWER (Golf/Vento '96-on)

E 9 — Fresh air blower switch
L 16 — Fresh air controls light bulb
N 24 — Series resistance with overheating fuse
S 24 — Overheating fuse/heater (8 Amp.)
T 1 — Connector single, on resistance for fresh air blower
T 4 — Connector 4 pin, on resistance for fresh air blower

T 8c — Connector 8 pin, behind dash panel, centre
V 2 — Fresh air blower
43 — Earth point, A pillar, right lower
80 — Earth connection – 1 –, in wiring loom for instruments

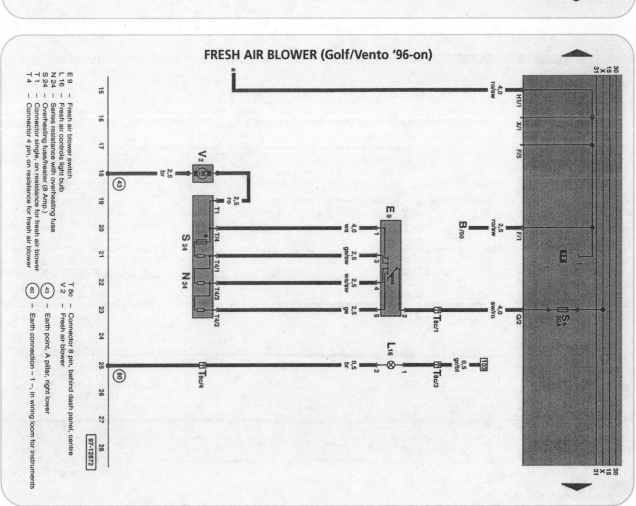

HEATED REAR WINDOW, HEATED OUTSIDE MIRROR, NUMBER PLATE LIGHTS (Golf/Vento '96-on)

INTERIOR LIGHT, DOOR CONTACT SWITCHES, BUZZER FOR LIGHTS LEFT ON (Golf/Vento '96-on)

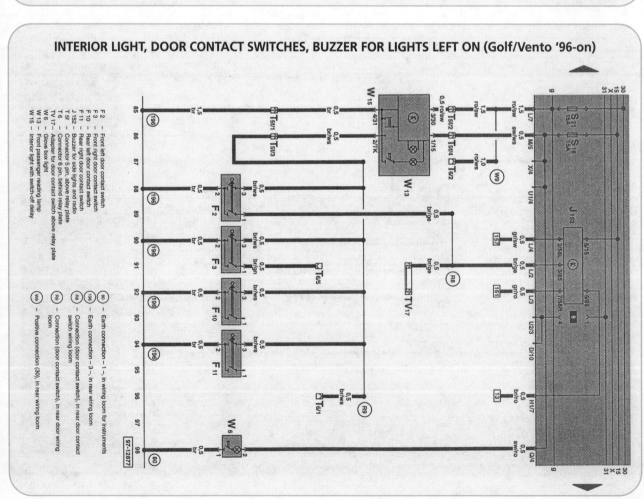

E 15 – Switch for rear window
F 34 – Warning contact for brake fluid level
K 10 – Warning lamp for rear window
L 39 – Bulb for heated rear window switch light
T 5e – Connector 5 pin, on rear cross panel
T 5g – Connector 5 pin, in tailgate
T 6 – Connector 6 pin
X 1 – Number plate light
Z 1 – Heated rear window
Z 4 – Heated outside mirror (drivers side)
Z 5 – Heated outside mirror (passengers side)

Z6 – Plus connection (X), in window heating loom
Z5 – Connection, in window heating loom
W11 – Connection (58), in tailgate loom
190 – Earth connection – 3 –, in rear loom
125 – Earth connection – 3 –, in headlight loom
98 – Earth connection, in tailgate loom
80 – Earth connection – 1 –, in dash loom

F 2 – Front left door contact switch
F 3 – Front right door contact switch
F 10 – Rear left door contact switch
F 11 – Rear right door contact switch
J 152 – Buzzer for side lights and radio
T 5f – Connector 5 pin, above relay plate
T 6 – Connector 6 pin, behind relay plate
TV 17 – Adapter for door contact switch above relay plate
W 6 – Glove box light
W 13 – Front passenger reading lamp
W 15 – Interior light with switch-off delay

W9 – Positive connection (30), in rear wiring loom
R9 – Connection (door contact switch), in rear door wiring loom
R8 – Connection (door contact switch), in rear door contact switch wiring loom
190 – Earth connection – 3 –, in rear wiring loom
98 – Earth connection – 3 –, in rear wiring loom
80 – Earth connection – 1 –, in wiring loom for instruments

LUGGAGE BOOT LIGHT, RADIO, ASHTRAY LIGHT (Golf/Vento '96-on)

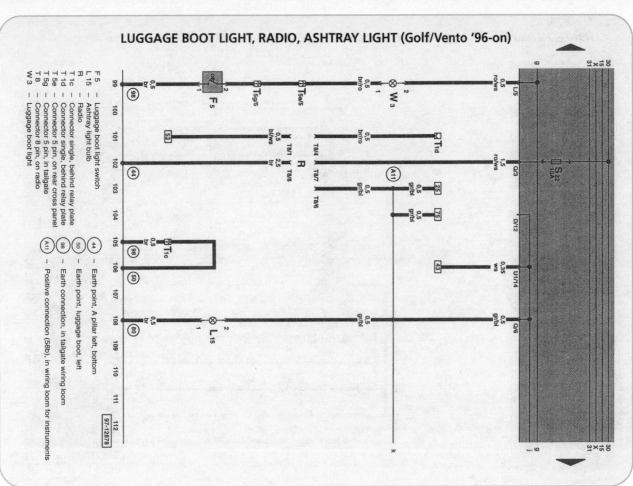

F 5 – Luggage boot light switch
L 15 – Ashtray light bulb
R – Radio
T 1c – Connector single, behind relay plate
T 1d – Connector single, behind relay plate
T 5e – Connector 5 pin, on rear cross panel
T 5g – Connector 5 pin, in tailgate
T 8 – Connector 8 pin, on radio
W 3 – Luggage boot light

(44) – Earth point, A pillar left, bottom
(50) – Earth point, luggage boot, left
(98) – Earth connection, in tailgate wiring loom
(A11) – Positive connection (58b), in wiring loom for instruments

HEADLIGHTS, SIDE LIGHTS, SWITCH FOR HEADLIGHT DIPPER AND FLASHER (Golf/Vento '96-on)

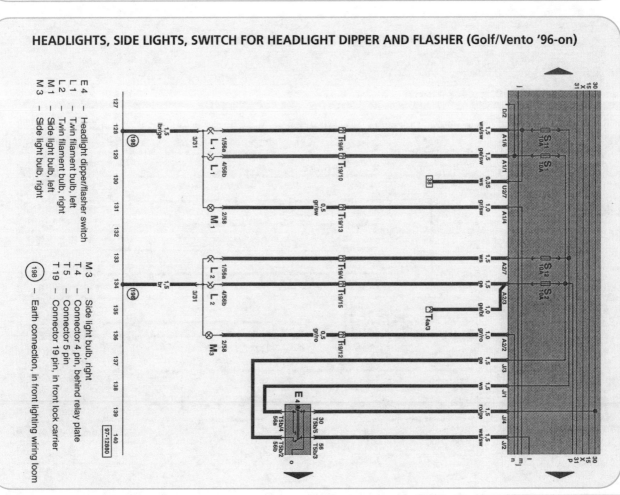

E 4 – Headlight dipper/flasher switch
L 1 – Twin filament bulb, left
L 2 – Twin filament bulb, right
M 1 – Side light bulb, left
M 3 – Side light bulb, right

M 3 – Side light bulb, right
T 4 – Connector 4 pin, behind relay plate
T 5 – Connector 5 pin
T 19 – Connector 19 pin, in front lock carrier

(198) – Earth connection, in front lighting wiring loom

TURN SIGNALS AND HAZARD WARNING LIGHT SYSTEM, PARKING LIGHT SWITCH (Golf/Vento '96-on)

E 2 — Turn signal switch
E 3 — Hazard warning light switch
E 19 — Parking light switch
J 2 — Hazard warning light relay
K 6 — Hazard warning light system warning lamp
T 4c — Connector 4 pin
T 5g — Connector 5 pin
T 7a — Connector 7 pin

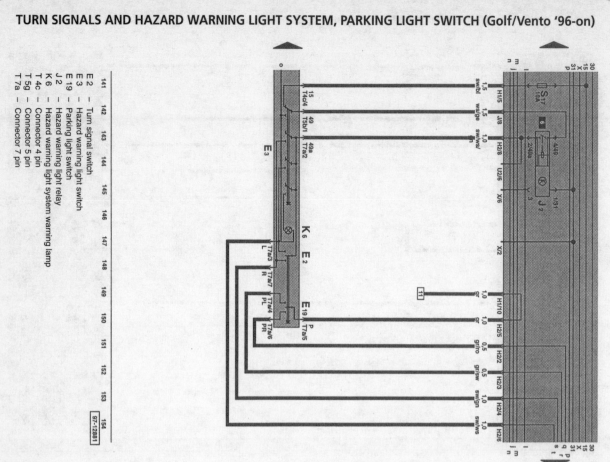

TURN SIGNAL, TAIL-LIGHT (Golf/Vento '96-on)

M 2 — Tail light bulb, right.
M 4 — Tail light bulb, left.
M 5 — Turn signal bulb, front left.
M 6 — Turn signal bulb, rear left.
M 7 — Turn signal bulb, rear right.
M 8 — Turn signal bulb, front right.
T 2n — Connector 2 pin, behind left suspension turret.
T 2n — Connector 2 pin, behind right suspension turret.
T 5d — Connector 5 pin, on tail light, left.
T 8d — Connector 8 pin, on tail light, left.
T 8e — Connector 8 pin, on tail light, right.
T 19 — Connector 19 pin, behind radiator grille, right.

C19 — Connection (turn signal, right), in headlight wiring harness.
C20 — Connection (left turn signal), in headlight wiring harness.
63 — Earth point, bulb holder, tail light, left.
64 — Earth point, bulb holder, tail light, right.
119 — Earth connection -1-, in headlight wiring harness.
197 — Earth connection -2-, in headlight wiring harness.
198 — Earth connection, in front lighting wiring harness.

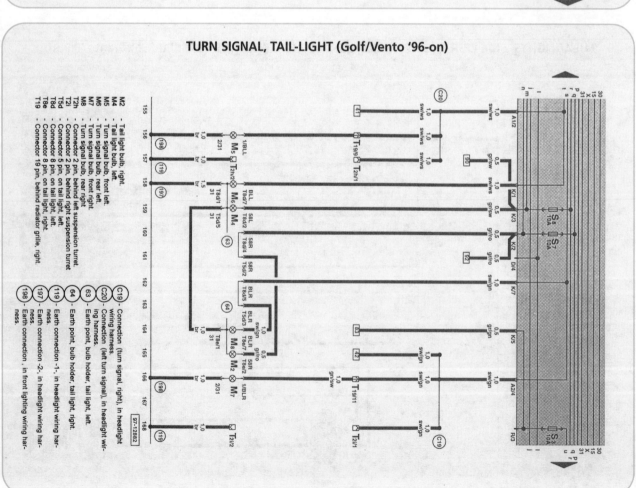

LIGHTING SWITCH, REAR FOG LIGHT (Golf/Vento '96-on)

E1 - Lighting switch.
E20 - Switch and instrument illumination control.
K4 - Side light warning lamp.
K13 - Rear fog light warning lamp.
L9 - Lighting switch illumination bulb.
L20 - Rear fog light bulb.
T3a - Connector 3 pin.
T8d - Connector 8 pin, on left tail light.
T19 - Connector 19 pin, in front lock carrier.

64 - Earth point, bulb holder, right tail light.
119 - Earth connection -1-, in headlight wiring harness.
198 - Earth connection, in front lighting wiring harness.

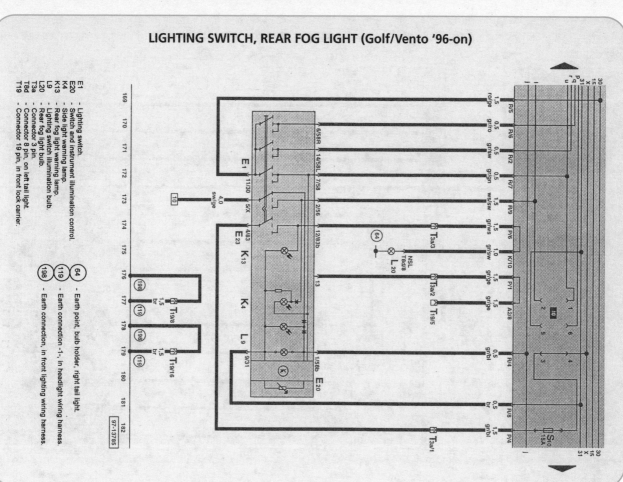

REVERSING LIGHTS, DUAL TONE HORN (Golf/Vento '96-on)

F4 - Reversing lights light switch.
H1 - Horn / dual tone horn.
J4 - Dual tone horn relay.
M16 - Reversing light bulb, left.
M17 - Reversing light bulb, right.
T5d - Connector 5 pin.
T8d - Connector 8 pin.
T8e - Connector 8 pin.
T19 - Connector 19 pin.

63 - Earth point, bulb holder, left tail light.
64 - Earth point, bulb holder, right tail light.
129 - Earth connection in dual tone horn wiring harness.
C13 - Positive connection in dual tone horn wiring harness.

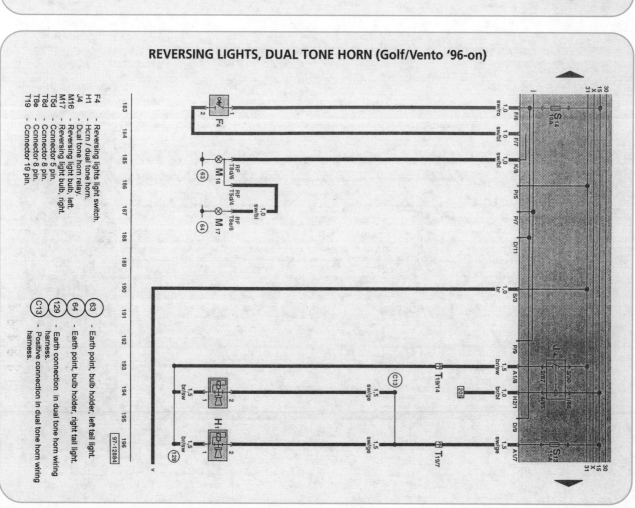

WINDSCREEN WASH/WIPE SYSTEM (Golf/Vento '96-on)

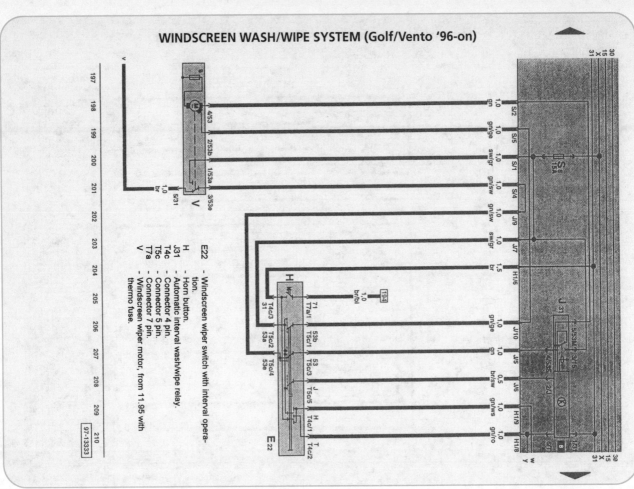

E22 – Windscreen wiper switch with interval opera-
tion.
H – Horn button.
J31 – Automatic interval wash/wipe relay.
T4c – Connector 4 pin.
T5c – Connector 5 pin.
T7a – Connector 7 pin.
V – Windscreen wiper motor, from 11.95 with
thermo fuse.

97-13333

REAR WINDOW WIPE/WASH SYSTEM, BRAKE LIGHTS (Golf/Vento '96-on)

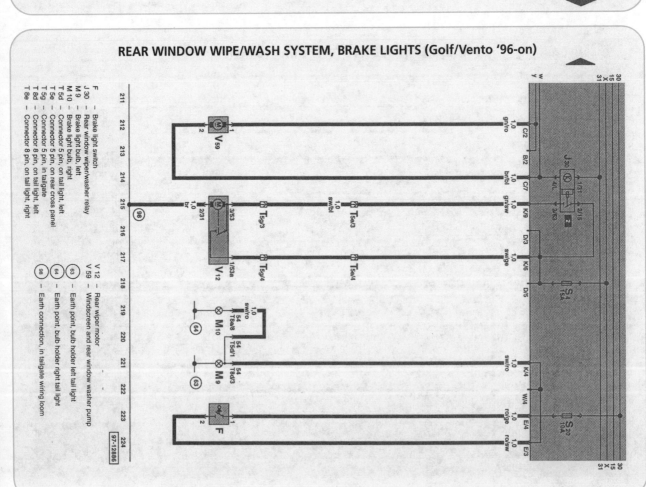

F – Brake light switch
J30 – Rear window wiper/washer relay
M9 – Brake light bulb, left
M10 – Brake light bulb, right
T5d – Connector 5 pin, on tail light, right
T5e – Connector 5 pin, on rear cross panel
T5g – Connector 5 pin, in tailgate
T8d – Connector 8 pin, on tail light, left
T8e – Connector 8 pin, on tail light, right

V12 – Rear wiper motor
V59 – Windscreen and rear window washer pump

63 – Earth point, bulb holder left tail light
64 – Earth point, bulb holder right tail light
98 – Earth connection, in tailgate wiring loom

97-12886

INJECTION SYSTEM CONTROL UNIT, IGNITION SYSTEM, LAMBDA PROBE - 1.4 AND 1.6 LITRE ENGINES
Golf/Vento '96-on

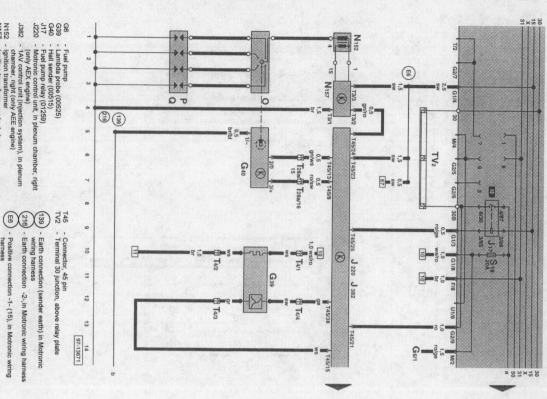

CONTROL UNIT FOR INJECTION SYSTEM, KNOCK SENSOR, SENDERS FOR COOLANT AND INTAKE AIR
TEMPERATURE - 1.4 AND 1.6 LITRE ENGINES (Golf/Vento '96-on)

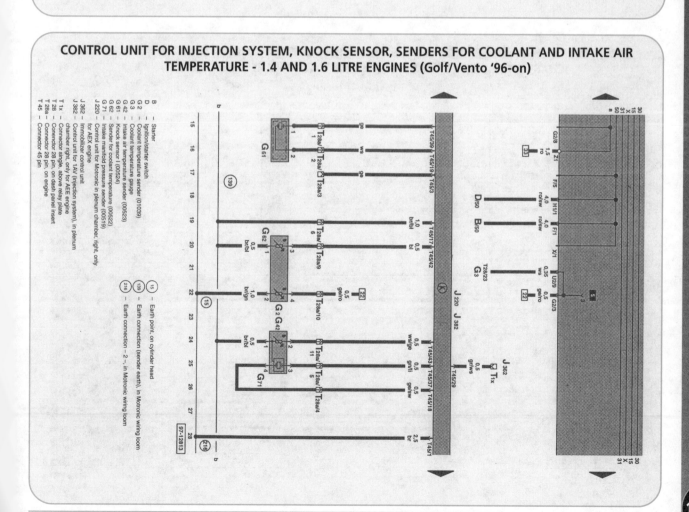

CONTROL UNIT FOR INJECTION SYSTEM, INJECTORS, THROTTLE VALVE POSITIONER, IDLE SWITCH, THROTTLE POSITIONER-POTENTIOMETER - 1.4 AND 1.6 LITRE ENGINES (Golf/Vento '96-on)

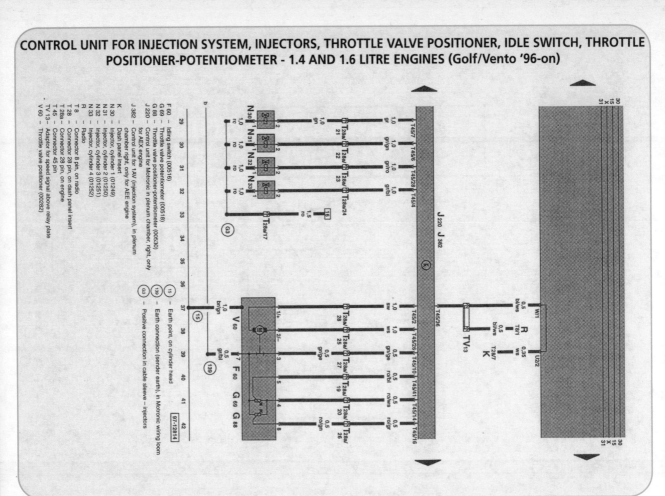

CONTROL UNIT FOR INJECTION SYSTEM, ENGINE SPEED SENDER, SOLENOID VALVE FOR ACTIVATED CHARCOAL FILTER SYSTEM - 1.4 AND 1.6 LITRE ENGINES (Golf/Vento '96-on)

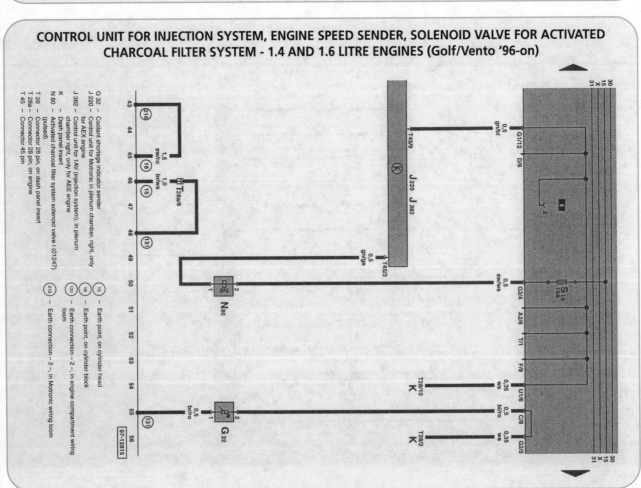

OIL PRESSURE SWITCH, SENDER FOR SPEEDOMETER - 1.4 AND 1.6 LITRE ENGINES (Golf/Vento '96-on)

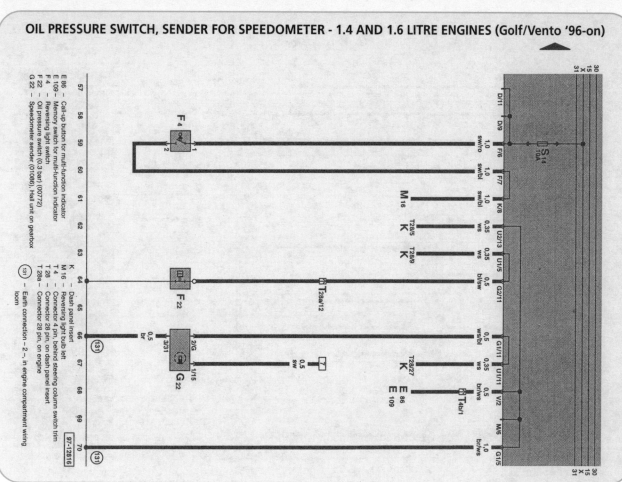

E 86 — Call-up button for multi-function indicator
E 109 — Memory switch for multi-function indicator
F 4 — Reversing light switch
F 22 — Oil pressure switch (0.3 bar) (00772)
G 22 — Speedometer sender (0.1086), Hall unit on gearbox

K — Dash panel insert
M 16 — Reversing light bulb left
T 4 — Connector 4 pin, behind steering column switch trim
T 28 — Connector 28 pin, on dash panel insert
T 28a — Connector 28 pin, on engine

131 — Earth connection – 2 –, in engine compartment wiring loom

97-12816

GENERATOR, STARTER – 1.9D ENGINE (Golf/Vento '96-on)

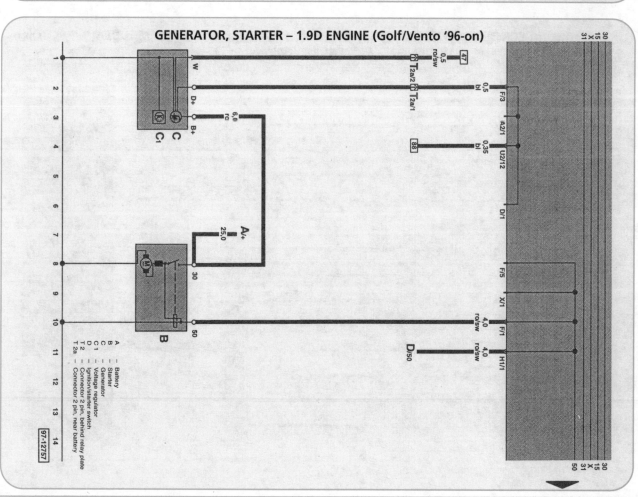

A — Battery
B — Starter
C — Generator
C 1 — Voltage regulator
D — Ignition/starter switch
T 2 — Connector pin, behind relay plate
T 2a — Connector 2 pin, near battery

97-12757

CONTROL UNIT FOR DIRECT INJECTION SYSTEM, ENGINE SPEED SENDER, AIR MASS METER - 1.9D ENGINE
(Golf/Vento '96-on)

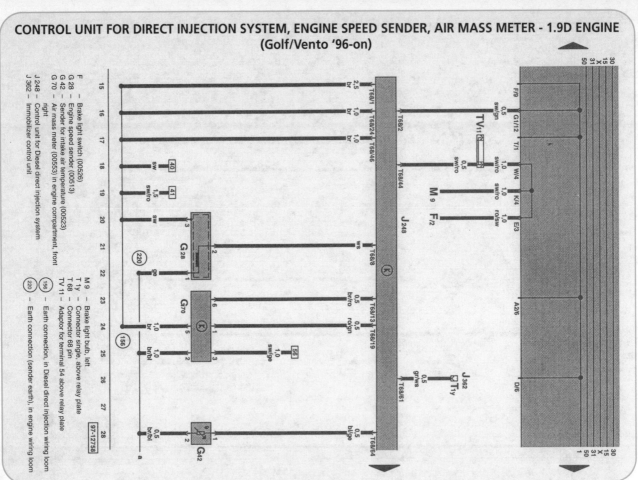

F   – Brake light switch (00526)
G 28 – Engine speed sender (00513)
G 42 – Sender for intake air temperature (00523)
G 70 – Air mass meter (00553) in engine compartment, front right
J 248 – Control unit for Diesel direct injection system
J 362 – Immobilizer control unit

M 9   – Brake light bulb, left
T 1y – Connector single, above relay plate
T 68 – Connector 68 pin
TV 11 – Adaptor for terminal 54 above relay plate

(220) – Earth connection, in Diesel direct injection wiring loom
(150) – Earth connection (sender earth), in engine wiring loom

97-12758

CONTROL UNIT FOR DIRECT INJECTION SYSTEM, SENDERS FOR NEEDLE LIFT AND MODULATING PISTON MOVEMENT - 1.9D ENGINE (Golf/Vento '96-on)

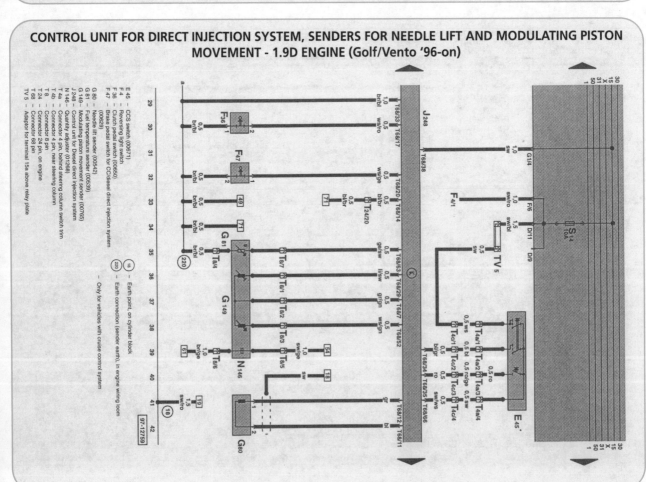

E 45 – CCS switch (00671)
F 4   – Reversing light switch
F 36 – Fuel temperature sender (00539)
F 47 – Brake pedal switch for CC/diesel direct injection system
G 80 – Needle lift sender (00542)
G 81 – Modulating piston movement sender (00765)
G 149 – Clutch pedal switch (00560)
J 248 – Control unit for Diesel direct injection system
N 146 – Quantity adjuster (01268)

T 4a – Connector 4 pin, near steering column switch trim
T 4b – Connector 4 pin, behind steering column switch trim
T 8   – Connector 8 pin
T 24 – Connector 24 pin, on engine
T 68 – Connector 68 pin
TV 5 – Adaptor for terminal 15a above relay plate

(18) – Earth point, on cylinder block
(220) – Earth connection (sender earth), in engine wiring loom

* – Only for vehicles with cruise control system

97-12759

DIESEL DIRECT INJECTION SYSTEM CONTROL UNIT, ACCELERATOR PEDAL POSITION SENDER, EXHAUST GAS RECIRCULATION VALVE, COOLANT SYSTEM GLOW PLUGS - 1.9D ENGINE (Golf/Vento '96-on)

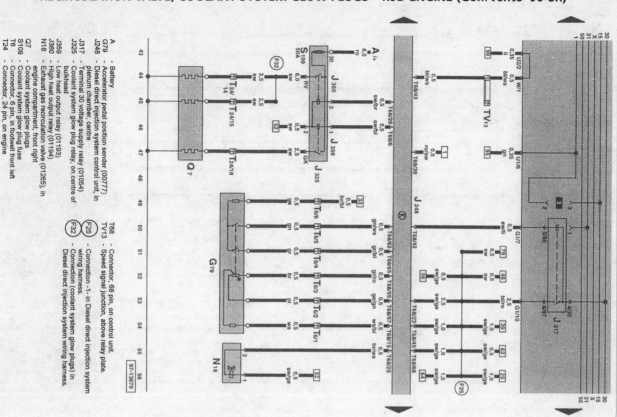

A - Battery
G79 - Accelerator pedal position sender (00777)
J248 - Diesel direct injection system control unit, in plenum chamber, centre
J317 - Terminal 30 voltage supply relay (01054)
J325 - Coolant system glow plug relay, on centre of bulkhead
J359 - Low heat output relay (01193)
J360 - High heat output relay (01194)
N18 - Exhaust gas recirculation valve (01265), in engine compartment, front right
Q7 - Coolant system glow plugs
S109 - Coolant system glow plug fuse
T6 - Connector, 6 pin, in footwell front left
T24 - Connector, 24 pin, on engine
T68 - Connector, 68 pin, on control unit
TV13 - Speed signal junction, above relay plate
F25 - Connection -1- in Diesel direct injection system wiring harness.
F32 - Connection (coolant system glow plugs) in Diesel direct injection system wiring harness.

97-13679

DIESEL DIRECT INJECTION SYSTEM CONTROL UNIT, GLOW PLUG RELAY, COMMENCE OF INJECTION VALVE, FUEL SHUT-OFF VALVE, VALVE FOR THROTTLE VALVE - 1.9D ENGINE (Golf/Vento '96-on)

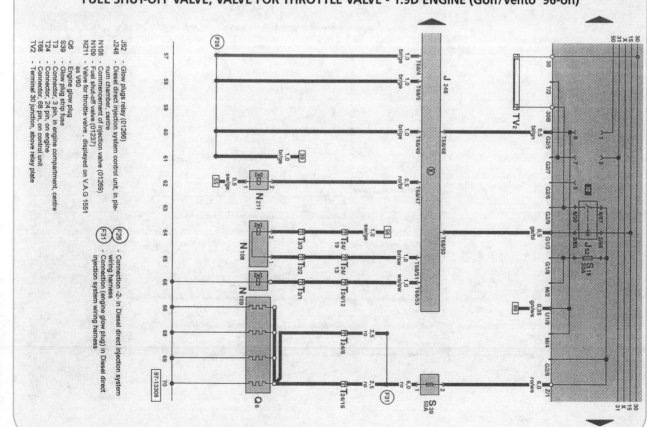

J52 - Glow plugs relay (01266)
J248 - Diesel direct injection system control unit, in plenum chamber, centre
N108 - Commencement of injection valve (01269)
N109 - Fuel shut-off valve (01237)
N211 - Valve for throttle valve (01237), displayed on V.A.G 1551 as V60
Q6 - Engine glow plug
S39 - Glow plug strip fuse
T3 - Connector, 3 pin, in engine compartment, centre
T24 - Connector, 24 pin, on engine
T68 - Connector, 68 pin, on control unit
TV2 - Terminal 30 junction, above relay plate
F26 - Connection -2- in Diesel direct injection system wiring harness
F31 - Connection (engine glow plug) in Diesel direct injection system wiring harness

97-13308

SENDER FOR ENGINE TEMPERATURE, OIL PRESSURE SWITCH, SPEEDO SENDER - 1.9D ENGINE
(Golf/Vento '96-on)

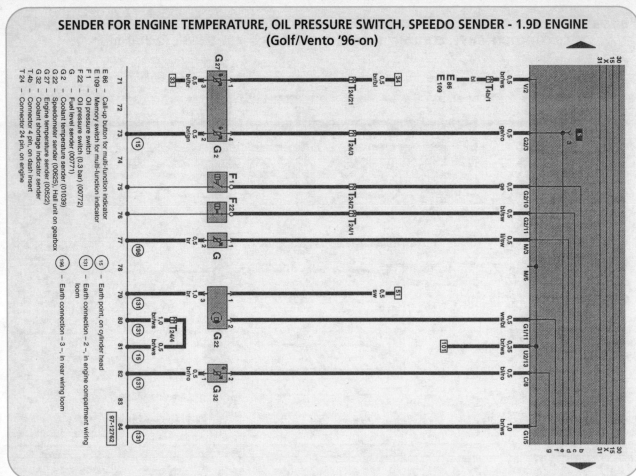

E 86 – Call-up button for multi-function indicator
E 109 – Memory switch for multi-function indicator
F 1 – Oil pressure switch
F 22 – Oil pressure switch (0.3 bar) (00772)
G – Fuel level sender (00771)
G 2 – Coolant temperature sender (01039)
G 22 – Speedometer sender (00625), Hall unit on gearbox
G 27 – Engine temperature sender (00522)
G 32 – Coolant shortage indicator sender
T 4d – Connector 4 pin, on dash insert
T 24 – Connector 24 pin, on engine

⑮ – Earth point, on cylinder head
⑬¹ – Earth connection – 2 –, in engine compartment wiring loom
⑲⁶ – Earth connection – 3 –, in rear wiring loom

GENERATOR, STARTER, FUEL PUMP, FUEL LEVEL SENDER – 2.8 LITRE ENGINE (Golf/Vento '96-on)

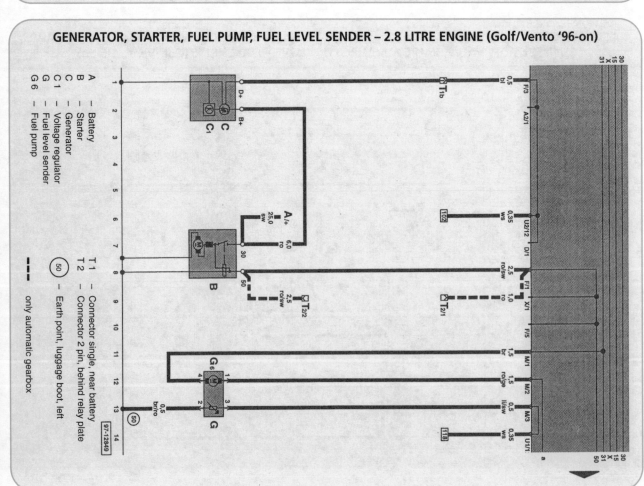

A – Battery
B – Starter
C – Generator
C 1 – Voltage regulator
G – Fuel level sender
G 6 – Fuel pump

T 1 – Connector single, near battery
T 2 – Connector 2 pin, behind relay plate
㊿ – Earth point, luggage boot, left
‐ ‐ ‐ – only automatic gearbox

CONTROL UNIT FOR MOTRONIC, IGNITION SYSTEM, LAMBDA PROBE – 2.8 LITRE ENGINE (Golf/Vento '96-on)

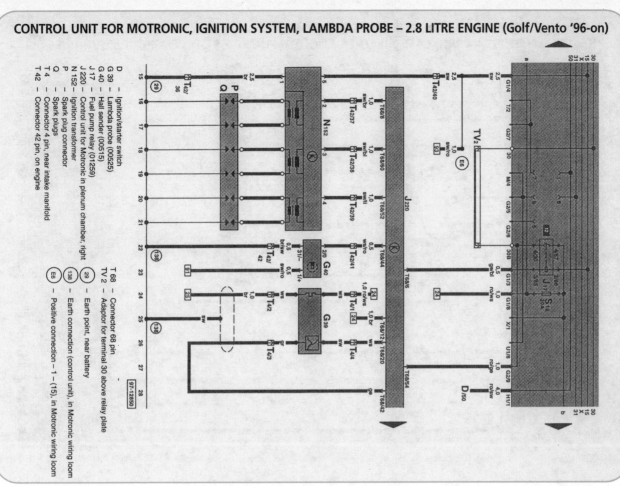

CONTROL UNIT FOR MOTRONIC, KNOCK SENSORS, THROTTLE VALVE POTENTIOMETER, SENDER FOR INTAKE MANIFOLD TEMPERATURE, AIR MASS METER – 2.8 LITRE ENGINE (Golf/Vento '96-on)

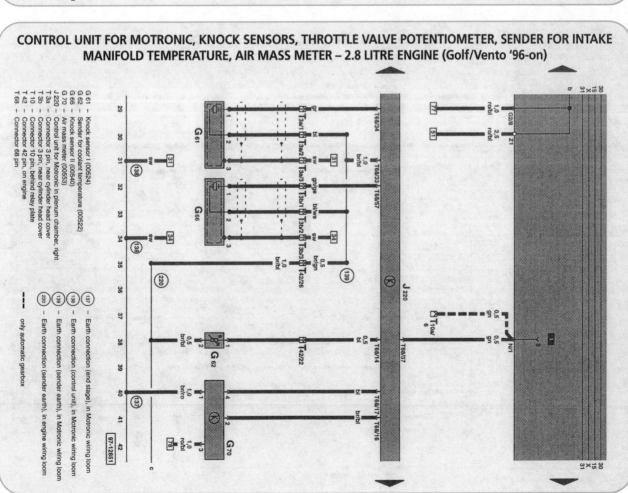

CONTROL UNIT FOR MOTRONIC, ENGINE SPEED SENDER, SOLENOID VALVE FOR ACTIVATED CHARCOAL FILTER, HEATER ELEMENT FOR CRANKCASE BREATHER, COOLANT PUMP – 2.8 LITRE ENGINE (Golf/Vento '96-on)

RELAY FOR BELT WARNING SYSTEM, BELT SWITCH DRIVER'S SIDE (Golf/Vento '96-on)

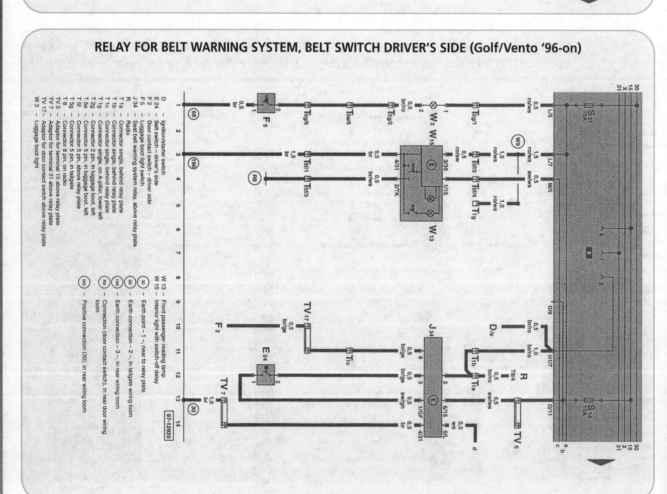

WARNING LIGHT FOR SEAT BELT WARNING SYSTEM (Golf/Vento '96-on)

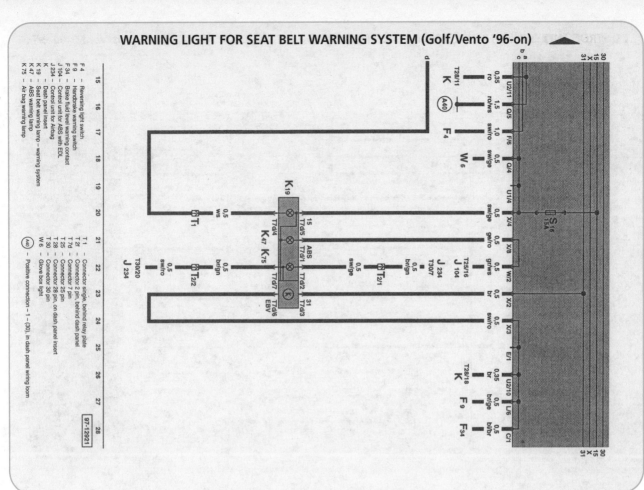

F 4 — Reversing light switch
F 9 — Handbrake warning switch
F 34 — Brake fluid level warning contact
J 104 — Control unit for ABS with EDL
J 234 — Control unit for Airbag
K 19 — Dash panel insert
K 47 — Seat belt warning lamp
K 75 — ABS warning lamp

T 1 — Connector single, behind relay plate
T 2 — Connector 2 pin, behind dash panel
T 7d — Connector 7 pin
T 25 — Connector 25 pin
T 28 — Connector 28 pin, on dash panel insert
T 30 — Connector 30 pin
W 6 — Glove box light

(A40) — Positive connection – 1 – (30), in dash panel wiring loom

97-12921

ALTERNATOR, STARTER, FUEL PUMP, FUEL GAUGE SENDER (Golf/Vento '96-on)

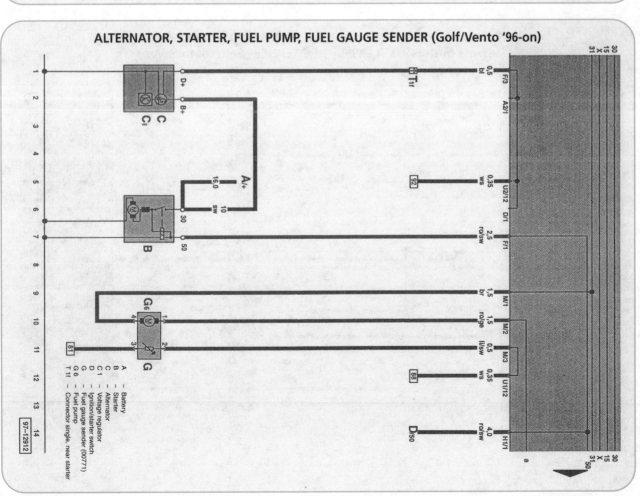

A — Battery
B — Starter
C — Alternator
C 1 — Voltage regulator
D — Ignition/starter switch
G — Fuel gauge sender (00771)
G 6 — Fuel pump
T 11 — Connector single, near starter

97-12912

15-22

SIMOS CONTROL UNIT, IGNITION SYSTEM, ENGINE SPEED SENDER, KNOCK SENSOR (Golf/Vento '96-on)

G 28 - Engine speed sensor (00513).
G40 - Hall sender (00515).
G61 - Knock sensor.
J361 - Simos control unit, in plenum chamber, right.
N152 - Ignition transformer.
N157 - Ignition transformer output stage.
O - Distributor.
P - Spark plug connector.
Q - Spark plug.
T3 - Connector, 3 pin.
T3c - Connector, 3 pin, near starter.
T3g - Connector, 3 pin, near starter.
T28 - Connector, 28 pin, on cylinder head, left.
T68 - Connector, 68 pin.

220 - Earth connection (sender earth), in engine wiring harness.
246 - Earth connection, in Simos wiring harness

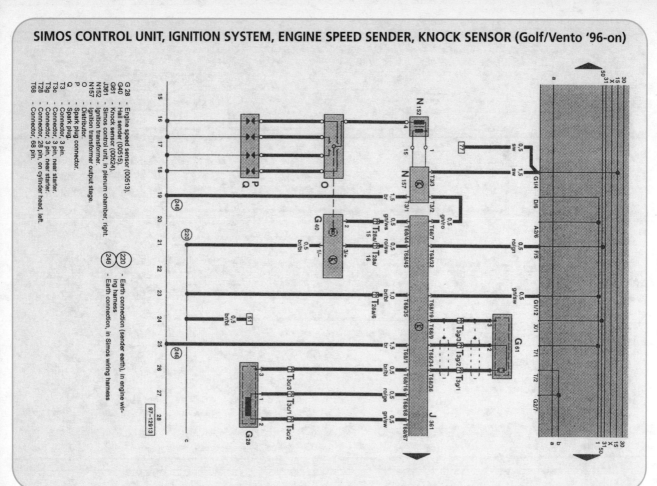

97-12913

SIMOS CONTROL UNIT, LAMBDA PROBE, COOLANT TEMPERATURE SENDER, INTAKE MANIFOLD TEMPERATURE SENDER (Golf/Vento '96-on)

G2 - Coolant temperature sender.
G39 - Lambda probe (00525).
G42 - Intake manifold temperature sender (00523).
G62 - Coolant temperature sender (00522).
J17 - Fuel pump relay (0125V).
J361 - Simos control unit, in plenum chamber, right.
T1n - Connector, single, behind relay plate.
T2n - Connector, 2 pin, behind relay plate, air conditioner
connection.
T4 - Connector, 4 pin, near exhaust manifold.
T6 - Connector, 6 pin, air conditioner connection.

T28a - Connector, 28 pin, on cylinder head, left.
T68 - Connector, 68 pin.
TV2 - Junction box for terminal 30, behind relay plate.
18 - Earth point on engine block.
220 - Earth connection (sender earth), in engine wiring
harness.

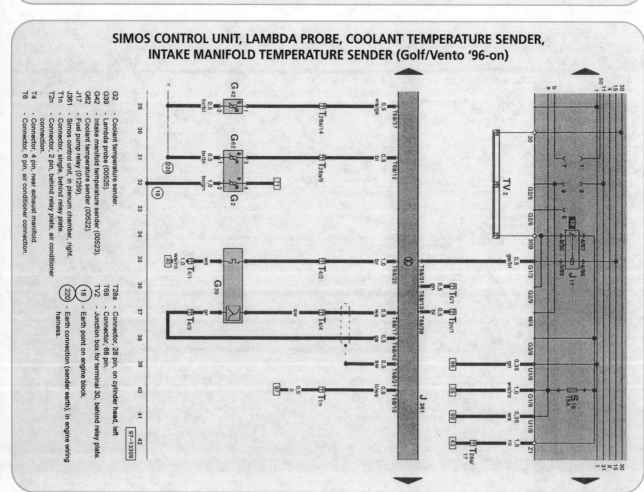

97-13309

SIMOS CONTROL UNIT, INJECTORS, AIR MASS METER, THROTTLE VALVE CONTROL PART
(Golf/Vento '96-on)

F60 - Idling speed switch (00516).
G69 - Throttle valve potentiometer (00518).
G70 - Air mass meter (00520).
G88 - Throttle valve positioner potentiometer (00530).
J338 - Throttle valve control part.
J363 - Simos current supply relay.
N30 - Injector, No. 1 cylinder (01249).
N31 - Injector, No. 2 cylinder (01250).
N32 - Injector, No. 3 cylinder (01251).
N33 - Injector, No. 4 cylinder (01252).
V60 - Throttle valve positioner (00282).

T28a - Connector, 28 pin, on cylinder head, left.
T68 - Connector, 68 pin.
(G3) - Positive connection in injector wiring harness.
(13) - Earth point, in engine compartment right.
(246) - Earth connection in Simos wiring harness.

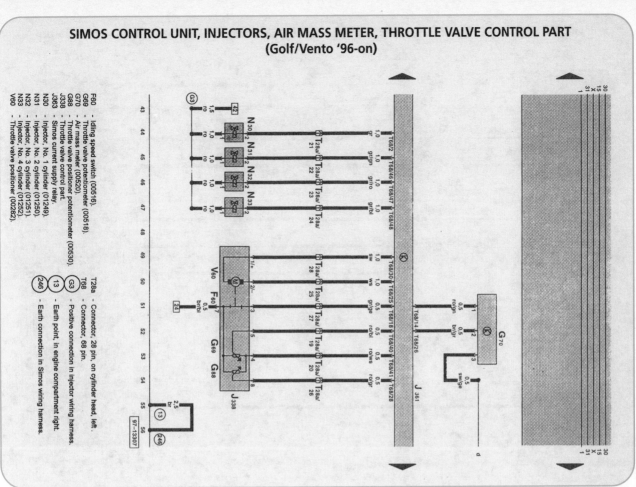

97-13307

SIMOS CONTROL UNIT, ACTIVATED CHARCOAL FILTER SYSTEM SOLENOID VALVE (Golf/Vento '96-on)

F87 - Radiator fan run-on thermo-switch.
J293 - Radiator fan control unit, in engine compart-
       ment, left.
J362 - Immobilizer control unit, behind dash panel,
       left.
J363 - Simos current supply relay.
N80 - Activated charcoal filter solenoid valve 1
       (01247) (pulsed).
N156 - Twin path intake manifold switch-over valve
       (01243)
R   - Radio.
T1   - Connector, single.
T2w - Connector, 2 pin, behind relay plate.
T4I - Connector, 4 pin, on radiator fan control unit.

T6   - Connector, 6 pin, on immobilizer control unit.
T8   - Connector, 8 pin, on radio.
TV13 - Junction box for speed signal, above relay
       plate.
(E30) - Connection (87) in engine wiring harness.
(G9) - Positive connection in Simos wiring harness.

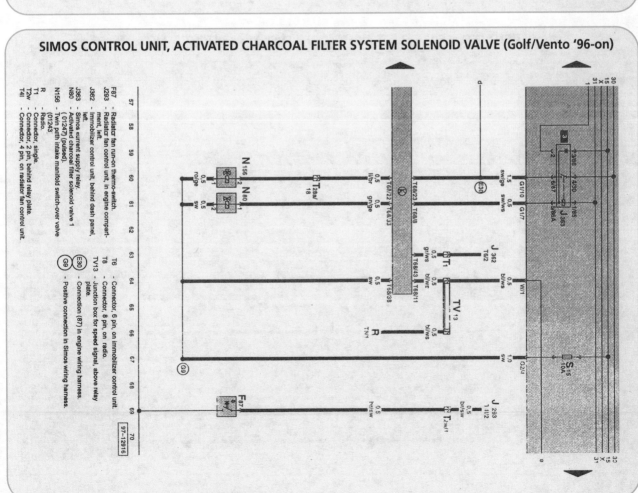

97-12916

OIL TEMPERATURE SENDER, OIL PRESSURE SWITCH, SPEEDOMETER SENDER (Golf/Vento '96-on)

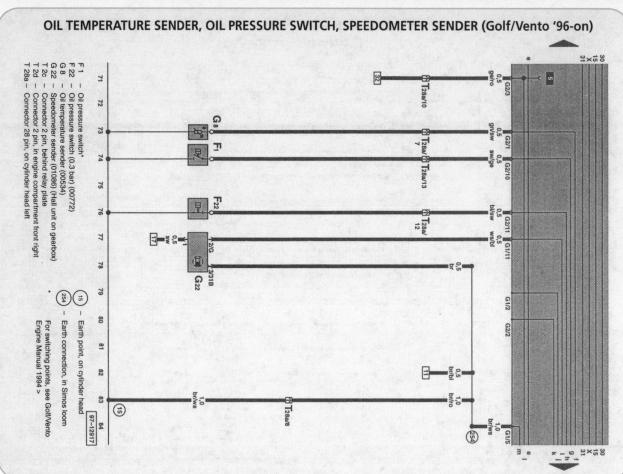

F 1 — Oil pressure switch*
F 22 — Oil pressure switch (0.3 bar) (00772)
G 8 — Oil temperature sender (00534)
G 22 — Speedometer sender (01086) (Hall unit on gearbox)
T 2c — Connector 2 pin, behind relay plate
T 2d — Connector 2 pin, in engine compartment front right
T 28a — Connector 28 pin, on cylinder head left

15 — Earth point, on cylinder head
254 — Earth connection, in Simos loom

* For switching points, see Golf/Vento Engine Manual 1994 >

BRAKE LIGHT LEFT, BRAKE LIGHT RIGHT, HIGH LEVEL BRAKE LIGHT (Golf/Vento '96-on)

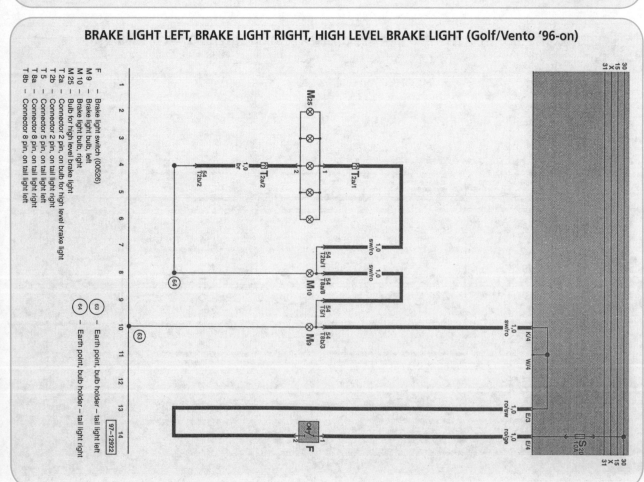

F — Brake light switch (00526)
M 9 — Brake light bulb, left
M 10 — Brake light bulb, right
M 25 — Bulb for high level brake light
T 2a — Connector 2 pin, on bulb for high level brake light
T 2b — Connector 2 pin, on tail light right
T 5 — Connector 5 pin, on tail light right
T 8a — Connector 8 pin, on tail light right
T 8b — Connector 8 pin, on tail light left

63 — Earth point, bulb holder – tail light left
64 — Earth point, bulb holder – tail light right

STARTER, ALTERNATOR, RADIATOR FAN – 1.9TD ENGINE (Golf/Vento '96-on)

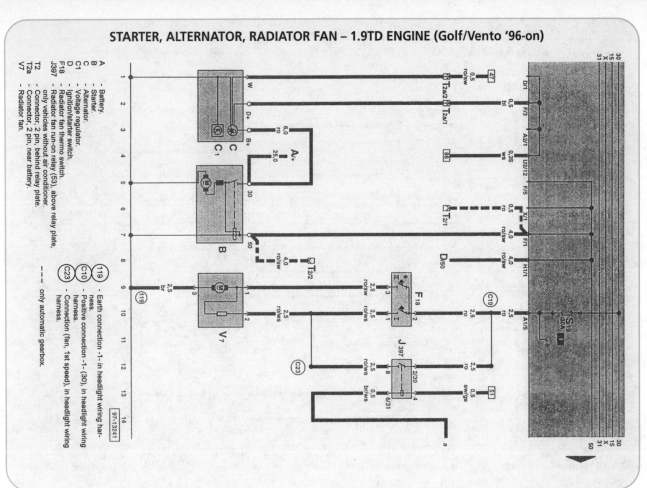

DIESEL DIRECT INJECTION SYSTEM CONTROL UNIT, ENGINE SPEED SENDER, AIR MASS METER – 1.9TD ENGINE (Golf/Vento '96-on)

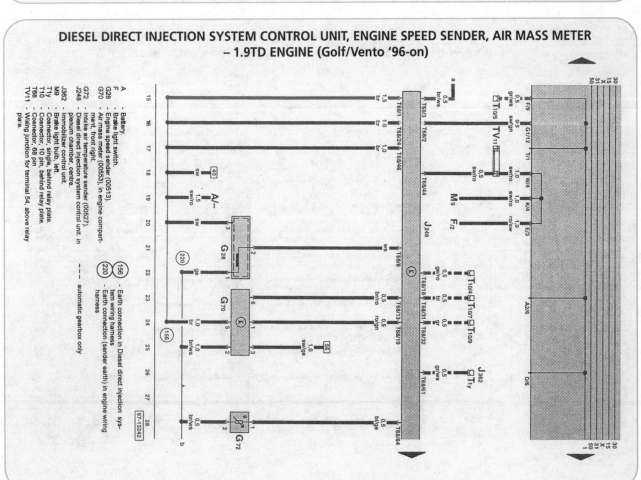

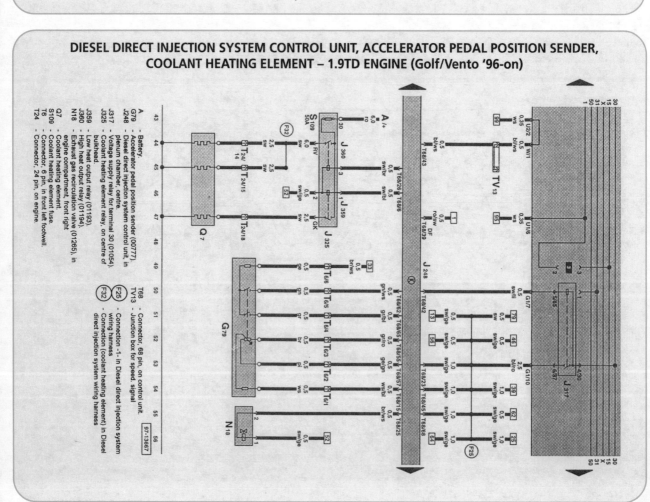

DIESEL DIRECT INJECTION SYSTEM CONTROL UNIT, NEEDLE LIFT SENDER, MODULATING PISTON MOVEMENT SENDER – 1.9TD ENGINE (Golf/Vento '96-on)

E45 - Cruise control system (CCS) switch.
F4 - Reversing light switch.
F36 - Clutch pedal switch (00650).
F47 - Brake pedal switch for CCS/Diesel direct injection system (00629).
G80 - Needle lift sender (00542).
G81 - Fuel temperature sender (00539).
G149 - Modulating piston movement sender (00765).
J248 - Diesel direct injection system control unit, in plenum chamber, centre.
N146 - Quantity adjuster (01268).
T4a - Connector, 4 pin, behind steering column switch trim.
T4b - Connector, 4 pin, next to steering column.

T8 - Connector, 8 pin.
T10 - Connector, 10 pin, behind relay plate.
T24 - Connector, 24 pin, on engine.
T68 - Connector, 68 pin on control unit.

(220) - Earth connection (sender earth), in engine wiring harness.

- - - only automatic gearbox.

* - only vehicles with cruise control system.

97-14354

DIESEL DIRECT INJECTION SYSTEM CONTROL UNIT, ACCELERATOR PEDAL POSITION SENDER, COOLANT HEATING ELEMENT – 1.9TD ENGINE (Golf/Vento '96-on)

A - Battery.
G79 - Accelerator pedal position sender (00777).
J248 - Diesel direct injection system control unit, in plenum chamber, centre.
J317 - Voltage supply relay for terminal 30 (01054).
J325 - Coolant heating element relay, on centre of bulkhead.
J359 - Low heat output relay (01193).
J360 - High heat output relay (01194).
N18 - Exhaust gas recirculation valve (01265), in engine compartment, front right.
Q7 - Coolant heating element.
S109 - Coolant heating element fuse.
T6 - Connector, 6 pin, in front left footwell.
T24 - Connector, 24 pin, on engine.

T68 - Connector, 68 pin, on control unit.
TV13 - Junction box for speed, signal

(F25) - Connection -1- in Diesel direct injection system wiring harness.
(F32) - Connection (coolant heating element) in Diesel direct injection system wiring harness.

97-13667

15-27

DIESEL DIRECT INJECTION SYSTEM CONTROL UNIT, FUEL SHUT-OFF VALVE, ENGINE GLOW PLUGS - 1.9TD Engine (Golf/Vento '96-on)

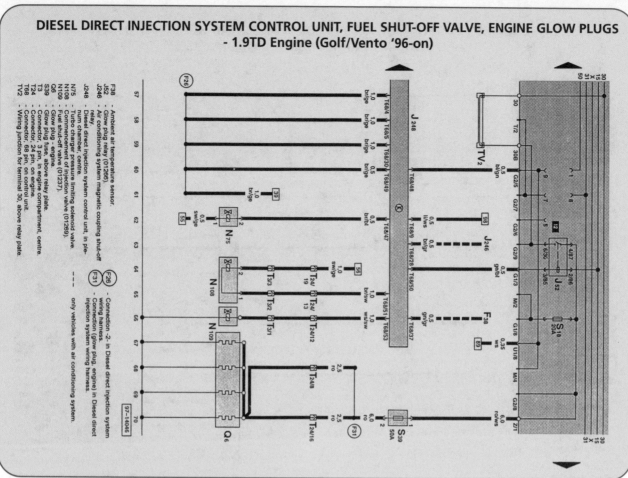

F38 - Ambient air temperature sensor.
J52 - Glow plug relay (01266).
J246 - Air conditioning system magnetic coupling shut-off relay.
J248 - Diesel direct injection system control unit, in plenum chamber, centre.
N75 - Turbo charger pressure limiting solenoid valve.
N108 - Commencement of injection valve (01269).
N109 - Fuel shut-off valve (01237).
Q6 - Glow plug - engine.
S39 - Glow plug fuse, above relay plate.
T3 - Connector, 3 pin, in engine compartment, centre.
T24 - Connector, 24 pin, on engine.
T68 - Connector, 68 pin, on control unit.
TV2 - Wiring junction for terminal 30, above relay plate.

F26 - Connection -2- in Diesel direct injection system wiring harness.
F31 - Connection (glow plug, engine) in Diesel direct injection system wiring harness.

--- only vehicles with air conditioning system.

ENGINE TEMPERATURE SENDER, OIL PRESSURE SWITCH, SPEEDOMETER SENDER - 1.9TD Engine (Golf/Vento '96-on)

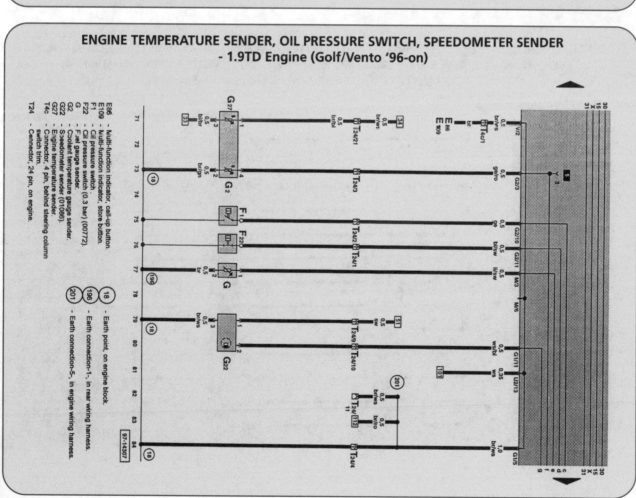

E86 - Multi-function indicator, call-up button.
E109 - Multi-function indicator, store button.
F1 - Oil pressure switch.
F22 - Oil pressure switch (0.3 bar) (00772).
G - Fuel gauge sender.
G2 - Coolant temperature gauge sender.
G22 - Speedometer gauge sender.
G27 - Engine temperature sender (01086).
T4c - Connector, 4 pin, behind steering column switch trim.
T24 - Connector, 24 pin, on engine.

18 - Earth point, on engine block.
186 - Earth connection-1-, in rear wiring harness.
201 - Earth connection-5-, in engine wiring harness.

MONO-MOTRONIC CONTROL UNIT, ALTERNATOR, STARTER, INTAKE MANIFOLD PREHEATING
– 1.8 MONO-MOTRONIC ENGINE (Golf/Vento '95-on)

MONO-MOTRONIC CONTROL UNIT, THROTTLE VALVE POTENTIOMETER, INTAKE AIR TEMPERATURE SENDER, COOLANT TEMPERATURE SENDER, IDLING SPEED SWITCH, THROTTLE VALVE POSITIONER
– 1.8 MONO-MOTRONIC ENGINE (Golf/Vento '95-on)

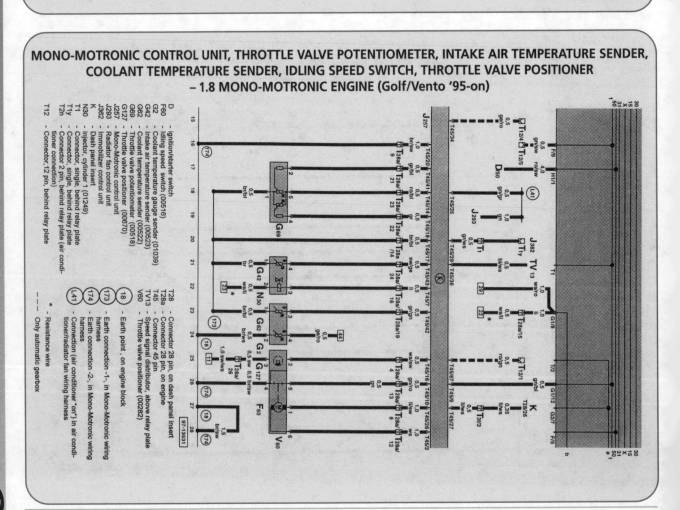

MONO-MOTRONIC CONTROL UNIT, LAMBDA PROBE, IGNITION SYSTEM, FUEL PUMP
– 1.8 MONO-MOTRONIC ENGINE (Golf/Vento '95-on)

OIL PRESSURE SWITCH, OIL TEMPERATURE SENDER, SPEEDOMETER SENDER
– 1.8 MONO-MOTRONIC ENGINE (Golf/Vento '95-on)

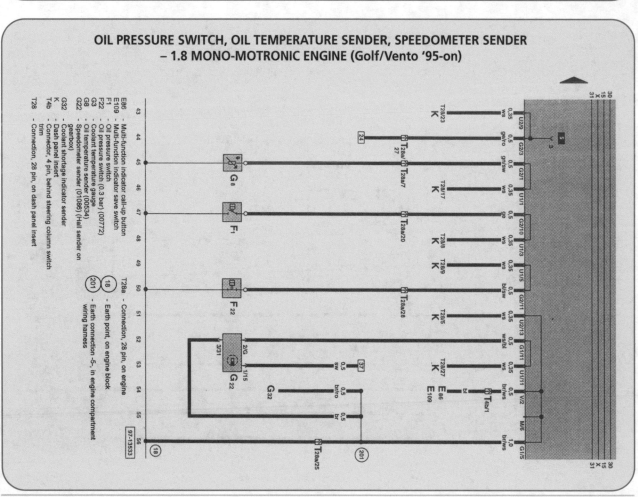

IGNITION/STARTER SWITCH, IMMOBILIZER (Polo '95-on)

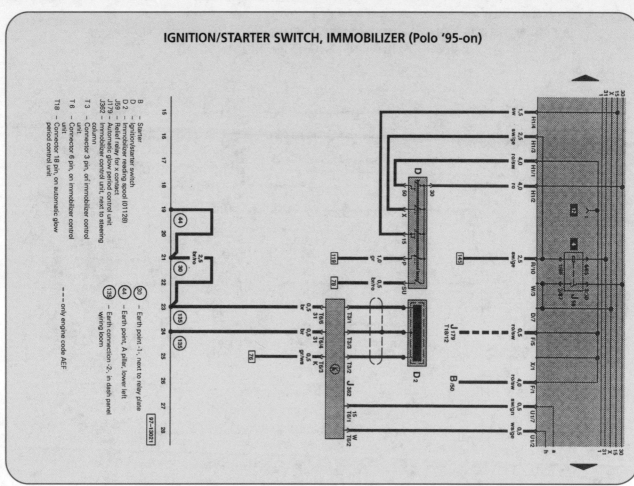

B   – Starter
D   – Ignition/starter switch
D 2   – Immobilizer reading spool (01128)
J59   – Relief relay for x contact
J179   – Automatic glow period control unit
J362   – Immobilizer control unit, next to steering
         column
T 3   – Connector 3 pin, on immobilizer control
         unit
T 6   – Connector 6 pin, on immobilizer control
         unit
T18   – Connector 18 pin, on automatic glow
         period control unit

30 – Earth point -1-, next to relay plate
44 – Earth point, A pillar, lower left
135 – Earth connection -2-, in dash panel
        wiring loom

– – – only engine code AEF

97-13021

INTERIOR LIGHT, LUGGAGE COMPARTMENT LIGHT, HANDBRAKE WARNING SWITCH
AND BRAKE FLUID LEVEL SWITCH (Polo '95-on)

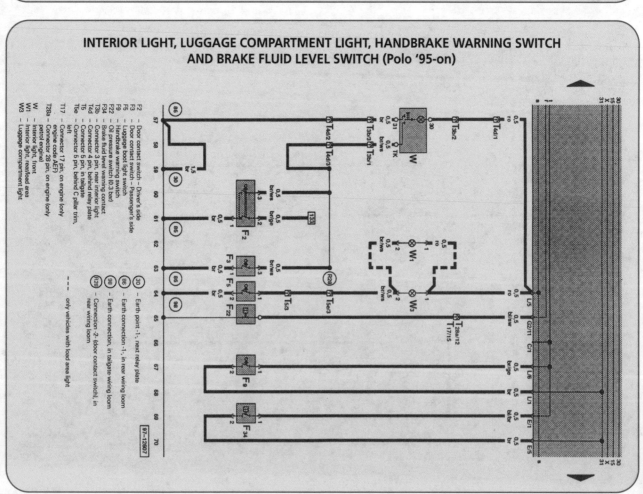

F2   – Door contact switch – Driver's side
F3   – Door contact switch – Passenger's side
F5   – Luggage boot light switch
F9   – Handbrake warning switch
F22 – Oil pressure switch (0.3 bar)
F34 – Brake fluid level warning contact
T3b – Connector 3 pin, near interior light
T4d – Connector 4 pin, behind relay plate
T5   – Connector 5 pin, in tailgate
T5e – Connector 5 pin, behind C pillar trim,
        left
T17 – Connector 17 pin, on engine (only
        engine code AEF)
T28a – Connector 28 pin, on engine (only
        petrol engine)
W   – Interior light, front
W1   – Interior light, rear/load area
W3   – Luggage compartment light

30 – Earth point -1-, next to relay plate
86 – Earth connection -1-, in rear wiring loom
98 – Earth connection, in rear wiring loom
28 – Connection -2- (door contact switch), in
        rear wiring loom

– – – only vehicles with load area light

97-12607

HEADLIGHTS, SIDE LIGHT (Polo '95-on)

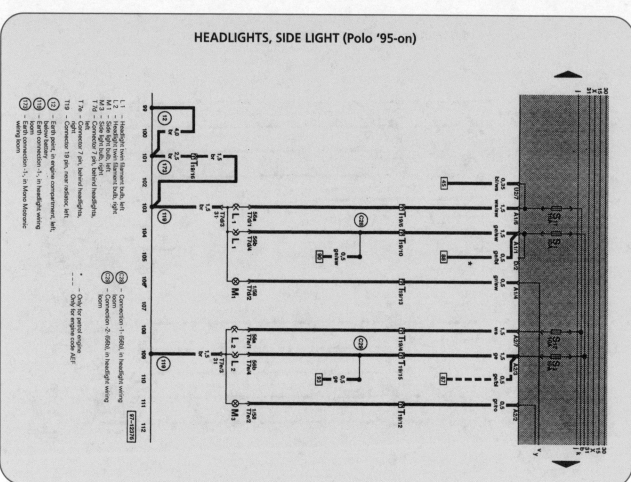

L1 – Headlight twin filament bulb, left
L2 – Headlight twin filament bulb, left
M1 – Side light bulb, left
M3 – Side light bulb, right
T7d – Connector 7 pin, behind headlights, left
T7e – Connector 7 pin, behind headlights, right
T19 – Connector 19 pin, near radiator, left
(12) – Earth point, in engine compartment, left, below battery
(119) – Earth connection -1-, in headlight wiring loom
(119) – Earth connection -1-, in headlight wiring loom
(173) – Earth connection -1-, in Mono Motronic wiring loom

(28) – Connection -1- (56b), in headlight wiring
(29) – Connection -2- (56b), in headlight wiring loom

• – Only for petrol engine
— — — Only for engine code AEF

97-12376

HEADLIGHT DIPPER/FLASHER SWITCH, TURN SIGNAL SWITCH, PARKING LIGHT SWITCH (Polo '95-on)

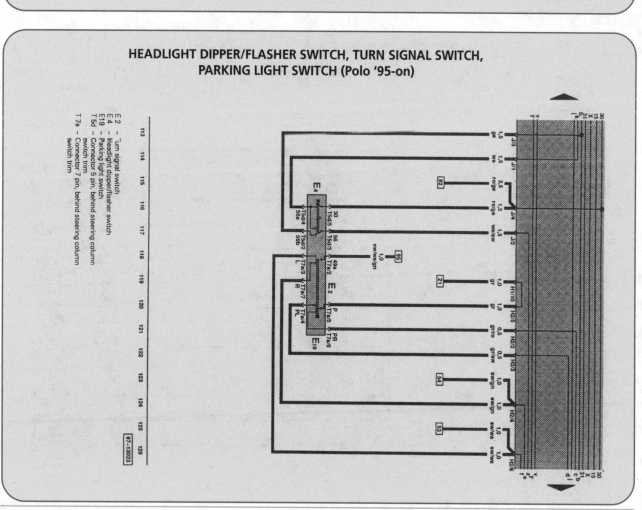

E2 – Turn signal switch
E4 – Headlight dipper/flasher switch
E19 – Parking light switch
T5d – Connector 5 pin, behind steering column switch trim
T7a – Connector 7 pin, behind steering column switch trim

97-13023

TURN SIGNAL, BRAKE LIGHT, TAIL-LIGHT (Polo '95-on)

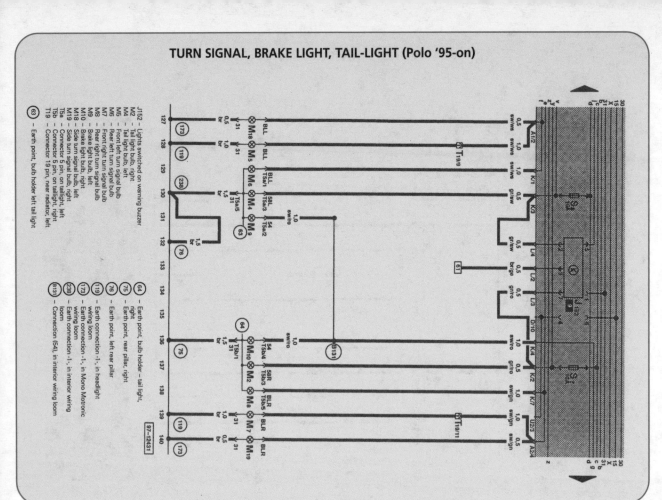

J152 – Lights switched on warning buzzer
M2 – Tail light bulb, right
M4 – Tail light bulb, left
M5 – Front left turn signal bulb
M6 – Rear left turn signal bulb
M7 – Front right turn signal bulb
M8 – Rear right turn signal bulb
M9 – Brake light bulb, left
M10 – Brake light bulb, right
M18 – Side turn signal bulb, left
M19 – Side turn signal bulb, right
T5a – Connector 5 pin, on taillight, left
T5b – Connector 5 pin, on taillight, right
T19 – Connector 19 pin, near radiator, left

63 – Earth point, bulb holder left tail light

64 – Earth point, bulb holder – tail light, right
75 – Earth point, rear pillar
76 – Earth point, left rear pillar
119 – Earth connection -1-, in headlight wiring loom
173 – Earth connection -1-, in Mono Motronic wiring loom
238 – Earth connection -1-, in interior wiring loom
B131 – Connection (54), in interior wiring loom

LIGHTING SWITCH, REAR FOG LIGHT (Polo '95-on)

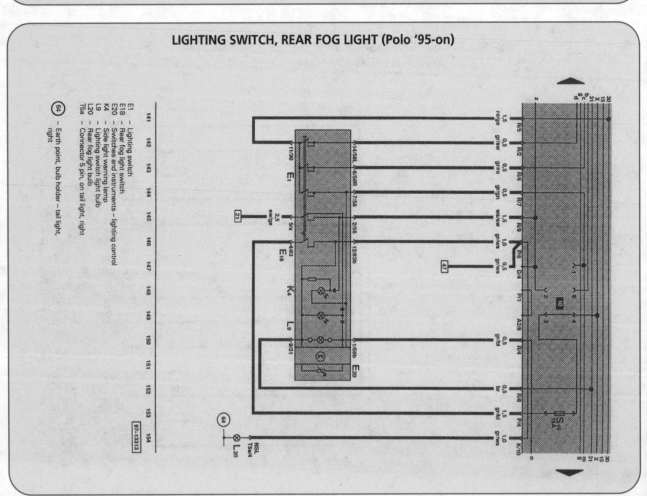

E1 – Lighting switch
E18 – Rear fog light switch
E20 – Switches and instruments – lighting control
K4 – Side light warning lamp
L9 – Lighting switch light bulb
L20 – Rear fog light bulb
T5a – Connector 5 pin, on tail light, right

64 – Earth point, bulb holder – tail light, right

BRAKE LIGHT SWITCH, NUMBER PLATE LIGHT, HEATED WINDSCREEN WASHER JETS (Polo '95-on)

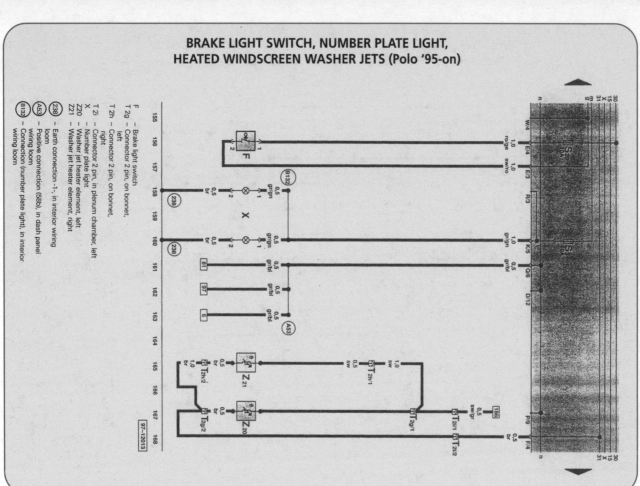

F – Brake light switch
T 2g – Connector 2 pin, on bonnet, left
T 2h – Connector 2 pin, on bonnet, right
T 2i – Connector 2 pin, in plenum chamber, left
X – Number plate light
Z20 – Washer jet heater element, left
Z21 – Washer jet heater element, right
(238) – Earth connection -1-, in interior loom
(A53) – Positive connection (58b), in dash panel
(B132) – Connection (number plate light), in interior wiring loom

97–12013

REVERSING LIGHT, HEATED REAR WINDOW, HORN (Polo '95-on)

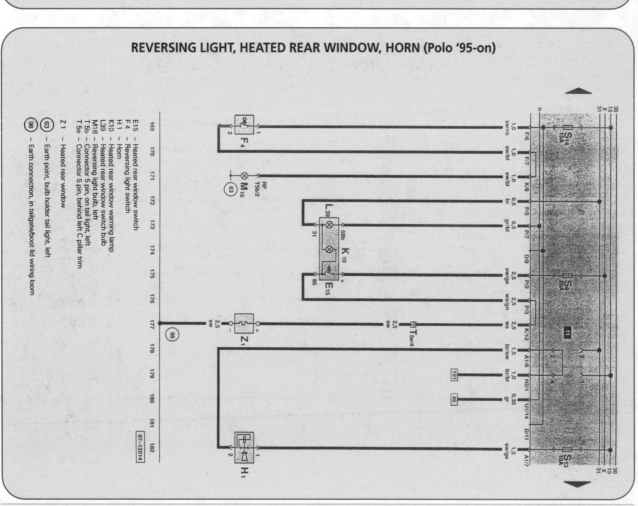

E15 – Heated rear window switch
F 4 – Reversing light switch
H 1 – Horn
K10 – Heated rear window warning lamp
L39 – Heated rear window switch bulb
M16 – Reversing light bulb, left
T 5b – Connector 5 pin, on tail light, left
T 5e – Connector 5 pin, behind left C pillar trim
Z1 – Heated rear window
(63) – Earth point, bulb holder tail light, left
(98) – Earth connection, in tailgate/boot lid wiring loom

97–12014

15-34

WINDOW LIFTER SWITCH IN DRIVER'S DOOR, CONTROL UNIT AND MOTOR FOR FRONT LEFT WINDOW LIFTER (Golf/Vento '96-on)

WINDOW LIFTER SWITCH IN REAR LEFT DOOR, CONTROL UNIT AND MOTOR FOR REAR LEFT WINDOW LIFTER (Golf/Vento '96-on)

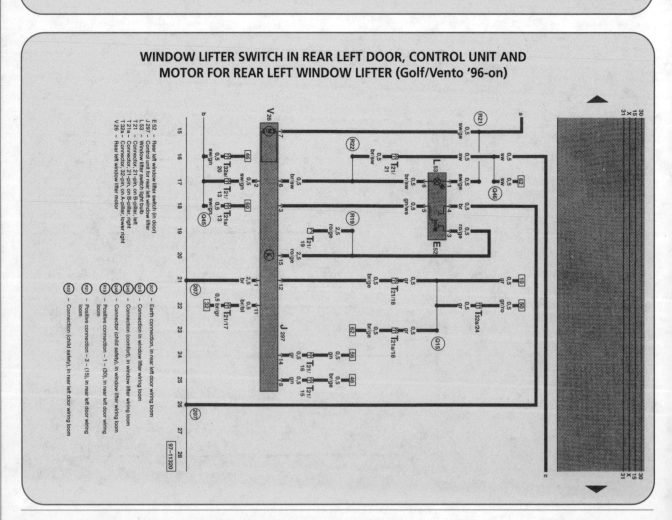

SWITCH AND ISOLATION SWITCH FOR REAR WINDOW LIFTERS (Golf/Vento '96-on)

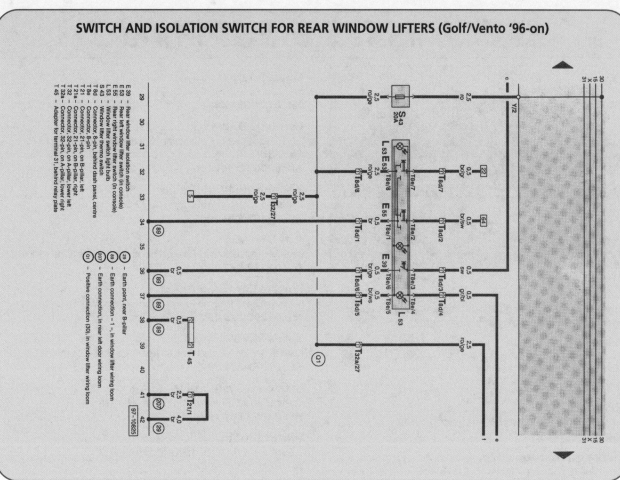

E 39 – Rear window lifter isolation switch
E 53 – Rear left window lifter switch
E 55 – Rear right window lifter switch (in console)
L 53 – Window lifter switch light bulb
S 43 – Window lifter thermo switch
T 8d – Connector, 8-pin, behind dash panel, centre
T 8e – Connector, 8-pin
T 21 – Connector, 8-pin
T 21a – Connector, 21-pin, on A-pillar, lower left
T 32 – Connector, 32-pin, on A-pillar, lower left
T 32a – Connector, 32-pin, on A-pillar, lower right
T 45 – Adapter for terminal 31, behind relay plate

⊕ – Earth point, near B-pillar
⑧ – Earth connection – 1 –, in window lifter wiring loom
㉚ – Earth connection, in rear left door wiring loom
⑤ – Positive connection (30), in window lifter wiring loom

97–10825

WINDOW LIFTER SWITCH IN FRONT PASSENGER DOOR, CONTROL UNIT AND MOTOR FOR FRONT RIGHT WINDOW LIFTER (Golf/Vento '96-on)

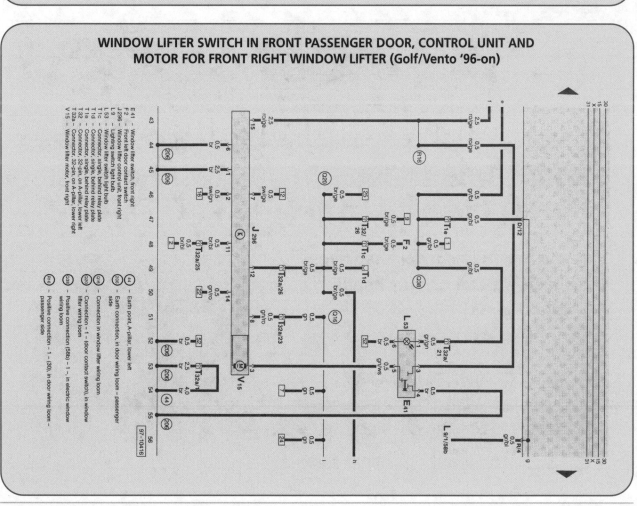

E 41 – Window lifter switch, front right
F 2 – Front left door contact switch
J 296 – Window lifter control unit, front right
L 9 – Lighting switch light bulb
L 53 – Window lifter switch light bulb
T 1c – Connector, single, behind relay plate
T 1d – Connector, single, behind relay plate
T 1e – Connector, single, behind relay plate
T 32 – Connector, 32-pin, on A-pillar, lower left
T 32a – Connector, 32-pin, on A-pillar, lower right
V 15 – Window lifter motor, front right

㊹ – Earth point, A-pillar, lower left
⑳⑥ – Earth connection, in door wiring loom – passenger side
㉑⑥ – Connection – 1 – (door contact switch), in window lifter wiring loom
㉓⑧ – Positive connection in window lifter wiring loom
㈤⑧ – Positive connection (58b) – 1 –, in door wiring loom – passenger side
R16 – Positive connection – 1 – (30), in door wiring loom – passenger side

97–10416

SPECIALISTS & SUPPLIERS

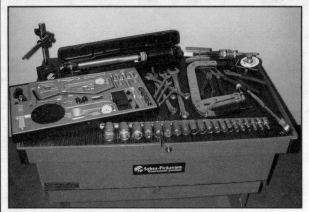

Autoglass Ltd.
Autoglass operate the well-known, nation-wide call-out service for emergency glass replacement. Ring Freephone **0800 363 636** for details of your local branch.

Robert Bosch Ltd.
Broadwater Park, North Orbital Road, Denham, Uxbridge, Middx, UB9 5HJ
Tel: 01895 838 360

Castrol (UK) Ltd.
Castrol BSS, Pipers Way, Swindon, Wilts, SN3 1RE
Tel: 01793 512 712

Clarke International Ltd.
Hemnall Street, Epping, Essex, CM16 4LG
Tel: 01992 565 300

Dunlop Tyres Ltd.
Fort Dunlop, Birmingham, B24 9QT
Tel: 0121 384 4444

Hastings Direct
Conquest House, Collington Avenue, Bexhill-on-Sea, TN39 3NQ
Tel: 0800 00 1066

Hammerite Products Ltd.
Prudhoe, Northumberland, NE42 6LP
Tel: 01661 830 000

Just VW Audi
Breakers Yard, Moat Road, Theberton, Suffolk, IP16 4RS
Tel: 01728 833 600

Potters Car Dismantlers
3 Sandy Lane, Titton, Stourport-on-Severn, Worcs, DY13 9PZ
Tel: 01299 823 134

Sykes-Pickavant Ltd.
Church Bridge Works, Walsall Road, Cannock, Staffs, WS11 3JR
Tel: 01253 784 800

Tecalemit Systems Ltd.
Estover Road, Plymouth, Devon, PL6 7PS
Tel: 01752 775 781

Wurth UK Ltd.
1 Centurion Way, Erith, Kent, DA18 4AE
Tel: 0870 5 98 78 41

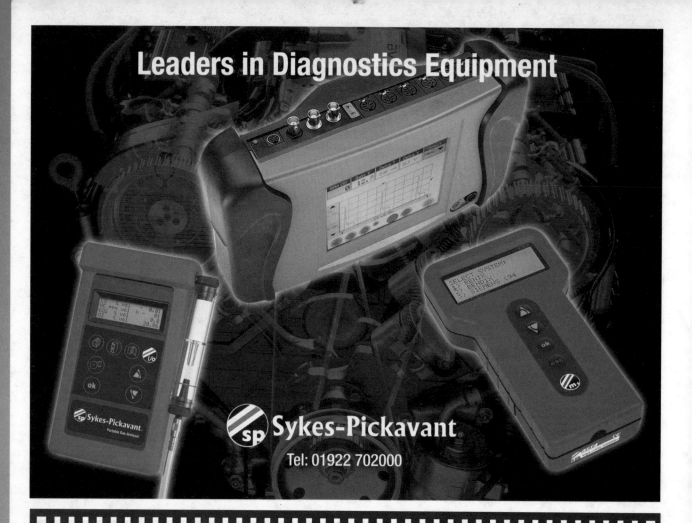